Quantum of Shale
Round the Tracks

Jeff Scott

Methanol Press

> ***Something sharp and rusty on their tongues again,***
> ***something more he'd hoped to spare them:***
> ***new bedside silences for visiting hours,***
> ***new definitions for never, for over.***

Michael Donaghy (1954-2004)
From 'The Swear Box'
Collected Poems (Picador 2009)

First published in Great Britain by
Methanol Press
2 Tidy Street
Brighton
East Sussex BN1 4EL

For a complete catalogue of current and forthcoming publications please write to the address above, or visit our website at www.methanolpress.com

Text and photographs copyright © Jeff Scott, 2009
Jeff Scott has asserted his right to be identified as the author of this Work in accordance with the Copyright, Designs and Patents Act 1988. All rights reserved. No part of this publication may be reproduced, stored in a retrieval system or transmitted in any form or by any means, whether electronic or mechanical, including photocopying, recording or otherwise, without the prior permission in writing of the copyright owners or publisher.
The publishers have made every effort to contact all copyright holders. If proper acknowledgement has not been made, we ask copyright holders to contact us.

ISBN 978-0-9553103-7-9
A catalogue for this book is available from the British Library

(Hardly suffering) Editor: Michael Payne
Word Wrangler: Graham Russel
Stenographer: Vy Shepherd
Book & Cover Design: Vicky Holtham
Cover Photograph: Jeff Scott

Printed in the UK by Lightning Source

i.m.

Stefan Usansky

1944-2009

This book is dedicated to the memory of Stefan Usansky.

Stef served in organizations, and among his friends, as a kind of social glue. This is the role you might expect from a man who was deeply curious about all kinds of people. He brought this passion as a point of pride to a number of different intense interests: among these were family, friends, work, Manchester United, Israel, sport, and his own geographical and cultural origins. Invariably he found much in life to love and much that made him laugh.

Stef treated all his friends and acquaintances similarly. He took delight in our successes, cheerfully comforted us when we stumbled, enjoyed our company, but, most importantly of all, remained steadfast and totally loyal. Some might say this loyalty occasionally crossed the line into blind partisanship, yet ultimately it was this same loyalty that drew you to him and caused you to want his approval.

It's easy to be sentimental about the dead because they are not here to contradict us. Stef had his quirks and idiosyncrasies, like everyone else. But what Stef truly had in abundance was an ability to live life to the full and the idea of half-heartedness remained unknown to him.

Around the time of the retirement that he so richly deserved, illness unfairly returned. After this diagnosis and through the years that followed, Stef manifested his love of life through optimism, strength, and endurance. He triumphed over the deleterious symptoms of his cancer by asserting his continued commitment to those values in his life that had brought him that far in the course of life's way, rather than succumb to the painful and humiliating details of his disease.

Stef appears in some of the chapters of my previous books during our visits to Poole, Belle Vue, and Buxton. On those trips he managed to see many different facets of speedway. As a proud son of Manchester, he went to Belle Vue Speedway in its glory Hyde Road era. He didn't need to be prompted to fondly recall many vivid memories from the time of his salad days.

Stef always had so many memories, stories, and tales; a laugh and a smile were always close. In life as well as illness he taught me very much. I'm determined to emulate his optimism, courtesy, and zest.

His enduring memorial will be the positive power of his friendship and character to impel those he knew towards the good, long after his death.

Rest in Peace, Stef.

CONTENTS

Chapter 1.	**Coventry:** *"You have to look after them and keep them happy!"*	7
Chapter 2.	**High Beech:** *"Don't worry, it'll soon empty out, most of these have to go for an afternoon nap shortly!"*	13
Chapter 3.	**Sittingbourne:** *"His stance on the bike is exactly the same as his dad's!"*	16
Chapter 4.	**King's Lynn v. Ipswich:** *"Can you tell us what you just told the lads on the truck about the last race without the expletives?"*	19
Chapter 5.	**Ipswich v. King's Lynn:** *"Oh! Wow! Look at the new programme board!"*	26
Chapter 6.	**Reading v. Stoke:** *"You've clearly got a good mother – is she attractive?"*	28
Chapter 7.	**Rye House:** *"Unless you've felt the burn of the tyre on your leg you really have no idea what it's like to ride a bike competitively."*	33
Chapter 8.	**Swindon v. Poole:** *"With hindsight, 1984 really was a turning point for the sport and everything has changed since then!"*	41
Chapter 9.	**Eastbourne v. Wolves:** *"We'll have to put it in a jig, straighten the diamonds where it's bent and the forks aren't 100 percent, but I'm sure we can fix it!"*	49
Chapter 10.	**Mildenhall v. Scunthorpe:** *"We even had a tug-o-war between the mascots – best of three – 'cause they even had a bear with them."*	53
Chapter 11.	**Reading v. Edinburgh:** *"Britain's sexiest mascot and also the most expensive!"*	62
Chapter 12.	**Isle of Wight v. Sheffield:** *"We're all committed to speedway but everyone else isn't."*	67
Chapter 13	**Ipswich v. Peterborough:** *"Last year he asked Zibi Suchecki if he had the right to be here."*	74
Chapter 14.	**Cardiff GP:** *"Inside they'll be able to buy non-flammable air horns."*	79
Chapter 15.	**Birmingham v. King's Lynn:** *"They must want to get it on 'cause they're suctioning the water off the track."*	88
Chapter 16.	**Coventry v. Poole:** *"He looks like he's done 15 rounds with Amir Khan. What with his nose and his Cornish accent, he's even harder to understand!"*	97
Chapter 17.	**Sittingbourne v. Scunthorpe:** *"It's not asking a lot to get 50 more, is it?"*	102
Chapter 18.	**Plymouth v. Weymouth:** *"If you'd signed it, you'd be contractually obliged not to fraternise with the riders."*	107
Chapter 19.	**Weymouth v. Plymouth:** *"Save £4 with this Leaflet* (Terms and Conditions Apply)"*	115
Chapter 20.	**Reading v. Edinburgh:** *"I bumped into two Reading fans there – we struggle to get them to Workington but we can get them to Sweden!"*	122
Chapter 21.	**King's Lynn v. Somerset:** *"You're Dave Cheshire's son, I can tell by your eyes."*	129
Chapter 22.	**Sheffield:** *"We cancelled at 10 o'clock because of the weather and the forecast is for more rain at 6 or 7 o'clock."*	136
Chapter 23	**Sheffield:** *"If you want to copy Darren – be encouraging!"*	141
Chapter 24.	**Wolverhampton v. Eastbourne:** *"I did my spell pushing - everybody does!"*	146

Chapter 25.	**Redcar v. Workington:** *"Where are all the rakers?"*	154
Chapter 26.	**Edinburgh v. Redcar:** *"He's conscious but has damage to his foot or ankle!"*	162
Chapter 27.	**Workington:** *"I said, 'They want you to wear women's clothes!'"*	168
Chapter 28.	**Newcastle v Sheffield:** *"The riders don't turn round the corners but slide round counter steering with the steering wheel and sliding the back end around."*	178
Chapter 29.	**Belle Vue:** *"Ove Fundin and Peter Collins are inside now signing autographs!"*	185
Chapter 30.	**Poole v Eastbourne:** *"Why are they watering the centre green?*	190
Chapter 31.	**Kidlington:** *"We're of the view – if the stadium was available – we think there'd be Oxford speedway!"*	196
Chapter 32.	**Lakeside v Swindon:** *"When we saw how their number 7 was riding, well!"*	202
Chapter 33.	**Oxford v Wimbledon:** *"I don't have very many nice words for the GRA!"*	211
Chapter 34.	**Scunthorpe v Glasgow:** *"We've not really beaten anyone by a big score."*	216
Chapter 35.	**Edinburgh v. Somerset:** *"He actually gated ahead and then let the others through!"*	225
Chapter 36.	**Berwick v. Somerset:** *"Oh, you've brought a bag to put your goggles in!"*	231
Chapter 37.	**Glasgow v. Berwick:** *"Hey, laddie, keep the throttle open more today!"*	238
Chapter 38.	**Buxton v. Weymouth:** *"We're the only track with such a varied selection of animal droppings."*	244
Chapter 39.	**Stoke v. Redcar:** *"Hit me! Big Ty? Big Ty! Hit it! Hit it! You gotta appreciate that!"*	252
Chapter 40.	**Sheffield v. Scunthorpe:** *"His wife Angie Collins used to cut my hair – when I had hair."*	259
Chapter 41.	**Scunthorpe v. Rye House:** *"She certainly wasn't a full-fat Goth – perhaps a Goth-lite."*	264
Chapter 42.	**Sheffield/PLRC:** *"I've no idea who's gonna win, mate! It could be any one of ten."*	270
Chapter 43.	**Peterborough v Wolverhampton:** *"Please write any additional comments on reverse."*	276
Chapter 44.	**Rye House/CLRC:** *"'Ere Lisa, pose for a photo so you can be on the cover of his next book!"*	285
Chapter 45.	**Sittingbourne v. Rye House:** *"Poised on the brink of adequacy."*	293
Chapter 46.	**Reading v. Redcar:** *"You know, in a year and a half here, I haven't actually met Barbara Horley."*	298
Chapter 47.	**Somerset v. Edinburgh:** *"I've dug out an old hat in case we need it to celebrate!"*	304
Chapter 48.	**Reading:** *"You must have very many happy memories?"*	311

Introduction

The book you have in your hand continues my examination of the question 'what is speedway?' that I embarked on when I travelled to every track in the country in 2005, 2006 and 2007. This odyssey resulted in the publication of the books *Showered in Shale, Shifting Shale* and *Concrete for Breakfast*. So this is really more of the same but also something different. *Quantum of Shale* is also not a club history nor the (auto) biography of a rider but a snapshot and my personal journey round every stadium that staged the sport in Britain – this time during 2008. Again, it was a pleasure to be able to have a reason to visit every track in the country, often more than once albeit slightly tempered by another summer of wet weather. Though I could only write about what I encountered, I have again tried to capture some of the characters that make up some parts of the speedway world as well as vaguely attempt to delve beneath the surface of what I've seen. All of life was there at speedway in our nation and many people went out of their way to be kind, tell me their thoughts on speedway or comment on my books. What notionally started out as a philosophical quest has continued to take a somewhat anthropological turn but, hey, that's apparently the shadow that falls between the idea and the action.

Anyway, when writing this book I have tried to adhere to the lessons I was given previously by my editor, mentor, advisor and writing coach Michael Payne as well as encouragement from the late Michael Donaghy who suggested I write about what I know or love.

Sadly, anyone familiar with my blog or my previous books will know that I'm not adverse to some pointless navel-gazing, pretentiousness and facetiousness. Nonetheless, I hope that you can forgive these faults and mostly enjoy the chance to travel to the tracks again in my company as much as I relished the visits.

Lastly, without the riders prepared to risk their lives on high-powered bikes without brakes on various different tracks – for our entertainment and to make their living – there would be no sport to watch in this country. In our everyday lives, we often take our own mortality for granted and, equally, we make light of speedway injuries as part and parcel of the sport. The 2008 season was another poor one for serious injuries in the UK and, clothed in their racing gear, unlike their loved ones, we often forget that every rider is someone's brother, son, partner, husband or father. Hopefully we can all remember this every time a critical comment nearly passes our lips without need of further injury to remind us of the real situation.

There you have it. I hope that you enjoy your journey.

Brighton
10th June 2009

CHAPTER 1.

Coventry:
"You have to look after them and keep them happy!"

9th February

With the new speedway season only four weeks away, the chance to get back into the swing of things arrives in the Midlands. Well, to be exact, at the Coventry Sports Connexion Centre in Ryton-on-Dunsmore. Usually this sports centre on the outskirts of Coventry is the regular weekend home for dog shows, car boot sales and is also famous as the Coventry City FC 'Sky Blues' training ground conceived and implemented by Jimmy Hill. However, this particular Saturday – after the long dark winter nights of the close season – it leaves speedway fans spoilt for choice with two different events taking place simultaneously at the same location. Inside a spacious sports hall is the 2008 Speedway and Grasstrack Show that, the pre-show advertising in the *Speedway Star* boasts, will enable you to casually mingle with riders – albeit only ones from Coventry – as well as have your photo taken with the Eazy Oils Racer girls. The advert in the *Star* foregrounds the lure of these girls dressed in tightly fitted clothes and claims that fans should "Come along and start your 2008 season!!!". The attractions on offer include the aforementioned team stand of the Coventry Bees ("2007 Treble Champions") as well as trade stands, bar and catering, rider stands (unnamed) and rider merchandise, along with a bouncy castle, magic carpet ride and a disco. Even with all this on offer, parking remains free, children get in at absolutely no charge and adults only have to part with £2.50. If this wasn't already enough, also in the sports centre next door is the Speedway Memorabilia Fayre and Auction organised by Nick Barber with the help of his family – brother Johnny, sister Bev and mum Molly. It's not quite the memorabilia extravaganza on the size and scale of their November event though, nonetheless, there's an extensive range of speedway memorabilia merchandise from the 1930s onwards. In fact, there's a cornucopia of programmes, books, photos, paintings and the like displayed on the various exhibition stands of the fayre itself. Stored in the adjacent room are yet more treasured items that everyone can bid for later in the white heat of the auction.

I arrive early and immediately make my way upstairs to the exhibition area where, with unhurried professional ease, Johnny Barber is midxway through the task of laying out his merchandise attractively. I've barely come through the door when we're joined by another early bird in the form of the vastly experienced and hugely knowledgeable Colin Pratt, currently Coventry Bees promoter but also a true speedway legend. Though, as a modest man, he's naturally too shy ever to acknowledge, let alone claim, the pretension of legendary status for himself. Usually taciturn, an innocuous question from Johnny about the forthcoming 2008 season provokes Colin to let rip about the introduction of the new (and peculiar) team building points limit of 38.85 for Elite League teams during the 2008 season. The upshot of the introduction of this reduced level has – more than at any other club – badly affected the Coventry Bees team line up. During the winter close season, they've had to decide which of their three leaders from their treble-winning roster to let go. In the final analysis they chose to retain Chris Harris and Rory Schlein and, after considerable angst, the talismanic Scott Nicholls has reluctantly been allowed to leave the Bees to go on loan to Eastbourne (though, at one point, until the Eagles rearranged their team line up, it looked like Scott might be frozen out of the 2008 Elite League altogether). Though it's months since news of the new limits broke and some time since this difficult decision was made, the need to actually have to make it clearly still rankles with Colin. "Just because some wally can't run his business we have to suffer! I agree that there has to be some kind of rider control, but we built up our side by looking after the riders on and off the track! You've got to respect the riders and they've got to respect you, otherwise it just don't work! We suffered before, just 'cause some other people can't run their damn business. We lost Hamill and Hancock and now we've damn well suffered again! Who else has paid out £36,000, £26,000 and £20,000 on full transfers? We signed Rory Schlein and built him up. Look at Chris Harris, he went from the Conference League to the Elite League but two years ago he was struggling with a low average. We talked to him and treated him right. The driving from Cornwall was killing him so we put him up at [his mechanic] Chris Anderson's place and we still paid him his driving money, and now look at him two and a half years later!"

Passionate rant over, Colin attentively shuffles through the merchandise on Johnny's stall with some care and shows considerable interest in some of the programmes. Both men fall into an easy conversation about the collection of speedway memorabilia that Colin himself has at home. These include an assortment of race jackets, including one from Harringay[1] in the 1940s and a prized Rye House Rockets race bib from 1977. Though his club have their own stand in the sports centre next door, his early start and curiosity have lured Colin to the Collectors' Fayre to sift through some of the memorabilia before the public officially arrive. "This used to be really good here – before your time – but some of them got a bit silly at the hotel and got banned!" Johnny nods along in agreement, "I heard they were letting off fire extinguishers and that". Often guarded in public, this morning Colin remains on a roll, "I know we're local but it's pathetic that we're the only club who are here today![2] I get up every day at half-five to drive to Coventry: we're a professionally run club for 24 hours a day, seven days a week."

Johnny sympathises, "The trouble is, new promoters come in and throw a load of money at a rider and say 'there you go!' Look at Ipswich, I know they're my local club, but they built up Danny King from the Conference League to the Elite League and then Peterborough just came in and took him!"

Johnny has found a receptive audience in Colin, "That's what I mean! You have to look after them and keep them happy! Everyone in the club is important – everyone – no matter what they do!" It's suddenly become a rather sincere speedway version of *Grumpy Old Men*, "You can't say it's like that anymore," Johnny replies, shaking his head. "Look at us at Peterborough, we were there 10 years and then we heard in November from a fan who rang us saying, 'sorry to hear you're not doing the trackshop'. No one took the time to ring us up and say to us, 'thank you for all you've done but we've decided to go with someone else'. That's the way it is nowadays!"

"It wasn't like that before you started but that's the way it's gone!" says disgruntled Colin, as he moves off purposefully next door to quickly survey the goodies on offer in the auction room for sale later.

A large number of treasures have been readied to go under the auctioneer's hammer. To facilitate review and their subsequent purchase, they've been carefully placed in a large number of easy-to-access brown boxes on a row of tables. Shortly afterwards, the viewing area will be massively congested when a keenly knowledgeable cohort of would-be purchasers gather (once they reach the head of the queue) to carefully inspect the specific items of merchandise they can request from Nick's staff at their leisure prior to the auction itself. I've come to the Fayre to catch up with people and to gossip but also to try to sell some copies of the 2008 edition of the *Methanol Press Speedway Yearbook* edited by Speedway historian Robert Bamford. He's the sport's most prolific and best-selling author widely known for his expertise and legendary attention to detail. You can't even attempt to produce an authoritative *Yearbook* filled with stats and other information on an intermittent or annual basis unless you have an innate fastidiousness as well as a gift for record keeping. Though it's a whole new experience for me in publishing terms, this isn't the first *Speedway Yearbook* that Robert Bamford has ever produced since he previously used to publish these with Tempus. They're a company widely known in the publishing industry for their local history books. However, in recent years, since they've been bought and sold on a couple of occasions this has led to a rumble of dissatisfaction among some of their authors. Robert is one of these disgruntled authors who felt that the upheaval caused by ongoing ownership changes led to them to take their commercial eye off the ball with regard to his books in both marketing and sales terms as well as allegedly causing some delay in the payment of royalty cheques. Whatever the cause or accuracy of the various author complaints, all this is in the past for Robert who brought his pet project to Methanol Press for the 2008 edition. It's the first book not actually written by myself published by Methanol Press, so I've had some rather attractive large-scale posters produced to Blu-Tak onto the walls of the stairs that lead up to the Fayre. Initial interest in the book is keen and sales are comparatively brisk. This remains the case for the first couple of months of publication which, personally, I put down to pre-season excitement but also the fact that a large number of people take a statistically driven approach to their enjoyment of speedway. It's hardly a

---

[1] "Harringay" is the speedway spelling though apparently political correctness has subsequently altered this to "Haringey".

[2] King's Lynn speedway would also be in attendance at the Speedway and Grasstrack Fayre next door represented by Buster Chapman and Nathan Hollands.

surprise that speedway fans love statistics, given the complexity of the rules and scorecard. Let alone the fact that the use of rider averages allows meaningful comparisons to be established between different clubs (and riders). Though the natural constituency of a speedway memorabilia fayre necessarily means that those with an interest in speedway's past aren't necessarily going to want to purchase a book about the speedway present, nonetheless, some still purchase Robert's latest book to add to their burgeoning speedway book collections.

With the Fayre at either venue yet to officially open, I have a brief reconnaissance next door. If on *Star Trek* they invariably set the phasers to stun, then the heating system inside the sports hall has been set to kill (even though the outside ambient air temperature is already noticeably warm for the time of year). Given my discomfort at the heat, I wonder how awful this temperature would feel if you were actually tried to use the building for its real sporting purposes? Like so many sports halls, the building looks like a large shed from the outside, while inside there's a huge amount of space dedicated to each stallholder with more than enough left over to house many more display stands should demand to exhibit there have been considerably higher. Afterwards, on the speedway forums, some visitors expressed regret that all the speedway clubs in the country – with the notable exceptions of Coventry and King's Lynn – just couldn't be bothered to turn up with a stand. Though, to be fair, in true chicken-and-egg fashion the fans also didn't really show up in any great numbers either! The stallholders who did attend had various products to sell. Some would be bought by the die-hard fans (speedway jackets and the like) while other items on display (such as helmets and oils) were primarily aimed at the riders. Any rider who bothered to put in an appearance was always going to attract considerable interest. During my brief visit I spotted Chris Harris, Rory Schlein, Brendan Johnson (and his dad Dave), as well as David Howe (who was based at his own grandiosely named David Howe Racing stall rather than on the imaginary stand that represented his local club, Wolverhampton, who are locally based but conspicuous by their absence).

It wasn't so long ago that the British Speedway Promoters' Association fronted by Jim Lynch organised their own pre-season exhibition at the nearby Stoneleigh National Agricultural Centre. This event attracted such a decent crowd that there was wild talk of a regular indoor event but, in typical speedway fashion, this came to naught. Sadly the days when the BSPA could be bothered to organise such an event to advertise their wares to the media and the fans alike have long since passed into the dim mists of time. If pressed for an explanation, a mix of financial considerations and the ineffectiveness of the event to garner substantial media or fan interest is usually cited as the primary reason behind the decision to no longer bother with it. To be fair to the BSPA, the fans that usually turn up at such events are already die-hard speedway followers so this additional promotional outlay is unlikely to result in extra revenues through the turnstiles come the start of the season. To a greater or lesser extent, all trade associations provide a convenient umbrella organisation under which a variety of different and competing businesses (who happen to be in the same industry) can present themselves together to outline their real or ostensible needs to the outside world. In this case, for the sport of speedway, the BSPA provides governance, strategic vision along with advocacy of members' aims and objectives. Whichever way you look at it, the

Bargains galore

BSPA members should either support this event or, alternatively, organise something more meaningful in its place. Clearly geographic considerations play their part in lack of interest from speedway clubs (along with time and cost) but it's nonetheless symptomatic of the respect in which the fans, sponsors and media are held that the trade association of a mature sport – that finds itself within an increasingly competitive overall sports environment – chooses not to make a song and dance about either its own appeal or unique attractions. We all know that the raw fact that speedway takes place somewhere every night of the week across a geographically disparate area during the spring, summer and autumn months adds to the difficult complexity of easily and effectively communicating its appeal. It would good to be able to claim that every speedway club effectively promoted their events locally and regionally via the print and broadcast media but, the reality remains that it would easier to count on one hand those clubs that consistently show such skill and/or application (or, even, a media-friendly relationship). Inertia at a national, trade association and regional level isn't usually viewed as a recipe for long-term growth or financial health.

Someone with the good sense and entrepreneurial acumen to consider attendance (albeit a last-minute decision) at such an event is Buster Chapman, hard-working promoter from King's Lynn speedway. Though hardly a stone's throw away from Coventry (unlike many other clubs located much more conveniently for Ryton), Buster has driven over with Nathan Hollands in order to put the best foot forward for the sport generally and his own club in particular. While he helps unload the display stands and materials from the distinctively liveried King's Lynn speedway black van, Buster reveals that he doesn't really expect any earth-shattering results from the day, "Even if only a couple of people start coming along to the Norfolk Arena regularly having seen us at this Fayre, then it will have more than covered the cost of the petrol and the exhibition charge! Obviously, we're here to promote the club but we're also here to promote *Powerslide*, which is what we call our training schools. We have 16 bikes, four of them new ones and Shaun Tacey has done all the engines, so they really are the business. We only decided to come yesterday and it's costing me 200 quid to do this. But, if we get some extra customers at the *Powerslide* or coming along regularly to the speedway, then it'll be more than worthwhile!"

Community relations are extremely close to Buster's heart and, within the sport, King's Lynn speedway club is quite rightly lauded for the effectiveness of their community work via their innovative and acclaimed King's Lynn Speedway Study Centre. "We're the only motor sport involved in Study Centres – there's no Formula 1 involvement or anything from MotoGP! I went to an event at Wembley. It was full of the Manchester Uniteds, Arsenals and Tottenhams of this world. There were big wigs, champagne and nice food and we were there – little old King's Lynn! I was so proud! The BSPA, like the government, don't help at all. They say, 'it's all right for you, you own your own stadium!' But, that's not the point. I paid for everything! The building, the staff, all the computers and equipment, everything! We get all the wild kids. I love the disabled and children, the orphaned, those that have been chucked out of home or who do nicking – anyone! And you know, the teachers say they didn't wanna know at school, and now they study maths, computers, and geography. It helps straighten them out! I'm so proud. Jonathan said, 'Let's kick it into touch,' but I didn't wanna 'cause it's something I love! Being really part of the community and helping them kids! At the event at Wembley, Peter Scudamore said some lovely things and went out of his way to mention us. In our area we work closely with Norwich City and they've been very helpful. Together I think we're really playing our part in Norfolk. I'd be classified as 'not educated' from a qualification point of view. I don't have no CSEs or nothing but that's not intelligence! You can have all the qualifications and still be hopeless. Inspiring young people, no matter who they are, is so satisfying! Not being funny [names substantial sum of money] is neither here nor there for me but, being part of the community and making a difference, well I just can't put it into words! Being able to be able to make a difference is something beyond money! Next month [March 2008] we'll have a visit from two Sports Ministers and the Education Minister to look at the King's Lynn Speedway Study Centre! It really is something to be part of that and to be making a difference!" Flushed with pride and enthusiasm, Buster shoots back off to the van to help Nathan carry in yet more of the boxes of display equipment.

Elsewhere in the hall, there's quite a commotion when the Eazy Oils Racer girls arrive in their tight-fitting lycra cat suits, specially styled to look like speedway kevlars (though, obviously, the real things are made of an altogether thicker material to provide greater safety protection). I imagine, apart from the attraction of the riders, most people will want to have their photographs taken with these girls. I don't have time to do that, but I do get to speak to the charming Malcolm Blythe from the Coventry trackshop. Like Colin Pratt, he's not best pleased with the reduction in the points limit thrust upon his beloved Coventry Bees for the 2008 season agreed upon at the BSPA annual conference. "It's become the Coventry and Swindon training track nowadays. Other clubs who can't do what we do, end up with our riders! It can't be right. Two days before it was announced, Mr Sandhu and Chris Van Straaten met and he was told it was most likely gonna be a 40-point limit. Yet, two days later, it was 38.5. Then Mr Sandhu learnt that Chris Van Straaten had already signed five riders with that limit in mind! If I was Mr Sandhu, I wouldn't be at all happy and I think that's why he's taken a back seat this year and Allen Trump has taken over the promoter's licence. I think we've got a good side but it's definitely weaker than the side that won everything last year! We'll just have to see how we go – it's really too early to say at this point."

Back over at the Collectors' Fayre there's already quite a crowd of people who look like they ceased to be strangers to the Garden Centre some time back and are more than happy to avidly look through the merchandise in the Fayre area. At a long line of tables next door, there's already a studious hush as people patiently study the assorted memorabilia of yesteryear in silent, almost total, absorption. A regular stallholder at these events, Martin Dadswell from the Eastbourne trackshop, has a quick wit and an impressive repertoire of insults that he delights to practise in my company. The composition of the 2008 Eastbourne Eagles team has already been revealed apart from the mystery rider who will occupy the vital number 7 reserve team slot. Martin tells me confidently, "Dave Mason is gonna be our new number 7!" In fact, such is the rumour and misinformation during the winter months of any close season, it turns out Dave Mason would be Lewis Bridger's mechanic and the final Eagles team place would be taken by James Brundle. Stood by my book display I get a good chance to study the clientele, watch the world go by, overhear conversations and have a brief word with passing friends or customers. One man tells me, "I remember my first meeting at King's Lynn with Terry Betts and Malcolm Simmons," before he goes off into a lengthy reminiscence of how great speedway used to be. I make a brief trip to the Sports Centre car park (where sadly this week there is no car boot sale) to meet Bob Tasker who's the Chief Executive Officer of a DVD multimedia speedway empire based in the North East of England. In old money, we'd know him as a man who makes speedway meetings videos from his back bedroom and kitchen. He has the exclusive rights to film a variety of speedway clubs (and record their meetings for posterity) including Redcar, Newcastle and Workington. He's kindly agreed to pick up some book stock on behalf of Graham Platten who runs the Berwick speedway trackshop and also doubles up as their speedway photographer. Our talk quickly moves from speedway matters to football and he makes my day when he refers to Newcastle United Football Club as "The Britney Spears of Football!"

When I return to my stall, continuing the Newcastle theme, I notice that Johnny Barber serves a man who's a George English lookalike. While we know there's a David or Victoria Beckham lookalike market, whether or not there's sufficient demand for someone who looks like George English has yet to be established. This chap would definitely fit the bill should demand suddenly pick up. On the subject of identity, a man called Nigel Bird who's nearly lost his voice comes to my stall and says, "Are you Robert Bamford? I've never met him and I've always wanted to meet him! I've sent him lots of information now and again and it would have been a delight if you were him." Sadly, I'm not Robert and Nigel has no interest in the George English lookalike. Someone who's instantly recognisable is Robert Peasley. I watch him concentratedly search through a mountain of programmes that he alternates with frequent glances inside one of the two notebooks he clutches tightly in his free hand. Later I learn, his little red notebook lists his *Speedway Star* collection, while the little blue notebook covers his programmes collection. "I've looked at the auction but, for once, there's really nothing I want to buy. Well, I bought a 1955 Southampton v. Oxford programme for £22 in November and there's another one for sale but it's not as good as mine 'cause it's got a photo missing! If it's going for £4 or something, I might get it later." The closure of Oxford Speedway club and confirmation over the winter that there will definitely be no rescue for the club during the 2008 season (or, possibly, longer) has hit many loyal supporters, like Rob, hard. "I'm definitely not going to Swindon and Reading. I'm not supporting the local clubs, I'm probably going to go to Scunthorpe. Well, I'm sure I'll go to quite a few clubs as I won't be able to keep away from watching speedway but I'm not sure where yet. It'll be strange not to be working on the programme each week during the season, let alone not seeing any racing in Oxford."

The charming John Jarvis, co-author along with Robert Bamford of the best-selling and enthralling *Homes of Speedway*, has come to the Fayre with his wife. Given that his house is already full of memorabilia, I imagine she'll be keen to ensure that he purchases absolutely nothing else. Still within her earshot, John pointedly tells me in a loud voice, "I'm here just to sell my library of sports grounds books at auction!" With the published time of the auction nearly upon us, large numbers of people have already made their way through next door to politely jostle and bagsy a well-positioned seat close to the front in good time for the bidding to start. Trevor James, the Bolton fan who runs the adjacent programme stall to my stand, tells me, "I've had a good day but today is my last ever 'cause you just can't pick up the stock any more. Nick Barber is the first port of call for anyone with programmes to sell nowadays. I can't knock him, it's his business. I can't buy in bulk like I used to! It's just singles nowadays. I'm gonna get rid of the clutter and do something else. I've had a good run!"

Also on his way through to the auction is the affable, modest and knowledgeable Tony Steele, widely regarded as the best speedway referee in the world. I congratulate him on the fact that he has once again been chosen to be part of the roster of officials in charge of the Grand Prix events during 2008. "I didn't get my international licence to just officiate at Grands Prix as I've told you before! Last year (2007) I got to see many of the different places all round the world where they race speedway not just the Grands Prix and that's what it's all about, isn't it, really?"

Rather like people slow down to watch an accident when passing in the opposite lane on a motorway, so it is with speedway auctions where everyone crowds into the room in order to watch other people bid even if they don't actually intend to do so themselves. Concentration levels are high and the atmosphere is one of hushed reverential silence. The auction is very professionally run and managed by the Barbers, who fully deserve the 10% buyer's commission they earn from the sale of each lot. The lot number on the first item is called and Nick Barber summarily describes it before he asks, "Am I bid £10 for it?" I decide not to wait for the many hours that the auction will take to complete amongst an audience of speedway fans whose primary interest rests in the memorabilia and artefacts of yesteryear. As I carry one of my boxes down the stairs, I overhear some stallholders chatter as one nods toward a pile of old magazines. "I don't mind if he chucks them out after he buys them, he won't be able to sell them to anyone else!" At the Speedway and Grasstrack Fayre next door, the temperature still remains incredibly high but the crowds low. Those that have come wander round, linger by the various stalls or chat in aisles wide enough for a cash-and-carry wholesaler. In the absence of the vast majority of speedway teams and riders who ply their trade in this country, the event has the air of an afterthought or something where the central attraction is conspicuously notable only by its absence. Polo mints might be popular and marketed as a sweet without a centre. However, you have to worry how long such an event like this can continue without the support of the vast majority of the clubs who stage sport in this country.

9th February Coventry: Speedway and Grasstrack Show

CHAPTER 2.

High Beech:
"Don't worry, it'll soon empty out, most of these have to go for an afternoon nap shortly!"

17th February

Once again, the King's Oak Hotel in Epping Forest is the location chosen to celebrate the anniversary of speedway's inception in this country at High Beech on February 17th 1928. The event is actually held exceptionally near the very spot that first dirt track meeting was ever run at in this country. Indeed, you can still pick out the overgrown oval circuit behind the hotel and walk the banked mud perimeter that would have been the public viewing areas. This year it's the eightieth anniversary and, though this is the sort of milestone that in any other sport would have the various clubs and governing body milking the media publicity for all that it's worth, the speedway authorities in this country take a completely different approach. Their attitude is so low key that they effectively ignore it! As usual, enthusiasts like Terry Stone and his 'Men in Black' will be on hand to warm up their Douglas, Rudge and JAP speedway bikes while, inside the bar area of the hotel, there will be the Collectors' Fayre organised by Rye House and Peterborough Trackshop Manager, Andy Griggs. On display will be various items of memorabilia including such treasures as team body colours, programmes, paintings, photographs, and badges along with assorted videos and magazines. My close reading of the *Speedway Star* (issue dated February 9th) reveals buried in the small print on page 37, "this year the anniversary is being supported by the Paradise Wildlife Park Speedway Museum". Upon arrival in the exhibition, area it's not immediately apparent how this generous support will actually manifest itself, though it is difficult to escape noticing the large Speedway Museum stall.

During previous visits to this anniversary celebration, I gathered that the regular clientele who traipse to Epping Forest would primarily be gentlemen of more advanced years. Each year the overall mood of those lured to attend on a Sunday morning could best be characterised as a mix of wistful longing nostalgia for the certainties, smells and glories of yesteryear. It's an outlook leavened with an air of celebration at the basic fact that they (and their memories) have survived this long and that they're still capable enough to meet, gossip and catch up with similarly minded friends. All the speedway stallholders you'd expect to find at such an event are in attendance. These include organiser Andy Griggs, Nick and Johnny Barber, Martin Dadswell and Alan Boniface as well as John Rich and Bill Gimbeth who've been seconded by Dave Rattenberry to man his stall. Apart from Methanol Press, Tony MacDonald and Susie Muir have taken a stall for all the various *Backtrack* books and magazines. They have a "Books Special Offer", which sees the cover price of their entire backlist catalogue discounted to a price of £10 each per book. There's a further special offer that if you buy any two books you will then get *Sliding Into Hell*, John Berry's speedway novel absolutely free!

On my stall, Robert Bamford's just published *Yearbook* attracts the attention of Derek Barclay, "I must buy the *Yearbook* as it's the only book you've published where you're not slagging me off!" Following the Dons demise in 2005, the ex-Wimbledon programme editor has moved on to pastures new and informs me "now that Buzz [Burrows] is there, I'm writing for the Stoke programme again. Though I have a press pass, I'm not sure I'll get in past Caroline [Tattum]. Buzz's wife is Caroline's sister! I suppose I could mention that but I'm not sure it'll help me. I'll take a programme and say 'look what I'm doing for free every week for your club,!' [pause] I think I'll call Dave beforehand to sort it out." Shortly afterwards, Nick Barber asks, "What is it with the Wimbledon fans and Buzz Burrows? He's just an average Conference League rider." I'm happy to provide some insight, "I think you'll find it was the sheer excitement of his all-action racing style at the self-acclaimed 'best track in the country' that prompts this adulation!" My explanation elicits a 'harrumph' and "What! First out of the gate wins?"

The Master of Ceremonies at the High Beech anniversary event is the cheerfully optimistic Craig Saul who, during the speedway season, effortlessly imparts a huge amount of interesting and insightful speedway information over the public-address systems of both Rye House and Peterborough Speedway clubs. Away from his speedway duties, he's also the Press Officer and announcer at Barnet Football Club. Last season he'd also had the honour to "share" the microphone with the King's Lynn speedway uber presenter, Mike Bennett at several of the Super7even meetings. Occasionally, he'd got some uninterrupted air time, most notably at the Premier League Pairs meeting staged at Somerset the evening before the 2007 Cardiff Grand Prix. That night Craig entertained the crowd without his partner in crime since Mike, along with his distinctive Butlins Redcoat style jacket, were stuck in heavy traffic, [like many fans] until heat 8. Upon arrival at the Oak Tree Arena, there had been some embarrassment for Craig when the regular Somerset Presenter/Announcer, Dave Lewis, only discovered at that point that he'd been replaced by the organisers and wasn't required to do the presentation. If the event had been held in Hoddesdon, Craig knows that such a breakdown in communication from the management wouldn't have been an issue since Len Silver prides himself on an extremely professionally run operation throughout all departments of his speedway business. "Len looks after everyone at the club very well – whether they're riders, helpers or staff!"

Rye House speedway club is the closest speedway track to the High Beech event so, understandably, they're comparatively well represented among the fans that attend this event. While she sends her husband, Eddie, away to enjoy looking at the stalls and the vintage bikes, wheelchair-bound Rockets' fan Elizabeth Tarling speaks highly of the attitude of Berwick promoter, Peter Waite. "When we went to Berwick, I was at the other side of the stadium to him and he came all the way over to speak to me and asked if I was alright and could he get me anything. He's the only promoter who has ever spoken to me! What a lovely man! I think he should be applauded for keeping the club going, particularly when so many riders don't want to travel up there every week to ride. I speak as I find and he should be applauded for keeping Berwick alive – it's a lovely track! At Berwick, I could watch on the back straight – I had a really good view up above the action. Some of the Rye fans moan about how awful it is there, but I don't think so! I tell my husband to go off and wander like I used to do before I was in this. I don't like him standing there, while I sit. If all tracks had viewing facilities like they do at Berwick, it would be a lot easier for someone like me to really see what was going on!"

Ian Glover, Sittingbourne Start Marshal, has come along to enjoy the anniversary celebrations, albeit without the colourful checked trousers that he wears on any Sunday race day in Kent (or any Friday at Lakeside) during the speedway season. One name that invariably springs to mind when considering the 80 years of history that speedway has in this country is, inevitably, Wimbledon speedway: "Plough Lane was an awkward track to get around when it was the authentic one, nevermind the one laid out on tarmac. Buzz really had that [latter-day] track figured out so, no wonder, he was unbeatable round there against any Conference League rider! One time I just went there to watch the meeting – Graham Arnold was Clerk of the Course – and the ref [1] had been taken ill on the motorway on the way there. I used to do the reffing in the old third division so they suggested I step in. I got the agreement of both of the team managers – Dingle Brown and Bryn Williams – and they rang Jim McGregor [ASR (Association of Speedway Referees) allocations secretary] who approved it all. I said I wasn't going to put up with any messing about. First race there was a crash on the first bend and I said all four back. The phone immediately rang and it was Bryn complaining, saying I didn't know what I was doing and I'd made the wrong decision! I said, 'You agreed that you'd abide by my decisions!' The ref's box there was like the dugout at a football match. It was so low down and, ideally, at speedway you need to be looking down! There were hanging baskets, flowers and everything – three riders would go into the corner but you'd only see two of them come out. It was a nightmare! They rang referee Chris Gay who was on a beach in Southend and asked him to rush there. He got there about heat 8 and said, 'you carry on, I'll just watch you.' He took over for the last few and the phone rings with Bryn complaining about all four back not knowing it was Chris in charge. Bryn said 'look here, Ian, blah blah blah blah blah'. Chris just let him talk. I did exclude some riders. There was tapes touching and everything; it was terrible, but also completely memorable!"

No auction of speedway memorabilia or any event that deals with speedway's history would be complete without the attendance of Allen Trump. He's a man whose name apparently legally cannot appear in the speedway press

---

[1] These officials were actually known as 'stewards' rather than as referees, since this was also a training league for the officials as well as for the riders. Of current licensed SCB officials, Paul Carrington and Mick Bates progressed/qualified via this training route to the chagrin of some older referees who felt that they weren't properly qualified since they'd not undergone the traditional formal qualifying regime.

High Beech: *"Don't worry, it'll soon empty out, most of these have to got for an afternoon nap shortly!"*

without the words 'millionaire businessman' in the same or adjacent sentence. Last year Allen got to swim in the speedway promotional shallow end when he promoted the sport at the Conference League level in Oxford. After another sudden surprise closure of that club, Allen has moved further up the country and league structure to take on promotional duties at the Coventry Bees. Despite his admittance to the inner sanctum of the British speedway hierarchy, he still has some pertinent questions: "Who was at the Speedway Fayre last weekend? Coventry Speedway with Chris Harris, Rory Schlein, Colin Platt and me all with proper stands? Buster was there for King's Lynn too, though without a proper stand, but apart from that, who was there? Today I brought Sam Ermolenko[2] along but, again, there's nobody else! All the promoters care about is their own business – simple as that! They're not interested in history or tradition! Their club is as far as it goes. The BSPA pretends to be an Association but everyone just looks out for themselves and not the overall interests of the sport. Look at the people here today, they're all very keen but there aren't many of them. This year is the eightieth anniversary of speedway starting in this country and you'd think that we could make a lot more of it than this!" After these brief but passionate words Allen moves off to rejoin Sam Ermolenko who now has the avuncular Bert Harkins by his side. There are many riders from yesteryear in the crowd, but I'm too young to recognise let alone name them. Stood by my table as they survey the small but crowded exhibition area, a man remarks to his friend, "don't worry, it'll soon empty out, most of these have to go for an afternoon nap shortly!"

Martin Dadswell prepares his display

One sugar for Bill Gimbeth and John Rich

17th February High Beech 80th Anniversary Celebration

---

[2] In fact, Sam attended as Allen's business partner because of a project they were working on together at the time. Allen Trump is also probably (one of) the biggest speedway memorabilia collectors in the entire country. He simply loves the collectables, especially photos. Some other financially secure collectors envy him because, in auction, he can automatically outbid them for any item. He just keeps his hand up and outbids any normal non-millionaire rival! At the end of speedway auctions, he has been known to hand over cheques for thousands. Consequently, Allen is a rarity in promotional circles since he has a keen appreciation for the history and previous culture(s) of speedway's bygone days, unlike the majority of his latter-day BSPA fellow promoters!

High Beech: *"Don't worry, it'll soon empty out, most of these have to got for an afternoon nap shortly!"*

CHAPTER 3.

Sittingbourne:
"His stance on the bike is exactly the same as his dad's!"

2nd March

The programme for the St John Ambulance Trophy and the Nathan Gaymer Memorial Trophy proudly proclaims that Sittingbourne Speedway Club specialise "In Amateur Speedway Activities". They do this at the Old Gun Site in Raspberry Hill Lane, at Iwade, near Sittingbourne in Kent. Using the description 'programme' is probably putting things a bit strongly since the line ups for the St John Ambulance Trophy and the Nathan Gaymer Memorial Trophy have been copied onto a lime-green piece of A4 paper. Nonetheless, all the information is there and the chance to see at least 30 heats of speedway racing has drawn a good-sized crowd to the track on a cold, blustery but sunny morning. Apart from the race line-ups, great play has also been made about the "easy access" from the Sheppey Bridge junction of the A249. Although, the diehard Sittingbourne loyalists who regularly come to watch their speedway here would probably make the journey irrespective of its ease or difficulty. Built on the time, effort and enthusiasm of numerous volunteers, everything looks to be in place as last-minute preparations occur throughout various locations within the stadium grounds. On the centre green, Start Marshal Ian Glover struggles against the wind as he places the various coloured flags into position while, inevitably, wearing his trademark checked trousers.

I set up my bookstall close to the windowed hut that serves as the refreshment kiosk here. Always popular on any race day, the driving wind forces more fans than usual to stay inside to linger more appreciatively in the shelter and warmth of its environs. My position gives me an ideal view over the senior track but also, if I glance behind me in the opposite direction, I can also see the junior racing track. Today, as usual when there's racing on the senior track, this is used as an additional car park for various riders' vans and other assorted vehicles. Thousands of people – even me, in fact – have now taken their first tentative turns of the wheels of a high-powered speedway bike on the training tracks at Sittingbourne. Nowadays this is done under the expert eye of training instructors Stuart Lee-Amies, Paul Heller and Ken Hubble. Unlike me, many people take to riding a speedway bike like a duck to water. Rather like the triumphant return from a successful fishing trip or a notable game of golf, the desire to tell people about what you've achieved or your overall experience is incredibly strong. Stood by my table, a man called Frank is one such gleeful evangelist for the speedway training experience at Sittingbourne. "I ride with the older boys. We've all got used to each other now, plus we all want to get to work on a Monday. [Nods towards the senior race track in front of us]. Whereas the youngsters they don't think about it or the need for elbow room and just go for it. Trouble is they don't have much spatial awareness. You only get that by bumping into things and they certainly do that a lot! When people stand on this side of the fence they're full of opinions about what the riders – and the promoters – should do. But once you get on that track, it all falls away and is irrelevant compared to the racing! Until you've tried it you just don't know."

Shortly afterwards, Sittingbourne Speedway Club's Press Officer (and contributor to the Stoke Speedway programme), Derek Barclay, stops for a word. Our talk quickly turns from speedway to other matters, in this instance my new Sunderland photo book, *Banter & Bustle*. It's a kind of football version of *Shale Britannia*. Never afraid to stereotype, Derek tells me authoritatively, "They're all criminals in Sunderland, aren't they?" News that the football Premier League at one point threatened to reserve the option to sue me over the inclusion of photographs taken inside football stadiums on match day (but not featuring the match itself) Derek laughs and says, "that's a step up from Ian Perkin!" Away from the track Derek is a long-time fanatical supporter of the sadly now defunct Wimbledon Speedway Club and also a leading advocate of the skill and thrills provided by veteran speedway rider Buzz Burrows on the CL version of the track. He is also a regular contributor to the *British Speedway Forum* and in this week's (March 1st) has written the Sittingbourne Crusaders track review of 2007. Derek has an engaging writing style but has inadvertently landed himself in hot water on Internet forums with his identification of and written comments about the so-called "season low" of an away defeat for the Crusaders at Oxford Speedway. He'd written, "The latter [defeat was sad] not just for the size of the 50-point gap, but that so little respect had been forthcoming from the hosts who seemed very bitter about the one-point defeat they'd suffered out in Kent just a week earlier." Comments upon an away loss of 71-21 would usually attract little further analysis except during the quiet months of the close season when fans, desperate for speedway news, scour the Bible of the sport to slake their methanol cravings. Such club overviews are presented as the authoritative gloss of the previous season (in this case 2007). Like Derek, I wasn't at the meeting so can't really comment on the attitude or otherwise of the Oxford fans, riders and management. However, people who were there have subsequently highlighted that traffic chaos on the M40 meant that Crusaders rider Harland Cook was delayed when he became snarled in said traffic. In order to allow Harland time to get to the stadium, the Oxford club took the decision to run a couple of second-half races at the start of the meeting to ensure that the Sittingbourne side weren't further weakened during the early heats by the late arrival of one of their riders. This flexible approach doesn't seem indicative of a club keen to win at all costs let alone one that failed to show their rivals "respect".

Dance of the deckchairs

If the *British Speedway Forum* attracts forthright opinions, then another site called the Weird World of Subedei is an Internet forum where posters comment on speedway matters with remarkable frankness. Indeed, the common language of men and a refreshing cynicism percolates throughout the various topics discussed by its members on this forum. They even have an award called the "Flapperjack of the Week". This isn't an award that anyone in speedway would necessarily go out of their way to covet. The FotW award has been previously won by many luminaries with connections to the shale and these include characters like John Postlethwaite, Nigel Pearson, Kelvin Tatum MBE and Haringey Council. To this list of august names, can now be added that of Derek Barclay. Anyone who rushes to their dictionary to check the exact meaning of the word "Flapperjack" will be sadly disappointed as I suspect your dictionary, like mine, offers no direct translation. Suffice to say, certain words shouldn't be used in polite company or, even, on the Internet. So, instead, in a weird example of a kind of speedway version of metonymy on this website a coded alternative word is used to stand in place of the more explicitly descriptive word that the posters would really like to use. The choice of winner usually requires lengthy debate amongst the forum posters about the relative merits/demerits of various alternative candidates. Ultimately the bad grace of his comment wins Derek the "week 34–week 35" FotW award.

Pre race manoeuvres

Such matters are irrelevant to the fans in attendance today since we've all come to enjoy a bumper afternoon of racing. One of the joys of speedway is the large number of people you get to meet who share your love and passion for the sport. Today I'm privileged to meet one of the country's leading blues musicians, South London based Bard of Bromley, Billy Jenkins who's here along with his wife (and poet) Jill Tritton. After I published my first book *Showered in Shale* and toured the country trying to sell it (while also writing my blog), Billy got in touch via e-mail to offer his congratulations, sympathy and support. Since then Billy has taken it upon himself to fulfil many roles ranging from advisor through to agony aunt. He has also very kindly read and commented upon every single word of my subsequent books, *Shifting Shale* and *Concrete for Breakfast*. This is a mammoth and time-consuming task that he has undertaken voluntarily and without payment (along with my other generous advisors, Caroline Tidmarsh and Vy Shepherd). His eye for repetition, his knowledge of the sport and keen appreciation of technical detail has been invaluable in ensuring my howlers are kept to a minimum and help make the manuscripts what they are. It's a genuine surprise and pleasure

Billy Jenkins

Sittingbourne: *"His stance on the bike is exactly the same as his dad's!"*

to finally get to meet him. Apart from his musical work, Billy is a Humanist Funeral Officiant for the Britsh Humanist Association. In old money, this means that Billy conducts their funeral services for the inreasing number of people who don't wish to have a religious ceremony. Wrapped up against the cold, Billy's eye is immediately caught by one of the riders listed as taking part in the St John Ambulance Trophy. "Oh good, Marc Bibby – do you think he's the son of Jack Bibby – the old Crayford Highwayman rider! I loved him as a second half rider at Hackney who always really tried but never quite made it. Actually he did make it to the team but didn't get anywhere really. He had a lovely leg-trailing style!"

This afternoon we are treated to the alternating races of the St John Ambulance Trophy and the Nathan Gaymer Memorial Trophy. As usual, since this is Sittingbourne Speedway, there are a number of keen but less youthful riders out on the shale this afternoon along with teenagers. One of these riders in heat 1 is indeed Jack Bibby, who wears the green helmet and rides what looks like an old JAP bike that repeatedly stalls before it gets to the start line. Fortunately for him, Start Marshal Ian Glover is on hand to push him until the engine fires back into life. Over the loudspeakers Derek Barclay informs us about one competitor, whose name I don't quite catch, "the total age of bike and rider is 110 years." Once the tapes rise, like the rest of the field, Jack Bibby takes it tentatively into the first corner but then quickly gains enough confidence to have a neck-and-neck race with Chris Neame for the next four laps. They ride so closely and evenly together that you imagine they're part of some formation speedway display team who've spent so long together they've managed to almost synchronize their every movement into perfect harmony. Though not conducted at the breakneck speed of the professionals, this heat 1 battle in the St John Ambulance Trophy has lit Billy's imagination. Jack's son Marc also competes for the same trophy and during heat 7 Billy exclaims, "His stance on the bike is exactly the same as his dad's!" A short while later Billy spots one of the helmetless rider heroes of his youth, "Blimey! Jack Bibby is like an old man! I suppose he is 'cause he was a youngster when he rode for the Crayford Kestrels, which was around 1977–1978, so it's been a while!"

When not transfixed by the racing or engaging conversation with Billy and Jill, I'm stood by my books answering occasional questions posed by passers by. Over the tannoy, Derek Barclay tells the assembled crowd, "Over there on the trellis table is Jeff Scott with Robert Bamford's latest *Speedway Yearbook*. It's better than it has been in other years and his other books in which he slags me off for some reason! I don't know why?" There isn't a rush of purchasers but I'm joined by a passer-by called Robin, who's happy to reminisce about his experiences watching speedway: "Me mum used to do the St John Ambulance at Hackney so I've been brought up with it. Barry Thomas was my idol and I was sitting 10 yards away when Vic Harding got killed in front of me at Hackney. So I know it's dangerous! When I rode at King's Lynn with that mad Norwegian, what's his name? – Olle Nygren – it was fantastic! Me mate had just had a messy divorce and couldn't see his kids so he said 'I don't care if I get hurt', so I said, 'what about trying speedway?' So we came here. When Graham [Arnold] did it, he could just go for it but with Paul [Heller] things changed and he put the emphasis on safety – you have to! Everything you've learnt on a motorbike previously you have to do the opposite of. So, rather than slow down at a corner, you speed up! If you slow down you straighten up and find the fence. It's more dangerous to do that anyway. We stopped in the end. Me mate broke his collarbone after he fell off after I fell and he caught my front peg. I've known him since we were kids but the competitiveness of it all was coming between us! It was great fun but, when it became more cut throat between us, there was no point carrying on then."

Ironically in a trophy competition designed to raise money for the St John Ambulance (as a thank you for all their efforts), one of the riders is prostrate on the track receiving lengthy treatment. Before the meeting, Sittingbourne Incident Recorder, Chris Golding, had joked, "If they're dead we'll chuck them over the fence, if not we'll give them some treatment!" While we wait for the action to start again, Derek Barclay holds forth at great length. He regales the crowd with a welter of statistics and observations. Due to the planning permission conditions in operation at the Old Gun Site, there are no musical interludes. Music at speedway isn't something you don't consciously miss until you suddenly notice its absence or wonder why the gap between each race has started to drag slightly. Luckily, Derek is on hand to fill the silences. Sometimes accurately and sometimes not if judged by his apologies for some inadvertent, ongoing errors. "One of the facts I got wrong, I said," is the remark that prefaces one such lengthy correction, before he concludes, "and it's so unusual for me to get anything wrong, isn't it?" The clearly audible sound of laughter from his colleagues in the officials' box perched (on an old WWII military gun emplacement) high above the Sittingbourne Speedway start line echoes through the stadium over the public-address system.

2nd March
St John Ambulance Trophy Winner: Charlie Heatley
Nathan Gaymer Memorial Trophy Winner: Jerran Hart

Sittingbourne: *"His stance on the bike is exactly the same as his dad's!"*

CHAPTER 4.
King's Lynn v. Ipswich:
"Can you tell us what you just told the lads on the truck about the last race, without the expletives?"

12th March

Since Easter falls in March this year, the 2008 speedway season can start before March 15th. The fifth day of the 2008 speedway season (after it was brought forward to start on March 8th) has drawn me to East Anglia where a strong, chill wind blows metaphorically through speedway and also literally through the Norfolk Arena. Rule changes agreed over the winter mean that the aggregate bonus point has been abolished and replaced with the incentive of 3 points for an away win. Another innovation that came out of the BSPA Annual Conference was the decision to introduce the concept of promotion and relegation between the Elite and Premier Leagues. Based on the performances of 2007, it wouldn't be a complete surprise to find that both King's Lynn and Ipswich race in the inaugural meetings for this new qualification system. Popular opinion has it that the introduction of this end of season contest is purely a cosmetic exercise but also a useful money-spinning opportunity (rumoured to be worth £100,000+) to entice a large crowd to end-of-season play-off matches for the EL promotions who have struggled at the bottom of the table. A late-season boost to finances sounds a compelling enough reason for its implementation since, realistically, the strength and depth of any Elite League team – even at the end of a motivation-sapping poor season – should be more than enough to see off any erstwhile Premier League competitor (assuming they have both the inclination and interest to make a serious attempt to gain promotion to the senior tier of British speedway). The proof will be in the pudding but an Inter-League challenge between these two East Anglian rivals definitely provides an engaging season opener.

It's the first time that the Ipswich Witches have returned to the Norfolk Arena to race competitively in more than five years. Previous meetings have seen feelings run high between riders and track staff with Shane Parker (then of King's Lynn) famously trying to hijack the Foxhall Heath tractor to grade the Ipswich track. Albeit without success since he couldn't get the vehicle in gear and his erstwhile helper, Buster Chapman, was unceremoniously rugby tackled by Witches staff before he could offer any meaningful suggestions about operating procedures. While these incidents are fondly recalled in their programme notes (and pictured on its front cover), Keith and Jonathan Chapman also look forward to the possibility of a successful 2008 season in all competitions. They relish the possibility that they might record 100 successive home wins in competitive Premier League meetings. They also hold out hopes that they might retain the KO Cup for a fourth successive season and the Premier Trophy for a third. The management of King's Lynn speedway definitely promote their club to their local area aggressively and, while hyperbole is always part of the equation, the team they have assembled for this season indicates that many if not all these goals remain achievable.

Invariably, whenever you visit the Norfolk Arena, further investments have seen changes made to the stadium infrastructure. Though I have no detailed list of these, it's clear that the club have started to tarmac the stadium car park and also, very noticeably, further decorated the now rather spruce home-straight bar. The bar building itself now features a new glass side door that enables easier access from the area just after the entrance turnstiles. The club programme seller, Nannette, has already set out a substantial pile of programmes under the roof of a shelter adjacent to the bar, its new door and, of course, the stadium trackshop. The trackshop remains located inside a ski-chalet-type wooden building that wouldn't look out of place on a skiing holiday to the French Alps organised by Rye House promoter Len Silver. Bustling past on his way to duties unknown in another part of the stadium, a preoccupied Buster Chapman has little time for small talk and responds to my question as to his general health with a terse, "I'm freakin' terrible – this wind is a nightmare!"

Inside the warmth of the trackshop, Johnny Barber and Mike Moseley have already resumed their familiar positions behind the display counter piled high with the latest King's Lynn logoed and branded merchandise. The talk of the shop is the "new look King's Lynn Wulfsport jacket" which has been designed to exacting specifications by fashionable co-promoter and man-about-town, Jonathan Chapman. He has definitely designed a truly distinctive garment drawn from the Macey Gray School of Dress Sense ("It was like she'd been spun round 10 times, blindfolded and thrown into pantomime wardrobe and told, whatever you land on you'll wear on stage tonight"). However these jackets were inspired, my mother would definitely view such garments as "fashion items" rather than must have accessories you'd purchase to ensure that you keep dry and warm. Whatever its insulation quality, the jacket already definitely attracts strong reactions. Sadly for Enjay Designs (who, Mike Moseley tells us in his slightly partisan programme notes, "provide superb ranges of merchandise" and "are now the largest company of their kind in Great Britain") the new range of King's Lynn 2008 shirts they also produced for the Press and Practice Day were immediately rejected by Jonathan Chapman. Apparently because the club nickname hadn't quite been presented on the garment to his complete satisfaction, "the word Stars had a yellow border and he absolutely demanded a white border saying, 'we're trying to build a bloody brand here, you know!' He then found further fault with the shirt – seemingly the Banham Poultry Ltd logo was too small!"

For their own amusement, each week Mike and Johnny forecast the likely score prior to the meeting. For this inter-league challenge meeting Mike nominates 38-52, whereas Johnny goes for a 45-all draw. Johnny is sceptical, "If it's 38-52 they'll [the Ipswich riders] get a rocket up their arse from John Louis 'cause it'll kill the gate. It would be a disaster. I dunno – 'cause I'm a promoter's son – I can say that. They'd much prefer a 2-point win for King's Lynn so that all the Ipswich fans and all the King's Lynn fans turn up in force. Before Ipswich win, of course!" My news that Buster already looks worn down by the stress of the first meeting prompts sympathetic comment from Johnny, "no promoter is ever happy past the first meeting of the season 'cause everyone hassles them from then on!"

In a multimedia age, just sending a press release to the local newspaper will no longer cut it when so many people access their information online. Jonathan Chapman produces a relentless stream of breathlessly excited press releases throughout the season and the glamour of this East Anglian Derby meeting between Ipswich and King's Lynn has attracted a large BBC van with white satellite dishes to the club car park. Someone I gather must be a reporter of some kind (judged by the headphones and microphone he carries in his hand) accosts Jonathan Chapman and demands, "Can you turn the music down a bit? I'm not saying off – but down a bit – so we can record a piece for tonight!" The quality of the loudspeaker system is another investment the Chapmans can quite rightly feel proud of at their club since, unlike the strain on your ears often enforced at many other tracks in the country, there is absolutely no danger that we won't be able to hear announcements, *bon mots* from Mike Bennett or savour the music. Jonathan smiles at the request and asks, "Are you *BBC Radio Norfolk*?" Shrinking from the misapprehension and any possible connection with Alan Partridge, the headphoned man from *BBC Look East* snaps back, "No! We're the telly!" On the subject of lavish photographic work and slick presentations, DVD entrepreneur and club presenter Mike Bennett stops by my bookstall to enquire, "tell me, what on earth are you doing here tonight?" My reply that "it's the excitement and 'cause it's invigorating", fails to convince him. Mike shakes his head, "why don't you choose another adjective! [Shivers theatrically] They say it's a summer sport!"

It appears anyone who is anyone has a microphone in their hand tonight. Mike clutches his tightly while he takes the opportunity to promote my wares over the public-address system to the small number of people who have bothered to make their way into the stadium since the gates opened 10 minutes ago. "Jeff is here with his *Yearbook* – I'll be plugging it profusely all night 'cause I've got a copy!" Jonathan Chapman gleefully shouts to Mike Bennett as he passes, "There's your biggest fan there!" Mike Bennett displays great interest in the gratis, new look version of Robert Bamford's *2008 Speedway Yearbook*, so I jovially remark, "it must be nice that one of my books contains no disparaging comments about you!" The self-imagined master of repartee – quick as a flash – replies that he doesn't suffer from catagelophobia, "it's water off a duck's back to me! You've got to remember I've been in this business for 20 years so I've developed the skin of a rhino and know that I'm lower in people's esteem than an estate agent!" Earlier I'd heard Jonathan say you now needed a dongle at the Norfolk Arena and I wonder if this might be Mike's nickname in these parts? Shortly afterwards, Jonathan beckons Mike over and they move away to conduct their subsequent conspiratorial conversation in greater privacy. Quite what exactly they talk about will remain an eternal mystery but two minutes later the rhino-skinned Master of Ceremonies says over the tannoy, "I forgot to mention, the trackshop has some fantastic fashionable brand new jackets this year and beenie hats! They're especially good on the follicly challenged." Over the loudspeakers each week, Mike gives the strong impression that he'd walk a million miles for one of his own smiles.

Jonathan Chapman is in ebullient mood about prospects for the season ahead. "Sounds funny, but I'm even more excited about our prospects now that Rusty has come here. He's fitted in well, looks good on the track and I love it when we can turn round a rider no one else wants! We haven't failed doing that yet and I love it!" Jonathan sports the new-look King's Lynn anorak and is clearly proud enough to do an Anthea Redfern-style twirl. "Do you like the design of the jacket? I done it! If Wulfsport had done it I doubt it would have looked so good! They normally have the badge on the front in the centre and, when you open it when it gets warmer, you can't see who it is! Whereas you can read 'Stars' on this one! I'll get all our sponsors on the sleeves and also get all our championships on it![1]. And I'm also gonna get a memorial notice to Ashley Jones put on. I reckon the fans will love them! It should be a big crowd tonight – the weather's been good all day although this wind's a bit cold."

Blimey, is it speedway already?

Inside the warmth of trackshop Johnny playfully remarks, "I hear the Sultan of Cheese has mentioned the *Yearbook*." Talk of the *Yearbook* prompts Mike Moseley to ask, "Do you know about all the mistakes in the *Yearbook*?" Even though I'm the publisher, I genuinely haven't heard any feedback about so-called errors. I quiz Mike further and hear news of a deeper, structural problem. "There has been a problem with the way that some of the refs record tapes offence exclusions. Many of them have been putting down "T" in the programmes, which means excluded for a tapes offence [Actually, Appendix E of the Rulebook says this should be recorded as "E"] and counts as a ride. Whereas, when riders have been excluded under the two-minute warning or for delaying the start, they should have put down "M" [Actually, Appendix E of the Rulebook says this should be recorded as "N2"] to be correct and that doesn't count as a ride. So when the programmes get sent to the BSPA presumably they get collated incorrectly into the results and averages. I don't know how many times this has happened but Rob Bamford will know and be able to tell you!" All SCB officials have now compulsorily embraced technology in their work. However, rumour has it, that the referee with fiercest resistance to adoption of the new-fangled laptop technology to reduce 'unforced' errors, ironically also has the most indecipherable handwriting – step forward: Dave Dowling.

New anoraks on the centre green

If the ability of the referees to fill out their programmes correctly causes doubt then Mike Moseley also has concerns about the scorecard in the new-look King's Lynn programme. I don't wish to sound like the pernickety, design 'guru' Howard Jones (the regular reviewer of programme layout typography and design who writes in the) but Mike quite correctly highlights that the use of colour in the new-look 2008 King's Lynn version of this document makes it almost impossible to make legible changes to the team line-up. Obviously, this is only important should, perchance, this change. This is not an issue for

[1] At the rate they've won trophies over recent years, they'll need enough sleeves to fit an octopus.

King's Lynn v. Ipswich: *"Can you tell us what you just told the lads on the truck about the last race, without the expletives?"*

tonight's meeting but, in the normal run of things, speedway line-ups regularly alter. These changes can be for many reasons, ranging from injury to the latest altered averages. Should there have been any reason to do so, making changes would be almost impossible for either team line-up. The programme presents the King's Lynn riders in white letters on a solid black background while, for the Ipswich team, we have yellow letters on a royal blue background. "I have to ask, how are you supposed to make team changes on that?" declares Mike rhetorically as he waves his programme around for additional dramatic effect.

Suddenly the car park looks full, there's a queue at the turnstiles and demand for the programmes is high. So much so that Nannette and her helper have very little time to rest let alone chat. Given it's the first meeting of the season after a speedwayless winter, many people want to have a cheery but brief word as they shuffle along the line to purchase either the programme or the raffle tickets. One fan with a cricked neck offers us all some of his chocolate-covered Brazil nuts ("Take two, they're moreish"). With little time left before the tapes fly up to start another season, Mike Bennett enthuses over the tannoy, "It's been a long old winter but we're BACK and welcoming our old friends from Ipswich. We've missed you!" After more verbiage and piffle, we're treated to an interview with Jonathan Chapman who uncontroversially informs us, "The boys in the pits are so up for it and for putting on a good show!" Keen to enter into the banter, Ipswich promoter John Louis when interviewed remarks, "He's always looking for a bit of an advantage, it's so dark on our side of the pits that poor old Chris [Louis] can't see what he's doing! A bloke came to look at it but then went away again without fixing it! I think Jonathan wants to save a bit of electricity." At the sound of his name being taken in vain, the ebullient Jonathan butts in to rebut allegations of parsimoniousness, "John must realise we haven't done it deliberately. Dunno why he's complaining about the lights here when there ain't no lights down there [Foxhall Heath] anyway!" Keen to throw off (as yet unstated) accusations that this is a meaningless warm-up fixture, John Louis intones his reply in the bored manner of a man reading a prepared speech, "We're really going to go for it! If the riders don't give it 100%, they're the ones who'll regret it when we get home!" Sounds like it could be smacked bottoms, no tea and straight to bed for any miscreants in the Ipswich team.

Never afraid to ask a platitudinous question or ten, Mike Bennett buttonholes King's Lynn Stars team manager, Rob Lyon, for his thoughts on the squad they've assembled for the 2008 season. "I think everyone has a little bit of improvement in them!" Talk of the need for improvement doesn't bother Mike Bennett, let alone throw him off his platitudinous stride and, even though a wheel has yet to be turned, he tells us with faux authority, "There's already a great team spirit in the pits – seeing Kevin [Doolan] with a smile on his face lifts everybody!" Luxuriating in the glow of the Aussies' smile and vibrant team spirit, Rob Lyon then adds, "this is the best one-to-seven I've ever worked with, I think!" Amazing how these things can look so obvious before the riders have turned a wheel, let alone had a competitive race. The subject of excitement and keenly contested racing is a topic close to Mike Bennett's heart. Indeed, it underpins every waking moment of the staff at his burgeoning multimedia empire, "The DVD of last season is the best double DVD we've ever produced! The two discs contain all the action from last season and it's on sale now!"

Long-time King's Lynn speedway fan, Pete Brennan, continues to amaze with his tenacity to resist his apparently terminal illness. He moves his wheelchair conspiratorially close to my table to theatrically whisper, "Do you know anyone who wants to come and take a photo of my living room? The walls are lined with photographs. I've met them all: Split Waterman, Peter Craven, Ove Fundin MBE, all the greats! The only two I didn't like were Tommy Price, who was rude to me when I was five (I'll never forget it, you could sense how mean he was) – and Anders Michanek, who once knocked a kid over who was waiting for his autograph and he didn't even look round, let alone say sorry!" Though pride would probably be the wrong word, Pete flourishes a letter on hospital-headed notepaper from his pocket written by his heart surgeon/consultant. It covers quite a few complicated health issues but the phrase that really leaps out from the page says, "his condition is inoperable." Fortunately, the Norfolk Arena is one of the country's most wheelchair-friendly speedway stadiums so Pete can wheel away to find one of the many good vantage points from which wheelchair-bound supporters can enjoy the spectacle of the racing.

The parade truck makes its way onto the track and, as it slowly circles the circuit, Mike Bennett (who's also on board) keeps up a running commentary while the riders wave to the fans, "No changes in the programme which is great! All the riders are as per programme – how often can you say that?" Reaction to the parade truck is too muted for Mike's satisfaction, "Come on! Come on! Clap your hands! It'll keep you warm." A polite ripple of applause greets this

---

King's Lynn v. Ipswich: *"Can you tell us what you just told the lads on the truck about the last race, without the expletives?"*

suggestion. Since the racing hasn't yet started, it is legally permissible to take a photograph with a flash camera from the terraces and, even though there are 14 riders on the parade truck, Mike Bennett naturally assumes that the majority of photographs will be of him. "Look, an Ipswich flasher – there's lots of those! Come on! Nobody is making any noise for the riders." Though the riders look keen to head back to the comparative warmth of the pits, they still have the formality of Mike Bennett's lengthy introduction of them to the catatonic crowd. "Trust me this will be the quickest parade in history ever!" The Ipswich riders get comparatively short shrift before Mike embarks on a lengthy encomium about each King's Lynn rider that eventually finishes with a paean of praise to returning Australian Kevin Doolan. "He's got a real determination to get us back into the Elite League, that's why he's come back here: Kevin Doolan!"

No sooner have the riders retreated back to the pits than the first two-minute warning of the season at the Norfolk Arena is sounded by referee Jim Lawrence. All four riders proceed in an easterly direction from the pits to the start line – Tomas Topinka and Shaun Tacey will get the King's Lynn season under way, while Robert Miskowiak (whose name Mike pronounces as "MICK-CO-WEE-ACK") is partnered by his Ipswich colleague Piotr Swiderski. Rather unnecessarily we're then told, "The action is kicking off tonight with heat number 1, as usual." It's a revelation that's followed up a few moments later with yet more mind-boggling news, "So, off we go, on what is – on paper – a very interesting clash!" The first race of the season features yet another win at the Norfolk Arena for track specialist Tomas Topinka and, with Shaun Tacey last, the points are shared. From a home fans' perspective, the entertainment levels will sharply drop from this point onwards because the Ipswich Witches then go on to record 10 heat advantages (in sharp contrast to the home team's meagre single heat advantage). Stuck out on the centre green or in the pits every week, Mike Bennett clearly harbours some suspicions that his words of wisdom will be regularly drowned out by the CD player operative located in the referee's box perched high in the grandstand. "Tell you what we'll try this year, I'll do a dedication, and you'll turn the music off! [music blares incredibly loudly] Oh, OK, we won't turn it off!"

Judged by how the riders struggle to control their machines, either they failed to get enough pre-season practice in to settle back into a smooth groove or, alternatively, track conditions work against them. It soon becomes apparent that the track is the cause of their collective difficulties. Never one to shirk responsibility, Buster Chapman is soon on the centre green to apologise and explain, "Sorry about the track but we have had extreme weather conditions. There's a lot of dust in this wind. Sorry about that, it [the wind] didn't start today until about 2 p.m. We would have put water down but the riders didn't want it as it would turn to ice and be very dangerous for them to ride." One rider who immediately stands out as likely to race round the track in somewhat harum-scarum fashion – whatever the conditions – is Kozza Smith. "All action" would be words you would use to describe his approach to travel at speed on a speedway bike. Clearly he has latent ability and promise on a bike as well as judged by the way he beats the experienced Steve Johnston for third place in heat 3. This race also sees Kevin Doolan head his erstwhile rival (and ex-team mate) Chris Louis, though any hope of a King's Lynn fightback held out by this heat advantage disappears almost at the moment it materialises. If the track causes some riders difficulty, then the start tapes are no less easy to cope with. Simon Lambert gets his helmet stuck in them during the initial attempt to run heat 4 and, though Lambert would win many marks for artistic merit, referee Jim Lawrence still has no choice but to exclude him. To shelter from the biting wind I rush back to the trackshop while over the tannoy Mike Bennett describes the merits of Robert Bamford's *Yearbook*, "it says here 'it's an indispensable guide'". Johnny Barber laughs, "That's a bit sarcastic isn't it?" The club's Community Liaison Officer, Nathan Hollands, joins us in the trackshop where he models the XXL sized version of the King's Lynn 2008 anorak and sings its praises, "What I like about it is that there's tons of room for a jumper underneath it!" Talk soon turns to the track and Johnny gnomically notes, "The fact that the riders didn't want the track watered says it all!"

To entertain but also distract us from the cold, Mike Bennett interviews Kevin Doolan, albeit only to quiz about the future prospects of his fellow Australian and team mate, Kozza Smith. Mike correctly notes, "You just want to keep him on the bike!" In fact, by his own calculations Kozza would fall 70 times during the 2008 season. Reluctant to criticise someone still in search of his metaphorical feet within the sport and who's a recent arrival into this country, Kevin contents himself with an assertive "He'll get there!" Shaun Tacey further demonstrates that conditions remain tricky when he falls on the apex of the last bend on the second lap of heat 6. It doesn't cost King's Lynn any points since Shaun had already been relegated to the back of the field. In the referee's box, after he's confirmed the result,

King's Lynn v. Ipswich: *"Can you tell us what you just told the lads on the truck about the last race, without the expletives?"*

Edwin Overland sympathises: "A very awkward-looking fall for Shaun Tacey there!"

Back in the trackshop Jonathan Chapman – the Giovanni Versace of speedway jacket design – has rushed in to quiz Johnny and Mike about sales volumes of the new anoraks. "How are the jackets going?" Not wishing to give too much away, Johnny reveals "they're going well despite the gold lettering." Despite the fact that to the neutral onlooker the majority of Ipswich riders look considerably sharper from the gate, Jonathan is already quick to admire what he has seen from the Lynn riders. "I tell you what – Topinka and Doolan are going to be 11-point men in the Premium League this year – no one is gonna touch them!" While Jonathan helps himself to one of the new King's Lynn beenie hats, a fan bursts in to demand, "Do you have any gloves?" Never afraid to highlight a lost sales opportunity Jonathan also chimes in, "Yeah, why haven't we got any gloves?" Rarely one to leave home without the application of a reasonable amount of hair gel (or exotically coloured hair dye), Jonathan Chapman is often seen at a speedway track with an attractive girl by his side. Tonight is no exception and, to smooth her speedway education, Jonathan introduces her to me with a nonchalant, "Jeff writes books and I'm in them all!" His latest lady friend looks less than impressed. "Why?" Crestfallen, her beau changes the subject, "There's really no answer to that! Come on, I don't want to miss this race!"

The rerun of heat 6 sees Jarek Hampel easily beat Tomas Topinka from the gate. In fact, Hampel looks a class apart all evening and rides to a supremely untroubled maximum 15 points from his five rides. The Ipswich Witches pile on the agony with a maximum heat win in heat 7 engineered by the partnership of Steve Johnston and Chris Louis, who have an impressive combined age of 76 years. I tell Johnny that I'm hopeful that the next race will see the start of the King's Lynn fightback in the form of a race win from 'Lambo Rambo'. "You mean 'Rambo Lambo', get it right mate – Mike Bennett's copyrighted it. It's better than the 'Nerminator' – Daniel Nermark went up to him and said 'Actually, mate I hate that, can you stop using it?' and we never heard it again after that!"

On the centre green, Mike Bennett has managed to corner Ipswich reserve Chris Schramm for a brief interview and, somehow, manages to resist the urge to coin an unwanted moniker for the Essex-born rider. "If I'd stayed in the Premier League, I'd have got a lot older. I wanted to double up so couldn't so this is the best option." Ever keen to showcase his razor-like wit and parade his speedway knowledge, Mike Bennett asks another of his trademark carefully researched questions. "A lot of the Elite League tracks will be completely new to you, won't they?" A nonplussed but polite Schramm covers his goof, "Ah yeh, well, I've been to all of them before except Belle Vue!" Moments later, temporarily without anyone to quiz, Mike says the first thing that comes into his head and thereby, inadvertently, reveals his own unique take on the Jonathan Chapman designed King's Lynn Wulfsport anoraks, "I can say the jacket is wind resistant but doesn't keep you warm!" On a cold night, an unreserved recommendation like that really should ensure the fans flock to buy them from the trackshop.

Things have got so bad on the interviewee front that Mike is soon reduced to quoting things that he's read in the local press, "It said in the local paper that Chris Louis was offered the job of England Manager but turned it down to concentrate on his riding – and good luck to him." With heat 13 nearly upon us, Mike does his duty and name checks the race sponsor. "McCartney Food Services – a new sponsor for this season – for all your Catering and Janitorial Needs." I have to say that if you decided to start a new business that linked together two distinct and separate skills areas, then catering and janitorial work wouldn't exactly immediately strike you as a marriage made in heaven! Nonetheless, there might be some sort of bizarre business logic in this decision but, sadly, Mike is unable to enlighten us. One thing is for sure, any company that sponsors their local speedway club – no matter how recondite their products or services are – deserve to be supported or, at least, applauded. The early failure to water the track has – by this late stage of the evening – made this part of Norfolk closely resemble the Gobi Desert in a sandstorm, albeit without the camels. The combination of a strong wind and flying grit creates a dust storm that batters the riders and fans alike. It's definitely not a night to savour a sherbet Dip Dab. Packing the minor places in heat 13 allows King's Lynn to gain a modicum of success in the shape of their second drawn heat in succession. That said, Jarek Hampel wins by the country mile ahead of Tomas Topinka who's usually invincible around the Norfolk Arena during most Premier League meetings. This drawn heat result has an element of good fortune about it since Miskowiak has an engine failure on the third bend of the third lap when lying second.

With the score at a somewhat embarrassing 30-50, back in the trackshop a smiling Johnny Barber exclaims, "So maybe speedway isn't fixed!" The young Australian Kozza Smith has been good value all evening and further illustrates his future potential in heat 14 when – on the first lap – he forces his way up the inside of Chris Schramm and ruthlessly drives him towards the fence to gain second place. Once ahead Smith is difficult to pass since he fails to ride anything like a consistent line for the remainder of the race. The race winner is Steve Johnston whose victory is commented upon approvingly by Edwin Overland, "he enjoyed that one in a nervous sort of way". Even though the meeting had ended as a contest much earlier in the night, the line-up for the nominated heat 15 pits the King's Lynn top two of Topinka and Doolan against Hampel and Swiderski for the Witches. As he ambles from the trackshop to the edge of the track to look through the highest fence in British speedway, Johnny Barber notes, "Hampel's out in [heat] 15, he must be on flat money tonight!" The few fans that have already left the stadium in order to beat the rush out of the crowded car park miss out on a superb exhibition of competitive speedway racing. Keen to restore his battered pride on the night, Tomas Topinka shoves Hampel aggressively in the first corner to gain the lead. Hampel proceeds to patiently track him for the next three laps and wait for the opportunity to pass. Oblivious to the duel ahead, Kevin Doolan initially leads Swiderski before the Pole powers under him on the third bend. The third bend is to prove popular since, on the final lap, Hampel also uses it to blast under Topinka for the lead and, thereby, create a gap so large that Swiderski is nearly able to follow him through it. As they trundle back from the safety fence to the trackshop Mike Moseley wittily notes "It must be your first away win in 20 years!" Johnny is having none of it: "We won at Mildenhall two years ago."

Mike Bennett proceeds to entertains the fans that still linger inside the stadium with frequent mentions of the DVD from tonight's encounter that will shortly be available from his company. The last race would definitely be worth watching again, but quite what pent-up demand there will be from King's Lynn fans keen to watch a repeat of their 34-58 defeat remains unclear. Whatever their collective inclinations, subliminal advertising isn't the Bennett way so we're treated to frequent almost Tourette-like explanations about the various features of said forthcoming DVD. [I count four mentions in less than five minutes].

To break up the commercial advertising Mike brings his customary charm and diplomacy to bear in a post-meeting interview with Tomas Topinka. "Can you tell us what you just told the lads on the truck about the last race, without the expletives?" This line of questioning provokes no meaningful response so, instead, Mike tries a follow-up question. "Three and half laps in front of Jarek Hampel and you nearly did it!" "But I didn't!" replies a slightly exasperated-sounding Topinka. Less than sympathetic Mike replies, "Yeah – 'cause you stuffed it up!"

Despite the heavy defeat, an upbeat Johnny Barber believes that King's Lynn have assembled a side to challenge for Premier League honours during the 2008 season. "Tomas Topinka and Kevin Doolan will always score highly. Shaun – once he gets used to the track again – will score 5 or 6 every week with some 9s or 10s as well. Kozza Smith is gonna score or fall! And he will fall less often as the season progresses. John Oliver just needs to get his confidence back after his injuries and Simon Lambert always tries hard and can go well here. So the only question mark is, really, how will Rusty Harrison do?"

12th March King's Lynn v. Ipswich (Inter-League Challenge) 34-58

CHAPTER 5.

Ipswich v. King's Lynn:
"Oh! Wow! Look at the new programme board!"

13th March

Refreshed after a restful night and fortifying breakfast at one of the country's great but reasonably priced bed-and-breakfast establishments (Lower Farm at Harpley, near King's Lynn), I drive cross-country for the return Inter-League Challenge fixture at Foxhall Heath. There is no wind in Ipswich, but thick dark clouds fill the sky from early afternoon. Inside the stadium, the Barber family have already dressed the trackshop with many new items of 2008 Witches merchandise displayed prominently to attract the eyes of eager Ipswich fans. Judged by the light drizzle that starts to fall before 4 o'clock, the likelihood that any of these will be let into the stadium already looks extremely remote though some of them have already arrived in the car park to wait patiently in their vehicles.

Felixstowe-based Nick Barber has joined his brother Johnny on trackshop duty, "Chris [Louis] says he will be happy with 900 tonight. They'll run tomorrow if it gets rained off!" Diminutive Ipswich Promoter John Louis purposefully walks past the trackshop and, as he goes up the stairs of the building diagonally opposite, calls out, "They say it'll rain till around 6.30 or 7.00 and then we'll have some dry!" The always dapperly dressed and invariably quick-witted Ipswich presenter, Kevin Long, has ducked into the trackshop to shelter out of the light drizzle. He takes a meteorologically optimistic point of view, "The darkest of the clouds aren't over the stadium anymore! But, the wind has dropped, so it's not blowing them through, just like at the Press and Practice." This isn't good news since the Press and Practice Day was abandoned. Nick Barber has a slightly hangdog expression and morosely mutters to no one in particular, "Utter bastard, isn't it?" Contrary to the received opinion held by everyone else, Johnny's weather forecast research indicates a fine evening, "I must be looking at the wrong weather!" The idea of a postponement until the next evening doesn't really delight Nick, "They say the weather forecast is even worse for tomorrow!" Keen to consider the practical details Johnny details the options: "It takes them 45 minutes to lay the track so, as long as it's dry when they do it, we should be alright."

Any trackshop worth their salt will spend the winter months ensuring they have sourced attractive merchandise for the new season ahead. If all speedway fans were like 24-year-old Junior Witches team leader, Nicola Thorpe, then the speedway trackshop business would boom and always be recession proof. She dashes into the trackshop out of the drizzle and asks rhetorically, "How good is this rain then?" When she catches her first sight of the glorious new season's merchandise laid out on the trackshop tables Nicola's face lights up as though Christmas has unexpectedly come early. She squeals loudly, "Oh! Wow! Look at the new programme board!" Clutching the board excitedly she moves on to fondle the new club race jacket, "I won't be buying the new anorak. I don't like the white Witches logo, only the black one." To my untutored eye, the new Ipswich race jacket is festooned with sponsors' logos including the *Evening Star*, Turnkey, Anglia Will Hire, Ambassador Lift Trucks and Result Performance. Nicola's father Pete – who does the programme and is the secretary of the sports club – follows closely behind his daughter and watches proudly as she cannons around the trackshop unable to decide which item of merchandise to enthuse over or savour next. Holding an anorak up for closer inspection she exclaims, "Look, Dad, Nick has found a 3XL." Ever practical Pete asks, "Have you got any scissors to cut the sleeves back?" only to be admonished by his daughter, "Oh Dad! That's the fashion! Oh Dad, how much money have you got on you? Apart from the £300 I owe you from last night?!" Nicola turns to Johnny sat behind the counter "You know, if there's any merchandise with Jarek on it, I'm buying it!" Clearly aiming for an outraged reaction, Johnny points to one of a forest of rider images on the table, "He's actually smiling there!" Militantly protective of her idols, Nicola retorts, "You leave Jarek alone! We're only at meeting one so no slagging Jarek or any of the other six off!" Johnny affects not to listen and retorts, "Jarek is going bald".

While Nicola is distracted by the latest version of the Ipswich hoodies available in the shop Johnny tells me conspiratorially in a loud theatrical whisper, "There's a place down the road called St Clements!" Talk of local mental institutions doesn't distract Nicola from her investigations. She holds a hoodie in the manner of the women you see on adverts after their favourite jumper has been treated with some wonder version of a fabric softener, "It's lovely, I love it, Nick! I love those beige ones! How much are these?" The £20 price meets her approval, "Huh, when's Dad about?" Nicola expertly sifts through the latest version of the Ipswich pens and demands, "Where is the Jarek pen I required? Ooh, I think his hair's not so receding in that one!" By all accounts Nicola takes her Junior Witch team leader role much more seriously than she takes the arrival of the new Ipswich speedway merchandise. Membership of the Junior Witches club is £6 per year. For this price you get a free welcome pack and a birthday card, plus, every week, one lucky member is chosen as mascot and also get to have their photo taken with a rider of their choice. This year Nicola's boyfriend Lewis has agreed to become a junior Witch team leader. Johnny chortles gleefully at the prospect, "He has to wear a pastel blue hoodie! I can't wait to see him in it, which is probably why Nicola says he needs a coat." Despite the extensive range of brightly coloured clothes on display the departure of the Nicola Thorpe whirlwind leaves the trackshop a significantly less vibrant place. Johnny smiles, "You should see her when we lose – not the best loser in the world!"

Speedway tonight

Although not exactly heavy, the rain remains constant. Despite this, an extremely optimistic man pops in to tell us, "They're saying on the radio the meeting is on!" Johnny kindly conducts a brief masterclass for me using the various items of merchandise on hand to illustrate/highlight the vagaries of their construction as well as the quality of the stitching or the fabric used. These are the sorts of essential details that would be missed by the casual speedway fan but noticed by those actually in the business. Johnny hasn't liked what he's seen at the Reading Racers online trackshop, "Those beige caps must cost 75p each and the embroidery is £1 max. They're on sale at £12 with a winged wheel but no mention of the Reading Racers!" If the ratio of the unit manufacturing price to selling price of the Reading caps is a concern then the decision during the winter to award the Programme of the Year to Workington, really beggars his belief. "I can't see how that is but then Howard Jones has his own agenda, never mind that he does the Stoke programme." All further discussions are cut short when (at 18.10) news filters over from the speedway office adjacent to the pits that the meeting has been postponed until tomorrow night. Hopefully without the drizzle, the chance to see their beloved Witches in action for the first time this season will draw a substantial crowd from the local area to see them beat their erstwhile East Anglian rivals King's Lynn. It's a prospect whose appeal will be strengthened by the appearance of Jason Crump as a guest for the Premier League team.

13th March Ipswich v. King's Lynn (Inter-League Challenge) Postponed

CHAPTER 6.

Reading v. Stoke:
"You've clearly got a good mother – is she attractive?"

2nd June

The last-ever Premier League visit of the Stoke Potters to Smallmead Stadium in Berkshire isn't a fixture guaranteed to attract a large crowd though, on this particular early June evening, numbers have been swelled by the arrival of Wimbledon fans keen to see the Ronnie Moore Trophy Match Race which will conclude the meeting. This commemorative race has been organised by Wimbledon Speedway Plc in addition to their sponsorship of the meeting. Undoubtedly the choice of Reading Speedway as the venue to celebrate the 80th anniversary of Wimbledon Speedway club was a peculiar one probably driven by practical considerations such as its proximity to London, the cost of sponsorship, the need to celebrate such a significant milestone and the place in the Stoke Easy-Rider Potters team occupied by Dermot Mark "Buzz" Burrows. For many Wimbledon fans that thrilled to the sight of Conference League racing at Plough Lane, Buzz Burrows typifies the excitement of the years between 2002 and 2005. Each era of speedway has its own heroes and a club like Wimbledon – with its glittering 80-year history – will inevitably attract heated debate about which rider was the greatest ever to grace the distinctive red-and-gold race bib of the club. Obviously I don't have others' expertise, but I would imagine Ronnie Moore or Barry Briggs (to name but two riders) would have greater claim to the best all-time rider title. Still, each age has its heroes and Buzz was very much that man for the Conference League era.

However, you take your kicks where you can, so – in the absence of anniversary celebrations at the clubs' true home of Plough Lane – the grandiosely named Wimbledon Speedway Plc should be congratulated for marking this momentous occasion in some manner. Reading Speedway are grateful for the sponsorship and upon arrival Racers co-promoter Malcolm Holloway tells me, "They're only having one race between Buzz and someone else – Buzz will definitely win unless he has an engine failure! They brought a trophy and everything!" Malcolm's down-to-earth description of the finale of the Stoke meeting is interrupted when he shouts some last-minute instructions across to Commercial Manager, Paul Oughton, as he passes by in the distance. "They brought 20 guests and I said they could sit in the grandstand bar and maybe have a sandwich or something!" Some unkind souls on the Internet forums have questioned whether a race between Buzz Burrows and Barrie Evans (who both currently ride for tonight's visitors Stoke) is an appropriate or prestigious enough way to mark the anniversary of one of speedway's great clubs. Unofficial Reading speedway historian and author, Arnie Gibbons, ironically notes, "It's a big occasion, a match race between the two visiting team's reserves!" When I remind him that Buzz has progressed from the reserve berth into the team proper to occupy the number 2 race jacket and that Barrie rides at number 4 for Stoke, Arnie corrects himself, "Oh, second strings then!"

Sadly, the 80th anniversary doesn't excite the *Speedway Star* enough to give it any sensible coverage and many Reading fans in attendance will be otherwise preoccupied with the ongoing saga of the potential move of the club from Smallmead to the nearby Island Road site. Sadly, the site of the proposed new location remains resolutely untouched and Reading Racers co-promoter, Mark Legg, has been forced to acknowledge that racing looks unlikely to start there in June 2009 as originally intended. After he appealed for their continued patience, Mark then requested all Reading speedway fans support their club to the hilt for the remainder of the 2008 season and to try come along to as many meetings at Smallmead as possible. Obviously comparisons are invidious. When speedway ends at Smallmead the stadium will be demolished while, since the Plough Lane facility still remains in use for sports (albeit other than speedway), Wimbledon speedway fans do not have the same degree of closure. At the time of their departure from their spiritual home in 2005 following the breakdown of rental negotiations with the GRA, Wimbledon Speedway Plc chairman Ian Perkin propounded the idea that the 'forced' departure of the speedway club was a prelude to the likely redevelopment of the site by GRA owners, Capital Risk Partners. Three years later this forecast still remains a potential possible outcome but clearly Mystic Meg has little to fear from Ian as a potential replacement. The various details of the club's departure from Plough Lane in 2005 has been rehearsed various times by many different people without alteration of the fact that the Plc incarnation of the club still sadly remains homeless. The increasingly unquestioned orthodoxy of the Plc's victimisation by the GRA has built up over time and, despite what some see as strategic negotiation errors, angry believers often denounce all those who dare depart from this script as troublemakers, fools or apostates. The GRA have yet to comment publically.

Whatever your point of view, it's certainly true that without the commitment of Ian Perkin and that of fellow directors of the Plc (along with a host of committed and willing volunteers) fans of the club wouldn't have been able to savour the Conference League years at Plough Lane if they hadn't taken on the responsibility to run it (after the departure of those who'd bravely reintroduced it). Indeed, the patina of history burnishes the memory of Plough Lane and memories of visits there are cherished by many speedway fans who were fortunate enough to thrill at the racing served up there (whatever the era of its vintage). In his programme notes, Ian Perkin highlights that the first-ever meeting took place at Wimbledon Stadium on Monday May 28th 1928 and, excluding the war years, there followed 63 years of uninterrupted speedway at the venue until it closed in 1991. Eleven years later, it was initially resurrected by Steve Ribbons and Dave Croucher who quickly passed the baton on to Wimbledon Speedway Plc. Many enjoyable meetings followed until the last-ever meeting at the club (The Laurels Championship) was won by Buzz Burrows. The speedway bug quickly bit many who went to Plough Lane in the pomp of its real glory years. Plc Chairman Ian Perkin was no exception. He first went to a meeting at Wimbledon in 1962 (as a 10-year-old) and saw the staging of the Internationale. The roster of riders on display that Bank Holiday included key speedway figures of the era such as Ronnie Moore, Barry Briggs, Ove Fundin, Peter Craven and Bjorn Knutsson as well as the soon-to-retire Split Waterman along with riders in brightly coloured leathers like Mike Broadbank (in red racing apparel) and Nigel Boocock (in light blue). Who wouldn't have their passions stirred and imagination lit by such an experience? Throughout his years following the club, sadly Ian conspicuously failed to see Wimbledon become League champions though they did get close to Conference League victory in 2005 under his management team. The last league championship title actually won by the club was in 1961.

Every Monday, Commercial Manager Paul Oughton is to be found stood with his colleague Ross Marks by the entrance turnstiles. Once there they encourage youngsters to join the Junior Racers scheme aimed at children aged at 11 and under. During a break in the flow of arrivals through the gates, I quiz Paul about the costs and benefits of speedway meeting sponsorship at Reading. "It's usually £400 to sponsor a meeting and you can bring along 10 guests. They all get VIP entry, programmes, the chance to have a guided walk around the pits, a table in the Racers lounge as well as a buffet and, of course, announcements about their sponsorship over the public-address system throughout the night. They can also go to the centre green and watch some races and, unlike tonight when they brought their own trophy to present, the meeting sponsor can present the 'rider of the night' award. I'm looking forward to it – when Buzz rode here for us he was great! He looked so youthful on a bike." The referee for tonight's meeting is the highly respected Tony Steele. Recently he's found his attendance in an official capacity at meeting appears to act as a jinx on proceedings, "There have been 23 crashes in my last two meetings, which were the Copenhagen Grand Prix and Rye House v. Birmingham on Saturday. And I mean real crashes not just falling off!"

With the start of the meeting only a few minutes away a posse of start-line girls

Dale Fontaine in the pits

Behind the scenes

Tensions build before the match race

Reading v. Stoke: *"You've clearly got a good mother – is she attractive?"*

pass us and prompt Paul to exclaim to Ross, "Umm! We've got a new blonde one tonight!" Quite how he spots this when three of the girls have blonde hair is something of a mystery. Still, if sponsors and possible commercial partners also get paid this level of detailed close attention, then the club will laugh all the way to the bank. On the subject of mirth, a regular feature of the Smallmead race night is the banter between Reading Racers announcer Bob Radford located in the referee's box above the start line and roving club presenter Paul Hunsdon. He's the man whom I've dubbed speedway's most optimistic man in light of his ongoing campaign to find, interview and possibly romance attractive child-rearing Reading speedway fans in their 30s (euphemistically known in men's lifestyle magazines as Milfs). When not zealously pursuing his apparently endless one-man priapic quest, Paul breaks off from his campaign to banter with Bob over the loudspeaker system on race night on a wide variety of matters, speedway and otherwise. Tonight, the immediate question in hand is how to correctly pronounce riders' names. The presentational team at Reading are so conscientious that they even find time to debate the exact pronunciation of riders' names who aren't actually at the stadium or due to ride. It's attention to detail that's typical of their approach to their work but also a refreshing change from some other tracks around the country where any bizarre phonetic pronunciation will suffice. Tonight the object their debate is actually to be found within the confines of the Smallmead stadium. Bob Radford wonders aloud about Stoke reserve Jesper Kristiansen, "I'm not sure whether to call him Yesber or Jessber." Ever-pragmatic Paul Hunsdon makes an executive decision, "you call him 'Yesber' and I'll call him 'Jessber'."

If Asian betting syndicates were to bet on speedway rather than football matches then a rich source of income could be wagers placed on the number and frequency of the track grades at Smallmead on any chosen race night. One positive legacy of the John Postlethwaite Bulldogs era has been the upgrade in tractor quality. The small shiny red one waits until after the fourth heat with the scores tied at 12 apiece to take to the track. Modern equipment in use at Smallmead stands out from the norm and, as the tractor circles the race track, Paul helpfully explains, "We must apologise for a little bit of dust tonight but you'll understand why we didn't put any water down 'cause everyone kept saying it was gonna rain this afternoon but it didn't!" He then goes on to outline the details of the later match race for the Ronnie Moore Trophy, "We have two Stoke riders with Wimbledon connections who'll be racing for a trophy and we'd like to extend a very warm welcome to Ian Perkins and Wimbledon this evening."

The first race after the track grade (heat 5) sees the Racers third consecutive race advantage and they take the lead for the first time. It's a supremacy they won't relinquish for the rest of the evening. Any casual observer of this race would have seen Ulrich Ostergaard win with some ease closely followed by his frequently inconsistent race partner, Tomas Suchanek. Buzz Burrows appears to treat the race as the opportunity to practise his match-racing tactics and technique against guest team mate Kauko Nieminen whom he kept behind him throughout by frequent, almost telepathic, positional changes on the track. It was an exhibition of riding skill that excited Bob Radford if not his notional race partner, "Buzz had an exciting ride back there in third place." Next time out Buzz calls on his vast racing experience to snatch a third place from Reading reserve Nicki Glanz on the last corner. Paul Hunsdon sings his praises, "Some very intelligent riding from Ben Barker's partner, Buzz Burrows, on the last bend!" High up in the referee's box perched on top of the home-straight grandstand Bob echoes these sentiments in his inimitable own way, "yes, he gets a bonus point. If you're a bonus-point aficionado and collect those sorts of things."

Ever keen to help his presentational partner in crime with his Milf hunt, Bob Radford quizzes 16-year-old Nathan who's come along to help out in the commentary box this evening.

[BR] "You've clearly got a good mother – is she attractive?"

[Nathan] "Not really."

[BR] "Oh, that's a shame, Paul Hunsdon likes young mothers! Paul, you've been very quiet this evening, have you gone off with Nathan's mother?"

[PH] "No, I'm with Wacky Racer." [the club mascot]

[BR] "I thought you liked ladies in their late 30s?"

[PH] "No! No! You've got that all wrong and you'll have to be quiet, my girlfriend might be in earshot."

The Potters Nieminen–Burrows partnership gets another outing in heat 11 when the Finnish rider is sent out with a black-

and-white helmet colour for the widely anticipated tactical ride. Fortunately for the nascent Stoke Potters fightback, Nieminen gates with alacrity from the tapes (and proceeds to win the race) before Buzz even gets half a chance to block his every move to pass. The race for second place between Tom P. Madsen and Burrows is worth the admission money alone and, given how the riders battle with each other neck-and-neck throughout the four laps, you can't help but wonder if, perhaps, another rider could substitute for Barry Evans to ensure a competitive match race in the Ronnie Moore Trophy that will conclude the evening. With the Racers lead suddenly narrowed to only 5 points, heat 12 comes to a dramatic stop when Klaus Jakobsen locks up on the fourth bend second time round and causes Nicki Glanz who's close behind to take urgent evasive action and crash. Though the Stoke rider is quite correctly excluded, a clearly discomforted Nicki Glanz spends considerable time lain on the track surface receiving the patient ministrations of the medical team. Bob Radford is quick to inform us over the tannoy, "Let's hope it's just funny elbow – what is the phrase for that?" Stood over the fallen young rider, Paul interrupts him from track side to update the crowd on the medical situation, "In fact it's Nicki's right ankle that's giving him the problem though it's not too far away from the elbow!" Minutes later we're told, "apart from the bang on his right ankle Nicki has hurt his left shoulder a little bit."

The banter over the public-address system soon turns to talk of look-alikes and Paul confesses, "I'm often mistaken in the street for Shane Lynch [from Boyzone] but that's a different story." With trademark rapier-like wit Bob responds, "Even though it was Mr Gobey [track electrician and music co-ordinator] who identified Nicki's ankle as his elbow he thinks it was Bet Lynch not Shane Lynch you were mistaken for!" The jollity continues when Bob Radford asks, "Tony Steele has a question for you – was it you who lost Reading their sponsor?" Quite what the basis of this question is I don't know but Paul Hunsdon immediately bites back, "It wasn't! And I have a message for Tony Steele. I was on the phone to [game show contestant] Phil Morris who was at Rye House on Saturday where he led heat 1 but found himself with a broken collarbone and an exclusion. Which hurt much more than the elbow injury he received but I mustn't mention who the ref was!" A casual glance in the *Speedway Star* confirms Tony Steele as the referee for said fixture between Rye House and Birmingham at Hoddesdon. The match report (by Pete Hill) described the opening heat that saw both Adam Roynon and Phil Morris subsequently both lost to the meeting through injury. "Morris, tucked into second place, came under pressure from Robert Mear and just as the Rye House man looked to have pulled in front, the Welshman went down on the third bend. Roynon, who after a slow start was just getting in contact, had little option but to lay down his machine in an attempt to avoid his fallen colleague." All this talk of ex-Reading riders distracts us from the sight of Nicki Glanz as he slowly hobbles back to the pits. In true resolute speedway rider fashion, Nicki is quickly back in the saddle and manages a third place in the rerun.

The interval invariably features the legendary raffle draw conducted with aplomb by Master of Ceremonies, Paul Hunsdon. He skilfully manages to alternate between building crowd anticipation levels about the business at hand and his ongoing pursuit to find the woman of his dreams. Never afraid to stoke the anticipation levels of the crowd to fever pitch, Paul claims "£85 – it's a life-changing sum for someone!" With dreams of untold wealth cunningly dangled too late to buy a raffle ticket, I temporarily lose concentration and fail to discover whether one of the raffle tickets "on the buff" (as Paul likes to mysteriously refer to some unidentified colour) wins. Though I do notice Mr Hunsdon use his best Tadley accent to say "Bettina from BAYZING-STOWK". Anxious to learn how their evening is going, I make my way to join a small group of Wimbledon fans stood on the steps of the section of the home-straight grandstand that overlooks the first bend. Should a fire officer be in attendance, I would imagine he would take the view that the area outside the fire doors should be kept clear. However, on a night when Wimbledon Speedway Plc sponsors the meeting no one would be so churlish to raise this matter. Stood among a group of likeminded men of certain age, ex Wimbledon speedway Programme Editor, Derek Barclay, is clearly in his element. Derek saw his first speedway meeting at Wimbledon Stadium in 1974, 12 years after Ian Perkin, but freakishly for his first-ever Plough Lane visit also attended the Internationale (which, by then, had been renamed by its sponsor the Wills Internationale). Entranced ever since by his first trip to the hallowed portals Derek later recalls in print, "it was the most magnificent venue and the most thrilling racing, under lights and in front of a packed Bank Holiday crowd … I still get goose-bumps recalling it now!" Despite this auspicious introduction to the sport at the venue, Derek cites the Conference League era as "forever his favourite of all times" because of the "family nature of the South London Club." It's hardly a secret that Derek is a huge fan of the "amazing Buzz Burrows" whom he claims without question is "one of the most exciting riders EVER to ride in the colours of the London club."

Though now deprived of the chance to see Wimbledon race in contemporary British speedway, Derek has recently adopted the Stoke Potters as his Premier League club and, whenever possible, takes the chance to see them ride to watch his hero Buzz Burrows thrill the fans at Loomer Road or at other speedway venues throughout the country. Stood on the periphery of the group in conversation with a man in a jacket who tightly grips a trophy in his hand is Wimbledon Plc Chairman Ian Perkin. He's dressed casually for the occasion in black jeans-type trousers and a coloured shirt that more artistically minded types might describe as a concrete grey/blue colour. Mr Perkin looks more prosperous than I recall and I wonder if he's seen the article in today's *Sun* prompted by comments allegedly issued by "Taliban warlords" headlined "We'll Kill Anyone Who Eats a Biscuit." This exclusive and disturbing news report has been brought to the newspaper from Helmand Province by their 'investigative' reporter Jerome Starkey and features a picture of a custard cream biscuit with the photo caption "Fatal…custard cream." Before we can even think about an exchange of pleasantries, Ian purposefully heads off to the centre green with the smartly jacketed man in charge of the Ronnie Moore Trophy just prior to the start of heat 13. Since photographic arrangements haven't been formally confirmed, a conscientious and slightly panicked Derek Barclay asks if I would be kind enough to arrange for the Reading Racers club photographer Les Aubrey to capture a post-race trophy presentation.

In the commentary box, Bob Radford listens to my enquiry and, ever practical, suggests that it would be easier if I went out to the centre green myself and ask the always cheerfully helpful Les if he could do the photographic honours and record said event for posterity. Latent demand apparently already exists for these photos. Though the *Evening Standard* should be where they appear this has proved not to be the case in the recent past. Nonetheless, Derek feels sure the *Surrey Comet* newspaper and the *South London Press* (home of alleged Dons apostate and veteran speedway reporter, John Hyam) would wish to use such photographs to accompany their reports on the Plc-organised match race for the Ronnie Moore Trophy that tonight will mark the 80th anniversary of the club. Personally I love any excuse to go to the centre green so it's hardly a sacrifice to make my way out there to stand in close proximity to Ian Perkin on his big night and also chat to Les Aubrey. By the time I arrive, Ian Perkin has already had the foresight to arrange some photographs with him, "Some bloke – called Perkins, is it? – has already asked me!" The last two races of the Premier League meeting flash by literally and metaphorically when viewed from the centre green and, predictably enough, Reading run out comfortable winners 54-41.

Absorbed in his thoughts, Ian Perkin awaits the on-track arrival of Buzz and Barrie for their match race. Once the riders are on hand at the start gate, the Plc Chairman and Perry Atwood conduct the toss for gate positions with minimal ceremony. Stood close by with his roving microphone, Paul Hunsdon softly intones over the public-address system with the hushed profundity I expect he reserves for investitures, snooker commentary or unexpected news of divorce proceedings: "And we've got Ian Perkin, the former Wimbledon promoter as well as two riders with Stoke connections, sorry two Stoke riders with Wimbledon connections. Not sure who the bloke is with him though? He looks like Ted Bovis of *Hi-De-Hi*!" Quick as a flash Bob Radford retorts, "It's Robbie Coltrane!" Quite whether the presentational team should take the mickey out of the meeting sponsors – as they burnish the metaphorical flame of their club's memory and await the opportunity to mark 80 years of speedway at Wimbledon with a match race – isn't a question I can answer. Fortunately, Ian and Perry are so caught up in the occasion and absorbed in the race proceedings that I doubt they notice. Predictably enough, Buzz Burrows gains an easy tapes-to-flag victory in the slowest time of the evening, 65.27 seconds. In the absence of other events, say, like a gun salute to commemorate the anniversary of 80 years of Wimbledon speedway, it would be churlish to claim that this was not a fitting tribute to one of speedway's all-time great British clubs, albeit one with greater hint of whimper than bang. Just as beauty is in the eye of the beholder, I'm sure that the Wimbledon fans drawn to these celebrations at Smallmead all enjoyed their trip down memory lane, the chance to convivially renew acquaintances with old friends and would take great satisfaction that they were actually there to commemorate their beloved club. Doubtless discussions and reminiscences continued in the bar beyond closing time and, given the slight make-do and mend nature of the event, the bonhomie of these friendly *ad hoc* celebrations do, in so many ways, typify the present state and collegiate nature of speedway.

2nd June Reading v. Stoke (Premier League) 54-41
The Ronnie Moore Trophy Match Race Winner: Dermot Mark "Buzz" Burrows

Reading v. Stoke: *"You've clearly got a good mother – is she attractive?"*

CHAPTER 7.

Rye House:

"Unless you've felt the burn of the tyre on your leg you really have no idea what it's like to ride a bike competitively"

15th June

Rye House Speedway Club stage the 2008 FIM Individual World Junior Championship Semi-Final at Hoddesdon on the last Sunday before Midsummer's Day. This meeting is what it says on the tin – namely, one of the two meetings from which eight riders will qualify for the Grand Final of the Under 21 World Championship to be held in Pardubice in the Czech Republic at the start of October. Clearly young riders are the lifeblood of the sport and the field for today's meeting is drawn from three different continents (America, Europe and Australasia). Obviously, all the riders will race to win though, in reality, the real strategy will be to ensure qualification through a top-eight place finish. Some of the riders in the field are very familiar to British Speedway fans because they already ply their trade in this country. Whereas others appear far more exotic since they've only really been experienced via reports of speedway meetings held in faraway places. Speedway, much more than football, has a long tradition of familiarising British people with a wide variety of exotic foreign sounding place names and surnames. This afternoon's meeting is no exception. At a casual glance many of the riders on display appear to have unpronounceable names and, if this were a game of scrabble, the use of Mateusz Szczepaniak's name – whose father Greg rode for the Leicester Lions in 1976 – would definitely score highly! Many speedway announcers struggle with even the most basic of rider names but, this afternoon, we're fortunate to have one of the most diligent and well researched presenters in the business on duty – Craig Saul. Craig doesn't come from the Speedway School where you just turn up and wing it with a series of increasingly bizarre pronunciations but has, in fact, diligently researched the correct intonation and pronunciation of all the riders likely to be on display. You often hear plaudits expressed by fans and speedway workers alike regarding the quality of Craig's work. Dave Rattenberry echoes the opinion of many, "That Craig Saul is an excellent presenter!"

The Rye House promoter Len Silver sets great store by young rider development at his speedway club. He puts his money where his mouth is and runs both Premier and Conference League sides. Arguably, the Conference League version fails to wash its face economically in attendance terms but, with good money to be made for the club through the bars and catering facilities, this clearly is a financial commitment that Len Silver is prepared to make to benefit the sport in general. It's not entirely altruistic since the CL has provided a conveyor belt of young riders for the main Rockets team. Seemingly almost every year, the new PL reserves are generally products from the home grown Conference League Raiders – so, to his credit and benefit, Len doesn't have to spend money on unnecessary signing or loan fees for new riders. Invariably, any promoter will tell you that they are delighted to stage a special one-off meeting but, in the case of this FIM Under-21 World Championship Semi-Final, Len's delight appears genuine. Indeed, Len spent a lot of time and money to ensure that the Rye House track got accredited and licensed at FIM level[1] A promoter of the old school, Len Silver runs race-day presentations with ruthless efficiency and a strong hint of military precision, judged by the way that the neatly uniformed track staff march out in regimented military style (with Colonel Silver at their head) just prior to the start of the meeting. Len doesn't require any second invitation to wander down memory lane and the meeting programme allows him to give full rein to his reminiscences. In a two-page article entitled "BEING YOUNG IS NOTHING NEW", Len looks back at various youngsters who, though of tender years,

---

[1] Len ran the U21 Quarter-Final in 2007 and the Semi-Final in 2008 on the understanding that he would stage the 2009 Final. Unfortunately for him, the BSPA undermined this agreement when they instead decided to accept the right to stage the GP Challenge at Coventry. The consequence of this decision meant that the 2009 U21 Final would now, instead, be staged in Croatia rather than Hertfordshire.

have made their mark on the world stage. Ronnie Moore still remains the youngest-ever rider to reach a world final (at the age of 17 in 1950). Len marvels at the fact that nowadays we can see riders as young as 14 compete in Academy League while 15-year-olds can ride at the Conference League level. Little or nothing is without historic precedent, "this concept is certainly not new although these days it is far more common than in the past. If we look back to pre-war (1932 to 1939) or early post-war years, working class lads did not have the money to go into expensive motor sports so riders tended to be a bit older [before they started]."

Many people have Chris Holder as their pre-meeting favourite. He's a rising Australian star of the future who now plies his trade at Poole in the Elite League, after he'd served a couple of years speedway apprenticeship racing for the Isle of Wight. Last season he finished runner up to Emil Sajfutdinov in this competition and, since this will be his last year of eligibility for the Under-21 World Championship, he'll look to go one better. That said, the task at hand today is solely qualification. Two hours before the scheduled start time (2 p.m.) the car park already looks full with impressive queues stretched outside the entrance turnstiles ("credit cards accepted"). Once I'm inside, it's a shock to see how full the stadium already looks. Even when space on the terraces isn't at a premium, usual practice is to immediately scuttle with your garden furniture, blankets and bags to your favourite spot to reserve the ideal vantage point. The configuration of the track and terraces at Rye House stadium allows you to overlook almost any section of its surface. I decide to base myself in the main grandstand, overlook the start line and sit next to well-travelled Eagles fan Sid Greatley. Like so many other keen fans of a certain age, Sid has journeyed widely to watch his beloved sport. He's regularly found at speedway tracks throughout the country and not just those where his beloved Eastbourne Eagles visit. Recently retired, Sid will now be able to really indulge himself and add to the million miles he claims he has already covered to follow speedway. The rear and side windows of Sid's trusty car are festooned with so many no longer fashionable stickers, that you have to assume he only uses the wing mirrors to see any vehicles behind him. Though he claims to be a speed merchant between points A and B, whenever I pass him his car definitely travels sedately. For a while I did beep my horn, flash my lights and wave whenever I passed him though, subsequently, I realised this didn't help me stand out from the majority of road users Sid encounters. Still, the pleasure will be all mine as the meeting unfolds while we sit together in our moulded plastic seats set into the concrete of the grandstand.

Once through the turnstiles, the first person I encounter is Hazal Naylor and immediately address with the immortal words, "hello Heather." Invariably stressed and perpetually busy on race day Hazal retorts, "it's Hazal!" I prefer to get my first gaff of the day over with quickly and, after I've delivered hot off the press copies of my new book *Concrete for Breakfast* to Andy Griggs in the trackshop, I wander down to the pits in search of Peter Oakes. There's impressive security at the pit gate in the form of an officious older gentleman who has perfected the slightly distant air of Sergeant Wilson during one of Captain Mainwaring's addresses to the platoon. He clearly delights to frustrate would-be interlopers keen to con their way into the pits to hobnob with the riders, mechanics and officials. After some vigorous hand signals, I attract Peter's attention and, as he arrives at the pit gate, a smiling Len Silver approaches from the other direction. Len proudly and expansively waves his arm through 180 degrees at the stadium around us as if we've stumbled upon the Hanging Gardens of Babylon or are extras in the crowd scene from *Evita*. Without preamble, Len immediately quizzes the Coventry team manager: "You're a good observer of people and speedway meetings. Look at all the people sitting down – you can tell they don't come to speedway regularly. They're in all the right places but would usually be standing, if they came regularly! We're gonna do well today. Not that we haven't worked hard for it mind! Lots of them are local people and, hopefully, they'll like what they see and come back again!" After he's drunk in the full glory of the situation, Peter politely responds, "Have you advertised it a lot locally?" Happy to initiate Peter into the ways of the world in the modern electronic age, Len replies as though he's having to converse with a slightly deaf but reclusive neighbour, "Yes, of course! But the Internet is where everyone looks for information nowadays so advertising locally isn't as important as it used to be!" Len then chit-chats distractedly as though weighed down by the thought of the many other things he could or should be doing. Before he bustles off in distinctive diminutive fashion into the pits, I enquire whether he'll throw the traditional Rye House race-day £1 coin into the crowd as per usual. The honour of the opportunity to stage this prestigious FIM meeting is so grand for the club that Len has unilaterally doubled his investment. "They'll have my guts for garters if I don't toss the TWO POUND coin into the crowd! It's the TWO POUND coin we use to toss for gate positions in team meetings but, we don't do that for individual meetings, as the gate positions are already assigned for each race!"

Rye House: *"Unless you've felt the burn of the tyre on your leg you really have no idea what it's like to ride a bike competitively"*

During his conversation with Peter, Len revealed that he was doing his autobiography. Richard Madeley's allegedly apocryphal remark springs to mind: "So tell me about the autobiography; what it's about?" Len's narrative wouldn't only cover his lengthy speedway career but would also include many other events from his varied life, such as his evacuation during the Second World War, his national service and business career. Though my mental image of Len late at night with a quill is hard to shake off, I ask Peter if he's ever thought of writing his autobiography. Within speedway circles, Peter Oakes is well known as a multi-tasker. He not only works as a promoter and/or team manager but he combines these activities with his talent as an author and journalist. His newspaper background and experiences would provide a story in itself. Peter still regularly contributes to the *Daily Star* and is a journalistic veteran of the lamented Fleet Street era of newspaper publishing, that's now sadly gone the way of all flesh. Peter personally experienced the radical overhaul of working practices within the newspaper industry since he was on the staff when Eddie Shah launched his second newspaper venture *The Post*. "I worked on Eddie Shah's second national newspaper *The Post* when it launched but only lasted 13 weeks in 1988 (I think) and then closed down. The editor was the late Lloyd Turner. He was the editor of the *Daily Star* when they carried the stories of Lord Archer and the prostitute, Monica Coughlin, for which Archer got libel damages but then was later convicted and jailed for perjury. I was assistant editor (features) on the paper, which was basically the fourth in command. We worked at offices in Warrington and one famous story is how a fortnight before Christmas staff, who were working in excess of 12 hours a day to produce Christmas specials, Shah himself came round the office at around 1am to wish everyone well. The FOLLOWING morning (around 10 a.m. on, I am fairly sure, December 11) all the executives had a call to say the paper had closed with immediate effect. Along with every other executive I had a long-term contract (I think it was two years' notice period – enough to tempt most of us to leave secure jobs) but we were told if we didn't agree to accept very short redundancy terms Shah would liquidate everything and we'd get a penny in the pound if we were lucky! About a dozen of us carried on working for nothing over the next month in the hope of completing a sale to an interested company but it all fell through when it was discovered there were no assets – every bit of furniture, every computer, etc. was on rental and the *Post* owned absolutely nothing!" The most revolutionary contribution Eddie Shah made to the newspaper industry was to pioneer computer photo-setting and full-colour offset printing (at *Today* newspaper) during an era when national newspapers still used linotype machines and letterpress. Some of the technology he utilised has had a significant ongoing impact within the industry.

Peter modestly claims that no one would have an interest in his life story. Though that might be true of the newspaper revolution, so many other stories from his life would resonate beyond the speedway community. Much more a Liverpudlian than a Scouser, brief highlights from Peter's life include: he fought with John Lennon at school; he was offered his first reefer (as I believe they call them) by Jimi Hendrix; he broke the worldwide exclusive story of the Welsh invisible fighting fish; he persuaded Priscilla Black to change her name to Cilla Black; arguably he wrote the first 'kiss and tell' that featured Kathy Etchingham's story, Jimi Hendrix's girlfriend, shortly after the musician's death (Peter recalls the interview was conducted "at a Cambridge hotel where they served steaks

Dave Rattenberry and John Rich wheeler deal in the car park

Andy Griggs in his trackshop

on wooden plates"); he knew Marc Bolan when he had straight hair (actually I made this one up); and was banned from Swansea Football Club by a certain John Toshack. All this and we've hardly scratched the surface of Peter's stories from his Fleet Street heyday. Before I can learn any more, the gate marshal reminds us the meeting starts in 10 minutes. Clearly a compelling book remains to be written.

Minutes prior to the rider introductions and parade, the stadium appears impressively full. I scuttle back to my seat in the grandstand but, instead, find that Sid hasn't quite understood my request. Admittedly, "please mind my bag for a few minutes" probably has some latitude for interpretation but I couldn't predict that Sid would let someone else sit there. The smug but sour old age pensioner in question steadfastly refuses to move. With the grandstand now apparently full, I am lucky to spot another spare seat. It is free because in front of it a large post partially obscures some parts of the track and, what track you can see, is partially blocked by spectators bobbing about by the greyhound track fence. Nonetheless, any spare seat is a found treasure moments before the meeting starts. However, it does have the benefit that it is next to two rather glamorous-looking women in designer sunglasses. After Craig Saul eloquently introduces the riders and impresses with his command of some difficult pronunciations, the first race is surprisingly won by Linus Eklof rather than the pre-meeting favourite Chris Holder (or 'Chirs' Holder as it appears in the programme). Perhaps the Australian was discombobulated by the copiously watered track? Though the programme advertises that "the track will be graded every fourth race" no mention is made of the formation display of water bowsers we witness in action throughout the afternoon. Judged by the frequency of their bowser usage, you'd suspect the speedway club have been incentivised to completely drain the nearby River Lea.

To my untutored eye, the contours of the Hoddesdon track traditionally favour riders who start from the inside gates though, in recent years, the dramatic burr that used to so affect riders unused to its topology appears to have been pretty much eliminated. Nonetheless, the need to command the race from the first turn is pre-eminent at any speedway track, particularly when early points on the board can smooth the qualification process. Heat 2 illustrates this point when a dramatic start to the race sees the red-helmeted 18 year-old Kim Nilsson (whose father, Tommy, rode for Len at Hackney in the mid-70s) struggle to even turn his bike. Instead, he careens on straight through to the apex of the bend where he knocks into the white-helmeted William Lawson. This unexpected contact then fires the Scot into the fence, though not before he's also tangled with Eastbourne's Lewis Bridger. The only rider to evade the clash of man and machine initiated by Kim Nilsson is Tobias Busch who escapes still on board his equipment. Sadly Kim Nilsson is excluded for his efforts and also lies prone on the track for a considerable time surrounded by medical staff. After a 25-minute delay, he's whisked off in an ambulance and takes no further part in the meeting, thereby precluding his ambition to fly the Swedish flag in the FIM Speedway Junior World Championship Final in Pardubice. The sight of an empty track (except for the injured rider, medical staff and ambulance) proves irresistible to the bowser driver who sets off again in his truck to re-water the track before the rerun of heat 2. The lady next to me echoes my thoughts, "It's not like it's dusty or anything, is it?" In fact, we're all wrong since William Lawson raises impressive quantities of dust in the rerun of the second heat when he wins comfortably ahead of Lewis Bridger.

No sooner has the race finished than, once again, the bowser is back out on the track working its liquid magic. The lady next to me notes, "To be fair, it does look a bit dusty." Behind her glamorous designer sunglasses, the lady next to me turns out to be Claudia Stchmann, wife of Jan. A perceptive analyst of the sport, its hierarchies, participants and foibles, Jan rode in British speedway for many years (as well as in Sweden, Denmark and Poland). He now rejoices in the official title of National Coach, Speedway, Danmarks Motor Union. Like her husband, Claudia has flown in this morning from last night's GP in Copenhagen. Before the third heat gets under way, the always informative Craig Saul reminds us over the public-address system, "Ricky Wells is technically still a New Zealander; remember that if he wins!" It's useful information given he's listed as a United States rider in the programme. The next moment Craig appears to imagine he's been transported to the Lord Mayor's Banquet and has to inject melodrama and delight into proceedings, "Ladies and gentlemen: I give you Tai Woffinden!" Given how keen Craig was to clarify Ricky's complex nationality issues, it's notable that similar explanations aren't forthcoming for Tai. It's not so long ago that Tai hadn't yet "made up his mind" whether he would ride at senior level for Great Britain or Australia. Long before Zola Budd ran in the Olympics under a British passport (though she was clearly South African), the world of sports nationalities had become a murky business. Even within speedway we have Bristol-born Jason Crump proud to speak in Strine and be a militantly patriotic Australian. Similarly accented Scunthorpe-born Tai (who was also brought up in Australia) has elected to ride for the country of his father's birth, Great Britain. Given the notional shortage of British young rider talent, it's useful that such a gifted rider as Tai has sensibly chosen to represent this sceptred isle. Loud applause greets Tai's arrival onto the track and also his departure from it after his race win in 56.95 seconds. In between, Tai makes light of the difficult gate 4 start position (only Chris Holder and Morten Risager will win a race from this gate) when he powers towards the first bend only to then make a smooth cut back and drive underneath all his putative rivals for the lead before he's even exited the second bend. With pride that mixes patriotism along with delight that a Rye House rider presently excels on a world stage, Craig notes, "What a tremendous cut back on the first bend by Tai!"

Throughout the afternoon, the finish of any race appears to be the signal for the bowser to again circuit the Hoddesdon raceway. Though it's a typical English summer's day with considerable amount of cloud and occasional sun, Claudia Stæchmann and her friend Elaine Herbert studiously keep their eyes hidden behind their designer sunglasses even though we're sat under the shade of the grandstand roof. Later, Claudia says that she wears prescription lenses but that they're to keep the dust out of her eyes. Over the tannoy, the news that Kim Nilsson has withdrawn from the meeting with suspected concussion is confirmed. Claudia and Elaine are both "Comets girls" and, are so quick to inform me "we're from Cumbria!", that you'd suspect they work for the tourist board. Though Claudia then confesses "when I met Jan Stæchmann he rode for Stoke so I became a bit of a Stokie, duck!"

Heat 4 confirms the high calibre nature of the racing on display and, towards the end of the meeting with qualification at stake, definitely no quarter is given or asked. The surprise package of the day turns out to be Troy Batchelor, who produces a fine performance. Things nearly don't start as he would have planned in the fourth heat when only a last-bend cutback and race for the line enables him to snatch the victory from the stylish-looking Morten Risager. The afternoon heat (albeit without the sunshine) continues to dry the track and requires the astonishingly frequent ministrations of the overworked Hoddesdon bowser. As early as the end of heat 6 a blue groove appears on the first bend, prompting Claudia to note, "There we are – we're getting more like the Grand Prix – a blue groove has appeared!" With a rock-hard surface and the traditional lack of shale, it's always going to be difficult to avoid. The seventh heat sees Chris Holder confirm his status as a pre-meeting favourite with a win, but only after a breathtaking overtake by the young Australian past Morten Risager on the fourth bend of the opening lap. The crowd and Claudia Stæchmann gasp audibly as he thrillingly squeezes through an apparently non-existent gap. The excitement also overwhelms Craig Saul who breathlessly exclaims afterwards, "and a win for second in last year's event for Craig Holder!" From a British perspective, it is a worry to see a somewhat out-of-sorts Lewis Bridger trail in at the back. Ecstatic reactions again became the order of the day when the home crowd's favourite *Wunderkind* Tai Woffinden comfortably wins heat 8 by well over a quarter of a lap. The only threat to his supremacy is the rider himself when his enthusiastic post-race wheelie celebration nearly ends in tears. With confirmation of the news that Tai is now a Works Jawa rider, the quality of his engines will consistently match his undoubted virtuoso talent on a speedway bike. Less-garlanded mortals like Eastbourne reserve and possible Swedish star of the future Simon Gustafsson remain adulationless,

Crowds gather

Rider parade (with flags)

particularly after he runs a last in heat 9 after a first-bend close inspection of the safety fence in the manner of a slow-motion circus 'Wall of Death' display.

The three races prior to the scheduled interval break go according to expected form. The crowd whoops with delight at Tai Woffinden's win in heat 10, followed home by Mr Consistent (aka Morten Risager) who claims his third consecutive second place. Heat 11 sees an easy win for Chris Holder, and Troy Batchelor maintains his exhilarating form with yet another victory in the 12th race that has Lewis Bridger again finishing last. Third place goes fortuitously to a rider destined throughout his career to be known as "Robert Kasprzak – brother of Krzysztof" after Lewis executes a spectacular first-lap 360 degree turn on the apex of the third and fourth bend. Things are never dull on the track (or off it) with Lewis and it's a testament to his exceptional motorcycling ability that he somehow remains on his bike, albeit relegated to the rear of the field.

Though the increasingly visible blue line doesn't appear to be having any affect on the quality of the racing we witness, the interval break sees yet more thorough dousing of the track to keep the ongoing dust problem at bay. Previously we've only been treated to appearances of the big tank bowser but the interval sees this supplemented with the small bowser along with another tractor that pulls a small tank of water. If this formation doesn't resolve the dust problem, nothing will. Craig Saul has a busy interval with announcements celebrating Father's Day, "Lots of dads being proclaimed 'the Best Dad in Town'; and here's another 'best dad'!" Many young children seem to run off their energy while others succumb to the timeless lure of the sand-covered dog track. Claudia points out, "It's amazing how much fun kids can have with sand." It's a thought echoed by her friend Elaine, "Yeah, they couldn't give a monkeys about the bikes." Ingenious children improvise with discarded beer glasses to make their sandcastles though my news that "it's the dog-track sand" has both ladies pull quizzical expressions.

This longer gap in proceedings allows me to quiz Claudia Stæchmann about her unique behind-the-scenes perspective on the speedway scene. She takes a very sympathetic view of the pressures involved if you work in speedway as a younger rider. "They're often boys in a man's world! It's a hard lifestyle – or lack of it, really – the travel, the injuries, the sports psychology. Unless you've done it, you just don't know what's involved! Or, as they say, unless you've felt the burn of the tyre on your leg you really have no idea what it's like to ride a bike competitively! Let alone know what it's like to put in the punishing hours of travel required to compete at the highest level in Britain, Poland, Sweden and Denmark. Have you ever been on a speedway bike? Once I'd been on one (and felt the sheer power of the thing), I completely realised how dangerous what Jan did was! I went on one on the sands at Lawson's Farm[2] just before I got my road licence. I'd never been on a proper bike as an adult – my Dad has always been involved in motor sport so, obviously, I grew up around them so I always had a little pee-wee or something to bomb about on – but, really, I knew nothing about them. It was a real eye opener! Speedway riders get treated differently in different countries. Team Danmark supports their riders with their diet, fitness, physiotherapy and psychology and this is all part of the armoury, if you like, of the modern speedway rider. I'm so pleased Jan no longer does it but he's definitely a better manager for knowing what the riders are going through!"

"Nowadays the travel is immense. Top riders compete in all the major leagues, ride in the GPs and also race in Russia. Nicki Pedersen goes via Japan to Vladivostok as that's the most compatible route to get there. It's four days away to a totally different time zone. He has to race when he gets there and it's totally exhausting. Then there's the injuries themselves, the recovery from them and the psychological impact that that has upon a rider. Look at Kenneth Bjerre: he was cycling three days after having a pin in his leg – I'd still be in bed! But the riders force their bodies to the limits, just to get back on the saddle again! Things are much more professional now but it doesn't get away from the physicality of the sport or the lack of lifestyle it involves. Nowadays diet has become another important component of any top speedway rider's preparations. I think Nicki only has 7% body fat and Charlie Gjedde has 9% body fat. Many fans just don't really know what's involved since they only see the riders turn up at their track in their country and race. It all looks very glamorous but, behind the scenes, it's relentlessly demanding!"

"I don't look at the forums because so many people there just don't know what they're talking about. I only went on

[2] "Many people know where that is and, now, that young Richard Lawson – who used to ride professional motocross – has started riding for the Workington Comets, even more will shortly! He did a few laps at Derwent Park and the rest, as they say, is history."

Rye House: *"Unless you've felt the burn of the tyre on your leg you really have no idea what it's like to ride a bike competitively"*

a forum once when I voted for the Stoke Rider of the Year – obviously I voted for Jan – it was when I was still trying to get a ring on my finger! [smiles] When you look at other motorsports – like rallying and Formula 1 – and what they get paid, most speedway riders are paupers. In the Elite League, there seems to be a problem balancing the books. Though, obviously, some riders' pay is very attractive, that's not the case for everyone. That said, while there's a culture of brown envelopes or, I should say, when there's a perception of such a culture existing then there's always going to be inequalities between the riders. Some people say all promoters are wankers! But, there's so many good ones but, equally, one of them called my mum a c*** – how dare he call my mum that when she isn't! – when she was chasing him for unpaid bills. So yes, some promoters are arseholes but, on the whole, they're the exception! Look at Dave Tattum and Stoke Speedway. It's a nice club with nice fans and they always pay on time. Contrary to some people's perceptions, he really cares about his club and the riders. When Garry [Stead] was injured, Dave was beside himself and, people say, he nearly gave up! Jan thinks very highly of Stoke and always likes to send his young Danes there."

"I think that, maybe, there's a cultural difference between the different nationalities of the speedway riders. Jan would tell me that the Danish national characteristic is to be tidy and fastidious (Jan's house was immaculate until I arrived and created a storm there). Whereas other nationalities have a reputation for being more happy-go-lucky. Something that could help the sport in this country would be if *Sky* took what they do presenting the sport and its riders to an even higher level. When we watch Swedish TV, they do more interviews with the riders and they also do really interesting things like film the riders at their homes when they're off-duty. You get a much better idea of the man behind the rider that way and it genuinely makes for interesting television. Recently they interviewed Andreas Jonsson on his lake – I know they all live on lakes – but seeing his place you got a real idea of who he was and how he lived, not just where he lived."

"Given I'm Jan's wife, I get to go to all the speedway meetings I want and get to go behind the scenes. It's a privilege to do so and one that I don't take for granted. Everyone always says how dangerous it can be and, though injuries are part and parcel of taking part, it's not something that you get used to. Inevitably, Jan has seen his friends get hurt and that's not something that many people see at their place of work, is it? In some ways, this sort of meeting – when the youngsters are still really keen and going for it – is the most enjoyable! There can be something soul-destroying about maximums at this level, but not today. Tai maybe just thought he could turn up and win. But, now, he's realised that there are lots of other talented young riders who are as keen – or just as keen – as he is!"

The first race after the interval is a do-or-die affair for Lewis Bridger who needs a win to have any realistic chance of qualification. Easier said than done with Tai Woffinden next to him in the blue helmet colour but the Bexhill-based rider appears suddenly rejuvenated and storms to victory (though there are some mutters afterwards that this was a predetermined race fix agreed amongst the British riders). Lewis rarely needs any excuse to engage in some celebratory wheelies and, as gifted a rider though as he is, Tai definitely needs some further wheelie practice if judged by his efforts on the back straight. In third place is Grzegorz Zengota who, due to his exceptional form on the practice day, has been the talk of the terraces prior to the meeting as a possible "dark horse". The next three races are won by this afternoon's form riders – Troy Batchelor, Chris Holder and Morten Risager (whose win has Claudia clap enthusiastically and remark "Morten's really up for it!"). Morten then also wins his final race to ensure his comfortable qualification for the Final in the Czech Republic. The new version Lewis Bridger also continues to be a rider transformed and wins heat 17 to rescue a situation where, with only 2 points from three races, qualification looked unlikely. Afterwards Lewis remarks, "after three races I wanted to go home. I haven't been round Rye House for a year and a half and I didn't have a clue what sort of setups to go there with. Even though the foreigners are used to big tracks, they are also used to getting their bikes dialled in to slick tracks like that. I basically thought that was it after three rides. I had a lot of help from [Eagles co-promoter] Martin Hagon. He was up there and he was great with me. I couldn't have had anything better. If I hadn't qualified then I would have wasted a year of my career. I dug deep, went out and had two wins, and I managed to do it."

A pre-meeting glance through the programme would quickly have identified heat 19 as theoretically the most exciting race of the day. So it proves! With the exception of William Lawson, the triumvirate of Holder, Woffinden and Batchelor have all already qualified for the October final and, therefore, could reasonably be expected to take their hand off the gas. In the event we are treated to an exhibition of pulsating racing from three bright young speedway talents. Local favourite Tai Woffinden fails to gate and finds himself last into the first corner before he calls upon his track craft (and local knowledge) to swoop past Holder and Lawson in pursuit of the race leader Troy Batchelor. A ding-dong battle for second place ensues as Chris Holder rides forcefully past Woffinden only for Tai to then return the favour at the start of the last lap. Comfortably ahead for the majority of the race, Troy Batchelor is nearly caught on the line after an exhilarating swoop round the outside by Woffinden who fails to snatch a victory by the width of a tyre (to the simultaneous delight and disappointment of the partisan crowd). Though a last in this race, other results over the last four heats go in his favour, and mean that William Lawson becomes the third British rider to qualify for the Final along with Lewis Bridger and Tai Woffinden. After an afternoon of high quality racing, all that remains is the third place run off between Holder and Risager (won by the Australian) followed by a three rider run-off for ninth place won by Simon Gustafsson to ensure he will occupy the coveted reserve position at Pardubice. Though Troy Batchelor is the surprise package at the meeting, the overall standard on display is extremely high and definitely justifies optimism for the future, if there is upcoming young rider talent like this. In the car park afterwards I overhear two older speedway fans relive some of the exciting moments of the races they've just witnessed: "I can't remember the last time I saw a Grand Prix meeting as exciting as that one!"

15th June 2008
FIM Individual World Junior Championship, Semi-Final Winner: Troy Bachelor (and speedway)

Rye House: *"Unless you've felt the burn of the tyre on your leg you really have no idea what it's like to ride a bike competitively"*

CHAPTER 8.

Swindon v. Poole:
"With hindsight, 1984 really was a turning point for the sport and everything has changed since then!"

19th June

Wayne Russell, son of club owner and Swindon Robins promoter Terry Russell, has kindly agreed I can launch my latest book *Concrete for Breakfast* at Abbey Stadium. Wayne has followed in his father's footsteps in the speedway world and he helps ensure the smooth day-to-day running of the club. Whether it's modesty or an oversight, if you look inside the Swindon Robins programme you will see an impressively comprehensive roll call of staff without mention of his name. Anyone who is anyone appears to be listed including the Reserve Clerk of the Course (Andrew Reynolds), Club Sports Therapist (the wonderfully named Karen Pantry, known to all as Flo) and even the Electronics Scoreboard Operator (Jordan Satchel). Many other people make up the backbone of this organisation are also listed but, judged by his absence, Wayne appears to hold no formal responsibilities at the club or enjoys a position too difficult to define! News of my book launch via the good offices of the newly appointed Swindon Press Officer and Programme Editor (Chris Seaward) have quickly reached *BBC Radio Wiltshire*. They have requested an early-morning interview for the day of the launch. The oft-quoted Andy Warhol famously claimed everyone would enjoy 15 minutes of fame though, in my case, it has been abridged to 5 minutes on *BBC Radio Wiltshire*. My interview was delayed by the previous item that, in true Alan Partridge-esque fashion, featured an in-depth interview with the Wiltshire-based people who would supply 50,000 Bibles to the Olympics in Beijing. Fascinating stuff that closed with the observation from the Bible printer, "I expect we'll need a reprint! It's not just the athletes who need to get in touch with God!" The journalists on the programme are very familiar with Swindon Speedway Club but, though they had done some pre-interview research, the segment failed to start auspiciously when I was introduced as "Jeff Smith."

The ostensibly big news around Abbey Stadium in recent weeks has been the decision of the Speedway Grand Prix organisers (BSI/IMG) to ignore the claims of Mads Korneliussen for the wildcard berth at the Danish Grand Prix to be held indoors in Copenhagen. Always a passionate man, Alun 'Rosco' Rossiter has made the case for Mads – the much-improved Swindon number 3 – to be invited. His protests fall on deaf ears when the organisers nominate Kenneth Bjerre. This is a story that has refusesd to die in the Swindon area and Rosco fumes at the injustice where Mads' recent domestic success against top-line riders (for example, his triumph over Grand Prix star Hans Andersen round the Blunsdon track) fails to translate into an appearance on the international stage. Ultimately, the majority of riders are selected for the Speedway Grand Prix on a grace-and-favour basis and, as always with patronage, there is no chance of appeal. Whatever the specific reasons why Korneliussen was overlooked, unusually Alun decided to employ wit rather than anger on the Robins club website. "We've come to the conclusion that his off-track appearance could be the reason. Maybe if he was to have a slicker haircut and have a [smarter all round presence] then maybe the international bigwigs would begin to take him more seriously." Events move on quickly and students from the Hair and Beauty Department at Swindon College offer to groom Mads. They propose to give him a selection of hair and beauty treatments at their North Star Campus. Studiously ignoring his own 'need for help' in this area, Rosco welcomes the offer. "If it takes a grooming session to get Mads noticed, then so be it. It's more productive than simply doing nothing and Mads is willing to do whatever it takes to be recognised – even if it means cutting off that wispy blonde hair!"

Actually just making your way to the Abbey Stadium is fun nowadays since the ongoing road works ensure that the road layout appears to be reconfigured every time you visit. At Poole Speedway they show sufficient promotional ingenuity to advertise the club on the local car park exit barrier and, if Swindon were to find some uniquely Wiltshire way of advertising the attraction of their speedway, then a small advert on some of the thousands of fluorescent traffic bollards that surround the stadium they would reach an impressive captive audience. One of the first people

I spot upon my arrival at the Abbey Stadium is Club Commercial Manager Paul Oughton who undertakes a similar important role for the Reading Racers. I quiz him about the earlier grooming session for Mads. "To promote the event we worked closely with Karen Barber who is the Programme Area Manager at Swindon College. She arranged for the students to give Mads a haircut, manicure and pedicure. They tried to make his haircut look a bit smooth but Mads wasn't having it! There was lots of press attention; we had Points West (telly) the Club Website, the *Swindon Advertiser* (the local paper), *BBC Radio Swindon*, *MTV*, the Mads Korneliussen fan club, *BBC Oxford TV* and *GWR*, which I think stands for 'goes wrong regularly'. I don't think Swindon College expected so much attention but we're delighted here at Swindon Speedway that we can build a relationship with them that works both ways! Speaking as the Commercial Department we're delighted."

Paul takes the commercial work for the Swindon Robins seriously and part of his job description is to be relentlessly enthusiastic. Even he goes a little OTT with the hyperbole when he claims to me, "We're the new glamour club!" Whatever the veracity of this claim, youth is certainly to the fore – both in the team and in some departments off the track, "We've a Commercial Manager who's 30 [Paul worryingly talking about himself in the third person] and a Press Officer who's 23 [Chris Seaward]". In common with Reading where he also works, there are a welter of attention-seeking initiatives from Paul and the boffins in the Commercial Department at Swindon. One such popular initiative is the renowned Swindon Legends' Lounge. Demand for this facility is at such a fever pitch that Paul has had to prepare an advice letter, "Due to the high amount of interest in the Lounge from next week on I do need to know if you have extra guests or if you would like to book an additional table well in advance of the event so that as many people can enjoy the thrilling action as possible." Like many in this book, it's a long but significant sentence without any punctuation at all! Even though there are still many hours before the tapes rise, as if to illustrate the incredible popularity of the conference facilities at the club, there is a huge cheer from within the grandstand bar directly above our heads. "There's a staff meeting of some sort – it's a commercial night and a local company have booked themselves in. In fact we have two groups tonight and towards the end of the summer, possibly the end of August we're going to have Speedway Speed Dating!" This could be the unmissable spectacle of any speedway summer both from the point of view of who the clientele who turn up and, even more wonderfully, the repartee you could overhear. Given the age profile and unique dress sense of the average speedway fan, this would be an event I'd definitely pay good money to watch, let alone be involved in!

I quickly set up my table under the lee of the home-straight grandstand adjacent to the yellow-hashed marked floor that designate the fire escape access-way at the bottom of the steep stairs that lead down from the Legends' Lounge, grandstand bar and toilets. In front of my position, the track staff are conscientiously hard at work with last-minute preparations to the air fence and track. I fall into conversation with Steve who, in new money, is part of the "Stadium Facilities Management Team". In old money, he's a sweeper and rubbish collector at the club. Presently, he's fussing over a couple of the black plastic dustbins I've cheekily moved to clear space for my table. The new arrangement of two bins together elicits a theatrical tut and glare but, once he has rearranged the bins to his satisfaction Steve tells me, "I worry that Reading is gonna shut down! No one's saying nothing but, Prudential own the land and it only stays open 'cause of the extensions they keep getting granted. Crowds have fallen off dramatically too! I said to Malcolm [Holloway] 'what's going on with them? You must be really struggling financially?' That previous bloke messed up things by changing the name and the race night but they've dropped off even further from the seven or eight hundred they always used to get. I can tell from the amount of rubbish I pick up afterwards. At Swindon, I get four bin bags full but at Reading I'm lucky to get half a bag nowadays! Don't get me wrong, speedway people use the bins – until they're full – dog people are much messier. Though, someone throws a lot of paper on the floor every week by the start line at Reading. As I say, I reckon it's gonna close! No building is happening elsewhere at that other place either. Even the dog crowds are falling off. Well, they have a really big Saturday night but there's no one there on a Wednesday and a Thursday!"

With my table laid out in its full glory, Rosco wanders down the grandstand stairs in his distinctive red Robins anorak deep in conversation with club owner and co-promoter Gary Patchett. The distinctive cover of *Concrete for Breakfast* that features the Sexy7even girls along with Christopher Henry Van Stratten sporting film-star sunglasses, immediately catches Alun's eye. Rosco looks at the book briefly and introduces me to Gary. Initially I'm surprised that even he knew my name but subsequently realise it's emblazoned all over the cover of the book. They wander off as yet more

---

Swindon v. Poole: *"With hindsight, 1984 really was a turning point for the sport and everything has changed since then!"*

cheering is audible from upstairs in the grandstand bar area. Tonight is book launch night and, sadly, some traditions are hard to break (although I would like to) so it's a disappointment when – just like happened at Somerset when I launched *Showered in Shale* in 2006 – a book is stolen from my stand before the gates have even opened, thereby eliminating the loyal fans of the Swindon Robins from any subsequent police enquiries. Though irked, I decide to take the theft as a bizarre form of compliment. Luckily Steve Davies, referee Margaret Vardy's partner, is on hand to entertain with reminisences about the fact that Margaret alleges I misquoted her in my first book *Showered in Shale* when I reported some disparaging general comments she subsequently denied all knowledge of ever mentioning. Steve chortles at the thought, "It's rare someone crosses her and she forgives them!" On a subsequent trip to the Isle of Wight, they extracted some revenge and doctored my publicity board (while it was in Dave Rattenberry's car boot) to read: "The biggest load of pretentious rubbish I've ever read – Margaret Vardy". Steve's a keen, long-time speedway fan who frequently travels with Margaret when she's on official duty and also elsewhere together to just watch as normal fans. I've never been quite able to place who Steve reminds me of until I realise that he's the Midlands version of Mr Yateman (the verger played by Edward Sinclair in *Dad's Army*). "Fabio's in the old town is superb. It's really excellent! We've got a table booked there for quarter past ten." Steve has recently seen the speedway at Stoke and admires the all-action style of Dermot Mark Burrows. "Buzz is Buzz! Brilliant sometimes but, other times, he rides like a 15-year-old rearing at the starts and then turning 360s on the bend. It's never dull when you watch him!" Afterwards I consult the Trip Advisor website for more information on Fabio's. Customer feedback ranges from praise ("this is our favourite restaurant in Swindon … not a pizza in sight. Instead, the biggest selection of fish dishes I've seen outside of a speciality fish restaurant") to backhanded damnation ("the food used to be lovely").

Bob Fisher waits for the rush

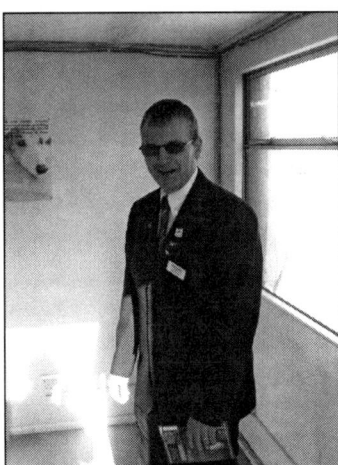
Trevor Claridge, member of the Hospitality Care Team

Speedway meetings are rarely short of interesting characters with stories to tell. Burma Star veteran Fred Martin and his wheelchair-bound friend Eunice inform me they're regulars at Sheffield, Scunthorpe and Belle Vue. Fred sings the praises of Ricky Ashworth whom he rang for help the night prior to a cremation service at Blackley in Manchester. The deceased's dying request was to have a speedway bike on display at the crematorium and Ricky was only too happy to step in the breach when asked. In his 80s, I gather that Fred Martin invariably finds the best in everyone and likes to acknowledge kindness, "Apparently Ben Hopwood also turned up with his bike at the funeral – it's amazing the nice things that people do for people, isn't it?"

To while away the time prior to the racing, Rosco is interviewed over the public-address system. Though he acknowledges the truism that Swindon presently confound their so-called 'critics' (in reality the individual club columnists of the *Speedway Star* who had the temerity to forecast that they'd struggle this season) and currently lead the Elite League table after 17 matches, Rosco is far from happy. The first leg of the KO Cup quarter-final at Poole that Swindon lost 53-40 hasn't improved his outlook on life. Another frustration is the injury to their in form young Australian, Troy Batchelor. "It's very frustrating! Troy is a tough cookie. Tomorrow he's going to Harley Street to see an elbow specialist that Jason Crump recommended as the best in the business. After last night, I must say – it's a bit negative – but we were a two and a half man

Swindon Speedway Office

Swindon v. Poole: *"With hindsight, 1984 really was a turning point for the sport and everything has changed since then!"*

team down there. Leigh scored 18 and Mads did his bit while James Wright chipped away. We're without Troy again [tonight] so will be running rider replacement and I'll be hoping for a lot better performance from some of the riders. [pause] They know who they are!" A glance at the racecard confirms these unnamed but possibly underperforming riders as Seb Alden (3 points from five rides), Travis McGowan (paid 2 points from five rides) and Manuel Hauzinger (paid 2 points from three rides). Rosco's grumbles are arguably well founded since Pirates are presently weakened by the loss of Magnus 'Zorro' Zetterstrom who was replaced at reserve by Poole number 8 rider, Jordan Frampton. Jordan's contribution was paid 2 points. At the end of the 2007 season, when the wheels comprehensively fell off the Robins championship campaign wagon during the Elite League play-offs, Rosco subsequently alluded to a lack of team spirit allegedly brought on by the pernicious influence (or lack of it) of his Polish riders. Despite the lack of Polish riders and the fact that Swindon Robins team went away to bond prior to the start of the 2008 season, there are murmurs off that all still isn't well with collective team spirit. However, if judged by comments in the press, publicly team spirit and bonhomie oozes from the pores of every Robins rider team and everyone sports smiles that wouldn't disgrace synchronised swimmers.

Whatever the reality of the situation, greater consistency and better results are required by the Swindon speedway management. Indeed, if their 2008 season was to kick on, then the Robins talismanic captain Leigh Adams will have to continue to excel and, hopefully, inspire his less-talented team mates. Predictably, the Aussie comfortably wins the first race but is followed home by Pirates pairing of Chris Holder and Freddie Eriksson who, worryingly, don't even need to bother to team ride to keep the out-of-form Seb Alden trailed off at the back in fourth place. If a drawn heat isn't quite what Doctor Rossiter ordered, then a fall and exclusion for Manuel Hauzinger during the first attempt to run heat 2 won't help his mood. If there were marks for artistic impression, then Manuel would score highly for his dramatic crash test of the second-bend air fence (when third). Sod's Law immediately applies in the rerun when James Wright, race leader first time out, only manages second when given the chance to try again. Though he pressures and threatens to overtake Daniel Davidsson throughout, he just doesn't quite manage to generate the speed to charge past his Pirates rival.

All authors, not just speedway ones, invariably expect their book to be a best-seller. Hopefully, praise will subsequently be showered on the book, its quality lauded to the heavens and the author garlanded with rose petals (or their equivalent) wherever they travel! My experience hasn't quite lived up to these grandiose expectations and, though tonight's Quarter Final KO Cup Second Leg, sees my book launched onto an unsuspecting speedway public, arguably one of the best speedway books of the 2008 season was launched just three nights previously at Smallmead Stadium in Reading. Notionally significant for the Reading v. Mildenhall Premier League encounter staged that night, in reality it will go down in the annals of history as the night that unofficial Reading Racers speedway club historian, Arnie Gibbons, launched his meticulously researched 40-year history of the club, *Tears and Glory: The Winged Wheel Story*. As a Reading fan, it's a book I've been dying to see published and, setting my partisan opinion aside (I had helped advise Arnie on the project), it's truly a speedway book after my own heart! In *Tears and Glory*, Arnie cleverly mixes the bread-and-butter facts and figures that make up any speedway club history with a wonderful array of extraneous information about the club, its riders and characters as well as the town of Reading itself. All of this is leavened with Arnie's understated wit allied to an unusual feature in a speedway history book, namely how he cleverly interweaves significant political and cultural events from outside the cloistered rarefied world of speedway into the main story.

The back cover blurb on any book is hugely important and anyone who picks up *Tears and Glory* couldn't help but be intrigued when they read Arnie's outline. "Walk outs, sit downs, fights, crashes, drugs, shopping, law suits, battles for control, transfer requests – all the drama is there." Indeed it is! Along with all the facts and figures that you'd expect from someone as authoritative and fastidious as Mr Gibbons. In speedway, as in life, triumph usually isn't too far removed from tragedy and in this case the book is dedicated to Reg, Pat and Bill but also to two Racers who lost their lives racing, "Geoff and Denny, proud wearers of the Winged Wheel."

Before the third race Arnie sidles up to my stall and, if he were a dog, he'd definitely have had two tails. His natural pride in publication and sight of bound copies available for the public consumption has been further haloed by the sales triumph of the launch evening itself, where it sold 51 copies. In addition, Internet sales totalled 11, Arnie sold three direct himself, major UK book distributor Gardners ordered a couple of copies and WH Smith's in Reading

Swindon v. Poole: *"With hindsight, 1984 really was a turning point for the sport and everything has changed since then!"*

town centre have bought 10 copies on a sale or return basis. Seventy-seven copies in one fell swoop are certainly more than I've ever managed and already Arnie's book could be seen as the speedway book sales sensation of the 2008 summer! Unlikely to directly experience fatherhood, Arnie's pride definitely has some equivalence with that of delight in a first-born. I don't imagine that Arnie would even be this delighted if the world turned upside down and his beloved Liberal Democrats became the Government of this country (though power sharing with the Tories after the next election might even see this, until recently, unlikely eventuality still happen). As if it combines an *aide memoire* with a comfort blanket, Arnie tightly clutches a copy of *Tears and Glory* and, in the manner of a vicar referring to a well-thumbed copy of his Bible in mid sermon, throughout the meeting he glances into the sacred book to reconfirm what he has just remembered or previously written. After months of intense effort, unsurprisingly for the remaining months of the speedway season *Tears and Glory* will be the prism through which Arnie either sees or interprets the live speedway action that unfolds in front of him.

"I'm amazed you can get blasé after just one night!" he tells me with my launch night sales presently standing at one copy sold and one copy stolen. "I try to take a different approach to each chapter. For example, the one on 1984 is really about the collapse of speedway. It's the longest chapter and covers such things as: the bribe scandal, the fact that four teams rode permanently with a guest and, of course, the Michael Lee fiasco! Never mind that the number of teams dropped from 16 to 11 just like that! In 1982 the Denny Pyeatt crash at Hackney is the story of the year. While, in 1992, Reading had 13 matches in a row in October and rode almost half a season in that one month. It was an incredible proportion of our total matches. If you're going to try to write an interesting history book – it's boring just saying that one meeting followed another and we scored xyz or the other. By finding a turning point or significant event for each season, I think I've managed to avoid that. With hindsight, 1984 really was a turning point for the sport and everything has changed since then!"

I'm really not sure what the collective noun for a group of three authors stood together at a speedway meeting should be. It's definitely a question that required an answer when Swindon speedway author, Graham Morris, joins us. He's used print-on-demand publishers Lulu to publish his masterwork, *Swindon Speedway: The Year That Ended in a Seven*.[1] The book covers the (ultimately traumatic) previous season's [2007] Robins campaign that saw them installed as pre-season favourites to lift the Elite League championship title only to miss out in the final analysis. If they'd won, sales would have prospered, particularly given this milestone was last achieved in 1967.

Back on the track, Swindon embark on a run of three drawn heats, although heat 5 would have been a 5-1 to the home team if, on the first bend, Mads Korneliusson had not taken his partner Travis McGowan for an enforced close inspection of the air safety fence. Travis has to use all his skill to ensure that he doesn't complete the inspection with a comprehensive test of his crash capabilities, but it nonetheless relegates him to last place.

Between races Graham and Arnie banter. "I'm reading your book at the moment", confesses Arnie, "I must say the Reading fan in me enjoys reading about Swindon not doing very well!" Pointedly quizzed by Graham about Swindon victories at Smallmead, Arnie expertly turns to page 251 of his own book (with impressive and accomplished ease) to quickly reveal that four out of Reading's biggest seven home defeats were actually against Swindon (and included

---

[1] Graham's book is a witty blow-by-blow account of the whole of the 2007 season that, somewhat bizarrely, has a first chapter entitled July 2006. After this strange start in chronology terms, the book follows a traditional month-by-month journey through the season – highlighting the key moments – before in-depth chapters on the Play-off Semi-Final and the two-legged Elite League Final. The book closes with a chapter about a deflated October 2007 that's followed by a review of the 2007 results and statistics. The book also has occasional examples of the type of speedway photographs that I love. One such appears on page 19 and features some parked cars (with the new Blunsdon by-pass in the background) with the rather wonderful caption, "The ever-shrinking Abbey Stadium car park". I'm not sure what they put in the water in this part of Wiltshire but Swindon speedway club have more authors than some teams have capable riders. They're usually called Graham apart, of course, from the prolific Robert Bamford – until recently Press Officer for the Swindon Robins – who, though he modestly wouldn't claim this himself, is the best-selling speedway author of his generation. Robert has a prodigious number of books to his name in print and these include his renowned *Yearbooks*, *The Homes of Speedway* (co-authored with John Jarvis) as well as too many club histories to list or name individually. Another recent but also marvellously prolific addition to the Swindon speedway publishing pantheon is Graham Cooke, creator of the charming and frequently wonderfully revealing *Blunsdon Blog*. In his blog, Graham takes us behind-the-scenes and provides a window on the hidden but essential curatorial aspect of speedway. The site has been rewarded with over a million visitors. If you haven't already visited this online treasure, then you should do so or alternatively indulge yourself with a purchase of either *The Year of the Blog* or *The Blunsdon Bloggers' Tour of Sweden 2007*. Obviously, if a blog has been created or a book produced then, logically, this aspect of the sport no longer remains hidden! Not only does the reader learn about successful track curation but a slew of stories and characters also leap out from the screen (or off the page). In the hands of a lesser writer than Graham Cooke – the dedication, humour, tenacity, skill and common humanity really wouldn't shine through so touchingly as it does.

Swindon v. Poole: *"With hindsight, 1984 really was a turning point for the sport and everything has changed since then!"*

the then record home defeat in 2000 of 32-58 though, sadly, this was bested in the last-ever team meeting at Smallmead by Redcar 33-60). Things pick up for the Robins in heat 6 when Leigh Adams expertly shepherds his out-of-form partner Seb Alden home for maximum heat win. It's a masterly display of team riding by Leigh Adams but nearly doesn't happen when Alden overcooks it on the last bend to almost but not quite allow Davey Watt through at the line. Keen to accentuate the positive, over the tannoy we're told, "I give you Leigh Adams!" Earlier I'd quizzed Wayne Russell in his office about the reasons behind why Leigh Adams always refers to himself in the plural when interviewed on television. Wayne defended the use of the royal "we" with a quick-witted and almost believable explanation, "He means 'his team' of mechanics and, of course, the rest of the riders. He's a real team man, Leigh!"

With the Robins lead only a slender 2 points (but still 11 points behind on aggregate) Mads Korneliussen appears to get a flier from the tapes to which he then adds some much-needed steel when he aggressively takes the closely following Bjarne Pedersen to the fence. The drawn heat doesn't do much for the prospects of the Robins but doesn't stop Arnie who again feverishly flicks through his book. "You wouldn't think he was the brother of Tim Korneliussen, one of the worst riders ever to ride for Reading! He rode eight matches for an average of 1.04 (gaining 6 points from 22 rides). Tim even ran Brendon Mackay close – he has an all time running career average of 0.94 (34 rides full paid 8 points)." In an attempt to distract the Swindon faithful from their likely exit from the cup, the Robins equivalent of speedway royalty Leigh Adams is quizzed about the recent Danish Grand Prix: "I started good and felt I was on the right page, though a couple of gate falls set me back. We'll forget about that now and concentrate on Cardiff. It just keeps getting bigger and bigger and the atmosphere is unbelievable!"

Though bodily in Blunsdon, Arnie's imagination has taken him away to his garage where a pile of boxes that contain his newly printed book are stored, "I'm surprised by how little space they take up in the garage!" The research throughout his book is excellent but, as previously mentioned, it's the small details that delight. Arnie's trawl through the local Reading papers (which were then the *Standard* and the *Chronicle*) in 1936 revealed that the participants at the Huntley and Palmer's Recreation Club Gala thrilled over the competitors of the "Pretty Ankle Competition". In July 1936 news broke in the press of a further attempt to stage speedway at Tilehurst, though Arnie's eye had been caught by a report headline "Six Tons of Bovril Stolen." Arnie had also bravely given a copy to the person most likely to be his sternest critic – his mother – whose initial reaction was to comment, "[long pause] Wow, you've done well and I like the footnotes."

Heat 7 actually marks the start of four consecutive drawn heats to further stymie chances of a Robins fightback. Things could have gone better in heat 8 when Seb Alden gets out of shape on the second bend and relegates himself from second to fourth. Enthusiastic but polite Robins fan Darcia Gingell passes and bats off my observation ("if I were a Swindon fan I'd be pretty upset with the way things are going") with well-practised diplomacy, "we'll win but not by enough points to go through, sadly!" Arnie cuttingly puts Alden's failure to score into context, "Once in a while they gate and look like a speedway rider, the rest of the time they don't!" Arnie confesses to Graham that he'd had to tread carefully while he compiled his book. He'd framed phrases judiciously and chosen his quotations cautiously. "I had permission from the *Speedway Plus* website to quote from something about Reg Fearman on there – but it was best to err on the side of caution as Reg can reputedly be quite litigious minded." Temporarily distracted from insights into the genesis of *The Winged Wheel Story*, Graham Morris opens my book and exclaims, "The first word I saw was orgasm!" It's not a word that typifies my book. Heat 11 sees Robins team manager Alun 'Rosco' Rossiter shuffle his options and give Troy Batchelor's rider replacement ride to Travis McGowan. Arnie tuts in touching surprise, "I see Rosco's failed to make the astute team change: i.e. bring in James Wright and have Hauzinger take the rider replacement ride in heat 13, where he'll come last!" When I quiz Graham, "Are your riders allowed to win?" He responds philosophically, "Nah, only if Leigh Adams goes with them." Surprisingly keen to defend the misfiring Robins against light irony, Arnie wades in "To be fair, they provided the majority of the heat winners so far, it just doesn't feel like it!" Graham has been bitten by the writing bug and admits that he's started work on a book about the team of 1967 – the last time the Robins had a championship winning side. With effortless encyclopaedic knowledge, Arnie proceeds to name the full line up of the Robins victorious team without pause and concludes with, "That was quite impressive!" Rather than acknowledge it was so, Graham prefers to throw Arnie a further (hopefully) difficult question, "Who was the number 8 then?"

On the centre green, there's a bigger crowd than some clubs actually get on the terraces and nearby to us a group

Swindon v. Poole: *"With hindsight, 1984 really was a turning point for the sport and everything has changed since then!"*

of heavily tanned half-pissed young blokes struggle to use the air horns they've purchased from the nearby Barbers' trackshop. While they might be virgin air horn users, they clearly fancy themselves as gifted singers between shouty conversations peppered with an extremely high swear word quotient. The tactical "blunder" that Arnie identified proves costly in heat 11 when the Pirates level the meeting score at 33 apiece with a snatched 2-4 heat win. Though an aggregate points victory is still theoretically mathematically possible for Swindon with four races to go, it looks highly unlikely unless you are a supremely optimistic Robins fan. Nonetheless heat 12 signals the start of a brief fightback. In the initial attempt to run the race, Jordan Frampton gets excluded after a fall and most neutral observers would expect Bjarne Pedersen is now odds on to win the rerun heat against the partnership of James Wright and Mads Korneliussen. However, in speedway things don't always go as predicted or scripted. Bjarne leads from the tapes but, on the second bend of the second lap, James Wright defies convention and overtakes the Pirates rider. This prompts a rare but huge cheer from the torpid home-straight grandstand crowd as well as a vigorous clap of the hands from Arnie. Similarly inspired, Mads Korneliussen rides a wide line from the final bend to the finish line to pass the chequered flag ahead of Bjarne to yet more unalloyed delight from the Robins faithful.

Graham Cooke and Steve Davies

Graham Morris chooses this moment to bid Arnie goodbye with a handshake and, as he tries to leave, gets his foot embarrassingly and rather clumsily caught on the corner of my table to scatter a large pile of my newly printed books onto the floor. The fightback by Swindon shows greater coordination and continued in the next race when James Wright defies the grumbles of his Wiltshire critics to gate with speed and considerable aplomb. Showing the great spatial awareness of a master craftsman at work, in a glance Leigh Adams immediately appreciates the situation and uses skill and experience to cunningly block the fast charges of Chris Holder. Adams then proceeds to team ride his junior partner home. It's a masterclass in which the canny Australian apparently senses or predicts every twist and turn of the skilled rival behind him. Unable to find parallels from his book, Arnie does the permutations, "This could be a last-heat decider yet! If Wright and McGowan get a 4-2 in the next one – which is doable – and Mads and Adams get a 5-1 in the last – which is plausible – that would be a change of tempo!" Completely caught up in the moment, when the race starts Arnie bellows, "Go on Travis!" a few times before the realisation dawns, "God, I'm cheering for Swindon – help!" Things suddenly look fantastic for the Robins and, with a third consecutive maximum heat score tantalisingly close, James Wright punctures the mood when he badly lifts on the back straight of the last lap of the penultimate heat to allow Adam Skornicki past. With some disappointment, Arnie observes, "Wright's tiring, isn't he?" Close by the group of suntanned drunk blokes have gained greater competence on their air horns but haven't quite sussed the unspoken etiquette and nuances of their use. They parp along at irregular intervals – often during the less exciting parts of the race – and repeatedly shriek in almost homo-erotic unison, "You've got to fight for your right to party!" For whatever reason, they need no second invitation to paint the home-straight grandstand red – massive cigars are soon lit but these prove to be premature (though the assumption they had any idea what the scoreline is a wild one). At least, the Robins have creditably taken the aggregate result to a notional last-heat decider. 10 points

Book display (minus 1)

Filling in the programme

Swindon v. Poole: *"With hindsight, 1984 really was a turning point for the sport and everything has changed since then!"*

up on the night and suddenly trailing off by only 3 points on aggregate; the chance to progress to the semi-final briefly tantalises until the power pairing of Holder and Pedersen for the Pirates shows astute tactical awareness by keeping Korneliussen locked at the rear of the field (after they allow Leigh Adams to blast off and away into the distance).

The last few heats of the meeting definitely excite and, even more significantly, I can now say that I was there to witness that once Arnie's book was safely published, he could reveal his true colours as a closet Robins fan ("in my defence, it was Travis"). Some of the crowd immediately dash away to the car park keen to thread their way back through the slalom of traffic cones and the latest complex road layout that surrounds the stadium. Others linger to hear the centre-green post-meeting interviews. Leigh Adams top scored with a five-ride paid maximum, while James Wright was deservedly nominated as "Man of the Match" for his 14-point haul (from six rides) from the reserve berth. His performance showcased his undoubted talent and he was aided on the night by some fast starts and occasional overtakes. The lack of these attributes on a consistent basis has caused rumbles of discontent from certain sections of the Abbey Stadium terraces. They say there are two schools of motivation when someone hasn't done as well as you thought they might. Current management thinking indicates that you should accentuate the positive and focus attention on what your employee has achieved or delivered. The other much less favoured and much more demotivational approach is to highlight these real or perceived failings publicly. The latter would appear to be the Swindon way if judged by Clive Fisher's interview with Seb Alden over the public-address system. "Is it your head or is it the bike? You keep winning and then coming last, winning and then coming half a lap behind in the next race. You've got to change – 'cause time's running out and there could be changes!" Few of us would like to hear this level of bluntness at work about ourselves. Sebastian gives a creditably mild-mannered reply, "We'll see what happens," though he's betrayed by his body language as he stomps back to the pits. Where, if I were him, like some other riders need less encouragement to do, I'd throw a few spanners around. Manuel Hauzinger who has raced to a three-ride zero also gets some motivational Clive Fisher treatment. "Are we angry with him?" Clive ponders rhetorically, "Of course we're not, we're just unhappy for you." In a typical speedway scene, the riders linger patiently to sign autographs and pose for photographs by the start-line fence. I buttonhole the passing Wayne Russell for his opinion on tonight's events, "If James hadn't lifted in heat 14 or, if Mads had gated in gate 15, we'd have won! But, as Leigh said, we lost it last night!" A slightly downcast Darcia Gingell passes with her friend Holly who reveals, "I missed a red carpet event at the O2 to be here watching us. Still, once you've seen one red carpet event you've been to them all!"

19th June Swindon v. Poole (KO Cup Quarter Final, Second Leg) 50-40

CHAPTER 9.

Eastbourne v. Wolves:

"We'll have to put it in a jig, straighten the diamonds where it's bent and the forks aren't 100 percent, but I'm sure we can fix it!"

21st June

Midsummer's night sees the second meeting in six days held at Arlington, this time the KO Cup Quarter Final first-leg clash between Eastbourne and Wolves. A poor start to the season in the Elite League has seen Wolverhampton firmly rooted at the foot of the table so, in normal circumstances, you would expect that they would be trying to engineer a cup run to keep their supporters' interest in the season alive. Sadly, even before a wheel had been turned, this looks unlikely because of the injury sustained by their star number 1 rider Fredrik Lindgren during the recent Danish Grand Prix. The injury occurred after a dramatic incident with Ales Dryml and, after such a spectacular crash, it was a reassurance to learn that the young rider had not sustained serious career-threatening injuries.

If this crash had been dramatic then the talk of the Eastbourne pits and terraces was the heat 14 crash on Monday night that saw Cameron Woodward somersault over the wooden section of the Arlington back-straight safety fence and yet somehow still manage to get up and walk away without serious damage. The crash occurred during the televised *Sky Sports* Elite League A clash between the Eagles and their recently resurgent local rivals, the Lakeside Hammers. It was a spectacular 'off' and reminiscent of a horror crash in almost the same place some years back by David Norris (when he also narrowly missed a parked tractor). It happened around about the point on the back straight when the riders have reached maximum speed prior to their swooping entry into the third corner. Viewed from the terraces it appeared that Joonas Kylmakorpi had "turned right" on his younger Australian rival at the very moment the rider drew alongside to try to pass him. After some time laid out on the track, immediately after his return to the pits that was certainly the perspective taken on the incident by Cameron Woodward when interviewed live on *Sky* television (and also when interviewed by Eastbourne presenter, Kevin Coombes). The report in the local newspaper, the *Sports Argus* noted, "Woodward was scathing in his criticism of the Finn for shutting the door on him on the outside line. The Lakeside reserve didn't emerge from the incident unscathed since he again dislocated his troublesome shoulder and had to visit hospital in order to have it put back into place." After some time for reflection and subsequent study of the television replays at home, the riders' union soon reasserted itself and Cameron was much more guarded and philosophical in his reaction than he was in the heat of the moment. "I think he came out to stop me but it wasn't really careless. He was just trying to win the race. It's racing. I had a few bruises and some skin came off. I've got a sore wrist and knee but nothing really. I'm glad I didn't dislocate my shoulder like he did." It definitely looked a horribly serious incident on the night to shocked onlookers and the severity of the incident could be gauged by the live broadcast reaction of *Sky* commentator, Kelvin Tatum. Not only did appear genuinely lost for words (even his trademark mock profound or garbled ones) but wore an ashen shocked expression on his face until Cameron finally rose from the shale back to his feet. Brian Owen, the hard-working *Argus* sports reporter, could understand why, in the cold light of day, Cameron had revised his initial highly critical opinion. "No wonder *Sky* loves speedway – they get right in there following a crash and get reactions people make in the heat of the moment when they're still dazed! Other sports just wouldn't let it happen. They'd want control because [instant reaction] doesn't always represent the club or the sport in the best light. Mind you, speedway people don't seem to care!"

I quizzed Cameron's mechanic Ashley Wooller for his version of events. "I've seen quite a few people do it [fly over the fence] and you think 'Oh, freak!' as they forward somersault and the bike goes over. Norris used to do that!

Loads of people have, including Nicki. Cam was really in the wars that night because in heat 3, Tomicek's engine struck him in the middle of his back protector. Another shame was that the big crash happened on the bike Cam had just borrowed from Edward. We'll have to put it in a jig, straighten the diamonds where it's bent and the forks aren't 100 percent, but I'm sure we can fix it!" Clearly this had proved to be the case since Edward Kennett's mechanic, Chris Geer, had just unloaded Edward's bikes along with other vital equipment from his van and brought them to his bay in the pits for the Wolverhampton meeting when Ashley jovially called over "How's our bike then?" Ashley refused to be drawn on whether there was any intent by Joonas Kylmakorpi prior to the incident, "You just can't say, but I think not! Though the ref thought he was to blame 'cause he excluded him!" Ashley's wife, Eastbourne Eagles club physio Jane Wooller adds, "We chatted to Cameron that night after he'd packed up and he said, 'After the smash I shut my eyes and thought, blimey, I'm on this bike for a long time!' I said, "You shut your eyes!?" And Martin Dugard said 'We all do!'"

If this late meeting incident could, ultimately, be overlooked and marked down to experience then the comments of Lakeside owner Stuart Douglas after his team's 51-39 defeat couldn't be so easily discounted. Afterwards he fulminated, "People will say I'm a bad loser and I'll admit that I often am a bad loser, but this is more from a general speedway point of view then when we're on *Sky* we should be working hard to make doubly sure there's an entertaining meeting. After that match, I feel sorry for *Sky*, the people watching it and also a little sorry for myself. The track for the first half of the meeting was a disgrace considering it was going out live on telly. They might as well have run it on concrete. If you didn't pop out at the gate – and admittedly we didn't – then you weren't going anywhere … I wouldn't be surprised if it was done just for us, but it could be a club policy that started recently. I'm disappointed that we lost but I'm also disappointed for the sport that the result was so important to Eastbourne that they prepared a track like that." Renowned for his track curatorial abilities, Bob Dugard explained the situation behind the track he'd prepared for the Lakeside meeting to the *Sports Argus*, "the circuit was dry and not exactly in tip top shape. The preparations had been complicated by late afternoon rain and the ongoing threat of showers borne out by the weather forecast and the cloudy sky." Bob then continued, "I think the comments show his naivety as a promoter. Heat 1 was won in 55.6 seconds. That's not far off the track record. Riders were lifting coming off both corners so you can't say there's no dirt there. The race times were consistent all the way through. If you know about speedway, that tells you all you need to know. To be honest, his comments have left me completely confused. The fact is his riders were not good enough on the night."

With two meetings in quick succession and with opponents Wolverhampton weakened by the need to use rider replacement for their GP star rider Freddie Lindgren, it's hardly a surprise that the KO Cup quarter final hasn't inspired Eastbourne's faithful to attend in significant numbers. This is a disappointing outcome for the co-promotional team of Martin Hagon and Bob Dugard who, at the end of the season, revealed the break-even attendance figure at the club to be 1,350 fans. Though the car park looks reasonably full, many people travel without passengers and this visually appeared to be borne out with many gaps on the far from packed terraces. The lack of fans along with the reduced quality of the opposition makes this doubly bad news for the home promotional team since against a weakened side many Eastbourne riders are likely to score a bumper number of points and therefore get a bumper pay night!

Obviously enough, referees travel all round the country to officiate at speedway meetings. Given their minimal pay (and reimbursed expenses), anyone who dedicates their time to work as a speedway referee must do so for the love of the sport and the chance of involvement in speedway rather than the financial rewards. This must definitely be the case when you factor in the abuse they frequently get from the fans along with the promoters and riders. One perk of the job is a BSPA pass, which should allow entry to all speedway tracks in the country. Even when they're not officially on duty, many referees can't stay away from speedway meetings and I often bump into officials, particularly Tony Steele, Margaret Vardy, Christina Turnbull, Chris Gay and Chris Durno with his son (Tom). Tonight Chris has driven down from his home in Solihull just to take in this KO Cup clash. I can't quite believe that while he's prepared to take a 350 mile plus round trip to watch the meeting, it appears that many local fans haven't been motivated or bothered enough to put in similar effort. "Early season there was a note from Chris Van Stratten saying crowds were down massively in the first few months. He blamed the weather but we all know it's the recession! Speedway is a luxury and luxuries are the first to go. Look at tonight, I'm shocked by the size of the crowd! It has to be less than a

---

Eastbourne v. Wolves: *"We'll have to put it in a jig, straighten the diamonds where it's bent and the forks aren't 100 percent, but I'm sure we can fix it!"*

thousand! It's a fine night and a cup match – admittedly without Lindgren – but it's still shocking!"

Even though the Eagles aren't presently the strongest Elite League team in British speedway this season, they've recently had successive home victories. They start the Wolves fixture in confident mood with a comfortable 5-1 win. You can never take anything for granted in speedway as the second heat illustrates when an engine failure for Kenneth Hansen robs the visitors of a drawn heat. The combination of a weakened team and occasional bad luck sets the tone for Wolverhampton who then slump in the face of powerful and confident riding from the Eagles team that sees them gain heat advantages in the next four races to take a comfortable 26-10 lead after six races.

While Bob Dugard patiently grades the track on his trusty tractor, Eagles presenter Kevin Coombes has his work cut out to entertain the crowd with some rider interviews and observations. Kevin takes the chance to quiz Edward Kennett about Stuart Douglas's reported comments on the quality of the Eastbourne circuit. He opens their dialogue with a rhetorical question, "How dare he? Arena's not exactly the best track in the country, is it?" With the Cardiff Grand Prix only a week away, conversation soon turns to this blue riband event in South Wales. Kevin and Edward will both be there in their respective capacities of presenter and rider. Uncontroversially Edward reveals that his GP master plan would be based on a simple strategy "to keep focused, give a hundred percent and race all four laps!" All his equipment has been prepared in advance, even the bike temporarily borrowed and recently crashed by Cameron Woodward. ("My good friend Kamikaze Cameron as we now call him has already mended it!"). Brief interview over, Edward departs to prepare for the seventh heat where Wolverhampton team manager Peter Adams sends Niels-Kristian Iversen out in a black-and-white helmet for a tactical ride to try and restore some balance to the scoreline. Over the public-address system Kevin Coombes continues to look forward to Cardiff, "We're proud to do the presentation work at the GP. It's only a few years ago that Eddie used to help hand out the sweets and now he's riding there in front of 40-50 thousand people. We're very proud of him!"

It would appear Edward has hit peak form at just the right time if judged by the way he comfortably races to his second win of the night in heat 7. Based on tonight's display, second place for Iversen comparatively represents something of a triumph for the Wolverhampton team. Things further improve for the visitors in the next race when Ales Dryml races to their first heat win of the night, albeit pressured throughout by Lewis Bridger. The odd drawn heat is neither here nor there given the superiority of the Eagles and normal service resumes when the next race results in the third Eagles 5-1 of the night. It's also the third consecutive race win for the suddenly rejuvenated Lee Richardson. The race gods are clearly looking kindly upon locally based Rico tonight because he's even managed to have his mandatory engine failure after he's crossed the line for victory (as he did in heat 5). With a cricket score already a foregone conclusion, Kevin Coombes takes to the public-address system to talk up prospects for the return leg at Monmore with optimism in his voice: "I had a word with Peter Adams earlier and he says although they've had a few home defeats the racing has been exciting by all accounts. When the new averages come into force on 1st July there's going to be a few changes. They

Riders of the future

Arlington trackshop

Bob Dugard supervises start gate preparations

Eastbourne v. Wolves: *"We'll have to put it in a jig, straighten the diamonds where it's bent and the forks aren't 100 percent, but I'm sure we can fix it!"*

have a low team average so – if they could bring in riders like Matej Zagar or even Nicki Pedersen – they could really start to go places! Stranger things have happened and that's speedway!"

During the interval break, the Wolves team get brief respite and Nick Barber in the Eastbourne trackshop also looks to the positive side of events, "A big home win is good for crowds! Fans enjoy it as a change and it brings people back!" Shortly afterwards, the Eastbourne riders resume where they left off and provide the race winners in all the remaining races, except for heat 14 when Nicolai Klindt provides Wolverhampton's second race victory of the night. Scott Nicholls and Lee Richardson both comfortably race to paid maximums, while Edward Kennett gets a full maximum. Lewis Bridger gains the points that his all-action racing style deserves but sometimes doesn't quite achieve. While Eagles reserve Simon Gustafsson reaps the benefit of his 15-lap mid-afternoon practice session with paid 7 points. The home team performance is so strong that they only run one last place during the meeting (James Brundle in heat 12). As the riders come round on the Meridian Marquees truck for their victory parade to celebrate their easy 62-30 victory Judy Hazelden gets slightly carried away, "32 points should be enough at Wolves – if not, they want shooting. If they don't win, I'll run through Horam naked!" Next to her, daughter Karen harrumphs, "Let's hope they don't then!" As the sparse crowd dash away to the car park without bothering to linger at the trackshop, Nick Barber shrugs philosophically, "Neither Nicholls nor Richardson will get an easier maximum this season." While it's a comfortable win on the night it's definitely not good financial news for the co-promotional team of Bob Dugard and Martin Hagon. That's the considered opinion of Paul Bailey who, until recently, masterminded the club finances for the Eastbourne Eagles under previous promoter, Bob Brimson: "That's an expensive night on a low crowd!"

21st June Eastbourne v. Wolverhampton (KO Cup Quarter Final, First Leg) 62-30

Eastbourne v. Wolves: *"We'll have to put it in a jig, straighten the diamonds where it's bent and the forks aren't 100 percent, but I'm sure we can fix it!"*

CHAPTER 10.

Mildenhall v. Scunthorpe:
"We even had a tug-o-war between the mascots – best of three –'cause they even had a bear with them"

22nd June

Though we're only a day past midsummer, the Mildenhall speedway season 2008 already looks less than stellar. The league table supposedly doesn't lie and prior to the meeting with the Scunthorpe Scorpions, the Tigers were the runaway weakest team in the league having already raced to 12 defeats. The tone for a difficult season was set when Mildenhall lost their first League meeting of the season at home to Berwick 29-61. Many further losses followed and, after the recent 35-58 home loss to the Redcar Bears, there had been a 'clear the air' post-meeting press conference inside the stadium's Fenman Bar. All seven riders plus promoter Simon Barton, team manager Laurence Rogers and a large number of fans attended. If souls hadn't exactly been bared, then frank words had definitely been spoken during this post-mortem. Tigers captain Kaj Laukkanen had confessed that the team spirit had gone awol, promoter Simon Barton lamented that there "just wasn't enough fight or effort" and claims from the floor that Laurence Rogers was waffling led to him to briefly walk out of the press conference. Mildenhall then found themselves faced with a few potentially difficult away meetings. They'd got tonked by Reading at Smallmead but, by the end of the week, they managed to surprise Scunthorpe and themselves when they took the Scorpions to a last-heat decider at the Eddie Wright Raceway.

If it presently wasn't exactly a bed of roses for Mildenhall Fen Tigers then the same can't be said for Premier League newcomers Scunthorpe Scorpions. Upon arrival in the stadium car park, I am greeted by bright sunshine and eddies of dust blown by the strong warm wind. I've hardly parked before Rob Godfrey pulls alongside in his Land Rover with his wife Gail. Since their narrow home victory over the Tigers on Friday, the Scorpions have travelled to Rye House and lost but, nonetheless, Rob remains upbeat about the lay of the land in his part of the speedway world. "The racing has been the best I've ever seen at our place! I know I'm biased but, our lot aren't good starters, so they've been coming from behind. It's much easier to be a success in the Premier League than it is in the Conference. Our crowds are up – we've had some high and some low – but even the lowest have been better than the Conference League last year. It's also easier to sack the riders in the Premier League! Before you'd think, I'll give them a few more rides. But this is a business and it's their job so, if they're not doing it, then I have to make changes! That said, we've got a side that can win more often now. Last year we were getting 60s all the time, whereas this season it's been over 50 once, I think, and all 48s and 47s which isn't good for my heart but exciting for the fans to watch! Last week, we had a last-heat decider with Mildenhall which surprised us but they both went on parade afterwards 'cause it was so good. Today we're gonna take them apart!"

Some of Rob's riders have already arrived in the pits and he hurries off to catch up with them. Meanwhile, I've been joined by the hyperactive and perpetually curious Michael who briefly completely fails to recognise who I am. Once he's remembered, Michael helpfully helps carry a box of books from the car park to the shaded display area in the grandstand adjacent to the trackshop located between the refreshment kiosks and the bar. Our walk takes us through the pits entrance gate, down the deep shade of the tunnel cum accessway that runs through the impressive home-straight grandstand and almost out onto the track. We avoid venturing onto the track and instead take a sharp right through the sun-bleached pits area to head up the concrete steps of the first- and second-bend grandstand. The combination of the bright sunshine and the strong warm wind makes the shade of the grandstand the ideal location from which to watch this afternoon's speedway. The door of the Fenman Bar is open but inside it's completely deserted, except for the new fangled type of collapsible display poster that showcases a vicious looking tiger image and features the words, "No Brakes – No Fear – No Mercy!" In the interests of accuracy, based on this season's performance so far, it should also say, "No Points".

I've arrived so early that Johnny Barber has yet to arrive in the Barbermobile aka the Enjay Designs small white van. When he does arrive, Johnny struggles with the various boxes and the heat. Never one to resist a sit down in the shade, once the stock has been completely unloaded and stacked, he patiently starts to lay out the merchandise on his display tables or Blu-Tak the posters and photographs to the brick walls as well as hang up assorted items of Tigers-branded merchandise. Throughout this process Michael shadows his every move and alternates between getting under Johnny's feet or else he fingers the stock with a mix of curiosity, fascination and desire. He ignores the welter of photos, pens, cups, badges and caps but, instead, is most taken with the black felt-lined GP riders' badge board, 10 badges wide by 15 badges deep. There is a horizontal line of badges – appropriate to their race bib number and national flag – for each (regular) rider from the 2008 Grand Prix series. For example, the number 4 race bib is worn this season by Tomasz Gollob, so his tabard-effect badge features a white background and a red border with the Polish flag at its centre topped and tailed with his name above said flag and his number below it. All badges follow the same design template, so the badge for honorary Pole, Rune Holta features a similar colour scheme but occupies the seventh row on the felt-lined badge board. Below that is the Scott Nicholls badge (red border, blue background with the Union Jack flag at its centre) emblazoned with his race number (8) and, beneath that row of badges, the Chris Harris badge appears with a large sized number 9. A sign written in felt tip on a small card says, "GP rider badges £2". Michael would clearly like to purchase one of these badges but isn't sure which rider he should favour so, instead, continually checks with Johnny, "How much are they?" The constant reassurance that they cost £2 each is, obviously, food for thought but not action.

Though it's still quite some time before the turnstiles open to admit the fans, I'm surprised to see a large group of people pass from the vicinity of the area of the entrance turnstiles and walk briskly in the sunshine past the pits home-straight stand. I double check with Johnny whether the gates have opened early only to be told, "No, funnily enough, they're the helpers! There's often more of them than the fans!" With nothing left to do, I make my way down to the away section of the pits area and chat to Magnus Karlsson's mechanic, the always affable Paul Henry. Based in Hull, Paul cuts a distinctive figure based on his height and general stature all set off with a mane of blonde highlighted hair distinctively styled in true late-70s roadie bouffant fashion. One of the other mechanics (or perhaps a rider's sponsor or father) joshes with him, "You're looking tired!" Distractedly Paul nods towards Magnus Karlsson who lulls in a nearby chair in T-shirt and jeans, "So is he!" In fact Magnus looks relaxed and fresh, despite the warmth of the day and the possible stress of the races that lies ahead for him. If there were justice in the world, this shouldn't be the case since, after the previous night's Rye House meeting, he'd enjoyed himself so much that, eventually, he'd briefly spoken to God on the great white telephone. One of the joys of youth is the ability to nonchalantly brush off the deleterious after-affects of boisterous celebrations and their associated technicolour yawns.

Mostly bathed in bright sunshine, the track has a variegated colour where it hasn't been watered consistently. The surface looks dusty and light coloured in places and, where it has been watered by the bowser pulled by a blue tractor that slowly circles the West Row circuit, it's taken on a deep dark mud brown colour. Mildenhall have a guest track curator this afternoon, in the form of Sheffield and Scunthorpe speedway's vastly experienced trackman, Graham Trollope. On closer inspection, even the recently watered sections of the track appear to be drying inconsistently. By the low wall that separates the pits area from the dog track and the solid (stock car) crash barrier topped with a wire fence that borders the race track itself, a man stood on his own intently studies the steady progress of the tractor as it slowly wends its way round the circuit. I'm not sure that I would be as completely absorbed in such a spectacle but, it transpires that he has a professional and nostalgic interest in this activity, since he used to be the trackman at West Row. I don't catch his name but he tells me rather authoritatively, "With the sun and wind like this the track is gonna get patchy. Some sections of it are thick and wet and others are dry and dusty – it's really not gonna be ideal for racing at all! It would be much better if it was one or the other! But, when the riders go from thick and wet to dry and dusty, it throws them off completely and makes controlling the bike a nightmare. There's not much you can do about it as a trackman. They're trying to flood it at the moment but it's really not going to make much difference. This is one of the fastest drying tracks in the country so, as quick as they put the water down, it'll get soaked up. It's different at King's Lynn because there it's half a mile from the river and close to the sea so, as the tide rises, so does the water table and the moisture comes up through the surface. The same can't be said of here!"

Back at the trackshop Johnny has been joined by Mildenhall and Ipswich speedway presenter Kevin Long. Despite

---

Mildenhall v. Scunthorpe: *"We even had a tug-o-war between the mascots – best of three –'cause they even had a bear with them"*

the fact that it's a scorchingly hot afternoon, Kevin looks remarkably cool and dapper even when dressed in a formal white jacket worn over his brightly coloured collared shirt. Always a snappily dressed man who likes to err just this side of dandyish, Kevin's brow and recently shaven head betray no sign of the dampness that appears to afflict everyone else even though we all wear far fewer layers of clothing. Kevin needs no second invitation to recall the drama of the previous week's post-meeting press conference, "There were open questions from the floor to Simon (Barton), Laurence (Rogers) and all the riders. Usually there's only a couple of them but, last week, they were all up there. It gives people the chance to emerge from behind their keyboards and ask the questions they want answers to directly. Laurence kept saying 'When the riders click'. If he said this once he said it 10 times even though some of these wouldn't click if they wore tap-dancing shoes. At one point, a fan told Laurence off for waffling. It's hard to know what to do when someone's accusing you of having more waffle than McCain's so Laurence left for a bit. You can understand why the fans are getting frustrated! Mildenhall have yet to win this season – well, they beat King's Lynn in a challenge meeting, I think, maybe it was a Premier Trophy meeting, but they definitely haven't won in the Premier League yet! What with the injuries, the team changes and the fact that the riders say the track is different for each and every home meeting, I doubt it's gonna change this afternoon! Even though we're not winning, the diehard fans still come along without fail! We had a great crowd last week for the Redcar meeting though they did bring quite a lot of fans. We even had a tug-o-war between the mascots – best of three –because they even had a bear with them. We had Di [Farmer] in her tiger outfit. She won, of course, but I think he let her!" Discussion then moves onto the merits of reserve Henning Loof who, by all accounts, is a nice bloke who lives in the local area. Sadly he's struggled to deliver the points on anything like a regular basis. Nowadays, no conversation about Henning can avoid the fact that away from the track he works as a male nanny.

Poster

Tractor goes round and round with the bowser

When the racing gets under way it's quickly apparent that the strong (but warm) wind plays havoc with the tapes. A recent televised fixture on *Sky* had Alun 'Rosco' Rossiter rather ridiculously complain that the wind had blown the tapes onto Leigh Adams's wheel (at a point when climatic conditions in the stadium had wind strength merely at susurration levels). Heaven knows what he would say if faced with this afternoon's blustery conditions at West Row. The tricky tapes situation isn't helped by the wind direction. It blows strongly from the first bend towards the fourth bend and, thereby, forces the tapes back onto the wheels of the riders as they attempt to line up. When the Start Marshal eventually has all the riders just about into position and the race is under the referee's orders then, really weirdly, a female member of the track staff very noticeably attired in a bright orange coat rushes out onto the track to order the riders to get into their gate positions correctly! It's a surreal moment, let alone that either a rush of conscientiousness or bossiness has led her to feel that she somehow has the right to even intervene! The race gets as far as the second bend without incident before Michal Rajkowski hits a bump in mid-bend and his bike takes off uncontrollably and throws a surprised rider to the shale. Referee Barbara Horley doesn't stop the race and this continues with the remainder of the riders all looking somewhat uncomfortable on their machines and just about in control of them! On the third bend of the

Mildenhall v. Scunthorpe: *"We even had a tug-o-war between the mascots – best of three –'cause they even had a bear with them"*

penultimate lap, Richard Hall falls and, after a brief delay, remounts to rejoin the pursuit of Jan Graversen who labours with some form of technical difficulty. Nonetheless, Jan just about manages to coast over the line for a second place, albeit only fractionally ahead of the hard-chasing Hall. The Scunthorpe 'Henderson Insurance' Scorpions lead from the off and fail to relinquish this advantage for the remainder of the afternoon. Over the public-address system Kevin Long looks on the bright side and, although the stadium doesn't exactly look packed, he's effusive in his congratulations, "It's great to see so many of you here this afternoon on this very windy but sunny day!" Kevin then re-confirms the evidence of our own eyes, "It's a very windy day so the track has taken on lots of extra water, making track conditions difficult."

I'm told that the woman on the centre green who wears the bright orange coat is Alison Owens and she rejoices in the moniker of Trackstaff Supervisor. During the meeting, she's effectively a glorified flag marshal, albeit one (if judged by the frequency of her interventions) with definite aspirations to take on the duties of the Start Marshal. With the strong wind still very problematic and the tapes billowing everywhere, Alison takes it upon herself to marshal the two inside gates occupied by Henning Loof (gate 1) and Ben Powell (gate 2). The Scunthorpe rider is the main object of her attention, though she fusses around and hassles him without any notable sign of success. When the race finally gets under way, the riders again appear to battle their machines and the track rather than each other. Though no one exhibits a smooth riding technique, Byron Bekker wins easily. After he's skulked at the rear of the field for most of the race, Ben Powell eventually rouses himself to dash for the line from the last bend and almost snatches third place from Mark Baseby. This last gasp effort plays havoc with his bike control on the warm-down lap. While Ben just about avoids the fence, Kevin explains the decision behind the unusual sight of two starting gates in action this afternoon, "We've installed a second starting gate – literally behind the start line – as the wind keeps blowing the tapes onto the riders' wheels and we don't want the Alun Rossiter wind-blowing excuse!" It's rare you see two starting mechanisms in use and, ever-vigilant but also curious, Scunthorpe promoter Rob Godfrey and Scorpions team manager Kenny Smith needs no second invitation to stride out to give it and the track a thorough inspection during a temporary delay in proceedings. Kevin's mission to explain continues, "We do need the tape a little bit tighter, obviously, there was a lot of slack in that knicker elastic and it's been causing problems in the wind!"

On the track the collective scratching of heads continues with the addition of more participants from the Mildenhall management. During the delay we're entertained with news of the 50/50 draw, "We've seen some very healthy prizes this season topping £100 so don't forget, the more tickets you buy the higher the prize." In the shade of the first-bend grandstand a large contingent of Scunthorpe fans add to the atmosphere and entertain themselves with some good-natured banter. Sat in the deep shade of the trackshop area, Johnny Barber jokes that the orange-coated flag marshal has escaped from Guantanamo Bay. Speedway historian Arnie Gibbons has ventured along to West Row and stands clutching his new book *Tears and Glory* in the manner of a security blanket. Sales and interest in this title continue, "Reading lending library have already ordered a copy!" The meeting resumes and the Scunthorpe faithful are rewarded with a victory for Viktor Bergstrom, who's closely followed by Magnus Karlsson with Tigers guest Tomas Suchanek badly trailed off in third place. Conditions remain difficult as evidenced by exciting Mildenhall reserve, Mark Baseby, who initially appears to master the surface sufficiently to overtake Emiliano Sanchez only to throw it away in bizarre fashion on the third corner one lap later. Mark showcases an elegant slow-motion Wall of Death type manoeuvre when he mounts the third-bend kickboard before, as the bike speed fades, he falls into a forlorn heap at the exit of the bend.

Quite what needs to be done to the track isn't exactly apparent but, while whatever that might be is figured out, the tractor does extensive remedial work. Notoriously the West Row stadium was built on a potato field and, in a burst of nostalgic track curation, it appears the tractor driver is keen to recreate the potato-field look this afternoon by patiently gouging the track surface. Kevin Long fills the time with a foray to the merchandising area to give us an update on the current mood in the pits or, more accurately, the current mood on the track. Since, once again, pretty well anybody who is anybody from either team has relocated themselves out onto the track, where they chat in earnest conspiratorial gaggles or walk slowly around with eyes intensely fixed on the surface as if they're part of a police forensic search for clues in a murder enquiry. Riders kick the surface, team managers gesticulate and assorted track staff listen interestedly. Kevin huffs, "The wind is blowing the tapes a metre back towards the fourth bend and Scunthorpe have been worrying about infringements and rolling as well as the state of the track. It got to the stage

---

Mildenhall v. Scunthorpe: *"We even had a tug-o-war between the mascots – best of three –'cause they even had a bear with them"*

where they [Rob Godfrey and Kenny Smith] were almost suggesting they wouldn't go out until the remedial work was done to the surface. Complaints about the tapes were a load of bollocks – no one ever really looks at the tapes, anyway – everyone looks at the pins and the mechanism. With the wind and sun like this it's difficult to put right! There's a particular area of concern as you come out of the second bend where it's deep and boggy. Obviously, when it's deep and difficult that's not ideal for speedway!" While the riders, mechanics and team managers linger, the tractor transforms the problematic second-bend surface from ostensibly smooth into the suddenly *de rigueur* ploughed field effect. Quite how this will help remains a mystery. Quizzed on the contribution of the orange-coated lady, Kevin notes, "That's Alison, she runs around like a loony!" From behind his trackshop table, Johnny Barber watches the curation work phlegmatically and takes some consolation from the 7-17 score line. "This is a good one. We're only 10 points down. Which, by our standards, recently, isn't too bad! It's a very sunny afternoon – admittedly with a strong wind – but a lot of people have still come out to enjoy themselves at the speedway." Kevin switches his microphone back on and, over the public-address system, updates the crowd on further progress. "We do officially have our interval now while the track work continues. As you might have noticed, the consistency of the surface is causing the riders some problems! There's a very slick dry bit and then it gets very sticky and deep, particularly down this end [bends 1 and 2]. It's a track of two halves and we're trying to progress the meeting as quickly as we can – once the track staff have done their work." The tractor driver is keen to entertain and reverse circles round the track to continue to effect the promised remedial repairs.

Fresh tyres

On track discussions

Contributor to the Berwick and King's Lynn programmes, Mike Moseley, has come along to West Row stadium to enjoy the sunshine and an afternoon of speedway before his polyps operation the next day. "Laurence Rogers was the first out there trying to paper over the cracks in case anyone would think it was the team that was awful rather than the track! The Scunthorpe riders certainly seem to be coping with it okay." Full-time policeman and part-time speedway photographer, Phil Hilton, provides another first hand account of the havoc at the start gate, "Kaj [Laukkanen] wanted to put a bollard out to stop the tapes flying back. He claimed, 'the Start Marshal can take it away just before the tapes rise', but Trevor Swales said he couldn't."[1] Meanwhile, Kevin Long has found Mildenhall team manager, Laurence Rogers, and pesters him for an update, "Things should be sorted shortly. That's not waffle! Maybe there is something in it that the first bend is difficult but [waves towards the track] he's a great trackman and, if we just let him get on with it and improve things, maybe we can pull those 10 points back when we get started again!" The words have barely left Laurence's mouth before Kevin squeals, "Is that a bike I can hear?" During the track grade and inspection the orange-coated Alison Owens was left without riders to hassle at the start line and kicked her heels for 30 minutes along with her other less hyperactive orange-coated colleagues on the centre green. In fact, at Mildenhall speedway club, there are more people in fluorescent clothing on the circuit than you often find in a late-night motorway road repair team. Keen to assert herself, just at the moment all four riders

[1] This is specifically outlawed in the SCB regulations. A rule change made to the SCB Rulebook shortly after Chris Louis was struck on the head by a metal tapes holder in Poland.

collectively rev their bikes to a maximum under the referee's order, Alison lunges and dramatically picks up a red flag (but doesn't wave it). Johnny notes sardonically, "She's making sure the red flag works!"

During the speedway close season, the pages of the *Speedway Star* treat us to individual track reviews. Said articles also include in-depth (but sometimes partisan) comment upon each individual club's programmes. Judge Howard Jones indulges his quest for improved design flair with an examination of apparently mission-critical factors like page layout and paragraph indentation. This season, it's a shame Howard's creative analysis won't extend to any consideration of the Mildenhall 2008 tabards since they'd provide a rich source of material for his finely tuned judgements. To my untrained and artistically untutored eye, the Tigers tabards incorporate a design feature of strong vertical black lines that – when viewed from the stands as the riders flash past – cause the numbers on the rider race bibs read incongruously as 111, 121, 131 and so on.

Michal Rajkowski wins heat 6 and temporarily gives the Mildenhall Barmy Army something to cheer though a massed trumpet of air horns is more the order of the day. The next race sees Henning Loof explore his own unique way round the track with a virtuoso straight line dash from the start gate to the bend 1 fence without the bother or requirement of any sustained attempt to turn. The remaining riders in the race battle with the track and continue without him. In the trackshop Johnny harrumphs about track conditions, "Dunno who that bloke was that you were talking to earlier but, whoever he was, bring him back!" Mildenhall's sole representative since the first bend, Jan Graversen fights the good fight, battles manfully but can only finish second, while Scunthorpe move into a 14-28 lead. Keen to provide entertainment for the home section of the crowd, Kevin Long informs them over the public-address system, "Rumours of a new signing – there's no truth that it's Hans Andersen! Who's [here] enjoying the meeting from the pits with Trevor Swales and Mick Bratley this afternoon!" Laurence Rogers has delayed the obligatory Mildenhall Tigers weekly use of the black-and-white helmet until it can be potentially both effective and properly savoured. After an extended three heat wait for its use, the anticipation proves worthwhile when Michal Rajkowski wins his second consecutive race (heat 8) in the distinctive but frequently seen round these parts headgear. Further entertainment is provided during this race by Mark Baseby who's persistence sadly fails to advance him from fourth place when his efforts come to naught with a last-bend crash into the apex of the fence that appears to badly bash his back. Kevin confirms the evidence of our own eyes and informs us "Once again, Mark Baseby giving his all with his never-say-die attitude."

This latest Tigers heat win is the signal for yet another round of extensive track-grading work and, once again, the tractor driver takes to the track for some lengthy repairs. During another impromptu interval, the 50/50 draw for £146 is conducted with the help of visitor and star rider Hans Andersen. Kevin wonders aloud, "I hope the supporters' club can afford Hans Andersen doing the raffle draw because he can't come cheap!" The excitement of the draw builds to a crescendo when the second prize goes to the holder of the yellow ticket ("yellow like your sexy race suits in the GP") while the main prize is won by someone with a lucky pink version ("he's pulled out a pink ticket appropriately enough for him!"). With the draw completed, Kevin retreats from the pits to the trackshop area to watch the further ministrations of the tractor to the race surface, "Unbelievable, having waited 20 minutes for the track to dry out, now we're watering it!" Grand Prix badge rider sales have proved a hit this afternoon and can probably be used to judge riders' popularity in the same way that opinion polls try to establish who's going to win the next election. Kevin Long is a keen advocate of this analytical framework, "You can judge the most popular GP riders by the badge sales – there's only one Scott Nicholls badge left – unless Johnny's put them all in his pocket?!" The lone Scott Nicholls badge sells almost as soon as the words leave Kevin's mouth. Before he retreats back to the pits Kevin asks, "Is my wit too quick for you to keep writing it all down?"

The subsequent track-surface work is clearly to the liking of the Mildenhall Fen Tigers – well at least to Kaj Laukkanen, Michal Rajkowski and guest Tomas Suchanek – since they then combine together for a further two consecutive heat wins. Astonishingly this reduces the chasm of the original points deficit to a mere 5 points with the score comparatively poised by recent West Row standards at 29-34. The real drama of the meeting then arrives on the first bend of heat 11 when a combative first corner sees Jan Graversen exit the second bend with a lead that he then fails to relinquish. Throughout the afternoon, Graversen has ridden determinedly and with some aggression. Another prime example of his will-to-win is the manoeuvre that takes him between Henning Loof and Carl Wilkinson as they race between the first and second bends at the start of heat 11. Since there are no fallers, there is no reason for the referee Barbara

---

Mildenhall v. Scunthorpe: *"We even had a tug-o-war between the mascots – best of three – 'cause they even had a bear with them"*

Horley to call a halt to the race. Nonetheless, you didn't have to be an expert on body language to quickly realise that Carl Wilkinson is less than happy with the young Dane apparently almost taking his wheel on the first bend of the race. When you wear a crash helmet and wish to strongly communicate with someone who also wears a crash helmet, then the subtlety and nuance of your conversation will necessarily be lost. Not that this bothers Carl Wilkinson as he flashes past the chequered flag as if intent on competing in a fifth lap of a race. At such speed, he soon catches up with Jan Graversen on the second bend and proceeds to outline his deficiencies before he then bolts to the pit gate to prepare to continue the discussion while the Dane completes his celebration lap.

In fact, quite a crowd of people from both sides of the pits has spontaneously gathered – readied and keen – to carry on *ad hoc* discussions in the pit lane and the pit area. Any fan located on the first-bend grandstand gets a panoramic view of the pits dispute, something that involves mechanics, helpers and riders from both teams as well as managers and promoters. The ferocity of these animated discussions are such that Barbara Horley is soon on her way from the referee's box to instil some calm. "Our referee Barbara Horley – in every sense of the word – is coming down!" Bolstered by the notional automatic authority of her position as match referee, Barbara also works in education so can quickly identify and control juvenile behaviour. Easy to spot in a crowd of riders and mechanics in his distinctive white jacket, Kevin Long provides a running commentary on events in the pits. "Barbara has invited Laurence and some of the Scorpions officials into the pits office – she's stopped short of pulling the blind down!" The updates then break off while Kevin then has a passionate and animated conversation with Scorpions team manager, Kenny Smith. We're too far away to hear the specifics of Kenny's points but it's safe to say that with his ponytail flying and his arms flailing animatedly that he doesn't appear overly happy with the Mildenhall presenter. Sight of this bollocking prompts the Tigers Barmy Army to offer words of encouragement ("Hit him, Longie!") and imaginative chants of support ("Longie! Longie!"). In the heat of the moment, pretty well everyone has an opinion and is keen to get involved. Richard Hall's mechanic [aka his dad] offers Trevor, Mildenhall Pits Steward a chance to resolve matters with pistols at dawn or, at least, some philosophical debate elsewhere. Afterwards Trevor makes light of their discussions, "He did have a few words and I will be going outside later – so you never know our paths might cross again!" His debate with Kenny Smith over, Kevin then resumes his description of events but specific details are scanty. Basically we learn that the confidential discussions in the office have concluded and that the management of both teams have been sent back to their respective sides of the pit area. Probably with use of the naughty step, extra homework and the threat of detention afterwards.

While Barbara makes her way back to the referee's box, Kevin leaves the pits for the comparative calm of the trackshop area. "I don't know what Barbara Horley has said – she hasn't spoken to me. If they came here often they'd know that Jan Graversen does that every week on the first corner. He forgets to turn every week! I see my job as explaining to the fans that can't see what I see or know – so, when the managers were called to the referee's office, obviously I'd talk about that. Kenny Smith said to me I was inciting the crowd and I said I was just doing my job as the announcer, as he should just do his as the team

Crowded pits

Victory parade

manager rather than bother about mine! I told him 'there were two sides of the stadium that can't see and won't know what is happening or why there is another delay!' I pointed out his side were 14 points up and now they're only 5 points up so, perhaps, that requires his attention!" Three hours into the meeting, the 12th heat of the afternoon/evening starts but quickly stops again when Mark Baseby's all-action style sees him confront the bend-three fence once more. The rerun is comfortably won by Finnish rider Kaj Laukkanen (in what will be his last appearance with the club), though there's still some drama at the line when the flag marshal struggles to unfurl the chequered flag fully, so can only wave it in peculiarly contorted fashion. Yet more track curation then ensues. Arnie Gibbons notes: "There's a hell of a blue groove on the third and fourth bends! Unusually it starts by the third-bend fence and then heads on round tracing the contour of the centre green." It really is an impressive example of the genre.

For once during the 2008 season, the speedway gods briefly look down kindly upon the Mildenhall Tigers and permit a run of form from heat 5 onward that produces an unbeaten sequence of race advantages (five) and drawn heats (three). This comparatively amazing run of good fortune ends by the second bend of heat 12 when Jan Graversen smashes into the fence. His sudden demise delights an older lady with bleached blonde hair who leaps to her feet in jubilation at sight of his misfortune. Some other Scunthorpe fans also celebrate his fall but with less enthusiasm than the bottle blonde who shrieks, "Aaah, he's hurt his bum!" Fellow fans then question whether her delight in reality hides her secret aspirations for romance ("I'm not that desperate"). The rerun has Emiliano Sanchez and Richard Hall race away from ex-Belle Vue rider Michal Rajkowski for a 1-5 heat advantage that secures them the three league points awarded for an away victory. As the Scunthorpe riders cross the finish line, said older lady leaps like a young salmon desperate to spawn upstream. These celebrations are statistically premature since the Scorpions can theoretically still be overhauled. Arnie Gibbons studies his programme closely and correctly points this out to me before the start of heat 14, "Logically there should be a tactical substitute for Henning Loof. Their hope of winning with one is small and non-existent without one! The first time Henning Loof visited Smallmead with Somerset, [Reading uber-fan] Nick Dyer posted on the forum that he was 'the worst rider he's ever seen' and the next day Henning posted, 'I was trying'. The next time he came, he had one race where he went from first to last. He has the look of a rider who'll score points because other riders will decide not to pass due to the danger involved! Thierry Hilaire – who rode for Long Eaton, Milton Keynes and, possibly, Sheffield – was another who springs to mind. As does Tim Hunt, of course!" The tactical substitution Arnie foreshadowed is made by Mildenhall team manager, Laurence Rogers, but though Jan Graversen starts he is unable to make up the chasm of the initial 15-metre handicap and trails in last.

The rider selection for heat 15 causes some debate and Arnie wonders if they'll be a first-bend rematch for Jan Graversen and Carl Wilkinson. "Wilkinson is eligible for heat 15! There's no doubt he got a bit of a stuffing on the first bend of heat 11 but, sometimes, these things happen!" A fan called David Palmer comes to my table to pointedly highlight the impact the "poor" state of the track has had on the quality of the entertainment on offer this afternoon, "That race where Mildenhall got 5-1 wasn't racing at all, was it? They were going so slow! I go to all the Scunny away meetings that are local – Sheffield, Redcar, everywhere really, except Scotland and Rye House – and that wasn't racing!" Another fan (from Mildenhall) overhears our conversation and, as if I have some personal responsibility for the track, gives me both barrels of his twopenneth worth. "They don't know how to set it up – Robbie Kessler said that last week – it's a different track every week and hard to ride for the home riders! While the away riders come in with an open mind and set up their bikes as they see it." It's quite a vexed topic of conversation and a question that definitely bothers the Mildenhall fans around the trackshop area, "Trackman Huggy wasn't here which doesn't make it easy. He prepares a very fair track which negates any possible home bias." A cursory glance at the track prior to heat 15 can't help but reveal a huge blue groove at both ends of the circuit.² The final race of the meeting looks likely to be close until Michal Rajkowski hits the notorious third-bend bump (during the second lap) and suffers the trauma of the loss position while he clings desperately to his machine. Though the result is definitely not in doubt,

² Graham Trollope was later to comment on his curatorial experience at West Row. "I stood in at Mildenhall for their track man, Huggy, when he was away. I just went in on spec and it was 'there's the sprayer, there's the grader, off you go'. But the material they use has a fair bit of clay in it, which I'm not as used to, and I found it awkward to work with. No one told me any way in particular how to do it, and they just left me to it. I'd not used the stuff before and I was just thrown in at the deep end. Because of that, I ended up over-watering it a little bit, which made a tramline where it was too wet, but fortunately it sorted itself out in the end."

Mildenhall v. Scunthorpe: *"We even had a tug-o-war between the mascots – best of three –'cause they even had a bear with them"*

the Scunthorpe fan (with the bleached blonde hair) leaps and writhes with enthusiasm at the advantage gained for the Scorpions from this mishap in her distinctive salmon spawning upstream fashion.

After a lengthy meeting, there's an impressive rush in one direction to the Fenman Bar to secure the best seats for the press conference while, in the other, there's a bolt for the car park. Mildenhall team manager, Laurence Rogers, finds time for a few words en route to the press conference. He's dismissive of suggestions of deliberate intent during the controversial heat 11, "Like I would tell my riders to fence people – after I've had a rider [Casper Wortmann] fighting for his life in intensive care this year!" In the pits Magnus Karlsson's mechanic, Paul Henry, views the situation differently, "You don't use tactics like that to win unless you're desperate! The Danes are all like it!" On my subsequent trip down the grandstand steps towards the car park, I pass a determined-looking Rob Godfrey on his way up the stairs towards the Fenman Bar and the press conference. One Mildenhall fan told me afterwards that Rob temporary interrupted it, "to wave his finger at Laurence." I'm still loading boxes in the car park when a still agitated Rob Godfrey returns. He acknowledges heated words were exchanged in the pits after the heat 11 Graversen/Wilkinson incident. "What I said was a response to his [Laurence Rogers] premeditated instruction to put Carl Wilkinson in the fence. He was heard! I only said if the ref wasn't gonna sort it, I would instruct my riders to do the same! It's a shit promotion at a shit club with a shit presentation. If that's what they have to do to win – then they must be desperate! There're a number of incidents that we ignored. I'm really not happy with that approach to speedway. I dunno what I can do but I wouldn't do that myself. I can't imagine being that desperate!"[3]

22nd June Mildenhall v. Scunthorpe (Premier League) 40-53

---

[3] It was a meeting that brimmed with tension and controversy though, unusually, the *Matrix* didn't quite fully reassert itself in the *Speedway Star* reports afterwards (if you read between the lines). Laurence Rogers dismissed dirty-riding accusations levelled against Jan Graversen, "Carl Wilkinson is a pretty tough customer himself; he just came off second best in a hard first bend with Jan." Rob Godfrey took the view, "the match on Sunday was rather spoiled for me by Mildenhall maybe trying just a little too hard. Nobody wants to see injuries but someone was going to get injured if that carried on because we were being taken to the fence at times." The meeting report itself in the results section of the magazine (written by Randall Butt) noted the "Heat (and hot air) generated by the incidents" and also quoted Carl Wilkinson, "It was a clear case of trying to nail somebody; he came off his line and then straightened out on me." While, apprised of these comments, Jan Graversen retorted, "It was nothing like that. I was almost a bike length in front at the bend so I was making the turn I wanted."

Mildenhall v. Scunthorpe: *"We even had a tug-o-war between the mascots – best of three – 'cause they even had a bear with them"*

CHAPTER 11.

Reading v. Edinburgh:
"Britain's sexiest mascot and also the most expensive!"

23rd June

A warm but cloudy evening brings the Edinburgh Monarchs to Berkshire for the second leg of the Premier Trophy semi-final. It's the kind of evening that would count as summery in Scotland though you know that later (when the sun disappears behind the derelict grandstand on the back straight) temperatures at Smallmead will drop rapidly. The first leg at Armadale saw Mark Lemon top score for Reading with 10 points and the Monarchs run out comfortable victors by 22 points. Racers team manager Tim Sugar predicts, "We'll win – but not by 22 points. It would have been a lot closer but Mark Lemon fell off when leading on a tactical ride at their place." A passing fan chips in with "I can make a prediction now – we're not going to win the Cup!" Whatever the result tonight, co-promoter Malcolm 'Mad Wellie' Holloway is "absent because of his heart attack!" Malcolm's myocardial infarction happened five days ago on the return journey from the Racers Premier League fixture at the Redcar Bears on Teesside. Not only did he have the good fortune to survive this traumatic event but, as a resident of Basingstoke, the visiting consultant heart surgeon at Basingstoke General Hospital is Mr (Anthony Charles) De Souza from the Royal Brompton Hospital in West London. De Souza is a plain-speaking, highly regarded and giftedly skilful surgeon who had brilliantly operated on my mother Mary the previous month (for a different type of heart condition). Inside the match programme Malcolm airs some trenchant views on the performance of the team on the recent mini Northern Tour that took them to Edinburgh, Berwick and Newcastle. In print he can only describe this politely as "a disgrace". Though the riders redeemed themselves on the final night of the Northern Tour at Newcastle, Malcolm still wrote ominously (though he subsequently didn't act upon his threat) about the need "to look at things with a view to strengthening up".

The promoters at the club have kindly agreed that I can have a signing session this evening for my latest book. Whether the Racers faithful still have the budget or the appetite for further reading matter after Arnie's successful launch of *Tears and Glory* remains to be seen. Malcolm says a few kind words in his column and, also doing his part to promote my presence in the stadium, is Reading speedway announcer Bob Radford. Justifiably highly regarded in the sport for his experience, knowledge, insight and skill as a performer – Bob also has a keen eye for detail and a comical conversational manner as well as a quick wit that ranges from the sharp to the sarcastic. "This evening we're honoured by the presence of a minor celebrity with the emphasis on the word minor in the form of the eccentric speedway author Jeff Scott, whose latest book is called *Concrete for Breakfast*. He's kept it under a quarter of a million words this time! It's a very good, if somewhat eccentric read – his books take a bit of getting into but, once you do, you can't put them down! If you don't know him personally, don't worry, most people don't! It's a shame that referee Christina Turnbull isn't here tonight because Jeff gets on very well with her and enjoys being her occasional escort." In my capacity as guest Writer in Residence at Reading speedway my most recent blog described Bob at work in his lair (aka the referee's box) overlooking the track. "The vastly experienced, renowned and justifiably well-regarded club announcer, Bob Radford (61), who lounges in his chair coiled to spring into action with a witticism, *bon mots* or some infotainment over the tannoy. Off-air, he's even funnier and sharper – apparently combining in one person the skills found naturally in Paul Merton, Ronnie Barker (in Norman Stanley Fletcher *Porridge* mode) and Dale Winton." Later when I visit the referee's box he laughs mischievously, "Did you mind me getting my own back a bit? I hope you liked my 'occasional escort for Christina Turnbull' comment!"

It's quite an evening for authors at the stadium and unofficial club historian and *Tears and Glory* author Arnie Gibbons has dressed for the occasion in his favoured true colonial fashion. Given that he's a man who pays attention to the appearance of other people and the specifics of their attire, this is all too much for Bob Radford to resist and later we hear, "In the crowd tonight we have Arnie Gibbons who looks suspiciously like an Englishman abroad in a tropical country the way he's dressed tonight. You can just imagine him with mosquito repellent and a glass of Pimm's. I think his real name is Arnold [like Tony Blackburn's dog] but he's shortened it to be more like Arnie Schwarzenegger, like you do!" Arnie likes to dress for comfort and there's a famous photo of him on the *Guardian* website caught speaking passionately from the stage at a Liberal Democrat Conference that is captioned something along the lines of: "A delegate sports the Shopping at B&Q on a Saturday look."

In complete contrast, the smartly dressed Edinburgh promoter and team manager John Campbell is stood in the ice cream van queue for a "99". One of the real delights of speedway is the community nature of the sport and the close interaction between the performers and the fans. Though he speaks diffidently, John shouldn't be underestimated and is now the longest continuously serving promoter in British speedway. He has a shrewd appreciation of the foibles and idiosyncrasies of riders, fans and fellow promoters alike. After a disastrous 2007 season, the 2008 version of the Edinburgh Monarchs have performed so well so far this season that many people fancy them to gain many items of silverware. John sensibly dismisses such talk as premature but he will admit, "It's the best team I've ever seen and been involved with at Edinburgh. All of them are winners! They can't wait to race and there are no whingers. If it rains, they want to race and, if it doesn't, they want to race!" Congratulations are in order with news on the BSPA website that Edinburgh have been chosen to host a live *Sky Sports* broadcast in the near future. Some league promoters and team managers immediately spring to mind as the kind of people who love the glare of the TV lights and the notional celebrity it confers upon them. Based on what I know of him, I expect John would prefer a trip to the dentist in preference to a live broadcast on the television. He grimaces at my suggestion that he'll soon be a star on the telly, "Well, there are a few problems. To be exact, there are three problems. The dogs' race on a Monday night, we don't have planning permission, oh, and we can't get anyone to race against us! Apart from that it's a certainty that it's going ahead!" Except for their Premier League trip to the Isle of Wight, this is the furthest south the Monarchs will have to venture during the speedway season. Like his attitude to most topics, John remains phlegmatic about distances, "We've gotta come back here in a few weeks for a league meeting but we reckon we'll get back in about five and a half hours tonight, which isn't too bad." One thing that you can always say about the Edinburgh fans is that they travel widely in support of their team and often in significant numbers. During the Scottish "holiday fortnight", the Edinburgh supporters' club will definitely organise a week away to (weather and fixture lists permitting) take in a speedway meeting on every single night of the week. Not all of these meetings will actually involve Edinburgh racing, but the enthusiasm of the Monarchs fans won't be dimmed by that fact. I catch a few words with well-travelled Edinburgh fan Norrie Tait who tells me that rising star and Monarchs number 2, Thomas H. Jonasson recently forgot to bring along his steel shoe to their away meeting at Birmingham, "he only noticed in the first corner but that's speedway riders for you!"

By Edinburgh standards, they haven't brought as many fans along to the meeting as usual but there's still a reasonable crowd of them at their traditional spot on the grass bank of the third bend. From there they can overlook the activity in the pits and also on the track. Many clubs would be delighted if this

They're off

Sunny Smallmead

Yummy

Reading v. Edinburgh: *"Britain's sexiest mascot and also the most expensive!"*

number of fans would dedicatedly travel hundreds of miles to watch them ride. Given this is a one-off isolated fixture and not part of any multi-date tour, it's impressive. My stand attracts little custom though an astute and rather charming Polish man called Michala buys three books – for friends in Vancouver and Poland along with himself. We have a peculiar conversation where he speaks to me in Polish and I reply in English. He's clearly used to people misunderstanding the spelling and pronunciation of the dedications he requires. Arnie Gibbons stops for a few brief words en route to further interact with his public. "Nick Dyer did a nice piece in the *Reading Chronicle*!" The man next to him says, "Last Tuesday there was a piece in the *Evening Post* and the other week you made it into the *Newbury Weekly News*, along with the report on the Birmingham meeting and a photo. It's the biggest article I've ever seen in there!"

A regular feature of race night at Smallmead is the banter between announcer Bob Radford (located in the referee's box) and roving presenter Paul Hunsdon. Bob has just returned from a seven-day cruise to Norway and has brought his partner in crime a gift. "I've bought you a troll. He looks like Andy Povey – only a tad more attractive!" The cut and thrust of their conversation is a taste I've acquired (and relish). We might be treated to bigger helpings tonight, given that Bob reports, "Our referee tonight – Chris Gay – is delayed in traffic on the M25 at the moment!" Even though Chris drives a comfortable executive car, delays on the M25 can exacerbate even the most even-tempered of men. Thankfully he arrives around 7 o'clock and, with years of experience as speedway official, he quickly performs all the routine but obligatory essential duties required by the SCB before any speedway meeting can commence. In the meantime Bob Radford is trying to get to the bottom of the peculiar world of foreign riders' names. "Do we know what the 'H' stands for in Thomas H. Jonasson? And have we found out what the 'P' in Tom P. Madsen stands for?" Tadley-based Paul Hunsdon has almost done his homework, "Yes! It's something quite magnificent like Paarup!" Later when I check Robert Bamford's authoritative speedway *Yearbook 2008* to find this information, I discover that Thomas isn't listed since this is his first season in Britain. My guess is the 'H' stands for Hagar but I stand to be corrected. Quite a few of the riders have exotic middle names. Mads Korneliussen rejoices in "Klit", Kaj Laukkanen hasn't exactly shouted about "Pekka" and Leigh Lanham definitely doesn't strike me as a "Stefan". Charlie Gjedde sounds like he's been named after an explorer "Rasmussen", while Hans Andersen's "Norgaard" sounds exotic to non-Danish ears. Unless you were to read the *Yearbook* carefully (or attend an election they were involved in), it's unlikely that you'd ever discover some of these exotic monikers. Mark Royston Gregory Loram has certain nobility while Luke Alex James Priest has biblical (or rock group) resonances.

Out on the track names, like reputations, count for naught when Mark Lemon and Chris Mills combine to hammer in a first-heat 5-1. Second place for Reading number 2 Chris Mills moved his evening unto a much better footing after his late arrival at the stadium due to the aforesaid jams on the M25. Dale Fontaine is the sponsor of the second heat and, when given half a chance, performs his 'Echoes of Elvis Tribute Show'. Bob Radford's clearly been impressed by what he'd heard ("Dale Fontaine who sang so wonderfully for you a few weeks ago") but is even more impressed by the elegant all-action style of Andrew Tully who wins the race in a time of 60.74 seconds ("He was certainly fast and rode a magnificent line!"). Sadly for the Monarchs, their young Australian reserve Aaron Summers trails in last but allows Bob to issue a correction on behalf of his partner with the roving mic, "It's Aaron Summers not Ann Summers as Paul mistakenly claimed!" With the Racers already 4 points to the good on the night, presently located on the centre green Paul Hunsdon has confidence flow through his veins at the sight of the line-up for heat 3. Though we can only just about hear him say "The big O is just doing a practice start," above the deafening roar of Ostergaard's engine. In 2007, the Dane switched mid-season from Birmingham to Workington under something of a cloud though, so far, he has been a reliable and talismanic rider for the Racers during their 2008 campaign. Though, of late, he hasn't quite lived up to his own exalted high standards Paul senses improvement, "Ulrich hasn't scored so many points in recent weeks but hopefully his bike problems are now sorted out." Also out to ride in this heat is the Soosh [Tomas Suchanek] and, for Edinburgh, Derek Sneddon and Matthew Wethers. Whether admired or otherwise, Sneddon often inspires strong feelings but tonight struggles to adapt to the Smallmead shale surface and quickly finds himself relegated to fourth place behind the unpredictable Tomas Suchanek. This takes the meeting score to 12-6, the aggregate deficit to 16 points prompting Paul Hunsdon to (prematurely) exalt, "We're slowly clawing back the deficit!"

If Paul is delighted with progress so far, then Bob Radford approaches ecstatic, "And we have the appearance of another star! At first we had Jeff Scott, then we had Mike Patrick and now – Wacky the Racer!" The mascot that Paul

Reading v. Edinburgh: *"Britain's sexiest mascot and also the most expensive!"*

Hunsdon dubs, "Britain's sexiest mascot and also the most expensive!" is notionally on duty to thrill the kids. But, in the same way that (on the telly in *Spooks*) the intelligence services invariably try to persuade enemy spies to 'turn' and become double agents, Paul has hatched his own cunning Baldrick-type plan. "We want the kids to come down to the start gate for the sweets and to bring their mums so that I can see them! So come on kids, bring your mums to get some sweets from Wacky!" Whatever Paul's plans for the evening, the Reading Racers ambitions to fight back are somewhat disrupted by Ryan Fisher's victory in the fourth heat. Previously the combative American rider Ryan couldn't contractually be spoken of or written about without the word "controversial" somewhere in the equation. However, since his move from Elite League Belle Vue to Scotland to ride in the Premier League for Edinburgh, he appears to have been rejuvenated judged by his recent impressive form and rediscovered enthusiasm for speedway. Though, more points and the bracing air of Scotland are clearly important factors in his transformation, behind the scenes it's the calming influence of his wife Daelyn (step-daughter of Mike Faria) who's credited as the firm hand of guidance behind his improvement.

The Racers fightback stalls further when William Lawson wins the fifth heat in enough style to have Bob Radford comment, "Yes, thank you, our man is developing into a fine rider!" Two drawn heats don't yet quite qualify as a stalled cup campaign but the need for Reading to gain some advantage from heat 6 is a priority. The race features four unbeaten riders under orders at the tapes and, in the initial attempt at completion, first-bend bunching sends the rider from gate 4, Andrew Tully, off for a close inspection of the air fence. The St John Ambulance team on the centre green spring into action, "Various people breaking into a trot there! Andrew looks okay and let's hope the fence is also okay so we can get back on with things." While the safety equipment is repaired and readied for action, Bob Radford gives us the slightly mysterious lowdown on Arnie's book from the perspective of ex-Reading promoter Pat Bliss, "She says 98 percent is excellent but she's not going to reveal the 2 percent she disagrees with – but, wisely says, most people wouldn't understand!" The rerun of the sixth heat again only progresses a short distance before referee Chris Gay slaps on the red lights to stop the race. "Well, once again, a rerun with a public warning for the rider in blue – Chris Mills – to sit still!" The riders quickly make their way back to the start line for a re-rerun that sees Chris Mills get a flier from gate 3 closely followed by Mark Lemon from the inside trap. However, things only look good for the Racers until the apex of the third and fourth bend when Ryan Fisher, attired in his distinctive stars and stripes kevlars, blasts past them both. At the rear of the field there's further trading of positions though, fortunately for Reading, Andrew Tully falls on a fourth bend of the second lap (when third) to allow the last placed Mark Lemon through to ensure the consolation of a drawn heat. With the successive drawn heats total now stood at three, the need for a maximum heat advantage is paramount but quickly fades when the Monarchs combination of Sneddon and Wethers gate with alacrity and proceed to win with some comfort (except for a self-inflicted brief flirtation with the fence by Wethers during the second lap). With an aggregate victory still a remote statistical possibility, Bob Radford approvingly spots that a member of the track staff team looks like Ivan Mauger, "He'll dine out for a week in Newbury on that one!" Before heat 8 starts, the Monarchs signal their intent to kill off the meeting as a contest when Andrew Tully replaces fellow reserve Aaron Summers. Though it's only his third ever ride at Smallmead, Thomas H. Jonasson wins elegantly with considerable ease. Among the Reading faithful the realisation dawns that his two earlier outings in the meeting merely served as reconnaissance rides to discover and master the contours, topology and racing lines of the Smallmead circuit. The ninth race starts with Bob Radford announcing, "Wacky the Racer socialising as referee Chris Gay presses the button." On the track Ulrich Ostergaard inflicts the first defeat of the evening upon Ryan Fisher and, with the Soosh in third, Reading reduce the aggregate deficit to an almost insurmountable 20 points.

Much more fascinated with events on the centre green than on-track action, Bob Radford thrills at the sight of legendary speedway photographer "Mike Patrick who carries the same weight as Tim Sugar and I on our stomachs but he has two cameras! And so has Chris Gay too. I remember when he was young. It happens to all of us in the end!" The tenth heat is a drawn but a race with some excitement provided by Mark Lemon who pressures Derek Sneddon for four laps (without success). It also features a Chris Mills dive under Matthew Wethers on the final bend to sneak through for the consolation third-place point. Thomas H. Jonasson storms to victory in the 11th heat to the admiration of Paul Hunsdon and many others in the stadium. "He took some time to weigh up the track! That's his second impressive win tonight and, if my maths are correct, Edinburgh are through to the final." In fact, theoretically four consecutive 5-nils would lead to a run-off but that's as likely as a lightning strike or Kate Moss arriving at Smallmead for a date with Paul.

During the interval, I catch up with Edinburgh's Mike Hunter who's predictably sat in the home-straight grandstand to appreciate the action. Supremely dedicated to his beloved Monarchs, Mike also writes the most perspicacious news and match reports in the *Speedway Star* every week. He also gives the best reason I heard all season for not buying my latest book, "I would buy one but we flew down and they're very strict on weight!" If the likelihood of victory has gone then the fans can take solace in the interval raffle draw that, this evening, has a consolation prize of the Cannon and Ball Live in Blackpool CD. When the racing resumes, we're treated to what Paul Hunsdon would frequently call throughout the season "a trademark swoop from the Big O". In this instance Ulrich's focus on individual success results in Nicki Glanz being pushed wide on the first bend of the second lap in order to create the necessary space for Ulrich to dash round Derek Sneddon to take the lead. The "Big O" exits from the second bend in a manner that mixes speed, power and the hint of a slight loss of control. Ulrich then rears massively before he gains enough composure to ease to victory by a considerable margin (then you have to say Derek Sneddon isn't quite the same calibre rider as the Dane). Even for a serial optimist, though the meeting result is a foregone conclusion, the often vital 13th heat is a bit of a shocker and typifies the Reading Racers season since the Racers line-up looks good on paper but fails to perform on the track! The race itself is won by Ryan Fisher, second place goes to a rider Paul suddenly starts to call "Bill Lawson", while Mark Lemon finishes trailed off in third with Tom P. Madsen marooned at the rear. Bob Radford chooses to focus his attention on other matters, "It must be getting chilly down there 'cause the big man [Paul Hunsdon] has put his jumper on – cashmere, probably!" Ever keen to talk about music, Bob treats us to a review of the concert recently seen by the Reading speedway soundman sat next to him, "Steve Go-bay saw Bruce Springsteen at the O2 – he's 59 years young and one of the few musicians better live than on record."

Sat in the grandstand with friends, Oxford speedway track curator Nobby Hall has ventured from Oxfordshire to the wilds of Berkshire for a much-needed fix of speedway. "I still have the keys to the stadium and go down there to see how things are every day! That way I can keep the track looking reasonably decent and ensure that it doesn't get covered in weeds. I have to say I'm a bit lost without the racing every week! I've only had the smell of methanol in my nostrils five times this season." With no need to exert themselves beyond going through the motions, the Monarchs register a heat disadvantage in heat 14 and then draw the final race to allow the Racers to run out face-saving winners 46-44 on the night. Bob Radford is magnanimous in victory, "I think we can say Edinburgh have been one of the most excellent sides we've had at Smallmead this season! There'll be no press conference because of the time curfew. There's a second half with lots of action with the quad bikes. Don't forget we're racing this Sunday at Smallmead – against Somerset in the KO Cup – and, if it's nice and warm, you can all come dressed like Arnie Gibbons did tonight. One final thing, Malcolm Holloway is seriously ill in hospital so, if you want to hand in cards, please do so at the speedway office. Or you can e-mail via the club website. Obviously, Malcolm won't be racing next Sunday afternoon as that would be last the thing he needs, hanging around on the sidecars!"

23rd June Reading v. Edinburgh (Premier Trophy, Semi-final) 46-44

CHAPTER 12.
Isle of Wight v. Sheffield:
"We're all committed to speedway but everyone else isn't"

24th June

The Portsmouth ferry terminal car park is bathed in sunshine but completely deserted of vehicles since they've all just been loaded onto the boat for the 3 o'clock sailing. Inside the ferry ticket office – which also serves as the Isle of Wight speedway muster station on every Tuesday afternoon during the season – I'm astonished to find that there is no sign of either promoter Dave Pavitt or team manager Dave Croucher. Only Roy Collins (or as Crouch tells me later, "We refer to him as ACU Sat Nav Roy, or soppy bollocks, whichever is the more appropriate") remains in the plastic seated waiting area. This is a surprise as I've arrived well ahead of time for the 4 o'clock ferry sailing. Roy, however, tells me: "They go at 3 o'clock now!" As he speaks, a shadow falls across the booking office windows caused by the arrival of a giant lorry transporter with a large ready-built bungalow on the back. It's definitely a step up from living in a caravan, though I doubt this single-storey dwelling is bound for the Smallbrook stadium where the club has planning permission for some of the riders live in caravans during the summer. How the bungalow stays on the lorry transporter is a bit of a mystery, given it protrudes at the sides and off the back. I'm only pleased that I won't get caught behind it on the narrow roads that surround the ferry port. A vehicle of this size, loaded in this manner couldn't travel quickly and it has arrived late for the 3 o'clock sailing. However, cargo in the form of freight (rather than humans) is so important to the Wightlink Ferry Company (and whoever expects its delivery at the other end) that, although the ferry had already started to sail away, it has now been recalled to pick up the bungalow. This is good news for me as I can join the Isle of Wight management team on the boat. And also good news for Dave Pavitt because Roy hands me a paper bag, "Pav says, 'can you take the doughnuts?'"

The ferry is a working vehicle which criss-crosses the Solent many times a day and I'm sure those working on board have long ago got inured to any notional thrill they might feel at yet another journey. While they might take each trip and their skills for granted, their ability to dock the boat smoothly and accurately never ceases to amaze me. While I wait for the re-docking to finish, the ferry staff show no interest in checking my ticket but are very keen that I remain behind the safety barrier some distance from the vessel. I joke, "Thank God my bungalow didn't miss the sailing" – only then to be quizzed where exactly I'm going to put it on the Island. The transporter lorry looks like a giant snail with the bungalow on its back and takes some skilled manoeuvring to position it correctly among the other much smaller vehicles already on the parking deck. By the time it's shipshape and Bristol fashion I've already made my way up the many narrow flights of ferry stairs to the café area where the Two Daves [Pavitt and Croucher], ex Islanders team manager Jed Stone and another man have already begun to slurp their coffees. After a brief "hello", Pav rips open the doughnut bag, seizes one and bites into it with relish, "Ugh, these are custard doughnuts not jam ones!" Ever keen to look on the bright side Crouch retorts, "They're less calorific and better for you!" Crouch then theatrically says in a stage whisper to the other men at the table, "Watch what you say, he's a journalist." Crouch is keen to see a copy of my latest book and, after he's studied it for a short while, rather proudly explains to his fellow travellers how the book got its title. "Chris [Holder] and Cory [Gathercole] had a massive smash in heat 13 at Glasgow and it looked so bad that I expected both to go to hospital. Holder was excluded and when Cory came back to the pits he was dazed and didn't know where he was! I asked if he was okay and wished to continue and he said 'don't worry Crouch, I've had my concrete for breakfast!" [1]

---

[1] Cory's predilection for offs had Swindon co-promoter Gary Patchett comment in the *Speedway Star*, "Cory simply has to cut back on the number of falls he takes. He even tends to talk too much about landing on his backside, and I wonder if it weighs too much on his own mind. Certainly you don't win races or earn money by landing on your backside!"

With the sun glistening off its surface, the short 20-minute ferry journey across the water that separates Portsmouth from Ryde is just the ideal length of time to have a coffee, a doughnut and a natter. The ins and outs of recent speedway news and events takes second place to sad talk about Newport speedway promoter Tim Stone's recent premature death, aged 54. Talk of heart attacks or reminders of mortality isn't usually welcome at any time but particularly among men of a certain age and girth. Pav shakes his head slowly to signify the magnitude of the loss before he continues, "In the industry we all thought Tim had the place on a peppercorn rent but it turns out he didn't. No one would have predicted he paid £30,000! How he kept it going I just don't know!" Crouch is similarly amazed, "He always grafted and put in a thousand per cent effort – he lived and breathed Newport speedway!" Pav's 'flabber' remains well and truly 'gasted'. "He had crowds the same size as we do – 350 or 400 – and now he's gone! We're just passing through. We're all just passing through! If he'd got a few more yards out of the [hospital] car park, they'd have saved him. I remember one time we went down [to Newport] and I was in the pits when I saw a bloke with a scaffolding pole with a padlock on the end chasing Paul Fry round the pits and nearly catching him with it. I dunno who the bloke was – probably an irate father, or husband or someint – but Paul did a runner and clearly wasn't coming back! Which was a result for us 'cause they'd have to use a Conference League rider in his place. But, unusually, Tim wasn't around in the pits but he was pacing about in the car park for ages. I didn't know at the time what he was doing but he was waiting for the track doctor to arrive, so he could nobble him. When the doctor comes in, Tim's already seen him and got Fry signed off with a "speedway related stress injury", so they can use rider replacement! I complained to the ref who knew what the situation was but they had the certificate and we couldn't do anything about it. We lost by a couple of points in the end." The mystery man at the table pipes up, "One time when I was there Bob Coles got pissed up and went out on Michael's bike in Michael's kevlars pretending to be him. I said to Michael, who was in the bar, 'your dad is out on the track on your bike and your kevlars'. He didn't get far before he crossed the centre green and crashed into the safety fence. Tim went with him to the hospital making sure he [retrospectively] signed all the insurance forms before he got to the emergency department." It's clear that all these men collectively look back on visits to Newport and their interactions with Tim Stone with great affection.

Talk of health matters has Pav suddenly turn to Jed. "Did you hear Mad Wellie [Malcolm Holloway] has had a heart attack? There's nothing of him – unlike us – so it was a complete shock! Running Reading must have been much more stressful than people thought!" Formerly putting his metaphorical promoter's hat on for a moment in response to my questions about prospects for the Islanders, Pav tells me, "We're ninth at the moment and aiming for the play-offs – that's the idea anyway! We've won all our home meetings and won away at Mildenhall, but everyone wins there. We've lost a couple we should've won – away at Reading and also at Berwick, where we lost by 2 points. We still have a few left we could win away, though." Crouch nods in agreement and confirms, "We said at the start of the season we knew we needed three or four [away wins] to be near the top. We were delighted when we won away at Mildenhall in April but everyone wins there, so it sort of don't count!"

It's my first trip to Smallbrook Stadium this season and, though the bright sunshine adds lustre, all appears pretty much as I remember it. On the track the egg-shell blue coloured bowser is hard at work watering the surface and, as befits the close links of the club with Down Under, an Australian flag flutters on a flagpole nearby to the entrance turnstiles. Away in the near distance, wafts of smoke from the first bend indicates that they've started to cook (or reheat) food inside the refreshment kiosk there. Inside the deserted clubhouse bar, there has been a revolution furniture-wise. Gone are the mix 'n' match tables, stools and chairs and, to replace them, there's now a sea of rather swish dining tables surrounded by posh high-backed white leather-covered chairs. This look wouldn't be out of place in an upmarket hotel and, I would imagine, is probably the most deluxe furniture at any speedway club in Britain. The overall affect is a positive one though it's a look that fits rather incongruously, given the rest of the building, bar area and carpet remains resolutely unaltered, let alone that it runs counter to the notoriously hand-to-mouth financial basis of the speedway club. Still, it's impressive and Pav, proud of how the place looks, explains "Jed Stone's company did all this – it looks really nice doesn't it?! We wouldn't be able to keep going without help like this! We've a flipchart now and people can have meetings here in comfort. We can do parties, 40ths, 50ths, anniversaries, whatever – anything! People can sit and dine in comfort. We also have six motorcycle rallies here every year and, without them, we just wouldn't be able to keep going! At the Rallies they all park on the centre green and camp. They get blotto every Friday, Saturday and Sunday until we throw them out [of the bar] at 2 a.m. The next day they're all back somehow!"

Isle of Wight v. Sheffield: *"We're all committed to speedway but everyone else isn't"*

Jed Stone is stood next to Pav while he delights in the new furniture and the survival of the Isle of Wight speedway club. It's a testament to good housekeeping and shrewd husbandry of limited resources that a small club like this just about keeps its head above water. Jed recalls, "When I was manager here, other team managers would say, 'how much longer is the interval?' and I'd check with Dave how many burgers there were left!" "You've got to manage what you've got!" chortles Pav. The question of the length of the interval is a commonly raised subject. Some people claim that it's engineered to ensure that the punters don't immediately rush off after the meeting to return to the mainland but, instead, linger to avail themselves of the (now luxurious furnished bar) facilities to enjoyably pass the time before they leave for the last ferry sailing. Crouch has also often been quizzed on this matter, "When people complain to me I say 'funny, others have said the interval isn't long enough to finish their burgers'. Actually I don't think anyone can fairly say that …"

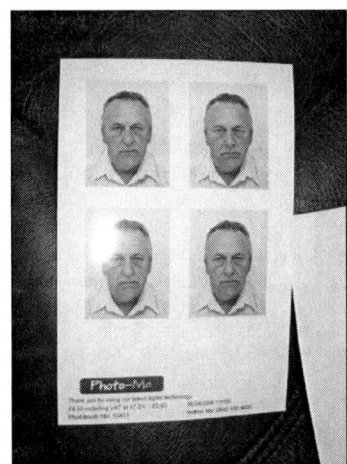

Wanted

Though today's Premier League visitors Sheffield also ride on a big fast circuit (albeit one without banking) Pav doesn't expect to suffer a defeat. "We've already beaten them once this season. Quite easily really [54-38] though, to be fair, they were on an 8-1, when Andre got excluded when Andrew [Bargh] fell off. If he'd been patient, he'd have definitely passed him on the next lap but he wasn't and that was it for them." Later Sheffield co-promoter Dave Hoggart gives me his version of this decisive incident from their recent KO Cup encounter: "Andrew shit himself and fell off with fright when he saw Andre charging up behind him! He locked up and, though Andre didn't touch him, he got excluded. From the ref's point of view [Jim Lawrence] the question is would he have fallen off without Andre? No he wouldn't! You don't have to touch him to get excluded. You could complain but the refs get so many decisions wrong there's no point!"

New furniture

Jed and Pav depart to the cluttered next-door speedway office and leave Crouch sat diligently on his own doing some speedway paperwork. Dave has a rich speedway pedigree and is the son of Bert Croucher, who was involved with Southampton speedway from 1947 onwards. "He was team captain for a number of years and was also the manager from 1956 to 1963, I think. In 1963 we used to get 17,000 people come along to Southampton speedway. Things were different then! When I was a kid in Southampton and my dad ran the track, we had a black-and-white telly with three channels. There was the pub, wrestling at the Guildhall on a Saturday, the dogs on a Friday or Saturday, the Mecca ballroom at the end of Southampton pier and there was your ABC and Odeon cinemas. Southampton didn't even have a nightclub in 1963 or maybe one just about to open. Anyway, Charlie Knott was the governor in those days – he really knew how to get people come along. He put on a good second half with six or seven proper races. Lots of clubs used to do a good second half but Charlie really put a lot of effort into organising interesting challenge matches or match races between the best riders in speedway. He would bring over Swedes just for the second half! Some nights you could have say, Southampton v. Wimbledon and we'd already have three world champions along and Charlie would bring down another two, like Peter Craven [Belle Vue] and Ove Fundin [Norwich], for some second-half match races. The equivalent these days would be a meeting of say us racing against Sheffield, if you like, and finding you've got a second-half match race between Tomasz Gollob and Nicki Pedersen. It really was a different time! It's different now. Each season you don't find speedway promoters saying that they're getting more [attendees] than last year! We have the same number of season ticket holders here but more of them are OAP concessions than they used to be. So those that started coming 10 years ago, when we opened, are ageing and we're not getting any youngsters. Everyone, even ignoring money is tight, has so much more choice of things to do nowadays that it's hard for speedway to compete. People often compare speedway prices (say £15) to football prices (say £35) but you get 90 minutes of soccer and speedway, let's be honest, is 15 minutes of racing. At some of them, say six maybe, it's follow my leader and not exactly packed with excitement. We're all committed to speedway but everyone else isn't – they have so many other things that they could do!"

Round by the start gate, the track surface gets considerable TLC from two very industrious track staff members. On closer inspection, the hard-working volunteers in question turn out to be Islanders club captain, Jason Bunyan – who douses the surface liberally with a hose – hard at work with his girlfriend, Rose Halfpenny, who attacks the surface with her rake. It would be safe to say that you don't see this at many speedway tracks in the country. Particular attention is given to the home straight, start-gate area and the first bend. They're watched, but not supervised, by Bryn Williams who's stood outside the referee's box drawing deeply on yet another much-needed cigarette. Nowadays smoking regulations dictate that Bryn can't share his hobby with the other occupants at work in the referee's box (although presently, they have all still to arrive). Something about Bryn immediately looks different to normal. In fact, he could fairly be described as having a 'newborn' slightly punk appearance because he's been shorn of all his hair. It's all been in a good cause since Bryn had been sponsored to shave his locks to raise funds for the Steve Johnston Testimonial meeting recently held at Coventry's Brandon Stadium. The tonsorial expert called up to do the honours was Billy 'Teasy-Weasy' Janniro who, judged by the finesse of his handiwork, either had to work with a very blunt shaver or suffered from a bad case of the DTs. Bryn nods towards the curatorial speedway team of Jason and Rose hard at work out on the track, "He likes to do the track himself with the best-looking mechanic in British speedway!" En route for the pits area Crouch has crossed the centre green and then, in his smart shoes, gingerly picks his way across the sodden shale surface to chat with the Islanders *ad hoc* but enthusiastic curatorial team. I have written elsewhere that Crouch is British speedway's equivalent of Howard Hughes, "I've quite an obsession with dust. I always argue with Bunyan about how much water he wants on! He complains, but I tell him: 'so long as it's safe I don't care what you think'. When holidaymakers come here with their kids, they don't want to go back covered in dust! They want to relax in the bar not wash the kids. Never mind that they don't have a washing machine when they're on holiday. When people ask them afterwards how it was, I want them to say how exciting the racing was, not how dirty they got!"

For the few Sheffield fans that have decided to travel to Smallbrook stadium, the meeting starts positively with an impressive win for Ricky Ashworth who heads home the strong Islanders pairing of Bunyan and Gathercole. Things take a turn for the worse for the Tigers in the next heat. Chris Holder's elder brother, James, who is partnered to maximum advantage by the Islander's New Zealander, Andrew Bargh, wins it. This initial arrangement of heat scores sets the tone for the early stages of the meeting, which then alternate between drawn heats and home-heat advantages. The third race starts eventfully when Islanders veteran rider Paul Fry gives a first-corner master-class on how to somersault with your bike. It is certainly a manoeuvre that impresses Bryn Williams in the commentary booth, "Paul Fry taking a spectacular tumble after a month out through injury. He's made of stern stuff! He's looking ruefully at his bike, good to see him up on his feet though he's down on his fortunes now!" Once the shaken and stirred Fry has been helped back to the pits and remounts his steed, the Isle of Wight's Glen Phillips then does the honours in the rerun to win the race comfortably ahead of Paul Cooper with a somewhat out-of-sorts Andre Compton comprehensively trailing off well at the rear of the field. Heat 5 sees the hardy Paul Fry back out on his bike in a race again won comfortably for the Tigers by Ricky Ashworth. It initially looks like Fry will complete four laps without reward but, on the penultimate corner, his Smallbrook track knowledge and many years of experience sees him draw level with Joel Parsons on the corner as a prelude to an overtake on the back-straight dash for the chequered flag. After the initial glitch in their first race of the meeting, the powerful Bunyan/Gathercole partnership combine to great effect in the sixth race to relegate Ben Wilson to the rear and take the scoreline to an already comfortable 23-13.

If the fightback was to ignite prior to full lift off, then it would have to start with Sheffield Tigers captain, Andre Compton. But, yet again, he labours to achieve anything except the slight improvement of a point for a distant third place ahead of the Islanders out of touch reserve Andrew Bargh. The Isle of Wight club has a long tradition of discovery and development with young Australian riders (with the option of the riders living in caravans at the stadium). The latest exports from Down Under, James Holder and Cory Gathercole, combined in the eighth heat to hammer in an impressive 5-1 maximum heat win. James Holder, who again shrugged off the pain from the hand injury that has dogged his season, won the race. Rather than take time out to have the operation that doctors have told him his injury requires, Holder prefers to race through the discomfort. Afterwards, marvelling at the all-action racing style of his Aussies, Dave Pavitt enthused, "They're typical Australians and give 100 per cent each and every race, win or lose." Tonight there's only one side likely to lose and that's definitely Sheffield who, judged by the way their heads collectively drop after their repeated late arrival into the first corner, effectively become a one-man team comprised of Ricky Ashworth (with occasional support from Ben Wilson).

No doubt to the displeasure of speedway's pits-based Howard Hughes [Dave Croucher], by the end of heat 8 eddies of dust drift from the track and blow over the fans. Though warm when the sun was shining, now that it has disappeared the air has a definite chill and dusty quality. After some TLC to the track and some cosmetic watering, heat 9 is about to get under way when referee Margaret Vardy suddenly slams on the red lights so that over the public-address system Bryn Williams can read out the registration of a recalcitrantly parked car ("So that it can be moved immediately as somebody wants to go to hospital!"). Bryn doesn't inform us of the exact nature of this medical drama (or the exact details of the parking infringement) but, after a few minutes' delay, in Mike Bennett-esque fashion he tells us, "There was a little bit of an emergency there". The short delay doesn't affect the concentration of the Islanders pair Glen Phillips and Paul Fry who dash away to record a comfortable maximum race win. On the warm-down lap, Glen Phillips tries to celebrate his victory with a wheelie but, while the spirit of triumphalism is there, the execution definitely isn't. The spectacle of this attempt enables Bryn Williams to get his trademark double entendre in much earlier in the meeting than normal, "… and Glen Phillips' wheelies are getting marginally better – by the end of the season, he'll be able to get it up properly."

With the meeting result pretty well beyond doubt, the real Andre Compton finally appears to have arrived and races from the tapes in smart fashion to lead the tenth race. However, though he looks to be back up to full pace, Cory Gathercole passes him in true home-rider Smallbrook fashion on the fourth bend of the initial lap. The rider with the most luxuriant mono-brow in speedway then finds a metaphorical tiger hot on his tail in the form of Islanders captain Jason Bunyan for the remainder of the race. Compton holds on for the remainder of these three laps to retain second place, despite a last-gasp dash to the line by Bunyan (on a section of the track he didn't water before the meeting). Apparently Sheffield team manager, Eric Boocock, owns a dice and heat 11 takes the last throw of said same when he nominates Ricky Ashworth to come out in the black-and-white helmet. It's a shrewd choice and Ashworth wins the race comfortably and, with Parsons third, the Tigers gain a heat advantage with the peculiar looking scoreline of 2-7. Announcing the race result, Bryn Williams allows himself to gleefully name-check his favourite race

Alan Sargent and a shorn Bryn Williams

Pre meeting track work from Jason B and Rose Halfpenny

sponsor a couple of times ("G J Aerials – For the best erection on the Island"), thereby taking his double-entendre count to a modest three.

With the scoreline at 42-27, the possibility of a Sheffield win remains mathematically possible until the next race sees Andre Compton trail in third behind Glen Phillips and James Holder. Though the fans in the stadium probably all realise that the Sheffield captain hasn't performed to his own usual high standards, we're completely unaware of any drama unfolding in the pits. Fortunately, it's in the nature of mobile phones that people can't speak into them without excessive volume, usually to either advise that they're on the train or alternatively to scream their half of the conversation in a manner that allows us all to vicariously share in the relative joy of the experience. Later, on the top of the weekly double-decker bus service back from the stadium to the ferry port, a young lady regales her listener with extensive gossip about the trials and tribulations of the Sheffield riders and mechanics on the road. We get an in-depth review of conversations, foibles, attitudes struck and even some context on what exactly the various protagonists wore when they said the things that they reportedly said. But, we [the occupants of the upper deck] also collectively learn, "Andre Compton stormed off after heat 12 in his van with all his gear on! He'd been arguing with his manager [which one we never learn] and then just loaded up his bike and left. [pause] Yeah. [pause] He'll get fined!"

Away from the track, Andre Compton is a successful businessman in the world of air conditioning and, for the last few seasons, has increasingly had to juggle the demands of his business commitments with his speedway career. Only 31, it was nonetheless a surprise during the 2008 close season to learn that Andre had reluctantly decided the time was right to retire from speedway (since he could no longer dedicate the time required to ensure he maintained his own high standards). It has also often been noted many times in speedway circles that any momentary loss of concentration massively increases the chance of injury.

Sheffield wasted little time before they announced during the close season that Ricky Ashworth would be their captain in 2009. Club promoter Neil Machin's comments at the time of appoinment appeared to highlight that the attitudes to the role might alter with the change in personnel. "[Ricky] knows what goes with the job and will lead by example ... it's easy to talk about team spirit, but that comes with like-mindedness compatibility and communication. Ricky will be good for the team and he wants to play a part in the whole structure of the club." These are requirements that few people would gainsay in any sport let alone speedway, though some Sheffield fans with slightly longer memories would appreciate the irony that Sean Wilson previously exhibited many of these qualities until peremptorily let go by the club.[2]

Most of the meeting I stand on the first bend with Dave Rattenbury, owner of a trackshop empire that extends from Wolverhampton to Redcar and includes Stoke, Buxton and Scunthorpe. The Isle of Wight used to be the most far-flung southerly outpost of his empire until the start of the 2008 season saw the club take back responsibility under their own wing. Dave had travelled down to the Island with his good friends Steve and Margaret Vardy to combine the spectacle of racing on the Island and to also chase up some outstanding monies from the gentleman who now runs the trackshop situated adjacent to the snack bar on the grass banks of the first bend. Though already equipped with a wad of money that wouldn't disgrace Harry Enfield in his 'Loadsamoney' incarnation, like many people, Dave quite rightly expects all monies owed to be paid promptly. I only wish that all trackshop owners would take this attitude without need for frequent reminders. In dogged pursuit of the outstanding monies, Dave frequently pops back and forth to the trackshop in the manner of a fast bowler returning to his marks and, in between times he watches the action or intersperses things with regular visits to the snack bar. Ostensibly bumbling, Dave must have been a detective in a previous life since little or nothing escapes his notice. The quality, variety and volume of the 2008 incarnation of the Isle of Wight Islanders speedway merchandise available for purchase from the trackshop doesn't excite him. "Their programme boards are shit – they just insert a sheet whereas mine are printed." With a practised eye born of many years of experience in the manufacture and sale of speedway merchandise, Dave then gives a comprehensive rundown on the quality (lack of), prominence and unit manufacturing cost variances

[2] Andre Compton would have a change of heart about his retirement during the close season. "I hope people can understand that I wasn't always giving it 100 per cent because I felt I was approaching the end of the road, but it's [relaxation during the winter] given me time to focus and I'm ready to go for it again and give it everything I've got."

Isle of Wight v. Sheffield: *"We're all committed to speedway but everyone else isn't"* (compared to retail price) of pretty well every item on display in the shop. It would be safe to say that Dave won't switch from his supplier or rush to add these product ranges to the shops in his empire.

They say you should always save the best till last and this would appear to be the code that Cory Gathercole lives by, if judged by the magnificent way he goes from last to first in the final heat when he bursts past Ashworth and Wilson as well as his colleague Phillips. This would have been spectacular watched from anywhere in the stadium but, like many others, I took in this spectacle from the upper deck of the double-decker bus that, prior to a prompt departure, handily overlooks the first corner. No sooner have the riders completed their victory celebration lap than the driver shoots off down the country lanes and residential roads of the Island at breakneck speed as though on a promise back at the depot. It's a cool and pleasant evening, so the stroll from the depot along the exposed wooden pier to the SeaCat terminal is comfortably reviving.

One of the enduring fascinations of speedway is the close relationship between fans and participants and the fact that the Sheffield management team of Eric Boocock, Neil Machin and Dave Hoggart also patiently wait their time in the queue to board the SeaCat is indicative of the down-to-earth, community nature of the sport. They talk among themselves but also, (unlike, say, Premiership footballers they're not a breed apart) happily chat away with the fans. It's clearly a journey that the management team have undertaken many times and the brevity of the 15-minute SeaCat crossing from the Island to Portsmouth is in marked contrast to the length of the night-time drive back to Sheffield. The 54-39 defeat hasn't left any of them exactly delighted but it's some aspects of a wider malaise within the sport that most concern a somewhat care-worn Neil Machin. He still can't quite believe that the 2008 Rulebook no longer contains the aggregate bonus point regulation, "Only four promoters voted for the best rule ever introduced in speedway. They say turkeys don't vote for Christmas but it now appears that they do! Maybe the BSPA should be renamed the British Stop Speedway Public Attending!" Another exasperation for Neil can be the attitude and approach of the riders, "When we get chimps on bikes all our problems will be solved!" Behind the mask of his cynical jokes and slightly downcast outlook, the reality is that Neil is worried about the future. "It's sad that speedway nowadays is getting like the Moto GP – where you have to have money just to compete, never mind succeed! I never thought speedway would get to that stage where sponsorship backing or rich parents makes the difference between who does well and who doesn't. We always had bikes that were roughly similar, so ability was the difference. Nowadays, it's all the tuning and other stuff that makes the real winners and to do that you need money. Even if the boy next door is brilliant, he's going to struggle without the investment and backup. That can't be good for the sport in the long term!"

Rather than dwell on real or imagined ills within the sport, Neil switches the conversation to talk about my latest book. He enquires about the provenance of its title and then says, somewhat elliptically, "I'm sure concrete is a word that will come up more in speedway this year."

Politely I say, "Really? I think I get your meaning."

Neil smiles, "I doubt it – but just listen out!"

24th June Isle of Wight v. Sheffield (Premier League) 54-39

CHAPTER 13.

Ipswich v. Peterborough:
"Last year he asked Zibi Suchecki if he had the right to be here."

26th June

The derby clash between Ipswich and Peterborough invariably attracts a large crowd to the Foxhall Stadium and, with two days to go prior to the Cardiff Grand Prix, those who turn up will get one last chance to see Hans Andersen hone his skills on the Suffolk track. So far, the Peterborough 'Muscle Finesse' Panthers haven't enjoyed the best of seasons judged by their lowly seventh place in the league table. More unusually, this season Ipswich have managed to cast off their wooden spoon status of recent years and presently look like they could press for a place in the play-offs. Last season, thoughts of such an eventuality would have the men in white coats question your sanity but, even with talismanic long-serving captain Chris Louis on the side lines with injury, possible glory definitely appears a realistic possibility.

Something that still might hamper the possibility of eventual qualification for the Witches was the 43-50 early season home defeat to the Swindon Robins suffered on April 14th. Though this was two and a half months ago, the sense of injustice from that evening still burns deeply in promoter John Louis's breast. In a nutshell, Sheffield's Joel Parsons rode at reserve for the Robins despite the fact that his average factually (and according to the Rules) made him ineligible. Interestingly Swindon don't see it that way and claim that, prior to the meeting, they received dispensation to confirm his eligibility from the SCB Management Committee. People often say it's whom you know and not what you know that counts in life and, on this occasion, the combination of whom you know and what you know proved vital when Parsons was given this late permission by the authorities to ride. Though it would appear an arcane administrative matter to outsiders that the BSPA failed to issue an amended "interim" average for Parsons until it was too late to change their choice of guest, this run of events eventually had an impact on the final scoreline. Understandably, Swindon ran with the hares and hunted with the hounds when they also lined up Shaun Tacey to possibly replace Parsons, the Robins can, with what passes for a clear conscience in speedway, claim that they had authorisation for their actions. At the time John Louis fulminated, "I am absolutely disgusted; the rules are crystal clear and were in use last season." If this were a murder trial (rather than speedway), then the matter would currently be *sub judice* and reporting would be restricted while we await news of the deliberations. But, because this is speedway, a painfully slow moving review/enquiry got under way though, the man in charge of it (Graham Reeve) successfully managed to prevaricate until the play-off stage of the season had been reached – always for ostensibly 'valid' reasons – to ensure any contentiousness from the result had been thoroughly dissipated and nullified. In the same way that Stalin would send people to Siberia rather than admit culpability, so it will be when the BSPA finally conclude that Swindon had permission for their actions and, therefore, broke no rules. Despite that the words in the relevant section of the Rulebook if viewed from an independent and/or common sense point of view appear to indicate that they had.

The fact that the fabled BSPA carpet will once again be lifted and serious matters swept underneath it is no consolation to a distinctly peeved John Louis. "This isn't a freakin' joke! They [Swindon] went down two routes. One of them was [Alun Rossiter] who rang Shaun Tacey at 20 past 4 and told him to load his van for the meeting. Whereas the other route was taken by Terry Russell – the Chairman of the BSPA – who rang his mate Graham Reeve, who wears two hats as head of the referees and a referee himself. The meeting steward that night was Mick Bates (they have those at *Sky-* televised meetings in the pits along with the normal referee in the box, who was Chris Gay) I didn't speak to him. I did speak to Chris Gay, the referee, who told me that was the decision and it had been taken out of his hands by his boss, Graham Reeve. Not that he said or could say anything but, like some of the refs I've spoken to afterwards, he knew it wasn't fair or within the rules! Swindon saying they didn't make a song and dance about it is not relevant as they're not going to say 'look at us', are they? After they've stolen the points! It really makes speedway look a freakin' joke. Let's just pick a team, say Lakeside, they could finish third – a couple of points behind Swindon at the end of the season – and get robbed of a top two place in the play-offs. Those two meetings at home could be worth a pretty penny [the Ipswich paper, the *Evening Star* places a value of £50,000 on each of these meetings]. It really stinks!"

John then patiently explains to me that even if natural justice was done and Parsons had his results expunged then, unlike how common sense would dictate, the various rider placings wouldn't be amended but would remain fixed as they were [albeit without Parsons]. For example, the heat 2 result on the night was Kroner, Parsons, Schramm, and Alden. If this were to be amended then the result would now read Kroner, No one, Schramm and Alden. Discussion of this further piece of madness from the complex but sometimes occasionally daft Rulebook doesn't exactly thrill John Louis. "Well a draw would be better than what we got – which was freak all! While Swindon got 3 points they shouldn't have – just because of who they are! It really doesn't do anything other than make speedway look freakin' silly! No wonder we struggle for credibility with outsiders. Not doing the paperwork is really no excuse. Angela from the BSPA office shouldn't be ringing up to say he couldn't ride with his average, it should say so in the paperwork." Already this season problems with the paperwork have required that the green sheets have had to be retrospectively corrected.

Before he leaves the turnstile area and retreats to the speedway office, John takes a brief trip down memory lane to calm his sense of injustice. "I started in 1970 when I rode in the British League II, which was our second league. Then I rode in the British League from 1972 until I retired in 1984. I wasn't involved for some years although I did one meeting at King's Lynn. I haven't kept the records and, if you know of anyone who has, I'd be delighted to know. I have a number of questions about my own career. Has anyone been more successful as a rider for England in the World Team Cup? How many times did I captain England? And how many times did we win the World Team Cup? Is there a more successful team than England in the World Team Cup? What was my total number of appearances? I really don't know the answers to these questions but I would be curious to find out!"

No sooner has John Louis left than Steve Johnston turns up to shoot the breeze with Johnny Barber in the trackshop. The previous Sunday his testimonial meeting had been staged at Coventry's Brandon stadium and, though you couldn't move for Australians in the pits, the meeting was won by Scott Nicholls when he headed home Jason Crump and Leigh Adams in the last race of the meeting. Thankfully, Johnno is old school enough to be a traditionalist and had the winner decided by their scores from the meeting rather than other modern fancier ways to find the victor. Always lively and cheerful, Johnno tells me, "It was a really good day – sunny and no one got injured!" Obviously, the key to any testimonial meeting is the size of the crowd and Johnno quickly qualifies Internet reports, "I wouldn't say a big crowd, I'd say a good crowd!"

Rider badges

Bev and Molly Barber

First corner action

Ipswich v. Peterborough: *"Last year he asked Zibi Suchecki if he had the right to be here."*

It's a warm but slightly overcast afternoon and every member of the Barber family with a speedway connection has been drawn to Foxhall Heath. Nick Barber supervises but also helps his brother Johnny, mother Molly and his sister Bev lay out a huge variety of Ipswich branded merchandise and memorabilia in the shop and around it on the nearby display tables. Later the father of the family, Colin, will also arrive to chain smoke and watch from the terraces that overlook the first bend. In addition to the Witches merchandise, there is also quite a range of GP related speedway collectables. Again, my eye is caught by the specially produced GP rider badges that are laid out in an attractive fashion on a coloured display board and take pride of place at the front of the shop. Johnny tells me, "We've got the rights to do the speedway World Team Cup memorabilia and Jim Lynch has asked for his jacket to say 'Team GB Manager – Jim Lynch'. Probably in case he forgets!"[1] I'm midway through my suggestion that, "maybe you could do matching gloves on a string along with left and right printed on them for him?" when I'm brusquely interrupted by a man in a florescent jacket. This man turns out to be a member of the security staff (called Len) and quite aggressively he asks, "Excuse me, do you have the right to be in the stadium?" Fortunately I do and Len retreats muttering "I had to ask, didn't I?" Johnny laughs, "You're in good company – last year he asked Zibi Suchecki if he had the right to be here." Recognising who should or shouldn't be inside any stadium is a difficult task and a skill that usually comes with experience. At Eastbourne, since Sheila Mansell's sudden departure from the pits gate, the new security man who replaced her has initially struggled to tell staff or riders from potential gatecrashers. Until he gets to know the Eagles riders they'll be quizzed every time they pass through en route to the pits and, for the recent meeting against Swindon, Leigh Adams was asked three separate times if he had the right to be there.

Though meetings with Peterborough are often quite combative affairs, talk among the staff prior to the turnstiles opening centres upon the highly charged meeting last Sunday between Mildenhall and Scunthorpe. The dapperly dressed Kevin Long is the presenter at both West Row and Foxhall Heath stadiums and needs no second invitation to reminisce. "There was food left in the referee's box from the week before and as it was a very hot day it had suffered. So I announced over the tannoy, 'There's a slight delay 'cause Barbara's box is infected with flies.' Mark Baseby cracked up. I think that's why he kept falling off all afternoon. Later Mark said to me, 'She keeps excluding me all the time, I'm sure she wants to shag me!'" However, the tension in the pits was ignited at the meeting by the heat 11 first-corner clash of Jan Graversen and Carl Wilkinson rather than the lascivious thoughts held by the match official Barbara Horley. Trevor Brame was in the pits when feelings ran high, "Richard Hall was going mental and I had a discussion with his father. He was very close to being reported to the ref for threatening me to go outside. I told him to take a deep breath and calm down. It all started with Kaj Laukkanen's mechanic, Ray Pike, and Kenny Smith disagreeing. Carl Wilkinson shouted, 'you tried to nail me! You tried to nail me!' Jan said 'I didn't! I was in front and I had the right to choose my line'. Rob Godfrey took objection and then they tried to calm him down. Whatever Kevin Long said I haven't a clue but Kenny Smith didn't like it. Blayne [Scroggins] was saying to them [the Mildenhall riders], 'Come on, you've got them now, take advantage!' Scunthorpe got all stressed out and wound themselves up. They didn't want to be the first team that lost to Mildenhall this season. As it turned out, they didn't. Some of them complained about the track but Wilko said it right when he said, 'It's just a bit of dirt – power through it!' Usually the track would be done by Huggy but he was away on a golf weekend, I think."

With my display table adjacent to the programme booth (and, sadly, a lot less popular), just as each race is about to start I rush from my table to the edge of the terraces to watch. This mirrors the (male) members of Barber family – well Nick and Johnny – who time their rush back and forth, like waves crashing on the shore, to stand next to their father Colin just at the moment the tapes rise. Tonight, Ipswich have altered their regular line-up to ride without Piotr Swiderski (for whom they operate rider replacement) and Chris Louis, whom they've replaced with guest Rory Schlein. The top end of the Peterborough line-up holds greater promise on paper since they ride with a powerful heat leader trio of Hans Andersen, Kenneth Bjerre and Danny King. Strength at reserve can make all the difference to any speedway team and Ipswich appear to have the slight edge with their Johnston–Schramm combination compared to the Panthers pair of Risager–Harrison. However, elaborate theories count for nought when the highly-regarded Hans Andersen trails back in third place from the first bend of heat 1. Usually, this would be the signal for

[1] Ipswich *Evening Star* speedway reporter, Mike Bacon, will comment on this jacket on his pithy weekly blog shortly afterwards. "There was poor old Jim Lynch wandering round the pits in a jacket which looked like it had been shoplifted from Wilkinsons and had his name printed on the back at some back street shop in Scarborough."

him to stalk and pass his determined but hapless opponents but, on this occasion, he appears lacklustre and out of sorts. Possibly the Sunday trip to Mildenhall has infected him with a virulent strain of the West Row virus that condemns its carriers to third or fourth place in the majority of races they compete in. The second race has Peterborough fight back with a race advantage that brings the scores back to a manageable 7-5. The third heat – sponsored by Warren Heath Cars (who pride themselves on their affordability and proximity to Sainsbury's) – provides an easy win for Rory Schlein. Jarek Hampel isn't every Ipswich fan's cup of tea and when he temporarily trails in third place behind Kenneth Bjerre a quickly exasperated Witches fan close to me shouts, "Come on, he's got a broken leg!" But just like Kryptonite disempowers Superman, no sooner have these words been uttered than Hampel goes haywire. Rather than broadside round the first corner of the third lap, Hampel hammers straight out wide to the fence, hugs its contours and thereby enables Claus Vissing to easily pass him. Finally stirred into action, Hampel nearly catches the Dane on the fourth bend before he immediately repeats his weird corner manoeuvre at the start of lap four to definitively relegate himself to a rather forlorn fourth place. Fortunately for the ire of the easily irked Ipswich fan nearby, the heat is nonetheless drawn.

The fifth heat sees another poor start for Hans that he then continues in that fashion trailed off listlessly in a distant third place behind the Witches pair of Hampel and Schlein. Nick Barber phlegmatically remarks, "I think he's on bike number 10 – it's certainly not his number 1 bike!" Whether his best equipment or not is already in Cardiff for the Grand Prix remains a moot point when Andersen grinds to a halt with an engine failure. Fans of both teams could be tempted to think that Hans is "saving himself" for the rigours of the Cardiff event but, only a few weeks later, rumours that all is not well in the Panthers camp gain confirmation. We subsequently learn that Peterborough promoter Colin Horton had allegedly failed to pay Hans Andersen on time as agreed. With a significant five-figure backlog of payments already in place by the time of the Ipswich meeting, it would be understandable if this were a possible cause of demotivation for the rider. However, one man's demoralisation is another man's joy so Ipswich fans are cock-a-hoop with the turn of events – something that Kevin Long echoes gleefully over the public-address system, "Hans Andersen on the receiving end of another Ipswich 5-1!"

Rumour on the terraces about Chris Louis has it that the Witches will abandon their use of rider replacement and could instead soon include the lost man of British speedway, Matej Ferjan, in their team. This possibility doesn't impress Witches fan, Jason Colthorpe: "That's just what we need to replace Chris Louis – a rider that wins when he gates, sticks to the inside and is hopeless away!" Jason has a number of exasperations and one of these is the variable form of Piotr Swiderski. Apparently, he's a rider that has a tendency to win when he gates but often doesn't demonstrate the fighting qualities required to come from the rear that speedway fans everywhere like to see in their team's riders. "We don't think Swiderski is a Pole because he can't pass!" Tonight's guest Rory Schlein has exceeded the expectations of many Ipswich fans including Jason ("can I retract that about Schlein?"). Kevin Long congratulates the Australian in a pit-side interview, "Guests don't usually give their all but you have already had two wins … if you fancy riding for Mildenhall they need some help!"

Tonight the team that will require help looks likely to be the Panthers. Through the middle section of the meeting Peterborough keep the scoreline to a manageable 6-point deficit helped by the fact that Ipswich reserve Chris Schramm appears to have an off night. After a disappointing last place, Kevin Long tells us "Chris Schramm giving 110 per cent as usual!" Not quite as dreaded as a vote of confidence from the chairman in football, whenever you hear about any rider "giving their all" you can guarantee they haven't won the race! Rory Schlein confirms the perspicacity of John Louis's decision to book him as a guest when he rides to a paid win behind the suddenly rejuvenated Jarek Hampel. The Ipswich fans savour the maximum heat advantage and take the opportunity to loudly remind Danny King in rude fashion that they 'don't really miss him at the Foxhall track' and, perhaps, his move to the East of England showground wasn't the inspired career move he hailed it to be at the time of his departure. If the get up and go has got up and gone from the Panthers, then the Witches compound their misery and quickly ram in another maximum heat score when Kroner and Johnston combine to best Peterborough's Bjerre and Vissing. With the scores at 37-23, the meeting is some distance away from finely poised and Nick Barber observes with some understatement, "This isn't that exciting is it?"

With victory almost assured, the only real clouds on the horizon are literal rather than metaphorical. Part-time weatherman Kevin Long updates us on local climactic conditions, "It's raining really hard [10 miles away] in Stowmarket apparently so referee Paul Carrington will keep us on the move!" Some other people on the move are the meeting's sponsors who've joined Kevin on the centre green to drink in the action along with their escort Julie Last, Ipswich's Advertising Manager. With the deficit difficult to make up, Hans Andersen appears in heat 12 with a black-and-white coloured helmet to try and redeem the situation. Sadly for the Panthers fans he can only finish second behind Robert Miskowiak. Out again two heats later, Hans finally wins a race (ahead of rider replacement Jarek Hampel). A key factor in their comfortable win is that the rider replacement facility is used to good effect by the Ipswich to gain 9 paid 10 points. Though, they're also helped by paid 12 points from guest Rory Schlein whose tally would have been even higher but for engine failure on the penultimate corner of the last lap of heat 15. Though Hans Andersen does ride in the last heat he finishes trailed off in last place. It's a completely forgettable night for him and, though 8 points from five rides would satisfy some lesser riders, it falls well below his exalted standard. Like many others in the team, he has merely gone through the motions during this derby meeting and, though at Foxhall Heath in person, in spirit – like his pay cheque – he's been absent!

26th June Ipswich v. Peterborough (Elite League) 54-38

Ipswich v. Peterborough: *"Last year he asked Zibi Suchecki if he had the right to be here."*

CHAPTER 14.

Cardiff GP:
"Inside they'll be able to buy non-flammable air horns."

28th June

We're repeatedly told on *Sky Sports* and in the *Speedway Star* that the Cardiff Grand Prix is the highlight of the speedway calendar. BSI aren't ever afraid to increase the hyperbole so proclaim Cardiff as the "Home of World Championship Speedway". You can't deny there's a good atmosphere but, year-in-and-year-out, the racing takes place on a rickety, sub-standard track surface that makes this grandiose claim harder and harder to substantiate. Within British Speedway, you can't deny that the Cardiff GP is the fat boy in the canoe. It's definitely true that it is the best-attended speedway event of the year in Britain (and worldwide), never mind that the quality of the stadium and atmosphere generated make it stand out. Prior to the big event itself, the speedway merchandising event of the year is the Speedway Fayre held annually next door in the bar of Cardiff Rugby Club. The sport of rugby (rather than speedway) is so centrally important to the national psyche of the Welsh that they have two stadiums adjacent to each other in the centre of their capital city.

As recently as 2005, there used to be rival Speedway fayres held prior to the Grand Prix but one of these has gone the way of all flesh and, by popular consent, Nick Barber's event has emerged triumphant. The law of unintended consequences dictates that all the stallholders, irrespective of their relative fitness or desire for exercise, compulsorily have to endure the Nick Barber Keep Fit Plan in order to display their wares at the Fayre. This regime basically requires that you hump all the stuff (merchandise, marketing materials etc.) you've brought from your vehicle in the Rugby Club car park, up the two flights of back stairs and through the French windows into the spacious bar area. Nick changes the position of my stall to a different location during the set-up and I'm initially happy to move, although this subsequently turns out to be a bad idea when the late-arriving stallholder immediately next door erects a fence-sized display of race jackets. If Phil Spector perfected the "wall of sound" then the wall of tabards adjacent to my stall means people definitely fail to notice my display. Pete Ballinger from *Clean Cut Videos* does his best to alert people to our general whereabouts with endless loops of the brand new (launched at Cardiff) Chris Harris DVD burbling from his television. "It's the best 20 races from 2007-2008, excluding the 2007 GP, as the rights were too expensive to purchase for that. We're running a Chris Harris competition to select his top three races – to win a set of Coventry 2007 DVDs! We should do very well with the DVD and, if he wins again tonight, we'll go round all the bars in Cardiff and sell off all our stock!" With the television volume set at 'kill' I am able to enjoy the sight and histrionic commentary of repeated Chris Harris race wins. By mid-afternoon, when Pete returns to his stall, I've been reduced to shouting, "Quick Pete, Chris Harris is in the lead again!" Only to be matter-of-factly told, "That's the gist of the DVD!" After I've listened endlessly to the excitable soundtrack, I could tell the man behind the microphone wasn't Mike Bennett and, whoever it was, they were heavily influenced in work by the style perfected by Nigel Pearson on *Sky Sports*. Impossible to believe, but they were arguably much more excitable than Nigel and commentated upon each race as if permanently on the brink of an orgasm. It's definately the work of a seasoned professional, given the predictable conclusion of each race and the need to remain on the cusp of ecstasy for the 60 seconds of each race after the tapes rise. Based on this showcase of his fluency, a career in porn movie overdubs possibly beckons for David Rowe.

The talk of the Fayre centres on the controversial end to the previous night's Premier League Pairs meeting held at Somerset. Until 2007, the traditional curtain raiser for the Cardiff GP for fans and merchandise stallholders alike was the Friday night meeting held in Newport. Since the event transferred to Somerset's Oak Tree Arena and went upmarket (to a Super7even event) Mike Golding and his partner Anita Lewis have taken the sensible but unpopular commercial view that they wish to maximise their own revenues from the bumper crowd via their shop and so banned all other stallholders from the event (though I was always welcome to attend any other Somerset speedway meeting). Despair at the comparative lack of choice among stalls wasn't the talking point but the rather bizarre refereeing decision that deprived the Reading Racers the chance to possibly lift the Pairs' crown. Like pretty well everyone there, Rob Peasley disagreed with the decision of referee Graham Flint, which saw Somerset rather than Reading progress through to the final to face Workington. "Lemo was definitely third. The Reading riders were riding round celebrating and the Somerset ones had gone off to the pits and the bloke on the centre green had even confirmed it. So we were all really surprised when the ref thought different! He was the only one in the stadium who did. Reading manager, Tim Sugar, wasn't very happy and got fined £300 for abusive language."

One joy of the Fayre (and of the Cardiff GP, in general) is the chance to bump into speedway people that you haven't seen for ages or people you have. With the Zimbabwean elections in the news, Johnny Barber wonders aloud if we could learn something from the administration of these elections. "Perhaps promoters could dip every fan's finger into indelible ink?" Talk of despots, tyrants and megalomaniacs naturally leads Johnny to ask, "Is [name redacted] the Robert Mugabe of speedway? For that matter, who is the George W. Bush of British speedway? Or the Tony Blair?" Whatever the answer to these important questions Johnny is adamant that the promoters frequently get an unfairly bad press from the fans. "The problem with speedway isn't the BSPA but often it's the fans! If you look on forums, prior to the [annual] November meeting it would be impossible to follow or implement all the contradictory suggestions given! If 16 of them shagged Kelly Brook they'd be criticised because it wasn't Tess Daly! They just can't win!"

Sue and Tim Scott (no relation) linger by my stall and confess, "He reads your book in the toilet. He's in there for ages – it's a man thing!" Arnie Gibbons also stops for a chat, while he clutches a wodge of cards, "They're my reference cards telling me what I have and haven't got!" *Tears and Glory* has had a positive review on the *Speedway Plus* website run by the hardworking and diligent Allan Melville. In his analysis, Allan accurately notes that the Reading Racers are "certainly not a club that one would list amongst the sport's glamour outfits". Arnie's masterwork is praised, "As a written history that flows well and is a genuinely entertaining read" and the review rightly highlights the way the book "puts the Racers' story into a wider historical context". A good example of this approach comes from the 1968 chapter when Arnie draws a telling comparison between the wage available to a petrol pump attendant and the pay rates riders could expect. It's very much a book you'd expect from a man who "did go to the last two meetings of the 1970 season". Page 159 of Arnie's book soon comes up in conversation and a glance at this page quickly sums up the appeal of the book in a nutshell since it's packed with interesting snippets. The year in question was 1993 and we learn: Jan Andersen scored 5519.5 points during his Racers career; Hans Nielsen highlighted that proposals to control rider wages would mean a pay cut "from £60,000 to £35,000"; while Smallmead's crowds averaged around 1,300 that season with an adult admission charge of £5. Arnie's footnote states, "Most fans underestimate the scale of the overheads a promoter has to cover. Insurance, BSPA fees, rental, interest and administration costs all mount up. I base this on my experience as an accountant (and I have acted for a speedway promotion)." It's often held that speedway historians (and their books) can often be as dull as dishwater but, the cultured Arnie proudly bucks the trend, "I did get a reference to *Waiting for Godot* in my book. I did think about mentioning Vladimir and Estragon standing on the second bend at Smallmead but I thought that might go over people's heads!" Talk of Samuel Beckett's play reminds me of the graffiti I saw on my first day at university on the wall outside the bar at my student residence, 'Back in 5 minutes – Godot'. Not exactly funny but symptomatic of students' desperate desire (and mine) to parade their erudition and literary knowledge. Quirkier still, the gents toilet walls in the library contained the sort of comments you'd experience in public conveniences everywhere but also had the plaintive gem, 'Am I the only QPR supporter on campus?' An experienced Agony Uncle had carefully written a helpful comment underneath, 'No, there's plenty more turds in the cow field'.

Tobi Kroner's mechanic John Carpenter stops by at my stall for a chat. John, like Tobi, hasn't quite got over the fact that the young German rider relegated Hans Andersen to third place in the first heat of the Witches/Panthers clash on Thursday night. "He beat Hans and that gave him real confidence! You should hear the stories I have travelling with the German rider for two years! Before we went to Belle Vue recently he called me on the mobile to say, 'I can't go, I have animals in the house'. I rushed round thinking they'd be squirrels or rats and they were ants!" Pete from *Clean Cut Videos* has taken a break and has been temporarily replaced by the taciturn but glamorous Jodie Lowry who usually works on a concession stall inside the Coventry trackshop selling ostentatiously branded rider merchandise. No sooner has she sat down than Allen Trump, the Coventry promoter, stops by, picks up a copy of the DVD and jokes, "I hope it's not a DVD of Bomber's best races this season – it would only take two and a half minutes!" Allen then studies the sleeve notes and asks a few questions about the product before he moves off empty handed. Sales professionalism dictated Jodie smiled sweetly throughout but pointedly notes, "I love Avtar, Mr Sandhu!"

Any speedway merchandising or memorabilia fayre run by the Barber family will inevitably have Phil Hilton on hand to help in some capacity. On race night at selected speedway tracks he's a photographer, while away from the shale, he's a long-serving police officer. The impressive blue line that developed at West Row the previous weekend had caught his imagination. "I took a photo of the third and fourth bend and was going to send it to the *Speedway Star* saying – 'M11 extension running through West Row!' But I didn't 'cause you don't want to kick people when they're down; at least, not if they're going to get up!" Like me, over the years Phil has noticed that the organisers, less than subtly, like to extract as much dosh as humanly possible from the speedway fans that each year loyally flock to watch the Cardiff Grand Prix. Though there is a confusing range of pre-booked and on-the-day-ticket options, the general impression is that ticket prices have increased markedly over the years while the catalogue-cum-programme (that, at one time, was included free with advance ticket bookings) now leaves only £3 change from a tenner. Though great play is made of its status a 'souvenir', it's not exactly filled with either new or scintillating information but is, essentially, a glorified racecard. Always anxious to further maximise their revenues, Phil tells me someone has had a masterstroke of a brainwave about air horns. "The shit is really gonna hit the fan later as the stadium have banned flammable air horns. These are the ones that Nick sells! They've been perfectly fine all the other years but not this year. Security is going to stop people as they go in. Inside they'll be able to buy non-flammable air horns. Something really stinks about that!" It's a weird world when the organisers get bent out of shape by the risks posed by air horns to an unsuspecting public, yet happily prepare a track that cuts up so much and so quickly that many experts (and riders) consider it dangerous to ride! Nick (like other trackshop owners throughout the country) has sold his traditional kind of air horn in good faith without prior knowledge of this late sudden change in policy for the Cardiff Millennium Stadium. You don't have to be a qualified detective to figure out that whoever is the supplier of the newly authorised 'correct' air horns available inside the stadium stand to financially benefit from this sudden change of policy. Any business that can extract further income from their customers and dress their profit motive up as a health and safety issue will invariably do so. I don't recall any recent fires at speedway meetings at any track in Britain (that have involved air horns). Honestly straightforward in his dealings with the speedway public, Nick quickly offered a full refund to anyone who returned their air horns. Later, once inside the stadium, a fluorescent-jacketed steward hands out free ear plugs from a large bag he'd brought along, "I'm disgusted they charge people for them at this event when there's such an incredible noise!"

Volunteer member of the Swindon track curatorial team, Graham Cooke, helps behind the scenes at the Cardiff GP. Obviously, strange hours and hard work are necessarily involved but it provides Graham with enviable access to riders and officials as they make their preparations for the big night. Graham's *Blunsdon Blog* has rightly attracted over a million visitors and his account of

Steve and Tai Girdwood

Childminder Nick Barber

Cardiff GP: *"Inside they'll be able to buy non-flammable air horns."*

the Cardiff experience (along with the photos) brilliantly breaks away from the often platudinous coverage and boosterism provided by rival sources of information. His blog is compulsory reading for any true speedway fan. With expertise gained from his love of the sport as well as his recent years behind the scenes, Graham has some strong opinions and predictions. "They just shouldn't have a practice the day beforehand! It's three and a half hours of the riders really hitting the same spot of the track. It's bound to suffer! They completely re-laid it and really packed it down, but it's still not ideal! I think Crump is really up for it tonight! Gollob didn't look interested and I don't know what Edward Kennett was doing at all!"

When I take my seat in the nosebleed section of the Millennium Stadium that overlooks the second bend, it's immediately noticeable how many seats yet again remain unfilled this year. Despite relentless almost year-round promotion, BSI hasn't been able to better the 2002 attendance figure of 42,000.[1] Though this event generates huge income for the organisers (significantly more than any other Grand Prix), the primary audience for this spectacle remains sat at home with a television. Whatever people may think about BSI/IMG, one thing that can't be denied is that they know how to manage and package the appearance of speedway for the television screen. With this in mind, they've craftily masked the true extent of the empty spaces in this arena with the canny tactic of corralling the crowd into key sections that will then make the stadium appear packed to the gunwales when notionally 'panoramic' shots are shown on television. *Sky Sports* has 11 cameras and 200 staff at the event to ensure it looks perfect on the screen. In order to also foster the supposedly spontaneous outburst of patriotism, free Union flags have been provided and placed under every seat in the section of the second bend where I'm sat. As usual, Kevin Coombes ramps up the entertainment levels through the communication of his own excitement about the event as well as through appeals to our patriotism or through the pre-identification of possible pantomime villains. Consequently, you'd be a hard-hearted person not to be tempted to pick up your Union flag and wave it at some point during the evening. Many fans have also brought their own (larger) flags to display or wave, usually to show their support for their favourite rider or highlight their pride in their national allegiance. However, the reality is that the flags provided under our seats are corporate flags there to facilitate a 'spontaneous' demonstration of *faux* nationalism. Notionally supplied for our fun on the night in the stadium but really calculatingly there to create a specific televisual effect of rampant patriotism on the screen. As usual, BSI aren't quite sure whether they want to treat the fans as bit-part players in a night at the funfair, an evening at the Eurovision Song Contest or valued members of the audience at the 'Last Night of the Proms'. Whatever the intention, viewed with the sound down these pictures will inevitably communicate the impression that the stadium is filled with patriots keen to enjoy the notional 'carnival' atmosphere to the full. Some fans have already spent many hours in the bars and, therefore, need little or no encouragement to become more overwrought than they already are! In front of my seat, a histrionic woman in a predominantly white cowboy hat with Flag of St George motif set off by an ill-fitted but matching top sits on the back of her seat. She manages to bob and weave to obscure much of my view. Keen to dance around on the seat back as if it's been electrified, she needs no second invitation to leap to her feet whenever encouraged to do so by Kevin Coombes to greet the arrival on track of an English rider. Luckily, there are only three "Brits" at Cardiff and only two of them permanently in the GP (due to sensible commercial favouritism rather than their performances), nowadays. Her patriotic fervour reaches an early crescendo from the first heat onwards after Scott Nicholls trundles up to the tapes to ride to a disappointingly predictable third place. This comparatively poor performance doesn't stop Mrs Cowboy Hat's loud screams throughout though, as the race finishes, her absent partner returns with a tray of lagers to be greeted with sudden invective and foul language.

It's a no-brainer to move from my original position to another section of the stadium, given the large choice of empty sections all around my original position. I decide to choose the deserted section that overlooks the first corner that provides a great view of the first-bend exit, though some idiot five rows below tries to obscure my view with enthusiastic use of his giant Polish flag. Eventually, the alcohol rather than the on-track action overcomes his enthusiasm. Behind me there's a camera gantry with a couple of cameramen who skilfully operate a remote control camera suspended on a 15-metre black pole. Their job is to film the second-bend crowd reactions and those along the back

---

[1] Afterwards we unofficially learn that 2008 set a new record with a marginal increase to 42,187. However, doubts remain whether this headline figure refers solely to customers who paid for their entry to the Cardiff GP. Even more interestingly, attendance figures for every GP meeting held in 2008 remained, at the time of writing, unpublished. Though it's impossible to know, suspicions remain that this is a policy decision to mask evidence of the variable overall popularity of the series. While concerns have been raised as to the strategic vision and managerial abilities of the BSI leadership, prior to the IMG purchase the attendance figures for all their SGPs were previously published.

Cardiff GP: *"Inside they'll be able to buy non-flammable air horns."*

straight. Looked at on the television later, they really frame the picture with professional perfection and magnificently create the impression that not only is the section extremely crowded but also that it's peopled with flag-waving patriots. Though we're only yards away, our vast section is empty and noticeably unatmospheric.

One aspect of the modern stadium experience is the profligate use of giant video screens. Given that a large number of the crowd are so high up above the track that they can't really see the action in any detail, these screens have become a vital part of enjoyment and notional spectacle of the Cardiff Grand Prix. Though, you feel you're almost watching a DVD of the event you actually attend, it does give us all the chance to watch the nuances of the action. The first race gives early indications that the track will, yet again this year, prove problematic for the riders. One person who has already previously proven that he thrives on the difficult track conditions at Cardiff is Coventry's Chris Harris who, to ecstatic reaction, wins heat 2. He thereby becomes the first British speedway rider to win a Grand Prix race this season. It's a sign of the relative decline of British speedway that it has taken 94 races for a victor to come these shores. Pre-meeting publicity from BSI implies that they've mastered the art of laying indoor track surfaces. Sadly, the early heats see many different riders suddenly struggle for control of their machines when their bikes strike the various unpredictable lumps and bumps apparently randomly scattered throughout the circuit. It is to be quite a night for Polish referee Marek Wojaczek. He spectacularly fails to justify his appointment to officiate at two further forthcoming Grand Prix meetings, let alone the Cardiff one. Though it is minor in the context of his future transgressions, heat 6 sees the referee ignore some tape touching by Nicki Pedersen at the start of the race. Obviously, the rules state this is an infringement and Nicki should be excluded. In a theoretical world of ifs, ands, buts and maybes – this would deprive him of the third-place point he gains that later effectively ensures he qualifies for the semi-final race-offs. As it is, after he has got the benefit of the doubt, Nicki nearly gains greater reward when he dives under Tomasz Gollob on the fourth bend of the third lap but is subsequently deprived of second place when track bumps force him to throttle-off and allow the Pole to pass him. Like London buses, after we've waited all season for a British rider to win a Grand Prix race, heat 7 then sees Scott Nicholls take the chequered flag. Behind him, the 99th GP race of the season featured an enthralling battle between Andreas Jonsson and Krzysztof Kasprzak who dice with each other for second place over the last lap and a half of the race.

Eight riders qualify for the semi-finals of any Grand Prix with their qualification determined by the points they score during the 20 races of each Grand Prix meeting. During the height of the season there is a Grand Prix pretty well every fortnight so, even if we ignore the limited number of really world-class riders in the competition, inevitably there's a sense of repetition allied to a sneaking feeling that for many riders this is sometimes just another day at the office. The top riders in the world qualify for the knockout stages of the competition on a regular basis and, on the whole, go about their work with matter-of-fact professionalism. The laborious nature of the 20-race qualification stage is an organisational structure that doesn't necessarily maximise the entertainment on offer and, when allied to the difficulties of the Cardiff indoor track, consequently leads to a number of pedestrian follow-my-leader, strung-out-

Bomber DVD's and Jodie Lowry

Patriotic cowboy hat

Cardiff GP: *"Inside they'll be able to buy non-flammable air horns."*

like-a-line-of-washing type races. However, as the meeting draws to a close the effort levels of the riders over their last two races noticeably increases. That said, most people's 2008 world champion in waiting, Nicki Pedersen looks badly out of sorts during the early part of the meeting and this is confirmed in heat 15 when he goes backwards through the field during the race. His namesake Bjarne leads from the gate and, by the second bend of the second lap, Nicki has lost second place to Scott Nicholls before he concedes third place on the last bend of the race to the always bustlingly competitive Chris Harris. This leaves Nicki on a meagre 5 points and in dire need of a race win in his final outing to ensure his progress to the latter stages that have come almost as right to him over recent years.

Before the drama of Nicki's win-or-bust heat 17, the flag-waving sections of the crowd are treated to the possibility that a third British rider might even manage to take the Cardiff chequered flag. Edward Kennett leads heat 16 for two laps only to then find himself passed by Niels-Kristian Iversen and, subsequently, relegated to third place at the start of the fourth lap by Andreas Jonsson. After he's gated with alacrity, it would be fair to say that previous GP experience, knowledge of the track and superior equipment proves to be the subtle but key differences between Edward and the rival riders who pass him. Perched high in the stands, I get a bird's eye view of the controversial first-corner incident in the initial attempt to run heat 17. Leigh Adams fires away from the inside gate, only to have the slightly slower-starting Nicki Pedersen cut across the track from gate 4 and (appear to) knock the Australian off his machine as they vie for supremacy. In reality, Nicki has shown masterly control, brilliant spatial awareness and world championship standard gamesmanship. Nicki quickly appreciates that he has been bested by his rival into the corner and so, instinctively, reacts to gamble on the possibly better outcome of a rerun by deliberately placing his front wheel on Leigh Adams's back wheel. This effectively ensures that he is flung melodramatically from his machine. It's a calculated decision that we've all seen in races many times before when the second-placed rider to the corner decides to tumble from their machine in the hope that the referee will err on the side of caution and apply the infamous 'first-bend bunching' concept to order all four riders back for a rerun. Since Marek Wojaczek has already proved that he might struggle to apply the rules, Nicki must also know that he isn't a 'strong' official. Given second place won't be enough to ensure qualification a theatrical fall holds out the possibility of a subsequent win in the rerun and remains his best hope to further consolidate his campaign to become world champion. Calculated gamble made and, to give the referee enough time to consider the full enormity of his decision, Nicki stays down on the track at the apex of bends 1 and 2 for well over two minutes. To the disbelief of the crowd and the rider himself, rather than take the 'easy' route Wojaczek unbelievably excludes Leigh Adams from the rerun of the race! Quite how this can be when he was clearly first to the corner beggars our collective belief. On the giant screens suspended from the stadium roof, we get to see the dramatic crash replayed in its full glory from a variety of angles. A truism of the modern technology rich age is that too much information can prove as misleading or inconclusive as too little information. Three replays appear to show Nicki Pedersen is definitively the aggrieved party but, more revealingly, the straight-on camera shows that Leigh Adams was clearly in front and, therefore, theoretically should legitimately be able to broadside his bike at whatever angle or position on the track he chose. Eventually back on his feet, Nicki is booed enthusiastically by the Millennium Stadium crowd all the way back to the pits. Often cast as the villain due to his aggressive riding style (and success), Nicki's status as a pantomime villain is doubly emphasised when even the image of his face when flashed on the giant screens even gets booed. To be fair, the referee has been decisive and had the confidence to make a huge decision, albeit the wrong one! It's one that will alter the course and result of this meeting as well as the overall series. Up until the moment Nicki chose to engineer his fall, Leigh Adams looked certain to qualify for the semi-final while Pedersen is apparently just about to have his world championship ambitions dented by his premature elimination from Cardiff.

With only three riders in the rerun, Nicki Pedersen is serenaded with a cacophony of boos from the crowd as he makes his way round to his gate 4 start position. With strange synchronicity, the Dane flies from the tapes but, as he reaches the apex of the first corner, Rune Holta – who has temporarily lost control of his bike after it unexpectedly reared from the white line of the first bend – clips him from behind. Nicki falls in dramatic but ungainly fashion by the second-bend exit, while Holta's bike somersaults over the air fence. Nicki quickly extracts himself from the tangle of his machine, leaps to his feet and apparently thinks to remonstrate with Holta only to think better of it and instead collapses to the floor as though shot by a sniper. After another two minutes spent on said shale surface to recover his composure (and allow his bikes to be readied for the rerun in the pits), Nicki rises tentatively to his feet and is again booed in pantomime fashion. It's all too much for a fat man a few rows in front of me who aggressively proclaims

Cardiff GP: *"Inside they'll be able to buy non-flammable air horns."*

with exaggerated hand gestures (ones you don't ever get to see on the late-night programme repeats for the deaf) that Nicki is an onanist. With his shaven head and a body that threatens to break free from his tight figure-hugging top, the man reminds me of a sausage angrily trying to burst its skin while he semaphores imaginary planes into land on the steeply rolling deck of his very own aircraft carrier.

Love him or loathe him, there's no doubt that Nicki is always great box office! The re-rerun of heat 17 is reduced to a match race between the Dane and Andreas Jonsson. Predictably Nicki secures the 3 points he requires and, like the conclusion of all the other races, just as he crosses the line flames theatrically flare up from either side of the track. It's a result that guarantees mutually assured qualification for both riders. Ever the professional, before the next race, Kevin Coombes tells us "Learning all the time – Team GB star Edward Kennett." It's a comment that rings true when second-placed Edward is almost reeled in by Freddie Lindgren but then shows bravery and skill to hold off the close attentions of his rival as they dash from the final bend to the finish.

Key camera position

By now the unpredictability of the bumps and ruts on the track surface repeatedly cause unexpected havoc at random moments. There are some who think that an element of unpredictability adds to the spectacle but, from mid-meeting onwards, the ruts are plainly dangerous for the riders. Nothing illustrates this better than the dénouement of heat 19. The race line up showcases Nicholls, Crump, Hancock and Gollob. All except the Pole have already pretty well qualified though, obviously, the outcome will still influence their final points total and, therefore, their semi-final gate positions. Scott Nicholls leads the race until a second-lap mistake on the apex of bends 3 and 4 allows Jason Crump to power past him on the home straight. Skilled riders like these traverse the lumps and craters of the indoor surface with skill that makes the rutted surface look merely bumpy. However, experience, posture and ability on the bike can only take you so far. Crump then hits a bump as he enters the final corner, loses control of the slide, hammers into the home-straight fence which throws him awkwardly on top of his handlebars and, as he shoots diagonally across the track, Jason still somehow manages to cling onto his bike. That he wins the race is a testament to his nous, skill as a motorcyclist and balance but also to the quick reactions of Scott Nicholls who evades his wildly riding rival, despite closely following behind. That a rider of the calibre of Jason Crump can be thrown around on his highly powered machine and across the track like a rag doll speaks volumes for the not-so-hidden dangers of the badly rutted Cardiff surface. The poor preparation is ultimately not down to the skill of the curatorial team but, allegedly, installation time given and the materials chosen by the speedway Grand Prix organisers. Whichever way you look at it, the provision of a below-standard track surface demonstrates contempt for the performers and fans alike. However, they do have previous and, after all, the BSI televisual package is premised upon the drama of the thrills and the spills – shown lovingly in slow-motion replay – so, in this context, any additional carnage will merely add to the marketability of the product as well as the visual appeal of the highlights reel. The medium of television necessarily desensitises the viewers to the humanity of the people featured. Just like it's easy (or convenient) to forget that the victims of war, famine and disaster shown on our news screens are real flesh and blood human beings with parents, family and friends, so it is with kevlar-suited riders who

Camera pole

Cardiff GP: *"Inside they'll be able to buy non-flammable air horns."*

smash into air fences or tumble from their bikes.

The last qualifying race of the evening has a Demolition Derby quality to it. Chris Harris roars from the inside gate and badly clatters the blue-helmeted Hans Andersen on the second bend. However, the Dane shows skill, determination and practised natural ability on his bike to somehow stay on and continues to roar off down the back straight in pursuit of the first or second place he still needs to ensure qualification for the semi-finals. Unfortunately for Chris Harris, he is in the wars. No sooner has he survived the first-corner bump with Hans Andersen than Niels-Kristian Iversen (in yellow) hits the rutted bumps of the inside white line as he enters the third corner, loses control and clatters into Harris to take both riders in a tangle to the air fence. Even referee Marek Wojaczek can't exclude the wrong person here and Iversen quickly receives his marching orders. Despite sustaining a broken nose, along with leg and wrist injuries as well as a sore shoulder, Chris Harris picks himself up and groggily takes part in the rerun. His walk back to the pits is greeted with such patriotic rapture and ecstasy that tear gas and a water cannon might be needed to restore order. There's quite a delay before the riders return to the track for heat 20. To pass the time, a tune that features the chorus "life is life" blasts out deafeningly over the high-quality speaker system of the Millennium Stadium. The crowd parp their non-flammable air horns in time with the song. In terms of atmosphere and ethos, to all intents and purposes the speedway Grand Prix often resembles a giant speedway-themed version of the Eurovision Song Contest. In recent years BSI have shown that they aim for the populist or retro in their selection of musical artistes to provide the pre-meeting and interval entertainment, so it's hardly a surprise that Cardiff often feels like either a night in Germany or the Albanian qualifying round for Eurovision Contest entry. When the riders eventually line up for the rerun of heat 20, Andersen flies from the tape and, on the third bend, Harris is subjected to an aggressive manoeuvre by Kasprzak who forces him wide. Suffering with his injuries, Harris faces a number of options. He can bail out, shut off or, in typical Bomber fashion, blast round the outside in the rough stuff and keep the throttle full on. In trademark fashion he takes the third option with considerable aplomb to finish second and, thereby, definitively ensures his qualification for the semi-final stage.

While we wait for news of the semi-final gate positions, a small army of tractors takes to the circuit. The notion that their grading activities could smooth the track surface is, obviously, false and their endeavours must be primarily cosmetic, particularly given the sheer array of the unpredictable lumps and bumps that the riders find with unerring ease. While the tractors circle, the really important work also takes place – namely, the removal of the shale-splattered air-fence advertising signs. There's really no point for the sponsoring companies to lash out considerable expense on air-fence adverts only to find the company name and logo obscured by dirt. A small group of men work with speed and practised efficiency to strip away the signs from the air fence. These adverts must be attached in a way that allows them to be quickly ripped off in the manner of a magician's assistant's skirt. Once removed, another pristine version of the removed advert is unfurled and quickly fastened in place. The 'Nordic Bet' bend appears to have taken a complete splattering. To help this process, there's also a man with a large backpack that makes him look like a spaceman without a helmet. Rather than a jet propulsion system or air supply, his backpack appears to be a Hoover with a thin pipe that's used to efficiently clean the shale from the top of the air fence (although some claim he's actually there to re-inflate the airbags). Once all the advertisers' signs are brightly legible (rather than the track bump-free), the racing can recommence.

The first semi-final is almost immediately plunged into controversy. The red-helmeted Bjarne Pedersen roars from gate 1, makes the corner and goes into a broadside. From the outside gate Nicki Pedersen gets the drop on Hans Andersen, cuts across towards the inside line and yet again manages to get his front wheel just into the right position to ensure that he's melodramatically knocked off – this time by his fellow countryman and namesake Bjarne. The Polish referee doesn't manage to find and operate the red lights switch until the riders have progressed to the third bend, while behind them Nicki Pedersen stays prone on the track like an overturned beetle. It's a carbon copy of the incident that led to the exclusion of Leigh Adams and, to be fair to him, no one can say the referee isn't consistent in his decision-making since he quickly excludes Bjarne Pedersen. It's a decision that completely incenses the usually phlegmatic Bjarne, so much so that he temporarily forgets a key part of his televised speedway routine. Usually vanity dictates that, whenever Bjarne removes his helmet, he immediately hides his thinning hair underneath a cap for any subsequent interview. Tonight he's so vehement and righteously angry that this fastidious and strictly adhered to routine is completely forgotten so he can storm to the pits phone and remonstrate (to no avail) with the referee. On

Cardiff GP: *"Inside they'll be able to buy non-flammable air horns."*

the giant screens we get treated to a prime view of his expressive hand gestures and the increasing baldness he usually goes to such lengths to hide. Luckily the crowd have a pantomime villain to focus their ire upon and Nicki Pedersen is the chosen object of their contempt. Given it's actually the referee who makes these disputed decisions each time, its ultimately churlish to blame Nicki Pedersen who, if only for the crowd reaction alone, has good reason to feel aggrieved himself. The 1960s and 1970s saw a series of books published on the tactics and skills of gamesmanship (*The Art of Coarse Golf* etc.) and, if anyone were to pen a volume on the dark art of speedway gamesmanship and tactics, then one possible author would have to be Nicki Pedersen (though there are plenty of other worthy candidates). While other riders are equally capable of theatrical falls from their bikes, tonight we have been treated to a master-class in the art of hopeful deception by Nicki who has, on two different occasions, failed to make the gate by a fraction but 'engineered' a subsequent coming together in a manner that could make him look like the victim. To achieve this takes skill, control and nerve, never mind that it shows a willingness to gamble in pursuit of victory through shrewd gamesmanship. For these characteristics alone, at Cardiff Nicki has thrown down the gauntlet to his rivals and further double underlined his determination to retain his World Championship crown.

Nicki Pedersen makes no mistake second time out with an easy win from the tapes that befits his status as possible champion elect. Behind him there is a battle royale between Hans Andersen and Scott Nicholls. Ever since the World Team Cup Final a few years ago, there has been no love lost between these two riders as is illustrated in the second corner of the race when Scott powers hard underneath the Dane and drives him close to the fence. They then ride neck-and-neck as though locked together until the start of the second lap when Scott establishes the supremacy that will ensure his qualification for the final. The second semi-final suffers from successive unsatisfactory starts and the referee takes it upon himself to warn Andreas Jonsson. They say the definition of an alcoholic is someone who drinks the same amount as you do but whom you don't like. The same holds true for the definition of dirty riding – you call it competitive riding when you like the rider and dirty riding when you don't. On the *Sky* speedway coverage Sam Ermolenko (and to some extent Kelvin Tatum) have historically struggled to hide their contempt for Nicki's attitude on the track towards his fellow riders. When the race eventually gets under way, Jason Crump aggressively batters Greg Hancock for the first three corners in a manner that would win a points decision in boxing and tonight would have had Nicki Pedersen booed off the track. However, there is no audible response from the crowd, while Greg demonstrates resilience and determination to drive round the outside on the bumpy stuff to race to a comfortable win ahead of the Australian. Chris Harris wins the contest for third place and finishes with 10 points – his best Grand Prix score of the season so far.

With Scott Nicholls in the final, patriotic anticipation increases and the Union flags primarily supplied by BSI for the benefit of the television cameras are waved enthusiastically. No sooner have the riders come under orders than Scott Nicholls bursts unceremoniously through the tapes after the apparently premeditatedly decision that to predict their rise will be his only way to gain advantage over these high-calibre rivals. The rerun final race could have been another battle royale between Crump and Hancock but for the fact that the Australian takes the honours by virtue of the fact that he exits the first corner ahead. On the track almost as much as on his bike tonight, Nicki Pedersen falls from his machine and bounces down the home straight of the second lap. Though clearly in pain, Pedersen sportingly removes his bike from the track before he collapses in pain on the centre green. It is a gesture that fails to get applause from the crowd but ensures that the referee has no reason to stop the race or Jason Crump's triumphant charge to the chequered flag.

28th June Speedway Grand Prix (Cardiff) Winner: Jason Crump

Cardiff GP: *"Inside they'll be able to buy non-flammable air horns."*

CHAPTER 15.

Birmingham v. King's Lynn:

"They must want to get it on 'cause they're suctioning the water off the track."

2nd July

Luckily I can travel mid afternoon to Birmingham so the notorious M6 traffic jams have yet to really kick in by the time I turn off the motorway to head for Perry Barr Stadium. It's hardly a surprise to see thick black clouds over the grandstand roof given that by the end of May the Brummies had already called off seven home meetings. The month of June then saw no abandonments and, given the industriousness with which the track staff sluice water from the track, they're keen to ensure that this meeting proceeds. Birmingham Speedway trackshop owner Nick Barber surveys the scene, "They must want to get it on 'cause they're suctioning the water off the track." They also spruce up the inside white line of the circuit so, if this were *Thunderbirds*, soon all systems will be go!

If the mid afternoon's skies over England's second city are filled with leaden-coloured clouds, then they're metaphorically even darker over the British economy. *BBC Radio 4's* lunchtime news programme, *The World at One*, is a catalogue of almost unrelenting gloom during my drive over. Lowlights include Marks & Spencer's profit warning (that saw their shares fall 20 per cent), Builders Taylor Woodrow announce a dramatic fall in new house building demand and, unrelatedly Alan Sugar stands down as Amstrad Chairman. To mark the event, he's interviewed by Martha Carney and, famed for 'calling it as it is', Siralun isn't exactly a ray of sunshine when he forecasts four years of hard times ahead "before the market turns". There's always a temptation to look for scapegoats and Siralun leaves us in no doubt where to place the blame: "Our American cousins went a bit wild and our banks got involved 'cause they wanted some of the action!" Elsewhere in Siralun's empire, the latest winner of the *Apprentice*, Lee "that's what I'm talking about" McQueen, somehow manages to miss his first day at work. It's not the best way to start a £100,000 per annum job and it would be fun to be a fly on the wall when Siralun discusses it with him. When I switch radio stations, to find something more cheerful, the local radio station forecasts heavy rain in the Birmingham and West Midlands area!

Quite what the forthcoming recession holds for speedway is far from clear but, one thing is certain, many speedway clubs have already endured a difficult start to the 2008 season. The period between the Cardiff Grand Prix weekend and the start of the summer holiday season is often a lull in the speedway calendar. Many fans splurge their money on their trip to Cardiff and then, subsequently, cut back on their regular weekly visits to their local speedway track for the following few weeks afterwards. The downstairs bar area of the home-straight grandstand at Perry Barr stadium houses two trackshops close together and Nick's sister, Bev Barber, works industriously to set out neat lines of model riders along with a huge array of yellow-and-red Brummies merchandise. It's the second season back in existence for this incarnation of the club. This difficult second year is often a test for the financial business plan of the club and the Brummies promotional team will have to attempt to retain the enthusiasm of the fans and, hopefully, maintain attendance levels. Fewer fans also means fewer potential customers for the trackshop. Last season, a casual glance around the stadium appeared to indicate that everyone had bought at least one item of yellow-and-red merchandise with a giant Brummies "B" emblazoned upon it. This season, the fans remain festooned in Brummies branded clothing of the 2007 variety, so trackshop sales aren't as buoyant. Later Nick Barber confides that takings at Perry Barr stadium have fallen by 75 per cent. "The first year everyone wanted to get everything and this year it's different!" Other parts of his trackshop empire still perform above market conditions, "Ipswich is up, Swindon always does well and King's Lynn is slightly down – Mildenhall is always small!" Not only does each shop perform differently but also the cost base varies dramatically. "At Birmingham it costs me three times what I have to pay at Belle Vue. Here I've got two staff working for me and they don't do it for charity so – what with the rent, fuel and staff costs –

I'm gonna have to consider the future carefully. At Ipswich suddenly everyone wants to wear the colours again and, at Belle Vue, [the promoters] love the stuff we've done, so that's good!"

A casual glance over the stall that Bev manages shows that the range and choice of products available has increased to include various styles of Brummies caps, knapsacks, sweatshirts, pit shirts, anoraks and umbrellas. There are even junior race bibs (at £12.50 a set), rider models and, a nice touch, casual tops with riders' names and numbers on including Birko (6), Roberts (8), Lyons (3) and Roynon (5). Not only have the Brummies been remarkably unfortunate with postponements (three of these against King's Lynn!) but they've been even unluckier with injuries! A casual glance through the racecard tonight indicates that many of these rider-specific items might struggle to sell since there are just as many guests as there are contracted Birmingham riders on show this evening. The Brummies will operate rider replacement for Adam Roynon and will have guests at number 2 (Chris Mills), number 3 (Andre Compton) and number 6 (Paul Clews). In marked contrast the King's Lynn Money Centre Stars still line up with their complete team and this presently bodes well for their trophy credentials. Despite the efforts of the ground staff, heavy rain in the area has created enough surface water on the track to ensure that this would be a lateral hazard should Perry Barr stadium ever become a golf course. They'll have a lengthy afternoon's work ahead on the track before the turnstiles open.

Innovative tree photo

Trackshops take a lot more skill, patience and visual flair to set out than you'd imagine and, if the soothsayers are to be believed, then difficult economic times ahead will impact on all areas of our lives including the world of speedway. While Nick and Bev continue to busy themselves, I look over the latest editions of the various speedway magazines stocked to try to establish exactly what you get for your money. The *Speedway Star* (28th June 2008 edition) is the bible of the sport and costs £2.60 each week if you buy it from a (track)shop, though you can save money if you take out an annual £100 UK subscription ("pay £1.92p per issue including first class postage" for it to be "delivered to your door"). In the last year the Surbiton-based office of the magazine has moved a few doors away and, unrelatedly, inside the magazine the layout has altered along with the type of paper used. Doubtless this makes it easier to lay out and typeset every week and also, I would imagine, makes the paper cheaper to purchase and also the magazine cheaper to mail. Pinegen Ltd prints the *Speedway Star* and also produces various important speedway programmes for BSPA-shared events like the Super7even series but also for the BSI-run SGP. Some staff members also have tasks to perform for the SGP series. The *Speedway Star*'s managing editor, Philip Rising is SGP Press Officer and so is a comparatively big cheese within its hierarchy. Subscriptions manager, all-round good bloke and Chelsea season-ticket holder, Dave Fairbrother is often seen on our television screens at SGP events with responsibility for placing the semi-final and final chosen gate positions onto a board erected for this purpose close to the pits. Often dapperly dressed for live TV, Dave's administrative role smoothes the wheels of the event and also kind of makes him speedway's equivalent of Carol Vorderman. Judged by the number of reports he writes, *Speedway Star* editor Richard Clark attends many SGPs as does chief photographer Mike Patrick and, probably less frequently, so does Scunthorpe speedway obsessive and *Star* deputy editor, Andrew Skeels. The long and the short of this close, hybrid but independent commercial reporting relationship

Cornucopia of Brummies merchandise

means that throughout the season the preamble, pre-meeting and post-meeting analysis of the SGP can sometimes appear to occupy disproportionate space within the magazine. Some promoters have (quietly) expressed concern that this departs from what they view as its primary reporting focus, namely the various leagues of British speedway. Looked at in snapshot terms the issue I study has a page count of 64 pages and a photo of a triumphant Scott Nicholls on its cover with a caption that optimistically announces, "I do believe I can do it". Coverage of the Grand Prix dominates and takes up nearly 30 per cent of the magazine (18 pages). The bulk of the remainder of the issue I look at is as follows: News (4 pages); Elite League (5 pages); Premier League (8 pages); Conference League (3 pages); PL Pairs (3 pages); and British speedway results (8 pages). There are also 6½ pages of adverts while space is also given to Grasstrack (2 pages); Gossip including Fantasy League information (2 pages) plus International and results (8½ pages).

The most interesting and simultaneously occasionally laughable feature in the whole magazine is a three-page interview with Paul Bellamy who rejoices in the grandiose job title of "Managing Director of BSI (Speedway)." His organisational role is described in glowing terms in this article, "Paul Bellamy is the link between Benfield and the new rights owners IMG and has as much responsibility on his shoulders as anyone this weekend, probably more than anyone." Rumoured to be almost as modest as fellow BSI visionary John Postlethwaite, the interview is nonetheless a fascinating insight into the workings, business philosophy, strategy and opinions of Mr Bellamy. He mixes business platitudes with wild assertion and some comments that strike the casual reader as plain wrong. Nick Barber is amazed by how far he's come in the sport so quickly, "It's only a few years ago that Paul Bellamy was counting the T-shirts after a big event at Eastbourne and now he's the Managing Director of BSI (Speedway)." The interview quickly skates onto thin ice when Paul Bellamy decides to offer prognostications about what is best for British speedway, apparently conveniently forgetting that when in charge of Reading Speedway, BSI (Reading) haemorrhaged cash and yet still struggled to organise a trip to the pub. Interviewer Richard Clark rather cannily explicitly queries whether these sincerely held opinions are influenced by commercial interests and necessarily coloured by what Clark elegantly terms "conflict of interests". Rather disingenuously Bellamy replies, "It's not on our part, there's only a conflict of interest with promoters in this country ... the conflict of interest isn't on our part, some promoters, not all of them, in the UK are complaining about it, but they've got to get their own act together first ... they have to sort out what night they're racing and do something about their stadiums. And there's a lot of speedway as well, possibly too much. Around Easter time there could be four meetings in a week – madness." Glamorously though the SGP is packaged, whether or not a competition primarily composed of 'invitation only' riders who race alternate weekends in 10 different locations (often on inferior tracks) qualifies him to offer such opinions remains a moot point. While Mr Bellamy claims relative impartiality without apparent irony, whether the SGP is organised and constituted in a fashion the speedway public wants to see sadly isn't subjected to similar analysis.

In charge of a greater number of trackshops than his competitors, Nick Barber is ideally placed to give some perspective on the volume of *Speedway Stars* sold on average each week. He won't divulge confidential commercial information, however, I do gather that the general trackshop trading environment isn't exactly rosy and, obviously, magazine sales are part of that overall equation. To a certain extent, since they aren't a big-ticket item, fans remain quite happy to spend the few pounds required for discretionary items like pens, magazines and badges. Nonetheless, when money is tight, fans either don't go to the meetings every week or closely monitor their expenditure. Food and/or drink often remain popular at tracks but, in an Internet age where information is readily available elsewhere, the *Speedway Star* might not necessarily remain an essential meeting purchase even if it provides the only real, comprehensive and historical record of note about British speedway. "Before we took over at Workington [trackshop], the *Star* used to sell 1,500 copies a week under Mitch Graham – but there was a year without a shop and any memorabilia and the *Star* subscriptions went up massively! I know as many people don't go along to watch the Comets race nowadays and, now, we only sell 6-10 copies a week at Workington!"

If sales have got tighter for the *Speedway Star* then the truism that nostalgia isn't what it used to be must surely spell trouble for Tony McDonald the canny magazine publisher behind *Backtrack* and *Vintage Speedway Magazine*. In a move that must count as either brilliantly strategic or brave, Tony has chosen to launch a new speedway magazine entitled *Classic Speedway*. Issue number 1 (dated Spring 2008) comes at "A special launch price of £2", though the cost rises to £3.50 for subsequent issues. It's a small format, 48-page magazine that's predominantly black-and-white

Birmingham v. King's Lynn: *"They must want to get it on 'cause they're suctioning the water off the track."*

with four colour pages. The arrival of *Classic Speedway* also signals the demise of Vintage Speedway Magazine and this fact is acknowledged in the small print that states "*Classic Speedway* incorporating *Vintage Speedway Magazine*". Sixty issues of *Vintage Speedway Magazine* were produced since it launched in 1993 until its closure and simultaneous incorporation into the new magazine 15 years later. The introductory message from Tony Mac and Susie Muir states, "It's a change we have not taken lightly." The new magazine retains some popular features and writers, "John Chaplin, Ian Hoskins and John Hyam are still with us, plus Letters and Chequered Flag." Choosing their words carefully, the editors reveal their sense of expectation about the magazine, "what we hope will become required reading for all supporters and connoisseurs of our great sport with a sense of history."

Looked at as an outsider, there's a possible segmentation problem ahead since previously *Vintage Speedway Magazine* and *Backtrack* appealed to totally separate and distinct markets. With the publication of *Classic Speedway*, these boundaries have now become blurred since the date focus of the new magazine will be "Post War II to early seventies". There are also some other continuity and cross-pollination issues, as signalled by the six-page interview with Olle Nygren, "In the second and final part of his interview, Tony McDonald hears talk of danger." One danger that we don't hear talk of is the reaction of the subscribers who now find they'll have to purchase this magazine to learn the conclusion of an interview started in the final issue of *Vintage Speedway Magazine*. If this wasn't already confusion enough, Martin Neal conducts a two-page interview with Bruce Cribb that ends with the comment. "If you want to read more about Bruce Cribb and the rest of his British racing career, including his time at Cradley Heath, Wolverhampton, Berwick and Exeter, then be sure not to miss Issue 26 of *Backtrack*." When I used to work in textbook publishing, commercial necessity dictated that we sometimes brought out a new edition of a popular textbook halfway through the academic year. Invariably, this caused much gnashing of teeth among the lecturers when they had to amend and update their lessons to take account of the additional information contained in the book. It caused even greater dissatisfaction among the customers (students) since some of them had purchased the superseded edition of a book that was now effectively redundant and no longer completely applicable to their course. In the business, we called this a "forced roll" and the inevitable result was (at best) a slightly disrupted relationship with our key clients (the lecturers) and at worst, dramatic loss of sales during the next year caused by resentment at our high-handed behaviour. While the similarities aren't exact, subscribers to *Vintage Speedway Magazine* now find the metaphorical rug pulled from underneath their feet and, if they are to fully enjoy the Olle Nygren and Bruce Cribb interviews, they'll now have to purchase two separate magazines! Only time will tell whether the magazine succeeds but clearly the publishers are aware of possible problems since they also take the opportunity to announce that they will be "holding one year subscriptions at the *Vintage Speedway Magazine* level of £12 for four issues". The content of the inaugural issue itself is varied and includes a six-page interview with Ivan Mauger; two pages on the museum, reunions and health news plus diary dates; a single page of "Name that Track"; a six-page interview with Neil Street conducted by Martin Neal; two pages of classic images; two pages on 1948/1958/1968; two pages on Ian Hoskins; two pages of letters; an

Cloudy skies and Bev texting

Blue drink and a pint of lager

Birmingham v. King's Lynn: *"They must want to get it on 'cause they're suctioning the water off the track."*

advert that trumpets "LAST EVER ISSUE OF VINTAGE SPEEDWAY MAGAZINE – don't be without this collectors' item!" Plus a single page of Chequered Flag that features the obituaries of Cecil Bailey (four paragraphs) and Cyril J. Hart (eight paragraphs). To retain the feel of a magazine within a magazine, there are five grey tinted pages that use the *Vintage Speedway Magazine* logo and these feature John Chaplin who writes about Vic Huxley as well as some book reviews, namely Trevor Davies's Warzone Speedway and Norman Jacobs's *Out of the Frying Pan: The Story of New Cross Speedway* (published by Stadia, an imprint of The History Press Ltd). The front cover features a photo of Ivan Mauger (when riding for Belle Vue) while the back cover foregrounds a really weird photo of Olle Nygren with a West Ham race tabard and a tree branch across his face that looks as though it has been surgically implanted.[1]

Nick Barber has *Classic Speedway* prominently displayed next to its sister publication *Backtrack* and knows from experience that every publication has its own shelf life, "We ran *Speedway Collectors' Club magazine* for eight or nine years until it ran its course. We did it for love not a profit but we called it a day 'cause we were just going over the same ground. This is bound to be a problem with any magazine let alone a history one. I imagine Tony [McDonald] is hoping that people will buy both *Backtrack* and *Classic Speedway* but I worry they won't plus the photos in *Backtrack* have a heavy bias towards London and the South East 'cause Tony bought all Alf Weedon's negatives. We used to sell 500 of each *Backtrack* but now it's 200 though, they're not all lost, as some of those will have gone to subscriptions!"

Yogi Berra the baseball player and manager famed for his unique, pithy quotations, once remarked "it's déjà vu all over again" though he hadn't seen the latest issue of *Backtrack* magazine (May/June 2008, Issue 26). Splashed across the coloured cover are shouty headlines and photographs that advertise interviews with Terry Betts ("Our big exclusive!"), Neil Street ("on his role in the four-valve revolution") and Bruce Cribb ("on his hard-man image"). The front cover copy doesn't reveal that 12.5% of the 48 pages are given over to adverts (five of these six pages will be for *Backtrack* magazines and books) but does promise us Bobby McNeil, John Berry, Jan Verner, Wags, Mike Wilding, Defunct track (Boston), Coventry in pictures, Rod Haynes and Mike Bennett. My eye is immediately caught by the promise of some Speedway Wags but the three-page "Wives and Girlfriends" feature article inside doesn't fulfil its latent prurient promise. In fact, these historical photographs feature attractive women who happen to be involved with speedway riders rather than individuals who seek out highly paid footballers because they seek conspicuous consumption, thrive on licentious behaviour or the excessive use of recreational stimulants. Also inside the magazine is the "Taking the Mic" feature that provides some much-needed background information on the talented speedway presenter Mike Bennett as well as some straightforward questions that allows Mike to talk about something he loves – himself! From this feature we learn, "These days Mike and partner Tracey run a media training business which takes them all over the world. Mike retired from speedway for several years because he'd "simply had enough" but was then tempted back in 2004 by Keith Chapman at King's Lynn. Bitten by the bug again, he is now the regular centre-green presenter at the Norfolk Arena and also took the microphone at some of last year's super7 meetings." You'll have to buy the magazine (don't forget it's Issue 26) to learn Mike's stimulating answers to the questions posed. My eye was caught by the discussion of the hypersensitivity shown by some people to Mike's extensive repartee and banter, "some of the promoters take what I say personally, which is a shame, as it's all tongue in cheek." Nick Barber doesn't share the joy of my discovery of this interview. "One thing is for certain – and you can quote me on this – that he'll definitely give this issue of *Backtrack* plenty of plugs at King's Lynn this Friday! So it'll be DVDs and *Backtrack* this week. Funnily enough, Mike missed doing the DVD for the King's Lynn v. Birmingham meeting where the unbeaten home record went [after 99 meetings] 'cause he was in Papua New Guinea! He sure gets around doing media training." In times of recession, it's a delight to learn that Mike's media credentials continue to impress in the obscurer far-flung parts of the world and that he makes a contribution to British exports!

Though the dark clouds remain, other parts of the sky have brightened considerably and, having driven from Felixstowe to Birmingham on many occasions only to then have the meeting postponed, Nick claps his hands delightedly in admiration of curatorial efforts. "You know they gonna get it on! Now they've suctioned off the water

---

[1] Quite what led to the choice of this photograph isn't clear but the next issue of the magazine also features some impressive shrubbery along with a rider of yesteryear. You have to wonder if publisher Tony McDonald wants to expand his magazine empire further and surreptitiously market a speedway-related gardening magazine by the back door!

Birmingham v. King's Lynn: *"They must want to get it on 'cause they're suctioning the water off the track."*

the track looks lovely and it's gonna be really grippy tonight!" Sister Beverley is also delighted though for different reasons. She does the speedway updates at Birmingham for the Internet, "Thank God there's no silly names like Rajkowski and the like tonight. They always beat the predictive texts!" When I praise the variety and display of the merchandise on offer Bev tells me, "They go mad for the mini riders here. I know some tracks they don't, but here they do!" Cardiff has taken a lot out of her. "I always feel deflated after Cardiff. Johnny [brother] says he's not going to take me again 'cause all I do is sit in the £65 seats and hide behind my programme when Scott rides and rely on the crowd noise to tell me what's going on! On the forums, people are moaning about people booing Nicki Pedersen. He's big enough to take it and I think he enjoys it! It's a pantomime really so it just adds to the atmosphere. People say it means you're gloating in riders getting injured. Obviously, you feel bad afterwards if they have but, really, when one of the 'villains' like Nicki bites the dust it adds to the theatre of it all! When Scott and Bomber passed him you couldn't ask for a better roar anywhere!" Bill Gimbeth helps out with Bev's section of the trackshop but isn't as optimistic with his meteorological outlook, "Oh no! Look at them black clouds coming over – the wind's blowing them this way too! It's King's Lynn, so it's bound to rain!"

Next week's meeting v Island

Midlands-based speedway officials are attracted to Birmingham speedway on race night like bees to pollen. Famous international speedway referee Tony Steele passes and I press him for reaction to the recent Cardiff performance of his Polish colleague. Ever diplomatic, Tony notes, "If I was being fair, it's hard to see from the ref's box at Cardiff who is leading. Nicki moved in as much as Leigh moved out – so I'd have had all four back though, the rules say, you exclude the rider who caused the stoppage. And that was the rider on the floor! Obviously, his decisions have had a major bearing on the destination of the Grand Prix. Once Nicki knew he could get away with it – he did! The second time it happened, you couldn't give the benefit of the doubt. Don't forget there were a couple of other decisions you could look at – the one where Nicki touched the tapes. And also the one where the referee gave Hancock a win when it should've been Adams – so he would have had the 8 points he needed to qualify and it wouldn't have mattered what happened in that heat with Nicki!" But for Tony's love of insurance, trains and speedway, he would have been an ideal British Ambassador for the Diplomatic Service. Affable Solihull referee Chris Durno is also here along with his son Tom. After a glance at the brightening skies he nonetheless predicts, "The Brummies don't do well when it rains!"

Ambulance TV

The sunshine that breaks through at 7 o'clock could lead you to ignore the later forecast of rain. Experienced promoters Graham and Denise Drury ensure the meeting is pushed through quickly and, from the centre green, announcer Chris Simpson confirms, "There'll be no parade tonight we'll go straight to the racing at 19.45. It's sunny now but we don't know for how long! We've already had seven [out of eighteen] Birmingham home meetings cancelled already this season and three of those have been against King's Lynn, four if you include the away meeting." Last season (2007) the usual presenter at Perry Barr was the experienced Peter Yorke but, this season, Chris Simpson has taken over and throws himself into the breach with much greater enthusiasm, "The riders are out a bit early unto the track – they'll have to wait 'cause we can't start racing until 7.45." No sooner has the first heat started than Craig Watson (on a rider-replacement ride for the injured Adam Roynon) falls on the first corner only to wait on the track surface for a red light that never comes from referee Graham Flint. Watson remounts disconsolately and immediately retires onto the centre green, while on track Kevin Doolan and Shaun Tacey storm to a maximum heat advantage. King's Lynn then repeat the medicine in the next race when Brummies captain James Birkenshaw retires and third place goes to Birmingham guest reserve, Paul Clews. Another guest, Andre Compton, quickly restores some pride for the Brummies when he wins the third heat ahead of King's Lynn's highly regarded Tomas Topinka.

Never afraid to verbalise the obvious, Chris Simpson informs us over the public-address system, "The Brummies are already looking for a big response from the riders – can they find it in heat 4?" Sadly for the home fans the answer is a resounding "no" since the injury jinx that has decimated the Birmingham team strikes yet again, this time on the second bend of the last lap of the fourth race. The all-action King's Lynn reserve Kozza Smith tracks and pressures Brummies stand-in captain James Birkenshaw for a lap and a half until they get in a massive tangle on the penultimate bend. Though the Australian is quickly to his feet it is clear from the reactions of the centre-green medical staff (and also how quickly they call the ambulance) that things don't look too clever for the fallen Birkenshaw. Referee Graham Flint awards the race and the consequences of this crash delay the meeting for half an hour. Metaphorical dark clouds have gathered over the hopes of silverware for the Brummies and the sky darkens further to mirror the mood of the fans and promotional team alike.

The next day I learn that the sight of yet another one of her riders injured on the track reduced Denise Drury to tears. Dressed in their snappy kevlars and crash helmets, it's often easy to forget that beneath their race suits riders are real people made of fragile flesh and bone. Though injuries are part and parcel of the sport, even for seasoned professionals like Denise their impact can't always be rationalised away.[2]

Because Perry Barr stadium is a modern, state-of-the-art dog track, you can watch the on-track action inside the grandstand bar on a wide selection of wall-mounted television screens. Consequently, we're shown a lengthy series of pictures that feature fluorescent-jacketed St John Ambulance staff as they fuss round the hidden but prostrate Birkenshaw. Chris Simpson updates us, "Birko is fully conscious and talking to the medical staff. Once we know more, we'll keep you updated!" The lady on the DVD stall frets at the ongoing iniquity of the situation, "Have we got bloody anyone left? He was captain tonight! You have to wonder if we're jinxed?" With her arms folded on the front counter of the trackshop, Bev Barber suggests, "I think we need to exorcise this place!" While we await further news, fans queue outside on the terraces for some of the most expensive ice creams in speedway (£1.50 for a small '99' and £2 for a medium one!) or listen to news of tonight's raffle draw (the owner of the winning yellow ticket is entitled to a £20 voucher for the trackshop). Eventually James Birkenshaw gets lifted into the ambulance before it slowly leaves the track at a funereal pace. Eventually we're told "Birko is with the doctor and he will go with him to the hospital. SCB Medical Advisor Dr Andrew Butler is in the stadium and will take over this evening. Although, there will be a slight delay, while he signs the necessary paperwork." The majority of fans stand patiently outside on the tarmac in front of the home-straight grandstand. Inside Bev reveals that away from the track she's a care worker who works with old people who suffer with dementia. Like many people in the caring professions, Bev's only paid the minimum wage and has to do other work to supplement her income, "The problem is I'm a middle-aged woman who needs to earn £300 a week. I'd love to be self-employed, like the rest of my family, but I just can't do that financially!"

After the extended delay, the five-man Brummies quickly find themselves further points behind when Kevin Doolan equals the track record of 56.6 seconds to win the fifth race and take the score to 10-20. Although 10 races still remain, Birmingham promoter and team manager, Graham Drury, is forced to explore his tactical options and brings in Andre Compton in a black-and-white helmet colour for heat 6. It's a shrewd move that's unexpectedly snookered from the gate. Nick Barber notes, "Rusty Harrison who usually doesn't do anything – is ahead!" Harrison goes on to win though the Brummies 5-3 heat advantage massages the overall scores to a slightly more acceptable 15-23. Nick views Harrison's win as further confirmation of the perceptive rider management undertaken by the King's Lynn promotional team, "Last year Rusty Harrison retired 'cause he was no good. He goes to King's Lynn and then they

[2] The next night SCB Official Chris Durno reveals that James Birkenshaw's injury distressed the riders and the officials at Perry Barr stadium: "Poor Birko kept saying [on the track and in the ambulance] to the Drurys: 'Don't tell me mum! Please don't tell me mum!' Denise Drury burst into tears when he said that! I think all the injuries have got too much for her this season and this just did it for her."

Birmingham v. King's Lynn: *"They must want to get it on 'cause they're suctioning the water off the track."*

resurrect him. They often do that with riders others don't fancy!" Normal service for the visitors is almost immediately resumed but for a last-lap engine failure for race leader Tomas Topinka. For the second successive race Craig Watson is gifted a point he otherwise might not have gained and the sight of him trailed off in third irks Nick, "How bloody embarrassing, Paul Clews is way ahead of Watson. I'd chop him if I were Graham Drury! So far all of Watson's points are gifted. At this rate it'll be at least a 20-point defeat!" By now the forecast rain has started to spit on and, ever keen to hammer home the obvious, Chris Simpson informs us, "It's officially spitting on the centre green." No sooner has his voice died away than another screeching voice bursts over the tannoy (à la *Little Britain*) to take the Mickey: "It's spitting! It's spitting! Everybody in!" While the riders line up for the next race at the tapes, the spits progress to slightly heavier and Nick looks beseechingly to the sky, "Maybe there is a God? If it's rained off now it scrubs the result and there's no refunds!" Shaun Tacey flies from the tapes to win the race ("What a gate that was!") closely followed by his enthusiastic but slightly wild, team mate Kozza Smith ("Here comes Kozza") who blasts magnificently past Paul Clews. Still just as likely to fall off as to excite, Kozza has enough time to make an elementary error (on the last bend) and, thereby, let Paul Clews through for second on the line.

The ninth heat sees Rusty Harrison finally bested by a 'home' rider in the form of Andre Compton who wins quite comfortably. Sadly for the Brummies, Lee Smart is marooned in last place on his way to an unwanted five-ride minimum of nil points. Nick Barber has identified some issues that potentially hold Lee Smart back – including power-to-weight ratios and racing tactics, "Smart's a bit lardy! He misses the gate by 10 yards then rides an extra 50 yards further round the outside. It's not gonna happen, is it?" The next race line up of Clews and Mills versus the King's Lynn combination of Topinka and Lambert excites Nick but the race nearly doesn't get under way when the two-minute warning expires before Paul Clews has even come onto the track. Suddenly keen to rely on the power of suggestion to ensure that referee Graham Flint doesn't exclude Clews, centre-green announcer Chris Simpson pipes up with a far from subtle "Paul Clews has just about made it!" at the very moment he appears at the pit gate. Though 'let off' his exclusion and allowed to line up for the race, it makes little difference since Tomas Topinka then proceeds to give a team-riding master-class from second place as he shepherds home Simon Lambert for all four laps of the race. It's an impressive and skilful riding demonstration that has Nick purr approvingly, "The old fox does it again!" With Chris Mills and Lee Smart both out of sorts, it's also a race result that takes the overall score to 25-37. You don't have to be an expert to know that a Brummies fightback looks highly unlikely. The next race features yet another race win for Kevin Doolan (who rides to a 15-point maximum by the end of the evening) though the heat is drawn after Shaun Tacey gates terribly and then backs off from the idea of overtaking Paul Clews on the third bend. Second-placed Craig Watson actually earns his 2 points and, from that moment on, shows a surge in form and confidence for the remainder of the night.

The flexible approach to the enforcement of the two-minute warning by the referee soon prevails for Paul Clews yet again. With Compton besting Topinka and Clews in third the Brummies reduce the deficit with a 4-2 and prompts Bev Barber to observe, "Bloody hell another heat advantage!" The meeting then trundles to a predictable conclusion before it ends with the finale of a drawn heat just as the rain starts to lash down. Announcer Chris Simpson does try to engender the hint of a fervent attitude among the fans, "We didn't have a Brummies war cry last week – give us a B....[continues]....who's the unluckiest team for injuries!? BRUMMIES!" Judged by the lacklustre response, they're not exactly happy with the latest result. Bev Barber is delighted to spot Sam Ermolenko at Perry Barr stadium, "Did you see Sam Ermolenko is here? I love Sam!" The fans that stop by my book display table for a chat on their way from the stadium are knowledgeable enough to factor in the catalogue of injuries at the club into their immediate reactions. Not that I'm ever likely to throw my leg over a speedway bike but I still receive advice on the best way to excel at Perry Barr. "The best way to ride the track is tight to the first corner, then mid track at the apex, drift to the fence and then go round the outside for bends three and four. It took Doolan no time at all to figure that out!" The rain disappears as soon as it's begun and a mystery rider takes to the track for a practice. I'm proudly told by a Brummies fan, "He would have challenged Lyons! It's hard to believe that 10 weeks ago he was lying on the track, isn't it?"

Keen to alert me to the dangers of the dangerous speeds achieved by traffic on the dual carriageway outside the stadium, Tony Steele helpfully advises that I avoid any life-threatening manoeuvres by going down the road and then turning left by the pub. These directions will apparently take me back onto a dual carriageway that quickly leads to the M6 motorway. Sadly, I either misunderstand the directions or miss the turn so end up completely lost. I ask for directions from some passers-by and receive some contradictory instructions that allow me to circle a couple of traffic light junctions repeatedly. Though it's well after 10 p.m., I spot a police van parked by a late-night Price Buster convenience store. With my car on double yellow lines and with my hazard lights on I rush over to a policewoman who's preoccupied winding yellow and black striped tapes round the trees of the car park. My cheery "Good evening, officer!" elicits a barked "What do you want?" Though I explain I'm lost and in need of directions, it's to no real avail since I'm brusquely told to follow City Centre signs that I've previously completely failed to find. "Just look for the City Centre signs – I don't have time to talk now, someone's just been murdered!" Because discretion is the better part of valour, I need no second invitation to rush back to my car. Nearly an hour later, after I've driven through a part of Birmingham that reminds me of the Bronx (foreboding tower blocks, fast-moving flash cars plus pockets of intimidating men on street corners), I eventually join the M6 and its late-night traffic jams caused by ongoing road repairs.

2nd July Birmingham v. King's Lynn (Premier League) 38-54

Birmingham v. King's Lynn: *"They must want to get it on 'cause they're suctioning the water off the track."*

CHAPTER 16.

Coventry v. Poole:
"He looks like he's done 15 rounds with Amir Khan. What with his nose and his Cornish accent, he's even harder to understand!"

4th July

The Coventry Trackshop is known for the range and variety of its Bees-branded merchandise. There's something for every Coventry fan, usually at attractive prices. There are stuffed Bees (£8.50/£5.50), baseball caps (£10/£9/£7), Bees satchels (£10.50), Bees shoulder bags (£15.95), rider photos, fridge magnets (£1.50), Bees trolley key rings (£2) Bees car stickers (£3), sew-on badges (from 50p), Bees bookmarks (£2) and even a unique but lovely Bees tray cover (£3.95). There's a full range of Bees clothing, ranging from fancy Bees pit shirts (£49.95) via Bees team shirts (£37.50) to Bees coloured T-shirts (now £9.95). Every single item in the shop has a highly visible and brightly coloured price sticker. The only item without a price sticker takes pride of place at the centre of the shop – a signed action painting of Chris "Bomber" Harris by local artist Garry Booth. Trackshop manager, Joyce Blythe matter-of-factly informs me that it's worth £300 but could possibly be mine if I buy a £2 raffle ticket. "By having a raffle the ordinary everyday sports supporter gets an equal chance to win the painting rather than any one person outbidding everyone else 'cause they've got the most money!" All the proceeds from the raffle are going to cancer research and there's no doubt that the lucky winner would gain a work of art that would stand out in any room, maybe even more than it does in the trackshop where the predominant colours are yellow and black. Another item not on sale in the trackshop is a black-and-gold neck brace and so Joyce has to make do with the traditional vanilla coloured one. I'm not sure how she sustained her injury but she tells everyone who asks (and many people do), "Malcolm surprised me by jumping on me from the wardrobe!"

It's a warm sunny American Independence Day and the shade of the trackshop provides a welcome respite from the heat. Joyce diligently fine-tunes the layout and display of the stock while her husband Malcolm busies himself readying the books and magazines. Later Ray 'Brummie' Billingsley and Malcolm will sell them from their booth located in the lee of the main grandstand adjacent to the entrance, turnstiles and programme stall. Tonight's Elite League meeting has the 2007 Elite League champions Coventry take on many people's favourite to be the 2008 champions, Poole. The cornerstone of last season's success was the Bees consistent home form at fortress Brandon allied to some crucial victories on the road. It was also built on the backbone of a settled squad but, during the close season, the revised overall maximum team average totals for 2008 saw the Bees have to lose the talismanic Scott Nicholls from their side. Compounding this forced change, 2008 has also seen the Bees suffer a variety of rider injuries. A brief glance at the meeting programme confirms the make do and mend line-up that will take to the track for Coventry this evening. Number 1, Chris Harris, is out with the injuries he sustained at last weekend's Cardiff Grand Prix and three of the remaining four top five positions in the team are occupied by guest riders in the form of Tai Woffinden, Fredrik Lindgren and Piotr Swiderski. Billy Janniro is also absent through injury, while Simon Stead and Rory Schlein aren't available because of the Grand Prix qualifiers. Malcolm isn't optimistic "We've got a Colin Pratt Select racing for us tonight!" Though excited to see Tai Woffinden race for the Bees ("what's he like?"), Malcolm's concerned about the lack of Coventry-owned riders on display. "Of the three Coventry riders racing tonight only Olly Allen is owned by the club. We have two reserves who aren't club assets – Andreas Messing belongs to Arena and Stan Burza belongs to Berwick. Bomber definitely couldn't ride after the time he's had recently. He looks like he's done 15 rounds with Amir Khan. What with his nose and his Cornish accent, he's even harder to understand!" Joyce chips in, "Much as I love Chris Harris and Scott Nicholls, we'd be better off without the GP riders in the Elite League."

If the interference of the speedway Grand Prix hasn't been a completely positive influence on British speedway then it's also prompted Malcolm to ponder some other questions. "We want to know why the green helmets have gone back to white for the Grands Prix so how come we still have them? I know Murdoch's *Sky* insisted we change so we could see them better, but that's rubbish!" Something else that's generally agreed to be rubbish was the state of the track again this year at Cardiff. In his Viewpoint column in the programme Colin Pratt raises a nuanced point about track complaints there. "It's hard to get it right, and you're only as good as your materials but it did cause quite a few incidents and it was fortunate that nobody was seriously hurt." It's widely acknowledged that the logistics involved to build the indoor track at the Cardiff Millennium Stadium is an incredible feat of ingenuity and engineering. It takes 130 lorries to transport 2,600 tons of chalk shale from the local area. The suppliers kindly mill the shale to the specification demanded by the organisers. In an ideal world, to make this chalk shale bind properly, approximately 500 tons of clay should be mixed into it. However, if this happened, the quarry that supplies the shale wouldn't then take this adulterated shale back afterwards! Clearly shale quality is important and ultimately affects the type of racing surface produced. Other suppliers do exist elsewhere in the UK, notably in Cornwall (where they have clay-based shale) or in Derbyshire where the best shale in the business – limestone shale – is readily available. Whatever the shale used, it's clear that for some time that the Cardiff track hasn't lived up to the demanding standards of the riders (and spectators). Interestingly, the speedway Grand Prix organisers do use limestone-based shale from Derbyshire at Parken Stadium and, with a five-year contract, they have found storage between its annual use indoors at the speedway.

Until required in the pits, Colin Pratt prefers to lurk in his lair (otherwise known as the speedway office) rather than promenade around the stadium. That said, an hour or so before the tapes rise, he does make a brief foray past the trackshop sales booth and my table to destinations unknown. As he passes, he spots Martin Horsley who is the club announcer and the junior partner to the leading light of the presentational team, experienced man on the mike, Peter Yorke. Though a man of few words, Colin advises Martin, "Don't get too excited tonight, otherwise you start shouting!" Martin explains, "I can't hear what it sounds like!" Only for Colin to remind him, "It's too loud." Advice for one half of the presentational team is cut short when Colin jovially calls out to an unidentified rider, "You're no good in Sweden, you're no good in Poland – where are you going good?" They leave deep in conversation and I just about catch a snatch of Colin as he earnestly explains, "There's nothing on the inside."

Solihull-based speedway referee Chris Durno arrives with his son Tom. Though he's not here to officiate, Chris rarely misses the opportunity to view speedway meetings in his local area. He too takes the view that tonight's contest is "Poole versus a Colin Pratt Select – this is gonna be an away win in the 50 points area. Nowadays, Birmingham has become our local track. There was some amazing racing during April and May but then they put on a meeting against Somerset where they'd over-watered the track and it was coming up in lumps. It was far from exciting to watch and I think some of those that were there that night have yet to come back to see another meeting!" Since he's the only referee handy I decide to quiz him about the mistake by Graham Flint in the Premier League Pairs semi-final that deprived the Reading Racers of their just deserts and the opportunity to contest the silverware. "Flint laughed it off and couldn't care about the criticism – he wouldn't talk to Tim Sugar on the night and isn't going to start doing so now." A chip off the old block, Tom Durno is extremely well versed in the ins and outs of speedway, speedway riders and their club sides throughout Europe. He tells me that contrary to some people's claims, "Tai [Woffinden] has ridden here before – he got 9 points!" Earlier I'd been in the trackshop when Chris and Tom first arrived and popped in to say hello. The conversation turned to Redcar promoter Glyn Taylor's decision to drop Gary 'Havvy' Havelock from the Redcar team when he refused to help the precarious finances of the club by agreeing a new reduced rate of payment for the rest of the season. Joyce Blythe understands his position, "I don't blame him for refusing a pay cut!" Her husband Malcolm views the situation differently and demurs, "Well, it was either less money or no money at all!" The idea that some riders are to blame for the excessive signing-on fees and points money they are paid by promoters is a frequently rehearsed theme among speedway fans. They usually blame the recipient of the payments rather than the person who decides to pay them those 'excessive' sums. Chris Durno puts the Havelock situation into some context, "They say he was on Elite League wages in the Premier League. That's why he didn't have to ride in Poland or Sweden 'cause he could make a good living riding for Redcar!"

While "Bomber" Harris was in the news at the Cardiff Grand Prix, one unexpected star of the event and its television

---

Coventry v. Poole: *"He looks like he's done 15 rounds with Amir Khan. What with his nose and his Cornish accent, he's even harder to understand!"*

coverage was his mechanic Ted "The Bear" when he tripped unexpectedly and fell in front of a live audience. When I've previously watched him work with Harris in the pits he's clearly a fast worker and enjoys an excellent working relationship with the Grand Prix star. Though I don't know him at all, I wrongly expected that he owned a good sense of humour so, when he passed my stall, I called, "Mind the step". Ted stopped and theatrically held his sides, "Ho ho!" and continued until a few strides away when he stopped and turned back to quite aggressively say, "How much did it cost you to go to Cardiff then? 'Cause it cost me nothing!" Ted then managed a few further steps before he again turned to deliver more *bon mots*, "Oh, I had a call from Ronaldo the next day telling me he's gonna teach me how to dive!" Later, Coventry fan and Steve Chilton would tell me, "Ted lives in our street – he's always looks like a proper mechanic to my mind!"

Just prior to the start of the race action I pack away my table and rush to the home-straight grandstand. Usually I'd expect it to be difficult to find a spare seat but this evening I'm spoilt for choice. The Coventry fan I sit next to is festooned in logoed clothing bought from the trackshop and tells me, "People are complaining about a side full of guests but I think it makes us stronger! With Swiderski, Lindgren and Woffinden I think we could do really well against Poole tonight." It's a prediction that looks a little misplaced after Magnus Zetterstrom and Chris Holder combine for a 5-1 in the first heat. Stood on the centre green watching the action is the somewhat battered Chris Harris. Peter Yorke snatches a brief interview with him before the start of the next race, "Not such a brilliant start, then! But it's doable, isn't it, Chris?" Ever phlegmatic and a man of few words Harris replies, "Well, it better be – otherwise I'll go back and kick 'em up the backsides!" Contrary to Chris Harris's expectations, things look like they are going to take a further turn for the worse. The Poole Pirates definitely look on for another maximum heat win until an engine failure for Daniel Davidsson on the third bend of the second lap robs them of their heat advantage. These rapid changes in fortune are all part of speedway's appeal. Whenever I've seen Chris Harris in person (or on the television), he always strikes me as a modest man who's ultimately really just one of the lads rather than imperiously aloof like some speedway riders are or can become. As if to confirm that his man-of-the-people attitude is genuine – and that he really is drawn from the same milieu as the fans – as soon as each race finishes Chris immediately fills in his programme (that features a vivid picture of his Cardiff facial injuries on its cover) in synchrony with the vast majority of the other diligent fans within the stadium.

If the Poole riders expect to romp to an easy victory they are surprised in heat 3 when Olly Allen and guest Fredrik Lindgren combine to hammer home a 5-1 win and thereby level the scores at 9 each. The next race then sees Swiderski gate with some alacrity and surprisingly beat Grand Prix rider Bjarne Pedersen. A fast start is the exception rather than the norm for the Coventry riders throughout the evening and, suddenly also infected by the Coventry malaise, Fredrik Lindgren makes a shocking start to heat 5, while Zorro and Chris Holder gate and zoom to the first corner ahead. Fortunately for the Bees, Magnus Zetterstrom fails to demonstrate the spatial awareness you'd expect of an experienced rider and thoughtlessly takes his younger partner extremely wide and almost into the second-bend air fence. This provides a gap wide enough for a police formation motorcycle team to pass through and Lindgren needs

Bomber painting

Trackshop satellite stall

Future NSSC guest

no second invitation to snatch the lead. Holder's natural skill on a bike ensures that he stays on but his excursion to inspect the inflatable furniture leaves him well adrift at the back of the race. Zorro does eventually deign to look round for his team mate but only just before he rushes from the fourth bend to the finish line. As a partisan, Peter Yorke must contractually watch a different race to the rest of us since he remarks "What about that from Freddie Lindgren? Not such a great start but boy did he make up for that with track craft!" If Zorro could come out in every race and ride his team mate into the fence then "track craft" will definitely see the Bees through to victory. The traditional order of things is restored in the sixth race when Bjarne Pedersen takes his rival Lindgren wide to the bend-two air fence for a close inspection, albeit accidentally, since he appears to take off after he hits a bump on the track. Tai Woffinden also manages to find his own bump but, in his case, it's located on the fourth corner and he temporarily locks up before he continues home for second place.

After a poor first ride, Davey Watt suddenly finds his gating gloves and wins the seventh heat comfortably and with Adam Skornicki in third, the Pirates 2-4 brings the scores level at 21 apiece. Peter Yorke isn't happy with the situation if judged by the fact that he decides to rouse the crowd with some controversial news about the Poole management team, "I didn't know that Matt Ford is an Aston Villa fan. I don't know why – but he's a big Villa fan!" I'm not sure that this allegiance is even common knowledge in Dorset where Matt Ford has invested in Bournemouth AFC. However, while it's not a long list, the roll call of celebrity fans who support Aston Villa include Prince William, Iain Duncan-Smith (ex-leader of the Conservative Party), violinist Nigel Kennedy, rock star Ozzy Osbourne, 1980s children's presenter Floella Benjamen and, now, also Matt Ford! I'm sure that Matt has been called many worse names. Another drawn heat follows before news of Matt Ford's football allegiances fully filters through to the pits. Before the ninth heat can start, the Bees track their not-so-secret weapon Piotr Swiderski who comes to the tapes and lines up with his fellow team mates Fredrik Lindgren and Olly Allen! If two's company and three a crowd, then this applies in spades amongst colleagues on the speedway track. Though, that said, three riders versus two would certainly give the Bees a significant advantage! But, sadly, since Swiderski isn't programmed to ride, the start marshal has to send him back to the pits without the intervention of referee, Stuart Wilson. Quick as a flash Peter Yorke jokes, "This is the way to beat Poole! He's [Swiderski] eager and keen to do well!" With only the regulation four riders on the track, the race eventually gets under way but quickly stops again when Olly Allen rears massively on the second bend and is thrown from his machine. One of the first people on the scene is Chris "Bomber" Harris who sprints at great speed from the pits to join his fallen colleague. Olly remains stricken on the track while the crowd are informed of the formality of his disqualification from the rerun. The crowd around me are pessimistic about the aggravation of being thrown from his machine will have caused to Olly's already damaged shoulder though, it must be noted, the incident would have been a lot worse but for the quick-thinking evasive action taken by Freddie Lindgren to avoid the fallen Bees rider. It's not a surprise when we learn shortly afterwards that Olly has withdrawn from the meeting. After a substantial delay and with only one Coventry rider in the race, Bjarne Pedersen's race win ensures a heat advantage that enables Poole to regain the lead. At this point the wheels comprehensively fall off the metaphorical Coventry wagon since the visitors go on a point-scoring bonanza and hammer home five maximum race advantages in the last six heats. The triumphal sequence for the Pirates is only briefly interrupted in the 12th heat when Freddy Lindgren wins in the black-and-white helmet colour. The possibility of sustained resistance is definitively ended after the 11th heat when Coventry are reduced to four fit riders on the night. Peter Yorke informs the crowd of the full extent of the horror story in the monotone of a drunken man grieving, "Bad news, Olly Allen has withdrawn, and more bad news, Tai Woffinden has also withdrawn 'cause he's aggravated a previous shoulder injury. When it happens with Coventry, it comes down a million per cent!"

A casual glance suggests Brandon stadium has more seats in its grandstand than any other British speedway track, though Poole, Birmingham or Belle Vue probably run them close. It's also possible to watch stood on the terrace steps in front of some sections of the home-straight grandstand. For a different point of view and so that I can run to my table at the interval, I stand next to a bloke who's there with his shy but sweet-looking son, Alec, who's kitted out in a Coventry Bees race tabard. Alec's dad is Karl Roberts who is not only a speedway fan but also the proud inventor of a speedway board game. They say the future is Orange but, in reality, the online digital realm is where the young people now look for their entertainment. Seizing upon the worldwide popularity of online games, Karl, along with Rob Searle and Dave Lambert, has spent considerable time and effort to invent an electronic game called "5-1

Coventry v. Poole: *"He looks like he's done 15 rounds with Amir Khan. What with his nose and his Cornish accent, he's even harder to understand!"*

Speedway Promoter". Their company WildKaRD Games, in conjunction with Methdesignz[1], has taken the trouble during the game's development to create an environment that tries to closely replicate the thrill and excitement of a speedway meeting. The game players can get the chance to manage the racing, choose the riders and experience the joys of the shale as though they were a heady mix of team manager and promoter. Gaming has wrought wonders for the popularity of almost any sport you care to name – from football to golf or basketball and American football. Karl tells me has wanted to go about things correctly and has therefore contacted the media/digital media rights holder for the BSPA and Speedway Great Britain. Because Karl and his friends have invented the game to promote the sport – no promoter they contacted initially refused to grant them use of their club names – rather than to make a profit he rather naively expected that his suggestion would be welcomed with open arms. This has not been the case, the rights holder "contacted us nine weeks ago with objections to our work and they promised me an answer in three weeks though I still haven't had one. Speaking to their legal team, they tell me they have an answer. But they need official confirmation of it and so can't tell me what the answer is at the moment! It's astonishing to think that you can go to the time and trouble of developing a game that you're sure will help bring the sport to a much wider audience only to not receive help from the media rights holders who are supposed to boost the visibility of the sport. Apart from the *Sky* contact they don't seem to be doing that good a job, do they? Obviously we didn't expect them to throw the rights round willy-nilly. We sent them a comprehensive legal document which would allow them to retain all rights to absolutely everything while, at the same time, giving us permission to go ahead with our game on a non-profit basis. Hopefully, we will hear from them eventually!"

The inevitable conclusion of the meeting isn't an enjoyable spectacle or experience unless you are a Poole Pirates fan. By my table outside the trackshop I get to hear a range of post-mortem opinions. One fan asks me "What do you think of that rubbish tonight?" but nips into the trackshop without waiting for an answer, while his wife stands outside nursing a damaged scaphoid sustained skiing ("a real speedway injury"). The knowledgeable and charming Wolves historian Mark Sawbridge has watched the fixture as a speedway neutral – or at least as neutral as you can be when you're a Wolves supporter watching a massive Coventry home defeat! Curiosity about the performance of Freddy Lindgren as a guest for the Bees as well as his natural love of speedway has drawn him to Brandon, "Did you notice Freddy did really well wearing a Coventry top but once he took it off he returned to his true Wolves form! Don't you think it's really sloppy taking the shirt off? If you saw 10 Sunderland players and one in blue you wouldn't be impressed! It's a shocking attention to detail that doesn't reflect well on anybody." Trackshop man Malcolm Blythe also isn't happy with what he's seen. "We were bloody pathetic. If that were the best team that Mr Trump and Mr Oakes could put together then I don't know what to say. I can't think of two words to describe it. We didn't even try towards the end. Mr Lindgren was a trier. Mr Swiderski only got 8 points from six rides. A fortnight ago for Belle Vue he got two wins from the gate plus another win, a third and a second. It could have been a lot worse if Poole had been really firing. Chris Holder never won a race all night and Skornicki had a poor night compared to how he goes round here – he needs to get a different bike or a new mechanic. Their only weak link was Daniel Davidsson, which is why we got rid of him! Obviously it was unfortunate we lost Olly Allen, then I doubt it would have made much difference even if we hadn't. I have to say that Zetterstrom is a revelation for them and I'm just pleased I'm here tomorrow night and not going to Eastbourne to watch us!"[2] The Coventry crowd disperses quickly and, as I pack up my table, Malcolm wonders philosophically, "Where's the water at Lakeside?"

4th July Coventry v. Poole (Elite League) 37-56

---

[1] For the latest information on developments and news of how to purchase the games go to www.methdesignz.co.uk

[2] Another important rider in this Poole victory, but not name-checked by Malcolm, was Davey Watt. Who, in contrast to the unavailable Simon Stead and Rory Schlein, chose to ride for his club and then make a dash the next morning to Motala in Sweden for the Grand Prix qualifying rounds. Sadly it was to prove an unwise decision when an overbooked KLM flight from Amsterdam to Linkoping meant that he was unable to make his connection having earlier flown in from Heathrow. Few airlines are famed for their customer service skills but, in my experience, even by industry standards KLM can be particularly intransigent when they 'try' to overcome travel/logistical difficulties. Overbooking is common airline practice but this was no consolation to Davey Watt who was unable to sign-on at the Grand Prix qualifying semi-final in time to take part in the meeting. Keen to keep his Grand Prix dreams alive, despite his self-imposed tight schedule, Watt flew instead to Stockholm and even considered hiring a helicopter to then fly from Stockholm to Linkoping but, in the end, admitted defeat. "To add insult to injury, the airline lost my engine. It was one of the most depressing days of my life," commented a chastened Watt afterwards.

Coventry v. Poole: *"He looks like he's done 15 rounds with Amir Khan. What with his nose and his Cornish accent, he's even harder to understand!"*

CHAPTER 17.

Sittingbourne v. Scunthorpe:
"It's not asking a lot to get 50 more, is it?"

6th July

Though initially there's sun in the sky, very strong winds and building dark clouds make this feel anything but a summer's day. In previous seasons the visit of Scunthorpe to Sittingbourne would encapsulate the gulf between two very distinctive approaches to racing that co-exist in the Conference League. On the one hand, there would be a team assembled to crush all in its path and, on the other, a team true to the ethos of a club whose aim is to bring on and develop rider talent rather than pursue silverware. However, it's a new season that has seen the Scunthorpe club matriculate to the Premier League but still also run a team in the Conference League. Consequently, while they still have a line up every other team in the Conference League would envy, they're no longer guaranteed odds on favourite to win practically every single meeting that they feature in. Nonetheless, they're still expected to win this encounter at the Old Gun Site but not by the extraordinary margins of yesteryear. Sensibly enough, promoter Rob Godfrey has a cost-effective strategic plan to use the Conference League team as a feeder club and that enables riders with potential and promise to make the step up into the Scunthorpe Premier League team. One way to foster that aim is the appointment of former long-time manager/promoter of Boston speedway, Malcolm Vasey, as their Conference League team manager. If this were horses, Malcolm would be a good judge of horse flesh but, since this is speedway, his extensive knowledge and experience of the Conference League level of racing in Britain will also prove invaluable for the club. In a funny way, this approach to their participation in the Conference League makes Scunthorpe more entertaining for neutrals to watch than when, in previous seasons, they pretty well swept all other clubs before them.

A regular feature of any Scunthorpe speedway meeting, home or away, is the presence of club Press Officer (and Programme Editor), Richard Hollingsworth. A modest but extremely knowledgeable man, who like many people involved in speedway, works long unpaid hours on behalf of the sport and club they love. Richard is a prolific writer and prodigious sender of press releases. Many of these arrive in the wee small hours of the morning. We're stood under darkening skies and survey the track before us. To my untutored eye it looks like they've sloshed an absolute ton of water onto the shale surface, if judged by the sheen of water that's just lain there. Richard views it differently, "There's a tendency for the track here to be under-watered." Sittingbourne aren't a sufficiently wealthy enough club to possess their own water bowser but, on a needs-must basis, have adapted a transit van with substantial water tanks that they fill from a well close to the trackshop. One condition of the licence under which Sittingbourne Speedway have permission to operate speedway in this part of Kent requires that they water the track on a very regular basis. Consequently, every meeting that you attend here features a white transit van as it endlessly circles the track to scatter its payload over the shale surface. Richard won't be drawn on his forecast of the final outcome of today's meeting but does note that a win will take Scunthorpe to the head of the Conference League table (albeit with the caveat that erstwhile rivals Plymouth, Boston and Redcar have ridden far fewer meetings). "This year we're going for the battling victories not the high scores of previous years!"

Sittingbourne speedway's hand-to-mouth existence is founded upon the hard work of volunteers as well as the regular paid use of its training track. Nonetheless, like any speedway club, crowd levels are hugely important financially. This season, like so many others before, it has suffered from a lack of crowd numbers. Eastbourne and Sittingbourne Programme Editor Mike Corby, who wears his deeply held enthusiasm and love of the sport lightly, takes a matter-of-fact view when I meet him in the car park. "It's one we need to win 'cause with Weymouth, Plymouth, Redcar and Stoke still to come it's difficult to see that we'll beat those. At home, I mean, 'cause we won't away! We lost to Buxton by 2 points – it was a brilliant meeting – and bringing the riders on is what it's all about really rather than winning! Our last meeting we had about 150 people. We need 200 to break even. It's not asking a lot to get 50 more, is it?"

The strong wind plays havoc with my book display set up by the first-bend clubhouse and, with ominous clouds being swept towards us, rider introductions are kept to an absolute minimum before they rush straight into the meeting. Though widely expected to be a much closer meeting than previous years, the first race gives little indication that this will be the case when visitors Byron Bekker and Stuart Parnaby race to a comfortable maximum heat advantage. If that signals that it is going to be a difficult afternoon for the home side then the rerun second heat confirms that is definitely the case. First time out, Daniel Berwick falls and is excluded and, in the three-man rerun, Marc Andrews for the Crusaders also falls and fails to finish the race. This gives the visitors a 0-5 race win and immediately took the score to an already insurmountable 1-10. You could argue that the absence through injury of the Saints vastly experienced heat leader Jonathan Bethell could possibly benefit the home side, given that the visitors will only operate rider replacement in his place. Indeed, taking Bethell's programmed ride in the third heat, Ricky Scarboro can only manage third, though with the race won by Scott Richardson, this hardly represents a disaster. The all-action Aaron Baseby has a tough battle to take second place and, to do so, he takes Ricky Scarboro to the fourth-bend fence on the second lap. Between races, I catch up with future world ladies speedway champion-in-waiting Chelsea Lee-Amies. "I sold my bike because it was too small for me but I'm gonna get another one! My dad [Stuart Lee-Amies] is Clerk of the Course here and my boyfriend is the club mascot." Stuart is a keen motorcyclist, who despite injury, has fought back to continue to ride speedway bikes for fun. He's another modest and extremely hard-working man who wears many hats at Sittingbourne including that of training instructor. Chelsea is extremely proud of his work in that capacity, "My dad's taught them all – Jerran Hart, Marc Owen, Lewis Bridger, Aaron Baseby and Marc Baseby." All of the Lee-Amies family are at Sittingbourne with the exception of Chelsea's mum. "Mum is working today so she can't be here but they both have Wednesdays off". Though she has her own friends, Chelsea takes her big sisterly duties seriously and, while her dad multi-tasks elsewhere in the stadium, she very capably minds her sisters Shannon and Mercedes.

Sittingbourne manage to draw the fourth heat but then, before at the start of the next race, Nathan Irwin completely demolishes the start tapes when he tries to anticipate when referee Christina Turnbull will release them. With some understatement, club announcer Derek Barclay tells us, "The tapes have got broken there and the referee has decided to exclude Nathan Irwin as the cause of the stoppage". The use of the word "broken" is a massive understatement given that Nathan has the complete set wrapped around his bike. It takes patient effort to untangle them and, though the Crusaders Daniel Berwick takes part in the rerun, the Saints race to yet another heat advantage to progress the score to 8-21. Though always likely to use the black-and-white helmet colour, talk of a much closer fixture had led me to expect that its appearance might arrive late in the meeting. However, needs must and the sixth heat sees an inspired Dean Felton take full advantage of this tactical option when he races to a much-needed first win of the afternoon for a Crusaders rider. His partner Alex Cunningham joins him in second place and the result sends Derek Barclay into controlled rapture. ("A brilliant win for Dean Felton in the black-and-white there"). The 8-1 heat advantage massages the scores to a much more acceptable 16-22. If this is the signal for a concerted Crusaders fightback then

"It says here ..."

Tegan walks Rose

the message doesn't get relayed to the pits because the visitors then ram in successive 5-1s (through the Bekker–Richardson and Irving–Parnaby partnerships). One man who takes extreme delight in every Scunthorpe race winner is their Team Manager, Malcolm Vasey, who dances with some abandon on the centre green as if offering an impromptu demonstration of how they really celebrate the carnival in Rio. He clearly relishes his work and the opportunity to dance. With Scunthorpe very much in charge with seven wins from the first eight races, there has to be concern that by the end of the meeting Malcolm's weirdly hypnotic war dances – speedway's equivalent of the Haka, albeit the Dad Dance version hailing from Lincolnshire – will have completely exhausted him. Though unlikely to get him much beyond the first round of *Strictly Come Dancing*, what Malcolm lacks in technical ability he more than makes up for in exuberance.

The home fans are well accustomed to the marmalisation of their team at the Old Gun Site (and elsewhere) so disgruntlement, if it surfaces at all, usually manifests itself as sardonic humour. However, the need for phlegmatic fortitude in the face of endless drubbings is cast aside in heat 9 with a comfortable win for Nathan Irwin and Aaron Baseby. The medicine might have continued in the 10th heat of the meeting – sponsored by the Vulcan Towing Centre – but the sudden possibility of a successive maximum heat win vanishes with a heavy fall for Alex Cunningham. Referee Christina Turnbull is left with no choice but to exclude the Crusader and rueful club announcer Derek Barclay observes, "Tremendous effort there, very nearly a 5-1 before well, a very unfortunate fall for Alex Cunningham having just got second place there!" I'm briefly joined by the sardonic but knowledgeable Steve Ribbons who remarks, "If we didn't have bad luck, we wouldn't have any luck!" Falls for the home riders have started to come thick and fast. The 11th heat sees Marc Andrews depart his machine and the referee awards yet another race as a well-deserved 1-5 for the visitors. A fan of speedway rather than just one club, prior to the stoppage Steve Ribbons had admired the riding skill of Stuart Parnaby of the Saints. "He's smooth, fast from the start – he looks bloody marvellous that Parnaby!" Along with Dave Croucher, Steve Ribbons was responsible for the reintroduction of speedway to Plough Lane although, having got the Wimbledon club back in action again, the management baton was subsequently passed on to others. Prior to his involvement at Wimbledon, Steve was the initial driving force behind the reintroduction of speedway at Rye House (Len Silver's autobiography covers some aspects of the events that led to Hoddesdon reopening for speedway). Despite these experiences, Steve remains keen to open and run another speedway club. He keeps a careful eye out for opportunities and remains alert enough to learn from his visits to speedway tracks throughout the country. "I went to Mildenhall v. Glasgow – what a place! Good crowd. Theoretically, it could have been close but Glasgow got three or four 5-1s and that was it. How it keeps going I don't know! The Pole [Michal Rajkowski] looked exciting but it didn't fill me with confidence they'd survive. The problem is when a track gets into trouble; the BSPA should have an emergency promoter, accountant and general team of people to ensure that the club can pull themselves together and the sport survive. But they don't! They just sit back and let other promoters go to the wall not really thinking of the implications for everybody else. The very worst thing that can happen in speedway from my point of view is for a track to either threaten to, or actually close mid season, and promoters can't keep going round with the begging bowl to the fans every year! That said, I'm hoping to be involved at another club shortly and that should really lift the lid on things! It's a green field site miles away from anywhere. But we need to get planning permission and we all know how difficult that can be! They have 25 acres at Norwich Rugby Club and budgeted properly – modelled on how they've done things at Plymouth – it could be a success. It's located at the end of the Norwich airport runway and under the flight path so we're confident of passing the noise test. However, the rugby committee want to discuss things among themselves and I'd like to think that [Buster] Chapman would view it as a positive. When I was talking of a track opening at Swaffham, he did object because he felt it was too close to King's Lynn. That's a shame, because I'd done a deal with Speedeworth's Roy Eaton to lease the place. Mind you, that was four years ago when I was speaking to him about that. His business was on a knife edge then so I'm not sure he would have welcomed the increased interest provided by Swaffham. Since then they've won championships and cups, so they'll have had a lot of money through the business, so maybe it'll be different now!" On the track yet another wrecked bike has been dragged back to the pits area. Steve Ribbons is in no doubt why so many Sittingbourne riders have fallen from their machines, "Graham [Arnold] has put down 20 tons of new shale. As is his wont – and it's caught the home riders out! You only need a light dusting on a track of this size."

The 11th heat sees the start of a run of four consecutive 5-1 heat advantages for the visitors. Obviously, this throws

Saints team manager, Malcolm Vasey, into an arm-twirling frenzy of samba dancing. Luckily, we all belong to the broad church that is speedway since, in some other sports, such exuberance would be seen as unnecessarily rubbing your opponents' nose in their defeat. The rerun 12th heat mathematically ensures Scunthorpe's triumph, though it takes until Byron Bekker's heat 13 victory for Malcolm to conduct his 'trademark celebration' and theatrically throw his baseball cap in the air to coincide with the very moment Byron crosses the finish line. Whatever the specifics of this victory, you have to wonder how Malcolm will choose to celebrate when Scunthorpe win something significant. Equally, given his many years at Boston, the opportunity for celebration has been a much rarer commodity there than it has, historically, recently been at Scunthorpe. In the commentary box Derek Barclay hints at his disapproval: "They've got an over-excited team manager!"

Niall (pronounced Neil) Strudwick studies the action

Though Sittingbourne speedway is run on love much more than ambition, many of their Conference League rivals have little time for such sentiment. To illustrate the point, the final race of the afternoon has the Saints track top scorers Scott Richardson and Byron Bekker rather than – with the victory beyond doubt – allow other less productive or skilled riders to experience the thrill of the nominated race. Derek Barclay matter-of-factly draws attention to this fact, "So, no let up from the Saints in heat 15 – we'll be seeing their top two." Stood by my table, Debbie Nottingham worries about the state of the Old Gun Site circuit. "The track is looking horrible!" Her fears prove well-founded when, at the start of the second lap, Aaron Baseby falls for the second consecutive race. Unlike the previous race, he doesn't immediately remount and rejoin the race but, instead, drags his machine from the track onto the centre green. A determined Dean Felton interrupts the visitors' run of maximum heat scores with second place to further highlight his performance as the top scorer for the Crusaders. Byron Bekker wins the race to end his afternoon with a paid maximum from six rides. The whole team, particularly Scott Richardson, has very capably supported him though the Saints strength in depth is illustrated by the fact that their lowest scorer, Michael Pickering, gained paid 6 from four rides. With the threatened rain now falling all that's left is for Derek Barclay to announce the results, pass on praise to riders ("Aaron is commended by the referee for getting off the track so quickly") and track staff alike "Thank you to the track staff!"

Bowser truck

I retreat to the shelter of the first-bend refreshment kiosk and chat briefly with Lakeside fan Roger Adams. As ever, his wife Angie Claydon wears a dress and, even though it's a Sunday, we can safely say that she's the only lady at Sittingbourne speedway to do so this afternoon. It turns out that Roger avidly collects a wide variety of items. Seven years ago he started to amass his speedway rider autograph collection and already has 325 of these. Roger also cuts rider photos from the *Speedway Star* and mounts them on white cards. His pride in careful presentation has seen him also amass 600 signed photos (so far). In addition, he has a tractor model collection ("at 1/43rd scale") to complement various other transport obsessions, notably with trains and buses ("every bus you've been on") plus, stranger still, water towers. Even more distinctively Roger has an extensive sack collection. "The oldest sack I ever had was from 1928. I once found a bundle of 300 sacks on the farm I worked on – I wish I'd kept them all now 'cause every single one was different!" Among the Sittingbourne fans in the glass-sided terrapin hut that serves as the refreshment

First bend viewed from the tea room

Graham Arnold

Riders line up and Malcolm Vasey (with cap)

area there are muted murmurs of surprise at the scale of the defeat to Scunthorpe. Afterwards, the disappointed team manager Chris Hunt echoes the thoughts of many loyal fans: "The performance from some of the team was unsatisfactory, almost to the point of being unacceptable and can't go on indefinitely. Dean Felton was, as ever, a great leader out there doing his level best to inspire a comeback after a truly awful start for the team by winning his tactical ride and young Alex Cunningham tried his heart out. Aaron Baseby also can't be faulted for his effort … but, though we had some hard luck stories along the way, overall the team performance can't be good enough to go down by over 30 points in a match both I and rival team manager Malcolm Vasey had down as a close encounter before the tapes went up."

6th July Sittingbourne v. Scunthorpe (Conference League) 32-60

CHAPTER 18.

Plymouth v. Weymouth:
"If you'd signed it, you'd be contractually obliged not to fraternise with the riders."

11th July

Though the RAC route planner details that Plymouth and Weymouth are based 104 miles apart, over recent years this still hasn't diminished the intensity of the Dorset/Devon rivalry. Given that there are only eight teams in the 2008 Conference League, the chance to do battle on a regular basis is never likely to be more than a few weeks away. If you ignore the Conference League Pairs and the Conference League Four-Team tournament, the Devils and the Wildcats will meet in the Conference League, Conference League Play-offs, Conference Trophy and Devon & Dorset Cup, as well as the KO Cup. It's third time lucky for the staging of the weather-delayed KO Cup Quarter Final first leg encounter at the St Boniface Arena in Plymouth, after initial attempts to stage the meeting were rained off in late June and early July. Not that the weather holds much promise when I set off in the Wildcatmobile (aka Jem Dicken's slightly battered car) driven by the Weymouth Team Manager accompanied by Weymouth Official Photographer and Press Officer, Julie Martin. Given how many times he's already driven there, Jem could be forgiven for driving on autopilot but the winding nature of the cross-country route taken means that his concentration levels have to remain high throughout the journey. Though it's one step short of travelling to a speedway meeting in a rider's van, it's definitely an honour to be able to ride to the meeting with some of the Weymouth club's cognoscenti. During the journey, among many other things talk turned to Luke Priest's recoveries from the severe injuries he sustained at Stoke that would have ended the career of lesser man. Jules notes that Luke "didn't practise on the anniversary date of his crash." With furrowed brow Jem retorts, "Obviously it still bothers him. If I'd known I'd have encouraged him to ride – it's the only way to really conquer it!" The personal tragedy suffered by Weymouth promoter Phil Bartlett and his family after news of the death from cancer of his 9-year-old daughter Hannah became public knowledge is also discussed. I gather that there will a memorial race tomorrow night at Weymouth and a fund-raising collection held. In order not to stifle the free-flow of the conversation, I've agreed not to repeat some colourful opinions and stories. It would be fair to say that both Jem and Jules hold forthright opinions on many of the rich tapestry of characters that make up Conference League speedway in this country. To the outside observer, they're clearly well used to each other's company and appear to have the slightly fractious relationship that you'd expect from an argumentative brother and sister or, perhaps, a long-married couple. Jules says, "We are like a married couple – we bicker and don't have sex!" They periodically fall out so don't always speak or even travel to the away meetings together but, with fences soon often mended, over the last few seasons they've certainly put in the miles together.

We arrive at the St Boniface Arena 90 or so minutes before the scheduled start time of 7.30 p.m. Jem tells me, "I dunno if they have a curfew, I think they do. They can't start the bikes till 7 p.m. and they definitely can't ride on the track till half seven so they warm up quarter of an hour and then have to wait to ride them!" With black clouds overhead, meteorological conditions don't look that positive and the likelihood of a third successive rain off could still happen. One problem with building a speedway track from scratch and its location on a rugby field that suffers from a low water table is, that without a substantial base, the track surface will be affected by surface water or flooding.[1] However, promoter Mike Bowden is a builder by trade so is well aware of the drainage issue and, indeed, has successfully worked round this for the past few seasons. Normally Jem would want to keep the scores tight in the first leg and then take advantage in the deciding leg at Weymouth. But, in typical speedway fashion, the second leg has been run first (because of the weather) and Weymouth only have a slender 2-point lead. Jem accentuates the

---

[1] Especially the third and fourth turn where water tends to collect and sit to make the bottom bend very soft. This is an issue that the SCB monitored very closely in 2008 after a number of adverse reports from rival promotions and riders.

positive, "We've lost away a few times against these but we're getting better here!" Like any team manager, Jem thinks ahead so rummages in his boot to find the black-and-white helmet colour, "doubt we'll need it but I'll take it just in case!" Talk turns to the identity of the SCB official for tonight's meeting, "So long as it's not Graham Flint – he can be a poor decision maker. Actually tonight we've got Dave Robinson so we might get the odd decision go our way!"

Jem heads to the pits area to start his team management duties and Jules follows to prepare her cameras or catch up with the riders. Jem jokes about the Weymouth speedway contract they have this season. "If you'd signed it, you'd be contractually obliged not to fraternise with the riders. You know that anyway! They all know that without me having to remind them!" Jules owns two cameras and two mobile phones that have buzzed and bleeped throughout the whole journey to Plymouth. Some of these communications are flirty texts from one of the rider's dads. "All I did was talk to him!" While they busy themselves elsewhere, I make my way up the slope to the pits gates entrance in search of the programme stall. Outside the locked entrance turnstiles, there's already quite a long queue of dedicated fans keen to stake their respective places inside the stadium. The very attractive admission prices (Adults £9, Disabled £7, OAPs £6 Child [5-16] £5, Children under-5 free) they have at Plymouth contribute to its appeal and, along with some success and close racing, are part of the equation behind the clubs' popularity. Like speedway fans everywhere, they've brought an impressive collection of garden furniture along with thermos flasks, sandwich boxes and the like. Because of the unique topography of St Boniface Arena, some fans have also cannily turned up with empty plastic crates to stand on. Slightly further away, three programme sellers stand in a small group and overlook a ditch full to the brim with storm water. Unlike the friendly outgoing programme seller I met on my first trip here, they're definitely not chatty and, I'm back through the pits gates, before I realise that I've purchased a programme dated 20th June supplemented with a black-and-white insert. Paying full price for an out-of-date speedway programme is one of the regular disappointments of a wet British summer but a quick glance inside this document reveals that its improved immeasurably since my last visit to Devon. Nowadays, it's a 24-page full colour affair packed with adverts but also a range of other articles and columns including contributions from chairman Mike Bowden and captain Seemond Stephens. There's also a gossip column and news section, an article on club history, action shots, a review of visiting riders, the fixture list, Plymouth rider averages along with the Nathan Stoneman (aged 11) Story as well as information on the Plymouth Mega-Ride (the UK's largest charity ride-out involving 8,000 bikers). Sensibly, the club see their programme as a key part of their regular interaction with their fans. Programme Editor, Gary Spiller, has clearly done them proud. Like many fans, Gary has been frustrated by the weather so far this season. "We've had four meetings off out of eight and one of those we did run was very soggy! You spend 15-20 hours doing the programme and then the meeting doesn't happen! You lose the will to live but then start over again."

By now Jem has been to the pits, done the track walk with the riders and returned to his vehicle for the last time before his evening's work really commences. He has a cunning motivational plan, "If I was Phil [Bartlett] I'd offer them an incentive – say £100 a man if they win. It'll motivate them but there'll be no danger of paying out! [pause] I've done the track walk and given the riders the chance to take the 'p' out of me!"

[Jules] – "Did you tell them how to ride the St Bumpyface track too? They'll tell you to get on the bike and show them!"

[Jem] – "I went on the bike after the meeting last week and didn't ride like a donkey. I wish I'd gone out before they'd roughed up the track. When they say the dirt's deep on the outside they're not joking! I nearly fell off and I was slowing down. Funny enough, Tom Brown's dad said we could do well if we roughed it up!"

Once the entrance turnstiles located in a bright red terrapin hut open, my book display table attracts some interest if not many sales. Most fans immediately shoot off to bagsy their favourite spot within the stadium but others linger by the DVD stall to chat or half-heartedly finger the merchandise. After weeks of torrential rain in the area, some fans are amazed that the fixture will go ahead. "They say yesterday bends 3 and 4 were under water! How he's got it on is amazing. I think we could struggle 'cause we've got a weakened side tonight. We'll see how strong the squad system is though, won't we? Last year, Mike Bowden said there'd be no doubling up riders and, yet, this year, he has two but never say never! We always do well against these here. You won't get good racing though, 'cause they don't do nothing with the track!" Weymouth number 2, Brendan Johnson also stops for a few words. He's an extremely polite young man and, like many people of his generation, he strikes me as mature and analytical. In his case, about his performances and ambitions. "I feel confident when I get to every track this season. I'm in the top 25 Conference League averages and feeling good everywhere I go. Last night at Swindon, I beat both of the new Aussies they have and that boosts you! That said, I'm just gonna keep my feet on the ground and be myself and do the best I can."

Though rumour has it that referee Dave Robinson will require photographic evidence to back up his track report for Colin Meredith if it cuts up later, the talk among the Plymouth fans has nothing to do with the surface but everything to do with the need to hammer their local rivals. It's two years since I came to a meeting at Plymouth and to the casual eye there appear to have been a number of improvements. These look to me to include the arrival of a new trackshop building, brightly painted yellow wooden terraces either side of the referee's box and what appears to be a handrail on the earth mounds that provide an elevated viewing section on the first bend. Much more noticeable than any change to the stadium infrastructure is the decline in crowd numbers. Though an attendance of this size would be welcome at many Premier League tracks (let alone Conference ones), compared to a couple of years ago, the popularity of the Devils has noticeably waned, particularly when you consider that this is a 'local' derby (albeit a regularly repeated one in 2008). However, if this represents the hardcore fan base that watch most meetings at the St Boniface Arena, then Mike Bowden's reputation as a promoter of an attractive and financially successful club remains well deserved. On the journey to Plymouth, Weymouth Team Manager Jem Dicken had been sceptical about the economics at the club, "With the money he [Mike Bowden] pays them I'm surprised he makes money!" Another thing you can say about Mike Bowden is that he's got a down-to-earth and avuncular presentational style, both when he introduces the teams and also when he welcomes the crowd. "And we're now back at the track for a dry Friday night and we'll see if we can't get through to meet Rye House here next Friday!" Comparison of the original racecard (from the programme dated 20th June) with this evening's shows that the Weymouth Doonans' Wildcats track the exact same 1-7 that they originally intended. While the Devils have replaced Jaimie Pickard at reserve with Danny Stoneman, moved Seemond Stephens to number 5 and switched Mark Simmonds to number 1. Or, at least, they would have, if he were here tonight. Mike Bowden rather sweetly explains that the Devils will run rider replacement for their absent number 1 because he's "taking his first holiday in 15 years".

Tonight the weather in this part of Devon can't quite make up its mind what to do – at 6 o'clock thick black clouds were overhead, by 7 o'clock the sun had broken through brightly and by 7.45 dark clouds had again begun to mass overhead. Whatever the weather situation, the meeting starts promptly at the advertised race time and, working together in unison, the riders, officials and referee fire through the initial heats with great rapidity. With a track length of 216 metres, the Devils definitely race on the shortest track in the country. It's difficult to distinguish the straights from the bends and the effect created – to an infrequent casual observer like myself – appears to be that the four riders frenziedly and almost continuously broadside their bikes. All speedway tracks have a home advantage and it's clear that the tight confines of this circuit require a special riding technique that Seemond Stephens has definitely mastered, if judged by the easy manner with which he zooms away to win the first race. Before he can do so there is a false start that sees Brendan Johnson

Fans queue

Riders vans

Plymouth v. Weymouth: *"If you'd signed it, you'd be contractually obliged not to fraternise with the riders."*

excluded for a tapes touching offence that he strongly disputes the veracity of afterwards. Seemond's winning time of 54.8 seconds is some distance outside the track record of 51.07 seconds set by Tai Woffinden in May 2007. With race times at other speedway tracks in Britain in the late 50s or early 60s, the kinds of time they announce at the St Boniface Arena sound strangely incongruous. Ex-Plymouth Devil, Tim Webster has his second outing of the meeting in heat 2 and proceeds to win it. Based on his exuberant celebration as he crosses the line, it clearly has great personal significance for him. After the first couple of heats have been drawn, Plymouth stamp their authority on the tie when Nicki Glanz and Tom Brown combine for a 5-1 race advantage that takes the score to 11-7 in a race sponsored by "Allan – a grateful supporter". Though the meeting is only 13 minutes old, we've already had three races! The fourth race sees dust levels increase significantly and also provides another race win for Seemond Stephens. Plymouth reserve Paul Starke has an eventful race – excluded from the initial running of the heat for a tapes offence, he then starts the rerun 15 metres back and, on a track of this perfectly formed size, it's almost an impossible distance to make up over other riders fortunate enough to start from the tapes. To compound matters, Paul tries so hard that he then falls but quickly remounts to gain additional valuable track time. Before the fifth race, a rather unique-looking grader circuits the track three times before the converted fire engine that serves as the Plymouth bowser proceeds to copiously water it. Stood next to me on the mound that overlooks the first bend is a proud granddad and a gaggle of grandchildren apparently on their first visit to speedway if his loud mobile phone conversation is anything to go by: "We're standing outside on a big mound but we're enjoying it!"

Like last season at Lakeside, there are an incredible number of photographers on the centre green (I counted seven at one point). Julie Martin is there in her distinctive white trousers and these contrast with the stylish bell-bottomed black trousers worn for the occasion by another taller lady photographer. Later I quiz Jules for more information, "I think she's from the local paper. I can tell that 'cause the speedway photographers jump around a lot more if they do it regularly!" Regular Devils fans will have become sated to a diet of 5-1s given the recent score lines here against Boston and tonight's visitors Weymouth. The fifth heat sees the Devils power pairing of Tom Brown and Nicki Glanz hammer home their second 5-1 of the night. It's a sight greeted with ecstatic screams of "5-1! 5-1! Michael we got a 5-1!" from an excitable lady next to me. Reasonably enough Michael asks, "What's the score?" Only to be told "Eh, I dunno, what's the score?" There are clearly a number of Wildcats fans dotted throughout the crowd as indicated by the muted cheer that greets Jay Herne's heat 6 win – something he achieves despite the close attentions of Nicki Glanz. A helpful man in front of me evangelises on behalf of the promptness of Conference League speedway, "This is the best to watch – the Premier League is too aggressive – whereas here we get very prompt racing and even prompter announcements of race times, plus riders who want to race and improve".

With little sunshine and a cool breeze, it's a surprise to see a topless rider in the pits. This might be partially explained by a prominent arm tattoo that should really be marked down as an artistic crime and lead to the arrest of his tattooist. It's cool enough for anoraks to be sported widely, though Pits Marshal and Plymouth's Speedway Website Forum Moderator, Darren Fletcher, wears a bright yellow shirt with the name Darren emblazoned across his shoulders. Given the Conference League is ostensibly a training ground for riders to take their first steps within the sport, often they don't always exhibit the smoothest of racing styles. At the St Boniface Arena even those with greater experience at senior level also bounce around on the intermittently bumpy surface of the racetrack. This is particularly noticeable on the third and fourth bends where pretty well all the competitors struggle for balance and control. If speedway were skiing, then this would be the equivalent of a mogul run. Though some of the Wildcats have benefited from regular visits this season, it's clear that they don't have the confidence of the home riders. In the eighth heat, Brendan Johnson bounces backwards from third into fourth after a struggle for bike control on the second bend during his third lap. Though he perseveres, this loss of position is difficult to make up in the 300-odd metres of the race that remains. 19-year-old Tim Webster who celebrates his second successive race win with yet more unalloyed delight wins the race. Later Julie Martin confides, "Tim Webster used to ride here but they kept dropping him. You could see how pleased he was to win here and prove something, whatever that is!" Out again immediately in the next race off gate 4, Tim Webster finds that Tom Brown has lined up incredibly close to him next door on gate 3. Webster attracts the attention of the Start Marshal to ask him to move Brown over. After some discussion with the official, Brown grudgingly retreats only to lines up in more or less the same position. A Plymouth fan next to me acknowledges the psychological gamesmanship, "He hasn't moved much, has he? I reckon about one inch or slightly less". Either keen to psyche out his opponent or irked by the request to move (possibly both), just as the riders come under

---

Plymouth v. Weymouth: *"If you'd signed it, you'd be contractually obliged not to fraternise with the riders."*

orders Tom Brown dramatically sticks out his elbows even further than would appear sensible to complete his pre-race intimidation of the Weymouth reserve. It's a sledge hammer tactic to crack a nut since Brown's quick reactions ensure that he gates a considerable distance ahead of his rival before he emphasises his complete mastery of his opponent with an aggressive drive out wide to the fence to block off the outside run that conspicuously fails to materialise. Nicki Glanz has also gated magnificently from the inside gate and the potent Devils Glanz-Brown partnership romps home for their third successive maximum heat advantage and progress the scoreline to 32-22.

Weymouth Team Manager, Jem Dicken, does after all have to use the black-and-white helmet he'd brought along. He chooses to give this garment to Andrew Bargh to wear in heat 10 where team mate Luke Priest'll partner him and the Plymouth Devils track the ultra-consistent Tom Brown (as rider replacement for Mark Simmonds) partnered by Jamie White-Williams. Both sets of riders definitely realise that this could be a significant turning point, both in the meeting and for the overall aggregate score. If Weymouth gain a maximum heat advantage then they'll be right back in the contest but, if this tactic fails, the possibility of an aggregate victory and their further progression to the semi-final of the KO Cup will diminish. Almost as soon as the race starts, the referee Dave Robinson puts on the red stop lights and gets the announcer to warn both Plymouth riders. "The referee says the rider in blue is to remain stationery at the start and the rider in red [Tom Brown] is to come up to the tapes a bit more promptly next time." In the rerun, Andrew Bargh makes a swift start from the tapes to keep the Wildcats slim hopes of aggregate victory alive, albeit with Tom Brown in hot pursuit. As they enter the last corner rather than take the safe option and settle for the points Tom tries a do-or-die dash for glory. Unfortunately he comes to grief and tumbles from his machine, ("Oh no, he tried too hard!") to allow Luke Priest to convert his third place into a vital second place. The boosted 1-8 score takes the score to 33-30 and reduces the aggregate lead for the Devils to a solitary point.

Fire engine bowser

Brendan Johnson reads after the meeting

The intensity on the track is suddenly echoed off it with quite a commotion away to my right and nearby to the cars parked in the vicinity of the entrance turnstiles. There are some shouts and people running before a tearful lady is surrounded and escorted to the pits area. During the brief fracas, staff ran and members of the Bowden family mill about while someone is told to run to the entrance gates to ensure that they are properly locked. The only phrase I can make out is yelled by another lady at one of the men: "You should have banned her!" It is difficult to see what has provoked the incident or, indeed, what exactly happened, given the distraction of the track action. Given the intensity of the emotions aroused, you'd immediately have to suspect that the unwelcome visitor can only possibly be a thief, black sheep of the family, disgruntled former business or romantic partner. Curious to discover what was really behind the sudden uproar, I step over to ask the programme sellers who've also been rubbernecking this brief drama. Sensibly children are taught the danger of strangers and it appears that this lesson has been well learnt by the programme sellers who deny any knowledge of any fracas, let alone insight into the reasons behind it or knowledge of any of the parties involved. Hardly a plausible or convincing denial! My curiosity clearly isn't welcome, but vanishes instantly with the sight of four riders lined up at the start gate ready for heat 11. Seemond Stephens again emerges victorious from his third race of the

Plymouth v. Weymouth: *"If you'd signed it, you'd be contractually obliged not to fraternise with the riders."*

evening while the Wildcats partnership pack the minor places to ensure a drawn heat that keeps the meeting delicately poised. Tipped off about my curiosity about the commotion, a man who resembles a junior version of Mike Bowden strides over and demands peremptorily, "Are you a spy? Or environmental or something?"

[JS] "No, I'm a guest of the club."

[MB Jr] "What are you writing?"

[JS] "Notes for my next book. Mike Bowden has given me permission to be here."

[MB Jr] "I'm Mike Bowden junior."

[JS] "I can see the family resemblance!"

[MB Jr] "What, the receding hairline?"

[JS] "No, the good looks!"

[MB Jr] "No offence meant. It was a family business! That's all! You know what families can be like. It was nothing at all."

I'm left to my own devices but I've clearly stood out from the crowd because of my curiosity and the apparently alien activity of my note taking. I'm joined by Jules whose hands shake with nerves as she smokes a crafty fag. "I just want to be at home and tell them we've won". Slightly discombobulated by my ostensible thought crime of curiosity, I ask Jules whether she noticed any commotion. "Naw, I was on the centre green screaming! But then, everything's weird at Plymouth. And you can quote me on that!" Heat 12 would be the decisive heat of the KO Cup quarter-finals. Tom Brown led from the gate with the Wildcats Webster and Priest behind him in second and third. If this race order were to remain then the heat will be drawn. However, Paul Starke, the Devils reserve with the number 7 race tabard has saved his best performance of the night for this vital race. First of all he picks off Luke Priest and then, on the last corner of the race, forces his way aggressively past Tim Webster to snatch second place on the line. The delight of the home crowd is unalloyed and the Devils aggregate advantage moved to a useful and probably insurmountable 5 points.

The hero of the hour Paul Starke is given a further opportunity to prove his mettle when given Mark Simmond's replacement ride in heat 13. The previously unbeaten Seemond Stephens flies from the third gate only to have to be stopped almost immediately when the referee illuminates the red lights. Via the announcer, referee Dave Robinson issues "A warning to all four riders to remain stationery at the start". At this news, Plymouth Chairman Mike Bowden strides theatrically towards the start gate to ostentatiously satisfy himself that there is no movement at the tapes for the rerun. A competitive race ensues but ends prematurely when Paul Starke falls on the second bend of the third lap and the race is awarded as a win to Seemond Stephens. Mike Bowden Junior returns briefly to apologise again, "I didn't mean to be rude. There was a lot going on! It's too long a story to go into."

The minimum requirement for Weymouth from the penultimate heat is a race advantage of some sort and this looks highly likely until the moment Nicki Glanz dives aggressively under Andrew Bargh on the third lap to seize the lead and ensure another drawn heat. The intermittent dust problem has continued throughout the meeting but, at the very moment of Nicki Glanz's race-winning manoeuvre, I get thwacked on the forehead with a large piece of shale some riders erroneously claim they don't bother with here! With one race to go, Plymouth are mathematically certain to race Rye House in the semi-finals of the KO Cup ("Even if we lose 5-0, we'll still go through!") The top-end strength of the Plymouth GT Motorcycles Silverline Devils is such that they can rest maximum man Seemond Stephens from the final race of the night and, instead, still track their power partnership of Tom Brown and Nicki Glanz. With regional pride and bragging rights at stake, the riders don't treat the race as a formality. Andrew Bargh manages to split Brown from Glanz and thereby breaks their sequence of maximum heat advantages. The Plymouth promotional team have packed 15, sometimes thrilling races, into 90 minutes and the crowd drifts away to the car park or the pits contentedly.

Optimism dictates that I ignore the darkness and continue to try to sell my books. Still in their kevlars and carrying their helmets, Wildcats riders Brendan Johnson and Kyle Newman stop by for a word. Never afraid to be self-critical, Brendan tells me, "That's the worst I've ever done here [1 paid 2]. I can't believe it! I was excluded in heat 1 incorrectly

Plymouth v. Weymouth: *"If you'd signed it, you'd be contractually obliged not to fraternise with the riders."*

when I didn't touch the tapes. I have to admit my head went down! It doesn't usually but I was stiff on the bike and everything. It's just so depressing! If I'm hard on myself, it's my way of motivating myself to do better. When we've been here before I've got 7 paid 9 and paid 8. When I was excluded first time out, I asked Jem to call the ref but he's a pussy. He shrugged and said it was too early to call.[2] At Oxford last year, Peter [Oakes] was on the phone – whether we won or lost – pressuring the ref! I just can't believe how bad I was but tomorrow night I'm really gonna make up for it with a big score!" Shortly afterwards Phil Bartlett pretends to run down me and my table with his car before he winds his window down to ask, "What are you doing here?" He's stuck in the slow-moving queue, so we chat for a few minutes. Phil is phlegmatic about the Wildcats elimination from the KO Cup and matter-of-fact about the death of his daughter Hannah, when I pass on my condolences. He switches the conversation to the arrival of the red crotchless knickers at his house addressed to Julie Martin that I featured in my last book, *Concrete for Breakfast*. "She didn't mind about the red knickers being in there. You know who sent them of course?"[I don't] "What, you still don't know who sent them to her? Well, I'll give you a clue. There's a popular film where the first name of an animated toy character is [name redacted]! So you should now find it pretty easy to find out!"

Raised viewing position

Since we're all part of the broad church of speedway many of us – fans, riders and management alike – head for much-needed refreshments at a nearby bar to celebrate (or drown sorrows). Some of the riders are too young to drink and, given that they wouldn't able to travel here let alone compete without the help of their parents, there's absolutely no likelihood that tonight will be the night that they'll start! The Plymouth Devils regularly frequent a Harvester-style pub with food on the menu, numerous television screens and a large car park. Those inside split into three factions: designated driver, designated drinker, and too young to drink. After some libations, we're soon back on the return journey to Weymouth – via a nearby garage where Jem buys a much-needed reheated pasty. The aggregate defeat is a definite disappointment but, after some consideration of the ins and outs of the thing, thoughts turn to possible revenge in the League meeting at Radipole Lane the next evening. The consensus in the car is that Weymouth, like Plymouth, would attach far greater importance to League success than they would to any other competition they can enter (or win) this season. Nonetheless, Jem imagines that they'll be delighted with the victory against their rivals and pleased to progress to the semi-finals. However, after a couple of weeks without any home meetings, he believes they wouldn't have been pleased with the size of the crowd. "It wasn't a big crowd for them. When they won their first meeting of the season it was rammed. You couldn't see any space anywhere!" The conversation lapses and Jules resumes control of the communications hub that is her two trilling mobile phones.

First corner and flyover

---

[2] Later Jem would comment, "You have to be very careful when you speak to any of the officials! It's all very well trying to put pressure on them but, it can work both ways, and they can just as well end up making decisions against you. They are under enough pressure as it is and, once they have made a decision, they never change their minds! Tonight the referee would have a better view than I would have so I would not doubt his integrity. If every decision was disputed, at every meeting, there soon wouldn't be any referees and thus no speedway! Riders should just concentrate on riding and let the team managers do what they think is right. Quite often I have complained to a referee about a decision on behalf of a rider knowing too well, in my own mind, that the referee is correct."

For many people involved in speedway, late-night drives are a fact of life. Invariably it's past midnight, there's a considerable distance to go to home and you're stuck in traffic queues through the late-night roadworks. Luckily we head back to Weymouth on a cross-country route, so delay from miles of fluorescent cones and workmen on the roads aren't an issue. However, pitch darkness, winding roads and the narrow high streets of country villages would be if I were at the wheel. Experienced on this route Jem takes it in his stride and, after some prompting, he explains something about his many years' involvement with Weymouth speedway. "I first went in 1974 and I've always been involved at the track. I've been a raker, a pusher, I spannered for Ian Humphreys, I used to put out the fence for the stockcars. I've done what needed to be done at the time it needed to be done. I was involved right up to the time we closed. The last year I can't really remember 'cause I was stood in the bar. When I looked at a photo of the team, I couldn't recognise half of them. You can't really compare them to now they're just different! Obviously riders stick in your mind, people like Martin Yeates. Once I heard the club was starting again I was never not going to be involved. There's three or four of us who work at the track – without us there wouldn't be a speedway club. Well, of course, there would because some others would probably do it! I spend three hours there every night and on a Saturday I work there from 8 a.m. until 11.30 p.m. Since we reopened at Weymouth I've been doing all sorts of things. Like put out the flags, stock the bar, hand out leaflets, pick up the rubbish, clean and paint the kick boards. There's no rules though, unless you do these things it don't look professional otherwise, does it? I write bits in the programme and put it all together and, of course, I'm the manager. When I tell them how to ride they don't listen but, if Boycie [Craig Boyce] tells them, they listen! But I suppose I haven't ridden, so that's understandable. I do my job and I try to motivate them. They're all different but it's something I've taken to! We've done a lot of work over the last few years. I'm a builder so I know the principles of building. A road and doing the track is just the same! If you haven't got a proper base you're lost 'cause the ground moves and you can never get a consistent surface. We have a clay base and we've put in drains. It was a massive job but has made a big difference. One day we had five or six feet of water lying on the track and I forked the drains – the ref said, 'this is off' but was amazed when we got it on. So, I'm the track curator and I know I'm biased, but I think our track is the best racing track! And the most entertaining one in the country! It takes a lot of hard work to get it that way. That's why I love the *Blunsdon Blog* because they're doing what we're doing! All clubs are run on the unpaid work of people like us. You see Phil [Bartlett] at 5.30 on a Saturday and then you don't see him till 5.30 the next Saturday. But, then he takes the financial responsibility! With holiday-makers we can double the crowd but, that's what we have to do over six weeks in the summer, if we're going to have half a chance of reducing any losses."

11th July Plymouth v. Weymouth (KO Cup Quarter-Final Second Leg) 51-42

CHAPTER 19.

Weymouth v. Plymouth:
"Save £4 with this Leaflet* (Terms and Conditions Apply)"

12th July

A question that's asked every year within speedway circles is 'how do we attract more fans to come along and watch speedway on a regular basis?' Whether economic times are good, bad or indifferent, if you can get those extra people to come through the turnstiles then it's going to have a massive positive impact on the financial health of the club. Recent years have seen new promoters arrive in the sport with great optimism that their marketing pizzazz and gung-ho attitude will miraculously get the punters through the gates. For every Stuart Douglas at Lakeside, there are a couple of John Postlethwaites (although no one else has failed on this scale in recent memory). Last season the longest-serving promoter in British speedway, Edinburgh's John Campbell, who has seen many newcomers arrive with unrealistic attitudes in his time, spoke with sagacity: "New promoters come in and think if they can spend a thousand pounds on some advertising and run with a board around town that the crowds will flood in – of course they don't! Getting 10 new speedway fans to come along is always the hardest thing to do." It's an immutable law of speedway that you can lose a hundred people off the gate much easier than you can gain 10! Quite how this circle can be squared remains something that clubs will always struggle to resolve, often innovatively, within their own local catchment area.

If the 'build it and they will come' school of thought promulgated by the film *A Field of Dreams* is discredited, then the "if you have success on the track the fans will come" philosophy has many adherents. Lakeside's go-ahead promoter, Jon Cook, puts this with trademark eloquence: "The majority of the fans go along to see their team win, and whilst they are successful, they will continue to support them. If they lose, then a few will get the hump and stop going, as they do anyway, and save their money as is their right." Even this commonsense and matter-of-fact outlook isn't an immutable law. Though the speedway season runs from March until October, many clubs have a narrow time window – basically during the school summer holidays – to maximise their attendances and turnover. This is probably a factor for all speedway clubs but definitely so for the clubs located in or near what could be considered holiday destinations. The exception that proves the rule is, of course, Poole where following the Pirates has long been woven into the fabric of the local community. Other clubs based close to holiday resorts (or campsites) know that they have transient audiences on their doorstep keen to enjoy themselves and armed with discretionary, disposable income. However, to actually convert that latent spending power into punters through the turnstiles remains difficult. King's Lynn speedway set great store by their campsite visits, while the Isle of Wight only just about keep their head above water because of their lack of summer holiday crowds. My local club Eastbourne have a holiday resort on their doorstep, yet holidaymakers apparently more often make their way to Arlington to watch the stockcars than they do the speedway. Some people claim that this is because of the frequency and visibility of the brightly coloured stockcar posters. Whatever the promotional gimmick or marketing tool is that excites the interest, the marketing truism that invariably applies is the one that says 50 per cent of all adverts work, but we just don't know which 50 per cent!

Weymouth Wildcats Speedway Club get good coverage in the local print and broadcast media and attract a loyal band of supporters to Radipole Lane on a regular basis. However, there isn't a sufficient number of diehard fans to guarantee the financial health of the club. The ongoing challenge for the Wildcats remains to draw the attention of day-trippers and holidaymakers to the existence of their club and, hopefully, thereby boost attendances. If or when they get there, club photographer Julie Martin is convinced that the speedway is a high-calibre, good-value and entertaining product. "Not being funny, we always have great meetings here! Maybe it's 'cause it's a smaller track no one can get away, you can always get past and there's always excitement and the odd incident. I'm biased I know but it really is always good every week!" Though, this is a genuine and sincerely meant testimony, the problem is still how to communicate this to holidaymakers. On the drive back from Plymouth last night, Wildcats team manager Jem Dicken somehow managed to persuade me that it would be fun to join him to walk along Weymouth seafront promenade and about the town centre wearing a sandwich board that advertises Weymouth Speedway. We'd also try to hand out leaflets to interested passers-by. In recent years, the use of sandwich boards in town and city centres throughout the country has diminished. Nowadays they're more often associated with the pseudo-religious messages like 'The End is Nigh', shops that sell dodgy discounted luggage, cheap calls abroad or bargain-basement furniture.

They say if you make your marketing messages unduly complex, then people often switch off before they've come to the crucial (but deeply hidden) bit. Down on the seafront promenade, luckily Jem hands me a sandwich board that strongly errs on the side of simplicity. On the recto side of the board there's an action photo topped and tailed by the words "Weymouth Speedway" and "Wessex Stadium Saturdays 7.15 p.m.". The verso side has two different action photos topped and tailed with the same text along with catchier copy in italicised letters, "0-60 miles per hour in under 3 seconds" as well as "No Brakes, No Fear". Apart from, our sandwich boards we also have a wodge of leaflets to hand people. Before we set off, Jem gives me some important advice. "Look out for the people in blue uniforms! It's not illegal, if they ask for it [the leaflet]. It's only illegal if you give it to them!" I gather that this is the speedway equivalent of a legal disclaimer should I find myself arrested on Weymouth seafront. I hadn't realised that speedway involved this kind of danger!

The leaflet itself is packed with information and asks rhetorically, "Are you ready to witness…Britains [sic] most spectacular sport?" If that accurately describes your intention, then you can "Save £4 with this leaflet". A quick look at the terms and conditions small print will slightly take the edge of your excitement when you read, "When presenting this leaflet at the turnstiles yourself and three other members of your party will receive £1 each off the full admission price. This discount cannot be used in conjunction with any other offers or special events promoted by other organisations." Obviously, it's incumbent upon marketing people to accentuate the positive but, no matter which way you look at it, even if you turn up on your own you'll still only get £1 off if you hand in said leaflet. These leaflets have been round for a while, so the main team sponsor is identified as the slightly mysterious and official-sounding HDBM [Harold Doonan (Building Materials) Ltd]. On the club tabards the main sponsor's name is put much more snappily as Doonans Sand & Gravel Wildcats. The club's media partners – *Wessex FM* and the *Dorset Echo* – are also highly visible on the coloured side of the leaflet. The verso side isn't printed in colour but is packed with dramatic sounding copy "Only the most talented motorcyclist can tame this type of beast, power sliding around the bends only centimeters [sic] away from their opponents." If this doesn't whet your appetite then there's also the news that, "With no brakes these motorbikes are travelling up to 65 miles per hour so sometimes things can go spectaculary [sic] wrong." A bit like the spelling, apparently. Helpfully, exact driving directions are also provided.[1] It just remains for Jem and I to give these leaflets away to as many people as we can interest while we walk around in our sandwich boards.

I already know through experience that giving away leaflets (on my books) can meet with resistance from speedway fans. To interest members of the general public who have no connection to speedway but innocently promenade on the seafront or rabidly shop in Weymouth town centre is altogether a different kettle of fish. One of the first people I hand a leaflet to is Ross Marks – we fail to recognise each other from our shared Reading Racers connections – and it turns out he used to be previously employed as Commercial Manager at Weymouth speedway. The fact that Ross is an early recipient causes much amusement for Julie and Jem. Julie has ventured down to the seafront with the blonde bundle of energy that is her daughter, Leah, but has sensibly refused to wear a sandwich board herself. Jem's down from the track as a brief respite from his extensive number of match-day duties at Radipole Lane. He sets off at a great pace along the Weymouth promenade. Once we get to the town centre, we divide to take separate streets and I find that some people are curious, so are happy enough to take a leaflet, whereas others react as if I've made an improper suggestion. Many people ask, "Is speedway still on nowadays?" After we've fought our way through the crowded streets of the town centre we retrace our steps before Jem heads back to the track. I wend my way back and rendezvous at the Black Dog pub where Jules has arranged to meet Weymouth riders Luke Priest and

[1] The next day at Reading, Paul Oughton will tell me, "you were giving away the wrong 'summer' leaflet at Weymouth – it should have the 'kids go free' one." Jem confirmed that we had both types of these leaflets with us that day.

Weymouth v. Plymouth: *"Save £4 with this Leaflet* (Terms and Conditions Apply)"*

Tim Webster. It's a popular and crowded pub with a wide variety of pub food on offer. With the arrival of sports science, sports psychology and nutritional experts, many top speedway riders have revolutionised their approach to their chosen occupation. As a sign of the times, at the 2008 Eastbourne Eagles Press and Practice Day, while the riders waited to pose for photographs on the centre green, talk among the younger ones among them focused on their comparative body fat percentages. Judged by their dining choices, these aren't issues that overly concern 23-year-old Luke Priest and 19-year-old Tim Webster who tuck into double burger & chips and chicken, chips & peas respectively. However, both make a concession to healthy living. Luke leaves his tomatoes while Tim scrapes the cheese and bacon from his chicken. They're of an age (and metabolism) that allows them to eat whatever they like with negligible consequences. Both tuck in with gusto and claim it will set them up nicely for tonight's speedway meeting over five hours later.

Sandwich boards

After they've eaten, Luke Priest volunteers to run us back from town in his van. Keen not to overdo things before their clash with the Devils, the lads turn down the chance of an ice cream from the renowned Rossi's emporium. Faced with a long walk along the seafront, Tim commandeers six-year-old Leah's mini scooter and proceeds to get pushed at great speed along the seafront by Luke. With this help, Tim reaches impressive speeds and cuts an incongruous figure perched on the tiny wheels of this child's scooter. He confirms his speedway talent and ability as well as demonstrates excellent control and balance when he leaps over various speed bumps en route to the van. Tim handles the scooter like a consummate professional, which prompts Jules to observe, "Can you imagine Jason Crump doing this before a big meeting?" It's my first trip inside a speedway rider's van and, with Luke and Tim upfront; Leah, Jules and myself use the spacious rear seat. Tim spends well over five minutes primping and preening his hair in the passenger side sunshade mirror. Eventually he achieves the required effect (though it looks no different to me). Luke enquires, "Why don't you have it like mine?" Contrary to the popular mythology of the tabloid press rants about modern-day youth, Luke and Tim are polite but quietly confident young men who are a credit to themselves (and their parents).

Nutritionally controlled pre-meeting meal

When we arrive at Radipole Lane a couple of hours later, the car park is already crowded with an impressive array of riders' vans. Many riders have already unloaded their bikes and equipment, while others are in the process of doing so. They say that workshop hours pay dividends in terms of additional points won on the track. Nonetheless, given the buzz and industry in the pits, the few hours before the tapes rise are also a vital part of any rider's mechanical and psychological preparations. The pits stall of each Weymouth rider is adorned with their photograph on the wall. Club photographer Julie Martin has kindly supplied these but, on a regular basis, she has to provide a new set of photographs because they suffer from wear and tear during the meetings. "The riders often deface them – well Karl Mason does and Brendan often becomes "Brenda" by the end of the night!"

Leah Martin and Jeff (as Jazzie B looks on)

Once the turnstiles open, my book display table attracts fans keen to stop and gossip. An older man comes up with a loss-leading publishing idea for me, "Why don't you do a book on riders born and bred in Devon and Cornwall – not Bristol – it would sell better than all these books here!" Shortly afterwards,

Weymouth v. Plymouth: *"Save £4 with this Leaflet* (Terms and Conditions Apply)"*

Plymouth Devils fan Evan is keen to emphasise an important aspect of local pride, "We always make much more noise than Weymouth here!" Another Plymouth fan tells me, "I hear Plymouth is for sale for £100,000" but is unable to substantiate the veracity of his claim when pressed for further information. Talk among some Weymouth fans focuses upon the need for quick revenge after last night's elimination from the KO Cup and stress is laid upon the 'greater' priority of the Conference League campaign for the Dorset club. They don't have to convince me but some fans are also keen to evangelise on the superiority of the racing served up at the Conference League level. "I think they [BSPA] just ignore our league and don't think about it. Though they ignore the Academy League more! It definitely needs looking at. Weymouth just can't go on scratching around with just eight or so proper fixtures and then scrambling around for some challenge meetings to fill the fixture list. On top of that, people don't have so much money and the cost of petrol means you have to pick and choose your meetings. Weymouth have been to Plymouth four times this season but I haven't been there at all yet. It's more that it isn't exciting, if I'm honest! You don't get many travelling fans in speedway – so you have to survive on your home gates!"

Widely travelled and highly knowledgeable speedway referee, Chris Durno, will officiate at tonight's meeting and is accompanied by his speedway-loving son, Tom. Chris relishes his official visits to Weymouth because of the quality of the racing served up but also the ideal position of the referee's box. Not only does it provide a panoramic view of the track but, if he pops out the back to stand at the top of the stairs, he can look down on the frenetic activity between the races in the pits below. In his opinion, this configuration is perfect and boosts the likelihood of an efficiently run speedway meeting. It's Weymouth's 12th meeting of the season and tonight's Conference League clash is sponsored by Ralph Tracey Plastering Services. Well, this is what we've just been told by Weymouth results announcer (and former Head of the National League in the 1980s) Alan Hodder, who must, surely, have the poshest voice in speedway! With his RP accent and old-fashioned manner of delivery, Alan appears to have modelled his microphone style on the voice-over narration used on Pathé newsreels regularly shown in cinemas until the late 1950s.

If the talk among Weymouth fans on the crowded Radipole Lane banking had been of revenge, then clearly, no one had bothered to tell Nicki Glanz and Kyle Hughes of the Devils who immediately storm to an impressive 5-1 in the first race. It isn't what the majority of fans want to see and prompts presenter Tim Helm to offer immediate oblique criticism of the Plymouth rider-recruitment policy in extenuation, "It just shows what riding in the Premier League can do for riders!" It almost sounds as if progression through the various tiers of British speedway is somehow not quite cricket, if you don't move on immediately from the Conference League once your talent develops. If it was quiet amongst the home fans after the first race then it becomes even more subdued after the second when a possible 5-1 reply from the Wildcats Tim Webster and Kyle Newman ends almost immediately with a fall for Kyle on the second bend. In Captain Mainwaringesque fashion, the lady next to me shouts with considerable feeling, "You silly boy!" Though 16-year-old Kyle remounts, the damage has already been done and he trails in last. Tim Webster's victory ensured a drawn heat but no reaction. This prompts Tim Helm to implore the assembled faithful: "Make a little bit of noise and clapping!"

A casual glance at tonight's racecard reveals that the Plymouth Devils don't have the power partnership of Tom Brown and Nicki Glanz wearing in the number 3 and 4 race bibs. Instead, they have Tom Brown paired with Jamie White-Williams in heats 3, 7 and 10. The claim that the Conference League throws up exciting race action in general (and at Radipole Lane in particular) is amply justified on the first lap of the third race. Tom Brown gates superbly from the inside only to have Luke Priest excitingly dice with him from the second to the fourth bend of the first lap. At this point the Birmingham-born Priest suddenly drops back to third and then falls before he remounts to trail home in last place. It's already highly impressive that Luke has shown the determination to come back from potentially life-threatening injuries. But it's also significant that he's recovered so well that the sight of Brown and Priest in full flow during the first lap – with no quarter given or asked – is worth the admission money alone. Given his father John Priest rode, Luke already has speedway credentials and this brave, albeit pointless, ride definitely double-underlines his pedigree. Though Plymouth have stretched their lead to 6 points, Tim Helm likes what he has seen: "What an excellent start to that race! With a first lap like that who needs Grands Prix?" If the third race showcased the quality of racing on display in the Conference League, then Kyle 'Silly Boy' Newman further confirms the high quality of entertainment on offer with a superb four-lap display in the fourth heat. After he's battled past the experienced

Weymouth v. Plymouth: *"Save £4 with this Leaflet* (Terms and Conditions Apply)"*

Plymouth captain, Seemond Stephens, to gain third place, Kyle then puts in a brilliant second and third lap during which he explores a variety of different lines to try and pass the Devils reserve Paul Starke. Throughout, the lady in pink to my left screams, "Come on Kyle!!" and is rewarded when the youngster sneaks past his rival with a brave last-ditch manoeuvre round the outside to snatch second place. It is a truly excellent race and, as he crosses the line, Kyle punches the air while the lady in pink celebrates with some dementedly delirious leaps of joy. One excellent race continues to follow another and the fifth heat sees Luke Priest lead for nearly two laps under great pressure from the Kyle Hughes of the Devils. Arguably trying slightly too hard, Priest then loses first place when he hits the third-bend fence second time round the circuit. However, Luke isn't easily beaten and soon resumes the duel alongside Kyle but again races just a fraction too hard to find himself with way too much speed as he starts the last lap and so, with grim inevitability, smashes into the apex of the fence. Referee Chris Durno has no choice but to stop the race and award it in favour of the Devils.

Scooter madness

Tonight, the Herne brothers appear to be involved in their own private competition to establish who can gate the quickest. Lee starts the sixth race impressively to beat the experienced Seemond Stephens but finishes with a fractionally slower time than his brother. The next race has Jamie White-Williams become the first Plymouth rider to fall this evening, up front his team mate Tom Brown wins the race and commemorates this with his distinctive aggressive but weird stare-at-the-crowd thing just before he crosses the finish line. It's a peculiar way to celebrate given his consistency at this level of racing but, it's safe to say, we'll probably see it again later. In the initial attempt to run heat 8, from the third gate Brendan Johnson rolls prior to the rise of the tapes and gets so much movement that he has to suddenly hold back from smashing them to smithereens. The previously unbeaten Plymouth number 2, Kyle Hughes, has greater predictive abilities but, unluckily, finds that referee Chris Durno has stopped the race. Second time out Brendan Johnson takes full advantage of his reprieve. Behind him, we're treated to the Battle of the Kyles. Second-placed Kyle (of the Newman variety) nearly jolts himself off his own bike as he starts his second lap and proceeds to successfully resist huge pressure from a determined Kyle (of the Hughes variety) despite one final aggressive swoop for the chequered flag. On the warm-down, 16-year-old Kyle [Newman] tries to acknowledge his opponent with a hand shake but 19-year-old Bath-born Kyle [Hughes] pointedly has none of it and, instead, speeds off. Once again, it's a race that reflects well on the riders involved and further confirms of the high calibre of the speedway racing served up tonight during this keenly anticipated derby clash staged at Weymouth's Radipole Lane stadium. Just as significantly, the maximum heat advantage ensures that scores are levelled at 24 each.

"Suits you, Sir!"

The Weymouth riders have reached a turning point in this contest although it doesn't initially appear so when Seemond Stephens leads the ninth heat for nearly three laps. Second-placed Wildcats skipper, Karl Mason, suddenly reveals exceptional acceleration to blast past the experienced Cornishman on the back straight. Then, in the race from the last corner to the line, Luke Priest somehow snatches second place with an outside blast past his rival. The Wildcats don't relinquish their lead from this point. Presenter Tim Helm can afford to be magnanimous in victory, "And congratulations to Seemond

Junior Referee-in-waiting Tom Durno

Stephens for a great race in his last season of Conference League racing!" Though this has been the 2008 season terrace chatter, talk of Seemond's retirement proves premature. It's also notable that whenever he isn't required on track or in the throes of preparation to do so, Seemond stands unobtrusively along with the fans on the terraces to quietly research and study the racing. He's the only rider from either team to do so! The balance of power shifts further when Lee Herne beats the always-combative Tom Brown in heat 10. Lee is so keen to succeed that he falls on the second bend of his warm-down lap to great hilarity from the crowd. The penultimate race before the interval starts in unsatisfactory fashion when Tim Webster falls on the first bend and, seconds afterwards, Kyle Hughes falls in a heap on the second bend. Kyle leaps immediately to his feet and appears unhappy with the paramedics, himself and also Jay Herne to whom he gestures in an uncomplimentary fashion. The rerun provides one of the few processional races of the evening. Nicki Glanz, who looks in a class of his own, showcases his smoothly effortless riding style to win it easily. With the self-critical Kyle Hughes third, this represents a mini fightback for Plymouth and reduces the score to 35-31. Tom Brown wins the next and celebrates with some donuts on the back straight and the fourth bend, his weird stare as well as his obligatory but peculiar trademark air punches of celebration. Obviously, he's highly delighted from a personal point of view but, given that Luke Priest and Kyle Newman pack the minor places, it's only a drawn heat so it really means little to the Devils from a team perspective.

The main feature of the interval break is a children's one-lap run round the track for a prize of a lollipop. A crowd of nearly 40 enthusiastic young runners line up at the tapes for the start of the race although, sensibly given our litigious society, they have to be warned, "Kids down at the start line – move back from the tapes otherwise you'll have your face taken off!" The race starts successfully at the first attempt and the winner runs home in an incredible 43 seconds. Understandably the field is soon strung out like a line of washing in the light of differences in age, size and levels of fitness. At the finish line, Phil Bartlett holds a clear plastic bucket of lollies and looks like speedway's equivalent of the Pied Piper of Hamelin. The majority of the Wildcats team have also come out to "garden" the start-gate area but soon find themselves overwhelmed by the sheer volume of children who finish the race. Phil Bartlett makes great show of waiting for the second last finisher to cross the line, gives this determined small boy the reward of his lolly and then heads back to the pits. Sadly Phil fails to notice that the last competitor has just about arrived at the apex of the last bend. She suddenly realises the full extent of her public social embarrassment, abandons her efforts and pulls up her hoodie (as if this makes her invisible) to try to sneak off the track unnoticed. Having overcome her self-consciousness of her size and fitness to take part, my heart goes out to her. Luckily, Phil isn't subsequently sued for the emotional trauma his actions have undoubtedly caused.

Chris Durno briefly stretches his legs outside the referee's box during the interval, "It's a good meeting and I'm enjoying it!" If he relishes this meeting, then the state of speedway gives him some pause. "There's 30 riders just controlling speedway in every country! They go round from country to country and keep young riders out the teams everywhere. They take all of the team places and all of the money. We might have an Elite League play-off Final between Poole and Lakeside with only one British rider and that's Leigh Lanham! And, he's hardly Team GB's brightest hope for the future! Unless the promoters see sense and stop wanting instant success, we're really going to struggle to survive! Crowds are down and there's no local riders for the fans to support!"

Shortly afterwards an Exeter fan alleges, "Seemond says he'd rather ride in a field than ride at Plymouth. It's not a proper track and someone will get hurt. At 39, he shouldn't be in the Conference League and it's a bit of beer money for him. He's always been a gater but this season he's started getting passed. He's got a young family and has to think of that too!" Shortly afterwards, the racing resumes and is watched from the centre green by Brendan Johnson and Kyle Newman who rather formally sit at a table to intently watch the race with their full-fat cans of Coke placed in front of them. Kyle then runs off as if he's just remembered he's left his tea in the oven ("I had to run off 'cause I remembered I had a race!") The Wildcats win is sealed in the penultimate race when the highly effective Weymouth Mason–Webster partnership combine for a maximum heat win. During the latter stages of the race – ever keen to capture the moment in a thoughtfully framed action photograph – Julie Martin shows an impressive turn of speed to sprint across the centre green from the second bend to the fourth. She's just in time to capture some photographs of an ecstatic Kyle Newman. The Weymouth fans greet the win with a roar, the riders continue to punch the air and Jem Dicken and Julie indulge in an impromptu brotherly and sisterly shoving match on the centre green. With the last race drawn, the Wildcats run out 49-41 victors and over the stadium speakers Tim Helm is gleeful, "Tell you what

Weymouth v. Plymouth: *"Save £4 with this Leaflet* (Terms and Conditions Apply)"

– it's our biggest-ever win over the Devils! Message from the referee, both teams have been an absolute credit to the sport!" Later we learn that Kyle Newman is deservedly rider of the night. Usually that would be that but tonight we have an additional race sponsored by Jill and John Roberts of Cleave Design. There's a trophy and prize money for a race that will be contested between the two highest points scorers of each team. Nicki Glanz wins this match race in honour of the memory of Phil and Jill Bartlett's daughter, Hannah "who recently lost her brave battle with cancer." Phil Bartlett thanks the crowd for their support and magnanimously tells Mike Bowden, "I'll go on record as saying what a great track you prepared last night!"

12th July Weymouth v. Plymouth (Conference League) 49-41

Heat 2 start

First bend bunching

Weymouth v. Plymouth: *"Save £4 with this Leaflet* (Terms and Conditions Apply)"*

CHAPTER 20.

Reading v. Edinburgh:
"I bumped into two Reading fans there – we struggle to get them to Workington but we can get them to Sweden!"

13th July

Sunday meetings at Smallmead are the exception rather than the rule. However, with the World Team Cup Semi-Final 'starring' Team GB being staged at Coventry on Monday night, then only a blind optimist would schedule against it. Consequently the Premier League fixture versus the Edinburgh Monarchs has sensibly been switched. The prospects for a Racers home victory don't exactly look healthy since the Monarchs have shown championship form at home and much verve away from Armadale. Only three weeks previously the Monarchs narrowly lost at Smallmead when, if the aggregate result hadn't already been beyond doubt, many suspected that they might well have ridden with more determination and won. The straw of comfort that the Racers only lost by 6 points in the Premier League at Armadale unfortunately ignores that Thomas H. Jonasson (from the Monarchs) was missing from that meeting.

In the sun-kissed commentary booth that provides panoramic views over the track, stadium and glistening spires of the nearby Green Park, experienced club announcer Bob Radford is again coiled like a panther ready to strike from his usual seat in the corner. Much given to reminiscences of the glories of yesteryear, Bob's quick wit and keen appreciation of people's foibles is never far from the surface. "We used to have well-paid top notch presenters and a poor loudspeaker system. Once a group of fans surrounded Bill Dore to complain and he famously said, 'You can see the racing can't you? What do you want to hear it for?' There's no answer to that!" Away from Smallmead, Bob lives in Swindon and keeps in regular contact with ex-Reading promoter Pat Bliss. "We're off to see *Mama Mia* the film and also off to see Manfred Mann. We have ticket numbers one and two. Pat's working nights doing data entry for the County Council so she can fit in her daughter's babysitting." Bob makes light of the famous chemistry that exists weekly between himself and amiable but priapic club presenter Paul Hunsdon. "Either it works or it doesn't! It's not for me to say. Though I think you definitely know if it doesn't! Because we have a different race night, it means the usual Wacky [Racer] and Rory's [Lion] are absent!" Though the usual occupants of the mascot costumes aren't available, judged by appearance it would be completely impossible for any fans to tell. Ever professional, over the tannoy system Bob bigs up the fixture and the quality of the opposition before he notes, "Wacky Racer is here, of course, the most unique mascot in British speedway!" Never one to miss the chance to pounce on unsuspecting prey, later Bob jovially promotes the work of speedway authors with Reading speedway connections, "Our Accountant in Residence Arnie Gibbons is here tonight. He usually dresses like a tourist in the Caribbean. His book comes highly recommended if you want to read about the club or you need a present to give away. Also here tonight is our guest Writer in Residence, Jeff Scott, who writes the most eccentric books in speedway. It's rather obvious he's had his hair done for this evening as it looks much blonder than it did last time!"

Elsewhere in the stadium inside the hallowed portals of the executive bar and dining room (aka the Racers Lounge) that also doubles as the press box, club Communications Manager, Andy Povey, Media Manager and Programme Editor, Robert Bamford, and the *Evening Post's* Sports Reporter Dave Wright are already in situ. Paul Hunsdon who has struggled with traffic on the way here joins them, "It's a nightmare getting out of Tadley with all the road works and the roundabouts they're building round the AWE!" Just like the search for Alan Sugar's Apprentice goes on, so does Paul Hunsdon's endlessly ambitious hunt for fit 30-something mums at Smallmead stadium. Hope springs eternal for Paul, most likely on the basis that a different race night might attract slightly different clientele to the stadium. You can't spend many minutes talking about speedway with anyone without the subject of the weather soon being on the agenda. Thanks to the Commercial Admin department, staffed by Paul Oughton, Paul Hunsdon and Ross Marks, Reading have joined the 21st century and launched their exciting text weather service. Personally since the number changed in mid June I haven't received any further communications on the state of the weather in Reading but, given the ubiquity of mobile phones nowadays, this seems a sensible way to contact fans who've registered to receive news of possible postponements. Much hilarity is enjoyed at the expense of the version of this service offered by Sheffield Speedway, who've (allegedly) recently contacted their fans with weather reports that were six weeks late. Paul Hunsdon looks on the bright side, "At least they're getting them!"

Some of the initiatives organised by Influx Marketing – aka the Commercial Department's Paul Oughton and Ross Marks – such as the Junior Racers club, have been met with widespread nods of approval. However, some of the recent initiatives have "apparently amazed the Reading management team". The back story is that, on the basis of their previous commercial work with Swindon and Somerset, co-promoter Mark Legg unilaterally appointed Influx Marketing on a one-year contract at Reading in an attempt to boost the commercial income of the club. So far, the number of initiatives started has been in inverse proportion to the income generated but not the confusion caused. These initiatives include the aforementioned text weather service, "Speedway in the community – Cash Back for Community Groups", the "Respect and Reward evening" along with the BOGOF offer for the Rye House Premier League fixture televised by *Sky*. [1]

Press Officer Robert Bamford tells me (as though speaking about somebody else) "who is known to be critical of these mad schemes" has quizzed Ross Marks about what exactly is going on. "I said to him 'you're coming out with one daft scheme after another – it's madness!' And he told me, 'you have to realise for every 20 daft schemes there might be a winner!' I also asked Paul Oughton who hasn't brought in one new sponsor this season what he was going to do to justify his well-paid contract for the year. Obviously, there's the schemes but then he asked me for some old programmes 'cause he was going to phone up old sponsors rather than visit or call on new businesses who hadn't sponsored the club previously! Malcolm Holloway and Paul Hunsdon have both brought in new sponsors and neither of them have a contract to do so. One thing that all these schemes have in common – apart from not getting anywhere, so far – is that they all generate pointless administration and paperwork! Paul's obsessed with 'data capture'! Quite what they're going to do with it, once they've captured it, I really don't know! The Cash Back for the Community Scheme is a case in point where the rules of the scheme are incredibly complicated involving specially coded tickets, collation of receipts and other stuff to take part in a scheme that's hard to explain and, of course, everyone has to fill out an application form! There aren't any application forms for the Respect and Reward evening for the various

[1] The press release for the community initiative took an optimistic perspective about a complex matter:

"READING SPEEDWAY is introducing a brand new Speedway in the Community scheme, namely 'Cash Back for Community Groups'. The scheme will give local youth and community groups the opportunity to gain cash back on their visit to Reading Speedway. This is the ideal chance for a community group to enjoy a fantastic action-packed evening out, whilst also raising funds for the group. The way the scheme will work is as follows: A youth/community group or school from the local surrounding area will be welcomed along to Reading Speedway for a particular race meeting of their choice. The group will be allocated a number of special coded community tickets, which they can give to their families and friends. The tickets will be assigned with a code exclusively referenced to that community group. When they come along to the meeting, the members and organisers will be permitted to gain entry for free and their friends or family members will hand their specified tickets in at the gate and then pay the normal admission price to get in.

The more friends and family members that attend with the group, then the more cash back the group will receive because these are the ones that will pay the admission price on entry. For every ticket that is handed in, 50 per cent of the admission entry fee will be given back to the group. This means that 50 per cent of the total admission fee given in by the group will go back to them and 50 per cent will go to Reading Speedway. The more people that attend from the group means more cash back gained from Reading Speedway!!

The superb advantages and benefits to your community/youth group are:

* A chance to enjoy the superb spectacle of Reading Speedway free-of-charge for the members and organisers of the community/youth group.

* An alternative way of fund raising for the group, using the growing medium of Reading Speedway.

* A fantastic night's entertainment for everyone involved with the group.

* A chance to gain awareness for your community group, using Reading Speedway and its various outlets.

BOOKINGS ARE BEING TAKEN NOW, SO FILL OUT AND SEND IN THE CASH BACK FOR COMMUNITY GROUPS APPLICATION FORM TO HAVE A CHANCE OF BEING PART OF THE SCHEME!!"

The press release for the Services initiative no less excitedly stated:

"READING SPEEDWAY has announced that they will be hosting a Respect and Reward evening on Monday 21 July 2008. For this special event, the Racers are inviting all members of the Services along for their Premier League meeting against Berwick Bandits, when they will be allowed to gain entry FREE of charge!! Services such as the NHS, Police, Fire, Territorial Army, Armed Forces and the RAF will only have to show their official identification and they will be permitted free entry into Smallmead Stadium as part of this Respect and Reward evening.

Yes, the club is inviting all of the Services along to come and enjoy an action-packed, high-octane, speedway meeting for FREE!!"

Reading v. Edinburgh: *"I bumped into two Reading fans there – we struggle to get them to Workington but we can get them to Sweden!"*

Services. It's not like we're based in Aldershot where they have the Army. In Reading we do have the police, fire and NHS services but we definitely don't have the Navy, the RAF or the Army. I can't remember ever seeing anyone in uniform at a speedway meeting unless they were volunteers or had been paid to do so.[2] I don't expect that anyone would try to pretend that they were a member of the Forces in order to get free entry but you don't know! Even the 'Beat the Starter' competition they have has a mechanism that often malfunctions! Quite what they'll come up with next is a mystery. They say Ross used to be a member of a Boy Band – he's now known as 'Pretty Boy Ross'. It was *Pop Idol* allegedly and I now see that they have a new gofer wearing a straw hat and open-toed sandals!"

Like the fans of so many clubs used to do, Edinburgh speedway fans still travel en masse to support their club. In this instance, on their Southern Tour. Since they're speedway fans as well as Edinburgh fans, on nights when the Monarchs aren't in action, they're happy to take in speedway wherever they can find it. Like every other recent Southern Tour, the Edinburgh supporters base themselves at their favourite hotel in Swindon and then travel around by coach from there. Until the shock premature death of Newport promoter Tim Stone and the subsequent demise of his proudly Welsh club, the original schedule would have seen them take in trips to Stoke, Newport, Reading and the Isle of Wight. Instead the itinerary has now become Stoke v. Redcar, Reading v. Edinburgh, Coventry (World Team Cup) and Isle of Wight v. Edinburgh. The tour was prefaced with their regular Friday night at Armadale where the Monarchs took on visitors Rye House in the Premier League. In recent years there has been some bad feeling between the teams and the consensus among the Monarchs fans is that they deserved their narrow 47-46 victory. Passionate Edinburgh fan Ronnie Trotter commented, "Mark Lemon didn't do so well for us as a guest on Friday. We only won by a point but then we did have Graham Flint as the referee – you know, the one who made a mess at the Pairs. Woffinden speared Jonasson – the bike and the rider went over the fence – so obviously it was all four back!"[3]

Ronnie is keen to stress that there is good team spirit among the 'Seven Musketeers' that make up the 2008 version of the Edinburgh Monarchs team. He's delighted that Ronnie Correy has no longer anything to do with the club. "Every week in the programme it was always money, money, money with him. He was a lazy little shit. His attitude seemed to be if I cou'dna beat these riders then I'll look down at my engine when I'm third and I'll give up. He cou'dna beat a carpet or our reserves!" However, Ronnie is disappointed that the Stoke fixture they intended to watch was postponed. "We went and learnt it was sunny on Friday and no rain on Saturday but still it was called off for a waterlogged track. It musta been really heavy on Thursday or maybe the Redcar at Sheffield result [45-45] worried them!"[4]

Of the 50 Monarchs fans on the Southern Tour, 27 of them have come along to Smallmead and congregated in their usual position on the grass banks of the third bend. This vantage point provides a good view of the track but also overlooks the hive of activity in the pits. The 2008 season has seen the introduction of end-of-season play-offs which will pit the winner of the Premier League play-offs against the loser of the Elite League relegation play-offs in a home-and-away clash to decide which of them actually rides in the top tier of British speedway in 2009. Ronnie tells me, "At the moment, if we went up we'd race against Wolves". Given that 'Doc' Bridgett track curates at both Armadale and Monmore Green, logically this would mean he would get to prepare/doctor both tracks. Ronnie's more worried about the financial viability of promotion rather than the shale the riders race on. "So, even though this year is a good year to go up for the big payment, our nearest club would then be Belle Vue and we'd lose the derbies against

---

[2] In the event nobody in a Police, Fire, Army, Territorial Army, Navy or RAF uniform was spotted in the stadium for the Premier League meeting against the Berwick Bandits. My light-hearted suggestion that the free-entry scheme be expanded to the emergency breakdown services of the AA and RAC wasn't acted upon!

[3] Modestly unassuming Mike Hunter writes the weekly match reports on Edinburgh fixtures for the *Speedway Star*. They're arguably the best written of all the meeting reports and, each week, it's a delight to savour the various subtle nuances they contain. His version of this incident runs as follows: "There was controversy in heat 10 as Jonasson made the start, but seemed to be brought down as Woffinden ran into him and launched his own machine over the fence. The 'all four' decision was generous to the young maestro who vaulted the fence to retrieve his bike." The words of each and every sentence are carefully chosen and every sentence comes weighted with serious freight. For example, "Chris Neath's Armadale record is patchy, especially when he spends so much time telling everyone that the match should be halted, but he is adept at nipping out at the start and that's what he did in heat 4."

[4] Commenting on the decision to call off the Redcar fixture early on Saturday due to an unfit track, the report by Neil Evans in the *Speedway Star* quotes Stoke promoter Dave Tatum. "The reason for calling off is purely because it had rained virtually every day for a week and we simply haven't been able to get on and repair the track. It's not particularly waterlogged or under water, it's just the surface is that heavy that we haven't been able to work it as it needs to be done. Calling it off is not because of the showers today. It's because of the amount of rain the track has taken all week and that has meant we have not been able to get machinery on it or do the necessary work before race day."

Reading v. Edinburgh: *"I bumped into two Reading fans there – we struggle to get them to Workington but we can get them to Sweden!"*

Glasgow plus the meetings against Workington, Newcastle and Berwick! So it wouldn't be economically viable to even think about."

Though this season the Racers management have rashly promised that each meeting would start promptly at the scheduled start time, Bob Radford advises us, "There'll be a slight delay for some additional paperwork to be completed." I imagine that this is BSPA paperwork rather than data capture requirements for the Commercial department. Sat in the shade of the main grandstand, Mike Hunter successfully downplays the championship credentials of the Monarchs and even the possibility that they may win at Smallmead this evening. "We'd like to have William [Lawson] in our team tonight rather than Krzysztof Stojanowski. Recently a few of the team have had a few knocks so we're not quite firing like we were! We need an experienced rider to calm them down but, though Ryan [Fisher] is the most experienced, he's even wilder than the youngsters!" Keen to pre-identify potential future problems, Mike posits the forthcoming home clash with Redcar as a possible danger. "We could have a close meeting with Redcar – they've got a strong team and they drew at a track [Sheffield] where they don't go well but they do go well round ours!" They'll also have their talismanic ex-world champion Gary Havelock in the team. "Gary Havelock earns the kind of money that closes speedway tracks! Fans pay to get in and that should be it. That said, if he was our rider I'd chip in!"

Robert Bamford and Andy Povey at work in the Smallmead executive bar and dining room

The meeting finally gets under way – or, at least, the riders are out on the track for their warm-up laps – but it appears that, no sooner have the riders taken to the track, than the track marshals have raised their red flags to indicate that the pre-meeting practice has closed. Reading's Chris Mills ignores the official who holds a red flag by the pits gate and decides that he deserves an extra lap to ensure that his often inconsistent gating gloves work properly. On the third bend, the Monarchs fans around me are irked by the ostensible favouritism but the officials ignore their loud cries of "Oi!". Ronnie Trotter ostentatiously glances round the Smallmead stadium to check the size of the crowd. It's safe to say that anyone who intends to come along tonight is, almost certainly, already here. "This is a really poor crowd! As it's not too long till you shut down, you'd think more people would come along! Our crowds have picked up, not that John Campbell [promoter] would say so. If it was a lock out, he'd still complain he'd had a bad night and about how much he'd had to pay the riders!"

Paul Hunsdon conducts another MILF hunt cum raffle (as Elvis looks on)

With the riders on their way out to the tapes for the start of the first race, I glance over to the pits viewing area where it appears there are two John Campbells! The original/real John Campbell is stood a yard ahead of his doppelganger, a dead ringer of a John Campbell look-alike. On closer inspection it appears that the upstart John Campbell is younger, less smartly attired and sports a slight comb-over. Prior to the meeting some Reading fans worried that Thomas H. Jonasson had definitely figured out the Smallmead track during his last visit (after he closed his first appearance in Berkshire with two comfortable wins). These fears prove well founded when he blasts from the tapes to win the heat comfortably. With William Lawson out with a shoulder injury, Edinburgh have called up the services of the Isle of Wight's, Krzysztof 'Stoj' Stojanowski, as their guest and his main contribution to the race is to puncture the second-bend air fence when he crashes into it on his final lap. Reading staff in the pits, the Racers fans on the third bend and the officials on

Reading v. Edinburgh: *"I bumped into two Reading fans there – we struggle to get them to Workington but we can get them to Sweden!"*

the centre green – particularly the flag marshal on the third bend who itches throughout the meeting to unfurl his red flag – all desperately try (without avail) to draw referee Mick Bates's attention to the rapid deflation of the air-fence panel. It's self-interest rather than a commendable attitude to safety that spurs their reaction in the vain hope that the referee will stop the race and order a rerun. Stylish on his bike, Jonasson looked extremely quick to the naked eye and a race time of 58.96 seconds soon confirms the evidence of our eyes. It's only 0.86 seconds outside the track record set by Per Jonsson in October 1987.[5]

Temporarily abandoning his 'milf' hunt, Paul Hunsdon ventures over to the Monarchs contingent on the third bend to conduct a vox pop with Gary Lough (aka King Jamie on the *British Speedway Forum*), "You usually have a lot to say on the Internet – what do you think tonight's score's going to be?" Gary straight bats the question, "I cannae predict a win over the tannoy, can I? On the Fans Forum I predicted a 48-44, so I cannae change now." With optimistic irony Paul replies, "We're unbeaten in the Premier League on *Sky*!" With air-fence repairs still under way Paul playfully issues the verbal equivalent of a shake of the head, "Don't you run into our own fence, we've only a few panels left!"

While we wait, the controversial heat 10 of the recent Monarchs meeting against Rye House meeting is loudly relived in its full glory by some fans who further confirm to themselves the iniquity of referee Graham Flint. "Tommy Allen was on the inside with Jonasson trying to shut the door as Tommy tried to push him out and Tai Woffinden caught his back wheel. That was all-four back but, when Sneddon went down in heat 15, he excluded him!" After the inflatable safety furniture has somehow been repaired, the Monarchs hammer in a second heat 5-1, through their reserve power partnership of Derek Sneddon and Aaron Summers. This gives the Monarchs a lead they don't relinquish. Edinburgh would've had more points on the board in the next race but for a moment of madness from their all-action American rider, Ryan Fisher. After he's stalked race leader Ulrich Ostergaard for three laps (and nearly caught him), as he exits the second bend on his final lap Ryan suddenly decides to batter his bike into the safety furniture rather than continue his hot pursuit. Settling for mediocrity bothers some people and Ryan is definitely from that school of thought. The inflatable fence does its job but the velocity of the impact is such that Fisher's bike bounces across the track and narrowly misses Andrew Tully. Luckily, Tomas Suchanek is so far behind that he can easily avoid the by now stationary bike. Ryan storms back to the pits in high dudgeon to yell, like King Lear, at the sky, the elements and himself before he dramatically punches his section of the pits wall upon return to his booth. A Monarchs lady fan appears to sum up the general mood, "He's an arse!" Ronnie Trotter is in no doubt about the problem, "He just doesnae know when to give up! He's lost so many points for us already this season. He should have settled for a 3-3 there! There was no need to be where he was! How many times does it have to cost him money to repair his bike before he realises?"

If Reading are to attempt to close the gap, then the sooner they start the better. Sadly heat 5 sees Ulrich Ostergaard fail to gate and, in his haste to catch the fast-starting Jonasson, he manages to clip his back wheel as he exits the second bend and clatters heavily into the traditional non-inflatable section of the safety fence. Viewed from my vantage point on the third bend, Ulrich's head goes over the fence and then bounces back as though it's spring loaded. The Monarchs fans are definitely of the hopeful opinion, "The referee should definitely award it 5-1 now – both Monarchs riders were clearly ahead!" Excluded for his trouble, Ulrich spends considerable time upon the shale being treated by a couple of paramedics. Eventually he gets to his feet and gingerly makes his way back to the pits and the shock of this sight prompts Paul Hunsdon into the sort of weird mispronunciation you'd expect from a third-rate ventriloquist ("Ulrich Osterstageer"). Ironically, in a heat sponsored by the Pangbourne Osteopathic Clinic, the rerun sees Tomas Suchanek gate second and clatter into Stojanowski. Referee Mick Bates orders all three back – a decision which further disgruntles the partisan Edinburgh fans ("he was pushed off by blue"). At the third attempt the race runs to completion and the Edinburgh pair race to another 5-1 heat advantage to extend the early score to 12-18. One 5-1 deserves another and Reading immediately hit back with their own maximum heat advantage from Mark Lemon and Tom P. Madsen. Warned first time out by the referee to sit still at the start, Derek Sneddon rides like a man possessed in the rerun but can only finish third. In fact, he does well to remain on his machine when in the vicinity of the Bermuda Triangle of the Smallmead second bend during both the first (forced out wide by Lemon) and second laps (by his own natural aggression).

[5] In fact, Jonasson's winning time was the fastest ever recorded at Premier League level at Smallmead Stadium

On track there's a flurry of drawn heats but drama off it, when one of the Monarchs lady fans collapses on the grass bank of the third bend close by to where a gardening dog had dug a small trench prior to the meeting. On the centre green, we can see compelling evidence that Reading speedway are clearly an Equal Opportunities employer when it comes to track volunteers since there's a lady raker in a black-and-white striped top on the third bend and yet another lady raker on the fourth! Shortly afterwards, the replacement Wacky Racer departs the pits and proceeds to patrol the tarpaulin-covered dog track escorted by his own Goth minder. Three successive drawn heats causes Bob Radford's mind to wander towards almost Hunsdon-like thoughts of Kim Wilde, "She can come and do my garden any time!" After a comfortable win in heat 7, the all-action Ryan Fisher then spends the first three laps of heat 10 manfully resisting the advances of the mighty Racers, Lemon and Madsen, before the red mist descends and yet another moment of madness sees him swoop out wide, lift and crash. Another Edinburgh 5-1 goes the way of all flesh and is transmogrified into a drawn heat. Everyone bathes in their mutual unhappiness, the fans with Ryan's cavalier approach and Ryan with himself as he struts back to the pits in high dudgeon. Ronnie Trotter's irked enough to rush to the wire fence overlooks the pits to shout, "You freaking arsehole, go back to America!" Ryan stops, looks up threateningly as though he contemplates whether to climb to the fence for a confrontation but, instead, contents himself with a shouted but evocative "What?!" Ryan then gestures his response with a clasp of his fists together before he fluidly twists them with his thumbs outside. It's all far too street or hip-hop for me to understand what exactly it means but, you don't need years in front of *Vision On* to gather it's not a compliment! Ryan's face is contorted with anger and his zeal for expressive communication continues with some flamboyant pushing of his tongue to the front of his mouth. It's all got very Ugly Bug Ball but, thankfully, by now the real John Campbell (rather than his look-alike) is alongside his gifted, but occasionally troubled, American rider to quietly whisper some calming words. Probably in the manner of a mating whale music CD, often played as background music during a relaxing massage. Ignoring John Campbell's equivalent of haunting whale or dolphin melodies, Ryan angrily strips off his Monarchs tabard, theatrically turns down his kevlars before he distracts us all from the effect of his own anger when he enters the wrong pits cubicle, exits again to the correct one and then melodramatically punches the wall. With a few deft blows, Ryan has artistically transformed the corrugated wall to the extent that it could almost be a late entry candidate for the Turner Prize. At this rate, they'll have to conduct emergency repairs Ryan's section of the corrugated pits wall as frequently as the second-bend air fence. In his match report posted on the Edinburgh speedway website afterwards, Mike Hunter elegantly summarises the said on-track incident. "It was a silly mistake but he is such a bold rider." To be fair, Ryan Fisher is a significant factor behind the widely held perception that Edinburgh are championship material. So, the fact that he can run a little wild, goes with the territory. It's often acknowledged that he's a much more placid and focused rider since his move from Belle Vue to Scotland. This is commonly attributed to the influence of his wife, Daelyn, who's the step-daughter of speedway notable, Mike Faria. Mike spent three seasons at Powderhall and, unlike his son-in-law, meets with Ronnie's approval, "He's one of the best riders we've ever had – a real Racer!"

With the scores still elegantly poised at 29-31, the 11th heat provides a collector's item double exclusion. In a bizarre first lap, the Racers Jamie Smith manages to fall on the third bend and, a fraction of a moment later, Chris Mills also falls. With the action right in front of us, the Edinburgh fans have no doubt how to adjudicate the double snafu: "That was two individual incidents and they should both be excluded!" Though he couldn't hear this judgement, referee Mick Bates agrees and takes the unusual step of excluding both home riders. It certainly proves he takes a scrupulous and independent approach to his work since you rarely see double exclusions, let alone double exclusion of home riders. All that remains is for Stojanowski and Jonasson to make sure that they actually race during the rerun to ensure they gain a rare 0-5 to take the score to 29-36 and definitively kill off the meeting as a contest. Ronnie has no doubt about the tactics the Edinburgh riders should pursue for the remainder of the meeting, "You just tuck in behind Ulrich Ostergaard and try to win the heats with Chris Mills in them!" The jet black clouds overhead reflect the dark mood of some nearby Reading fans whose smouldering sense of injustice bursts into flames with Mike Bates's decision to exclude Nicki Glanz after the initial attempt to run of heat 12. The incident in question saw Tully lock up in front of Glanz and left Swindon-born youngster nowhere to go other than to hit the deck. It's a common-or-garden speedway incident without premeditation or malice. A Reading fan with spittle frothing from his mouth squawks: "He locked up in front of him!" In the aggrieved manner of someone who felt he'd seen nothing illegal, Monarchs fan Ronnie Trotter remained phlegmatic: "It's all part of the game!" In the rerun, the world temporarily turns further upside down when Derek Sneddon out-gates Ulrich Ostergaard and leads him for a whole lap before the Dane

---

Reading v. Edinburgh: *"I bumped into two Reading fans there – we struggle to get them to Workington but we can get them to Sweden!"*

executes one of his trademark blasts round the outside. With the heat drawn, Monarchs fans take solace in that their comfortable 7-point lead wouldn't be subject to tactical options, "We didn't really want a 4-2 there!"

The interval raffle prizes are confirmed by Paul Hunsdon, "Third prize is *Tears and Glory* by Arnie Gibbons – I've just got to page 69 – and fourth prize is a painting of the Racers in action donated by super fan Ricky Knight." As usual, Bettina from Basingstoke hovers close by in the hope that Paul will select her to draw another of the prize-winning raffle tickets but, fickle as ever, Paul switches his attention to another youngster to help with the third prize draw. "Let's have a word with your brother, what's your name?" "Kaylie" "Oh, you're a girl! Is it too late to say sorry? It's your mum's fault for giving you a haircut like that!" [Kaylie's mum arrives] "Oh, hello, mum, it's your fault for giving her a haircut like that!" Having effectively stymied his own 'milf' hunt, Paul finishes the draw formalities quickly and then tries to excite the assembled crowd with news that Tim Webster, Russell Barnett and Danny Warwick will race in the second half. In the grandstand bar, a slim-line and extremely smartly dressed Reading co-promoter, Malcolm Holloway, sits with a table of friends. He makes light of his recent surgical procedures under the expert guidance of the highly regarded ace surgeon from the Royal Brompton, Mr de Souza. "Tell you what, I ain't freakin' dying yet!"

The racing resumes and all hopes of a possible Racers fightback are extinguished by the fourth Monarchs 5-1 (won by Derek Sneddon ahead of his race partner Ryan Fisher). Ryan clearly hasn't forgotten about the recent barracking he received from his own supporters on the third bend and, with hands as expressive as his, he needs no second invitation to clearly signal his thoughts during the final lap of the race. As a bonus, he showcases some complicated high-level charades gestures – impressive when you also have to control your bike – en route to the pits. The pits wall escapes unscathed. I run into Arnie Gibbons who has returned from the semi-final of the GP Qualifiers in Motala, "I bumped into two Reading fans there – we struggle to get them to Workington but we can get them to Sweden!" Though the meeting result is beyond doubt, in my opinion, referee Mick Bates then makes a howler when he fails to exclude Ulrich Ostergaard for his actions during the initial attempt to run the final race of the Premier League meeting. After his start from gate 4, Ulrich Ostergaard appears to deliberately fence Thomas H. Jonasson into the second-bend air fence. It's a crash that Paul Hunsdon correctly describes as a "horrendous spill" and the youngster is only saved from serious injury by the Smallmead air fence. The best construction that could be put on the incident is that Ulrich rode a racing line that compressed the available space outside Jonasson and thereby forced the following rider to either shut off or, through inexperience/bravado, continue. A less forgiving interpretation of the incident would view it as some form of retribution for the severe embarrassment Jonasson had caused the more experienced Dane on his home circuit throughout the evening. I watched the post-interval racing from the second bend and don't believe that it was accidental or just a racing 'incident'. Mike Hunter, who viewed the incident from his seat in the grandstand, was equally categorical. "I thought Ulrich Ostergaard should be excluded for that! I hope he [Jonasson] doesn't come out as he'll do the same again. I'm pleased with the result because we've been a bit shaky recently and we're better away than at home." In the rerun Ulrich Ostergaard rides a different, more appropriate racing line and, this time, Jonasson remains on his machine, albeit trailing behind race leader Mark Lemon. Ostergaard tracks, sizes up and passes his exciting-to-watch young rival on the last bend of the race to steal second place. The Racers maximum heat advantage massages the scoreline but can't hide the gulf in ability, let alone how convincingly the Edinburgh Monarchs have won, despite some thoughtless and expensive crashes from Ryan Fisher.

13th July Reading v. Edinburgh (Premier League) 41-48

Reading v. Edinburgh: *"I bumped into two Reading fans there – we struggle to get them to Workington but we can get them to Sweden!"*

CHAPTER 21.

King's Lynn v. Somerset:
"You're Dave Cheshire's son, I can tell by your eyes."

16th July

With over a third of the fixtures already completed, Premier League table toppers Somerset 'Sharp Retail Systems' Rebels visit the Norfolk Arena to take on the King's Lynn 'Money Centre' Stars. In recent years King's Lynn promotion, riders and fans have felt that they have a right to expect silverware in their trophy cabinet. The 2008 season has already shown them that both Somerset and Edinburgh won't let them have things all their own way. Always a difficult proposition at their home track, tonight the Stars lack race practice after three rain-offs in Norfolk over the last fortnight. Even if they're a little race rusty, they're nonetheless keen to become only the second team this season to defeat Somerset. With many hours to go before the tapes rise, Johnny Barber has already laid out the trackshop and is already in situ behind the counter. The concentration of King's Lynn Stars merchandise and memorabilia means that the shop is a sea of navy, gold and white. One item in particular stands out and catches my eye, namely a mug with the letters MILL emblazoned on the side. This prompts the obvious question, "Are you doing Tony Millard mugs now then?" Johnny shrugs, "Nah, we're not that desperate, they're Millennium Stadium ones." I enquire how much it would cost for Enjay Designs to manufacture a special run of 50 Mike Bennett mugs with the strapline, "I'd like to have an affair with myself!". Answer: about £3 each. I believe they'd be a great promotional gift idea to help promote speedway nationwide but Johnny remains sceptical, "You just don't help yourself, do you?" Johnny then ruins my night with the news that the "Sultan of Cheese", King's Lynn uber-presenter Mike Bennett won't be around to work the crowd into a lather this evening and will be replaced by his understudy Kevin Moore. This shock news is a huge disappointment since I'd keenly anticipated another evening when Mike relentlessly promotes his DVDs. I also hoped to hear him promote the slightly out-of-date but still fantastically readable May/June 2008 issue of *Backtrack*. This already should have found its way onto the bookshelf of any diligent speedway fan since it's packed with exciting interviews and includes one with Mike Bennett. ("Some of the promoters take what I say personally, which is a shame as it's all tongue in cheek"). For some reason what Charlie Brooker said of Philip on the *Apprentice* springs to mind: "he looks like he throws himself roughly on the bed each night, hungrily moving his hands all over his own body, trying to kiss himself deeply in the mouth."

The drive to Norfolk allows me the luxury of a listen to *Thinking Allowed* presented by Laurie Taylor on BBC Radio 4. They discuss the concept of acquired situational narcissism (ASM) and examine key differences between lies, boasts, and exaggerations. Coined by Cornell University's Professor of Psychiatry, Robert B. Millman, ASM is a clinical condition that tends to develop in late adolescence/adulthood. Fame, wealth and other trappings of celebrity usually bring it on. It's a narcissism for the modern age that's triggered and supported by a celebrity-obsessed society, where fans and the media support the idea that the susceptible individual is vastly more important than other people. Most people don't believe their own publicity but, those that do, can trigger a problem for themselves, particularly when it transforms a latent aspect of their character into a full-blown personality disorder. This can often lead to difficulty in relationships and erratic behaviour. Interestingly, the radio programme doesn't discuss disordered narcissism whose hallmark traits are a lack of empathy and difficulty grasping others emotional states (or their impact upon them). With his many years of experience in the sport, I had hoped to quiz Mike if he'd come across any characters who fitted this particular bill?

Johnny could help but is reluctant to be quoted in print. With a job that has him travel from track to track and trackshop to trackshop, Johnny is well used to a day-to-day existence that features lies, boasts and exaggeration. Nonetheless, he's keen to set himself ambitious personal goals, "I must have been feeling pretty rash 'cause I told my brother [Nick] that if I hadn't lost 10 stone by Cardiff next year [2009] he wouldn't have to pay me! I'm going to have to learn to love salad." Quite what is going on the BSI/IMG Speedway Grand Prix series is another vexatious subject. "I saw Simon Lambert beat Adrian Rymel three times round here the other week yet, on Monday night [in the Speedway World Cup], I saw him [Rymel] fly by Scott Nicholls. I wonder if that was the grippy track or the engine? I worry – but have no proof for my suspicions – that the GPs and the World Team Cup are irredeemably corrupt. I see that Scott has earned less than $20,000 from the GPs this year, so far, so he can't be doing it for the prize money!"

Absent presenters are everywhere nowadays including Mildenhall. "Michael Max stood in for Kevin the day after Cardiff. He tried not to be biased or boring but didn't succeed. Once you've got used to double entendres you notice when someone doesn't slip them in!"

[JS] "Did Glasgow win then?"

[JB] "Ha! Ha! What, an away team win at Mildenhall? I hear Ulrich has pulled out tonight at Birmingham with an injured hand. That will please Graham Drury. Apparently he's hired a team of faith healers to try and beat the Brummie curse jinx that they have there."

An extremely youthful Australian enters the trackshop and Johnny interrupts our conversation.

[JB] "Another Aussie! Which one are you?"

[Mystery Aussie] "I'm Matt Cheshire."

[JB] "You're Dave Cheshire's son, I can tell by your eyes. You've definitely got your dad's eyes!"

[JS] "Where are you from?"

[MC] "Perth."

[JS] "Maybe Perth is twinned with King's Lynn."

[JB] "How long are you over for?"

[MC] "A couple of weeks just to see what it's like before I come over properly. I'm 13!"

[JB] "Will you ride here later?"

[MC] "Yeah, it's my dad's favourite track."

[JB] "It's got some dirt. Later the Somerset riders will get out of their vans and cry at the sight of dirt."

[MC] "I went to Denmark and now we're here. I hope to have a spin tomorrow. Then we take the motor home back to Exeter and I hope to ride in the Under-15s at Redcar on Saturday."

Matt fingers quite a few items of stock but leaves the trackshop without a purchase. We resume our conversation. "We got the franchise to sell Team GB merchandise at Coventry for the World Team Cup after getting permission from Terry Russell. But we got stitched up by [name redacted] – well, [name redacted], who rang Nick half an hour before he set off to Coventry with all the merchandise saying 'You won't be able to sell anything here but come along and we'll talk about it.' When Nick got there, he asked how much the caps cost to make [£4] 'well we want the same mark-up as we get on ours! And we get them for £1.50 and sell them for 15 quid, so I'll offer you £1.80 to be fair.' There were tee-shirts and sweatshirts and everything. Nick wasn't happy and came back with most of them on principle!"

The King's Lynn side of the pits is already a hive of activity with Kozza Smith, John Oliver, Rusty Harrison and Shaun Tacey completely unloaded but at various stages of completion with their pre-meeting preparations. The Somerset side of the pits remains completely deserted but Somerset promoter Mike Golding's partner, Anita Lewis, has seized the chance to purchase some refreshments from the queue-less snack bar. Shaun Tacey is hard at work on the back sprocket of his bike and, while he works, gives some slightly downbeat insights into the wafer-thin speedway rider finances he experiences in the Premier League. "I'm scoring well but I'm not making it pay! I'm lucky that I ride with Tomas [Topinka] and we often get a 5-1. I also ride with Kevin [Doolan]. That first win pays for your travel at away meetings. You need 6 or 7 points just to break even nowadays, which is ridiculous! And that's only 'cause I do my

---

King's Lynn v. Somerset: *"You're Dave Cheshire's son, I can tell by your eyes."*

own engines. If I didn't and had an engine tuner, I just dunno how I'd feel about things! Vann [Shaun's son] is now into skiing – it's safer than this so I'm pleased – 'cause we live a few minutes away from Ipswich ski centre." I suggest that maybe Shaun should join Rye House because there's a dry ski slope in nearby Harlow plus their promoter Len Silver runs a successful ski company [Silver Ski] so he could probably get some attractive skiing holiday discounts. "I nearly did join Rye House once but the week away [team building] wasn't quite enough to persuade me!"[1]

King's Lynn co-promoter, Jonathan Chapman is the youngest person in such an influential position within British speedway. Over the last few years he's had some of his rough edges smoothed through experience but, nonetheless, still it's safe to say that he's been unafraid to question many of the certain certainties that traditionally make up a speedway promoter's outlook. He's tried new things, courted controversy and been prepared to see initiatives end in success or failure. If his impact were a balance sheet, then the positives of his approach and outlook significantly outweigh the real or perceived negatives. Within the small cadre of individuals who wield power within British speedway, one minute Jonathan is the brave, bright new future and the next minute completely out of favour. At present [16th July 2008] he's firmly located outside the tent pissing in. It's a situation that frustrates him. "Every day they [British Speedway Promoters Association] seem to shoot themselves in the foot. As an Association we should have a responsibility to promote the sport and run things properly. But, in many ways, it's not promoted properly. I love speedway! In my opinion the BSPA should stick together. Too many people have interests in their own favour – to benefit their own pocket! It will all come to a head one day. We've got economic downturn and there is a new breed of promoters. But they're frustrated with this management who need to do their own thing, when all they've done is FAIL! Whenever people find an excuse not to do something or look at new ideas, there's an opportunity! As a sport we need a joint effort. As an Association we should promote sport properly and that means doing things together. If you open a corner shop you don't have the same power as Tesco but, if you club together, you can change things! I rebranded the Super7even, it was lots of individual meetings but it's now recognised as the Super7even. If you group things together attractively, they can have more impact. We do lots of work in our community. If you had 27 speedway clubs working within their communities it would be a powerful sport! The fact that we're not is the Association's own fault. You can't blame each individual promoter. This season we've had a situation where one track has closed [Newport] through the unfortunate death of someone. We've had the Pairs meeting at Somerset where the Somerset hotline said it was rained off. This year the crowd was down. If people decided they wanted to go at the last minute and rang up, Somerset had left the old message on from the previous week. These are only small things. Unless speedway is promoted properly – and we should all fall in line – then it's gonna be difficult!"

Saddlebow Road track surface

Gentleman Shaun Tacey

[1] A week later Shaun Tacey scored paid 10 points against Scunthorpe and then commented in the *Speedway Star*, "I'm finding – and a lot of other guys as well – with the cost of diesel as it is, we need to be getting the points. It's costing a fortune filling up the van to go to away meetings and it's making the job very, very hard for us. It's been hard enough just to keep things going without paying off bills which you've incurred from the start of the season, getting the equipment you need to be competitive. It's a vicious circle, really, and these fuel costs are hitting everyone, the fans included. The sponsors? Yes please! I'm desperado!"

Once the turnstiles are open, although few people seem interested in buying a copy of my book without Mike Bennett there to promote it, many of them are happy to share their weirdly Alan Partridgesque stories about the absent presenter. "He used to run a disco called Mike Bennett International Roadshow – that's 'cause he once went to Wales. I think he was a relief DJ at *Hereward Radio* in Peterborough and, at one point, also worked for Hospital Radio in Scotland. He used to play tapes of his old radio shows at speedway meetings! When he was at Oxford in about 1987 he launched his own fan club – it only ever had one member! Boston fans took a T-shirt to Berwick for Dick Barrie and they used to rag him saying 'Mike Bennett's Number One fan'. But Dick refused to wear it saying, 'I can't wear it 'cause Mike Bennett's Number One fan is Mike Bennett!' When Wiggy was still around, a fan went up to Mike Bennett and said 'You know you're the only man in speedway who has a bigger nose than Wiggy!' Was it in *Backtrack* where Rob Grant said he was going to smack him one?" Whether these are apocryphal stories or bear some loose relationship to actual events, I'm unable to check with him.

Kevin Moore has temporarily replaced Mike as presenter. They say that dogs take on the characteristics of their owners and, most likely unconsciously, as his understudy, Kevin's prolonged exposure to Mike Bennett means that he has some, but not all, of the master's presentational quirks, characteristics and skills. This is immediately evidenced by his comments during the rider parade, "Well, it wouldn't be summer if there wasn't a black cloud overhead!" Each Somerset rider gets due acknowledgement but, compared to the fulsome praise for their King's Lynn counterparts, they get short shrift. We hear about all the Stars riders including John Oliver ("he gets really annoyed if he loses a race, let's hope he doesn't get annoyed tonight!") Simon Lambert ("and believe me those wheelies are improving!") and Tomas Topinka ("probably the busiest rider in the Premier League with all those guest bookings")." Though we can't see it from behind the safety fence, we're informed that King's Lynn have won the toss ("as usual Tomas picking gates two and four"). There's a brief interview with Stars Team Manager, Rob Lyon, who gives us some cod Zen philosophy Norfolk style, "There's 8 points up for grabs this week so we're going for all 8 points!" In the referee's box perched high above the start line, club announcer Edwin Overland is, by his own taciturn standards, extremely chatty tonight, "Big wins, tall scores, we love those! Fair enough, but we love to be tested and, with Somerset here, this is the one we've all been looking forward to!"

At my stall, Amanda Buckley-Taylor pops by to thank me for the photographs I'd taken when she posed with her idol Scott Nicholls last season. She proudly shows off the horseshoe tattoo on her neck/shoulders with the words "Scott Nicholls Racing." Amada smiles when I call her "Mrs Nicholls". "I wish! I've lost 13 stone altogether and he said I was looking good!" Inside the trackshop Johnny's friend from Mildenhall, Michael metaphorically gets under his feet.

[JB] "Michael, what have I told you? Four times today you've interrupted me when I'm serving a customer!"

[M] "I know."

[JB] "So what will I do?"

[M] "Ban me from the shop".

[JB] "Why shouldn't I ban you from the shop?"

[M] "If I stop interrupting."

[JB] "Well STOP interrupting!"

Over the stadium speakers we learn from Kevin Moore some apparently shock news about heat 2, "So many times the reserve race can be pivotal!" It's a message that hasn't percolated through to the Somerset side of the pits since the Rebels partnership of Brent Werner and Mathias Kroger are well beaten by Kozza Smith and John Oliver. Jonathan Chapman had told me earlier that Kozza's reputation goes before him, "I know riders still don't like overtaking him round the outside!" If things look bad for Somerset after two heats at 9-3, then after three races, things look even worse when Tomas Topinka and Simon Lambert combine for another 5-1. During the race, just at the moment he looked to have got to grips with the track surface, on the third bend Rebels Swedish number 3 Emil Kramer slid in slow motion into the wooden safety fence. Often the falls that look innocuous cause the most severe damage and so it appears in this case when the ambulance is quickly called out onto the track. Edwin Overland adopts his concerned voice, "I've got to say it's not looking good for Emil Kramer and it's not good news for Somerset." To

King's Lynn v. Somerset: *"You're Dave Cheshire's son, I can tell by your eyes."*

distract us from the on-track medical drama, after he's told us, "I love riding at number 1!" Kevin Doolan tries to talk the contest up to another Kevin (Moore), "We've got to get stuck in 'cause we know it's gonna be a touch match and, I think, we're really up for it." Keen to provide the Watergate-style investigative reporting that Mike Bennett has trained the Norfolk Arena crowd to expect, Kevin Moore isn't afraid to ask the difficult question, "I guess team spirit has never been better?" In the face of such an incisive question Kevin Doolan has no choice but to spill his guts, "Yeah, great!"

Talk of a tough meeting isn't reflected by the on-track experience. Heat 4 yields yet another 5-1 for the Stars and takes their lead to an already almost insurmountable 19-5. Edwin Overland has some exciting news that surely has worrying implications for the future financial health of Mike Bennett's DVD business. "Tonight's meeting is being filmed! Nothing unusual about that. But it's being shown again in the bar straight afterwards, which is unusual, for the first time here tonight!" Advance publicity that promised a close contest has drawn a large crowd to the Norfolk Arena. Indeed the programmes sold out (though, inserts are available) and over the loudspeaker system Kevin Moore desperately tries to talk up the notional difficulty of the meeting, "We can only repeat what we've said before – Somerset have only lost one match away, at Scunthorpe, this season!" While we wait for the fifth heat and the Somerset riders to rouse themselves from their collective torpor, we're treated to an interview with Richard Hellsen who still keeps reasonably close tabs on the sport ("I watch *Sky* and read the *Speedway Star*"). He reveals that, like elephants, speedway riders have excellent memories ("once you've ridden, you never forget but, nowadays, you feel a bit stiff the next day"). Richard also proffers the opinion, "I think there may be too much grip in the track!" The fifth heat results in the fourth successive maximum heat win for the Stars though it's notable for a fall by Jason Doyle on the last bend when marooned back in third place. It's an unfortunate end to the race for him and for Somerset since he's the only member of tonight's Rebels team who's so far looked at all comfortable on his bike or capable enough to race round the Norfolk Arena. No sooner has the race finished than Buster Chapman defends his track preparations. "I'm just amazed that Richard Hellsen says the track is grippy! It's slick actually, it's smooth, very consistent! I can't believe they've got good riders that aren't doing it. You can tell it's slick from the times – they're in the 60 seconds, it would be 57 if it were grippy. There's nothing wrong with the track whatsoever!"

The ceaseless quest for innovation and improvement at the Norfolk Arena has seen the club introduce the revolutionary concept of transponders attached to each speedway bikes so the split time for each individual lap can be transmitted onto the electronic scoreboard. Speedway fans across the country have been trained to look out for and respond to the heat times for a completed four-lap race. Whether or not there's a need to know or a demand for lap split times has yet to be firmly established but, judged by the weird figures flashed up on the electronic scoreboard, there still appear to be teething troubles with the equipment. For example, heat 3 split times are given as 30.84, 00.14, 14.98 and 14.68 while Edwin Overland gives the official time as 60.58. Heat 6 produces yet another heat maximum for the home riders – the fifth on the trot from what will turn out to be a sequence of nine successive 5-1s (11 in total) in a winning time of 61.61 seconds. The split times that appear

Scott Nicholls tattoo

Michael - keen Mildenhall fan

King's Lynn v. Somerset: *"You're Dave Cheshire's son, I can tell by your eyes."*

in bright red letters on the electronic scoreboard informed us the first lap was won in 31.45, the second lap 00.14 seconds (pretty quick), the third lap in 14.98 and the final lap in 15.04 seconds.

The eighth race has the Somerset riders awake from their collective slumber and actually start to fight for the points. Sadly Stephan Katt and Brent Werner have saved this rare example of concerted effort by Rebels riders for their own mini-race-within-a-race as they dash to the line in a fight for a distant third place. Announcements over the tannoy are plentiful but, notable by their absence, is any news about the availability of DVDs or *Backtrack* magazine. Inside the trackshop, Johnny tells me, "Mike Bennett promoted the *Backtrack* magazine saying '*Backtrack* is on sale and I'm interviewed in it' but he forgot to mention that some bloke called Terry Betts was also in it!" There are so many 'zeros' and 'ones' on the Somerset scorecard you could be forgiven for the thought that the Rebels were trying to amend the computer code used to generate the electronic scoreboard split times rather than contest this "Premier League – top of the table clash!" If they didn't have Jason Doyle, they would have been totally bereft. Just like one swallow doesn't make a summer, this poor performance doesn't necessarily disprove the validity of their championship credentials but would be a great disappointment for the few Rebels fans that have taken the trouble to travel to Norfolk to watch them. Rusty Harrison is extremely diplomatic when interviewed: "I think we've risen to the occasion just a little bit more than they have! I haven't ridden for a while. Everyone is up for it and everyone needs to earn some money!" Heat 10 has Shaun Tacey try to tantalise the opposition into a reaction (and inject a modicum excitement into proceedings) when he completely fails to make the gate. However, by the time he exits the fourth bend, Shaun has already clawed his way back through the field into second place, after an exciting third-bend manoeuvre that sees him overtake out-of-sorts Rebels Brent Werner and Mathias Kroger. Interviewed after this race with the 49-11 score reminiscent of mismatched Rugby League match, Jonathan Chapman praises one of the elder statesmen of the Stars: "Just gotta say, Tacey was just awesome in that last race! We're just awesome! Our riders are so focused and into what they have to do to win this league." Jonathan's ebullient mood soon overcomes his diplomacy. "I think they've got Jim Lynch guesting in the pits for them tonight! We have to respect Somerset – as they're a 50-point side – but, I think, on tonight's performance Mildenhall would put up a better show! I dunno if the Somerset management are going to apologise for their performance but, hand on heart, King's Lynn could never go to an away meeting and perform like this as the whole team would be sacked!" Moments later, calling upon his vast speedway experience announcer Edwin Overland gropes for greater context and diplomacy, "strong words from young Jonathan but, to be fair, I think we did all come along expecting something a little better from tonight's opposition!"

If Jonathan's words were intended to galvanise the opposition, then they have an immediate (albeit temporary) effect. Jason Doyle wins the 11th race in the black-and-white helmet colours but the 2-7 heat score can't really be described as any restoration of credibility since the woeful 51-18 scoreline belies this. No sooner has the Rebels fightback begun than it fades after yet another 5-1 for the Stars – this time from Tomas Topinka and Kozza Smith. It's not often you see riders do celebratory wheelies from the second bend of the last lap but such was Topinka's dominance that he was able to indulge in this luxury. Kevin Moore takes pride in Kozza's paid maximum: "He's been threatening to do it for some weeks but a fall has often deprived him of a full maximum!" A second place for Jason Doyle in heat 13 continues his one-man resistance to the King's Lynn onslaught and limits the home team to a mere 4-2 heat advantage. Normal service is then resumed in the penultimate race when it is won by Simon Lambert and, in the process, gains a deserved paid maximum. "If you take into account his matches for Boston, it's a long time since Simon Lambert was beaten by a member of the opposition." Edwin Overland is also in a state of shock, "against the League leaders – who'd have thought we'd have got the biggest win of the season at 20 to 8 this evening?" Sadly, from an entertainment point of view, the meeting was also almost over as a contest by that time!

They say always save the best till last and that lesson is confirmed when Kevin Doolan and Jason Doyle indulge in a battle royale on their last lap. Doolan passes Doyle on the first corner with a cutback, Doyle re-passes Doolan on the third bend and, with another cutback, Doolan passes him again on the fourth! With Jordan Frampton third, this is to be the only heat that Somerset draw all evening! To sum up the effort expended, it is fair to say that Somerset have ridden like six jigsaw pieces from six different puzzles. Cambridgeshire-based referee Barbara Horley has come along to the Norfolk Arena to be entertained but, like so many others on the night, will leave disappointed, "I was expecting an exciting meeting and that was dire!" Stood at the bottom of the steps that lead up to the referee's box Bryn

King's Lynn v. Somerset: *"You're Dave Cheshire's son, I can tell by your eyes."*

Williams draws heavily on a reviving post-meeting cigarette, "the only excitement was the last heat, oh, and the Tacey pass in heat 10!" Elsewhere Jonathan Chapman is unrepentant about his centre-green intervention on the microphone, "Somerset weren't happy about what I said but it picked the meeting up. It motivated Doyle to win a race for them and everyone stayed till heat 15, which was a great race! They said, 'Wait till you come to Somerset, we'll make sure you get a good welcome!' I said 'There's only two problems. One, I won't be going and two, we'd do a lot better than that', so really there's no comparison!"

16th July Kings Lynn v. Somerset (Premier League) 68-25

Hello sailor!

Home straight fence at dusk

CHAPTER 22.

Sheffield:
"We cancelled at 10 o'clock because of the weather and the forecast is for more rain at 6 or 7 o'clock."

17th July

After their mauling by King's Lynn and the injury to Emil Kramer, the Somerset Rebels wouldn't then relish a trip to the self-styled 'fastest speedway circuit in Britain', namely: Owlerton Stadium in Sheffield. After an uneventful drive from King's Lynn, I arrive inside the stadium grounds to discover almost eerie silence and absolutely none of the activity I would expect five hours before an important Premier League meeting. It's overcast and the sky is filled with clouds but the Met Office (along with the Internet forecaster Metcheck) promise a dry afternoon and evening. The track itself looks in perfect condition, albeit empty of tractors circling. Keen to find out more, I head to the Sheffield Speedway Office and find Neil Machin alone behind his desk speaking on the telephone and, simultaneously, studying the Rulebook. Neil also has a cigarette on the go as if the national workplace smoking ban never happened. Call over, the Sheffield speedway co-promoter casually jokes, "I might have known you were coming – as it's raining and the meeting is off! It was called off earlier at about 10 o'clock to save people travelling. It's a shame you didn't hear!" My hotel room is booked and paid for and so, since I already have the metaphorical ticket, I've no choice but to go along for the ride. I must admit it's 30 seconds since I stepped through the door but it definitely wasn't raining outside when I came into his office. Neil comes over all 'Michael Fish' with me, "We cancelled at 10 o'clock 'cause of the weather and the forecast is for more rain at 6 or 7 o'clock tonight." Neil definitely isn't his usual chipper self. Hardly a surprise given the recent shock tragic deaths of his close friends Darren and Sharon Boocock, who were killed on Friday July 4th in a road accident on the Maltby-Tickhill Road on the outskirts of Rotherham. Their funeral service will be held at Owlerton Stadium tomorrow. Grief at the shock news has been felt throughout the speedway world and weighs heavily on Neil. There are no easy words and no point to even attempt to find them. The speedway meeting against Somerset would have provided some, probably much needed, distraction but with the postponement, the stadium will certainly look in pristine, tip-top condition for the funeral tomorrow.

Despite his clear preoccupation, Neil makes a good host and, between the many phone calls, he draws deeply on a succession of cigarettes while he chats about the sport he knows and still often loves. Speedway, like life itself, is often shot through with sincerity and hypocrisy in equal measure and, in such a world, there's often no place or welcome for a candid man. Many speedway people pride themselves on their candour and, even by the standards of the sport, Neil is candid and plainly spoken to the point of bluntness. "This is a great stadium to work in. Without the greyhounds this stadium would be flattened. Massive revenue from gambling helps many stadiums throughout the country and they wouldn't open if they had to depend solely upon speedway. The fact of life is that speedway has to co-exist with other sports, like greyhounds. That's how it is! We do everything we can to let people in our local area know that we run on a Thursday and that the racing is fast and exciting here. We've got a big sign outside by the dual carriageway to catch the eye from the road. We've got a good relationship with the stadium landlords. In fact, I'd say we've got a better relationship than most 'cause we're on the same page more often than not. Since I've been here – the last 16 years – £10 million has been spent on the stadium because the landlords believe that they have to reinvest capital into the facilities. I'd say we have the best corporate facilities to market to businesses, even better than Poole. Speedway has been staged at this track forever. They laid down the speedway track in 1928 and it's been the same shape and size for the last 79 years. Our track is synonymous with close and exciting racing. I understand the place, and they understand speedway. One of the reasons why I'm still here is that I've always believed in the venue! Once upon a time, speedway revenues outweighed the greyhounds but that's no longer the case."

"The credit crunch brings out the cheating and sneaky elements in the sport – the elements that plague the sport –

but we've got a good business that we run well and have a fantastic stadium with landlords that are happy with us! You can never sit still and must change and adapt with fashion and the times. It's economically difficult at the moment but speedway should learn from other sports. Cricket has grown and changed itself and how it projects itself to the outside world and, most importantly, they've reinvented the product. In speedway we don't consider our patrons' existence in many aspects. We don't recreate things to attract new faces. Some people might dispute that. The way we structure and govern our sport relies upon majority voting. It's human nature that people will look after their own interests – often there's so much tunnel vision in the discussions we have. At last year's Annual Conference, it was perceived that some tracks had a home-track advantage. Without considering our patrons (and the new patrons we might wish to attract), we abolish the bonus point. In my opinion, it was the best rule we had and getting rid of it was one of the most unpopular things we've ever done! At Sheffield we used to sell meetings on the basis that while the result of the meeting wasn't in doubt it still meant something on aggregate. Only four tracks voted against its abolition – forgetting that, often, the bonus point took the meeting right up to the wire. A classic example is our [recent away] meeting at the Isle of Wight, which was dead and buried by heat 10. I think the riders lose a bit of urgency because of the bonus point going. It was considered [at the Annual Conference] on an opinionated basis without thinking of the ramifications of abandoning it. The shining light of the bonus point allowed us to enhance the package and sell a better product. It can't be denied that the bonus point gives an additional element of urgency to a meeting that otherwise would be over as a contest! Okay, last year, the only bonus point the 2007 Premier League champions dropped was to us when we snatched it in heat 15 at Rye House with a 4-2. The decision was a criminal act against speedway! I feel qualified to say that after 16 years. Len Silver, who has been in speedway all his life, was astounded. It's probably the most unpopular thing we've ever done and it was a decision probably taken without analysis. I think you'll find that, if they revisited the vote today, it would go a different way! We have to give ourselves every advantage to sell our product, to galvanise that interest on the terraces and get people there in the first place."

Cloudy sky

Rain forecast later

"If you've had a team thrashed out of sight it can't help but, then, some people just don't bother to go to the return fixture. We've always had piss-weak teams in speedway. Mildenhall are the present whipping boys – these crop up most years! It's not good for business but better than having no team at all in the league! All other sports when they change try to show progression, yet speedway goes backwards. Football introduced the penalty shoot-out, which is so popular. It gets attention; the fans like it and TV love it! Cricket looked at its old-fashioned product and realised that it would have to compete with other sports and appeal to a wider audience. They revamped the structure of their product, quite dramatically, and geared it towards a time when people can go along to it. Speedway has to measure its outgoings against the [economic] climate and provide a product we can demonstrate is value for money! We've all been to processional meetings where we think 'how can they get people here every week to watch this?' The bonus point helps that. One thing we lose when we lose crowd levels – apart from the revenues – is the atmosphere! You can't really get this with less than a thousand people as that number creates urgency, noise and banter. You get characters emerging from

---

Sheffield: *"We cancelled at 10 o'clock because of the weather and the forecast is for more rain at 6 or 7 o'clock."*

the terraces, who add to the whole thing, and you can present a product that's really entertaining! Once you've got over fifteen hundred, it really revs up further. We need to get back to grass roots 'cause we're in an economic downturn and people are careful about how they spend their money. As a sport we don't always help ourselves by not listening. There was the vote in the *Speedway Star* [in 2006] about tactical rides. There were fifteen hundred votes and 89 per cent wanted to get rid of the tactical rides, as it was generally perceived as a 'joke'! What do we do? We retain it! But adjust levels to 9 points in 2007 and then 10 points in 2008, but retain the tactical substitute ride at 8 points. Again, and this is typical, the implementation of the tactical ride was taken without examination as a pilot scheme in the KO Cup at Premier League level was waved aside. The Elite League adopted it in the name of commonality and we had to adopt it too."

I would ask Neil if he knows Yogi Berra's famous remark "we may be lost but we're making good time" but again we're interrupted, as we have been throughout our conversation, by the endless ringing of the phone. Neil adopts the attitude of an excited and informed telesales worker who treats each caller as though they're the only one to have asked about the status of the meeting. His voice is optimistic and, after he conveys his standard message, "We cancelled at 10 o'clock because of the weather and the forecast is for more rain at 6 or 7 o'clock" goes on to advise, "the next fixture at Owlerton will be the Premier League clash versus Newcastle." In the *Speedway Star*, Paul Rickett reported the postponement as the result of "another rain-hit Thursday. An overnight downpour left parts of the track under water and with the forecast for more heavy showers, there was no option other than to call the meeting off." Judged by the lack of precipitation outside the Sheffield Speedway Office, those blasted forecasters have misled the public again. When there's a brief respite from the phone calls, I quiz Neil on the fine weather. "There is gonna be a fine spell though the rain returns at 6 o'clock. 6 o'clock rain is the kiss of death, things go rapidly downhill from there. I can't tell you the number of calls I get when we've got a cloud in the sky – it's amazing. I even get calls the day before and from down the country if they've been having rain. But, that said, some of them that have been rained off shouldn't have been rained off! Birmingham freaked up their track. I'll put that differently; there can be track problems that can be seen as rain, like at Birmingham. Look at Redcar versus Sheffield. There was rain at 6 o'clock and it was called off at 6.20 and our fans drove back with clear skies in sunglasses. Unnecessary rain-offs are damaging to the whole problem of what we do. We have to stop educating people to think the odd shower means that it won't go ahead. There is the perception that some promoters think 'I'm cancelling 'cause people aren't turning up anyway'. The economic climate has made things hard and even I know what I think before I make a £50 round trip in the car. Speedway product in the summer is the period when there ain't no football and we get the improved weather. You can't do anything about the weather when it's against us but we've got to use our loaf. There should be more of an enquiry when meetings get cancelled not because of the weather. If people have confidence, they will travel – if not, they won't travel! Things like the bonus point are another reason not to travel. We are in the leisure industry and probably will be the first to feel the draught. With the economy, the wheels haven't fallen off the wagon yet but it could be five years before we recover. I've been in business a while and I've never experienced the sort of thing the world banks are experiencing right now."

Stadium manager, Ken Trench pops into the office and Neil tells me "He's the stadium manager but I always introduce him as the stadium owner!" Ken has arrived to confirm the arrangements for the Sharon and Darren Boocock funeral tomorrow. Neil tells Ken, "I'm going to the Chapel of Rest at 3.30 to organise things for tomorrow. There's a 12.30 service at the track and a wake in the Panorama Room – in between it's friends and family only to the Crematorium. It's freaking savage! Devastating! Like losing family and friends just in one phone call! It's tragic, there's just no other word for it – it's tragic! It's hard for us but what about their 12-year-old? There's gonna be some very dark times in the foreseeable future. It's freaking savage, mate." Neil invites me to come along and brushes off my objection that I don't have any suitable clothes with me. "Everybody's welcome, it doesn't matter what you look like or what you're dressed like. The service is open to everybody. The Crematorium is friends and family but, if you've got the time, come to the wake which is also here in the Panorama Room."

The phone rings and, for once, it's not a weather query! The call goes on for quite some time and I only hear the fragments from one side of the conversation. "Yeah, it's rained off." [Pause] "It's a disruption. We've got a bloody big job to do in the second part of the season." [Pause] "I know." [Pause] "We just haven't been there, we just haven't been good enough!" [Pause] "It ain't the same problem, it moves through the team like bloody wildfire!" [Pause]

Sheffield: *"We cancelled at 10 o'clock because of the weather and the forecast is for more rain at 6 or 7 o'clock."*

"Technical set-ups." [Pause] "Every track has home-track advantage. If you've got a bloody good team and they're buzzing, they'll be difficult to beat." [Pause] "To be top of the averages you have to be good home and away." [Pause] "It was s'posed to be Somerset. They got 25 away at King's Lynn, bloody rubbish!" [Pause] "There was a time 15 years ago when we used to dream of winning at home, you've got to have the team to do the job, don't ya?" [Pause] "Well, shit tends to put big scores by Paul Cooper's name and slick tracks don't!" [Pause] "And yeah, you're not the only one to identify that!" [Pause] "Andre Compton has more maximums at home than any other speedway rider in the Premier League! But, you're right, he's gone a bit off the boil and, I think, it's his mechanical team. We're in professional motor sports and, if you don't keep and maintain things, you fall behind!" [Pause] "Yeah, you assume that." [Pause] "Yeah, riders like Ben Wilson. They spend a lot more time in the workshop 'cause they're chasing his butt and want his job! He can be inconsistent too, still. Gets one point at Reading but 14 the next night at the Isle of Wight!" [Pause, draws deeply on his cigarette] "Why don't you help Lee Smethills and Kyle Hughes? [Pause] "When I can afford seven engines, I'll buy them all an engine and fuel. It will cost you 20 grand and you don't have to fall into bloody favouritism!" [Pause] "Well, the answer is, I often get asked this, and we're as good as the opposition allows us."

"The views I get over this phone! At least, you get some feedback – even if they're completely wrong! Where were we? Ah yeah. It's attention to detail and, if you don't get that right, things go wrong. The credibility of our sport is in our hands and, if we don't get the details right, it could be in jeopardy. There's the old saying 'credibility is like virginity – one cock up and it's gone!' For example, I don't do GPs. I went to the first-ever British GP at Hackney in 1995 and it was a complete freak up. I took major sponsors, took them to the restaurant at huge expense and we couldn't see the meeting from the restaurant – basic stuff. Some seats outside got wet 'cause of the roof. The PA system was a problem and parking was a nightmare. I damaged my own credibility with my sponsors going. With the GP nowadays it's very much an 'us' and 'them' situation between the FIM and the domestic product. There's no consideration at all! And hey, domestic product is really the nuts and bolts of what we do. Years ago, a rider wouldn't even think of going abroad if they had a British League meeting and, now, they've acquired this position where they expect a British promoter to cancel the meeting! Speedway riders are drawn from the society of which they're a part. The rewards of being World Champion mean that corners will be cut to win – on the track and off it! At the moment, some of them don't need British speedway like they used to, so, they're not gonna have the commitment – if they're here at all! I've never had any time for John Postlethwaite. I've always thought he was a complete arsehole based on my experience of a shared event at Sheffield. We staged the opening of the World Cup series about five years ago. He just sat in the BSI area, his feet on the desk and watched it on the telly. He didn't come out, didn't say 'hello' or shake anyone's hand. The tail wags the dog and, with the riders, we've lost discipline. An early decision should have been made to eradicate those problems. Someone with the arrogance of John Postlethwaite isn't going to listen. He went to Reading to show us all how to do it, he couldn't have made a bigger freak up if he tried! Then there's Paul Bellamy, who lives in the shadow of John Postlethwaite and all his knowledge. They've inflated everyone's costs with riders and failed to put people on the terraces. That's the most important thing – 'cause, ultimately, it makes all the problems go away!"

If the lobby to retain the bonus point enjoyed the success of a campaign for a clean-shaven Santa, then what exactly the structure of British speedway will be in 2009 is already the equivalent hot topic around the country. I quiz Neil on talk of some teams possibly breaking away. "Why the freak would you want to break away from your own Association? Rather than there even be talk of a breakaway, maybe we should redesign the BSPA to do what it says on the label! We're an Association so all members are equal members! Though, it's a little bit like *Animal Farm* – where some members are more equal than others. Our constitution states we're all equal. I've only ever wanted to be treated in an equal way. I don't want to manipulate or cheat to get an advantage. People talking about that [the breakaway] in a glib way doesn't address anything. Our Association is affiliated via the FIM to the RAC and to the ACU. People don't consider the ramifications. If we're not happy, we need to sort things out ourselves. If the decision-making process is flawed you change the decision-making process. I don't agree with some of the practices of our industry and, every time I suggest change, I end up with a fine. I'm never going to agree with a situation where people get individual and private benefits at the expense of the Association. The decision-making board are elected to protect the interest of the members, if they don't and we don't like what they do, we have to re-elect others. If then we don't like them, we have to blame ourselves. The management committee is there to protect the Association. It's

---

Sheffield: *"We cancelled at 10 o'clock because of the weather and the forecast is for more rain at 6 or 7 o'clock."*

a big responsibility. When I did it, I found myself doing things against the interests of my business but for the benefit of the sport. Creating rules is one thing; manipulation – interpreting them – is another! The manipulation of the written word and what it's supposed to mean goes on all the time. [Taps the SCB Promoter Guide on his desk] That's just to help – the important document is the SCB Rulebook. We do have to ask ourselves if there are too many rules. I know how our Rulebook came about. It was to eradicate every fiddle that every manager and promoter has developed over 40 years to gain advantage. Referees have to consult their Rulebooks just to sort a situation at the meeting, it's madness! We're in a simple sport. It's four blokes on motorbikes doing four laps round an oval! Willy-nilly modification of rules isn't the way to go and, if we lose that level of understanding on the terraces – and it all comes back to how many people you have on the terraces, that's the most important thing – and when we forget that we've forgotten everything!"

17th July Sheffield v. Somerset (Premier League) Postponed

Sheffield: *"We cancelled at 10 o'clock because of the weather and the forecast is for more rain at 6 or 7 o'clock."*

CHAPTER 23.

Sheffield:
"If you want to copy Darren – be encouraging!"

18th July

Notionally a summer's day, the Hillsborough area of Sheffield was dull, overcast and it was a day that friends and family wished weren't happening. Well over an hour before the service, the Owlerton Stadium car park was crowded and the mourners stood round in small sombre groups gathered together in the large area adjacent to the turnstiles. The stadium itself looked smart and well kept. The centre-green grass was lush, the track smooth, manicured and void of all activity. The spick and span emptiness of the stadium created an atmosphere of solemnity and, in the shadows of the home-straight grandstand, there was an air of mournful expectation. On the sloped floor of the terrace two parallel lines of 10 chairs were lined up with military precision to face the start-line area, slightly obscured by a presentation plinth located on top of the dog-track wall from which the minister would later speak and from where the eulogies would be given. With a bunch of flowers, lectern and microphone displayed on one side and, in pride of place on the other, was a gleaming solitary speedway bike dressed in the colours and logo of Darren Boocock's company OzChem. It dominated the plinth and was, clearly, a symbol of Darren's riding career but also of the help and inspiration he provided to a legion of other riders – from juniors to World Champions. The bike faced in the direction it would have to if it were to be ridden in a race round the Owlerton speedway track. Stood ceremonially on the plinth, it graphically signalled that Darren and Sharon's race had already run but also that they'd travelled far and fast in an incredibly short time. Laid by the front wheel was a large bouquet of flowers.

The service took place exactly two weeks after the tragedy and, even since the day before, Neil Machin appeared to have aged. Along with Dave Hoggart, he'd come round for a final check that everything is ready and perfectly in place. Dave looked shell-shocked and Neil seemed bereft as he stared at the scene in front of him. [Deep sigh] "Bloody hell!" he uttered, looking sightlessly into the distance.

[Dave, forcing a smile] "It's a first at Owlerton!"

[Neil] "It's one we could have done without!"

[Dave] "Everyone wanted it here."

[Neil, approaches empty line of chairs and rattles one absentmindedly] "Is there enough chairs?"

[Dave] "There's enough chairs."

Neil ran through a detailed checklist of questions with Dave in stream-of-consciousness fashion.

[Dave] "Don't worry; the Funeral Directors have done everything wonderfully!"

Lost in thought, Neil walked forward to look wistfully at the solitary speedway bike. Also on the podium, the minister conducted his last check of the lectern and established whether the microphone worked. Neil looked distant and walked off back in the direction of the Speedway Office, probably to keep himself distracted with other last-minute checks. He passed through the ever-increasing but already sizeable crowd that was gathering quietly by the turnstiles. Solicitous, even at a time of great stress, Dave Hoggart told me, "Neil is broken up! You won't get any sense from him today. If he says anything, he'll repeat himself!" Dave reassured me that the funeral service for Sharon and Darren is open to everyone and will be held without dress code. "Everyone is welcome at the service today. Those that have come in T-shirts were probably the closest to them! Equally, lots of other friends have come really dressed up. People can pay their respects however they like."

Six days after the shock news rocked family and friends, the Sheffield programme for the meeting versus Redcar – starring Darren's good friend Gary Havelock – contained a moving and sincere tribute from Neil "and all at Sheffield

Speedway". It read as follows:

"WORDS simply aren't enough to describe how everyone at Sheffield Speedway – and indeed EVERYONE throughout the speedway world – feels following the tragic deaths of Darren and Sharon Boocock.

Darren has been part of the fixtures and fittings here at Owlerton for many, many years – while Sharon was also a keen speedway fan, the couple having actually met here at Owlerton when Darren first came over from Australia's Gold Coast to try and make his way as a junior rider.

They were subsequently married 15 years ago and have a lovely son in 12 year-old Jack.

Last Friday's accident, on the Maltby-Tickhill Road on the outskirts of Rotherham stunned people around the globe.[1]

In short, Darren was one of speedway's great characters and the grief in the wake of the tragedy was a measure of just how much everyone thought of him.

He was like family to me and was a friend to everyone.

Of course, after hanging up his leathers through injury he went on to become an inspiration to a legion of top riders – helping out juniors right up to World Champions. Thursday nights just won't be the same.

His OzChem logo has been seen around the sport for several years with Darren having sponsored a legion of riders.

Grand Prix star Greg Hancock said this week that Darren touched the hearts and minds of so many people. He was bang on.

We will all miss Darren and Sharon so very much and our thoughts at this terrible time are with young Jack."

Neil and Dave were occupied elsewhere when the hearses arrived in stately fashion at the far side of Owlerton Stadium. At a snail's pace, they carefully took to the track and drove into position, one behind the other – adjacent to what would be the start-line area. The car park was as crowded as it would be on a race night. (Dave Hoggart remarked afterwards "It was a big enough crowd for us to hold a Conference League meeting!") Indeed, a huge crowd of people have gathered to patiently wait for the signal to move round to the home-straight grandstand to where the funeral service will take place. Conversation was muted. Some people were in tears, while others had a last-minute cigarette, exchanged hushed words or remained expressionless. It was a veritable Who's Who of Speedway, though the crowd was way too big to even attempt to begin to identify people, let alone that it would have been rude to stare at a time of great upset and grief. Barry Briggs was there, looking dapper, but sombre. I noticed many familiar faces among the mourners. I will have missed many speedway people amongst the throng, but the mourners included: Gary Havelock, Glyn Taylor, Steve Johnston, Andre Compton, Neil Collins, Chris Van Stratten, Colin Pratt, Ricky Ashworth, Carl Stonehewer, Sean Wilson and Laurence Rogers. At the back of a crush of people spread across the terrace, I found myself stood next to Nigel who'd watched the sport for 45 years since he went to his first meeting aged 6. "Nigel Boocock was my idol as a boy and I'm named after him. It runs in the family. I started at Long Eaton, then followed Leicester and then Long Eaton before I moved to Lincoln and started to watch Sheffield. My mum came to watch Sheffield a couple of times in 2007 – she was aged 81 when she died in November 2007." You instantly gathered from the size of the crowd, just how many different lives and networks both Darren and Sharon had touched in their lives. Nigel continued, "Darren didn't stand on ceremony and he certainly didn't

---

[1] The *Speedway Star* later reported: "A verdict of accidental death has been recorded after an inquest into the tragic crash which killed Darren and Sharon Boocock last July. It was a decision to overtake on a notorious road that cost the lives of both Darren and his pillion-passenger wife. Darren (40), the son of Nigel Boocock and friend to a catalogue of top riders, may have failed to spot the second of two identical articulated red lorries coming in the opposite direction on Tickhill Road, between Maltby and Tickhill on the outskirts of Rotherham. Seeing one lorry go past, Darren pulled out to overtake a slow-moving, high-sided Ford Transit and trailer on his Triumph Sprint bike and crashed head-on into the following wagon. As Darren braked hard, his machine slid under the wheels of the lorry, the driver braked and tried to avoid it, but the couple were killed almost instantly. According to an accident expert, Darren may have had a view across the fields of what was ahead and mixed up one heavy goods vehicle for the other. "The rider either did not see either of the goods vehicles or more likely only noted the second one and mistook this for the first lorry to pass him, thinking the road was clear," Pc Greg Beatson said at the inquest in Rotherham. "Unfortunately it wasn't, there was an identical vehicle in front." The two lorries, travelling about 150 to 200 yards apart, were not excessively close, he added. Pc Beatson added: "The rider may have seen one vehicle and assumed there was only one when in fact there were two." Recording a verdict of accidental death, coroner Fred Curtis said Darren's decision to overtake was "flawed" in all the circumstances. But he stressed that he was equally satisfied that the problem was not that he had been riding at high speed, but simply his decision to overtake.

Sheffield: *"If you want to copy Darren – be encouraging!"*

superstar it! On a Saturday he'd be at a Grand Prix and then, on the Thursday, he'd be helping second-halfers in the pits! He was just as at home with the best as he was with those that could hardly ride a bike! It's unusual to have such a sombre event in a place of great happiness but, given the person he was, I'm sure that's what Darren would have wanted!"

Pretty well everyone in attendance at the service appeared to have the stylish but understated cream coloured Order of Service provided by John Heath & Sons, the Sheffield-based funeral directors. It featured a colour photograph of Darren and Sharon on the cover and inside was the Order of Service, conducted by the Vicar of Owlerton, The Reverend Nick Dawson. Nick was definitely local and rejoiced in his work at the imposing church located on the opposite side of the car park to the stadium. Some mourners stared intently at the Order of Service throughout, as if to look up would somehow cause disruption. Others looked blankly lost in thoughtful grief, clutched their Order of Service and appeared not to see it or anything else. Family and friends filled the reserved rows of chairs specially placed in front of the plinth and the remainder of the crowd enveloped these mourners. Some of the people at the service had taken the day off, while others had clearly had come straight from work – whether it was from offices, shops or building sites. It was definitely standing room only in this section of Owlerton Stadium and, 10 minutes before the service begins, a dull and overcast day suddenly brightened when the sun broke through the cloud. It lifted the atmosphere and bathed the hearses in weak sunlight.

Poignant memorial

Difficult choices had been made for the funeral service itself from the hymns to the prayers and Bible readings. For those chosen to speak, what to say in the eulogies is an altogether more difficult task. The modern way of death and its commemoration is for music to be played but, before the first note sounded, the minister Nick Dawson asked us all to "come a little closer" and gently advised, "there's plenty of room on the other side of the chairs in this stadium." The funeral service got under way to the sound of Dido's *White Flag*, which played loudly over the speaker system. Whether it was the sound of the music, signalling that the service had started that finally confirmed Sharon and Darren's premature demise as hard fact, or the lyrics themselves, many mourners were suddenly in tears. To my right, one lady was inconsolable. Though the man with her offered comfort and the warmth of his presence, he was also quietly crying. The lyrics of the song suddenly sounded evocative and poignant as though somehow freshly crafted and written specially for Darren and Sharon. Over the stadium speaker system, Dido sang the opening line of her song, "I know you think that I shouldn't still love you" in slightly staccato fashion. It would have been a hard-hearted person who remained unmoved. I wouldn't care to speculate which of the other lyrics resonated the strongest with family or friends. There were many evocative commitments about love ("No I won't put up my hands and surrender"), there were affirmations of love, ("I'm in love and always will be") and also one that's just plain incorrect but with, the sudden finality of death, sounds poignantly evocative, "I know I left too much mess and destruction to come back again". Like Dido, many people would have "gone down with the ship" if it could have meant that Darren and Sharon could return but, instead, we were all caught in grief and reminded of our collective mortality.

Funeral cortège

Order of Service

The opening prayers were followed by the hymn *Abide With Me* written by H.F. Lyte (but wrongly attributed to W.H. Monk in the Order of Service). This hymn is a tribute to the love of the Lord in life and in death. We were then all treated to a eulogy given by Sharon Wadsworth on behalf of Darren's sisters Vicki and Mandi. If people weren't moved by their memories then they were certainly stirred by Sharon Wadsworth's moving and heartfelt tribute to Darren. Without notes all I can now recall from a wonderful address – that mixed humour, plain speaking and stoicism in the face of sudden loss – is that Darren was an enthusiastic and mischievous child. He had an Australian twang, "he was often in plaster as a child" and apparently, quite significantly, "he had a fascination with fire". He loved life without reservation – he relished fun and danger in equal proportions in the same enthusiastic way that he relished his friends. Darren was always wholehearted and his advice to go-karters he'd only met three months before typified him: "Forget Top 10 – aim for the podium!" The most fortunate event of his life was, we were told, the day that he met Sharon who completed him and also calmed him. Sharon Wadsworth said so much, so movingly in her eulogy that it's hard to pick out any one thing from a wealth of memories and reminiscences. One phrase that was hard to forget was "Your big or, should I say, elder sister said: 'You were my best brother, my only brother'…"

A friend and colleague of Sharon's, Sue Zahra-Hall then also gave a wonderful eulogy. It too was a heartfelt and moving speech that Sue prefaced with: "I make absolutely no apologies for going on at length." This was true in a sense but not anything that you'd notice, let alone apologise for, given its absorbing nature. We learnt many tiny but human details about Sharon's life. These included: her skill as a PA; how she remembered everyone at work; how she liked to work hard and play hard; her 104 words per minute; how she was dead easy to get on with but, also, how incredibly fondly she was recalled by her work colleagues. She was the life and soul of all and every party, whether birthdays, impromptu drinks with friends or traditional festivities like Christmas. She was Darren's soul mate and life partner, his helper and his friend. Sue had promised that she would not give in to her emotions. But, after she uttered the words, "The greatest honour of my life was when I was asked to be Jack's godmother" she broke down. How she managed to last that long was a testament to her determination to memorialise her friend with dignity and sincerity but, most of all, with a clarity that would try to capture the essence of Sharon in a way that combined broad brush strokes with meticulous detail. Neither speaker wore rose-coloured spectacles but only identified possible perceived 'faults' to magnify the brilliance of the complete package. If Darren got into scrapes and broke bones, then Sharon's downfall was her inability to cook. If you can laugh out loud at a funeral service – or, at least, feel like laughing out loud – then that's probably one of the sincerest signs of love, respect and common humanity at a time of great grief.

After the eulogies, the Bible reading was taken from the fine Psalm 139 ('Domine, probasti'). It is a moving psalm and contains many pithy quotations. *"Yea, the darkness hideth not from thee; but the night shineth as the day"* and *"Thine eyes did see my substance, yet being unperfect; and in thy book all my members were written, which in continuance were fashioned, when as yet there was none of them"*. Interestingly, this was the old King James Authorized Version rather than the new-fangled modern version that has prospered like a form of religious Leylandii. This psalm is also commonly truncated before verse 19 and its invariably inappropriate phrase, *"depart from me, ye bloody men"*. The minister then gave the address and this was as far from the norm or traditional expectation as the choice of Owlerton Stadium was as the venue for the funeral service location. The Reverend Nick Dawson spoke for some time. He demonstrated good oratorical skills, expressed his sympathies for the bereaved with compassion and, through his words, reverenced the deceased. In passing he mentioned that he'd lost his own daughter, Hannah, so could appreciate and sympathise with the pain of loss and bereavement felt by family or friends. In lesser hands, this sad personal experience could have been mawkish (or a cue for further tears) but the minister drew the powerful lesson that unexpected premature death, while a fact of life, was no less hard to bear. Clearly accustomed to conducting funeral events, the Reverend Nick Dawson used some stock phrases but, rather than sound stilted and churchly, in a speedway setting they somehow sounded typically Yorkshire! We heard how religion and belief in God was, "Not pie in the sky when you die but steak on your plate while you wait!" And at the end of his peroration, the minister provided a lesson for those who hadn't already learnt it and who wanted to take some hope from the tragic situation, "If you want to copy Darren – be encouraging!"

Prayers were followed by an adapted poem by David Harkins that advised, we can "smile because they have lived" and also suggested we can open our eyes to "see all that they have left". After the blessing, Dave Hoggart then had the unenviable task to read out what, in older less technologically advanced days, would be called telegrams. These were from Ivan 'Sprouts' Mauger as well as Nigel and Cynthia Boocock. After so many heartfelt speeches it's difficult to bring the words of others to life but Dave calls upon his presentational skills, to convey the sincerity of the messages. *Onward Christian Soldiers* closes the service. Some people sang with gusto, whereas others mouthed the words or stood lost in their own thoughts. For those that could remain behind, the instructions were "Please stay for refreshments. The family will join you following the private committal." And if wished, all donations should be made to the Bluebell Wood Children's Hospice.

In the back of the Order of Service, there was a message from Neil Machin headed "A MAN WHO IS RICH IN PERSONALITY WILL NEVER BE A POOR PERSON…".

It reads as follows:

"Darren and Sharon Boocock…I am privileged to have been a part of their lives – and of their family's lives – since their teenage years.

I've always walked a million miles in their shoes, always with an objective to be a positive and progressive influence on their lives.

I was proud to be the Best Man at their wedding 17 years ago and, like everyone here today, I have many stories, mostly humorous which, will last a lifetime.

Darren was always the extrovert, with unparalleled social and communication skills. He was the life and soul of any gathering, while Sharon was the stabilising influence. The 'handbrake'. A perfect partnership.

Jack Boocock will carry the family name forward for generations to come, with the same sparkle and enthusiasm, the same wit and humour that will always be the hallmark of our memory of Darren and Sharon."

18th July, Owlerton Stadium, Sheffield

CHAPTER 24.

Wolverhampton v. Eastbourne:
"I did my spell pushing – everybody does!"

21st July

A trip to Monmore Green to watch the Elite League B fixture between Wolverhampton and Eastbourne promised to feature close and exciting racing, particularly given that both teams race on similarly sized tracks. Politely referred to in the industry as 'technical' tracks – usually taken to mean small and difficult to ride (except by the home riders) – both circuits are famed for the quality of their track preparations undertaken by curatorial experts Bob Dugard and Alan 'Doc' Bridgett. Eastbourne still have an outside chance to compete in the end-of-season play-offs at the top of the Elite League, while (even though it's still a comparatively early stage of the season) Wolverhampton already look highly likely to feature in the relegation play-offs. If the season is to be extended into further possibly lucrative play days for the Eastbourne riders then this is a must-win meeting. Wolverhampton also need to emerge victorious as part of their campaign to avoid the possible embarrassment of participation in the inaugural (but lucrative) end-of-season play-offs.

My trip to Wolverhampton was given some additional context by the *Sun* newspaper, which warned, "Fellows beware if you go to Wolverhampton – it's the home of Britain's worst gold-diggers." In this, no doubt, highly selective and unrepresentative survey a staggering 22 per cent of the girls interviewed said they would rather date for money than love. They're clearly optimists since their ideal man apparently earns at least £300,000 a year! An Internet dating site the *Sun* identified as primarily "for the Rich" conducted the survey but they clearly haven't received any good quality marketing advice since they've lumbered themselves with the rather tawdry-sounding URL www.golddiggers.uk.com. My rudimentary understanding of so-called 'gold-diggers' is that should you be suitably wealthy then they would invariably find you without any need to log on to a website. The same article continued to be shocked at the rather common-sense news that "a quarter of all those girls" surveyed, "would not look at somebody who was skint." Even if you ignore the statistical size of this survey, I have reservations about its methodology, given the places it identified as 'gold-digger' central. Wolverhampton definitely wouldn't be the first name that sprang to my mind[1] but, then, neither would second-placed Plymouth. Belfast, Portsmouth and Glasgow closely follow in the survey results. Based on per capita income it's a surprise that the more chichi parts of, say, London, Bath or Edinburgh conspicuously fail to feature. If a speedway town was to be nominated in this survey, beforehand I would have guessed in would be Poole!

I arrive at Monmore Green Stadium just after 2 o'clock on a scorching hot summer's afternoon. I immediately report to the speedway office where I find the Wolves team manager, Peter Adams, in the shade and already hard at work behind a desk there. He advises that Chris Van Straaten won't arrive till about 5.15, when he'll be occupied with his preparations for the meeting. Though I'm early, Dave Rattenberry and John Rich clearly arrived much earlier since the frame of the trackshop has been erected, the plastic cladding sides and roof have been attached and the majority of stock has already been unloaded from their large white transit van. Dave's driven here in the van and his recently purchased rather deluxe Mercedes is conspicuous by its absence. John informs me "Gareth Rogers has just bought Dave's old car off him for £500. One of Gareth's relatives is in the business of cleaning them." Graham Williams, who also works in the Wolverhampton trackshop, arrives shortly afterwards to add his creative flair to the merchandise displays. While John Rich puts out the stock, Dave tells me, "Say what you like, Andy Griggs keeps a lovely looking trackshop! A bloke the other day was complaining to me about how bare the King's Lynn shop was. I always say it's best to stock quality merchandise 'cause then people'll be prepared to buy the stuff." My mother warned me years ago that politics are everywhere, "even cleaning toilets." Brief partisan analysis of his competitors over, Dave turns

[1] There's trouble on the horizon on the Black Country dating scene since a survey, a few weeks later, appeared in the *Sun* that claimed Wolverhampton men were the fourth 'Most Romantic' in the country. Hull was named as the place with the most romantic men.

his attention to the stock displays of his own trackshop and gestures at some wristbands as he instructs John Rich, "I don't think we need this cheap stuff out front here – we need some programme boards or something like that!" John retorts sharply, "You'd say that no matter what I put out!" The shop is festooned in the gold-and-black club colours of Wolverhampton speedway. Giant bulldog clips hold a selection of scarves in place on the stall pelmet. The "Wolverhampton Speedway" versions I'd expect have due prominence but there's also a Peter Karlsson scarf that features the Swedish flag. Whether Dave is merely selling off surplus inventory or has started a subtle campaign for Peter to rejoin the club isn't clear.

The stall definitely acts as a magnet for everyone who arrives early at the stadium whether they're on the staff or, later when the turnstiles open, one of the fans. Speedway is never short of characters or stories. Dave Rattenberry is always keen to point me in the direction of people with a wealth of speedway stories. I don't get to learn these from Graham Williams but do catch Kevin Davies, who's "a very, very, very, very big Sam Ermolenko fan." He first came to Monmore Green Stadium in 1968 and, for the last three or four years, he's been Pits Marshal. "Since 1984 I've done various things here, raking and stuff. I did my spell pushing – everybody does! We've got our own pushers down here for red, blue, green and yellow. I've never been able to ride a bike so I've kept my hand in by helping out in any way I can. We're a close-knit family here and that's part of the fun! What makes Monmore great is the good viewing, the fans are great and also the management is top notch. Winning the League and Cup double in 1996 stands out. Things have changed! Obviously, the speeds have got quicker and, from what I've seen, the originality has gone out of speedway! The chrome adverts they used to have on the farings – that used to gleam under the lights (I was only 10 when I first came) – have gone nowadays and, I think, we're poorer for it! It's hard to say who my favourite riders would be. When I first came here, it's a toss-up between Peter Vandenberg and Hassie Holmqvist (don't ask me how you spell it!). They were my heroes then, I can't tell you why. Sam Ermolenko is my ultimate hero! I got me son down here when he was 3 or 4 in 1986 (he's 26 this month) and Sam always had the time to speak to us and used to spot us everywhere. No matter how busy he was, he always had time for the fans and was always approachable. He rode here recently in the 80th Anniversary meeting and, I still say, he could do a job for somebody in the Premier League! But, after all the knocks he's had, it's probably best he doesn't take the risk now. Now, uh, uh no, I don't set my stall by anyone since Sam retired. I say, 'if they show up and are trying then that's what you want!' You don't need riders that go some places, don't gate and just tilt round – that's not very good! It's harder for the fans nowadays to go all over. Like everything else, it's the cost, isn't it? I used do meetings seven days a week but I couldn't afford to do that now!"

Like many people bitten by the speedway bug Kevin has a memorabilia collection that, in his case, specialises in speedway tabards. "I've just got the 80th Anniversary Lindgren tabard which is another for the collection. I have 25 or 26 tabards. I have Sam's last Wolves one down here, and his last but one American one (I think he only rode the qualifier in the World Team Cup). I think the Missus paid £170 for that American one! Most of them are from Testimonials: Knudsen, Steve Johnston and that. I did my staircase with them but, they got in the way, and people kept knocking them down. I have two of

Track tlc

John Rich with Freddie Lindgren fan, Kayleigh Jones

Wolverhampton v. Eastbourne: *"I did my spell pushing – everybody does!"*

Sam's race jackets from the League and Cup double (the spare ones) and George Stancl's." I ask Kevin whether Nicki Pedersen will ever return to Monmore Green. "I've got mixed feelings on that score. He has calmed down quite a bit. I've always got on well with him and my son, Chris, absolutely loves him! He's an out-and-out number 1 but, rumour has it, he's priced himself out of the market!" Clubs, like riders, endure their peaks and troughs, "This season hasn't started so well for us but, I think, they'll turn it round. To be honest with you, no matter what the score, we always get good speedway here. Proper racing and entertainment and track preparation! You can't say that of other places! It's that bad at Coventry I won't go there, as the racing is 'follow the leader' and a dust bowl. I only went to Steve Johnston's [Testimonial] meeting to get the tabard. I know I'm biased but you can't beat the speedway we get here at Wolverhampton."

Though Kevin has arrived many hours early, his duties in the pits require that he can't really hang around to gossip. Though the turnstiles have yet to open, there's already a gaggle of loyal Wolves fans gathered round the trackshop gossiping. One of them is Dave 'The Hat' Haddon who's a collector of speedway baseball caps. "I started collecting them in 1996 when I went to Czechoslovakia for the Golden Helmet. I bought about 40 and started from there. At home I don't have wallpaper, just baseball caps! At the moment I've got 7037 of them. It's not just speedway, I also have them for football, ice hockey, tennis, cricket, Formula 1, oh, and the Speedway Grand Prix. One of my favourites is Ayrton Senna's national cap. Really, I just love collecting them. At home, I've got a new fitted wardrobe in the spare bedroom full of them. I try to wear a different one to work each day [tonight he wears a Niels-Kristian Iversen STENA cap]. Unfortunately, I finish work a week on Wednesday. I'm a locksmith. I'm gonna have a holiday for the time being and then get me a little job.[2] The most I've paid for a cap was Michael Schumacher's, it was 50 quid and it has all the years round the peak when he won. I've been coming here since 1961, when I was 13. I missed the first two meetings and came to the MG Trophy, which was won by Ron Taylor. Monmore was the closest to where I lived. I've been to nearly all the tracks, apart from the new ones. Tommy Sweetman was my favourite rider when I first came here but the best rider Wolves have ever had here – without a doubt – is Sam Ermolenko. He was a brilliant rider and a brilliant team man. There's also been a few bad riders – the worst has to be Johan Fransden (in the '70s). He was Danish and he was rubbish! As I say, there's been a few bad riders but he stands out. I don't think it's proper speedway nowadays, it's just power! I much preferred the '60s and '70s. There was better speedway then. This year it's looking like relegation but, hopefully, we can pull out of it. I will still be here next year, come what may! I love the sport and I love the people. I'm a season-ticket holder. I've asked Dave to do me a cap for the 80th Anniversary but, he wouldn't do them, so I got the badge instead." Dave 'The Hat' breaks off our conversation to call over to Dave 'The Rat' Rattenberry, "Dave – get them caps done! Or, do me one!" Dave Rat makes no commitment or comment, except "Ha! Ha! Ha!"

There's a strict race-day regimen adhered to at Monmore Green Stadium so, by early evening, there's a queue of white riders' vans in the car park while they patiently wait for the pits entrance gates to open so they can gain admittance. Also in a queue in the sunshine are a substantial number of speedway fans who wait for the turnstiles to open. When they do, there's a rush of people towards the pits areas and also into the deluxe grandstand facilities that they boast at this stadium. Built to accommodate the greyhound punters in comfort and luxury, it's similar to the opulence provided at speedway clubs like Poole and Birmingham who also share stadiums primarily run for the purpose of greyhound racing. The always-friendly I.C.A. Crook (aka Mushy Pea), who shares trackshop duties at Buxton speedway with John Rich, stops by my book display for a chat. After he wanders off, rather shockingly John Rich informs me that he's made his mind up to retire from his duties in the Rattenberry speedway trackshop empire. "I'm 65 next July and, I always said, I was gonna retire at 65. I have some investments that mature when I'm 65 or 66, so I'll be all right. I didn't want to do half a season, so I'm retiring at the end of this season. I'll still do Buxton and help out but I'd prefer to use my free passes on the buses and trains to see people. Also, I can watch all the speedway meetings I want rather than work at them and miss some of the races! When I left school, I was a milkman before I worked in a factory. I didn't enjoy that and said I'd never go back but, then, I got a job driving and working in a factory. I did so much driving I was always out. I started at 6 or 6.30 in the morning and finished at 3 p.m. I went and

[2] Five lever mortice locks are the best. Some insurance companies won't insure you without them. They're supposed to be the most secure. Whether they are or not I don't know. But, it's £50 or £60 for a good one!"

Wolverhampton v. Eastbourne: *"I did my spell pushing – everybody does!"*

had my food at the factory to talk to people but I didn't work in there. I intend to enjoy my retirement like I always said I would!"

In-demand speedway presenter, technician and colour man, Shaun Leigh, stops for a few words. He's been disappointed by the performance of Team GB in the Speedway World Team Cup but, overall, enjoyed what he'd seen. "You'd have thought with so many Coventry 'track specialists' in the team that some of them could have done something on the night! I watched the WTC final on the Sunday morning and really enjoyed it. Riders were passing each other left and right and going for it! There was some really exciting racing. But, they went to the commercials after heat 21 and when they came back it was the presentation ceremony so we missed four heats completely. I don't know what *Sky* were playing at!" Wolverhampton's club inspires such passionate support that even newspaper seller Peter Blackwell has considerable knowledge, insight and expertise about speedway generally, let alone just his local club. To maximise attention (and, hopefully, sales), Peter has parked his bright red transit van at the bottom of one of the two sets of stairs that lead up into the entrance area of the posh grandstand. Not only is the vehicle an eye-catching bright red colour but also it's emblazoned with a distinctive giant image of the *Express and Star* newspaper. Like many local newspapers, they support the various teams and sports active within their readership area. Consequently, they give Wolverhampton speedway considerable coverage. Sadly, they no longer have the country's most elegant speedway writer, Tim Hamblin, regularly on the case (as their main speedway reporter) although he's not completely lost to the sport since he writes the "Media View" in the Wolves programme each week. Pete unloads a bright red metal stall from the side doors of the van and proceeds to do a brisk trade with tonight's edition of the *Express and Star*. "Sales have been good all season! I like coming here but, then, my son [Scott Blackwell] used to ride. He liked riding at King's Lynn, 'cause it was fast and safe and there was enough room for everyone. He's moved to Australia now. They don't get the rain-offs there but, sometimes, it's too hot to race! He was in Adelaide but has now moved to Queensland. We mean to visit him but haven't got around to it yet. But we will. No matter how Wolves do, the paper always gives them good coverage!"

A small but perfectly formed group of keenly dedicated Eastbourne fans have made the long journey up from the South Coast to see the Eagles ride in the West Midlands against Wolves. Andy Ling the father of the hard-working Eastbourne Eagles Press Officer, Kevin, is one of the fanatics who has travelled up from Sussex, as are Martin Dadswell and Alan Boniface from the Eagles trackshop. Whenever he can escape the sanatorium, Martin likes to see the Eagles ride in their away meetings though, sadly, this isn't as often as he'd like. On race night at Arlington, Martin arrives early and leaves late and, in between times, enjoys an obscured view of the action on the track. He also cleverly manages to hide his naturally sunny disposition behind the mask of his perpetually put upon and slightly lugubrious demeanour. The casual Freemasonry of speedway trackshop owners requires that Dave Rattenberry greet him fulsomely, like a long-lost friend who's arrived unexpectedly with a large cheque. Mischievously Dave exclaims, "Here's Martin Dadswell – Jeff Scott's biggest fan!" With a captive, critical audience only yards from his stall, Dave can't resist one of his favourite themes of the last few years – namely, how my books allegedly conspicuously fail to excite the punters ("The book just

The Eastbourne massive

Wolves Pits

isn't selling!"). Martin is a receptive audience and needs no second invitation to join in, "It's your worst yet; it's freakin' shite!" In an aggrieved tone of voice that verges on the high pitched, he loudly tells Dave Rat, "He's misquoted me again in it. I wouldn't call him numbnuts, would I? I'd call him a ****!" Keen to savour the legendary Monmore atmosphere they've journeyed so far to relish, Martin and Alan make their way onto the steps of the open terraces. They strategically base themselves where they can see the start/finish line, overlook the action on the first and second bends as well as have distant sight of some of the pits area activity. It's a lovely balmy evening for speedway and, though it's reasonably crowded, the terraces aren't completely full. Martin can't help but compare tonight with his memories of yesteryear, "It used to be intimidating here but it's not anymore!" I double-check that I can (accurately) quote him, "Put whatever you freaking want, ****! Don't suppose you've sold many of them, have you? I wouldn't worry about people nicking them, I'd worry about them putting them back!"

The Wolverhampton-Lakeside programme from July 7th is pressed into service for his meeting and, for our £2, we also get an insert for tonight's meeting which contains a racecard, some information on Eastbourne (along with a team photo) and the latest BSPA bulletin that features a brief interview with Ian Thomas (in which he expresses excitement about the forthcoming PL Four Team Tournament to be held at Workington). Even the insert requires correction since Ronnie Allen will be the SCB referee at tonight's meeting, instead of the listed Graham Flint. More importantly, Christian Hefenbrock won't ride, so Wolverhampton will operate rider replacement at number 4. The rider wasn't given permission to ride by the track doctor in light of the after-effects of a crash at the weekend. Eastbourne make a powerful start to the meeting with a first race 5-1 that has Scott Nicholls win in 55 seconds, the fastest time of the night. Most likely echoing the thoughts of many Wolves fans, Alan Boniface isn't impressed with Fredrik Lindgren's performance, "Freddy Lindgren must have left his World Cup bike at home tonight!" With Wolves challenge for Elite League silverware already on the critical list, the ambulance manoeuvres round the pits when there aren't even any fallen riders on the track. The gimlet-eyed Martin Dadswell squints into the distance. "Hello, the ambulance is coming out! Do they know something we don't?" It's a truism in speedway circles that strong reserves will provide any team with a strong springboard for track success and, since they've only six riders tonight, Wolves will need strong performances from Kenneth Hansen and/or Nicolai Klindt. In a race sponsored by Pitstop Mobile Tyre Service, the Wolves reserve partnership immediately bite back with a 5-1 to level the scores. For the majority of the first lap, Hansen rides like his bike has a handbrake before he suddenly scuttles past both Eastbourne riders to transform a possible drawn heat into a welcome maximum advantage. Alan Boniface isn't impressed with the race tactics shown by the Eastbourne riders, "They obviously didn't watch the first race, otherwise they'd know they'd only have to shut the inside line down! We might as well go home now." Hansen immediately gets another ride and bags an important third place ahead of Cameron Woodward to give Wolverhampton their second successive heat advantage and an early 10-8 lead. Well used to sudden changes in fortune, the Wolverhampton faithful don't bother to rouse themselves, let alone get too ecstatic. This lack of audible reaction proves well founded when Eastbourne immediately hit back with a race advantage in the next race to level the scores. They are helped in their task by an engine failure for Nicolai Klindt and enthusiastic Wolverhampton centre-green presenter Ian 'Porky' Jones helpfully informs Klindt, "I have to say buddy, Nicolai, your bike didn't sound too good when you let the clutch out!" Though this reminds me of Murray Walker's famous quote, "Are my eyes deceiving me, or does Senna's engine sound a little throaty?" We don't learn Klindt's reaction to this statement of the mechanically obvious.

Ever alert to nuance and fine detail, Martin Dadswell has closely studied the Monmore Green Stadium speedway safety equipment. "Their air fence doesn't start until half way round the [bend 1] corner!" He's also plugged into the inner sanctum of the speedway grapevine and, interpreting the distant tom-toms, informs us, "Did you hear Mildenhall technically went out of business last weekend? So Allen Trump bought the licence! They'll run until the end of the season and then use it at Exeter, if it opens!" An infectious but virulent strain of mechanical gremlins appear to be rife on the Wolverhampton side of the pits among their reserves and, in the fifth heat, Kenneth Hansen grinds to a halt. Fortunately, the race is won by Niels-Kristian Iversen (aka Puck) to ensure that the overall scores still remain tied. From the referee's box perched high in the home-straight grandstand but awkwardly positioned some yards ahead of the start/finish line, club announcer Peter Morrish tries to enthuse the Wolves fans with news of some exciting discount offers from the Trackshop, "Wolves T-shirts usually £9 but, tonight, they're a fiver!" With prices crashing, Alan Boniface decides to hold off on his Wolves memorabilia purchases, "I'll wait until they're £2!" The key match-up in the sixth heat pits Wolverhampton's Ales Dryml against Eastbourne's Simon Gustafsson. The Eastbourne

Wolverhampton v. Eastbourne: *"I did my spell pushing – everybody does!"*

youngster bests his more experienced rival who, in lacklustre fashion, trails round at the back of the field. Despite any obvious sign of an engine failure, from his vantage point on the centre green, 'Doctor' Ian Jones is keen to diagnose an epidemic of mechanical difficulties as the root cause of Wolverhampton's poor form, "The mechanical gremlins are plaguing us tonight!"

If some of the Wolverhampton riders look lacklustre then, in marked contrast, Eastbourne's Lee Richardson fizzes with vim and vigour. So much so, that he leads the (awarded) seventh race with considerable ease though the race is really only notable for the last lap exchanges between Cameron Woodward and Kenneth Hansen. On the second bend of the last lap, Hansen exploits the famous Monmore inside race line to sneak inside Woodward, only to have his Australian rival attempt to immediately return the favour on the third bend but, instead, massively clatter into his Hansen's back wheel to dramatically unseat them both. It's an immutable law for mechanics everywhere that, if there's a crash that involves their rider then it will definitely happen at the furthest point away from the pits. This holds true tonight for Ashley Wooller, Cameron's preternaturally calm mechanic and East Sussex's answer to Usain Bolt, who ostensibly runs but, in reality, makes comparatively stately progress towards the spot where Cameron has beached himself on the track. With the Eagles narrowly ahead going into heat 8, Start Marshal Keith Kershaw decides he isn't happy with where Simon Gustafsson has lined up on gate 1 and takes it upon himself to physically drag the rider's front wheel into a much more satisfactory position. Interestingly, the same Start Marshal doesn't deem it necessary to take such dramatic action with any Wolverhampton rider during the meeting! With the riders positioned perfectly, Eastbourne then power away from the tapes and romp home to another maximum heat win that extends their overall lead to 6 points. They're helped in no small part by the second successive retirement from Nicolai Klindt. With a glance towards the pits, Martin Dadswell is disgusted at the lack of team celebration, "Look at the Eastbourne side of the pits, not even a flicker of acknowledgement of the 5-1 apart from David Mason placing his hands together once! All the riders just turned their backs and walked off!"

The issue of team spirit is an ongoing and vexed one within speedway, given that all the riders are effectively self-employed individuals who often happen to ply their trade for a large number of teams dotted throughout Continental Europe. The situation is compounded by another harsh reality of speedway life, namely that – at the end of each season – many riders often find themselves shunted from one club to another like chattels without any consideration or loyalty shown by their employers. In this context it's understandable that you'd just want to concentrate on your own job and ensure that you do everything within your power to maximise your own earnings which, almost without exception, will be determined by the number of points that you score at any given meeting. The Wolverhampton side of the pits tonight is also notably unanimated. Like many other nights spent at Monmore Green stadium during the 2008 season it would transpire. When, during the close season Wolves promoter Chris Van Straaten trumpeted the return of Adam Skornicki to the club as "someone with charisma, character and the ability to put a smile on people's faces" he also revealed, "walking through our pits last season was often a depressing experience."

By the ninth heat Kenneth Hansen is already about to take his fifth ride of the night but it's another reserve that catches the eye, when James Brundle roars from the tapes to out-gate Niels-Kristian Iversen. His lead is short lived but, perhaps, a sign of what he could do at the Elite League level with greater experience and confidence. Though he's an Eagles fan, Alan Boniface isn't impressed with the lack of speed shown from the tapes by the Wolverhampton riders, "I think the greyhounds are getting out of the starts quicker than the Wolves riders!" On the centre green, Ian 'Porky' Jones doesn't have much to cheer about either so, when Lindgren leads the 10th race by 15 yards, he rather superfluously appeals to the catatonically quiet Monmore crowd, "Come on! Let's bring the boy home!" If the Wolves faithful harboured hopes that this will kickstart a fightback, then they are immediately dashed by the impressive Eagles pair of Scott Nicholls and Lewis Bridger who power to their second maximum heat advantage of the night and, thereby, further extend the Eastbourne advantage to a comfortable 10 points. More notable from a Wolverhampton perspective is the ongoing misfortune that besets their reserve riders in this race. First of all, Hansen is excluded under the two-minute warning and then, his replacement Nicolai Klindt, suffers this third successive retirement with his latest mechanical difficulty. They say hours in the workshop represent points on the track and, on this basis, Klindt's workshop must have some impressive cobwebs. With the last throw of his metaphorical dice Wolves Team Manager, Peter Adams, hands Niels-Kristian Iversen the black-and-white helmet colour in an attempt to claw back the deficit. At the start of the second lap, things look bleak for the Wolves with Richardson comfortably ahead and Klindt marooned at the back. However, Gustafsson then rears and gets so massively out of shape, it allows Klindt to pass him. Often happy to settle for the place he already has rather than battle for a better position, tonight's vigorous version of Lee Richardson has clearly had three Weetabix for breakfast. Indeed, he leads the race until Iversen aggressively cuts under him on the second bend of the last lap. Usually, at this point, the regular version Lee Richardson would automatically settle for second place and, with the scores as they are, this would definitely be the shrewd strategic option. However, tonight's ferociously red-blooded incarnation takes affront and accelerates massively down the back straight to determinedly blast under Iversen! Predictably this only serves to skittle himself from his own machine. Always keen to add his completely unnecessary commentary to the last lap, I'm pretty sure that Ian 'Porky' Jones blurts over the tannoy, "He's made a balls up!" Many referees would stop and award the race at this point – for the crash rather than the exclamation – plus exclude the fallen rider as the primary cause of the stoppage. However, Ronnie Allen is made of idiosyncratic stuff so, instead, lets the race wend its way to a conclusion before he retrospectively excludes Lee Richardson. The Wolves 8-1 resurrects the meeting as contest since it narrows the scoreline to 36-39.

The Wolverhampton fightback continues in the 13th heat with a Wolves 4-2 due, in no small part, to the way David Howe manages to keep Eastbourne's Monmore Green track specialist, Edward Kennett, locked down at the rear of the field. Ian 'Porky' Jones is appreciative of the notional spectacle, "That's good speedway". There's been so little to enthuse about this season that his thoughts are immediately echoed by Peter Morrish, "What fabulous speedway!" With scores suddenly close at 40-41, Martin Dadswell rails with the lyricism of King Lear, "It's freakin' pitiful! They just go to pieces! We will lose now!" His phone beeps with a message from a Lewis Bridger fan (rather than Trevor Nunn), "She's not even here and she knows we're gonna freakin' lose!"

To add to the suspense, the crucial heat 14 team then takes a number of attempts to complete. First time out Cameron Woodward falls on the first corner but referee Ronnie Allen surprisingly adjudges that first-bend bunching was the cause of the stoppage and orders all four riders back for a rerun. It's a decision that meets with Martin Dadswell's approval but not that of the Wolves management team if judged by reactions in the pits, "Yeah, well done referee! Look at Chris Van Straaten looking up at the referee!"

The rerun of the race sees Kenneth Hansen get caught underneath Cameron Woodward on the first bend and knock him from his machine. In some respects this incident looks pretty similar to the initial attempt to run the race but, with the remorseless passage of time (and possibly with sudden thoughts of mortality), on this occasion Ronnie Allen judges things differently and excludes Hansen. Cameron remains prostrate on the floor for some time though fortunately much closer to the pits than his previous 'off' so his mechanic, Ashley Wooller, doesn't have nearly so far to travel to collect his machine (nor does he have to run). The length of time the Australian spends on the shale irks a small boy close to me who remonstrates in a squeaky voice, "He could have got up!" The third attempt to run the race manages to avoid any hint of a first-bend incident and Eagles pair of Gustafsson and Woodward combine for a maximum heat advantage to guarantee a win for the visitors with one heat still to go in the meeting.

A Wolves heat win in the final race completes the formalities and Wolverhampton run out losers by a mere 3 points. During the 2008 season, Wolves will eventually lose eight home Elite League meetings by narrow margins and this, possibly, indicates they like to entertain but also keep their fans tantalised with thoughts of victory right until almost the end of any meeting. The Wolves faithful who funnel out of the stadium pass my book display but don't stop to purchase a copy. After diligently speaking to as many of the Wolves management and riders as possible after the meeting, the *Express and Star* ex-speedway reporter, Tim Hamblin, stops by to deny unsubstantiated reports that the injured Christian Hefenbrock had been signing the right breasts of overly keen admirers to recuperate. "That would be hard as he's not even here!" Characteristically, Tim sums the meeting up succinctly, "First, Wolves try to give it away, then Eastbourne pull back and then try to give it away! It's unfortunate Christian [Hefenbrock] couldn't ride as one or two of the other riders are not quite in top form. At some clubs they'd get lynched but, under the team management of Peter Adams, it's more considerate. He's from the school that prefers a quiet word and a hand on the shoulder to ranting and raving!" Club presenter Ian 'Porky' Jones passes by and complains that he's suffered abuse during the meeting from disgruntled Wolves fans. The swings and roundabouts of speedway fortunes inevitably ensure they rise almost as quick as they fall. Nonetheless, whether the faithful feel roused to abuse or

Wolverhampton v. Eastbourne: *"I did my spell pushing – everybody does!"*

driven to indifference, it's undeniably true that the last significant speedway silverware to darken the portals Monmore Green stadium came six years ago when the club, (controversially in some quarters) despite their second-placed finish to their league campaign, became the first club to be crowned Elite League champions. Though the Monmore Green Stadium track has been voted SRA Track of the Year in 2006 and runner-up in 2007, clearly the fans would prefer the acknowledged and highly regarded professionalism of the Wolves speedway organisation ensured that the trophy cabinet has to remain locked throughout the season.

21st July Wolverhampton v. Eastbourne (Elite League) 45-48

CHAPTER 25.

Redcar v. Workington:
"Where are all the rakers?"

24th July

The first leg of my own mini Northern Tour involves a 300+ mile drive from Brighton through the outskirts of Middlesbrough to the South Tees Motorsports Park (STMP), the relatively recently built home of the Redcar Bears. Most speedway riders lead a peripatetic existence and those who ply their trade in the Premier League find themselves perpetually driving the motorways, dual carriageways and 'A' roads of the British road network during the season. It's a tiring business and, when the riders arrive, they have to work rather than enjoy my good fortune of the chance to savour the ambience and atmosphere. It's a boiling hot day on the Costa del Teesside, so much so that I find Brian – a volunteer member of the track staff – sunning himself in the seat of his car ("we don't get much here so you have to take advantage"). There's a distinctive aroma in the air that I can't quite place but imagine has something to do with the industrial area that surrounds the home of Redcar speedway. On the distant horizon is the Riverside Stadium the home of Middlesbrough football club, the proud centrepiece of an area they're gradually regenerating with newly built (but often unoccupied) office blocks and apartments. It would be fair to say that the speedway club finds itself at the outer reaches of this regeneration area and isn't essential to its progress or success. A rust-covered metal hulk of a structure dominates the not-so-distant skyline and, judged by its sheer size, could (to the untutored eye) be either a bridge or an impressive piece of industrial lifting equipment. Brian has worked at the track all morning and, after he's soaked up a further few lunchtime rays of sunshine, will go home to Thornaby for some food before he returns to the STMP later. Things have changed and continue to change in and around Middlesbrough. Brian has noticed that the modernisation of the area ensures posh pronunciations are much more prevalent than they used to be. "People don't come from Yarm any more, they come from East Yarm!" He clearly relishes his work at the track and praises Bears promoter, Glyn Taylor, who's recently endured a rapid transformation from hero to villain amongst some supporters of the club: "Glyn is the hardest working man I know."

Apart from Redcar's assistant track curator Ian 'Jacko' Jackson who relentlessly circles the track on his tractor and Brian topping up his nonexistent tan, the stadium appears completely deserted. In the baking early afternoon heat, the rough rock that forms the surface of much of the stadium's grounds makes it appears almost volcanic. It would safe to say that since the Middlesbrough *Evening Gazette* dropped the bombshell (on 12th June) of the news that Redcar Bears owner Glyn Taylor had put the Redcar TLS Bears up for sale that aftershocks have reverberated around the town and throughout speedway generally. Glyn was understood to have completed his buy-out of the club from Chris Van Straaten earlier in the year and was widely believed to have paid a fee somewhere in the region of £169,000. By the time the purchase was completed, many Bears fans had already purchased their season tickets and the revenues this generated were allegedly retained by the previous owners. It was a situation that effectively left Glyn Taylor with many season-ticket holders he'd have to let into the stadium every week without any payment. Clearly, given the price allegedly achieved, Chris Van Straaten is a shrewd negotiator (or, conversely, Glyn a poor one), particularly given the metaphorical clouds that were already on the general economic horizon, let alone the speedway one. Even at the time of the sale, things didn't exactly look rosy and, since then, events had further clouded the situation.

They say that it costs around £16,500 to stage an Elite League meeting and that the cost of staging at Premier League has gradually crept up over the years to somewhere in the region of under £11,000 per meeting. You don't have to be a forensic accountant to quickly realise that, given average speedway attendance levels, that some clubs could face financial difficulty without the help of sponsorship or, in the Elite League, *Sky* contract payments. Even these would only defray the cost of a small number of meetings so – even at the highest levels of the sport in this country – there are potential significant financial shortfalls without further cost control or greater sponsorship. Though the football clubs of the Northeast region might be blessed with loyal fans and bumper attendance figures, the same definitely cannot be said of the speedway clubs from the area.

In this context, you can easily realise how the Redcar speedway business plan wouldn't have been robust at the outset, never mind after the weather intervened to cause some early-season postponements. Speaking honestly to the *Evening Gazette*, Glyn Taylor confessed, "I am not cut out for the job. It's far more difficult than I ever expected it to be so I'm done. I'm not dealing with the financial pressures. By that I mean I'm working 80 hours a week and I'm not sleeping at night. That can't go on. I need someone to buy the club from me or put in a cash injection of around £20,000. I need someone to take full financial control. If that doesn't happen, I'm going to have to close the club down." The club have only been back in the Premier League for a couple of seasons and Glyn Taylor played a hugely significant role in the transformation of a disused rubbish tip (adjacent to a karting site) into a reasonably popular and occasionally packed speedway stadium with a distinctive tightly banked track. Unluckily, a series of postponements at the start of the season meant that Glyn Taylor didn't have any gate revenue to offset running costs of the club, never mind the capital to service the debt taken on through the purchase. The logic of the situation required that the club would have to review all its compulsory and discretionary financial outgoings. The top wage earner at the club was ex world champion and Redcar Bears club captain, Gary 'Havvy' Havelock. Negotiations between Glyn and Gary didn't go well since, quite understandably, Havvy didn't wish to alter the contract he'd already signed for the whole 2008 season midway through the campaign. Consequently, after the home win against Scunthorpe on 3rd July, the club captain was sensationally released by his promoter only to be reinstated 24 hours later after the timely intervention of a hastily organised consortium of concerned supporters.

The famous Roller

Hospitality area

An already complicated and potentially fractious situation was tangled further by the fact that Gary's father, Brian Havelock, is also the Bears team manager and clearly has a relationship with both parties in dispute. After a quickly convened SOS [Save Our Skipper] meeting held at a local hotel in Middlesbrough, a newly formed consortium announced that Gary Havelock would continue to race for the club under Taylor's newly proposed pay terms with the shortfall in his pay packet made up by the members of said consortium. Brian Havelock explained the mechanics of the deal. "We reached an agreement whereby Gary has accepted what Glyn has offered, i.e. a guarantee per meeting, and I have got a consortium together of 14 people, looking like becoming 18, to foot the bill for the shortfall in his wages throughout July and August. At the end of August, everything reverts back to the original contract being honoured by Glyn … If Gary scores less than 9 – which is effectively what the guarantee covered – then the consortium is not involved." Glyn Taylor was also keen to put on the record the rationale behind his business decision. "I went to Gary and said that I'd been backed into a corner and that it was purely a financial decision – 'would you please take this pay cut?' Gary came back and said he wasn't able to accept it so I was left with no alternative but to release him because I couldn't afford to pay him his current wage demands. It's no secret that our crowds have been lower this season and everyone is suffering from the 'credit crunch'. It was never ever anything personal to do with me not being happy with Gary, it was purely financial. Both as promoter and as a person I stand by the ethic that if you can't pay for something, you don't have it. I never wanted to get into a situation where we owed anyone money. I spoke to a lot of other promoters and they confirmed that the deal I offered Gary was a very generous one. Full credit to Gary and Brian for going out and finding the sponsorship to make up the shortfall. I was expecting the reaction I got because Gary is an extremely popular personality in the Teesside area – the local, home-ground boy come good".

The affair provoked a flood of column inches locally and nationally and Gary Havelock was equally keen to put his side of the story, "Only last week Glyn telephoned me to ask if I could take a 30-40% pay cut. I asked for time to do my cash flow and I felt I could not afford this to maintain the level of equipment expected of me as a number 1 and I informed Glyn of this. I could have accepted a small cut if it had been for all team members but I had been singled out to bear the brunt of his financial predicament. Then after our win on Thursday night, Glyn simply told me that he couldn't afford for me to ride any more for Redcar. That was that – so much for having a contract! Oddly, my contract negotiations with Glyn at the start of the year were the shortest I have had in my career, he was extremely happy with my terms. Then, on Friday, Glyn rang me to ask if I could ride for Redcar at Workington because they couldn't get cover for me. Of course, I accepted; I knew we had a coach load of fans going and I couldn't let them or my home town club down." A highly motivated Gary Havelock then seized the opportunity to illustrate his importance at the club when he scored 16 points in the meeting at Derwent Park.

I expected I would bump into the friendly Glyn Taylor but didn't expect to broach this subject with him during my visit. With practically nobody in the stadium (other than 'Jacko' on his tractor), I decide to explore and when I pass the locked trackshop behind it I'm surprised to find a man – crouched by the doorway of the portacabin that serves as the home dressing room – leant forward being violently sick on the floor. The man is dressed in overalls and, rather diligently, projects his sickness towards the side of the building. When he stops and raises from a prone position, the violently ill man turns out to be Redcar owner and promoter, Glyn Taylor. "It must be the stress. I had to leave a meeting with the council to renegotiate the lease!" In the same way that you do if you fall over in public and someone asks 'are you alright?' Glyn claims to be "fine" now that he's finished being sick. That said, his financial problems continue to weigh heavily on his mind. "If I could walk away now, I'd never go to another speedway meeting! When I said the club was up for sale, the amount of abuse I got was phenomenal! I'm just an ordinary bloke. My dad [Chum Taylor] was in speedway, like I've been in speedway all my life – as a rider and, now as a promoter, I just want nothing to do with it! I work 80 hours a week on speedway and I'm just sick of it! I'm also a tuner three days a week and have a queue of 12 engines waiting. I do them when I can and I say to them 'If you're not happy you can go somewhere else'. Neil Machin told me 'look at what comes in and what goes out and, if you're making a loss, pull the plug'. I sort of admired Colin Horton 'cause he got out and paid most people, only the odd one got burned. Whereas Waggy went bankrupt and I got 17p for a £600 bill. He owed Greg Hancock and several other riders a lot of money, but everyone got paid only a fraction of what they were owed – except for the taxman, the VAT man, the banks and solicitors who all got paid in full! They say the new man at Workington has lost interest and, effectively, got out of speedway as he's handed the thing over to Ian Thomas. He allegedly wishes he'd never got into it – though, it's said he did have a tax bill of about £20 million last year, so his situation is a bit different."

"The thing I like most about the speedway track – it'll sound silly – is the wildlife! We get all sorts here, rabbits, foxes, moles. It's amazing! You should have a look at this place on Google Earth before we started work on it. We cleared 30 tons of debris from the centre green alone. It was a huge job to create this place but, I'd walk away, if I could! We had five weeks of rain-offs at the start of the season and we've never recovered financially but I put my heart and soul into it. In 2007, we used to get 1,200 fans and, in 2008, we get 600 to 650 fans. Last week it was 653 fans. The away fans have dropped off. Last week we had Sheffield and they brought about 30 people max. If we take £6k, I have to give a substantial amount straight to the VAT man. Everything costs. It's unbelievable! The cleaning is £50 a week. It costs 350 quid to empty the septic tank. I have to pay the staff. We spend 350 quid per meeting on shale – we've used 100 tons this year so far. We lose tons of shale over the fence! With the narrow back straight, it means they [the riders] have to go straight whereas, on the home straight, they just drift to the outside and blast the shale over the fence. The rent on the buildings is £2,300. I had to pay a four-figure sum to the BSPA for their services from February to August. It was £4k on the loudspeakers and it's £450 medical cover for each meeting. The tyres are £518 a meeting. I just spent £18,000 for two away and two home meetings. You can say it's £1,800 to £2,000 per meeting to the away team and that's just paying them the away points money of £35, £25 and £20. The worst of the lot are the riders! They just look at the money. Vans cost £150 each per month, there's £70 each in rent, never mind the airfares, signing-on fees, and all the other things! We've even had tractor repairs. I bought a new gearbox last week for 700 quid."

"People say more people would come if we had a grandstand – but who the freak is gonna pay for it? There's a council meeting to discuss a sports grant for the grandstand but that's not gonna happen. The riders shock me! We were supposed to be in the Fours [Final] this weekend but mine say 'I ain't gonna ride' or 'I can't 'cause I've got a wedding!' So we've got to pull out and Scunthorpe are in our place. Drains were £7,500 and the fencing is £3,000. When I explained the situation to Gary [Havelock] and suggested a pay cut, he told me to 'freak off!' Trying to cut our cloth to our suit was sensible. But, he didn't see it as his problem as he had a contract. It's not much good to you if you're sacked! Neil Machin is a very good friend – I used to room with him when I was a rider – and he says 'you have to make it pay'. I do the engine tuning, that's £100 each and I do some other things. Colin Horton wants me to look at his [Peterborough] track. It's full of clay so, either it binds together when they water it and is unrideable or, else, there's too much dirt and the bikes can't cope. I'm gonna go down on August 1st – they have a meeting on the 7th or the 8th – to look. My recommendation was to scrape off 15 tons and then put down 30 tons of the shale we use here from Bradford. Getting paid £150 plus petrol is nice but it's not gonna solve things! Peter Oakes asked about all the costs here 'cause he might think of taking over the licence. Maybe, I dunno? If it's not the costs, you'd be amazed at everything that goes on! The council have a noise meter here. It's radio signal controlled and takes a reading at every meeting!"

Home straight crowd

Under orders

We move over to the small tea area in the pits where assistant track curator (to Glyn), Ian 'Jacko' Jackson, joins us. Glyn asks, "It ain't gonna freakin' rain is it?" 'Jacko' doesn't think that it will but, after he learns Glyn has been sick, anxiously quizzes him about what he's eaten. "I left Manchester at 6 a.m. after me Weetabix and I've had a cup of coffee since, oh, and an apple." They're in agreement that the amount of shale that disappears over the fence each week is criminal. During the season, 'Jacko' has had discussions with the riders about the surface, "I did the track ultra slick and they complained! So the next week, I put more dirt on the track and the freakers were all over the place. They only moaned even more, so I just do what I want now and they'll just have to cope!" Glyn shows me the giant roller that they have at Redcar and he's proud to tell me just how well this bespoke, handmade piece of equipment performs. "The roller is my best invention! It's a steel drum surrounded with tyres. It weighs two to three tons. There's 100 gallons of oil inside the drums and remember that one gallon weighs 10 lbs." Talk of track preparation skill and expertise is a subject close to Glyn's heart. "The track at Cardiff needs some serious attention. The money BSI make from Cardiff is amazing and none of it comes back to help the sport! I know the bloke in Australia who fills the stadiums for all sorts of events in Oz – he just did it with horses – and he wanted to take over the GP there. But they wanted 17 flown in first-class and put up in the Hilton. That was a minimum of £50k for starters, though it was never gonna happen." Talk of stadium income returns us to problems closer to home, "I sometimes wish we just rented the stadium. George English [at Newcastle] pays a good value rent per week and that's it – no cleaning, no nothing! Oh well, the show must go on!"

While hugely concerned at the endless litany of costs you have to bear to run a Premier League speedway track, something that definitely still excites Glyn is working with his hands (and brain) to build things to solve specific and seemingly intractable problems. Later he proudly shows me a prototype of a "revolutionary silencer" that he's developed. "I'm gonna make them slimmer and quieter. The present one is supposed to be 102 decibels but really it's 112 decibels! Graham Reeve acknowledges that. My one is gonna be a lot quieter and slimmer and won't cost as much. The bikes will go just as well, if not better!" Tonight's visitors are Workington and Glyn remains hopeful that they might travel with a reasonable number of fans to the South Tees Motorsports Park, "An extra 50 people tonight wouldn't solve things but it would help!"

I can place my display table wherever I like within the stadium grounds, so choose next to the hospitality portacabin with its raised balcony that overlooks the first corner but also provides a panoramic view of the track. On the other side of this temporary building, Richard McGlade works in his burger van and we chat about the need for a proper book on the exploits of the hooligans – known as the "Casual Firm" – that used to follow Middlesbrough football club in the 1970s. He doesn't feel that Paul Debrick's book *The Brick* really captures the full essence or glory of their activities. "He wasn't as important as he claims he was!" Before the turnstiles open there's a good-sized queue of fans and the car park beyond fills up remarkably quickly. One of the first fans to stop for a chat by my table takes an optimistic view of the likely attendance levels tonight, "I come at the same time every week and I had to park two rows further back in the car park than usual. Still, Workington often bring a few with them!" Eastbourne uber-fan, Sid Greatley, has travelled up for the meeting and even talks about going to Edinburgh the next day (although he doesn't do so). He has always travelled widely to watch his speedway and, as ever, sports his shiny fluorescent blue Eagles anorak. He's just retired ("they can't do without me"), and optimistically believes that Eastbourne still might gain some silverware, "I reckon we're going to make the play-offs!" Sheffield supporter Philip Brown has come along with his dad, Paul. Philip soon questions a recent blog posting where I take BSI/IMG to task for the usuriously low level of pay rates given to riders in the Grand Prix. It's not a perspective he agrees with, "The FIM set the pay rates for the riders which has nothing to do with IMG or BSI! BSI are just good businessmen – so, if they maximise their revenues, it's nothing to be criticised or be ashamed of! Speedway needs better stadiums to attract the fans!" I confirm to Philip that I still don't buy the self-justifying argument put forward by BSI that erroneously claims quality of stadiums and stadium infrastructure will somehow automatically professionalize the sport, increase attendances or, even, automatically necessarily enhance the spectacle on the track. I note that the facilities at the Cardiff Millennium Stadium are excellent but, nonetheless, Cardiff remains a consistently poor track. Philip denies any relationship between track quality and the racing produced by indoor stadia, "Whilst at Gelsenkirchen, the riders said it was a good track but the racing was awful!" To my mind this confirms that temporary tracks built in deluxe stadia will, almost without exception, provide neither high quality or entertaining races. Philip's dad, Paul, believes that speedway can learn some valuable lessons from basketball, "Promoters need to promote speedway to new people with discount offers and the like rather than one extra free meeting – like they had at Lakeside – which won't bring them back to pay £15 each week. Basketball has been innovative and used discount vouchers to get people going regularly and hooked on the sport."

Because of the tight confines of the 271-metre banked STMP circuit, the racing often looks excitingly close. However, some sensitivity exists about this perception. Recently the club and local newspaper have been quick to strenuously defend their reputation against comments by George English that though the riders race close together there is "little or no passing". There's precious little evidence of neck-and-neck racing in the rerun of the first heat, which sees Daniel Nermark win comfortably ahead of local fans' favourite, Gary Havelock, in a time of 53.2 seconds to equal the track record held by Ricky Ashworth. From the centre green, Redcar Director of Operations, Gareth Rogers, studiously talks up Benji Compton's latent talent while the rider makes his way out onto the track for the second race of the night. "Well Benji got stuck in last night at Birmingham and his performance was appreciated by the 20 of so travelling fans stood in a little cluster there." This evening the fans take the chance to cheer Arlo Bugeja when he wins the second race. Keith McGhie (Jon Cook sound-alike, club announcer and dead ringer for my dentist) relays the race results enthusiastically and gives Bugeja the expansive moniker of the 'Adelaide Arrow'. Arlo often almost has more nicknames than points to his name. Keith also tells us, "The referee Jim Lawrence would like to commend John Branney for picking up so promptly on the pits bend!" Before the third race starts, Gareth returns to his overview of the previous night's meeting at Birmingham and alludes to mechanical problems for James Grieves as a potential explanation for the Bears narrow single-point defeat at Perry Barr Stadium. The third race of the night (finally) features a passing manoeuvre from Joe Haines who blasts past Chris Kerr on the opening corner of the last lap. It's a sight that exasperates the man in front of me, ("Ha'way Kerr!"). Redcar have two Australians in the fourth heat, the rider with the grandiose nickname (Arlo 'Adelaide Arrow' Bugeja) along with Ty Proctor, whom Keith McGhie introduces as "The Thunder from Down Under" apparently unaware that Rod Stewart's ex-wife Rachel Hunter used this very phrase to describe her orgasms. Ty does indeed thunder from the gate only to find himself soon passed by the experienced Carl Stonehewer on the back straight of the first lap. Ty returns the favour and regains the lead with a blast round the steep banking of the last bend at the end of the second lap. On the final lap John Branney suffers what Keith McGhie terms a "water to the eyes moment". Just as he cranks up his speed to pass Arlo Bugeja round the outside of the last bend, his progress is suddenly cut short when his chain suddenly snaps just at the moment he exits the bend to race towards the finish line. Branney does extremely well just to stay on his machine but gets, what my dad would euphemistically describe, as 'badly winded'. The first four races have seen the teams alternate 4-2s and this prompts Keith to observe, "So that pendulum swings once again!" Over the tannoy, we learn that stock clearance has been dressed up as a generous discount offer by the track shop management: "Dave Rattenberry tells me that Bears T-shirts that usually retail at £9 are on special offer tonight at £5!"

A couple of surprising 5-1 race results then follow. Given his imperious form in the first race, you'd expect Daniel Nermark to comfortably win the fifth but, instead, he falls and, thereby, effectively gifts Grieves and Kerr their maximum heat advantage. In the next race, you'd be equally confident beforehand that local track expert and fans' favourite Gary Havelock would triumph. But, instead, he trails home a surprising third behind the Comets combination of Carl Stonehewer and hardworking reserve Charles Wright. It appears that no sooner does one team establish a narrow lead than the other team immediately takes it back again. This pattern continues unabated in heats 7 and 8 when Workington briefly burst back into the lead (for the third time in the meeting) only to find themselves pegged back after the subsequent race. Understandably heat 8 starts without John Branney, and Keith McGhie confirms, somewhat euphemistically, "We understand 'winded' John Branney won't be coming out in the next heat after he hurt himself nearly dismounting from his bike and is seeking medical attention!" Charles Wright replaces him but finishes last (his only fourth place of the night) watched by his mum Lynn, stood among the start-line crowd. You could almost set your watch by Lynn Wright's attendance at any speedway meeting that features either of her sons (James or Charles). Before this race, Master of Ceremonies, Gareth Rogers, dutifully talked up the delicately poised nature of the meeting, "It's all getting very intriguing and exciting, as I said earlier!" Josh Auty wins ahead of Joe Haines after a very hard-fought corner that prompts Gareth to note, "There's a great rivalry and competitive rivalry between these good friends!" No sooner have these words left his mouth than – as they reach the third and fourth bend of the warm-down 'celebration' lap (lap 5) – Josh Auty dramatically decides to mete out his own justice to perceived aggressors. This takes the form of a sudden head butt for the yellow-helmeted Charles Wright. With bonhomie in short supply, this outburst of violent retribution forces a heartfelt but slightly schoolmasterly "Oh dear" from Gareth.

Workington have arrived at the STMP with a six-strong side and they run with rider replacement for Tony Reima (whom I've never seen ride and suspect could be a figment of Ian Thomas's imagination). The experienced Comets trio of Nermark, Nieminen and Stonehewer all look extremely impressive around the banked circuit and they're given good support by both Joe Haines and Charles Wright, though John 'winded' Branney has (obviously enough) looked slightly out of sorts. Still first impressions often count for naught and, so this proves in heat 9, when the Bears Grieves/Kerr combination ram home their second successive maximum heat win to ease Redcar into their first lead of the night at 29-25. Personally, I would have expected ex World Champion Gary Havelock to then consolidate their lead in the next race but, instead, he's well beaten by Kauko Nieminen, who rides with noticeable speed and grace. Wittily Gareth tells us, "Certainly Koko's no clown!" Keith McGhie disapproves of Nieminen's prompt return to the pits after his easy victory, "Opting again not to take your applause and congratulations!" Gareth decides to labour Keith's earlier clichéd metaphor, "That old pendulum swings again" while, perched in the referee's box, Keith obsesses about the "Hard but physical Kauko Nieminen".

It's easy to wander round the STMP circuit and watch the meeting from different vantage points along the home straight or round the first corner. I find myself stood next to the friendly and knowledgeable speedway couple, Mandy and Keith Mason. Mandy has followed speedway in the Teesside area for many years and used to go to

Cleveland Park. "I watched in the late '70s and early '80s. I was 14 when I first went in 1972 and we used to get the bus. I don't think there was any one rider who was my favourite, maybe Steve Wilcox, but really all of them were my favourites! I tried to scrounge a lift off friends to away meetings and, ever since it reopened here, we've been coming back." If life is full of mysteries, then Keith Mason might not have all the answers but he's keen to search them out. He definitely has the most incisive question of the night, namely: "Where are all the rakers?" Now that he's pointed this out, it's blindingly obvious that there are no raking skills on display at the South Tees Motorsports Park. Mandy is equally mystified by their absence, "We used to have them at Cleveland Park!" Given my conversation earlier with Glyn Taylor about lost shale, I expect any rakers would have to base themselves 10 yards back into the home-straight crowd to locate the shale that's scattered there off the track during each and every race meeting. If rakers were based on the centre green, they'd be a further unnecessary expense and merely there for decoration rather than any real effect.

The imperious form of Kauko Nieminen and Daniel Nermark in particular suggests that the Workington Comets should be strong contenders for the 2008 Premier League championship. However, the 11th race of the meeting is to provide an immediate and serious dent in their championship ambitions. The race features Australian prospect Ty Proctor and the fast-riding racer in the distinctive orange kevlars, Daniel Nermark. The 31-year-old Swede has 3 points to his name and could well have more but for his heat 5 fall, when he comes to grief in pursuit of James Grieves of the Bears. For the first three laps of heat 11 we are served up some exciting race action and, as the riders hammer down the back straight of the final lap, Ty Proctor holds a narrow lead by virtue of his speed on the bike. Daniel Nermark is in hot pursuit and, at the point of maximum velocity on the back straight, his bike appears to clip Proctor's back wheel. This causes Nermark's bike to further accelerate and zoom fish-tailing onwards until it smashes into the third-bend fence to fling the luckless Comets rider into the air like the proverbial rag doll. The fence appears to buckle and warp upon impact, though it withstands the blow. Whether Nermark will be so lucky looks unlikely after his mid-air somersault has him land with full impact upon his head/neck. It is one of those genuinely horrific crashes when the quest for speed for our entertainment crosses a line to sharply throw into relief the mortality of the participants. People immediately start to run from the banked pits towards the stricken rider, while the medical staff (in dark clothes rather than fluorescent ones) run from the opposite direction. On the centre green, Gareth Rogers reacts quickly to exclaim, "We've seen what's happened – Keith put some nice music on please!" It's a thoughtful but also simultaneously peculiar request given that "nice" music will be necessarily in the ear of the beholder (and won't distract Daniel Nermark from the pain of his injuries). After a brief delay for a suitable selection, Keith chooses to put on an R&B song. It blasts out over the loudspeakers and features the lyric, "It's been the longest without you". In the stunned crowd, we collectively hold our metaphorical breath while riders, track staff and medical personnel fuss around the stricken Nermark. The ambulance waits ominously on the track. In the toilets two young boys excitedly discuss what they just saw, "He didn't half hit that fence like!" "Yeah, he's probably dead!" Outside a man on a mobile phone breathlessly relays a blow-by-blow account of the crash, "You've never seen anyone go so fast, he was absolutely full pace!" After a short delay, Gareth informs us, "Daniel is in a semi-conscious state. Obviously he has to go to the James Cook Hospital where they will assess him. Of course, he has a history of having broken both femurs but, at the moment, he's not certain of what happened which is probably a good thing!" Redcar speedway fans are knowledgeable about their sport and remain relatively hushed as they patiently wait for further news of his injuries from the track. Keith McGhie intones a classic example of an informationless information message (that we're usually bombarded with on public transport), "There's a slight delay and we do, of course, appreciate your patience." Shortly afterwards Keith supplies some slightly more specific news, "It seems Daniel just about has movement everywhere but he is drifting in and out of consciousness. But, hopefully, his injuries aren't as serious as we first thought!"

If the huge impact of the crash has knocked the stuffing out of Daniel Nermark then it's also put a giant spanner in the works for Workington and, when the Bears race to a 4-2 in the rerun, it appears to have ended all likelihood of a Comets away win. With Nermark programmed to ride in heat 13 and also pretty certain to participate in heat 15, there's need for an instant reply. Kauko Nieminen immediately provides this in heat 12 when he magnificently passes James Grieves on the back straight to gain the lead and go on to win the race. With John Branney third, Comets have a 4-2 heat advantage that reduces their deficit on the night to just 2 points and rests the score at 37-35. Over the tannoy, Keith McGhie conducts his own master-class in Dadaist slogans, "The phone from the pits does ring!" Mindful of the 10 o'clock curfew at South Tees Motorsports Park, the remainder of the heats are rushed through quickly.

Gary Havelock's first win of the evening comes at a vital time in heat 13 and restores the Redcar lead to 4 points with two races to go. The penultimate heat only features riders aged below 25. It's won by Joe Haines but the excitement is the battle for second place. Charles Wright stalks the multiple nicknamed Arlo Bugeja throughout and waits to chose his moment for a decisive blast round the outside of his rival on the back straight of the last lap. The Comets maximum ties the scores at 42 apiece and brings the meeting to a cliffhanger finale of a last-heat decider. If the fast-starting Daniel Nermark had still been fit enough to ride then, just like heat 13, the outcome would probably have been different. Nonetheless, even without him, the Comets field an impressive combination of Stonehewer and Nieminen but, once Grieves escapes at the start (and Havelock occupies third place) a home win is always going to be the likely outcome. This is duly confirmed when Havelock steals second place on the line from Stonehewer to emphasise that the Bears have seized the last-gasp advantage. The 47-43 scoreline flatters the home team but they have ridden their luck. Their determination over the vital closing heats gains a win that consolidates their mid-table position in the Premier League. While some of the crowd sprint for the exit to try and beat the rush from the packed car park, Keith McGhie continues to console us, "We apologise for the unscheduled delay tonight but accidents and injuries are outside of our control!" Sid Greatley marvels at how Nermark escaped without catastrophic consequences: "I thought he was dead, you know!"

24th July Redcar v. Workington (Premier League) 47-43

CHAPTER 26.

Edinburgh v. Redcar:
"He's conscious but has damage to his foot or ankle!"

25th July

I arrive so early at Armadale Stadium that the front gates remain resolutely locked. When I peer through the gates, I can just about make out the top of a tractor as it slowly wends its way round the track. The Monarchs curatorial team have clearly locked themselves inside the stadium and, as a stranger to the various other access routes to the pits, I'm completely unable to gain entry. There's a high wooden fence, and perched on top of it by the entrance gate is a large sign that sings the virtues of the "Armadale Experience". The basic message is that you can watch speedway here every Friday from April to October and that Armadale Stadium is the home of the Edinburgh Monarchs where you can see "Speedway at its best!" Interestingly, the stadium has recently been re-designated Scotwaste Arena. This coincided with the arrival of the *Sky* television cameras to broadcast a live Monday night Premier League meeting from here but also, more importantly, acknowledges the importance of the club sponsor. It's not immediately apparent what (if any) changes this re-designation has wrought within the stadium and, judged from the vantage point of the stadium car park, the infrastructure changes have been minimal. Until recently it was hard to find a litterbin within the stadium but, if only to illustrate the expertise of their main sponsor, many have now been provided. Confusingly, at the back of the portacabin that serves as one of the stadium hospitality areas on speedway night, there is a bright blue eye-catching sign that proclaims "Keyline Broxburn sponsoring the Speedway Scottish Open". Monarchs promoter John Campbell arrives almost at the same time as a large number of his staff do so, suddenly, the gates are flung open and people busy themselves with their preparations for the evening's meeting. The programme table is readied, the lady at the gate flourishes the board with attached guest list so visitors like myself can sign in and the turnstile kiosks are prepared for when the entrance gates open sometime later. While I wait in the car park, there is a programme on *BBC Radio 4* about the rise of the automobile that includes the amazing statistic that 100,000 tons of manure was removed from London roads every year between 1890 and 1900. At that time, fly tipping as a concept didn't exist and the most commonly found objects (horseshoe nails) played havoc with the temperamental new-fangled machine of the future. Dead horses were also just left in the street and, while this sounds surprising to modern ears, I'm sure that the Scotwaste Company has many equally peculiar stories about the rubbish they collect.

Always welcoming and friendly, I briefly catch up with promoter John Campbell about what, so far, has been an extremely successful season for the Edinburgh Monarchs. With a good number of clouds in the sky, meteorology is a good starting point. "I think it has rained here every week [on a Friday] this season! For the last three weeks, it has rained in the area and always here sometime between 5.30 p.m. and 6.30 p.m. There's always a forecast of showers here! When we're down to the hard core – as we are in speedway at the moment – every single fan is critical! No promoter can be completely honest, it's always on until it's off but I would ring everyone personally if I could." John is a comparatively caring employer and worries about the long-term prospects of some riders he has employed or encountered after their speedway careers have finished. "Let's face it, a lot of these riders would be beach bums or just lounging around if they didn't ride speedway. The ones who have a job – and do this sensibly – can become quite wealthy! Sometimes I think, 'What happened to so and so?' 'cause he couldn't do anything and, then, you find he's not doing anything! Ryan [Fisher] has possibly 10 years here [in Britain] and possibly 15 years in America – I dunno what they get paid there – so he has to make a go of it! People said, 'Don't touch him with a barge pole.' He and his family, they've all been brilliant and courteous. He's one of the easiest people I've ever had to deal with! During the meetings, he gets worked up 'cause he's riding for himself and trying to prove other people wrong. Whereas Derek [Sneddon] and Andrew [Tully] have grown up here and ride for the team, whereas Ryan rides for himself. When he comes back angry to the pits, he's mad because he's been losing himself money. He's lost hundreds of pounds this season already. When he shouts at himself in the pits, we all can't help hearing it. I have a word with him and he says, 'But I'm only shouting at myself'. And I say, 'I know, but we can all hear it!' He's very honest to deal with. We considered him for two or three years and, despite everyone saying 'don't', we did and I'm pleased we did! People say he was a drunk and fat but I haven't seen him with a drink and, he says, he hasn't had a drink and I believe him. [His wife] Daelyn probably told him! He's helped us around here with a whole series of things. With Thomas's [Jonasson] engine which he fitted for no charge. Recently he sent us a list of everything I owed him and he owed us. It came to £50 I owed him. He just wanted to be straight! After Reading, Ryan said the next day that he'd learnt a lesson and it was never going to happen again and yet, that night at the Isle of Wight, he rode on his back wheel through the pits! People said I had to have a word with him – it's so narrow there between the pits area and the fence – I knew I had to have a word without anyone telling me! Usually he argues 'cause he's never wrong and is the best rider in the world, like many of them think! But even he said this time, 'I'm sorry' before I'd even said, 'you can't do that 'cause someone will get killed!'" Talk of trips to Reading inevitably brings up discussion of the closure of Smallmead and innocently I wonder "What's going to happen to the greyhounds?" John retorts quickly, "You can't say that! Don't say that! Look at all the problems we had with animal activists here 'cause of that!"

Closed

"I'm the longest continuously serving promoter in British speedway. Others have done it longer but not continuously. It's 25 years this year! I've been doing it since 1984 but, then, I'm one of Edinburgh's biggest fans. I'd be here anyway! There was a time last year, when I wondered if we'd ever win another meeting. Then you would've been sensible to think about giving up but things always change in speedway. People are saying nice things about us and how we're gonna win the League. But, you have to be here every week to see we've gone off the boil. If you look at the results, it will appear we haven't – we've still only lost four – but say, Andrew [Tully] scores 6 points before he was going into the lead in the other races and throwing points away. Now, he's not! It's nice about the *Sky* meeting and Terry Russell rang and said, 'You've been moaning so much about lack of recognition, you've got it!' I didn't moan for that but just to have what we'd done recognised! We're lucky in speedway, and at Edinburgh, to have the fans we have. But often, though they know a lot, they're not as knowledgeable as they think they are! For example, you have to admire Craig Watson. He's got so much metalwork in his shoulder or whatever, that he can't turn the bike anymore in the corners. Particularly on tight tracks like here or Birmingham – his home track! When we rode there in terrible conditions we won but many of them weren't up for it but couldn't really say so 'cause it was at theirs. Craig was up for it, though! Even in heat 13, when he was off gate 4, he could have quite legitimately – and without any cause for complaint – have dropped back and rode round the inside. But there he was, first at the corner. Everyone passed him in the race, of course, but you have to admire his determination!"

Parade truck

Our conversation switches to the topic of Daniel Nermark's crash the previous evening at Redcar. "If they'd had him, they'd have won! I'm not surprised to hear he's crashed badly because, when he rode here, I always thought he was an accident waiting to happen! 'cause of the way he locked up in the corners causing other riders to shut off. But, one day, someone would get sick of it and just ride straight through him and harpoon him. Ryan said that after he knocked

First bend grandstand crowd

Edinburgh v. Redcar: *"He's conscious but has damage to his foot or ankle!"*

Trent [Leverington] off, 'I harpooned him 'cause he was in the way.' The fact that Ryan was out of control didn't cross his mind! They laughed about it afterwards. Well, Ryan did, I doubt Trent did 'cause it would've cost him a couple of hundred pounds to put his bike right afterwards." John dismisses my presumption that success on the track has led to burgeoning numbers of fans through the turnstiles. "Unusually for speedway this season, our crowds are on par with last year! We had two average derby [v. Glasgow] crowds and apart from that we're definitely doing better than everyone else. This could be a big crowd tonight because Redcar will bring some – in fancy dress! The weather is good and the Edinburgh holiday [season] is now over, if you can believe that!"

With my bookstall in its traditional place on the patch of grass opposite the burger van – just at the point where fans have to pass to wander down to the back-straight grandstand or have to turn to head past the hospitality terrapin huts to get to the taller but squat first-bend grandstand – I chat with knowledgeable speedway historian Jim Henry about aircraft malfunctions: a conversation prompted by the news that he's off to Tunisia for a two-week holiday. Shortly afterwards, Gary Lough's dad, Alan stops by and tells me, "I told Gary to cool it on his criticisms of [name redacted]. He's a mean bastard, and could lash out! If he did, I'd have to hit him and then he'd be out of the team, ken. So, I told Gary to cool it for the good of the team in the League this year!" Though a generalisation, many Monarchs fan are keen not to tempt the gods so are studiously careful not to make predictions about how the season might end. Nonetheless, beneath their caution, there's a quiet confidence. Some fans express concern about the general number of crashes there has been this year at Armadale and in speedway generally.

Just before the racing starts, I pack my things away in a rush and head to my usual vantage point between the raised base of one of the hospitality portacabins and the first-bend grandstand. It provides an ideal spot from which to see the majority of the track, although the second bend is somewhat obscured by the wooden safety fence. As ever, it's an experience made all the more enjoyable by the opportunity to stand with passionate Edinburgh fan, Dougie Copland and his father, Bill. The meeting starts dramatically when Erskine-based SCB official Jim McGregor even-handedly excludes both Thomas H. Jonasson and Josh Auty under the two-minute time allowance. Dougie sighs, "The old miscommunication thing! That was a shambolic start!" With Jim McGregor's authority stamped on the meeting from the get-go, the Monarchs decide to replace Jonasson with Derek Sneddon, while the Bears exercise their option to start excluded Josh Auty from 15 metres back. The other two combatants in the race are ex-World Champion and Redcar fans' talisman Gary Havelock and Edinburgh's guest, Carl Stonehewer, who rides in place of the injured William Lawson. "No one can replace William Lawson round here. He's the real number 1 we needed in the team!" With a weakened Monarchs line-up, the fact that the Redcar Bears traditionally ride with some verve around Armadale doesn't fill Dougie with confidence. The rerun sees things take a severe turn for the worse when Derek Sneddon gates but then collides with his race partner, Carl 'Stoney' Stonehewer. In the 20 or so yards that they ride together, the chance to establish an intuitive almost telepathic understanding is limited. The crash has a certain inevitability and freeze-frame quality. Stoney appears to stare fixedly at the fence before he hits the wooden boards of the second bend extremely hard. A chunk is taken out of the fence, though whether that was Stoney or his bike is hard to tell. From my vantage point, the minutiae of what happens on the track is obscured by the wooden boards of the safety fence but, as if we're suddenly been invited to witness a peculiar mime from the Edinburgh Festival, gloved hands briefly hold the top of the fence but then, with exquisite comic timing, clutch at thin air before they fall away again. At the time of the incident Dougie exclaims, "Oh no, disaster!" Moments later, he is more philosophical, "Well, Derek did get in his way a bit. Stoney's so big now he can't manoeuvre! He didn't seem to ride his way out of that. Stoney's gonna stop coming here! He got injured in the Scottish Open last year and, the year before, guesting for Newport, [he crashed] on this same bend and hit his head." From his trackside vantage point, centre-green announcer Scott Wilson provides us with a brief but somewhat anatomically confused medical update, "He's conscious but has damage to his foot or his ankle!" Referee Jim McGregor decides to exclude Derek Sneddon. It's a decision that doesn't meet with Dougie's approval, "Do you think that was a bit harsh? He seemed just to drift. This was always going to be a hard meeting, anyway. Stoney could have got 8. And providing everyone pulled together – like we have this season – we could just about win, as Redcar always go well here. We've had a lot of injuries this season. Tai Woffinden came off here on bend two and Jack Roberts hit the metal post last week – legs akimbo on the post! He was lucky 'cause there's no covering!" In the re-rerun of the first heat, Edinburgh send out Aaron Summers to replace the injured Carl Stonehewer and he finishes in second place behind Gary Havelock. Dougie isn't convinced by what he's seen of the Redcar number one, "Last time Havvy was here, he was awful!"

Edinburgh v. Redcar: *"He's conscious but has damage to his foot or ankle!"*

The second heat showcases the essential beauty of speedway racing with a thrilling contest for third place between Aaron Summers and Arlo Bugeja. Summers further illustrates his liking for the Armadale circuit with successive copycat inside passes of his rival on the third bend of the last two laps. Like many Monarchs fans, Dougie has been impressed with Aaron Summers's progress but doesn't view this victory over Bugeja as his greatest scalp of the season. "That was a hard-fought race but I did hear the Redcar fans saying Bugeja was hopeless 'cause he can't even sit in the same place for four laps. He nearly fenced [team mate Chris] Kerr last night in heat 14 to let Wright through for a Workington 5-1!" The tone for tonight's meeting is set in the third race when the Monarchs Fisher and Tully quickly vanquish ex-Monarch James Grieves. Dougie's impressed, "That was brilliant by Ryan – he won it on the first lap when he stopped the run of Grieves! He knew he was going to pass round the outside and Tully is always good at sneaking through the inside." Although this is a triumphant season (so far) at the Scotwaste Arena, the relentless encroachment of the nearby housing estate gives pause for thought and remains an ominously dark architectural cloud on the horizon. However, where there is speedway, noise complaints are rarely far away and, consequently, (to the casual observer) recent investments in the stadium infrastructure sensibly appear to be minimal. Long-term uncertainty also stalks local rivals Glasgow who presently have their home at Saracen Park. Dougie isn't that sympathetic to their possible plight, "Glasgow could find a track anywhere – there's always a bit of rubble anywhere in the city. Edinburgh's different, it's a real struggle! You know it's bad when Edinburgh have to look at places like Stirling and Fife."

A second successive maximum heat advantage for the Monarchs through the Matthew Wethers and Aaron Summers partnership takes them into an 8-point lead and has Dougie purr his approval. "It's good just watching a team of youngsters! If someone has a bad night, someone else just dips in. Tell you what, Jeff, I've really enjoyed the racing this season! It's good after the dross of the last couple of seasons that we've had to watch before. Did I tell you I was getting a bit disillusioned with speedway? It was overkill – if you're doing a hundred matches a season! I used to go to Edinburgh, Glasgow and Berwick and the Dale Devils, when they ran, as well as occasional other matches. This season I'm just coming to Armadale and going to the away meetings at Berwick and Glasgow. So now I only get to see Tai Woffinden once and it's made a big difference! The team this season has breathed new life into me a wee bit!" The danger that the meeting has already slipped away from Redcar against a depleted Monarchs team, prompts Havvy to make a quicker start but nonetheless one that still finds him behind his partner Josh Auty. All eyes are fixed on Ryan Fisher ("here we go, Ryan's got his dander up!) as he proceeds to race neck-and-neck with Havvy before he dramatically drops back to third just at the moment Havvy blasts to the front. Temporarily stuck behind Auty, Fisher then scuttles his way past only for the youngster to come down ("Auty has crashed himself") on the third bend of the second lap. In the rerun of the race, Andrew Tully gates with alacrity while, from the outside gate, Havvy heads Fisher to the corner, and ostentatiously glances behind him before he locks up. With nowhere to go, Ryan clatters into his rival and shows good control to stay on his machine before he resumes his pursuit but finds himself relegated from contention in third place. "He totally impeded him! The old red mist came down but he was too far back." Already 10 points in arrears, the Redcar Bears team manager, Brian Havelock, passes the black-and-white helmet colour to young Australian Ty Proctor who, unfortunately, has no answer to the fast racing, wide line taken by Thomas H. Jonasson. "Thomas is bloody mad! He thinks it's Sheffield round here! You know he's got a Peter Carr engine fitted by Ryan Fisher?" After the double points tactical ride option has been frittered away, Redcar's Grieves and Kerr then hammer home a maximum heat advantage against the highly regarded Wethers/Sneddon combination. Rather than the signal to properly fire up their expected fightback, this is to prove to be a false dawn since the Monarchs reply in kind in successive heats to extend their lead after nine heats to a comfortable 35-21.

The invariably smartly dressed and studiously modest Allan Melville – webmaster of the excellent *Speedway Plus* website (the ultimate resource for speedway fans everywhere) – searches me out in the stadium. Like so many in the crowd, he's savoured the competitive racing we've been served up by the riders of both teams inside the Scotwaste Arena. The quality and variety of his website deserves many more than 3,000 plus hits it generates per day. However, not content to rest on his laurels, Allan continuously searches for innovations rather than settle for comfortable complacency. The quest to combine originality with insight applies just as much to the look and feel of the website as it does to the breadth, range and internationalism of the various features, interviews, excerpts, photographs and the just plain quirky material that's regularly posted there. It's been a slow burn but deserved success since Allan founded the site in October 2002. It's definitely a site that illustrates the sincerity and passion speedway inspires generally but is also a tribute to Allan's single-minded dedication and love of his sport. If the *Speedway Plus* website didn't already exist, you'd like to think it would still be invented. But then, without the dedication of someone so single-mindedly passionate as Allan, you've got to wonder if anyone else could achieve something that looks so professional or remains so absorbing from a content perspective.

The relentless march of success enjoyed during the last few heats by the Monarchs is brought to a temporary halt by James Grieves who's familiar with the peculiar contours and topography of the tight Armadale circuit from the one full season he rode for the club in 1999. Throughout the 57-odd seconds of the race, the never-say-die Thomas H. Jonasson pursues him with such flamboyance and reckless determination that he worries Dougie, "He looks like he's attached to Grieves's back wheel and, has so much speed, it's frightening. Just settle for it Thomas!" In the 11th heat, 23-year-old Matthew Wethers conscientiously tries to team ride his partner and Monarchs team captain, Derek Sneddon, home for four laps from second place. Wethers is a veteran of the Edinburgh club (since 2002) and, though he has superb knowledge of the contours and quirks of the Armadale track surface, Josh Auty rides brilliantly to somehow snatch second place with his last-gasp dash for the chequered flag. Impressive though this effort looks, it's already tarnished in Dougie's eyes, "Matthew was suffering from Derek going so slow otherwise he'd never have caught him!" Even more significantly, when you glance at the race line up, is the identity of the hapless fourth-placed rider, ex World Champ Gary Havelock. Except in the BSI Speedway Grand Prix series, speedway remains a young man's sport. At 39, Gary Havelock is 14 years senior to the next eldest person in the race, Derek Sneddon. Convinced Havelock lives on the faint aura of past glories, Dougie is scathing, "Havvy's perfected the old Neil Collins wiggle to pretend that he's going fast."

Summers and Tully start heat 12 with a master class in how to team ride (ahead of James Grieves). Summers appears to only have a shaky hold on first place, while Tully endeavours to block the hard- charging Grieves. Dougie isn't convinced, "I don't like this team-riding thing with Grieves behind. Just go! Andrew, Go! Grieves was riding a bit scary there!" In mid race, Dougie recalls his earlier valorisation of the team ethic shown this season by his beloved Monarchs, "See what I mean about someone always chipping in this season? Tonight it's Summers!" James Grieves isn't keen to concede defeat lightly, so repeatedly tries his favoured spot of the Armadale third bend to attempt to pass his rivals round the outside. On the second lap, Grieves has to urgently scrub off his momentum after he nearly hits the fence but, it's definitely the case of a lesson unlearnt, when he repeats the manoeuvre next time round in exactly the same place. Sadly, this time he flies into the safety fence, bounces back across the track and clatters his team mate, Benji Compton. The referee is left with no choice but to exclude Grieves and award the race. This ensures another home triumph with fully three races to go for a notionally depleted six-man Monarchs team. With only the pleasure of it to really race for, heat 13 has Havvy and Deek duel for pride (if not honour). They indulge in a battle royale for second place until the third-bend jinx this time strikes Sneddon, who clatters into the fence and comes down. With the third lap nearly completed, referee Jim McGregor again awards the race. In heat 14, Edinburgh record their sixth 5-1 of the night when Fisher and the hardy Sneddon combine during the penultimate race to stretch the scoreline to 53-33. Chris Kerr gets a consolation third place for the Redcar Bears and receives the sharp side of Dougie's tongue for his troubles, "Is that Chris 'I like it slick' Kerr? A fantastic result for Edinburgh under the circumstances!" Over the loudspeaker system, Scott Wilson blurts out some exciting news, "I've just heard from Somerset and the Monarchs are confirmed as the top of the Premier League tonight!" With the Monarchs rampant, Dougie's mind turns to travails of the less fortunate located elsewhere, namely Glasgow. "Glasgow have missed Shane Parker this season. He's been slowly coming back from illness and had something wrong with his bikes. On the *Easy Tiger* website, earlier in the season, there were even some Glasgow fans slagging him off! So much so, that Shane had to come on himself and put them right! I have this sick sense of humour that I'd like to see Shane ride here for one season to stick it up Glasgow!"

With the meeting beyond doubt a while back, Redcar proceed to massage the final scoreline with a heat advantage in the last race and, thereby, only suffer an 18-point defeat. Dougie notes, "It's an even better performance when you realise that the replacements for Stoney only got 4 points!" The Monarchs fans drift away cheerfully and sight of my book display attracts a disgruntled Redcar fan stops to mournfully confide, "I think the Cubs would have ridden better than the Bears here tonight! [pause] Though, 37 points would have been good two decades ago!" Later, affable speedway veteran, Dick Barrie, stops by for a word and, held in his hand like a prized trophy, he proudly clutches some newfangled technology. It's the first time that I've ever spotted a Blackberry at a speedway meeting, let alone in the possession of someone you would consider managerial! Dick holds it in a manner that implies pride in ownership but also suggests that it might be a radioactive explosive device. Only his second day of ownership, he hasn't quite got the hang of his new gizmo if judged by its ear-splitting ringtone and the way he barks "Hello! Hello? Hello!" into the suddenly lifeless equipment. Despite his best efforts, Dick fails to make a connection and, thereby, imitates Redcar's failure to gel tonight as a team.

25th July Edinburgh v. Redcar (Premier League) 55-37

Edinburgh v. Redcar: *"He's conscious but has damage to his foot or ankle!"*

CHAPTER 27.

Workington:

"I said, 'They want you to wear women's clothes!'"

26th July

The gods have decided to smile on the Cumbrian town of Workington so, three hours before the scheduled start time, the sun beats down in blistering fashion upon Derwent Park Stadium. Home of the Workington Comets, this evening the club will stage one of the prestigious Super7even BSPA shared events, namely the 2008 Premier League Four Team Championship (sponsored by Moss Bay Metals). Workington is a proper speedway town and it requires, whatever direction you take to travel there, that you pass through some splendidly spectacular countryside. Recent years have seen the Super7even events plagued by traffic difficulties and, in keeping with that tradition, there has been an accident on the A66. This is the main road many people use to access Workington (via the Lake District) and, as a result, by mid-afternoon it's blocked in both directions. To further complicate matters, this weekend the nearby town of Maryport stages the acclaimed Maryport Blues Festival. Billed as the UK's premier Blues event, it has taken place in Maryport since 1999. Its importance, recognition and success has grown exponentially over the years to the extent that every hotel, B&B, village hall and performance space has been fully booked or occupied for its duration from early Friday until late Sunday night. Even Workington promoter Ian Thomas was tempted to join the throng to go and see Chuck Berry. "He was on last night at 11 but it was too late for me! They get 60,000 or 70,000 people come along during the whole weekend." Ian made a good decision not to go to the concert, "Chuck Berry got panned. He was contracted to do an hour and, though he did that, he didn't do it enthusiastically. It's a high quality event plus the main attraction on another night was Jools Holland and some American bloke [Jimmie Vaughan], whose name I forget. People underestimate Cumbria – whether it's the coastline or the cultural events. Status Quo played at Whitehaven Rugby League club but, I had to miss it, 'cause it was a Saturday and I was at Workington. It hit our crowds too which is typical of my luck!" Maryport is a delightfully compact harbour town situated on the Solway Firth and definitely isn't of sufficient size to house all the Festival visitors or events. Consequently, this late July Saturday afternoon, Workington finds itself besieged by shoppers, hordes of Blues fans as well as a good number of the speedway variety. Though the area likes to boast to tourists about its Roman and Victorian heritage, the way of the modern world is such that everyone appears to prefer the shops, music or dawdling until the roar of speedway engines fill the air to historical tours of the defunct workings of the local coal mines, iron makers and ship builders.

There has been a revolution behind the scenes at Workington this season since local entrepreneur Keith Denham purchased the club from Kidderminster-based businessman, Tony Mole. While many of the essential fixtures and fittings remain unchanged – Ian Thomas and Carl Stonehewer are both at the club and the home-straight grandstand remains resolutely unaltered – there have been significant alterations to the size and shape of the track as well as the quality of the materials used. Keith Denham, the Chief Executive of Workington's main sponsors, Thomas Armstrong (Holdings) Limited explained the changes undertaken at the club to the *Speedway Star*. "The first priority was the track, and we have spent a great deal of time and effort moving all the shale from the track and grading it in order to get rid of all the large stones that were mixed in amongst it. Then we repaired the base before totally relaying the track. We have also widened the home straight by two metres. In addition, we have carried out extensive repairs to the safety fence and reconstructed the fence on the home straight so that it will hinge down, making it quicker to drop and re-erect for the Rugby League matches. We've completely overhauled the floodlights and replaced a lot of bulbs. There are now over 40 floodlight bulbs working so the lighting should be a lot brighter than last season. It has cost an arm and a leg to do that, but it will make a huge difference. The electrics have all been replaced. We have a new starting gate system with two sets of tapes in order to reduce any delays if there is a problem. It has only been used for one meeting, which was last year's Cardiff Grand Prix, so it's a great piece of kit. We have lined out the home and away pit areas, generally painted and tidied up the place and we have set up a new hospitality suite coming out of turn 2, which will also have a viewing balcony. There has been a lot more to do at the track than we expected and there have been over 3,000 man hours of work put in there during the close season ... In widening the home straight by two metres, along with the exit at turn 4 and entry into turn 1, the track is now set up to provide some very exciting high speed racing, which should be entertaining for the fans and that also means that the track now has straights and bends that meet the FIM standards for width."

Given these extensive changes and the upgrade of the track to FIM standards, it wasn't exactly a surprise when Workington were given the chance to stage the Four Team Tournament. Prior to his departure, Super7even event's organiser (on behalf of the BSPA), King's Lynn co-promoter Jonathan Chapman revealed he wasn't a huge fan of the meeting format. "The Four Team Tournament, to be honest if there's ever going to be an event which I hold my breath about, it's that. I'm not a fan of it. The concept of one rider from a team in every race in a team event is not something I like. And I think it drags on too long, but we're cutting the races down, back to the original 28 this year. It's a lot of riders to get to one place at one time, but it's worked very well at Workington. For a number of years, Ian Thomas pleaded for it to come back there; he felt it was the right place. The only thing I'm a little reserved about is the home advantage ... Workington has got track changes being made this year, how they'll turn out I don't know, but I sincerely hope it's a successful event."

Though he's got a huge number of tasks still to attend to, Ian Thomas kindly takes the time to leave his speedway office adjacent to the pits area/pits gate to give me a tour of the terraces and proudly show off the new hospitality area on the second bend. Ian explains, "We've only had it four weeks – we didn't open it for Mildenhall but the sponsors love it! They get treated really well by the ladies with the refreshments and, of course, by the club!" The hospitality room itself has a substantial number of tables and chairs. This afternoon each table is covered with an immaculately ironed white tablecloth and a lone refreshment lady is already hard at work. An impressively large buffet awaits it fate and remains fresh underneath its cling-film covers. Ian also takes me to the doorway of "the bar next door for the fans". This has been slightly reduced in size from its previous capacity on account of the building work that created the hospitality suite area. However, the *piece de resistance* of the whole second-bend development at Derwent Park Stadium is the outdoor viewing platform which, due to its elevation and length, provides a fantastic view that overlooks the first- and second-bend action as well as provides the ideal platform from which to appreciate the drama of the rest of the circuit. Ian claims, with only a hint of hyperbole, "Look at that – it's the best view in speedway! He [Keith Denham] damn well wanted the best for his sponsors and hospitality suite and the views from here are panoramic!" Though he's delighted with the facilities, Ian is, by his standards, gloomy about Workington's prospects in tonight's meeting. Many people's pre-meeting favourites, they have suddenly been hit by misfortune. "Stoney's riding but he's not fit! Until Thursday night [when Daniel Nermark got injured in a crash at Redcar], we'd have walked this but now we won't even make the final! Injury is a part of speedway but it's definitely gonna jeopardise our League bid. When Daniel crashed he landed on his neck. The First Aid man who got to him first said to me after he'd gone to hospital, he thought he was dead when he first got there!

Ian Thomas on the new balcony

Mary and Karen Kelly

Touch wood, we haven't had any bad crashes here this season. Obviously we've changed the shape and we took all the shale off and sieved it right through. That means, it's slick most weeks and, I think, there's not been so much overtaking. Crowds dropped off last year but, this season, it's evened out to well over a thousand or so each week. Good for most places but bad for here! To win things, you need to avoid injuries. As I say, touch wood, the doctor hasn't had his car out on the track all season. He has been on the track – when one rider did come off on bend 1 – but, before he got to him, the rider had got up!"

Given eight clubs will contest the Four Team Tournament, the Workington pits area has had to have a temporary extension added to accommodate all the additional riders. The regular pits have been subdivided and these stalls have been supplemented with tarpaulin-covered scaffolding poles to create covered temporary pit areas. On any normal race night, the maximum number of riders in the pits would be 16; whereas, for tonight's Four Team Tournament, there will be 37! Close by to the brightly painted programme stall, a table has already been laid out in preparation for the promised 'meet and greet the rider' sessions organised so that the fans can get autographs, pose for photographs with their idols or discuss the prospects ahead with them. Workington Speedway club boasts a trackshop housed inside a metal sea container and, given the expected large crowd this evening, this has been supplemented with another sea container cum temporary trackshop. It's been strategically placed near to the pits turnstiles on grassy scrubland that bordering the road that serves as entranceway to the car park. The trackshop is run in no-nonsense but friendly fashion by Liz Fleming ably helped by her partner Gary and their son Scott. For one night only, fans will have a double opportunity to buy speedway merchandise and memorabilia from two quirkily housed trackshops! Many fans have arrived early to make an afternoon of it in the Derwent Park Stadium car park (and also park their cars in the premium parking places close to the exit).

Before the later fancy-dress arrivals and below the high cloud of a sweltering afternoon, some fans contentedly sit inside their cars to watch the rich tapestry of characters from the world of speedway wander by. Sat patiently in their car (with the windows fully wound down) are Edinburgh Monarchs supporting mother and daughter, Mary and Karen Kelly. Mary first went to speedway in 1947 and the list of Scottish teams she reels off provides a potted mini history of post-war team and stadium changes north of the border. She's watched the Lanarkshire Eagles at Motherwell, the Ashfield Giants, the Glasgow Tigers at White City, the Edinburgh Monarchs at Meadowbank and now enjoys their latest iteration at Armadale. Mary's ideally placed to travel to both Scottish clubs of the modern era, "I'm 15 miles away from Armadale in Lanark and 30 miles from Glasgow." She has many happy memories and these include watching Peter Craven at Meadowbank. Mary can wistfully recall crowds of 30,000 people at White City but, as a staunch Monarchs fan, also confesses, "I tended to support Glasgow when Stevie Lawson rode for them." She doesn't like to claim that one era is superior to another but sees each in their separate context. "There used to be concrete start grids and when it was wet they skidded all over the place and, of course, the tracks were deeper. You remember that the racing was always closer but, maybe, it wasn't! Nowadays they have faster bikes and, sometimes, that can mean first out of the gate wins. One thing that could change is if they cut out some of the stupid rules they have now. The tactical ride rule is silly and it's hard to understand. Twice recently, I've taken new families along to the speedway and they can't get hold of the rules at all. But I also preferred the old one-off finals. The Millennium Stadium is a great facility to have but isn't a racer's track. The man-made tracks should be got rid of or made to the standard of Copenhagen. The tracks at world level nowadays are too slick." Also extremely passionate about speedway, her daughter Karen highlights, "We want to cheer for the British team but Jim Lynch and Scott Nicholls call it 'Team England!' Surely they know Willy Lawson was in the nominated squad? I dinnae know why Jim Lynch got it? The spirit was poor and you never saw all the British riders together." Mary is keen to praise the quality of the welcome and the family spirit found at Armadale. "A family sat behind us at the old Meadowbank in the '50s and she appeared last week at Armadale – she's 93!

[Karen] "The credit John Campbell gets is well-deserved! A lot of thought has gone into that side and it's really great! I like young Aaron Summers – he's quiet just sitting there and gets better every week. I just worry about all the houses."

[Mary] "We vowed we'd never come back here [Workington] after what happened the last time. There was some tension in the stands. There were five or six drunken Workington fans that kept standing on their seats every time their riders came out. We couldn't see a thing and a couple asked them to sit down. They didn't like it and threatened

Workington: *"I said, 'They want you to wear women's clothes!'"*

that they were gonna wait outside for us. In the end we went out through the offices. It's the only time in all my years at speedway that something like that happened. I'm sure with the new man in, Ian Thomas, things have changed! Back in the old days, we used to take our caravan to all the tracks and catch the coach from Manchester for the World Final! The banter was good. We were fans from different teams but [nods at a gaggle of Monarchs fans in kilts] people still try to have fun nowadays. But, it's still not quite the same."

Hard-working presenter and Buzz Lightyear look-alike, Michael Max passes and pointedly scotches wild rumours that Glasgow might not run in 2009. "There's absolutely no truth in the rumours! We've signed riders for next year already and have agreed with the landlords for next season. We could always do with a hundred more fans but so could everyone. It's amazing how these stories start!" I quiz Michael about whether he's the new Mildenhall presenter, "It's a bit far even for me to drive! I stepped in because they needed someone. I'm a professional and you do the job for whoever pays you!" By now, the entrance turnstiles have opened and the queue has subsided. Between the trackshop and the bright blue programme stall, fans have a chance to donate money to the Speedway Riders' Benevolent Fund. Rob Peasley and his dad Cliff are stood in their bright yellow clothing though, given the warmth of the sunshine, the lady helper with them stands out as overdressed in her yellow fleece top. Various riders will take it in turns to sit at the autograph table. One of them is Shaun Tacey and, while there's no queue, he makes an animated phone call. When the call is over, Shaun reminisces, "I used to ride here. I like the place but I don't miss the drive!"

Back outside the stadium wall at the satellite sea container that serves as the satellite trackshop today, there's a panic that they've lost this week's bundle of the *Speedway Star*. The avuncular Peterborough Programme Editor and keen Panthers fan, Steve Miles takes a bullish view of the recent travails at the East of England Showground. "Everything's fine. Oh, everything's not fine but we're surviving fingertip style and, obviously, will now ride without Hans Andersen!" Also mingling amongst the Workington 4TT crowd is Brian Oldham. He's part way through a mini-version of his Round the Tracks Speedway Tour though, this evening, without his better half, Celia. Last season he visited every track in the country to celebrate a golden anniversary of sorts – his 50th year of watching speedway in Britain. He's a passionate advocate for the sport and, over the years, has got to know many within speedway including riders and their families. "I spent about nine hours with the Woffies [Woffindens] at Scunthorpe yesterday. At half past 12, I had tea with Cynthia [Tai Woffinden's grandmother] and put the speedway world to rights! And by half 11 I was drinking beer and discussing clutch plates! Celia will be so jealous!" Shortly afterwards, a man who claims to be the Newcastle pits marshal [listed in their programme as Brian McBean] rails against the politics of the team selection for the 2008 Premier League Four Team Tournament. "It's a bloody joke! It's political, man. Even the teams that are here! They say you'll need to alter the [racecard] insert. Berwick have been replaced by Scunthorpe and Ostergaard, Nermark and Kramer are all out." He's keen to praise the Reading Racers website for their prompt coverage of the 'breaking news' of the A66 accident, particularly when the comparatively 'local' Newcastle Diamonds website hadn't covered it! A passing Monarchs fan called Stuart has other worries, "I just worry that Ryan will knock off three riders in the first corner at the Scottish Open and

Programme stall

SRBF Collection

it'll all be Monarchs."

Away to my left – at the cusp of my peripheral hearing – Peter Toogood and Neil Machin stand apart from the car park bustle on some grass- and nettle-covered wasteland to have a private but animated conversation. Both wear practical but deeply unfashionable sunglasses that make them look like they're about to audition for a middle-aged speedway version of *Men in Black*. With the hubbub of people and conversation around the trackshop and my stall, I can only catch fleeting snatches of their conversation. But, judged by Peter Toogood's arm waving and abandonment of his usual reticent demeanour, it's a topic he feels extremely passionate about. Like one in every hundred overheard mobile conversations, the brief snippets I do hear sound fascinating. "When he said 'You're nobody!' that really got to me! ... that was the total of it, no, listen! ... you know how I say things!" Eventually, after a long conversation during which Peter waves his arms enough to land a squadron of planes on the Navy's largest aircraft carrier, they move away and within half an hour the area where they stood is completely occupied by an overflow armada of riders' white vans. Mark Lemon unloads just the one bike from his van and, with his giant kitbag and impressively sized toolkit balanced precariously on the bike, he slowly wends his way to the pits gate entrance to join the rest of his Reading team mates. The Racers will be in action the next night at Glasgow so Workington is really just one leg of a mini Northern Tour for their representatives at Derwent Park this evening: Mark Lemon, Tom P. Madsen, Chris Mills, Tomas Suchanek and Jamie Smith. Team Manager, Tim Sugar, and Reading Webmaster, Andy Povey have joined them on their journey north.

A large contingent of well-behaved Edinburgh fans in kilts have already made their way into Derwent Park Stadium. Much closer to the scheduled start time a large contingent of sombrero-wearing Manchester Mexicans arrive in party mood clutching an impressive number of cans to queue at the turnstiles and make occasional forays to the trackshop to survey its stock. They all wear black 'stag do' T-shirts and have clearly arrived in Workington with the desire to party during the afternoon as well as enjoy the speedway. Liz in the trackshop isn't impressed, "If I was the Belle Vue promoter I'd ask them not to come into the stadium as they do nothing for the club image! If Keith Denham knew this was happening he'd confiscate their beer if not bar them!" Their arrival appears to have excited some local female interest and Liz notes sardonically, "I see all the Workington trollops have latched on to them already." Though worse for wear, one of the Manchester Mexicans remains enthusiastically on the pull: "Are you a local lass? I've never been north of Blackpool before! This is my first time this far north. This is an excellent track, isn't it? We've got a poxy little track but, at least, we get all the top boys!"

With many more riders in the pits than usual, the logistics of the rider parade and introductions take some organisation. The riders wait patiently by the pits gate and then crowd onto various modern-style open-top 4x4s for a slow circuit of the Derwent Park Stadium track and a brief wave to the crowd. They then return to the pits to wait for the widely advertised arrival of Miss Cumbria in a helicopter. Away from the speedway track, Workington promoter Ian Thomas is, of course, a "close-up magician". He's also a show-business impresario since he books and manages various types of entertainer through his company "The Ian Thomas Organisation". Apart from close-up magic, customers can book the bands, caricaturists, party bands, disco and comedians. Ian has often used his show business experience and expertise in his parallel speedway career. Indeed, over the years Ian has invited many personalities to speedway tracks where he has worked. These include Ken Dodd, Max Bygraves, Jim Bowen, Bill Maynard, Bill Crompton, various look-alikes (Del Boy, Prince Charles, James Bond, Matt Ford) Blondini ("blows himself up in a coffin"), Henry la Mothe ("belly-flopped from 20 feet into 12 inches of water – he was a support act for Evel Knievel – he must be dead now as he was 69 then"), Dan Limburger ("fell 60 feet on fire into six foot flames") and a one-man band who played 104 instruments while he ran the 100 metres in 14 seconds "though he fell over when he did it! It was a great thing to say though – '104 instruments'!" For tonight's 4TT meeting Ian has chosen to play the glamour card in the form of 18-year-old Natasha Cooper who presently holds the title of Miss Cumbria 2008. She beat nine other contestants in the final round of the Cumbrian regional competition held at the prestigious Armathwaite Hall country house. Born in Whitehaven, Natasha lives with her grandmother in Eskdale and studies for an IT degree at the Lakes College. Much keener on horses than speedway, the 5ft 8in brunette is about to make a grand entrance from the helicopter that presently hovers above Derwent Park Stadium. The green helicopter circles and makes a stately but textbook landing in the middle of the centre green. With the rotor blades still spinning, the riders (along with the crowd) wait expectantly for their first glimpse of the beauty queen. The door opens and out springs Peter Toogood! Given his diminutive stature, Peter rather melodramatically but unnecessarily ducks to avoid the rotating blades and then, ever the chivalrous gentleman, helps Miss Cumbria from the helicopter. Peter has clearly decided beforehand that a fear of compromising paparazzi photos allied to the exalted status of his position within speedway dictates that he keep a neutral fixed expression on his face. Harry Pearson's wonderful description of Newcastle's "rotund retail maverick" Mike Ashley immediately springs to mind ("wearing the sort of blank yet benign expression adopted by the Queen when attending a break-dancing display by disadvantaged youngsters"). When Natasha embarked on her quest to become Miss England and, thereby, possibly get to enter the Miss World beauty contest, little could she have imagined that her bookings/duties would include a trip to the speedway, let alone the joy of a helicopter ride with the Chairman of the British Speedway Promoters' Association! Andy Povey suggests that Peter's arrival would have made greater impact if he'd jumped commando style – in fatigues rather than knickerless – from the helicopter, though he doesn't specify whether this should be with or without a parachute. Peter's spectacular arrival is the ideal moment to quiz Neil Machin about his earlier highly animated conversation with the Chairman of the BSPA. Always quick-witted and canny, Neil provides a plausible explanation. "Peter Toogood said to me: 'I dunno why they wanted me to be here at quarter to six!' and I said, 'They want you to wear women's clothes!' He was 'freakin' hell! No! Women's clothes!' I think I'd touched a nerve! Rather than dress in women's clothes, he went in a chopper and got to touch Miss Cumbria instead!" His Sheffield partner in crime, Dave Hoggart, chimes in "They say the chopper pilot is a real nutter!" Shortly afterwards, Ian Thomas issues me with a brief staccato version of events for this chapter, "You got some copy about the helicopter? There are 28 races and we're aiming for quarter to ten. We've an extra doctor, ambulance and paramedic. Alright, Berwick didn't turn up but the few riders missing are all injured."

Mark Lemon unloads

Kilts

The withdrawal of the Berwick Bandits adds to the complexity of the programme since we now have an insert to fill out for the qualifying semi-finals and then we revert to the original programme itself for the Grand Final part of the meeting. In semi-final 1 the Workington Comets are pitted against the Somerset Rebels, Sheffield Tigers and Edinburgh Monarchs. While the second semi-final pits the King's Lynn Stars against the Newcastle Diamonds, Scunthorpe Scorpions and Reading Racers. During the semi-finals each rider has to take two rides while the races alternate with heat 1 of semi-final 1 followed by heat 1 of semi-final 2 and so on. The two top-scoring teams from each group will then contest the Grand Final during which each rider will race three times over a series of 12 races that comprise it. As previously noted, there is one rider from each side in every race (thankfully) with the traditional points-scoring system of 3 for a win, 2 for a second and 1 for a third. I'm privileged to be able to watch the action from the cordoned-off riders' area of the terraces that overlooks the first bend. While the new hospitality area might provide a panoramic view of the action, the riders' and guests' viewing area also provides a superb view of the action as the riders race away from the start line into the first corner. The basic requirement for any team in the semi-final stage of the competition is (obviously enough) to collectively rack up as many points as possible to ensure that they get to the next vital stage of the competition.

Consequently, there's an element of measured professionalism rather than thrilling harum-scarum action about these initial 'qualification' races. Frequently, the on-track action is brightened by the comments of event announcer Michael Max. Carl Stonehewer's decision to even take part in the meeting initially looks bravely optimistic, particularly when he trails in behind Jordan Frampton, Joel Parsons and Andrew Tully. Michael Max confirms the evidence of our own eyes, "Stoney battling hard with that obvious injury!" Always keen to make linkages that might excite the large contingent of Comets fans in attendance, the exhilarating win for Tomas Topinka in the opening heat of the other semi-final group prompts Michael to observe, "Workington fans keep a close eye on Tomas Topinka who's the Comets guest at Mildenhall tomorrow! A decision has yet to be taken as to whether Stoney will ride but it looks unlikely. There'll be a very special guest tomorrow at Mildenhall, someone who almost left this earth – Barry Burchett."

Always knowledgeable, before a fourth heat that features Brent Werner, Charles Wright, Ricky Ashworth and Ryan Fisher, Michael Max informs us, "This race features four speedway riders who have suffered injuries through entertaining the public." Notoriously hawkeyed, from the centre green, Michael is quick to notice, "As you can see, Charles Wright has no dirt deflector on his bike! Can someone please have a word with him!" Failure to ride with a dirt deflector is, of course, an excludable offence. The race is won by Ryan Fisher and this excites a response from the large contingent of travelling Monarchs fans, "The Edinburgh fans leap to their feet for Ryan Fisher – they like what they're seeing from this exciting rider!" Something that people don't like seeing – or more specifically, don't like smelling nowadays – is cigarette smoke. "Sorry to be a bit of a killjoy but, anyone smoking under the covered back-straight stand, isn't allowed to do so! It's against the law of the land, I'm afraid!" Magnus Karlsson's mechanic Paul Henry takes a brief but well-earned respite from his duties between Magnus's races. Many people think that Scunthorpe will definitely qualify for the Grand Final stage of the competition. When I draw this surmise to Paul's attention, it fails to fill his heart with joy, "Who the freak says that? We've [Magnus & Paul] got a nightmare week ahead without even more racing! We were at home last night, we're here today, riding for Glasgow tomorrow at Ashfield and then away for them at Reading on Monday and the Isle of Wight on Tuesday!" Shortly afterwards a conflicted Scunthorpe fan shouts out some encouragement for Richard Hall, "Go Rich!" and, then immediately afterwards, lambasts him for being "a stuck-up bastard." Over the tannoy John Walsh appeals for a car driver to return to their car, "There's a green Skoda – last time it was a green BMW – with its windows open!" A girl fan in the crowd behind me smirks, "No one would want to nick that! Come on, the worst thing that could happen is that someone could throw litter into it!"

If the ostensible magic of the 4TT competition is to be retained, then the crowd have to feel that there's some sort of mystery about who will qualify from each semi-final group. After five heats the scores are pretty even in the first semi-final group. In the second semi-final group it already appears that King's Lynn and Scunthorpe are definite to qualify for the final unless Newcastle and Reading significantly buck up their ideas. Michael Max explains the situation with a wonderful description, "Three heats left in the qualifying and every point is a prisoner!" This only really applies to the riders from Somerset, Workington, Sheffield and Edinburgh and, to double underline the point, Michael evocatively adds, "If there's engine failures, or a bad start, then it's bath time!" Bath time comes quickly for the Reading Racers though Michael offers them some words of consolation. "They've not qualified so, I'm afraid, it's to the bar!" Up to this point in the meeting, the racing hasn't exactly quickened the pulses but the crowd definitely fire to life when Carl Stonehewer shakes off the torpor of his first outing to give a master class in heat 7 in how to ride the Derwent Park Stadium circuit. Stoney does it with grace, elegance, speed and aplomb. Apart from a great ride, it also puts Workington through to the final and the crowd react accordingly. Like London buses, once there's been one thrilling ride another immediately follows and, in this case, Jason King shines for the Newcastle Diamonds when he blasts round the outside and under the arm of Shaun Tacey on the back straight. Only one race left, technically anyone can still win from the first semi-final group. Michael Max continues to stoke our collective interest, "Everything can happen in heat number 8". But, similar to our experience of the earlier part of the meeting, nothing much does happen unless, of course, you count an engine failure for Joe Haines as drama. Though, that said, Workington and Somerset manage to ease through to the final at the expense of the Sheffield Tigers and the Edinburgh Monarchs. Their elimination is the signal for the invariably dapper Sheffield promoter, Neil Machin, to discard his (mandatory) SCB jacket and immediately change into a natty tracksuit top. Reading Webmaster Andy Povey complains animatedly on his mobile phone about the execrable nature of the Racers performance: "We were shite – it's difficult to put a more positive spin on it than that!" Phone call over, Andy confides, "Reading were bad but the track was even worse!

Workington: *"I said, 'They want you to wear women's clothes!'"*

The only positive I can think of is that none of them were injured!" Normally complaints about the track would be drawn to the attention of Workington's veteran track curator Tony Swales but rumour has swept through the pits that he's been peremptorily released from his duties at the club by owner Keith Denham, allegedly after a discussion on curatorial philosophy and its implementation. Afterwards we're told, though Tony Swales could have left with immediate effect, he remained for the duration of the meeting to ensure that duties were carried out professionally and effectively.

There's an interval while the riders clean their equipment and mentally prepare for the Grand Final stage of the competition. United as one in the crowd, we can't complete filling in our programmes since it's not yet been clarified whether Scunthorpe or King's Lynn will race in the blue helmet colour or the yellow. Eventually, Michael Max informs us, "King's Lynn won the exciting toss of the coin challenge and will ride in the blue helmet colour." If the semi-finals lacked consistent race excitement then, sadly, the trend continues into the final which quickly becomes a three-horse race between Workington, King's Lynn and Somerset. On the centre green, Michael Max had to draw deeply upon his presentational experience and the vast array of ready drafted *bon mots* to vaguely thrill the crowd before we've reached the fifth heat. There's so little excitement even the programme is thrust centre stage in order to provide a modicum of drama, "The red lights are on! There may be a slight error in the programme!" Before the start of the next race, it's quickly apparent that the referee is flashing the lights in the mistaken belief that we're at a discotheque, "The red lights are on again. I'm not quite sure why? [pause] the red light is off!" I quiz the ex Workington Programme Editor, Tony Jackson, about potential reasons behind the lack of oomph in the race action, "They widened the straight so there's been less crashes. They've also sieved the track and that's taken some of the body from it, as it were. Also, everyone used to cut everyone's nose off on the last bend but that doesn't happen so much anymore. The sides are evenly matched but, if we'd had Daniel Nermark or if Stoney was fully fit then, I think, the Comets would have taken some beating tonight."

Awaiting Miss Cumbria

Kauko and Stoney

With three races to go, Somerset look favourites to win with apparently only Workington likely to challenge them. However, the structure of Fours racing means that you can hold destiny in your own hands but also that you sometimes requires the help of others to succeed. Over the final three races King's Lynn gain 7 points while Somerset only gain a solitary additional point to add to their cumulative total and thereby miss out on the chance of glory. When the last heat of the Grand Final finally arrives, our marathon of a 28-race evening is nearly at close though it's still mathematically possible for Workington, King's Lynn or Scunthorpe to triumph. There are a number of permutations but, ahead of their rivals by 2 and 3 points respectively, the Comets look clear favourites to win the trophy, particularly since Kauko Nieminen lines up for them off gate 1. Michael Max ponders rider motivation, "There's trophies for the top three from Miss Cumbria but, I think, it's the kisses that go with them that might make them more determined!" After two comfortable wins Kauko decides to reserve his one poor race of the night for the vital 12th heat. His last place finish would have given Somerset the crown if only Jason Doyle had won the race but, instead, with a win for Tomas Topinka [and third for Doyle] there will be a run off. In fact, permutations are so complex that we're suddenly

Workington: *"I said, 'They want you to wear women's clothes!'"*

all in need of access to a supercomputer. Somerset would have also taken part in the run-off if only Richard Hall hadn't snatched second place on the line from Jason Doyle. Immune to this sudden complexity, an overweight girl in the crowd isn't happy, "Kauko freakin' came last!" Defeat for the Comets appears an even more likely outcome when Tomas Topinka gates in the rerun of the run off. But, for a meeting conducted throughout in almost studiously gentlemanly fashion, Kauko suddenly discovers his hard-riding gloves to aggressively cut across Topinka on the back straight. Presented with this obstruction, King's Lynn's Czech rider has to decide whether to shut off or crash in the possible hope that the outrageously hard-riding Nieminen will subsequently be deemed to have committed an excludable offence by the referee. During a long season (or career), discretion will invariably be the better part of valour. Sensibly Topinka errs on the side of caution and cuts his speed. The sudden shocking harshness of Nieminen's aggressive manoeuvre ensures that Workington lift the 4TT trophy on their own track!

The meeting concludes with the traditional victory parade serenaded with comment and grumbles from the fans. Michael Max sends us off with, "Thanks a lot to each and every one of you!" Scunthorpe Press Officer, Richard Hollingsworth, notes, "Hall has been disappointing away – this has been his best away meeting this season. The racing we have at Scunny has been unbelievable! It was a shame there's been something wrong with the gates this meeting! You wouldn't think it would be that hard to sort out, would you?" Oxford fan-in-exile and Speedway Riders' Benevolent Fund collection activist, Rob Peasley highlights, "Only speedway would not have defending champions [Isle of Wight] at the meeting! It was a boring meeting but a dramatic ending! The problem was that the hottest day of the year is never good for speedway, especially with 28 races to run." Before he scurries off into the night, an older fan tells me, "It went to the last heat and there was a run-off. That's the magic of the Fours though, isn't it? All the jockeying for position and hoping that other teams help you!" After he's concluded his duties Michael Max, sums up his experience of the event in the dark gloom of the car park: "It was a fair finish to the meeting. I just spoke to Kauko afterwards and, he said, he had to cut him off like that 'cause it was a one-off race. If it had been a league match, he said, he wouldn't and would have left him room but tonight he couldn't!"

Because of the Blues Festival, I don't get to stay at the smoker's paradise that is the Waverley Hotel. In the bar of my hotel, I bump into Scunthorpe team manager Kenny Smith with his partner, Julie Harrowven, who's Marketing Manager for Scunthorpe speedway club. After the appearance of some honest comments from her in *Concrete for Breakfast*, Julie watches what she says around me, while Kenny remains his usual cheerful, outgoing and clubbable self. His hair is tied into his trademark ponytail though it's not quite as luxuriant as I remember it. "We were pleased to get to the final and recovered well after a poor start. Rob Lyon reacted weirdly to the request to toss a coin for helmet colours in the final. Tony Steele administered it. I called 'Heads' and Rob said 'It needs discussing!' Tony Steele pulled a weird look so, I said, 'You call' but Rob said 'It needs discussing!' I asked, 'What needs discussing?' and, then, Rob storms off. I then tell Tony Steele I was happy to have whatever colour Rob doesn't want and he thanked me." An ex-speedway rider himself, Kenny takes a practical and sympathetic approach to young men he manages directly as well as those he's previously worked with. "Josh [Auty] admits the choice of Redcar was poor and wishes he hadn't left. He's talented but, sometimes, doesn't do himself any favours. I spoke to Charles Wright at Redcar on Thursday and asked him, what had happened there. He told me, 'Auty had elbowed me first time out so I returned the favour'. I told him, 'Lots of people will elbow you,' and, he knows that, but replied, 'Yeah, but I don't like him!' At Scunthorpe Josh and Tai used to race all the time against each other when they were on the same team! I told them to ride as a team now and race each other in the World Final – as you'll have plenty of time then!" Kenny has a casual modesty about his own racing career and skill as a rider. He has some unrepeatable stories about riding with Malcolm 'Mad Wellie' Holloway and some good stories about his experiences with Dave Mullett. He's curious about what will happened to Reading speedway with the closure of Smallmead and also fondly recalls his days riding at Tilehurst. Various reminiscences from his time as a rider round the tracks blurt out, "I was taught how to ride at Exeter by Vaclav Verner. He said to aim at the fence and, then, brush your back wheel off it – woomph! Vaclav used to say his wheel only lasted eight meetings. We used to get up to all sorts. I remember Dave Kennett knocking me off (to break my wrist or arm) when he was really aiming to knock off second placed Dave Mullett – but I'd suddenly accelerated into that position! It's different now to when I was a rider with lots of new tracks that we didn't have then." Some of the new generation of tracks meet with approval but others don't. Julie hadn't been impressed on one Scunthorpe trip to the Peak District. "The track was very poor at Buxton." In the context of these conditions, Kenny took a consultative approach "I told our lot they didn't have to ride it if they didn't want to but they did!"

Workington: *"I said, 'They want you to wear women's clothes!'"*

Julie laughs, "The winner was the one that could hang on! I don't like Edinburgh either – it's too technical a track. Where else do riders have to shut off in bend 1? There's houses close by, a bar like a shed and reserved people on the programme and burger stalls."

Kenny identifies the promoter of a Conference League track who ran a shared event in his own inimitable fashion, "I used to ride with him so I know how crafty he is! All season they had crowds well over a thousand but reported 600 for that one! However, it's amazing how honest most people in speedway are. I got called to the gate at Scunny for a man who'd lost his wallet and I lent him £10 and the promoter said, 'You'll never see that again!' And I said, 'I'd have helped him anyway.' The next week I was called back to the gate and repaid my money, he paid his entrance fee twice and spoke to Julie about a donation [£75] to the Riders' Support Fund. I told him, 'Take your cheque back, it wasn't so you'd donate!' He wouldn't and the man even refused to give us his name ("just Alan") for listing in the programme."

26th July 2008 Premier League Four Team Championship Winner: Workington

CHAPTER 28.

Newcastle v. Sheffield:

"The riders don't turn round the corners but slide round counter steering with the steering wheel and sliding the back end around."

27 July

If you look at a map, the cross-country road from Workington to Newcastle should theoretically be a scenic drive and, even though it's lovely and sunny, the reality is somewhat different. Approximately half way you pass through Carlisle town centre and, after a drive past the football ground, I stop for a brief rest at Tesco. Speedway is a small world even in Tesco. Previously (in Oxford) I'd bumped into Greg Hancock at the tills and this morning I'm surprised to find Debbie Dixon by the sandwiches and fresh fruit sections. Her partner and Scunthorpe photographer, Steve, should (theoretically) be the hunter-gatherer but he's presently elsewhere. After last night's PL 4TT, they'd stayed the night in Carlisle because of accommodation shortages in the Workington area. Arguably this is the most exciting Tesco in the country because it's at this store they stage a weekly late-night naturist shopping hour (Tuesday 8-9 p.m.). It's a concept to boggle the mind and has me wonder aloud where exactly you get to put your Clubcard? Debbie doesn't have an answer or, if she has, is too diplomatic to speculate. If such an event were held at the Tesco in Hastings, then there's an outside possibility that speedway fans could have an unexpected encounter with Lee Richardson or Lewis Bridger. Debbie and Steve are going back off home and can't be persuaded to join me on my journey from the North West coast to the North East coast for the Diamonds versus Tigers Premier League fixture.

The Newcastle Diamonds speedway riders race in Byker every Sunday during the speedway season. Most weekends you'd be unlikely to get a suntan but to coincide with the visit of the Sheffield and the arrival inside the city limits of Neil Machin in his trademark sunglasses, the city has suddenly become the Costa del Tyne. Bucking the trend to rename stadiums after a sponsor, the Diamonds now race at the innovatively named Newcastle Stadium. Tonight's meeting will have a later start time than usual because the St John Ambulance emergency team have also spent the weekend providing emergency cover for the little-known Sunderland Air Show. Sadly, it won't rank as one of the more memorable stagings because the hot weather dragged in sea fog to envelope the city pretty well all weekend. Though atmospheric, the fog turned the event into a fiasco. Later I'm told by a fan, "Nothing flew Saturday and, on Sunday, there was one fly by in the fog. We couldn't see it, though we could hear it! So they changed the schedule, then the fog cleared and nothing was flying and, then, the fog came back – so that was it!" Whatever the weather, the St John Ambulance people have to remain in attendance in case of medical emergency.

Upon arrival, my first port of call is the portacabin adjacent to the pits area that houses the Newcastle Diamonds speedway office. Warm sunshine has possibly played havoc with my senses since, to my mind, it smells strongly of the salty seaside. Joan English gives this suggestion short shrift and sums up the season to date, "We started well but, like everyone else, we've had our share of injuries." With a raft of tasks and duties to attend to, the longest-serving Newcastle promoter in the club's history, George English always provides a warm welcome. He's understatedly knowledgeable but his wry wit is never far away. Last night the Diamonds acquitted themselves reasonably well at the Premier League Fours at Workington but failed to qualify for the final. Though he'll appear tonight, they'd had to ride the Fours without Josef 'Pepe' Franc who'd been recalled to the Czech Championships by his National Federation the ACCR. The logistical arrangements required to manage the complexity of modern speedway riders travel itineraries is a nightmare for all concerned. "The only place Pepe could find to fly in from the Czech Republic was Stansted. But, though the plane was only 12 minutes late (11.37), easyJet had lost his engine. Sean Stoddart had his good one lost by UPS earlier this season. I've put Pepe at number 3 just in case he's late." The club has something of a mini injury crisis at present and will operate rider replacement for Christian Henry (torn shoulder tendons).

They're also without Jerran Hart who was injured recently when he crashed with Byron Bekker in a Conference League meeting at Weymouth. Replacement riders can be a struggle to find and, only last week, George contacted 12 different Conference League riders to establish whether they would accept a booking to appear at Newcastle Stadium (aka Brough Park, in old money). In the end, the club tracked Johnny Grey because no one else was available. The reasons for not accepting the booking ranged from the credible to the fantastic and included "working", "no engines", being located "down south" and "not contactable." Tonight Scunthorpe's Jonathan Bethell will fill the reserve berth.

Like many within speedway, George is well aware that the fine line between financial success and failure rests on the ability of the club to attract additional fans to watch the speedway on a regular basis. "I trace it all back to the invention of the video recorder and how that spawned the home entertainment industry of video games, DVDs and the like. It has changed forever how people look on being entertained. Nowadays they want the spectacle to come to them so that they can consume it rather than going out to experience its rawness at somewhere like this! People say 'Isn't it great that you have Redcar now' but we've lost people from south of the river to them. They probably bring 200 people three times a season but, when I walk around the South Tees Motorsports Park, I can see about 50 of our fans. So 50 times 25 meetings a season is a big difference! We've started to run expensive radio adverts on *Galaxy* – a commercial radio station that now targets 20 to 25 year olds rather than teens – to try to attract more local young people. The future of speedway depends on exciting these youngsters and getting them to come along. That advert is going to run eight times a day from Wednesday to Sunday for six weeks." Later in the speedway office George fires up his laptop and proudly plays an excitingly breathless advert that definitely catches the ear. The voiceover includes phrases like "Bike on bike action", "Naught to sixty, faster than a Formula 1 racing car" and "Come along and watch the Diamonds shine!" The advert also makes great play of the attractive pricing at Newcastle Stadium on speedway race night, "£13 for adults" and "£3 for under 16s". "We're always looking for new ways to attract people so watch us. We had 23 Poles along after we advertised to the Polish community in Newcastle!" The vastly experienced Barry Wallace who's an important cog in the Diamonds match-day presentation team briefly interrupts our conversation. Barry quizzes George about the parameters of the interview he intends to have later with Jerran Hart. The distance Jerran is prepared to travel when presently out of speedway on the injury list impresses Barry, "It's a long way for him to come! He's supposed to be out for 8 to 10 weeks but you know the riders, particularly 17-year-old ones, they all want to come back sooner. I'm sure that's what he'll say. It was a nasty injury to the base of the spine so it's best to be careful!"

Though speedway appears at least once a week on satellite telly during the speedway season, whether it has resulted in any improvement in Premier League and Conference League speedway crowds is a moot point. George believes there could be some improvement, "I'm not a big fan of *Sky*. Whether they've benefited the sport or not is open to question. Rather like football, with *Sky* the thing that irritates me is that there's never a bad game, no matter how awful it is! Nigel [Pearson] will have someone shouting in his ear for him to say how wonderful it is. Still, he embarrassed himself when he said Freddie Lindgren had won the GP with the most points – whereas the winner is clearly

Crowds gather

Jonathan Bethell

Sean Stoddart

Newcastle v. Sheffield: *The riders don't turn round the corners but slide round counter steering with the steering wheel and sliding the back end around."*

the rider who wins the final itself! Still, *Sky* don't help themselves by choosing the wrong fixtures to televise. They seem to love seeing the best Elite team at home versus the worst one! Whereas, if anything, it should be the other way round. Last season they hardly showed Eastbourne when they had Nicki [Pedersen] there – the number one draw in the sport and world champion in waiting – but, this season, we've seen them [Eastbourne] about six times. Then there's their obsession with Leigh Adams – who I don't like, I like Nicki – I think he must be the most-interviewed rider in speedway ever!" A read through Graeme Paterson's Talking Point column in the Newcastle programme suggests he isn't a big fan of *Sky Sports* speedway's fair-haired pits bunny, Sarra Elgan. "That other woman who does the Elite League coverage. I've forgotten her name but you'll know the one I mean. The blonde one with the hair waving around like one of those badly dubbed adverts for Head & Shoulders. You know who I mean yet? She seems to just wander round the pits with a pair of headphones on, flirting with Alun Rossiter and smiling constantly at riders, asking the odd probing question like "Ooh you won that race, didn't ya? Eh? Was it good? Did ya like it? Was good that, wannit?"

George is delighted with the form, approach and attitude of the Newcastle 'Sapphire Engineering Diamonds number 5, Jason King. "He's moved up here 'cause his girlfriend is here and, when I heard that over the winter, I told him 'Seriously! Well, there's only one place you can ride.' He's been excellent for us – easy to work with, a great prospect and exciting to watch!" Our talk moves on to the recent Premier League Pairs at Somerset where Reading were robbed of their place in the final by a poor refereeing decision. "Graham Flint ignored me at the PL Fours last night; I think 'cause of my comments in the *Speedway Star* when I thought his decision ruined it!" I ask whether Reading team manager Tim Sugar will get his £300 fine back. "No! Because it'll have been deducted from Reading's monies on the night. If, say, the ref fines someone from Sheffield tonight, I have to withhold that from their money and send a cheque to the SCB for that amount. Our referee tonight is Craig Ackroyd – it's his last meeting as a single man!"

Comments George made in my book *Concrete for Breakfast* about the Redcar track have caused something of a storm in a teacup locally[1] and briefly manufactured some ersatz tension when none really exists. Hopefully, it will serve its purpose and increase numbers through the turnstiles. To this end, the 'contentious' quotes have been covered in Middlesbrough's local newspaper, the *Evening Gazette* and mentioned in a Redcar speedway press release. George makes light of the situation, "I hope you're not writing another book! Chris Van Straaten rang me a few weeks ago to ask me about my comments about the racing at Redcar in your book!" Talk of drama at Redcar speedway brings up the recent Daniel Nermark crash that George saw on TV, "I was surprised it was going into the corner rather than locking up in it! You must ask Bob [of *GRT Media*] about the difficulties he had with getting the BSPA to agree to release the pictures – of what had already been described in press statements – to the TV people who were going mad for it!"

A keenly observant man, George spots a flock of five young magpies swoop through the stadium. "You didn't used to see them and now they're everywhere! Usually you only see one or two together so, five together, is something. We had to take the foam off the top of the safety fence 'cause the birds kept pecking it off to use for their nests!" When not consumed by his work for Newcastle speedway, George is a long-suffering Newcastle United football fan and season-ticket holder. Sadly, for many Newcastle fans like George, trophies have been thin on the ground during his lifetime. "When Keegan arrived we had 31 coaches from the Sam Allardyce era! Before a game, Kevin Keegan saw the players bouncing on trampolines supervised by the trampolining coach! When Damien Duff went back at half time expecting to get a bollocking or instructions about what to do in the second half [during the Allardyce era], instead, the video technicians showed the players brief snatches of video from the first half! Quite what that was going to do to help, I'll leave you to imagine."

In the small kitchen directly outside the door of the speedway office, Irene Best is notable by her absence, not least because she oils the wheels of a successful meeting with an endless supply of cups of tea and coffee. Her son Robbie is the track curator at the club and rejoices in the grandiose title of Circuit Manager in the club programme. Later, I bump into Irene who, for the first time as long as she can remember, has had to miss some Diamonds meetings at

[1] After our meeting at the South Tees Motorsports Park against Mildenhall in August 2007 George commented, "The racing was like it always is here – three riders close together but little or no passing. It always looks good but people rarely get by! The banked bend looks the part but it serves no real purpose as you'd think it would from looking at it."

Newcastle v. Sheffield: *The riders don't turn round the corners but slide round counter steering with the steering wheel and sliding the back end around."*

Brough Park because of a bad back, "I can't remember when I last missed two meetings! We've had some great riders here, not like the rubbish we have nowadays. Is it just me or do the riders not get on so well with the fans nowadays? It was different in the late 40s or even in the mid 70s. Now they don't want to know! [pause] Did you see the World Team Cup? It was like seeing the Danish Diamonds – Kenneth Bjerre, Bjarne Pedersen and Nicki Pedersen all started here!"

On one of the tables outside the hut that houses as the Newcastle speedway office, Sheffield speedway's equivalent of the Three Amigos – Neil Machin, Dave Hoggart and Eric Boocock sit together to enjoy the sunshine. Dave Hoggart asks, "Are you following me round? I see you every night almost – I'll have to think of some new jokes!" I tell him there's no need since we all still like the old ones! The irascible Eric Boocock looks scornfully at the chips that Neil and Dave tuck into, "Is it eating like it was last night? Just looking after number one?" Inside tonight's Official Raceday Magazine there's an interview with Eric and in it we learn: his parents couldn't afford a middle name, times were hard but we were happy then and also, given I made the last bits up, that he was born in Dewsbury, Yorkshire. *Black Hawk Down* was the last film Eric watched at the cinema while his favourite meal is steak and chips (although he also likes salad). Eric failed his driving test three times and has a beige coloured bedroom carpet. He also isn't afraid to admit to musical crimes and confesses his all-time favourite song is 'Bridge Over Troubled Water' sung by Simon and Garfunkel. The memory card of his mobile phone is full, he sends as few text messages as possible each week ("maybe five at the most") and, when pressed, "Can't think of anything that really frightens me!" In person Eric tells me, "I'm alright, it's the rest of the freakers! They all keep getting older – oooh, everyone does except me – I just get younger by knocking a few years off!"

Since everyone will have to walk past to actually watch the meeting, I decide to place my display table in the welcome shade of the home-straight grandstand adjacent to the programme stall that's also handily located just inside the entrance turnstiles. The Diamonds programme is an innovative and extremely readable document that retails at £2.50 a copy. At sports events nowadays, they never sell you a programme but, instead, call it a magazine and at Newcastle Speedway they're no exception to that rule since theirs is called an "Official Raceday Magazine". In my opinion, given the variety and quality of articles inside, it actually lives up to this description. One of the magazine/programme sellers has a natty line in patter that he loudly proclaims as each and every fan comes through the turnstiles. Mostly he shouts, "Official Matchday Magazine – £2.50! Sunshade as well!" Occasionally, he varies his pitch to claims it can be used as a fly swatter. An older speedway fan stops for a chat, "Speedway manages to survive every year without any real money in the sport! It always seems to be on its last breath but still goes on. One time it won't and where will we be then? Lots of things you think will always go on – end! At the end of the month [August 2008], the North Shields to Bergen ferry is going to stop after 145 years! They're all booked up now but, then, it's gone! The only sailing left then will be to Amsterdam and that's wobbling."

The balmy warmth of the evening appears to have had little negative impact upon attendance levels and, after the rider parade, the start of the meeting is delayed by a 10-minute track grade! Club announcer Lawrence Heppell informs us of curatorial intentions, "What we're trying to do is scrape a surface that's a little bit loose." Given that every speedway track in the country survives on its hard core of regular fans, only a supreme optimist would decide that a lengthy exposition of the rules and routines of speedway would be necessary to fill the time delay caused by the track grade. However, tonight's announcer is that optimist and so proceeds to explain some of the rudiments of the sport at length, "The riders don't turn round the corners but slide round counter steering with the steering wheel and sliding the back end around." The crowd talk amongst themselves and possibly wonder if tonight will be the first time in 2008 that Newcastle finally get to use a tactical substitute in a Premier League meeting. In fact, this won't happen until heat 12 of their meeting with Scunthorpe on October 12th but, after the Newcastle Stadium track surface has received some impromptu tender loving care, the meeting finally gets under way. The first race is won by Ricky Ashworth in a slow time of 67 seconds. Paul Cooper only just fails to snatch second place when he can't quite sneak past a slow but steady George Stancl on the penultimate bend of the race. Keen to gain whatever fractional advantage he can, Newcastle team manager, George English, gives Jonathan Bethell, Christian Henry's rider replacement ride so that he can acclimatise to track conditions prior to the reserves' race, otherwise known as heat 2. It's a good plan but, sadly, Bethell quickly finds himself off the pace and marooned at the rear of the field. Jonathan then contrives to fall at the start of the last lap before he remounts to trundle home a considerable time after the

Newcastle v. Sheffield: *The riders don't turn round the corners but slide round counter steering with the steering wheel and sliding the back end around."*

remainder of the field have already finished. George English has kindly given me a pits pass so I'm able to stand by the new wooden fence that separates the mechanically interested Diamonds fans from the race-night hubbub of the pits. Stood by the fence, they get uninterrupted views of all the activity on the home side of the pits. However, the area is configured in such a way that whatever the majority of the Sheffield riders and mechanics get up to remains mostly out of sight around the corner. Though I have a pass, I don't venture that far and, instead, base myself by the plastic crash barriers that they use to demarcate the pits viewing area from the sharp end of race-night business – the rider berths.

Before the second heat, there's a further delay for yet more attention to be given to the track. In the interim, Jonathan Bethell brushes himself down but also tends to his equipment with the help and advice of his blonde-haired (female) assistant/mechanic. 35 minutes after the scheduled start time (6.30 p.m.), the second race starts and, spookily synchronistically, Jonathan falls off at an identical spot – once again at the start of the fourth lap! From the knot of keen fans stood attentively by the pits fence, there's a cry of "Oh! He's off again!" Like before, bike in hand, Jonathan leaps to his feet, remounts and trails home in fourth place. On his return to the pits he's slathered in shale, sports a face like thunder and has the drooped shoulders of a man resigned to a difficult evening's work. Stood where I am, it's quickly apparent that the Diamonds riders and mechanics collectively work closely together to ensure that they're all ideally prepared and motivated prior to each race. Throughout the meeting, if any rider encounters significant mechanical difficulties, then it's all hands to the pump while the team rally round to offer advice, support, and know-how. One young man in particular stands out (who turns out to be Jerran Hart) as he bops about the pits, laughs heartily, animatedly talks as well as enthusiastically helps fix things wherever he can. Sadly, the bonhomie and collective fervour that is the Diamonds team spirit doesn't apply to Jonathan who's shunned as though he's radioactive. That said and in fairness, Jonathan has a fixed stare off into the distance and a demeanour that exudes the strong hint that he should be left well alone while he contemplates what T.S. Eliot playfully termed the 'thousand sordid images of which his soul was constituted'.

The third race of the night, like those previously, is won by a Sheffield rider. Over the stadium loudspeaker system, Barry Wallace observes gnomically, "64.7 – so times are getting a little bit quicker!" In his report on the meeting in the *Speedway Star* Eric Thornton claims, "Early problems with the track made conditions ideal for riders with a grass track background". Quite who these riders are is a mystery until he identifies, "Sheffield's trio of former grass track champions, Ricky Ashworth, Paul Cooper and Andre Compton, who took the first three races with ease." When they're not in the thick of the pits action amongst their Tigers team, speedway's equivalent of Siamese twins, Neil Machin and Dave Hoggart, between races stand by a low brick wall at the edge of the pits. It provides an ideal vantage point from which to monitor the Sheffield section of the pits in one direction but also, in the other, view the start, first-corner action and the general panorama of the track. As though he's taking part in a cigarette commercial for mysteriously unexplained reasons being filmed tonight in Byker, Neil Machin stands with one foot on the wall, wreathed in smoke with a lit Longbeach cigarette between his fingers ("they're Australian!") He takes a phlegmatic view of track conditions, "This'll be fine! I doubt they'll be track records though!" Dave Hoggart nods his agreement, "The Newcastle riders were kicking off before the start saying it was too sloppy and, now, they've ridden it – they're even less happy! Our lot don't like it but, we won't complain as we don't like to freak up someone else's meeting. When the weather is like this, you need to flood the track the night before and, I mean, really flood it! And then, flood it again at 6 a.m. Then you water it throughout the day. They probably had the dogs here last night so that would delay things for them. At our place, ours [track staff] often get in at 3 or 4 a.m. in the morning to flood it. That's why you don't see dust at Sheffield. It's never easy when it's hot like this, mind!" Neil remains keen to reassure me further, "This'll be alright mate!" Dave wonders philosophically, "What can George English do when it's his riders complaining?"

The fourth heat sees a Newcastle Diamonds rider finally win a race and this is signals a mini fightback from the home team. Successive 4-2 heat advantages bring the scores to 15 apiece. In the sixth heat, George Stancl and Sean Stoddart take the lead on the first bend of the second lap and, back in the pits, Diamonds captain Richard Juul loudly exclaims, "That's more freakin' like it!" Upon their return to the pits, race winner Stoddart and veteran Stancl are enthusiastically congratulated by Richard Juul. He then theatrically claps a lot before he goes over to gee up Jason King who's stood by his lady mechanic as he patiently waits for the ongoing track care to end so he can venture out for the next race.

Newcastle v. Sheffield: *The riders don't turn round the corners but slide round counter steering with the steering wheel and sliding the back end around."*

To my mind, Jason isn't really the rider who needs the psychological boost of additional encouragement, it's his race partner Jonathan Bethell. Sure enough, Jason King reacts with a comfortable win ahead of Andre Compton, while Jonathan Bethell manages to race to the second bend of the third lap before he falls. Overcome by dejection, mechanical frailties or a mix of them both, this time Jonathan doesn't immediately remount but stands disconsolately with his bike on the centre green until the race finishes. After a performance like that, it is always highly likely that he will be replaced by Sean Stoddart, the more experienced and in-form Newcastle reserve for his final programmed race of the night. While the team spirit flows around him, Jonathan remains almost invisible, stood alone in his rider berth but still shows commendable professionalism to ensure his bike remains readied for race action rather than packed away in his van. Heat 9 provides Paul Cooper's fifth ride of the night and his third heat win takes his cumulative points total to an already impressive 12 points. Ben Wilson finishes second and this Tigers maximum heat advantage restores the scores to tied (27-27).

During the interval Dave Hoggart recalls his own trips of yesteryear to Sunderland. "I used to drive up to Sunderland from the South to watch the speedway and, when we drove down the street in Sunderland, people would come out and stare at the sight of a car going down the street – wondering who the freak had posh relatives! In the mid '70s people used to go to work on the bus or cycle or go on a motorbike and leave the car, if they had one, in the garage. They'd get it out on a Saturday morning to wash it and go on a trip on Sunday. That's all most could afford and it's not that long ago! Nowadays, people feel entitled to a car and expect to be able to drive wherever they please." I also catch a few more words with Kenny Smith about last night's PL Fours meeting at Workington, "They were taking bits off bikes and Tony Steele tried to hurry Ian Thomas a couple of times and Ian said, 'If you freaking do that again, I'll just grade the track!'"

Things start poorly for the Diamonds in heat 10 when George Stancl comes off in a slow-motion fall on the first bend. He lays theatrically on the track in expectation of a rerun decision that conspicuously fails to come. Before the 11th heat, Jonathan Bethell's dejection levels increase further when it's confirmed that he won't take part in his last programmed ride. At the end of the third lap of this race, Jason King passes Ricky Ashworth to alter what looked like a certain Sheffield 5-1 into a 4-2. A drawn heat follows and a 5-1 from the Jason King/George Stancl combination in the 13th yet again brings the scores level (39-39). All the real drama of the meeting then got compressed into heat 14. In the initial running of the heat, there's a crash on the second bend of the second lap when third-placed Joel Parsons runs into the back of Sean Stoddart and is excluded by the referee, Craig Ackroyd. Diamonds captain Richard Juul, who avoided the crash with a smart lay down, returns to the pits shouting "Who's out?" He can't hear the answer that Parsons has been excluded since he's so pumped up (let alone that his senses are dulled by his crash helmet). Out front when the initial attempt to run heat 14 is made, Paul Cooper comes out for the rerun and fiddles enthusiastically at the start line. Predictably enough, he's the only rider chosen to be badgered by the Start Marshal and, after his reprimand, though Cooper has barely re-lined up at the tapes they immediately rise and he finds himself relegated into third place on the first corner. The chase is then joined. Cooper manages to pass Richard Juul on the third bend of the third lap but, immediately comes to grief, and is excluded. The referee awards the race as a 5-0 to the Newcastle Diamonds to take the progressive score to 44-39. The third bend is the furthest point from the pits and, after Paul Cooper throws his yellow-covered helmet to the floor, the theatrically irked rider walks the length of the home straight on the centre green to the accompaniment of the crowd who delight in baiting him as he slowly hobbles past. Though he has a fixed scowl, Cooper appears to ignore the insults until he reaches the first bend when, suddenly, he dramatically suffers extreme temper loss. This manifests itself in a rush towards the safety fence where he points aggressively at an unknown critic and generally goes ballistic. He's ushered back to the pits in voluble high dudgeon by his manager, Eric Boocock. Scunthorpe Speedway Marketing Manager, Julie Harrowven, tells me afterwards, "It was a dull meeting until then. Funny, because only a minute beforehand a Sheffield fan had said how calm Paul was and how he didn't lose his temper. I knew he could!"

The last heat of the meeting is effectively a formality since the Diamonds only need any rider to finish third in order to gain the point they need to assure their victory. In fact, George Stancl wins and, with Jason King third, the Diamonds run out comfortable victors at 48-41. It's a scoreline that doesn't reflect the closeness of the meeting. Afterwards Neil Machin would comment in the *Speedway Star*, "We went to Newcastle and they didn't win the meeting – we lost it. It was the most frustrating night I think I've ever had. We had both Joel Parsons and Paul Cooper excluded –

Newcastle v. Sheffield: *The riders don't turn round the corners but slide round counter steering with the steering wheel and sliding the back end around."*

Paul crashing after having the spokes ripped out of his front wheel by a footrest – in heat 14 – and that was that. Before that Newcastle were beaten and then we just threw it away. That meeting was exactly what our season has been like all year. We just have not clicked and we haven't had the rub of the green at the right time." The Diamonds riders including Jonathan Bethell enjoy a celebratory victory walk along the length of the home straight on the tarpaulin-covered dog track. Lawrence Heppell conducts some centre-green interviews and we're told by high-scoring (paid 13 from seven rides) reserve Sean Stoddart, "Yes, it's not been easy [this season]. I've had some problems with my bikes and some small injuries." Though asked, Sean is unable to throw any light on the initial heat 14 crash that sees Joel Parsons excluded, "I didn't really see it. I could hear Joel coming up behind me and I could feel his wheel rubbing against me!" Keen to get to the bottom of things, Lawrence subsequently quizzes captain Richard Juul about this incident in the rerun of heat 14 and we're told in a surprisingly broad Geordie accent, "I don't know how eventful it was really. He [Cooper] was trying to go round me and I wasn't going to let him. It was one of those things!" Jerran Hart gets asked, "Maybe you could tell me what it was like watching the team?" Modestly, Jerran makes light of his contribution although, stood in the pits, I saw him industriously help (where possible) throughout the meeting. Most notably when he helped with Sean Stoddart's bike repairs prior to the rerun of heat 14. "That crash in heat 14, I suppose you all saw it. That was just like mine – them two, they're lucky that they walked away. Mine was going into the corner and theirs was coming out but, them two, were lucky!" Clear though that statement was, Lawrence Heppell feels that he has to translate Jerran's analysis for the remainder of the crowd lingering inside the stadium, "There you are – a first person insight shows you how fine the line is between walking away and going home in an ambulance!"

With the sun set, the meeting over and, while the rest of the home fans rush to race from the stadium to the car park, sales remain poor. Afterwards Joan English sympathises, "People really don't have the money!" Bob Tasker of *GRT Media* asks rhetorically, "A quiet night at the office for you then?" and laughs at my reply, "Barry Wallace promised that he'd mention I was here but the only mention Barry made of "Scott" was Scott Richardson who was in the first of the second half races!" Bob highlights the sheer volume of requests that have to be announced on race night, "Barry has an unenviable list of announcements to make, I don't know how remembers them all! I used to have an advert in the programme but I now sponsor heat 5 which really helps bump up mention of DVDs further up his list!" Like the occasionally intense rivalry that besets the speedway trackshop world, the British speedway DVD market is equally competitive among its various producers. Bob mischievously highlights that one of his erstwhile rivals took "29 days to get the 2008 PL Pairs DVD on sale. When you think how many people wanted to see that semi-final decision, it's amazing! If we'd been doing it, it would've been on sale within a day or two. For all my speedway DVDs, Dalbers [Andrew Dalby] voices the DVD from the *GRT* studio (i.e., it's our kitchen) after it's been in the editing suite (i.e., our back bedroom). Did you see the 2007 PL Pairs *ReRun* DVD? I've never thought of tying a camera to a dog and having it run round the place but, if I did, I think I'd then edit it!"[2]

27th July Newcastle v. Sheffield (Premier League) 48-41

[2] Interviewed by *GRT* afterwards on their DVD of the Sheffield meeting, George English slams his own track as "abysmal" and hints darkly, "we've had major discussions with the people who are looking after it, I'll say no more than that!" This straightforward interview is playfully interrupted by a tongue-in-cheek Paul Cooper who not only claims, "the track was cracking" but notes, "I was clearly knocked off". Paul then proceeds to publicly identify George English as "one of the most corrupt managers in speedway". George gives "that person Cooper" short shrift.

Newcastle v. Sheffield: *The riders don't turn round the corners but slide round counter steering with the steering wheel and sliding the back end around."*

CHAPTER 29.

Belle Vue:
"Ove Fundin and Peter Collins are inside now signing autographs!"

28th July

Though Belle Vue Speedway Club spent the majority of their history at the famous but sadly now defunct Hyde Road, the club actually held its first meeting on 28th July 1928 at the Greyhound Stadium on Kirkmanshulme Lane. By a circular quirk of history, this venue is now the current home of the Aces and the location for their 80th Anniversary celebrations! A brief trip down memory lane will always throw up plaudits for the crowds, atmosphere and racing at the old Hyde Road Stadium and will, invariably, also quickly lead to mentions of the many illustrious riders who have down the years worn the distinctive red, white and black Belle Vue Aces tabard. After 80 continuous years of racing it would be invidious to try and single out any one rider as 'Mr Belle Vue'. However, it's easy to span many speedway eras and quickly reel off all those riders who have become world champions while at the club: Jack Parker, Peter Craven, Ivan Mauger, Peter Collins and Jason Crump.

The current promotional team of David Gordon, Chris Morton and Gordon Pairman have planned an afternoon and evening event of celebration appropriate to the illustrious history of the club. There will be "back-straight viewing" from the top of double-decker buses parked on said back straight, a fun fayre, a "display of world championship winning machinery belonging to two of Belle Vue's most famous sons, Peter Craven and Peter Collins". For those with a nostalgic turn of mind, there'll be a "'Cavalcade of the Stars of Yesteryear' – An 'Open Top' Famous 53 Bus as you have never seen it before full of Ex-Aces riders"! The racing itself will be in two main parts. The first part of the meeting is billed as "Speedway through the 80s". Basically some races "featuring stars from past, present and future as we once again marvel at the sight and sounds of JAPs racing 'six at a time' for the first time ever at Belle Vue Stadium." There'll also be a demonstration ride by 1976 World Champion, Peter Collins as well as exhibition races from youngsters aged under 12 and 15. Finally, the racing proper will start and the modern-era riders will compete for the chance to win the Peter Craven Memorial Trophy. A high-class field of contemporary riders have been assembled as the club attempt to "recreate the ULTIMATE British League Riders Championship with some of the most famous and iconic clubs from speedway's glorious past." In plain English this means that every rider will wear a historic race tabard that represents some of the great but, sadly, now defunct clubs from more illustrious eras of speedway history. Clubs like the Bristol Bulldogs, Norwich Stars, Wembley Lions, Southampton Saints, West Ham Hammers, Cradley Heath Heathens, Odsal Tudors, Exeter Falcons and Wimbledon Dons will all be represented. Some of these illustrious clubs luckily still remain in existence and these include the Sheffield Tigers, Belle Vue Aces, Coventry Bees, Birmingham Brummies, Swindon Robins and Poole Pirates. With such a cornucopia of entertainment the admission price of £20 for adults sounds a bargain particularly when children aged under 12 (accompanied by an adult) get free entry. There's also a souvenir programme that contains a free Belle Vue key ring (£5), plus there's the added attraction of a Speedway Fayre outside the stadium.

I've come along to have a display of my books at said Speedway Fayre and, when I arrive in the Kirkmanshulme Stadium's car park, it's blisteringly hot but completely deserted except for a deflated 4-metre tall inflatable Belle Vue stick man. Once the noisy air pump starts up again, the inflatable figure towers above the car park and looks like an extra from a Pink Floyd concert. I half expect an accompanying soundtrack of 'We don't need no education' or, perhaps, a floating pig to complete the effect. Although it's an unusual sight and works perfectly well, once the expected large crowd starts to arrive and begin to queue patiently outside the entrance turnstiles, there surely won't be room to inflate this figure. This season, the Belle Vue trackshop is run by the affable Nick Barber and, while I wait for him and his brother Johnny to arrive, I nip into the apparently also deserted stadium via the pits gate entrance. The back straight is filled with buses and an exhibition of historic bikes are already readied for their later display but look forlorn since they miss the essential ingredient – a curious crowd of fans. The pits are completely deserted and devoid of all activity let alone riders though, eventually, I find some of the track staff have taken shelter in their warm but shaded hut. It's lunchtime and some of them have sandwiches and drinks from the nowadays almost ubiquitous Greggs bakery chain but, rather pleasingly, the majority of these workers have brought their own. Ex Workington trackman Tony Swales is sat among them and gives a broad-brush account of his dismissal from curatorial duties at the Comets on Saturday at the Premier League Fours. Clearly those sat in the hut are already familiar with the specific ins and outs of said event, so it takes place in a conversational shorthand. Tony speaks quietly and a loud machine has suddenly sprung into life close by, so it garbles the account for me. "It all started on the Friday, the Doc said 'we've had a plan for the last nine years [noise]' and Keith Denham said, 'don't worry, there's only one person in charge and it's not the tractor driver!'" There's mention of swear words in the presence of his daughter-in-law and, possibly a young child – which, in turn, led to a conversation reported in the tea hut along the lines of: "'It's up to you what you do!' 'Well I'll go!' 'Are you going before or after the meeting?' 'After!'" Apparently, when offered such a choice, this would have always been the only answer. Tony concludes this account, "So I could leave with me head held high knowing I'd done a professional job!"

I don't wish to intrude on private grief any longer so I head outside to find that Nick and Johnny Barber have drawn up in the Barbermobile to begin to unload their tables and stock. They've brought an impressive range of Belle Vue Aces branded merchandise and memorabilia that ranges from key rings to teddy bears, via clothing, caps and rider photographs. There's a smattering of books but also magazines and programmes from times gone by. My stall will be at the end of their display in the lee of the blue metal stadium wall emblazoned with giant yellow letters that say "Belle Vue Stadium". Before the turnstiles open, the Speedway Fayre will have a captive audience of fans as they queue to enter unless they have VIP tickets (which entitles them to gain access through the VIP entrance immediately at the edge of the Fayre). If it were to rain, we'd be able to just about shelter in the lee of the grandstand but, thankfully for all concerned, the weather gods have ensured it's a scorchingly hot sunny day for this 80th Anniversary meeting. The Belle Vue trackshop will be available in its usual place inside the stadium. Nonetheless, ever entrepreneurial, Nick is keen to strike while the iron is hot and encourage fans the chance to impulse buy prior to their arrival in the stadium. The stadium car park isn't an area where they'd usually hold a display. So, unlike normal Monday race nights, Nick and Johnny will have to work with what they've got – namely, the tarmac floor of the car park, a brick wall and windows of the ladies toilet – to create an attractive display. Nick hands over a giant Belle Vue flag to his brother with strict but vague instructions, "Johnny I need a bit of artistry!" After a few moments thought, Johnny inserts the flag into the only open window of the ladies toilet and hangs it from there. It should brighten up the visual appeal of the stall until, as Johnny phrases it, "Lucy [Aubrey] will be here later to add some much-needed glamour!"

[JS] "Some *joie de vivre*!"

[JB] "Just 'cause you've been in some posh paper, don't use some big words!"

[JS] "What, French?"

[JB] "I don't care if it's German. The word is definitely glamour!"

The anniversary celebration should serve a double purpose. On the one hand, it will commemorate the 80-year history of the club but, more importantly, from a commercial perspective, it will (hopefully) attract some of the stay-away fans from the Greater Manchester metropolitan area back to Belle Vue Speedway. Particularly since the sport will be showcased by this event so colourfully and attractively with its trademark family/community credentials to the fore. Legions of speedway fans have also been attracted from outside Lancashire and, throughout the day, it's easy to spot many speedway notable figures and luminaries. One of these is speedway writer, John Chaplin, who stops for an animated chat with Nick Barber, "Norman Jacobs says he printed 1,200 copies of his New Cross book and they've sold out!" Nick remains sceptical of this claim, "I doubt they've sold out – they've just run out of stock as some will be returned." Even though there are nearly two hours until the entrance gates open, the atmosphere verges on carnival and has infected many fans stood patiently in the sun-drenched stadium car park. Indeed, this particular part of the city suddenly seems continental in atmosphere and ethos since people are happy to queue, savour the shared experience and, generally, just chat in the sunshine or check out the stalls for hidden speedway treasures. Ken Eyre attracts significant interest when he conducts an impromptu signing session of his photographs.

Belle Vue: *"Ove Fundin and Peter Collins are inside now signing autographs!"*

Avuncular Scotsman, Bert Harkins, has left the tranquil calm of a friend's canal boat in Stafford in order to enjoy the Belle Vue anniversary celebrations. "I've gone from 2 mph to 60 mph and then I'm off to Prague at the weekend!" His meeting reports from the various Grands Prix that appear in the *Speedway Star* are often one of the highlight of their extensive coverage and, invariably, worth a read. Speedway celebrities, team and/or event sponsors, VIP ticket holders along with guests of the club don't have to bother with the delay of a queue but can enter straightaway via the VIP entrance. One of these privileged people is BSPA Chairman, Peter '*Pulp Fiction*' Toogood who, sports his trademark gangland style sunglasses and looks like an extra from *Reservoir Dogs*. Even without the sunglasses, you feel it would be impossible to make eye contact since Peter swaggers confidently through the crowd like a lauded prize fighter or, possibly, with the strong sense of entitlement felt by a junior member of the *Sopranos*.

Ex Workington editor, Tony Jackson, marvels how the vagaries of luck and mechanical failure drew a fine line between triumph and defeat at the Premier League Fours on Saturday night. "It's amazing that Somerset only got one point from their last three rides! Frampton's puncture cost them expensively. And, if Hall had passed Topinka, it would have been King's Lynn and Somerset in the runoff!" Sheffield co-promoter, David Hoggart, arrives shortly afterwards and will later work the crowd into frenzy over the loudspeakers. He's an important part of the presentational team for tonight's meeting but is keen to emphasise the thrill of last night's Newcastle versus Sheffield Premier League meeting, "It was a cracking meeting. It was a brilliant advert for the sport! It was close, the lead kept see-sawing and the races were unpredictable!" Shortly afterwards, Jonathan Bethell is also happy to discuss the meeting at Newcastle Stadium but it was an altogether different experience from his point of view, "I was freakin' crap! I don't know about anything else!"

The scorching sunshine guaranteed that any waverers would have no excuse to stay away but, given the field assembled, Jonathan Chapman (beforehand) wondered how many fans would come to the meeting. "I wasn't impressed by the field. I reckon they won't get more than 2,000 which wouldn't be good when you think we had 1,500 paying customers at King's Lynn versus Somerset." As it transpired, the crowd was substantial with the not always reliable estimates on the Internet message boards and forums varied widely between 3,000 and 4,000 fans. Apparently stress-free with only hours to go before the meeting commenced, Belle Vue co-promoter (and a man unafraid to proudly wear a kilt when the occasion demands), Gordon Pairman confessed, "The break-even point on this meeting is very high!" Though the meeting equally functions as an anniversary of the club, it's also provides a welcome opportunity to advertise the club's continued existence across the print and broadcast local media. Belle Vue Speedway Club are already regularly reported in the *Manchester Evening News*. However, the meeting would also receive healthy coverage from *BBC Radio Manchester*, *Channel M Television* and *Mercury*. On regular Belle Vue race nights, Gordon Pairman likes to do the parade introductions. "I've run out of superlatives for Jason so, I started saying, 'Three maximums – he's starting to cost us too much!' I said it again a few weeks later and, afterwards, Jason came up to me and said, 'Are you really worried about the money?' And I said, 'I've budgeted for you to score 14 points every meeting and would only be worried if you weren't!' For whatever reason, he

Nick Barber, Chris Morton and deflated giant Ace

Aces badges

Autograph hunters

Belle Vue: *"Ove Fundin and Peter Collins are inside now signing autographs!"*

Memorabilia arrives

Early arrivals stake their places

didn't gel at Poole. They chose Bjarne [Pedersen] and that was that. I don't think Jason was happy not to make the decision to leave and Matt had the Press Release [from Jason] pulled from the *Bournemouth Echo* 'cause he wasn't happy with it. But it's worked out well, as he's happy here! Everything works like clockwork. He knows everyone and everyone knows him. He insists on being in the centre of the pits so he can see exactly what is going on and can help, whenever he needs to do so. He's only doing eight meetings this year in Sweden. So, he can concentrate on Poland where he earns his money and do the business here at Belle Vue. This year he's looking good for the GPs – though you never know – and it would be nice to say he won it here in 2004, 2006, 2008 and 2009! But to successfully defend it, he needs to win it first! I think that being settled and comfortable in his League racing helps him in the GPs."[1]

My bookstall attracts little interest and this isn't exactly a surprise when the majority of the crowd have come along to take a trip down memory lane. Throughout the afternoon, speedway fans bring boxes of magazines, programmes and assorted memorabilia that they then try to sell to Nick Barber (in his guise as the undisputed King of Speedway Memorabilia auctions). There is the occasional significant item but mostly boxes are filled with magazines and programmes that have little or no resale value or that are already easily available in significant quantity. Nick treats every would-be seller with his customary charm, interest and politeness. Sometimes he pays a small fee for these treasures and, other times, their owners are happy to leave them without charge. Next to my table, boxes of *Speedway Stars* from the 1970s are dumped in a disorderly pile and, extremely humblingly, fans swarm excitedly round the newly brought pile of back issues as if guaranteed to find gold hidden inside the boxes. Many search with a barely controlled frenzy and, after they've searched through each box with eagerness, they have a look of satisfaction even if they come up empty handed. Throughout the day, I haven't felt that great and, what with the heat, I decide it would be best to go away to lie down rather than stay and watch the meeting. I do go inside to savour the atmosphere and hear Dave Hoggart excitedly exclaim over the loudspeaker system, "Ove Fundin and Peter Collins are inside now signing autographs!"

Afterwards, accounts in the press and even on the *British Speedway Forum* will be universally positive about what many found to be an often emotional and poignant evening's entertainment. For many, the highlights are the vintage number 53 buses and the troupe of 40 ex-riders from the club. The pre-meeting publicity claimed that a "top TV personality" would try "his luck on the 500 cc machine". This personality turned out to be someone I'd never heard of – Jason Done from a soap opera I was only vaguely familiar with called *Waterloo Road*. Salford-born Jason would notionally take to the track but, in fact, it would really be Lewis Bridger in disguise! Jason Crump was, of course, many people's pre-meeting favourite to win the Peter Craven Memorial Trophy but his chances of success ended within a few seconds of the start of the first race, when he collided with Ricky Ashworth and found himself forced onto the

---

[1] Jason Crump would ultimately decide to sit out British speedway for the 2009 season. The reason given wasn't disillusion but exhaustion brought on by his extensive speedway travel commitments. At a Glasgow Speedway supporters' club event, Gordon Pairman would praise Jason's commitment to Belle Vue, his decency as a man and also stress that Jason isn't the best-paid rider in Elite League speedway by quite some margin. Gordon Pairman would also joke, 'I've got two useless things with me tonight – a condom and Jason Crump's 2009 contract!'

Belle Vue: *"Ove Fundin and Peter Collins are inside now signing autographs!"*

centre green. This exclusion proved to be an insurmountable obstacle for him. The programmed field suffered some withdrawals: Carl Stonehewer withdrew through injury (replaced by Kevin Doolan) and Chris Holder who withdrew "ill" (replaced by Ben Wilson). Widely fancied Jurica Pavlic endured a torrid evening to finish joint 12th with only 3 points. Leigh Adams had to win a run-off with Scott Nicholls to lift this coveted trophy, after both riders had finished tied on 14 points. The minor places were occupied by Charlie Gjedde who was third, with Tai Woffinden fourth, Jason Crump fifth and Joe Screen sixth. Belle Vue co-promoter David Gordon commented afterwards, "It was quite emotional to see all these people who had turned out on such a special day. Such a lot of work had gone into this by a whole team of people and it couldn't have worked out better on a balmy summer's evening. There were a lot of new faces here and we gave them a great night's racing and entertainment. But we are here every week and now we want these people to come back to join the rest of our fantastic fans and play their part in the future of Belle Vue. The strength of the club is in its supporters. We can have the best team in the world but if it's not well supported it will fall flat on its face."

28th July Belle Vue: Peter Craven Memorial Trophy Winner: Leigh Adams

CHAPTER 30.

Poole v. Eastbourne:
"Why are they watering the centre green?"

30th July

After an early summer of rain-induced postponements, it's a pleasure to arrive at any speedway track in scorching hot sunshine. Wimborne Road, the home of Poole speedway has a fire station, railway line and rather tatty Conservative Club on its boundaries. The track itself is housed inside a stadium that boasts the only new building in the vicinity, namely the rather deluxe back-straight grandstand. In the car park, Weymouth's Conference League rider, Brendan Johnson is on his way to the pits with an ostentatiously bandaged hand, "They say it isn't broken but both my dad and I can feel the bone moving!" Even though I'm not a medical practitioner, Brendan is keen to demonstrate his hand injury and presses an impressive lump he sustained during his crash two weeks ago. Brendan's definitely an analytic, ambitious and thoughtful young man who closely considers his own performance and that of others. "I've struggled to find a partner who understands me on the track since Jon Armstrong got injured. It's affected my confidence! Before I knew where he was and where I should be, so we had a great understanding. Since then my form has been up and down and, 'cause I set myself high standards, that isn't good enough!" He opens the latest issue of the *Speedway Star* (straight to the correct page) to highlight his own standing in the Conference League averages. "I've dropped out of the top 25 by 0.01! I still do the Academy League but, in the last two Academy League meetings I rode, I've been knocked off by my partner. Often I wonder why I do them nowadays!"

After a walk through the back-straight grandstand bar and disco area towards the pits in search of Poole Press Officer, Gordie Day. He's widely seen as the best speedway Press Officer in British speedway and sets the standard by which all others are judged (and, unluckily for their clubs, often found wanting). Gordie wears his expertise lightly and, on any race day in Dorset, dashes hither and thither but always has time to have a few thoughtful words with pretty well everyone he encounters. When I find him, typically he's down the far end of the Poole pits deep in conversation with one of the rider's mechanics. He gradually works his way along the riders' bays and then has an animated chat with Poole team manager Neil 'Middlo' Middleditch. It appears that everyone at Poole Speedway this afternoon has some form of hand injury since Middlo also has a strapped-up wrist. It turns out his bandage is the result of a mountain bike injury. When riders hang up leathers, there's always the question of what to do with the void of excitement and thrills in their lives. Neil has obviously found success within speedway management and the family salvage business but the quest to replicate the buzz of his racing years has recently taken him to the challenge of some steep, rocky outcrops. "I just started mountain biking and, I'm not ashamed to say, I'm the slowest of the group I cycle with. But, I have the stamina to always finish! Some of them peak too early. We did 31 miles last weekend. I must say I like getting some of the gadgets. They even have a GPS nowadays – I don't have it myself – what it can tell you when riding and afterwards is amazing!"

While he's stood in conversation with Middlo, Magnus Zetterstrom makes a beeline for Gordie to ask, "Do you have the envelopes?" The way that some people like to exaggerate the professionalism and airbrush the reality of the sport nowadays, you'd imagine that every rider gets paid (without delay!) by direct debit into their bank account. So, it's good to see at, arguably, the country's number one club that cash still remains king and, the working man's tradition of carefully calculated weekly cash payments in brown envelopes, still continues. Poole's speedway's race-day King of the Counting House is promoter Matt Ford and he's based in his lair aka an office in the bowels of the old-fashioned home-straight grandstand. Gordie bustles out of the pits, through the pits gate, over the track and onto the centre green towards the gap that is the tractor access way on bend one. En route we bump into Scott Nicholls and his partner Sophie [Blake] going in the opposite direction. Scott has the pushchair and Sophie has their bonnie baby, Maya, in her arms, "We've been paddling in the sea at Bournemouth to try to tire this one out before tonight!" Scott is the talismanic Eastbourne number 1 who'll be required to perform at a high level tonight if the Eagles are to have any chance to contain the in-form Pirates. Conversation over, we carry on towards the grandstand where Matt Ford occupies his inner sanctum. Though highly influential within the sport, Matt only selectively interacts with the actual punters and this has led to rumours that he models himself on Major Major from *Catch 22*. Understandably, given Matt's reticence, let alone its race day and that there's money involved, Gordie doesn't invite me into the office. I wait outside close to the programme stall with the parents of a would-be sponsor who've just asked Gordon if he can let Matt know that they're outside waiting for the opportunity to speak with him about possible sponsorship opportunities. While Gordie's inside collecting the riders' and Zorro's pay packets, I chat to the parents of the would-be but actually absent sponsor who's not here because "it's his birthday and he runs a car hire firm". They're all dedicated Pirates fans. "We're both Poole season-ticket holders and have been coming since 1974. There's always a warm welcome at speedway and, particularly, here at Poole. Speedway is for anyone! Sure we banter and commiserate when they [rival fans] lose but it's friendly. We're off to donate some money to the Academy fund – these youngsters are the future! We always stay to watch them ride, it's a shame not everyone does. It must be disheartening for them when everyone rushes off after a meeting!"

Cameron Woodward and Maxwell Richards

Gordie returns to collect the sponsors and take them inside while I watch some of the super keen early arrivals at the stadium come through the turnstiles. It's a social as much as a tribal experience, so they chat animatedly while they queue to buy their programmes. Many people consider Poole Pirates to be the Manchester United of British speedway and, it would be hard to gainsay that opinion, based on the number of trophies won or the size of their crowds. For some, Poole is a rich man's playground with its beautiful but hugely expensive houses, stunning coastline and its harbour full of yachts. However, many other people from the town support the Pirates with fervour and a passion that belies the genteel surroundings of the local area. Poole are so popular with their fans that they have entrance turnstiles on either side of the stadium. I personally prefer the home-straight grandstand but seats there are at a premium since, sensibly, many of them are pre-reserved for season-ticket holders or are taken by early arrivals. Gordie returns with the would-be sponsors and their broad smiles tell their own story. Gordie waves them off with a few polite words and pleasantries before he continues his race-day meet and greets with various members of staff and the small knot of Poole fans that have congregated there to wait to have a word with him. After the breeze has been shot, with no time for the grass to grow under his feet, Gordie strides purposefully back across to the centre green and kindly poses for a photograph by one of the tractors parked there. Proud of the club, but offhandedly modest about his own contribution, Gordie takes me on my own track walk. Just to find the time for such a gesture is a mark of the man and it's a privilege I appreciate, particularly given how many other people he could be with and all the things he has to do. Gordie speaks frankly about some of the current issues facing the sport. "You should ask yourself all sorts of questions. For example, why haven't BSI been able to get more sponsors with national or internationally known brand names? They were close to getting Vodafone in 2005 – for the Team Speedway idea – but, once they heard that if Antonio Lindback got injured they had no replacement (unlike Formula 1 where they have the car and just get another driver), they walked away! I think when he arrived John Postlethwaite thought he'd become the Bernie Ecclestone

Gordie Day with tractor

Start girls in the pits

of Speedway but, once he got here, he realised there was no money in it! Sunseeker [makers of yachts, sports boats, performance motor-yachts and offshore cruisers] is the biggest company in Poole but they're not going to sponsor speedway as none of the crowd – the demographic, as they call it now – can afford a yacht! I don't want to be the bearer of bad news, but speedway's dying! Look how many Coventry had [on *Sky*] the other night! Clubs just can't survive on these crowds! Look at the crowds and what do you think the average age is? They're old! Possibly sixty plus, and we're all going to die. Fuel costs go up, admission prices, food, everything goes up, and the one thing that doesn't is the pension. Would you come and watch it every week if you had to pay? You have to ask how and why has speedway frittered away the gift of 10 years of prime-time coverage on *Sky*? It must tell you either something about the appeal of the sport or the people running it or, even, its wider appeal!"

"What's going to happen with Peterborough? If they go out of business, is promotion and relegation going to work? I don't think so! We need to adopt the system they have in baseball and football in the US. We should abolish the Elite League and Premier League and just have Northern and Southern Leagues. Then there are local derbies, each league has its own play-offs and the winners of each conference race-off to be overall champions. We also need to get the connection back with the clubs!" I ask whether Gordie means connection for the riders or the fans. "Both! If you look back in the past, the Poole team had five or six riders that would return each year. And some youngsters bubbling under who might, or might not, make it. You pretty well knew who the team would be without having to think about it! Nowadays, the riders change clubs so often we don't really know the make-up of the team, never mind the fans. When you go to Eastbourne, how many youngsters do you see? Everyone says we have lots of kids, but, they're brought by their grandparents not their parents. Speedway just isn't the main entertainment anymore! It is for a few people but they're not aged between 15 and 30 with lots of disposable income. These people would be the future of the sport! Or the future of whatever they decide to spend their money on. We all love and respect our present fans – they're our lifeblood – but they're ageing and times are tough! We're even struggling here this year and Poole is an essential and integral part of this community! Sure new clubs start and have big crowds in the first flush of enthusiasm, but, where will they be in five years? When Somerset first opened it had 3,000 but now it has 1,000. That is the trend over time – unless speedway reinvents itself as sexy and interesting for the youth and the young adults of today. Presently that just isn't happening. Look around you, speedway needs to sort itself out sooner rather than later. With the crowds there are nowadays, it can't support the level of cost. We need the excitement back! We want people to say 'I really want to see Eastbourne', not 'Oh, how many times have they been here this season already!' No matter what happens, we always do well here at Poole, but we need everyone else to be doing well if the sport as a whole is to survive! We do well because we have high standards. I remember Neil Street telling Jason off when he was winning all his races as a junior ("a good rider would have been under you then"). You have people who are prepared and want to pass on their knowledge. Chris Holder won't be having his name on the side of the van and thinking he's made it, 'cause he'll still have his feet on the ground. When he gets 12, Boycie or someone, will tell him he should have got 14. We know we do well here but if you look around [speedway] you can see things need to change, if we're all to have a future!"

In business they say when America catches a cold, the rest of the world gets 'flu. On that basis, if a club like Poole no longer experience consistently increased numbers through the turnstiles then the outlook for the rest of the teams (within the Elite League) won't necessarily be bright. Apart from the race action, Wednesday night in Poole also has the added attraction that fans are able to buy a copy of the *Speedway Star* hot off the presses. Judged by the vendor's comments, Mike Starman, it sounds like his experience at Wimborne Road bucks the national trend of flat or declining sales, "I won't say our sales are up, but, there won't be many tracks that can say they sell 110 every week!" Back in the pits the Poole riders, mechanics and staff seem in expansive frame of mind. It's entirely understandable given they no longer appear to have any weak link in their team, let alone that they currently fly high at the top of the Elite League table and remain most people's favourites to lift the championship trophy (if they perform as expected in the play-offs). On the Eastbourne side of the pits the mood is also good since they have a settled team and aren't hampered by any injuries. Cameron Woodward's mechanic, Ashley Wooller, is notable by his absence and his place with the spanners is taken by Eastbourne sponsor Richard Freemantle. When I enquire about Ashley's absence I'm told, "He has to do paid work and can't do every meeting on what Cameron pays him. [pause] Nothing!" Zilch, nada, nothing, is roughly what the Internet forums and the bookies expect Eastbourne to gain from this evening's encounter. Gordie Day is still here, there and everywhere so I enquire if he expects a comfortable victory tonight. Politeness and experience dictates that he effortlessly evades my question but does observe, "It all depends on which Lee Richardson turns up as to whether it'll be close tonight! If it's the 10-point one, it'll be close."

The Poole riders and guests' viewing area is a narrow pathway that slopes up from the pit gate towards the rougher ground of the second-bend terraces at Wimborne Road. If you face one way you can see the start/finish line and the majority of the first and second corner (except where it's obscured by the air fence). Or you can also look down the straight towards the third bend or towards the final bend. It's the ideal vantage position to view the track action and, if you turn round and look the other way, through the metal railings you can overlook the frenzied activity of the Poole Pirates pits area. That said, calm confidence of another day at the office (rather than frenzy) appears to be the order of the day for the Pirates riders and mechanics. The traditional rider parade is followed by a few quick laps of practice for both teams. Lewis Bridger decides to ignore the red flags held out by the marshals that signal the end of the warm up and, instead, does an extra illegal practice lap. Whether it's his throttle control or the fact that he's the only rider on the track, his engine suddenly sounds incredibly loud. Sat quietly in his wheelchair studying the programme is Eastbourne (and Sittingbourne's) Programme Editor, the friendly and knowledgeable Mick Corby, who mutters, "I didn't have to look up to see it was Lewis." In the eyes of the Wimborne Road track officials, Lewis further blots his copybook when he does a mini wheelie as he enters the pit lane. An exasperated Poole Pits Marshal shouts "Trevor!" Sadly, a few minutes later, the vim and vigour shown by Lewis on his practice lap evaporates when the race itself starts. Chris Holder wins the rerun of heat 1 in untroubled fashion followed by Magnus 'Zorro' Zetterstrom who's also attired in equally pristine condition kevlars. If you didn't know otherwise, the evidence of your eyes would suggest that Lewis obstructed Scott Nicholls when he raced him throughout the heat for the honour of third place (until he retired from the race). Ever phlegmatic, Mick Corby tuts, "I'd think Scott would be privately fuming! But, let's remember, Lewis is still a young man and learning his trade. Having watched him from the start of his career, I just always want him to do better! I'm sure that he will, given time." One maximum heat score begets another and the powerful reserve combination of Freddie Eriksson and Daniel Davidsson for the Pirates put their less-accomplished rivals to the sword. Even at this early stage of the meeting the score line tells its own story and, if the Eagles had a mountain to climb before a wheel had turned, then with the score at 10-2 the situation already looks a great deal worse. The 10-point Lee Richardson whom Gordie Day had spoken of has entered the building and come out onto the track, if evidenced by the stylish way he wins the third heat ahead of Davey Watt and Adam Skornicki. At the rear of the field and completely alone, Cameron Woodward chooses the last bend to execute a slow motion demi-pirouette and fall before he sheepishly remounts and heads back to the pits. Meanwhile Mick Corby's thoughts return to the recent Steve Heath Memorial Trophy meeting. "I've never been covered in so much muck as last Saturday at Arlington but, with Bob and Roy in charge, you only notice it because it's a total rarity! If only every track had people that skilled involved in track preparation."

Throughout the third heat, we'd been joined by Freddie Eriksson who stares so intently at the race you'd have to wonder if he was going to be interrogated

Bjarne Pedersen and Chris Holder

Quizzical Lee Richardson and Scott Nicholls

Guantanamo-style about it later in the evening. Freddie also wins the unofficial Hans Andersen Look-alike Competition with some ease. Last season, 21-year-old Edward Kennett had a full season in Pirates colours. Understandably he shows good track knowledge and capable track-craft in the fourth race but can still only finish second behind the fast-gating Bjarne Pedersen. The fifth heat is drawn and features another four-lap battling duel – this time for second rather than third – between team mates Scott Nicholls and Lewis Bridger. As if to double underline his thorough knowledge of the Wimborne Road racetrack, the sixth race sees Edward Kennett bravely pass Zorro through an apparently impossible gap as he exits the fourth bend on the first lap. Though he never looked likely to catch elegant and zippy Chris Holder a slight loss of concentration on the last bend of the race by Edward unfortunately allows Zorro back through to convert an acceptable 4-2 into a disastrous 5-1 loss for the Eagles.

Since the early part of the meeting, though the breeze remains almost imperceptible, eddies of shale dust have been scattered over the fans that pack the first and second bends of the Wimborne Road stadium. Also covered in a light film of shale dust, Mick Corby matter-of-factly sums up a litany of speedway stadium construction issues, "Speedway isn't always popular in stadiums because of the dust that get everywhere! If you build a purpose-built one, it's hard to know what other sports to cater for. If the track is ideal, there's not enough room for a football pitch inside or a stockcar track outside. Most speedway clubs are tenants of the stadiums they race in, so often the speedway tracks aren't the ideal shape either!" The seventh race has the new improved version of Lee Richardson don the black-and-white helmet colour though, just as the riders are about to come under orders, Cameron Woodward's bike stalls and he requires a push start from one of the handy track staff. While this scene plays out away the distance, I turn to his guest mechanic for the night, Richard Freemantle, to say, "There's never a mechanic when you need one, is there?" "Not a good one anyway!" he replies sardonically. The sound of four engines held at maximum revs fills the air, the tapes rise and Cameron Woodward immediately stalls to find himself becalmed on the start/finish line. Richard exclaims, "Freak!" Effectively almost a one-man team, Lee Richardson bosses Bjarne Pedersen as they exit the second bend and then dominates the rest of the race in truly imperious fashion from the comfort of the front. With double points for the win, the scores are massaged for the Eagles and progress to a fractionally more acceptable 28-17.

Without Scott Nicholls in heat 8, Lewis Bridger decides to race a Pirates rider (Zorro) instead but is unable to prevent his 36-year-old rival from the race win that brings his points total to an impressive paid 9 from three races. Like most racers, Lewis spends much of his time frighteningly close to the safety fence. Mick Corby observes, "At the end of the season Lewis has probably used gallons more fuel than any other rider! It's not just his wide line but all the other stuff – the wheelies, the turning round at the gate. Not really sure who can advise him. Shaun Tacey is good with the youngsters at King's Lynn. He gets them going and Lewis needs advice from someone like that – a mental coach who knows what they're talking about, so he can just focus on the job in hand rather than get distracted." Talk of young rider development reminds Mick that the Eagles cupboard is comparatively bare, "Did you know Eastbourne only have a small retained list of riders? [list of names redacted] Clubs like Eastbourne just can't compete with the Pooles, the Coventrys and the Rye Houses who sign everybody. We even had to pay a loan fee to Poole to use Tomas Suchanek at number 8 this season! I dunno how much. But, if you don't use your own assets, it's always gonna have a cost. All clubs, not just Eastbourne, need young riders coming through the ranks. That can be difficult when they don't always get the support they need, though young riders do at Eastbourne, of course. If only more clubs ran second halves like we do at Arlington. Though our efforts have to be applauded, it really doesn't help things when the Academy League fixtures weren't even completed in 2007."

Heat 9 results in another 5-1 for the Pirates, this time hammered home by Davey Watt and Adam Skornicki to take the scores to 37-20. Music blasts over the tannoy, "There can't be many tracks that have the Kaiser Chiefs as their signature music." Richard Freemantle joins us and now is, apparently, part-mechanic and part-detective, "I've taken a bit of dirt out of the fuel cap – the breather hole – or rather not in this case! At least, I hope that's it, as Cameron has a new engine tonight!" Before the first running of the 10th heat, Trevor Geer (the avuncular team manager of the Eagles) exudes his usual bonhomie and rather definitively states: "We need to fight back!" At the sound of such Churchillian ardour, I chip in with a supportive "The fightback starts here!" Only for a mystified Trevor to ask me, "Why, who's in it?" No sooner have the riders sped from the tapes than the red lights come on and all the riders slow to a halt except for Lewis Bridger, who battles round the outside of the rest of the field into the lead by the time he heads unopposed out of the exit of the second bend. With wit drier than a dry thing, Trevor notes, "He probably thought he was in the lead until he saw the red light! [pause] Did you notice how the red lights came on and flickered off and then came on again?" Maybe the Wimborne Road electrics are haunted? Whatever the explanation, it's certainly given Trevor the opportunity to wear a quizzical look on his face and left him with further food for thought in addition to the variable nature of his team's performance. A win for Chris Holder never looked in doubt, though he's followed home by the Eagles pair of Lee Richardson and Cameron Woodward who, astride a new engine with a dustless breather hole, completes four laps without the hint of a fall or mechanical difficulties. The race is watched intently throughout by Scott Nicholls whose hands are clasped on the wire fence as if he's tempted to climb it. Whether it's fatherhood, Eastbourne or age, Scott's hair is noticeably flecked with the first signs of grey hair!

Eddie and Scott

While we wait for more race action, Mick Corby's observational skills lead him to pose one of the great philosophical questions of the 2008 speedway season: "Why are they watering the centre green?" Luckily, I know the answer to this obstruse question: "They're cleaning the air-fence signs before they put them back up again!" Mick looks impressed, "That's clever, I've never seen that before!" Scott leaves us for a while to go out and compete in the 11th heat. He finishes second behind Bjarne Pedersen but manages to put some distance between himself and his most tenacious pursuer, Lewis Bridger. Shortly afterwards he's back again stood at the fence with a hard-bristled brush in his hand that he uses to industriously scrape shale from his kevlars. Out on the track, the riders come under orders at the start line and, while his right hand clasps the brush, Scott's left hand tenses and flicks in unison with the rise of the tapes! Given how crucial starts are in speedway for success and earnings, it's understandable that a professional rider would want to continually test, hone and synchronise their reactions. And what better way to test the reaction speed of your clutch hand than from the safety of the pits viewing area. Mick Corby doesn't share my surprise at this observation, "So many of them do that! I dunno if it's a natural thing or if they just can't help themselves!" The meeting quickly runs to its predictable conclusion and, although the hard-battling version of Lee Richardson scores 14 points, it's effectively a one-man effort for the Eagles that's reflected in the final scoreline of 60-33. Cameron Woodward is the only other Eastbourne rider to win a race (heat 14) and, afterwards, even the polite Poole fans struggle to find some positives to praise in the Eagles collective performance. Along with confidence, Poole have greater strength in depth and their riders take the opportunity to guarantee next week that their pay packets will bulge. Chris Holder races to an untroubled but nonetheless impressive five-ride maximum and every Pirate secures at least one paid win. The reserves for the Eagles, Simon Gustafsson and James Brundle, manage only a point between them but even their much more experienced team mates have struggled to make any impression upon this efficient and highly confident team of Poole riders.

Trevor Geer studies the action

30th July Poole v. Eastbourne (Elite League) 60-33

CHAPTER 31.

Kidlington:
"We're of the view – if the stadium was available – we think there'd be Oxford speedway!"

2nd August

Like many speedway fans I'd be delighted if I could still continue to watch speedway races in Oxford. However, this was not the case after the club nearly went out of existence during a tempestuous 2007. Even worse no speedway will be staged at Cowley Stadium during 2008 nor are there concrete proposals for its re-introduction in 2009. Because speedway is the type of sport that inspires great passion and loyalty among its supporters, many loyal Oxford fans continue to meet and raise funds on a regular basis. Many speedway clubs have active supporters' clubs and organise various activity evenings. They often have the advantage that their club continues to be active but, in the case of Oxford, they have to burnish the flame of their memories and take their speedway kicks wherever they can find them. They continue to find these in Kidlington where they combine a convivial evening along with some fundraising when they host a barbeque and bingo evening to coincide with every televised round of the Speedway Grand Prix.

The Oxford SOS supporters' group host these events in one of the many bars at Kidlington Green Social Club. I'm told that the Social Club is "massively supportive" and this is reciprocated by many the Oxford fans who have, in turn, become members of the KGSC. All major cities have an urban sprawl that slowly co-opts outlying areas into the conurbation. Consequently, Kidlington is close to Oxford and, though it remains a completely separate entity, as a visitor you're very aware that you're on the doorstep of the more famous city. I've been invited along by Nobby Hall and Rob Peasley to savour the atmosphere of Grand Prix night in Kidlington. They've kindly spoken to the organisers to get permission and, though I could watch the meeting at home, I've travelled over 100 miles just to enjoy the buzz created by these dedicated Oxford Speedway fans. Once you start to talk about a trip to Kidlington, it's amazing how many other people have connections with it. My good friend, the late Stefan Usansky, was as usual curious to learn more. Indeed, he could quickly and accurately describe from memory the exact location of Kidlington Green Social Club. In addition (though not useful to my trip) Stef could also describe the house that he'd lived in and was keen to stress he'd spent many happy years in Kidlington. With cancer restricting his ability to travel, he was hugely envious of my trip. The Social Club itself is a large unprepossessing building surrounded by a large car park that's part tarmac and part rough hewn ground. It looks like many of the trade union clubs dotted throughout provincial towns in Southern England that I visited as a child when taken by my father. Even before enter I'm confident it will have a snooker table, an area that can be converted into a dance floor, a large amount of seating and tables along with large bars serving keenly priced alcohol, simple but wholesome catering and a come-as-you-are ethos all served up with a warm welcome for regular patrons.

Given that it's a barbeque event, I make my way to rear of the building where they have a good-sized patio style garden area and a symmetrical line of four sturdy wooden benches. An impressive array of barbeque equipment has already been laid out but remains unlit. Inside the room adjacent to the patio, there's a bar plus an array of different-sized tables with chairs that have already been set up to face the giant screen. Next to the screen is an impressively large scoreboard that, later, will help us enjoy and understand the progression of this round of the Grand Prix. At the back of the room, there's a compact kitchen area, currently packed to the gunwales with all the various essentials needed for a successful barbeque. These include bumper packs of rolls, sausages, various other food stuffs and a good range of condiments. Allie Joyce, Richard Watson and Chris Brown are already hard at work with last-minute preparations for tonight's barbeque. I admire the mountain of food and wonder how many people will be coming along tonight. I'm told, "We'd rather have too much cooked than too little – especially as it's advertised as 'Eat as much as you like!'" Chris Brown kindly explains some of the history behind this longstanding event and outlines an update on the progress of their campaign to return speedway to Oxford in Cowley Stadium. "SOS in the first place was 'Save Our Speedway' and is now 'Support Our Speedway'. Before the 1999 season, Steve Purchase said he wasn't going to run anymore so Brian Hamilton started this organisation. There was a radio appeal and we had a night at the stadium, which raised a £10,000 donation that persuaded Purchase to carry on. From that night, the barbeques arose and started in 2000 and we haven't missed a GP since then! We're a flexible group – eight or nine people – there's Neil Cutting, Jason Newitt, Colin, Jackie and Laura Pollard, Richard Watson, Allie Joyce and myself. A lot of people pitch in and help. Our average attendance is 65 to 70 adults but it has varied between 19 and 120 (just after Colin Horton pulled out). Funny enough without speedway running, this has been our best year in numbers terms – it's been around the 70s and 80s! The Kidlington Green Social Club has been massively supportive and we've all joined it as members and we're helping the club by the takings through the bar. Rather than hand the cash over to the promoters – if they want something and ask us for it, we buy it! Our biggest investment was in 2005, when we bought road blade. It was a great big four-wheel thing that cost £6,000. It was asked for by Nigel Wagstaff and the club own it. We always said we wouldn't publish accounts, everyone knows that. At any event, we say how much we have made, what the money spent is and what the balance is that remains in the fund. It's in the region of £3,000 at the moment. I dread to think what we've raised over the years! Probably £2,500 to £3,000 per year. Not a single penny has been raised at the track – the OSSC [Oxford Speedway Supporters' Club] raises money at the track – we raise money at social events. To date we've never refused a request from any promoter!"

Cooking starts

In answer to the $64,000 question, 'when will Oxford return to Cowley Stadium?', Chris Brown replies with practised ease. "Now, there's a question! We have to remain hopeful in our efforts. We're of the view – if the stadium was available – we think there'd be Oxford speedway! Of course, there's the question of the [stadium owners] GRA's intentions. At one time, we thought they would flatten it and build houses on it! But, we approached the Council with our worries. They've been amazingly supportive. We had a public meeting here attended by the County Councillor for this ward – Val Smith – whose husband Andrew is the MP for Oxford – and two City Councillors, Rae Humberstone (who is from the ward) and Bob Timbs. He's from the neighbouring ward but is the portfolio holder for Sport and Leisure for Oxford City Council. It's a part-time job. I work for Unipart, just as Bob does. They gave me the opportunity to address the full City Council for 10 minutes and they've either come to our meetings or known about our meetings. The Council attended when Nick Andrews announced that he was resurrecting the nomadic speedway team. Obviously, we don't know what the future holds but, when it comes back, we'll be in a good position to support the promoter when he comes into Oxford. You've got to understand the history. My understanding is, that from the '70s when the stadium was sold, the Council bought it and put a covenant on it protecting it for sporting use! Providing the Council want to continue – there is a financial value to any covenant – then there won't be houses. But you've got to remember, it's not only speedway at the stadium. There's dogs, go-karts and a ladies' gym. They use the venue four nights for dogs and go-karts are there when they can. It's a seven-day venue really. I did,

Scoreboard

Food is served

Kidlington: *"We're of the view – if the stadium was available – we think there'd be Oxford speedway!"*

however, worry about the BAGS [Bookmakers' Afternoon Greyhound Service], which is beamed live to all the bookmakers. No one turns up to watch the racing but it allows them to bet in the shops. At the start of the season, they took it away and gave it to Belle Vue but it has now moved back to Oxford in early July. Horton's gym still sits idle at the stadium. Allen Trump owns all the equipment at Oxford. He purchased it from Horton and, obviously, it's movable but includes things like tractors, the start gate and an air fence (Allen bought Nigel Wagstaff's on eBay). The BSPA hold the licence. We all want it back and, hopefully, that's what we're gonna see! There is a question about profitability but, really, how many profitable speedway clubs are there?"

Also helping with the preparations and on hand for a chat is Richard Watson. "I've been the cameraman at Oxford speedway for 14 years – this would have been my 15th! I started in 1994 when I took over from Mick Posselwhite when he started to train as a ref. There was an appeal over the speakers and I knew Mick as a friend and he talked me into it! On race night you sit next to the referee and it's always interesting at Oxford because you get – what any referee will tell you – is the best view in speedway! Half the time you don't know who's in the race but, one advantage at Oxford, is that if the ref wants a replay they get it instantly. I started going to speedway in 1978-79. The first track I went to was Cradley Heath when a friend offered me a lift and I went with him. I lived in Gloucester and he went to Oxford too and, after a while, I started going too. This season with no speedway I've actually missed the filming and the editing more than the speedway. I also filmed at Buxton for the first three years. Most of the speedway film people know each other. *T2TV*, run by Ken Burnett, is the best. I think he's the most professional. He puts a lot more time into his editing and things. Take *ReRun* [Productions], I've nothing against *ReRun*, but he took on too many tracks and I think the quality suffered. Pete Ballinger is going the same way with his tracks. Coventry is Pete and he's also doing Peterborough and Wolves. He was doing Reading but, unofficially, I've heard he wasn't turning up there much. Most of us do work together and swap material for our highlights tapes! I don't know much about Mike Bennett and I've had no dealings with Bob Tasker at *GRT Media*. I know they're highly thought of but I've never dealt with them myself. Speedway could be more professional and well promoted like they do at Poole. In the past, I've been to Bournemouth and seen posters and a car announcing speedway. It would be good if they didn't change the rules year after year but they do. This season I've only watched on television, apart from the Cardiff GP and Steve Johnston's testimonial. I've filmed twice at Sittingbourne when Ken has had a fixture clash."

Though the paying customers have yet to arrive, the place has a buzz of activity. Frequent experience of organising this event ensures that everything gets accomplished in orderly fashion and that everyone has been allocated their specific tasks. Some people are general dogsbodies, others barbeque the food or help in the kitchen. One man tells me "I'm the potato salad technician". Another committee member is 30-year-old Jason Newitt. "I've done a bit of riding from 1996 to last year, mainly at Oxford. I was there for 10 years. I enjoy it, anyway, just the actual racing and helping other people out. Originally I was grass track in me youth and Peter Oakes asked me to go to Peterborough, when he was promoter. There are differences. At grass track you ain't got a fence, there's just the grass, a rope and a post and anywhere between 8 to 16 riders in a race. Grass tracks and speedway tracks are virtually the same apart from one is grass and one is shale. I've now got nothin' to do on speedway nights. I've had no offers to ride elsewhere so I've gone back to grass track. The problem with speedway is there's so many riders and not enough team places. People have to miss out. Hopefully, I've still got a few more years left in me on the speedway track!"

In the compact kitchen area, Allie Joyce works quickly with practised ease. "I've been going to speedway all my life. My parents took me along to Oxford when I was small and I just kept going. Probably about 30 years now – not that I remember the early years. My first memory is probably the Hans Nielsen era. Of course, I remember the good years when we were winning titles. I remember the social side – making friends, getting to know other kids. Mum and dad would go off and I would mess around with my friends. Whoops, I've just cut me finger! [matter-of-factly bathes it and covers with a blue plaster] Best not to bleed on the food. We've been to a few meetings this year but not nearly as many with Oxford not being around. Probably half a dozen, we've done a couple at Coventry. I go with Neil, the tall guy over there. He didn't know anything about speedway when I met him. He seems to enjoy it after he started coming along with me. I used to go to quite a lot of home and away meetings. Now we're trying to get to some of the tracks we haven't been to before – like the Isle of Wight, Stoke and Birmingham. Personally, I like the Premier League racing (and the Conference League when we're in it). It's better racing and there's more of a team atmosphere. With the top riders they just jet in and jet out of the country riding for a different team every night, so it's not the

---

Kidlington: *"We're of the view – if the stadium was available – we think there'd be Oxford speedway!"*

same! In the Conference League, you see the youngsters that you hope might come through and become the top riders of the future. I live in Abingdon, and Reading and Swindon are about the same distance but I haven't been to either this year. I've gone in the past as a neutral but, really, without Oxford we haven't kept in touch as we used to. We all want Oxford back! I haven't got a clue when that will be but we remain hopeful that something will happen! But, if it doesn't happen in a year or two, it decreases the chance of it happening. Back when I was a youngster, Simon Wigg was my hero. He stood out from the rest with his distinctive green leathers and his more outgoing personality. The local rival team was either Swindon or Reading, certainly Swindon and it's always nice to see bigger crowds come along for the local derbies. My sympathies are with Reading – you never think it's gonna happen and, then, it does. We've had a lot of promoters come in and out, some better than others! Let's hope the next one's the best one we've ever had! And let's hope the next one sticks round for a bit as well! I'm going to a few grass track meeting this year, following Jason [Newitt]. I have a soft spot for Crumpie – I dunno why, I just admire his attitude and the way he's never beaten. At any meeting, anywhere, he puts in 100 per cent and doesn't cry off and gives his all! I like Greg too. He was a really great bloke at Oxford. When he rode here, the whole room [at the barbeque] got behind Greg on GP night and, of course, I like Lubos Tomicek. He's a local lad, really, 'cause he lives with a local family and comes to the barbeques!"

Once the doors open there's a rush of people keen to reserve their favoured seats in front of the giant television screen. Some of the seats are set out theatre style while others are arranged around tables. To the right hand side of the screen the large old-style scoreboard of the type you used to see at racecourses stands ready and adapted to display the heat results. It's so tall a stepladder is needed. These events have been held for so long on GP night in Kidlington that they have invested in specially made Velcro-backed individual rider signs. This ensures we all know which riders wear which helmet colours in which races. Apart from the racing and the barbeque, there is a raffle, rider draw and, afterwards, some bingo. It's a packed evening of entertainment held in a convivial atmosphere. People clearly sit with each other regularly but I'm lucky enough to spot Brian and Celia Oldham at a table big enough for four so I join them for the night. They're both dedicated speedway fans who travel throughout Britain but also venture overseas to get their various experiences of speedway action. Brian chats about their recent trip to Belle Vue for the 80th Anniversary meeting. "It was a lot more exciting off the track than on it. There was a circus on the third bend, a display of old bikes in the pits that I could visit and 30 old double-decker buses. Belle Vue have been fantastic to us – last year they were great to us, they put us in the programme![1] It was a shame Ricky Ashworth knocked Jason [Crump] over the white line in the first race as that meant he couldn't win it! It was a straight world-final-like meeting. Tai did his usual trick at the end of the meeting, like he does at Rye House, he fell off while doing his wheelies!" Brian and Celia recommend staying at the Sport City hotel in Manchester since it's only a 10-minute walk from Kirkmanshulme Lane Stadium and can sometimes be booked ahead at a bargain rate of £15 per night! Brian wasn't happy with Nicki Pedersen's behaviour at the Cardiff Grand Prix. "I wrote to the *Speedway Star* but they refused to publish it. If we're not careful, we'll end up with a world champion who has won it by cheating!" My suggestion that allegations of gamesmanship aren't solely restricted to Nicki Pedersen and that – if he's prepared to take the risk and canny enough to choose the place to 'fall' and referee to try it on with – it's his risk to bear and he alone will have to live with the consequences of his choice. "I want to see your point but I wouldn't recommend [that approach]. He chooses which ref to try it on with to get away with it! Not Tony Steele, of course – we need to clone him!" Our conversation is interrupted, when the Grand Prix bursts into life. The volume is set at an incredibly loud level, apparently for those that are hard of hearing (or about to be so). Brain continues, "After the meeting at Leszno, when Nicki did exactly the same thing to Jason Crump, the crowd whistled when that ref excluded Jason Crump. The next day at the airport when asked why he did it Nicki Pedersen said 'Well sometimes you have to ride tactically!'" Commentator Nigel Pearson also isn't one of Brian's favourites, "That bloke is a twit, that bloody Pearson. He says everything for effect! For once, he got it right when he questioned what the ref was doing at Cardiff. We don't have *Sky* and, for those GPs we don't go to, we come here. It's ideal – a barbeque, nice atmosphere and supporting a good cause. We live a one hour drive away just south of Northampton, a bit more than a lasso throw away from Jason Crump."

As a dedicated and long-time speedway fan, Brian believes (like I do) that anyone who dares to throw their leg over a speedway bike for our entertainment should be respected as well as applauded. Over the years, he's also become good friends with a variety of riders, their families and friends. He's proud to be part of the 'in crowd' and, while he

Kidlington: *"We're of the view – if the stadium was available – we think there'd be Oxford speedway!"*

might occasionally hear some ripe stories, he definitely doesn't wish to repeat them. Sadly, just like there is good and bad in all walks of life (whether acknowledged or otherwise), there is good and bad in speedway – this applies equally to the fans, promoters, speedway authors, track staff or riders. When I suggested that (theoretically) some of the top riders might share some culpability in the comparative decline of Elite League level speedway in Britain, I quickly gather that Brian comes from a school of thought that exempts all riders from any possible critical analysis (on the basis of their decision to participate in this risky sport). In a schoolmasterly fashion he stubbornly refuses to consider or debate the concept, "I don't agree with you!" Soon he becomes much more categorical, "I refuse to discuss it!" Luckily, the volume on the telly remains set to kill so we're bathed in the distraction of the opinions of Steve 'Johnno' Johnston. "Sometimes gate number 1 can work well all night and sometimes it doesn't!" he illuminatingly tells us. Johnno has an infectious attitude and a unique style of pronunciation that is further emphasised by the twang of his Australian accent, "Bee-jar-neee doing the old hold his knee while his mechanic runs off with the bike!" Johnno is often too honest and cheerfully admits to us that his employer, *Sky Sports* (along the many armchair viewers) enjoy the thrills and spills of the high-speed crashes just as much as the competitive cut and thrust of first corner. "When you have racing like that, where it's tight [in the first corner] and there's a bit of a shove, everyone likes that!" Indeed, crashes and clashes provide the vital circus element that this most visual of mediums depends upon for its power and effect. Brian's recovered enough to talk speedway with me again. "For a long time I wasn't sure about *Sky* and I'm not convinced that they're good for speedway! Sure, they put a lot of money in, but, is it the right amount of money?" The sight of Tomasz Gollob on his way round to the start line prompts another observation, "I've grown to like Tomasz Gollob – I didn't like him at Hackney when Craig Boyce hit him."

The *Sky* coverage provides us with the usual concatenation of voices and opinions, some of them sensible and others much less so. From the warmth and comfort of the *Sky* studio located in an industrial estate in Middlesex, Sam Ermolenko admires the Marketa Stadium track in the Czech Republic, as it "Starts building a nice burm". This would sound even better if he could effect a stereotypical Clouseau-like French accent. On the screen, Leigh Adams is his usual taciturn self. In interviews he invariably manages to talk about himself in the third person and responds to questions as if he's talking to someone with educational difficulties, "We've got to get more of them – more wins!" After decades of speedway promoters everywhere keen to pretend that every race isn't over by the first corner, Chris Louis reveals his own simple philosophy, "You can't have theories in this game! You just make the start, get in front and go for the win!" Nigel Pearson loves to get excited at the least hint of an overtaking manoeuvre and this evening he adds a new attitude to his repertoire, when he gets highly excited by the mere sight of forward momentum, "Look at Leigh Adams, he's moving forward big style!" Johnno's never happier than when he mangles rider names and, in heat 8, he introduces us to "Tomas Loo-bow-check". Though he's forgotten more than I know about speedway, Brian still doesn't want to share his toys. "I've said what I mean and if you don't agree with it, I have nothing more to add!" The idea that riders might settle for position or, heaven forefend, manipulate their averages towards the end of a season, are an anathema to his speedway outlook: "I refuse to say any rider doesn't ever try 100 per cent. Anyone who throws their leg over a speedway bike deserves our utmost respect. The problem with [British] speedway is the rotten management!" In reality, we're agreed about the respect in which we both hold riders and acknowledge the incredible demands that they (voluntarily) place upon themselves by their choice of career. The threat of danger is ever present and, like any job you wish to excel in, it requires dedication. "Tai is a very determined young man. When I saw him at Scunthorpe [recently] he'd flown in from Sweden, watched a meeting and then at 11.30-12 o'clock at night was in the workshop!"

Darkness has fallen but, ever optimistic, I stand outside by my books where I'm joined by John White who has his own fond nostalgic memories of Oxford speedway. "I was trackman at Oxford from 1978 to 1989. I did the junior track and just sort of fell into it. The track we did is the one that Hans Nielsen set the track record on – 56.2 seconds in 1987. It was Oxford against Coventry and there'd been a lot of rain in the day. Many riders didn't fancy it but Hans said it was fine and would show them. When he came back he said, 'that track record would never be beat, 'cause a fraction more throttle would've put you in the fence!' We knew he was coming over the winter before he did and we got a message saying to meet him there one day in December at 2 p.m. We turned up at 1.45 and tidied the pits and, with speedway riders, you wouldn't expect them till 5. We noticed the Merc. At 2 on the dot, he was there with

[1] To celebrate his 50 years watching the sport Brian travelled to every track in Britain that staged speedway during 2007.

us and we walked every inch of the track. He'd only ridden it once but knew exactly how to ride it. We agreed how he would like to reconfigure it – we laid out hoses – and, while the oval remained the same, we pinched in each straight so that you could go wide going into the corner and go wider coming out. It was a golden era, then, with Wiggy and Hans! Once you've done it for years then, maybe, it's time to change? Once the accountants arrived and we had to put in chits for the diesel for the track and only got paid a month later, if we were lucky, you have to ask yourself what you're doing. We're just volunteer labour – all clubs survive on this – and you don't need that aggravation. Did you know the SCB has to licence everyone from the pits marshal to the announcer, yet anyone can do a track without regulation? When you think how important it is for riders' safety, it's incredible! We used to have lovely deep red shale whereas, nowadays, they use stuff that really isn't suited to producing good tracks and racing! Last year, the Elite League racing wasn't so special. How that man [Colin Horton], I can't bring myself to say his name, can get away with that I don't know! But, we all enjoyed the Conference League much more!"

They say never work with children or animals and, it sounds, like Johnno would like to add speedway riders to that list, "I was half way through a comment there and he [Holta] fell off and spoiled it!" Shortly afterwards Keith Heuwen makes a brave stab at trying to sum up the essence of our glorious sport, "This is speedway not Formula 1, so it's fairly low tech!" A close race between Scott Nicholls and Lucas Dryml in heat 20 prompts Johnno to find a surprise recreational analogy, "You couldn't have put a Rizla between those two!" A well-deserved Nicki Pedersen victory looks highly likely and Brian Oldham isn't happy, "Lean on and fall off, isn't it, Celia?! The whole thing is fiddled! The Danes all stick together – Hans helps Nicki and Ole makes sure the correct gates are watered!" Once the tapes fly, Hans Andersen locks down Jason Crump (Johnno notes, "The old Danish team riding") and Nicki escapes to claim victory. Interviewed afterwards, unlike many sportsmen Jason Crump doesn't look for excuses but, instead, blames himself, "I messed up in the semi-final and got the last pick of the gates [in the final] and missed out on the 200 grand [by failing to qualify for the Superprix!]"

With the televised Grand Prix concluded, Chris Brown does the honours on the "Find the Cheetah Draw for the chance to win £50!" The sweepstake for the GP winner has 10 winners – all with the lucky ticket that says 'Nicki Pedersen' – who get £8 each. The raffle draw has seven prizes and there's a steady stream of lucky fans to collect them. Chris Brown closes with, "Some thank yous. Thank you to all of you for coming. There's quite a bit of work goes into this so, thank you, to everyone that's helped and thank you to the Social Club for having us and to the people who brought the raffle prizes. Thank you to Jeff Scott for coming, his books look like a bit of fun – I'd a flick through earlier. Apologies for not having a programme tonight, but, the photocopier at work played up. Hopefully see you all here again for the next Grand Prix!" Some people drift off and others stay to chat and drink with friends. I retreat to gather up my books from the table in the patio garden outside the French windows of the bar. Brian and Celia stop by on their way to the car park and briefly relive how enjoyable Brian's tour of every track in the country last year was. Celia mentions, "I wrote to the *Speedway Star* to suggest Brian do an article on each club for his 50th speedway year tour [in 2007]. It was rejected by Richard Clark [*Speedway Star* editor] who said we already cover this!" In retrospect Brian's pleased he wasn't obligated to introduce any Watergate style investigative reporting to the magazine, "I'm pleased I didn't now, as I might have betrayed the confidences of some of my friendships. I really don't want to say what I know as I value my [speedway] friendships!" Oxford uber-fan Rob Peasley pops out for a word: "We live five or six miles from here and have *Sky*, but, this is as close as you can get to a speedway meeting without actually going!"

2nd August Czech Republic Speedway Grand Prix on *Sky* Winner (in Kidlington): Speedway

CHAPTER 32.

Lakeside v. Swindon:
"When we saw how their number 7 was riding, well!"

8th August

Football and speedway clubs traditionally tinker with their club names at their peril. Northern Premier league club Leigh Railway Mechanics Institute became Leigh Genesis under ambitious chairman Dominic Speakman (though Leigh doesn't have a railway station). When Chairman, John Batchelor, wanted to take over Mansfield Town he wanted to change their name to Harchester United (very Roy Race of him), while Jimmy Hill ditched the Coventry City nickname of the Bantams in favour of the Sky Blues. Somewhere along the line West Bromwich Albion became the Baggies rather than the Throstles, while Reading Football Club dropped their historic moniker of the Biscuitmen in favour of the unadventurously anodyne Royals. The new broom sweeps clean arrival into club management of Stuart Douglas and Jon Cook saw a revolution in Thurrock. Recently associated with underperformance in the Elite League, Arena Essex retained their nickname but the new management team immediately changed their club name to the comparatively more evocative Lakeside. The utility of this name doesn't come from a lake but rather from the fame of the nearby eponymous shopping centre of the same name (everyone roughly knows where it is, after all). Those that predicted this re-badging would signal only superficial cosmetic change were proved wrong since, under this new management team, the club transformed themselves from perennial Elite League wooden spoonists into potential champions or, at least, championship contenders. Obviously, the speedway track remains in the same location and some of the basic integral infrastructure also remains untouched. Nonetheless, the Cook–Douglas revolution has seen a transformation in the attitude of the club on and off the track and, in the publicity speak that the club excels at nowadays, there is a whole new spirit and culture about the place! Stuart Douglas made an apparently effortless transition from club sponsor to owner and, with the appointment of Jon Cook on an initial three-year contract, delivered a managerial masterstroke. Not only is Jon the (comparatively) young face of modern speedway promotion but he has a talent for quick analysis and plain speaking that's a breath of fresh air in the sport compared to the guarded, old school outlook of some of his fellow promoters. He's passionately committed to the Lakeside Hammers but also just passionate about the sport of speedway in general. Never one to shirk from calling a spade a spade, he's also an impassioned advocate of the entertainment and value that speedway offers in our information and entertainment rich contemporary world. In the club's rather deluxe programme, Stuart 'Stan' Douglas gives good copy and understandably he's delighted with his hire. "Therein lies the raison d'être behind Jon's honest and outspoken points of view – if you cut him, he bleeds methanol. His DNA helix contains that rare genetic code that allows him to take everything that is positive in this sport and use that to fight everything that is destructive. The man is born for speedway. He is a fantastic visionary for the sport, and the day Cookie is instrumental in the running of speedway in the UK, will be the first day that British speedway will start to reclaim its place in the world of our sport." Stan makes Jon sound like the speedway equivalent of Doctor Who meets Superman and the Large Hadron Collider.

Whatever the breadth of his capabilities, Jon Cook hasn't yet progressed to being able to influence the weather. When I arrive at the Lakeside Raceway the stadium, like the track, looks sodden. The traditional rush-hour horrors of the Dartford Tunnel crossing led me to set off early to avoid the usual Friday night tailbacks only to find that the credit crunch had finally had one beneficial effect, in this case, with a reduction in traffic volumes using this section of the M25. Consequently, I've arrived an astonishing six hours early at the track having chosen the spectacle of speedway at Lakeside over the razzmatazz of the Olympics opening ceremony. Listening to the radio on the journey to Thurrock, a man from County Sligo in the West of Ireland had used a rather elegant description to emphasise that utility frequently trumps looks, "Beauty doesn't boil the pot!" The immediate surroundings of the Lakeside Hammers aren't particularly scenic, but the bowl in which the track is located allows fans to view the race action from excellent vantage points at any point around its oval. Though some complain that speedway viewed from a distance always makes it look slower, the club have addressed this through their back-straight initiative that now sees crash barriers errected on the stock car track. New management saw the Essex club alter many practices, adopt a more positive attitude and add increased presentational flair to their approach. These developments included the transformation of the club logo, greater attention to marketing materials and the use of attractive signage. This early on race night, the stadium is practically deserted except for the pits where, inside a large sleek black four-wheel drive American style truck, Jon Cook is on his mobile phone. When the call finishes, unafraid to get his hands dirty, Jon busies himself with a key presentational task in the home section of the pits, namely ensuring that attractive photo boards are displayed in each of the various individual rider berths. Each board features an action photo of a Lakeside rider who's named in sufficiently large letters for anyone to be able to be read them from a considerable distance and, of course, attractive use is made of the club logo. A few years ago, the idea that the Lakeside Hammers would have a 100% home record at this stage of the season wouldn't be a likely prospect! Though it's the case they remain undefeated going into the meeting with Swindon, the fact that Jon Cook only puts up rider boards for Andreas Jonsson, Leigh Lanham, Jonas Davidsson and Adam Shields reveals that the team that will take to the track this evening won't be the full-strength Hammers team he'd like to track against this high-calibre opposition. Indeed, Lakeside will run rider replacement for the injured Joonas Kylmakorpi, have Chris Mills replace Lubos Tomicek and bring in club number 8, from Premier League Workington, Kauko Nieminen. He's so new to the Lakeside team that he's yet to get his own pits photo board. Jon notes with trademark wry understatement, "We've only four of our regular riders tonight because of injuries and international meetings, so, we'll be a different proposition." This isn't the first time that I've seen Jon actively involved in the pre-meeting preparations. Last season when I visited, he humped around numerous crash barriers on the back straight and this afternoon he's dressing the pits, "Unlike some promoters who sit in their offices and bark out orders, it's best to help out, isn't it?"

This is the second meeting in five days for the club at the Lakeside Raceway, after they easily saw off the Eastbourne Eagles in a *Sky Sports* televised fixture on Monday night. Jon is matter of fact, "It was a good result. As we got ahead, the fight went out of them, I thought." The hours before race night are never a good time to chit chat with promoters and Jon's phone rings so often that you could wonder if they also run a call centre at the club. It's an important call, since Jon ducks into his vehicle for privacy and then drives it to the far end of the track for even greater confidentiality. The trackman in the pits remarks, "I've never seen anyone on the phone as much as Jon. I wish I was that important and everyone called me all the time!" Minutes later, Jon drives away in his glistening black vehicle to continue his preparations from the speedway office. When I catch up with him there he's ensconced behind his desk, computer on and joined in his inner sanctum by the vastly experienced speedway presenter Bryn Williams. Jon jokes he'd rushed here because, "of another emergency not caused by me but by the speedway office!" Keen to manage my expectations and emphasise that it's going to be a difficult meeting, Jon stresses that four days in speedway can be an eternity, "Tonight will be very different [from Monday] as we only have four riders." The immediate difficulty looks like it could be the rain particularly as, since my arrival, there's been an irritating fine

Hello officer

Red sky at night – Pavlic's Delight

First bend tlc

drizzle. Jon notes phlegmatically, "This isn't proper rain," before he adds, "It's bound to rain as I've just bought some diving gear!" Maybe Jon can influence the weather after all since, shortly afterwards, the heavy rain he forecast arrives to further soak the track.

Once the rain subsides it's all hands to the metaphorical pump to tend to the sodden shale of the Lakeside Raceway. There's clearly visible lateral water on the first, second and fourth bends and, if you had to choose a word to sum up the situation, it would be damp. However the root and branch reconfiguration of the club has gone in lockstep with a whole new outlook and team spirit around the stadium. Consequently, Jon Cook is out there on the track with Gerald Richter and members of his staff at work together to clear excess water from the track surface. When not reviewing progress, speaking plainly, or putting metaphorical cats among pigeons, Jon Cook uses his column in the programme to educate the Lakeside fans that the old ways of doing things no longer exist. With a slightly peevish tone to his column the week after the Swindon meeting, Jon makes Lakeside's weather promise clear. "One thing I do want to establish once and for all to all those that perhaps don't understand is that this is a new Promotion with a new ethic and those that think we should have taken the opportunity to call the meeting off as we had suffered an hour's drizzle or that we should have called off in the morning in case we lost, need to understand one thing. We are professional and we are building you a club to be part of and proud of. Therefore we do things right. Plenty of speedway businesses and the sport itself have been damaged sometimes beyond repair with a string of early rain-offs – some without weather foundation all in the name of winning. We won't do that as it's not just gamesmanship it's cheating and cheating the sport and cheating the paying public who invariably lose interest in the end and don't attend at all. We will wait until the track is too wet to prepare for an 8 p.m. start every time and if that's 4, 5, 6 or 7 o'clock that's the way it will be. You can make your minds up if it's worth risking a trip but you do it in the knowledge that every effort will be made." Jon then goes on to dismiss the idea that the Lakeside team can't perform on a "heavy track" and cites the example of wins at Coventry and Ipswich to illustrate his contention.

While much-needed work on the sodden track continues, the charming 'Scary' Sheila La Sage blows past the club trackshop like a whirlwind en route towards the Supporters' Club terrapin hut on the first bend. Scary organises the raffle and the 50/50 draw as well as some of the coach trips. Tonight, for reasons that I'm not quite clear about, she's arrived in a police helmet and appropriately enough, shortly, will conduct interviews with some prospective start-line girls. "I'm interviewing some more tonight. They're not from a dance school or anything. We had some trouble with the last ones 'cause they wanted paying when the meetings were cancelled! You can hardly get paid when no one paying to come in through the gate, can you?" Though there are still thick black clouds overhead, always keen to look on the positive side of life Scary asserts against the evidence of our eyes, "It's getting brighter!" To justify her optimism, she points to a tiny patch of white sky in the direction of Stansted Airport, "and it looks fine over there!" Scary also has the coach travel to sort out to the Elite League Pairs meeting at Swindon and the ELRC at Birmingham shortly. "It's £26 to go on the coach to Swindon. I've got 14 people and also to Birmingham where I've got 18. Alan says it's a dangerous track 'cause of the solid fence. I don't know 'cause I haven't been! I have to speak to the coach companies. I was quoted £550 a coach but they claimed I'd been misquoted and it should have been £775. I think it's because they under quoted for Cardiff. We took three coaches there. Stuart booked two at £1,000 each and I had to get a third and I got it for £725." Jovial club announcer, Bob Miller passes and, after he's exchanged some banter with Scary, remarks, "It would be nice to win the League without guests! We would have won at Poole by all accounts if we hadn't lost Jonas. Tonight we've got AJ – he still hasn't had his baby – and tomorrow he's in Sweden. We've got Hans Andersen as a guest at Eastbourne tomorrow. On Monday night against them it looked good on *Sky*. I think Kelvin is good when he's talking about the racing and the bikes but he struggles when he has to talk about other things. Nigel [Pearson] says things people who follow speedway know is exaggerated but, I think, he has to say these things. Like when they're in the first bend, he always says 'If it stays like this, it'll be a 5-1' when, we all know, it'll probably change! We had the Royal Air Force sponsor us on Monday – what a brilliant sponsor to have and to be associated with! I don't think *Sky* mentioned it at all but everyone could see and pictures say more! I thought we looked really good on TV. The Eagles didn't fall away, we powered ahead!"

Though the rain has stopped, the renowned 1st Place Diner situated on the ground floor of the main grandstand remains hugely crowded. Though they're keen to advertise the fact that they do takeaways, sensibly everyone has decided avoid the damp to eat and drink indoors. It's a warm and welcoming place. The prices are keen, the

Lakeside v. Swindon: *"When we saw how their number 7 was riding, well!"*

atmosphere welcoming and the staff friendly. None more so than Tracy Manning who, like Stuart Douglas and Jon Cook, realises that to motivate your staff, you have to lead by example. Tracy is blonde, bubbly and hard working and takes a genuine enjoyment in people. Speedway attracts a rich tapestry of different character and personality types and, given that they also open during stockcar meetings, it's safe to say that the Diner attracts an eclectic but loyal clientele.

During the winter, the club announced that they had received a record number of season ticket applications and, you'd like to think, that success on the track would always be reflected with increased numbers through the turnstiles. Income from fans is only a part of the financial speedway story and, obviously, if any speedway club is to survive (let alone thrive), then they will also need substantial other income. This applies to all speedway clubs but, particularly, at the Elite League level where premium-brand riders often come with eye-watering price tags in wages, signing-on fees and travel among other expenditures. Lakeside nowadays race in the highest tier of speedway and some of their income is provided by the allegedly lucrative exclusive *Sky Sports* TV contract. Given Lakeside have improved considerably and this season track an even more attractive and competitive side, the number of appearances they make live on the television has increased and, thereby, further boosted their basic *Sky* monies. However, all these sources of income will already have been a budgeted part of their business plan and, if the club are to fulfil their stated on-track ambitions, then they'll also have to succeed off the track. The advent of inflatable air fences at the Elite League level provides increased rider safety but also gives every club with this equipment additional sponsorship and advertising opportunities. I can't be exactly sure, but it looks like there are 16 panels for hire on the first and second bends at Lakeside and a similar number available on the third and fourth bends. Part of the race-day preparations undertaken by the Lakeside curatorial team involves a pre-meeting (and mid-meeting) pressure wash of these air-fence panel adverts. There are a rich variety of sponsors on display here and these include the Royal Air Force, *Sky Sports*, *The Enquirer*, Eddie Grimstead, City Electrics, the mysterious SBZ Corporation, S&B Commercials and Teng Tools. There are also a number of other shale-splattered signs that my poor eyesight prevents me from identifying exactly – Quality something something Parts, another that looks like Bird's and one other valued sponsor whose company name remains completely unreadable. Though, I'm sure that before the meeting starts all these signs will all be washed, in pristine condition and legible, in the excitement of Jurica Pavlic's debut I forget to check.

In order to maximise their commercial revenues, the forward-thinking Lakeside management team have produced a large deluxe glossy brochure with an action photo of (I assume) Andreas Jonsson on its cover along with the club name and logo, mention of British Elite League Speedway and the strapline '2008 Season Commercial Opportunities'. In 2007 the quality of the Lakeside programme was such that it should have scooped all the awards (though it didn't) since it set the standards by which all other programmes in the country should be judged. It appears that the same design flair and expertise has gone into the design, layout, use of graphics and photos for this corporate brochure. As previously noted, Stuart Douglas gives good copy and the language of the brochure certainly reflects this facility with language. The introductory welcome from Stuart informs potential sponsors, "Speedway is currently on the cusp of a new renaissance, and with The Lakeside Hammers as the hottest new property in this non-stop action motor sport, we really do mean business. GROW WITH US IN 2008!" The copy proceeds to highlight the national and regional media coverage the club attracts, the opportunity for companies to "achieve extended brand awareness" and notes how the club has "rocketed up the top-flight speedway league in the UK, finishing a hugely successful fifth position." There are a range of "sponsorship and advertising solutions" to fit every corporate plan and budget. Ultimately, the product for sale is the speedway itself, which serves as an all-action backdrop to a "Great Friday night out for clients or staff, fed and watered at the Raceway Tavern, with exclusive balcony views across the Arena Essex Raceway, our home track." They say everyone has their price and this brochure provides a full menu of opportunities, some snappily written descriptions and, most importantly, specific prices (excluding VAT). For example, a full page of full colour advert in the programme costs £995 for the season while a half page is £595. The club note that this document is the "ONLY speedway programme in the country printed bespoke and full cover EVERY week." A circulation figure of 30,000 is given (I assume for the season), and the breathless copy emphasizes that the programme "achieves another 50% of that in total readership." When I used to swim every weekday in the wonderful outdoor pool in Hemel Hempstead, I remember that the sports centre used to boast that they received nearly quarter of a million visitors every year. Given my regular attendance, it turned out that I was, in fact, 250 visitors.

Lakeside v. Swindon: *"When we saw how their number 7 was riding, well!"*

The brochure also tells us that an air-fence banner for the season costs £1,100 and will be attached to a fence "adapted successfully from the World MotoGP series." The text of the brochure also sensibly notes that speedway action photos appear weekly in a "multitude of regional press throughout Essex and East London which, of course, represents a "MASSIVE readership". There's also great play made of the "glorious bonus" that (until they're clarted in shale) the banners will appear in "EVERY race" throughout the two-hour duration of a live broadcast on *Sky Sports*. Inevitably, there are also Centre Green 'A' Frame Hoardings for hire – those placed on the bends cost £1,000 while an 'A' Frame Hoarding by the start line is much more visible and, therefore, expensive so it's mysteriously quoted as "Price on Application." Like so many aspects of the club, the Lakeside website has also been revolutionised under the new management and is reported to receive 50,000 hits a month, while the fans' forum achieves 60,000 per month. The club offers "overall website advertising, page specific advertising, and a button link" for a price of £1,295 per year, thereby enabling any sponsoring company to get their message "in front of more than 12,000 potential customers a week." There are also a number of additional attractive sponsorship opportunities and, it would be safe to say, that the principal sponsor will gain fantastic support from the club and an extensive range of benefits. The club set out an attractive menu of options for would-be sponsors[1] How you exactly value the financial, commercial and reputational benefits of any sports sponsorship has vexed more expert minds than my own. However, though it's definitely above my pay grade to even attempt to quantify these benefits, it's incontrovertible that the price any sponsor puts on the value and benefits they reap through sponsorship is much more an art than a science. If one man's meat is another man's poison, then what exactly any company will get from their sponsorship, inevitably, falls into a grey area. However, speedway sponsors will definitely enjoy the comparatively regular oxygen of national

[1]

	Principal Sponsor POA	Corporate Sponsor £9995.00 + VAT	Associate Sponsor £4995.00 + VAT	Race Night Sponsor £995.00 + VAT
Company name incorporated into the Lakeside Hammers	✓			
Racesuits tailored to suit company name, logo, and colours	✓	✓ logo on		
The best racesuit and bike race cover locations for branding designed for premium TV exposure	✓			
Name and logo branding across all our press advertising	✓			
Sponsorship and extensive coverage on SKY SPORTS including personal appearance in front of cameras of company representa	✓			
Branding on all club retailing merchandise clothing range	✓			
Major branding on backboard for all television interviews	✓			
Branding on all club retailing merchandise clothing range	✓	✓ selected items	✓ selected items	
Trackside banners	4	2	1	0
Exclusive startline A frame advertising hoardings (the PRIME television site)	✓			
Limited edition Gold Card access passes	5	0	0	0
Complimentary Tickets	100	100	50	25
Full page, season long, programme advert		✓	✓	
Interactive link button on club website		✓ includes large ad	✓	
Company logo on tv interview backboard		✓	✓	
Sponsored meeting as part of package		✓ you choose	✓	
Programme advert for the night plus name on front cover				✓
Free Buffet at the Raceway Tavern				✓
Live interview with company representative in front of cowd[sic]				✓
Sponsors Rider of the Night presentation and photo for PR usage				✓

Lakeside v. Swindon: *"When we saw how their number 7 was riding, well!"*

publicity on satellite television and this should help raise the local/regional/national awareness of their brands[2].

In my opinion, what's most compelling about this brochure is the combination of great presentation and the marvellous language that it uses to sell the speedway proposition at Lakeside. If every club in the country produced a brochure like this, I find it hard to believe that more companies wouldn't wish to get involved with their local speedway club. The brochure concludes with a comprehensive list of all the people you should contact to further your possible interest. It also has a delightful collage of photographs of sponsors enjoying themselves at an evening at Lakeside. The 10-page brochure then closes with copy that should form a template for every speedway club in the country. "Our dedicated and enthusiastic hosts will guide you through the speedway protocol and make sure you are cheering on the right team. All our sponsors and clients are invited down into the pits area where you get to meet the riders, and have the finer points of this amazing sport illustrated for you – yes, it's true, these bikes that accelerate faster than a Formula 1 car really don't have any brakes. Meet the guys who negotiate these 180 degree bends flat out and present the bravest with their Rider of the Night reward."

Interestingly, a glance at another club document – the programme for tonights meeting – reveals that while the copy and features remain as just compelling (if not more so) as last season, the 2008 version doesn't appear to quite have the same page extent or general lustre in its paper/print quality. I don't want to get all Howard Jones but, possibly, they've switched paper supplier or use a different printer? Nonetheless, these minor cavils aside, inside the meeting programme there's much to entertain as well as a huge range of Hammers merchandise that can be ordered on-line or ordered in person at the hospitality suite situated at the entrance to the first bend. Some of the items on offer don't appear to have made it to the Alf Weedon run trackshop. The outgoing Justine does the work there on speedway race night and she notes, "We had a really big crowd on Monday, but they always make more of an effort to put on a show when the telly is here! It's been quiet tonight and we could do with more stuff but it's up to Alf. If he don't want to buy the things, as it's his money!" As usual albeit increasingly frail, Alf is in attendance but he only arrives after the trackshop stock has been set out and leaves well before the end of the meeting. He still has a keen eye for detail so offers various suggestions as to how the products on display in the small sales space of the trackshop could be better presented to the public. Justine makes the changes suggested. Alf is a natural salesman who has a keen eye for a bargain and also seeks value for money. "Advertising in the *Speedway Star* is a waste of money, I hope that you don't do it!" Nowadays Alf's speedway empire has shrunk to the shop at Lakeside but, at one point in his speedway career, Alf had trackshops dotted throughout the country and enjoyed a deserved reputation as a gifted speedway photographer round the tracks. "When I was number 1 in speedway, I used to sit next to the Mayor in Poland. They used to say, here's your reserved seat. And I could name the women at all the tracks I used to go to – Reading, Belle Vue, lots of them – I'm too old now but I had fun then and don't regret it!"

Sterling efforts by the track staff (along with Scary Sheila's correct forecast that bright weather was on its way to Thurrock from the Stansted airport area) enables the meeting to start promptly. Stood by my table of books adjacent to the trackshop I get the chance to randomly take the temperature of the Lakeside fans' opinions about the 2008 version of the Hammers and discuss the likelihood of silverware appearing in their trophy cabinet. For most fans, the recent wooden-spoon years in the Elite League have been quickly and/or studiously forgotten. Everyone is on message and appears to have bought into the suggested narrative that 2007 was a year of consolidation and 2008 is the year that the club really kick on. Some fans appear to have had their modesty chip disabled, in favour of an attitude of entitlement that slightly over-enthusiastically celebrates the present-day reinvigorated credentials of the club. Pride in recent achievement is both deserved and understandably celebrated, though the Hammers fans' trademark wry humility appears, in some quarters, to have mutated into its less attractive cousin, conceit. Though

---

[2] In the sports sponsorship industry, Formula 1 gives the most bang for your buck with a huge worldwide reach that's only bested by the (football) World Cup and the (Summer) Olympics. However, television is a medium best suited to *worldwide* brands that require *worldwide* exposure. You would have thought that the brains behind BSI/IMG, John Postlethwaite and Paul Bellamy, would know this blunt fact of advertising life already. However the lamentable and often almost laughably anonymous quality of the 'brands' associated with the SGP series (with, of course, rare exceptions) illustrates the difficulty of solving the audience/sell through conundrum for any sporting spectacle outside the top tier of really premium events. What audiences will register and remember, let alone what recognition brands will gain through what medium remains without truly independent, verifiable qualitative and quantitative analysis, and unanswered beyond meaningless platitudes. Does anyone watch the SGP and think, 'My, I must go out and purchase a lift from Meridian?' Does the sight of Leigh Adams as he flashes past an air-fence advert make any viewer really hanker to place a bet or get a new Pentel pen? The advantage and value of sponsorship and air-fence space advertising at, say, Lakeside is that the products valorised are much more suited to the locale and pockets of the people attracted to watch the club and, therefore, like to gain greater traction and benefit for their outlay.

Lakeside v. Swindon: *"When we saw how their number 7 was riding, well!"*

most people would readily acknowledge that racing high-powered bikes without brakes is likely to lead to injuries, a hard done by outlook seems to have sprung up amongst a small cadre of fans that Lakeside have been singled out by the gods to endure misfortunes and injuries that will rob them of their rightful claim upon the Elite League silverware. One fan goes out of his way to tell me, "The most important meeting is Monday at Wolverhampton." It's a claim he follows up with "Swindon lost last night so that's brilliant!" I translate this to mean that there are low expectations of a weakened Lakeside Hammers emerging triumphant from their "top of the table clash" with the Swindon Robins. The riders are introduced and we're given a pronunciation lesson regarding 19-year-old Robins reserve Jurica "Pav-Litch". It's a timely lesson, though we do subsequently all get many chances to rehearse his name throughout the meeting.

There's measured parping of air-horns as the Hammers riders take their bow and the sound builds to something that verges on a crescendo when we're introduced to "A real number 1 – Andreas Jonsson!" Arguably the number 1 to watch out for is Swindon's Leigh Adams. Not only is he widely acknowledged in speedway circles as 'Mr Consistent' but, given he spent three seasons (1993-1995) of his varied British career at the then Arena Essex, this Australian GP star definitely knows his way around this 'technical' track. Apart from the fact that his trademark dedication to the Robins team cause will ensure Leigh leads them from the front in their quest for 3 away points to boost their play-off credentials, tonight he also has the chance to become Swindon's all-time highest scorer and overtake Martin Ashby's points total of 5,476.5 (from 641 matches). Over the loudspeakers we're told, "Tonight you probably heard that it's 11 points to equal the historic Robins top scorer and 12 points to beat Martin Ashby. Hopefully he won't do it!" Predictably enough, Leigh's quest begins positively with a comfortable victory in heat 1.

It's traditional to say that all eyes are on Jurica Pavlic in the second race but, if they aren't when the riders come under the referee's orders, they certainly are once the tapes rise! In his first-ever ride at Lakeside (on a damp track), Jurica leads from the gate to win by a huge distance and only ever looks likely to concede his advantage when he rears massively as he comes out of bend 2 and nearly unseats himself. Lakeside number 8 Kauko Nieminen also impresses with his determined chase of the young Croatian. A fall for the out-of-sorts Travis McGowan leads referee Peter Clarke to award the third heat and, thereby, takes the Hammers into a narrow 2-point lead. With conditions far from ideal, the track staff take to the shale with some large bags of sawdust that they proceed to liberally spread on its surface. "As you can see, sawdust being spread about the entrances as it's still a bit slippy!" To prove that his comfortable victory was no fluke, Jurica Pavlic again wins impressively from the gate. His team mate Troy Batchelor rides like a novice at the rear of the field until a last-gasp dash to the line sees him snatch third place, when he slithers past Chris Mills. Bob Miller injects a hint of drama into his announcement of the race result, "Tight on the line, almost too tight to call but [pause] third in green, Troy Batchelor." There's further delay before heat 5 for more sawdust to be spread on the first bend and also deposited in healthy quantities on bends three and four. A man comes to my table with some feedback on my books, "People say that you're a bit long-winded but, as a speedway fan, I like that as it means there's more to read." Alf Weedon looks downcast, almost morose, and news that my sales have verged on non-existent fails to improve his mood, "There's just no money about, is there?" It's also good to catch up with the knowledgeable Peter Butcher the Sports Editor of the *Romford Recorder* who suggests some design improvements for my future books, "Have one big photo rather than three small irritating ones."

Anything Jurica Pavlic can do, Leigh Adams can equal, as he proves when he wins the fifth race comfortably from Jonas Davidsson. It's also something of a collectors' item as it features an engine failure for the ultra-consistent Hammers captain, Adam Shields. With only one point from two rides it's hardly a crisis but a nearby Lakeside fan can't believe the evidence of his eyes. "I've never known Adam have two engine failures on the trot [I must have missed the first] he's so reliable – a real backbone for our team! He scores 8 or 9 at least every meeting, home or away!" Later on another fan tells me, "Apparently Adam Shields doesn't have a mechanic tonight." Troy Batchelor wins the sixth race and Jurica Pavlic makes it three wins from three rides when he fires from the gate in heat 7 for yet another comfortable victory. It's clear to everyone in the stadium that we're in the presence of the (British) dawn of an exceptional speedway talent, particularly given that it's his first time at Lakeside and the damp sawdust-covered shale appears to cause more-experienced riders on both teams some difficulties with their control, direction and traction! Heat 8 is another exhibition of speedway racing skill from Jurica Pavlic. He wins by a street and prompts the announcer to observe, "He's on fire that boy!" The next race has the Adam Shields that the Hammers fans all know and love storm to a comfortable victory closely followed home by his team mate Jonas Davidsson. Amazingly it's only the second win of the night for a Hammers rider but actually the first time a Hammers rider has seen the chequered flag since Jonas Davidsson won the awarded third heat. This 5-1 gets an ecstatic reception from the Lakeside fans – the loudest cheer I've ever heard at Thurrock during a League meeting – and, even though they've had a total lack of heat winners, somehow Lakeside have cannily managed to even the scores at 27 apiece. Scary Sheila passes on her way to the pits where they're about to draw the raffle tickets. She's been shadowed all evening by Cameron Saveall, a polite young man who volunteered to help Scary on the Cardiff coach and has helped her ever since. They make a good combination – he's a quiet young man who seems older than his 13 years while Sheila's a voluble woman who's young at heart. Rose comes over with her new dog Tegan to worry about the ongoing Lakeside injury jinx-cum-rider crises: "Poor old Jonas has got himself injured again! If he's going to be out for more than 21 days, we'll have to try and get a replacement in. I know who I'd like – Peter Karlsson – he loves it here and, if his average is right I think he'll come!"

Before the start of heat 10, some Lakeside fans in front of me get aerated about the news that Leigh Adams – quite legitimately – will take a rider-replacement ride in place of missing Robins rider (with the second-highest average), Mads Korneliussen. Predictably enough, Leigh Adams storms to his third win of the night but the drawn heat ensures the score remains tied. Another Lakeside fan matter-of-factly recalls recent history at the club: "Ronnie Russell was a lovely guy but he tried to do everything himself, whereas we have two professionals here now!" Over the tannoy we're treated to an impromptu interview with Mark from S&B Commercials Plc who is tonight's meeting sponsor, though his company also sponsor the first and last heats. Judged by their banners on the air fence and in the programme, they could well be a corporate or associate sponsor of the Hammers. He delights in the opportunity to describe his company and we learn they're, "the Mercedes-Benz and Mitsubishi dealer for Thurrock and a number of other locations in Essex". Mark enjoys the club, relishes the racing and with him has, "a crowd of clients and friends in the bar!" Throughout his interview, the track staff work efficiently to replace some shale-splattered air-fence banners and replace them with clean ones.

Leigh Adams takes his programmed ride in the 11th heat. It's no surprise that he again wins in some style to become the highest all-time Swindon points scorer with 5,482.5 points from 467 appearances. This impressive total includes 102 maximums (48 full, 54 paid) though it leaves him some way behind Barry Briggs's maximums total of 147 (142 full, 5 paid). After the race, Adams celebrates while the riders with Workington connections, Kauko Nieminen and James Wright shake hands with each other. The irrepressibly cheerful Tracy Manning briefly leaves the 1st Place Diner to let me know about the trips she does nowadays with her friend Sara to see Lakeside race. "I've started going to the away meetings now. It's brilliant to actually see some racing and it's so enjoyable!" With Jurica Pavlic out front in the next race and Batchelor tucked behind him in second it looks highly likely that the Robins will stretch their 2-point lead. At least, it does until Shields and Nieminen both impressively pass the Australian to ensure that the race is drawn. Though the Robins are effectively a two-man opposition, both Adams and Pavlic look completely unlikely to be bested by any Lakeside rider. Adams wins heat 13 and Pavlic wins heat 14 to take his lifetime Lakeside career record to six rides, six wins. It's an amazing performance and, genuinely, breathtaking to witness! His win in the penultimate race of the night also lays to rest some grumbles from some Lakeside fans that he's only a gater since, for once, he completely fails to fly from the start. However, by the time he reaches the third bend, Jurica Pavlic has already roared round the outside of Jonas Davidsson to gain the lead.

Strangely enough, 5-1 in the last race could still see the Hammers snatch a draw but, this looks highly unlikely when Robins Team Manager, Alun Rossiter, nominates his dream partnership of Leigh Adams and Jurica Pavlic. In fact, it's Pavlic's first tough ride of the night since he has to battle his way past the bike and outstretched elbow of his captain and team mate, Leigh Adams! Pavlic passes round the outside of Adams like he's stood still with his (trademark) leg flailing behind him as he does so. Off the track at the trackshop, Justine slams the door shutters closed a split second after the tapes for heat 15 rise. The retrospective re-writing of history so beloved of speedway fans dictates that the record will show that Leigh Adams team rode with his young Croatian partner. Unless the evidence of my eyes deceived me, it genuinely appeared as if Adams was determined to brook no opposition from any other rider in the first corner, irrespective of their team colours. With the unbeaten home record dented, unlike some of his fellow promoters after a defeat, Jon Cook remains happy to give a post-meeting interview over the stadium loudspeakers.

Understandably, he looks to the future and summarises Lakeside's evening as "Just a bad night."

In his programme notes the next week Jon is more direct but simultaneously circumspect. "Our last home performance is one to forget. It may have been too much to hope to keep our 100% record in League racing but to lose in the manor we did was frankly shocking. To see two riders dominate proceedings to the extent of winning 12 of the 15 races is unprecedented and it hardly marks us down as favourites for a title this year. It's hard to explain what went wrong but even with that incredible statistic if it hadn't been for points thrown away with mechanical problems or riding mistakes we could have achieved a result. Pre-match, our team looked poor but in reality it was our experienced campaigners that came up short for varying reasons, which do no good to be aired in public. We win as a team and lose as one."

With his duties not yet over for the night, club announcer Bob Miller remains studiously philosophical, "Things didn't look good as we went into the meeting and then, when we saw how their number 7 was riding, well! We're about to run what we call our second half. We usually have it first but tonight it's second." Like the rest of the crowd, Peter Butcher of the *Romford Recorder* is amazed at what he's just seen. "Usually it's only Andres Jonsson who goes round here in 57 seconds but, tonight, there were many times like that! It also puts to rest any claims that Lakeside isn't a passing track for opposition riders. People near me said 'it's too early to say how good he is until he fails to gate'. Well, he put that to rest in heat 14 and then the people near me said 'no one has done well off gate four'. Then he wins heat 15 from there!" Shoreham-based Webmaster of *Allspeedway.tv*, Stuart Slaney, is equally amazed at Pavlic's performance, "He hasn't just been winning, he's been winning by miles! He made the track look easy but, to be honest, the racing hasn't been up to much" After the second-half races, fireworks close the meeting and thousands of miles away the Beijing opening ceremony starts with fractionally greater ceremony. It must be a topic on some people's mind because, as I leave, I overhear some fans discuss (erroneous) rumours that Lakeside speedway will cease to exist when it becomes an essential part of the 2012 Olympic Village.

8th August Lakeside v.Swindon (Elite League) 41-49

Pits sign

Lakeside v. Swindon: *"When we saw how their number 7 was riding, well!"*

CHAPTER 33.

Oxford v. Wimbledon:
"I don't have very many nice words for the GRA!"

11th August

The 80th anniversary of the first meeting at Wimbledon's Plough Lane Stadium and the 60th consecutive year of racing for Oxford prompts a poignant celebration of sorts. Particularly, given the stark context that both clubs are presently defunct and without a home track to race on each week. However, hope springs eternal for most speedway fans so the specially convened Conference League Anniversary Challenge match between Oxford and Wimbledon at Reading's Smallmead Stadium provides a welcome and special night for supporters of both clubs. The meeting has been organised by Nick Taylor (founder of the Independent Wimbledon Supporters' Club) to keep both teams in the spotlight but also to illustrate their solidarity after, as Nick puts it in his programme notes, "both teams currently find themselves homeless after being unceremoniously 'turfed out' of their bases by one company, the GRA (Greyhound Racing Association), their reason being that the 'events were not financially viable.'" In the absence of detailed written public statements from the GRA to specifically explain their actions at Plough Lane and Cowley Stadium, conspiracy theories have abounded to become the orthodoxy to explain their ostensible intentions. Whatever the ins and outs of the specific but noticeably different situations that applied to Wimbledon's departure in 2005 and Oxford's departure in 2007 from their respective stadiums, there's no doubt that this clash between select sides who'll represent Oxford and Wimbledon have stirred the collective imagination of fans not traditionally seen every week at Smallmead Stadium. Strangely, it's also the second time this season that Reading has been the location for a celebration of the Wimbledon 80th Anniversary. The ex-promoters at the club (Wimbledon Plc) had organised a match race between Buzz Burrows and Barrie Evans while tonight's event is organised by the Independent Wimbledon Supporters' Club. Over the last two years, this organisation has run a nomadic Wimbledon team, on the basis that in the absence of any development in the search for a new location from the Plc, this keeps the famous Wimbledon name alive and in the public eye. At least, that way the vast army of Dons fans occasionally still get the chance to see their club compete over 15 races. Whether you take the view that less is more (or, alternatively, more is more), in 2008 the Wimbledon name remains well and truly 'alive', even if the fact that there have been two separate meetings to celebrate the significance of the 80th anniversary indicates that, sadly, the Supporters' Club and Wimbledon Plc don't exactly work hand in glove. There's definitely something to be said for keeping a club's name in the public eye while a search for a regular base for them continues. In Oxford's case, the birth of the Oxford "TFSuccess.com" Cheetahs happened after Nick Andrews and his sponsor Ian Kirke joined forces to ensure a team to represent Oxford could take to the shale in 2008. Overall, the organisers clearly hope that not only will tonight's meeting provide a focus for both sets of homeless supporters but, also, that the publicity generated will somehow pressure the GRA. Cannily, the organisers invited the GRA but, in keeping with their reluctance to comment on their future intentions, no one from that organisation has deigned to attend.

There's a mix-and-match aspect to the make-up of both teams. Nonetheless, some of the riders who'll race tonight also appeared the last time Oxford and Wimbledon met each other at Cowley Stadium in 2005 in the Conference League. It was a top-of-the-table clash that saw a controversial mid-meeting exclusion for Wimbledon captain, Buzz Burrows, under the two-minute warning. This decision has been seen by some as the decisive turning point in a match (ultimately won by Oxford) and also a pivotal moment in a season that saw Oxford, ultimately, pip their rivals to the championship title by a solitary point. The worthiness (or otherwise) of Oxford's championship credentials has subsequently debated on the *British Speedway Forum* by many fans including erstwhile disputants, Robert Peasley and Derek Barclay. Both contribute columns to tonight's programme, though only Derek recalls this meeting at length. After he's noted an opinion for which others have been pilloried ("Conference incarnation [of Wimbledon] wasn't everyone's cup of tea") Derek's obnubilated memory asserts itself and he goes on to make the claim "it was, in many ways, the pragmatists of Oxford against the side most encapsulating the true spirit of the Conference, in

Wimbledon." As I understand it, the flame of the true spirit of the Conference League is actually seen as being burnished by clubs like Sittingbourne and Buxton. These are the type of clubs who consistently give youngsters their first chance in the sport without encumbering them with an overwhelming need to put silverware in the trophy cabinet in order to evidence their 'success'. Clubs that have a greater penchant and/or desire for glory tend to make regular team changes, use older more experienced riders and, generally, show less patience with inconsistent young men as they struggle to take their first tentative steps within the sport.[1] Whichever club holds most true to the spirit of the Conference League, they both definitely graced the competition with distinction. Sadly, they're both now homeless and Rob Peasley sensibly notes in his column, "the publicity generated by this meeting won't do any harm as the two clubs strive to achieve their No. 1 priority – a regular base to stage speedway once more. Let's hope that happens very soon."

The Smallmead pits area buzzes and I bump into Graham Arnold from Sittingbourne. "I ain't doin' it next year or any more, mate! I've busted myself up and can't do it any longer. I'll miss the last meeting of the season on September 7th 'cause I go into hospital on the 4th to have a camera put up me back. Dunno what they'll find – it's exploratory. They'll probably take another disc out and that'll be me! I've freaked meself up doing too much really." Oxford's Rob Peasley expects a good meeting and admires Wimbledon's top-end strength, "it's quite a coup for them having Buzz at number 1!" Referee Dave Robinson is extremely familiar with the pits since he was a mechanic at Smallmead before he ever went onto greater glory of officialdom. Dave missed the recently abandoned Racers meeting against the Somerset Rebels. "I wasn't at Reading last night as I was still drying myself out from Weymouth the night before. At 6.30 it was still rideable but then the heavens opened and that was it. They'd cut a gully in the first bend to help it all drain away but, obviously, you can't race with that there, so I made them fill it in!" Dave's interrupted by the sound of a bike as it falls down unaided five yards away, "That ain't supposed to happen! Things get broken like that!" There's also quite a strong Sittingbourne flavour to the pits tonight and their Start Marshal with the impressively Wild West facial hair, Terry Smith, will guest at the tapes in that capacity tonight. He's also well familiar with the Smallmead pits, "I worked here for three years in the mid-1980s, helping out by doing Start Marshal. I must go and change my shoes." I overhear somebody's father say to one of the riders, "I saw your brother with hair down to there [points to shoulders]. I said 'I don't know whether to fight you or fuck you!'" Over by the riders' changing rooms, the Clerk of the Course worries that the air fence might get battered tonight and, if it does, there's a slight possibility of an abandonment, "we only have two replacement air-fence panels!"

Nick Taylor, the impetus behind the independent Wimbledon Supporters' Club, surveys the pits proudly and can't wait for the action to start. He'd be even more delighted if the club had a venue to race at again. Though extensive research into venues by the Plc drew a blank, he praises Ian Perkin, "His heart's in the right place for Wimbledon!" The editor of the rather wonderful quarterly speedway magazine *The Voice*, Stuart Towner gives his own '70s flavour to the pits by wearing platform soles. This prompts Reading's unofficial historian Arnie Gibbons to note: "They do seem rather built up! Some exciting news, I sold my first book in Sweden to a Mr Per Jonsson!" Always to be relied upon for a balanced and informative perspective, Arnie ruminates upon the iniquitous behaviour of the stadium landlords at Oxford and Wimbledon. "You have to remember that if you see the GRA as a property development company, they'll take a long-term view of their assets and how they might develop them. So a sale of Plough Lane for redevelopment is the possibility that some have claimed it is. Quite when this might happen is open to question." Weymouth photographer Julie Martin snaps away in the pits but then breaks off for her traditional pre-meeting change of footwear (when she swaps her high-heeled sandals for some sensible but stylish plimsoll-cum-ballet shoes).

---

[1] A glance at the Oxford and Wimbledon teams from 2005 reveals that younger riders with less senior level experience were in the Oxford side rather than the Wimbledon one. The Cheetahs only had two riders born prior to 1985 with Premier League experience: Craig Branney (born 1982) and Chris Mills (born 1983). Wimbledon also only had two riders born before 1985 but actually had three with Premier League experience, namely: Mark Burrows (born 1964) and Scott James and Grant MacDonald (born 1979). Previous years saw the Dons track Chris Hunt (aged 39 in 2003) and Andre Cross (aged 37 in 2004). When I quizzed Rob about the make-up of the Oxford and Wimbledon teams he remembered. "Apart from Millsy and Branney, who were in their early 20s, the rest of the Oxford team were teenagers. Craig [Branney] lost his team place at Newcastle and came to Oxford in 2004 when he had nothing, whilst Waggy and Bryn [Williams] had brought Millsy on at King's Lynn, where Waggy had promoted before Oxford. Jamie Courtney and Ben Barker were given Premier League opportunities during the year 'cause they were good youngsters who'd developed riding Conference League, which is the idea! Wimbledon did have two riders with considerable experience in Buzz and Grant, although the latter was on his way back from injury and was still only in his mid-20s. Looking at the rest of the Wimbledon team [for older riders with PL experience] it wasn't too bad, but overall Oxford definitely had the younger and less-experienced side, which is contrary to what my old sparring partner Derek claimed in the programme!"

Oxford v. Wimbledon: *"I don't have very many nice words for the GRA!"*

In the commentary box Paul Hunsdon is amazed by the size of the crowd that's been drawn along to watch this meeting: "I thought there was only going to be one man and his dog here tonight. If I'd known there was going to be a crowd like this, I'd have stayed on the centre green!" Perhaps his keenness to remain trackside also has something to do with his ongoing search for yummy mummies at Smallmead though, sadly for him, tonight the "strangers" are most likely to be middle-aged blokes with beer guts and beards. Nonetheless, Paul remains wistfully optimistic, "Were you here for the Glasgow meeting? They had a really foxy fan – Donna was her name!" In the home-straight grandstand, a regular Racers fan looks to the bright side, "At least we're going to be spared Wacky Racer tonight!" The rider parade features an interview with Nick Taylor who's delighted to have the talismanic Dermot Mark 'Buzz' Burrows back in the Wimbledon team. "We've been lucky to get Buzz 'cause, if this was a Conference League track, he wouldn't be able to ride. But, since Reading are the staging club, we can as it's their meeting and they just happen to be putting it on for Oxford and Wimbledon." Fans sat near me view Buzz's participation cynically, "It'll be like old times for Buzz – taking candy from babies!" His friend next to him wonders, "Has Buzz knocked anyone off recently?" When the action starts, some form of unofficial handicapping must be in operation because Buzz is either mounted on a lead bike or one that markedly lacks sufficient power. When the tapes rise, the veteran rider is third into the corner and then spends the remainder of the four laps in an ostentatious but doomed challenge for second place behind the youngest rider on display, 16-year-old Brendan Johnson. We're treated to the full theatrical repertoire of positions on his bike showcased by Buzz to indicate that he's dead keen to zoom past but, sadly, the 44-year-old fails to generate the necessary speed required. Jamie Courtney wins the race comfortably to assuage Rob Peasley's pre-meeting anxiety, "Jamie, and Sam [Martin], haven't ridden for a while so might be a bit rusty". The maximum heat advantage won by Oxford in the first race of the night represents a surprise in the context of considered opinion on the comparative team strengths but is also short lived. Wimbledon look to have assembled a much stronger side on paper and this perception looks to have some basis in fact when they immediately reply with a 5-1 of their own in heat 2. It's a processional contest, though there is a brief modicum of excitement provided by the battle for third place when Adam Wrathall overtakes his team mate Marc Andrews (son of Oxford team manager Nick) on the second bend of the final lap. The early stages of the meeting see both teams then exchange 4-2s before Buzz returns to the fray in the fifth heat and struggle to retain his third place ahead of Ben Hopwood. Heat 6 sees Jay Herne take his second outing of the night and we're told that he has a secret weapon in the pits in the form of "Australian team manager, Craig Boyce." Clearly not overawed by his Weymouth team mate, Brendan Johnson gates and blasts round the outside of the whole field to lead comfortably until the last bend when the experienced Jay Herne sizes him up and fires past him to easily win the race to the chequered flag. During his centre-green interview, the new sponsor of Oxford speedway, Ian Kirke (of Training for Success.com), professes to be "choked" to see his beloved Cheetahs take to the track once more. First taken to see them by his dad 30 years previously, he "sincerely hopes that the size of the attendances will make the business case to convince the GRA to allow Oxford back to Sandy Lane in 2009!" It's a heartfelt interview that's made even more notable by his use of the word "bastard".

Racers tractor

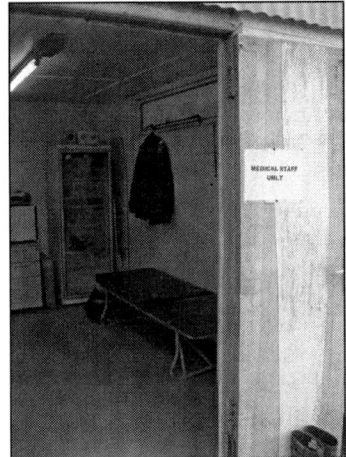

Medical room

Programmes attract good interest

Oxford v. Wimbledon: *"I don't have very many nice words for the GRA!"*

Locked in the commentary box away from the prospective 'talent', Paul Hunsdon advises that we have the wrong type of supporters' flags on display, "We have a request from pit lane – can the Wimbledon flag placed on the third bend be removed!" On the centre green, the guest presenter interviews Nick Taylor and optimistically enquires about the chances of a return to Plough Lane. Nick contents himself with an "I think not!" He then demonstrates commendable restraint when he refrains from any use of swear words, "I don't have very many nice words for the GRA!" Over the loudspeaker system, thank yous on behalf of the Nick Andrews speedway promotion are expressed and Paul Hunsdon passes on a message, "We have an announcement for Chris Brown and Rob Peasley – thanking you for all your efforts and nice to see you here at Smallmead, your old friend Nick Dyer." Congratulations are cut short by car park administration matters, "If you're the owner of a Citroen with the registration S301 EFC – you've left your window open, I wouldn't do that too often around here!"

At the midpoint of the meeting, Matt Wright and Terry Day secure a 5-1 for Wimbledon that gives them a lead that they don't relinquish for the rest of the meeting. After brilliant reflexes from the tapes in his previous race, this time Brendan Johnson makes a terrible start emphasised all the more by the way his front wheel waggles and sways dramatically during his first few yards progress towards the bend. Out in successive races, Terry Day follows up a paid win with a race win and, with Lee Strudwick second, suddenly the Dons appear to have established an invincible lead at 20-28. A stickler for exactitude, Paul Hunsdon informs us: "The rider replacement ride in heat 10 will be taken by Dermot Mark Burrows". It's an opportunity to revisit the 'eldest versus the youngest' clash and this time Burrows bests Johnson when he gates promptly to comfortably win the rerun of the heat. There's no rest for old bones since Buzz is out again in the next to struggle for supremacy against Sam Martin during the first two laps. They exchange passes in dashing fashion before experience conquers to gain Paul Hunsdon's heartfelt congratulations, "Well, a tremendous ride there from Buzz Burrows showing all his years of experience or was it youthful exuberance?" Oxford send Kyle Hughes out in a black-and-white helmet in the 12th heat. Their use of the tactical regulations nearly goes awry when Lee Strudwick leads the race before an engine failure gifts Kyle Hughes the win.

On the terraces, speedway's version of Memory Man, Arnie Gibbons, is doubtful whether the Conference League incarnation of Wimbledon encapsulates the ethos and spirit of youth development that many consider to be the cornerstone of the league. "Let's see, Oxford had Mills, Schramm, Hughes, the Branneys, Danny Norton but Wimbledon had Andre Cross, Buzz Burrows, Grant MacDonald, I'm not sure if Chris Hunt rode or not, I don't think he did, but he was a Milton Keynes junior in the 1980s! I also think Marc Norris rode for them briefly before he did his usual strop." Arnie glances around the Smallmead public, "There's a much more varied crowd here tonight!" While you can take an accountant away from his spreadsheets, you can't repress his natural desire to count. Arnie loves to try to estimate crowd sizes at speedway meetings, "With the usual disclaimer for margin of error, I'd say there were 570 people here tonight though some of them didn't pay to get in." Always with a fascinating fact at his fingertips, Arnie's pleased to see Kyle Hughes finally race at Smallmead. "He's been a Reading asset for two years and, I think, it's the first time he rode here. When Oxford's assets reverted to the BSPA, Postlethwaite bought a job lot in order to get Chris Mills back." If Arnie is THE authority on all things Reading for me, then he too also has his own authoritative sources, "I must check that with Nick Dyer." If Reading is Arnie's first love, then speedway is Arnie's true love. Consequently, during the speedway season he leads a peripatetic life, "I was at Sittingbourne yesterday and Derek Barclay's replacement as announcer was awful. He got everything wrong from the riders to the results and even the heat numbers!" Arnie's anxious about whether the Reading 'End of an Era' meeting will go ahead as planned on October 19th. Arnie's has already fretted about every scenario to foresee potential problems and has heard that the proposed date "clashes with a big greyhound meeting and, if it doesn't, the stadium demolition is due to start on October 20th!" He theorises that if the weather gods were to unfavourably intervene there'd be "no opportunity to rerun it!" Further complication is provided by the fact that "no one knows if there's a Young Shield this season. There's no official evidence to confirm that fact – which is a classic illustration of how pathetic speedway is – but, as there's no way we're gonna be in the top four, we should be one of the favourites to do well in that. So, we might have a real fixture pile up!"

Perched in his eyrie that overlooks the start line and centre green Paul Hunsdon finally spots a woman who fulfils his own exacting criteria, so he immediately extends an oral cuddle to her over the tannoy: "And a special welcome for the Weymouth Wildcats official photographer, Judy Martin." Out on the centre green, Julie Martin ignores the

Oxford v. Wimbledon: *"I don't have very many nice words for the GRA!"*

compliment given to her namesake "Judy" and concentrates on her own preparations for the start of the 13th heat. Often races are stopped by the red lights almost as soon as they've started but, in this instance, the race is halted by red lights before the race has had the chance to start! With Buzz Burrows hard at work digging for victory on gate 1, Paul Hunsdon informs us, "Could the Start Marshal remind Buzz Burrows that he's on gate 2!" Buzz switches gates and resumes his dig with renewed vigour. These preparations prove worthwhile when Buzz again gates to win and prompts Arnie to observe, "It's good to see these young riders with youthful enthusiasm!" Paul Hunsdon runs through the heat result that has just taken the scores to 36-45 and Arnie asks, "Two fine riders and Jay Herne did he just say?" The raffle prizes are drawn and Oxford track curator Nobby Hall wins the gift he never knew he wanted – an impressively large hamper of crockery! The Reading trackshop was already stripped of Reading Racers merchandise with any real lustre, significance or resale potential some weeks ago. Arnie already has a good stash at home, "There's no programme boards and only pink sweatshirts available in the trackshop now!" Arnie's about to go on holiday to the Lake District and while he's there he'll take in the Under-15 Championship at Northside (in Workington). "My partner suggested it – I think he plans the holidays around attractive speedway meetings to get me to go." Oxford massage the scoreline to a much more acceptable 43-50 with a last-heat 5-1, significantly helped by the Wimbledon team manager's decision to track Dons number 8, Martin Elliott (rather than Buzz Burrows). After a marked poor start, the rejuvenation of Buzz Burrows was such that you had to suspect either equipment problems or polite courtesy until his natural competitive urge and keen desire to always race to the max took over.

Excitement builds in the pits

11th August Oxford v. Wimbledon (Conference League Anniversary Challenge) 43-50

Sue Jackson-Scott, Stuart Towner and Terry Smith

CHAPTER 34.

Scunthorpe v. Glasgow:
"We've not really beaten anyone by a big score"

25th August

My decision to visit Scunthorpe for the August Bank Holiday double-header meeting versus the Glasgow Tigers and the Plymouth Devils means an early start from Brighton. The law of unintended consequences links both the 2012 London Olympics and Scunthorpe Speedway. My laughter nearly causes a car crash when the BBC Radio 4 *Today* programme carries news of the subsequent outrage caused by the film to promote London used during the closing ceremony of the 2008 Beijing Olympic Games. 'Visit London' had been commissioned by London Lord Mayor Boris Johnson to promote the joys of the capital city and produce an eight-minute promotional film that showcased its erstwhile glamour and cultural significance to millions of viewers around the world. The inclusion of the film during the spectacular closing ceremony of the Beijing Olympics would allow Britain as a country and London in particular to draw attention to our staging of the 2012 Olympic Games. All the usual images were included in this montage – the Queen, Buckingham Palace, Beefeaters at the Tower of London – plus the film also included many other images that highlighted London's notionally thriving cultural scene. The Royal Academy featured and, for a few brief moments, the camera lingered over various pictures hung there. Unfortunately this included Marcus Harvey's controversial portrait of the Moors Murderer Myra Hindley made up from multiple copies of children's handprints. It was vandalised when it first went on display during the 1997 Sensation Exhibition. The painting has lost none of its ability to shock if judged by the reactions of severe outrage visited upon the 'Visit London' team for their decision/temerity to showcase the glamour and cultural significance of London using images of Myra Hindley. Around the world, viewers must have already been shocked by the sight of a corpulent Jimmy Page as well as confused by the tableaux that included the footballer David Beckham, an open-top double-decker London Bus and London Mayor Boris Johnson. 'Visit London' had shown the Myra film many times without objection before tabloid complaints at its use during the Beijing Olympics closing ceremony prompted No. 10 Downing Street to issue an apology.[1]

Asked for his reaction by the *Today* programme about how 'Visit London' managed to represent Britain in the context of this spectacular closing ceremony, comedian Arthur Smith sympathised with the difficulty caused by time constraints and image choices. Arthur suggested that Boris Johnson caught exactly what Britain and its staging of the Olympics would all be about – blonde, shambolic and reeking of amateurism. If he'd been in charge, Arthur claimed that he'd have "chosen a mass march past of reality TV contestants and people with ASBOs" along with "a giant double-decker bus that no one was allowed to get on by the police." My conversation with Scunthorpe promoter Rob Godfrey upon arrival at the Normanby Road stadium indicates that he'd also probably include travellers in any such march past. The transformation of a brown field area of land on the outskirts of an industrial estate in Scunthorpe into a thriving speedway club has been a triumph of dedication, ingenuity and ambition. However, the site is also located close to an area designated for the use of travellers. In recent times, the club has enjoyed an uneasy relationship with their erstwhile neighbours. "The travellers got a tractor and chains and ripped the doors off the steel container. They stole the quad bikes and took the helmets but just threw them everywhere. They left the boots and the kevlars though. It's always been a travellers' site down the road. They all moved out in 2005 but only after they'd trashed the place! They took all the showers and toilets and everything from the washing block and even came back and took the generator. They left it a total mess. One family – the mum and dad plus three boys and a girl – have moved back. They couldn't get a council house in Scunthorpe because of all the damage they've caused. They have to have somewhere to live but you'd think they'd respect things?" Later I hear from other members of staff, "If these gyppos keep bothering us, Rob will throw in the towel!"

[1] That day's *Sun* reported the snafu in typically outraged and florid language. "A No. 10 source said the person responsible "should be fired". Winnie Johnson, mother of Moors victim Keith Bennett, was "stunned". She said: "Hindley is the symbol of evil – not a beacon of everything that's good about Britain."…A No. 10 source branded it a "total disgrace". Mr [Boris] Johnson was said to be "deeply disturbed" and immediately axed the film."

When it comes to this afternoon's PL/CL double-header meeting against Glasgow and Plymouth, Rob isn't quite sure if the speedway will triumph over other competing local attractions, let alone the Bank Holiday weather. "We've been getting big crowds here all season but there's lots going on in Scunthorpe today! The Queen's Arms in town – it used to be the steelworkers' pub – has got a gigantic rink outside in the car park and there's also an event in one of the parks. I don't know how that'll affect things but people who've come along this season will know how good the racing is that we have here!" I base my books table by the wooden hut that serves as the programme stall just inside the entrance turnstiles of the stadium. There are strong family connections throughout Scunthorpe Speedway club. The stall is run by Pat Hubbard – her husband, Peter, is Pits Marshal – and she's assisted this afternoon by Jackie Comerford ("I only come here now and then to assist") whose husband Martin is the club's Machine Examiner. Pat has been here from the outset of the Normanby Road incarnation of Scunthorpe speedway club. "I've been here since 2005 when we started and stood outside in the pouring rain. We had some friends who told us about the club starting, Rod Haynes, if you remember, he used to ride years ago for the Saints. Since it started, I've always sold the programmes. We didn't have this hut (which has been kindly donated) and I used to sit out there in the wind, rain or shine. We did have a gazebo but the wind took it away and shattered it. They've developed the stadium as they've gone along. The car park came first and then the bar – it's got room for a kitchen and people will be able to sit and eat and watch from there. There's a building for the riders to shower and change. I sell the programmes when we're here and we go to watch them away at Buxton, Sheffield and King's Lynn – anywhere my husband doesn't have to drive too far. He likes to get there and back in a day. I like the thrill of the racing and that smell, it's absolutely gorgeous! It's been a privilege to see these young lads come up – like Tai [Woffinden] and Andrew Tully – and know that they started here! It's lovely! My husband won Andrew Tully's kevlars in the raffle just after he finished here. It's stapled up in the bar so, we said to him, if he wants them back he can't have them 'cause they've got holes in. Apart from being the Pits Marshal, my husband [Peter] fills all the tea urns and opens the canteen and generally does some dogsbody things. My husband was here one day on his own when the gypsies started throwing stones at him [over the fence]. It got so bad that he stood on top of the referee's box so, that if they tried anything, they could only come up one at a time! When they broke in they took my granddaughter's quad bike. She can still hear it being ridden 'cause she knows the sound of the engine!" This area of the stadium suffers with a wasp infestation ("it's the rubbish, they love it!"). Pat and Jackie glance through my photograph book *Shale Britannia* and spot one photograph of Antonio Lindback, "Now that's a young man who went haywire and that's why they have to leave Tai alone, and little Joe Haines! They've got plenty of time [to develop] and don't need to be pushed." They hold the Scunthorpe riders in high esteem and are keen to let me know, "He's a nice young man that Byron [Bekker] – very polite! Lovely."

Scunthorpe's official photographer Steve Dixon stops by for a word and has a bit of a bee in his bonnet about how he perceives the trackshop owner Dave Rattenberry has behaved towards him. "You'd think if you came somewhere new you'd try to get on with the people already there! The first day, Dave Twattenbury was here, he put his arm round me and said, 'I'll see you're alright, Steve'. Whenever anyone says that you're always suspicious! I didn't know I needed seeing alright. I used to be happy – as official photographer – for the club and shop to sell my photos without payment 'cause I knew it was going to a good cause! Rattenberry said, 'I'll do you the same deal as I do with Claire Perkins [Stoke club photographer] 35p a photo to you and I'll sell them for 75p'. I don't care how much he sells them for. Then I hear he'd asked Claire to do some mugs with Scunthorpe riders on them so I rang and said 'what's going on?' And he said 'not to worry' 'cause he always did that but, if I'm the track photographer, he should ask me first, at least? I'd also heard he was getting photographers [four names redacted] to do Scunthorpe team photos and they do, even though they know I'm the photographer and wouldn't do it to them! Anyway, I said 'you said I'd be on the same deal as Claire but she gets 40p a photo'. 'I didn't say that' he said, when he did, but he also said 'you're on 30p a photo'. So, I said 'send all the photos back and pay me for what you've sold'. Counting them up it was £25 short so, I asked him for the money, but didn't get it. I sent him an email telling him what I thought of him and I mentioned it to Rob [Godfrey] but he just laughed. There's nothing he could do about it anyway!"

The last time I visited Scunthorpe, so many people at the track wore items of clothing with the initials TWR emblazoned across them that, I began to wonder, if these initials stood for an important local employer or perhaps a vital sponsor of the club? Maybe, even, this TWR was the Lincolnshire equivalent of Harley Davidson? Far from any connection with the automotive and aerospace industries, it turned out that TWR stood for Tai Woffinden Racing. Tai is the poster boy for all that they've achieved at Scunthorpe speedway since they reopened and, though he now rides for Rye House in the Premier League, he's still spoken of in reverentially hushed tones everywhere around the club. His grandmother Cynthia still works at the club and makes a mean cup of tea but, his impact at Normanby Road is such, that the fact that he started out here lends the club an aura that they understandably take great pride and satisfaction in. Tai has a hugely bright future ahead of him and, it's widely expected, that he'll soon take his rightful place in the upper echelons of the sport and/or at its pinnacle. The incidence of TWR clothing has, nonetheless, noticeably lessened from its 2007 peak and even his great admirer, the cheerful Barry 'Bazski' Preston, has turned up without these initials anywhere to be seen on his clothes. "I haven't done so much with Tai this year as I've been working and, anyway, he's been travelling all the time!" Bazski's speedway work nowadays is that of Music Man alongside Scunthorpe's presentational powerhouse, Shaun Leigh. Baz is characteristically modest about his abilities and how the job opportunity arose. "Shaun asked me to be the DJ 'cause he couldn't get anyone on a Friday. It's hard working with him 'cause he's a master DJ – that's his job! So, it's a real pressure! I've made a few mistakes but he's been very good. He said I can play what I like. He's not here today 'cause he's been let down by the bloke at Wolves, so he's had to go there. Graham will do it, instead, today and I'll do the music." Shortly afterwards Bazski's first record of the night is *Fanfare for the Common Man* by ELP. If nothing else, this betrays Bazski's roots as a speedway fan from the 1970s! Baz excitedly advises that I might like to go down to the pits to have a look at Richard Hall's Long Track trophies since they're temporarily on display there. Baz is also keen that I should broaden the outlook of my books, "You should do a book on life in the pits, as fans don't really know what goes on there or the pressures involved! Whether it's the Conference League or the Premier League, it's still really intense!" I tell Barry that (as Eastbourne Writer in Residence) I stood next to Nicki Pedersen – like a lemon – all last season in the pits at Arlington. He sympathises, "It's hard to get anything out of Nicki at the best of times, let alone when he's under pressure in the pits!"

Rob Godfrey's worries that alternative entertainment attractions in Scunthorpe city centre might hit the size of the gate proves unfounded since an impressive and continuous stream of people make their way through the turnstiles. Always heart warming to see – from any promoter's perspective – there's also the welcome sight of a large coach full of dedicated Glasgow Tigers fans. These fans stream off the coach and include Jim Fleming from Biggar. A passionate smoker and knowledgeable speedway fan, the necessary democracy of coach travel has let him down somewhat, "I thought we were going to stop at a service station on the way here so I could get some fags. But we stopped at a farm shop, which was no good!" Rather optimistically, Jim goes off in search of somewhere to buy some much-needed cigarettes. Shortly afterwards, Scunthorpe fan Paul makes a point to stop at my table to highlight the consistently great value offered by his club. "The racing is excellent here every week, it really is! I'm not just saying that. Now we're in the Premier League, it's always close and exciting. Last year I often left before the end as winning by miles wasn't fun to watch." It's certainly not the balmy weather that attracts the fans to the stadium since a strong Bank Holiday wind lifts up my table and blows it away. It blows so hard that the rope on the nearby flagpole flaps, rattles noisily and draws attention to the fact that there's no flag. Maybe it's been borrowed by the neighbours? My worry that the car park won't be big enough to hold all the vehicles is given short shrift by a girl in the programme booth, "The car park will be big enough if they park sensibly – that can be asking a lot though!" A talkative woman clutching a sweatshirt chatters while she buys a programme. She addresses the grown-ups while she looks at the little girl also on duty behind the counter. "I've got a sweater here, would it fit your little girl? [Girl smiles] There you go. It'll keep you warm when it gets cold later."

Away some distance from the turnstiles, the racing has started promptly close to the scheduled start time of 3 p.m. After only two heats, the meeting is effectively over as a contest with the score at 9-3. Richard Hall takes full advantage of what locals claim to be a 'grippy track' in the first race to establish a new track record of 56.39 seconds (he bests his own record by 0.51 seconds). Back in the team and almost returned to full fitness, despite the fact that he hasn't ridden for four months (until yesterday) is Shane Parker, the Glasgow Tigers talismanic captain. He wins the third race of the afternoon when eventually it gets run to completion at the third attempt. It could have turned out so differently since the initial attempt to run the heat saw Parker stuck in second until Anders Andersen fell on the third bend and got excluded for his troubles. The next attempt to complete heat 3 saw Emiliano Sanchez touch the tapes to earn an exclusion and, thereby, relegated himself 15 metres back for the next re-rerun. At the third time of asking, Shane made no mistake but, without another Glasgow Tiger in the race, a drawn heat was inevitable. Back at the turnstiles there's some debate about crowd levels. The comment "I'd say it's a crowd of 1,250 plus" gets short shrift

Scunthorpe v. Glasgow: *"We've not really beaten anyone by a big score"*

from the girl on the turnstile, "Dunno! I haven't counted the cash yet but there's less than for Sheffield, I'd say around 900."

Many people have remarked on the fact that start-line girls are an anachronism that really has no place in a modern world influenced by 21st-century sexual politics. Unfortunately, speedway isn't at the forefront of any equality, let alone radical feminism, and some clubs still set great store by their start-line girls. Coventry organise theirs in the manner of a dance troupe and the comely Sexy7even girls have taken kevlar tightness levels to an extreme degree never dreamt of (even by the trend-setting girls at Poole). Some clubs clearly employ the girls for the task at hand just because they're local speedway fans with connections to the club. Scunthorpe promoter Rob Godfrey is keen to be iconoclastic in a whole variety of ways that he runs his club and the chance to storm the citadels of entrenched male chauvinism has proved irresistible to him. Consequently, this afternoon at least, they have a start-line boy to supervise the green-helmeted riders. Perhaps this isn't just Rob Godfrey's contribution to sexual politics but a carefully conceived and cunning element of sports psychology employed to distract the various Glasgow riders to wear the green helmet colour? If, when they come under the referee's orders and their engines rev loudly, their mind suddenly wanders to ("bloody hell, I'm sure that was a start-line boy!") then that fractional second's advantage could prove crucial in the first turn and work to the advantage of the Scorpions riders. Heat 4 sees the promising young Australian reserve for the Tigers, Josh Grajczonek, (luckily in the yellow helmet colour) fly from the tapes only to be given a traditional Normanby Road welcome by Carl Wilkinson who passes him in the first corner with some gratuitous hard riding. Josh manages to cling on to second place until the penultimate bend of the last lap when Byron Bekker draws deeply on his track knowledge to overtake him. It's so thrilling that I rip the seam of my shorts.

Ref's box

Over by the tea and burger van, Sheffield speedway's equivalent of the Three Amigos (albeit without the hats and the distinctive flourish of thrusting their hips forward in unison) have congregated to enjoy yet another much-needed cigarette. Well, Neil Machin and Eric Boocock have while, close by, Dave Hoggart gets in the teas. Inside the refreshment kiosk, Cynthia Woffinden works quickly and capably in sweltering conditions. Neil Machin offers his own paean of praise to his geographically nearest rivals: "This is the best racing in British speedway [pause], generally. It was excellent when we were here." With the score already at 21-9, Dave Hoggart has been disappointed by the level of effort shown by the Glasgow Tigers, "I expected them to be a bit more spirited!" As the words leave his mouth, the tapes rise for the sixth race. Viktor Bergstrom rears massively as he exits the second bend only to get clattered by the pursuing Glasgow rider, though both riders stay on their machines. Dave Hoggart exhales loudly, "Freaking hell, here we go!" The start of the seventh race gives me the chance to point out the revolutionary start-line boy initiative to Neil Machin, "Freak – they have as well!" Heat 7 also gives the Glasgow Tigers faithful an early opportunity to see Shane Parker come out in the black-and-white helmet colour. He wears this tactical garment with some distinction and is awarded the race win, after Carl Wilkinson is excluded for unfair riding. The grippy state of the track appears to play havoc with Viktor Bergstrom's control of his bike. His machine is clearly drawn inexorably towards the fence and, if it's possible to describe it as such, he rides the fence wildly throughout but still

Longtrack trophies and pushchair

somehow manages to retain second place behind his "polite" team partner Byron Bekker. Sheffield's recent form gives Dave Hoggart some cause for concern, "We've lost three in a week – it couldn't have happened at a worse time. It's been a shite year! The lads just haven't done it as a team. We can't blame officialdom, it's just not clicking as a team!" I might be wrong but somehow I sense that the Sheffield Tigers haven't quite gelled as a team. In heat 8 (and already his fourth ride of the night) Josh Grajczonek is admonished by referee Graham Flint. At least that's what the announcer said, "I can tell you Josh Grajczonek has been warned by the referee for delaying the start, so the next time he does that we'll tie his shoe-laces together!"

Though I haven't heard anyone barrack him but, by the 10th heat, the green start-line boy has started to look somewhat sheepish and project an air of reticence as if he now wished he wasn't there. He also shows a marked lack of willingness to conform since he's the only start-line person to refuse to carry (or twirl) an umbrella. Apart from the support given by Robert Ksiezak, Shane Parker is effectively a one-man team for the Glasgow Tigers. He further illustrates his consummate skill on the bike when he effortlessly passes Richard Hall and Viktor Bergstrom on the first corner of the 10th race. Richard Hall chases him hard throughout but never looks likely to catch Shane and then, afterwards, ignores the generous offer of a congratulatory handshake. Stood underneath the referee's box, Scunthorpe Press Officer and Programme Editor, Richard Hollingsworth, is amazed that I've chosen to come along to the one Scunthorpe speedway fixture of the season where the opposition have failed to keep the scores close. "We've not really beaten anyone by a big score. 53-40 is our second biggest win but, today, I half predicted it would be a big score!"

The last lap of the 11th heat illustrates the difference in attitude to this meeting shown by each team. Carl Wilkinson, the harum-scarum number 5 for the Scorpions has, until that point, garnered a win and an exclusion (for unfair riding), yet his determination to grab more points remains undimmed. After he's stalked Robert Ksiezak for three laps, Carl finally sees his opportunity to blast past his prey on the second bend of the last lap and zooms away (with great aggression) to win the race. In fact, he's so keen to triumph that he continues to race until he exits the second bend of the fifth lap, apparently unaware that nowadays speedway races are only staged over four laps. Richard Hollingsworth is delighted with the win and has a brief blow in the plastic trumpet he already has hung around his neck for this very purpose. Richard's commitment to Scunthorpe speedway is exceptional. "I last missed a meeting in 1983! It was easy some years not to miss them as we weren't riding! The last one I missed was the Super National at Weymouth – the end-of-season play-offs in 1983. I went to all of 1984 and all the ones we rode in 1985 as well as the Challenge we had at Boston in 2003. I've been to every Conference League and Premier League meeting at home and away for Scunthorpe. I missed the Conference League Pairs this year as we had an Amateur meeting here the following day."

As the riders take up their positions in their respective start gates for the 12th heat sponsored by the Altered Image Unisex Salon, Richard wonders aloud, "Is anyone gonna beat Parker today?" Shane proceeds to win with some ease so, the definitive answer, appears to be 'No'. After the race had finished, Richard Hollingsworth gives voice to his thoughts, "Was that their first proper heat advantage?" The next race sees Glasgow Tigers captain Trent Leverington shake off his torpor to zoom from the gate accompanied by Robert Ksiezak. Unfortunately for the coachload of Tigers fans in the stadium, the Scorpions captain Richard Hall refuses to accept second best. He passes Leverington on the fourth bend through sheer force of will but also decides to lean on him just before he nips past. By the time Hall has reached the second bend of the second lap, he's undertaken Ksiezak and stormed away from his erstwhile rivals. The Scorpions also have Carl 'The Beast' Wilkinson in this race and – in the manner of stealing candy from a baby – he has little difficulty taking the third place point. Always fair-minded Richard Hollingsworth noted, "Trent rode well in heat 13 but got no points!"

In the sky over Scunthorpe, two groups of four Red Arrows fly past in formation and briefly add further lustre to the speedway event below them. With the exception of Smallmead on the Concorde flight path (until, like the stadium, it was taken out of service) or Mildenhall, Rob Godfrey must be one of the few promoters in the country able to organise such a glamorous fly-past. The double-header meeting then suffers a double medical delay. On the track in heat 14 Emiliano Sanchez proceeds to entertain with a third-bend slow-motion fall but spoils the apparently contrived look of his spill when he lies on the shale in considerable pain. Emiliano's move to Scunthorpe in a straight switch for fellow struggler Andrew Moore hasn't quite turned out as the rider or the promotional team expected.

The hope was that the chance to ride at Scunthorpe would provide the metaphorical kiss of life to the twilight years of his British speedway racing career. However, his season has failed to ignite and (to carry on the medical analogy) the expectations of the Scorpions has metaphorically cut off the blood flow to his throttle hand like a tourniquet. Almost in complete synchrony with Sanchez's fall onto the shale, off the track a corpulent man dramatically falls to the floor in front of the trackshop doorway. The crowd reaction to this possible medical emergency is to stand round, gawp and stare as well as ponder how they're going to pass the time of the delay without access to the array of bargains displayed within the trackshop! The only person to react quickly to the situation is Eric Boocock who raises the alarm in true Milk Tray man style when he climbs the ladder up to the referee's box to demand that they immediately appeal over the speaker system for some of the on-site medical staff to rush to the collapsed man's aid. Eric belies his years and what looks like a 40-a-day habit to climb the stairs with athleticism. Invariably casually poised like a panther about to strike, despite his age, you definitely still wouldn't choose to argue with Eric. He's certainly able to move with greater ease than the medical staff who are hampered by their bulky equipment and, if judged by their gait, the weight of their fluorescent clothing. By the time they arrive on the scene, the man has sat up on the step at the entrance to the trackshop and his girth ensures that he comprehensively blocks the doorway. John Rich, Dave Rattenberry and a customer are trapped inside like speedway prisoners of conscience. Scunthorpe Scorpions Advertising Manager, Julie Harrowven, recognises the bloke as a troublemaker from only a minute or so beforehand. "That's the man who just gave me a mouthful when I asked him to move from the hospitality suite. I told him, 'It's a private party' and he wasn't very happy – though I asked him politely!" Combined with the alcohol he'd already consumed, the sting of his eviction from the hospitality suite must have played havoc with the man's blood pressure and, after a short walk from the panoramic views of the suite terrace area to the trackshop half way down the back straight, it had clearly got all too much for him.

Pits preparations

Sheffield Speedway massive

With unexpected drama below, the referee's box temporarily empties of staff and we're joined at the bottom of the stairs by club Incident Recorder, Dave Palmer. Though this man's collapse isn't technically part of his job description and won't require notification on the BSPA paperwork, like many others in the crowd he's curious to have a quick look. However, unless something spectacular happens, once you've seen medical staff in bright yellow clothing treat one fallen victim you've seen them all. Nonetheless, Barry 'Bazski' Preston temporarily abandons his musical duties to have a quick rubberneck and matter-of-factly explains the ambulance procedures at Scunthorpe speedway. "They usually call the County ambulance and let them come and collect!" Julie Harrowven suddenly wakes up to the fact that I'm there with my notebook, "You're dangerous! I'm not standing by you anymore. I haven't forgiven you!" Julie turns to Dave Palmer: "Have you seen what he's done to me?" Dave hasn't seen *Concrete for Breakfast* so Julie explains that the Sittingbourne/Scunthorpe chapter contains some of her trenchant criticisms of Christina Turnbull's ability. However, nowadays things have moved on and opinions change, "I had a problem a while back with Christina Turnbull but I'm over that now! We had a meeting at Weymouth when she'd first started. All the riders came to the line and one of theirs elbowed ours to the floor and she just let the race go on.

Scunthorpe v. Glasgow: *"We've not really beaten anyone by a big score"*

Afterwards she knew she'd done wrong 'cause she spoke to Kenny about it." During each season, Dave Palmer gets to watch every referee at close quarters and witness their control of a meeting first-hand since he's sat right next to them in the referee's box at Scunthorpe. Dave is quick to defend Christina, "She's improved and is a really good ref! Definitely the best female referee!" Not quite as much of a radical feminist as Rob Godfrey, Julie isn't convinced, "They shouldn't have lady referees! No! They should only have referees who are ex-riders!" The sexual politics of speedway officialdom aside, it's clear we're going to be in for a long delay to help the fallen man who didn't want to leave the hospitality suite terrace. In case we need emergency fried food supplies for Dave Rattenberry while he's trapped inside the trackshop, the refreshment kiosk is fortuitously adjacent so we all have the reassurance that he's unlikely to starve. The job of incident recorder also has its hidden dangers. "A while back, the last time he came – for a meeting against Sheffield – Graham Flint [referee] fell on me. The chair just gave way." While we wait, Richard Hollingsworth fiddles with the plastic horn he religiously blows after every race to congratulate both home and away riders as they begin to celebrate their triumph with an additional parade lap. I quiz him how he got into speedway. "I first went to Ashby Ville in 1979. When it folded in Scunthorpe [in 1985], I drifted away from the sport fairly quickly but, I finally got my wife to go to a meeting with me in 2001 or 2002, when we were on holiday in Northumberland – we went to Berwick. Then we really got into the sport again or, I did! And then Scunthorpe came along. This is definitely my favourite track!" I ask Richard where else he likes, "That's a very tricky question. Glasgow, Stoke, there seems to be decent racing in those places!" Though you wouldn't believe it looking at him, Baz has an even longer history with Scunthorpe Speedway club and has been going since he was 12. "Me dad first brought me. I grew up in Scunny. I'm not sure now who the meeting was against but it was at Quibell Park." I double check the spelling only to learn from Baz, "Quibell Park – it's said QWHY-BALL PARK, you southerners don't know how to say it!"

After a 25-minute delay, the racing finally recommences and though Sanchez has been excluded, Scorpions reserve Ben Powell still wins to gain a drawn heat and progress the scores to 53-34. Over the loudspeaker system we're unsurprisingly informed that Glasgow have nominated the only two riders who've displayed any vim or vigour this afternoon to compete in the nominated heat 15 – namely, Shane Parker and Robert Ksiezak. News that Scunthorpe will be represented by Magnus Karlsson and Carl Wilkinson causes Richard to exclaim, "How did they come up with that?" The question is asked and immediately answered by the fan, "Rumour is Richard Hall has already packed his stuff up!" Neither of them are convinced by my suggestion that, as a neutral observer, "for excitement Wilkinson should ride and Bergstrom should too if you want someone to hang off the fence for a race." Away on the fourth bend Jim Fleming takes full advantage of the fact that Scunthorpe remains a speedway track you can still smoke at. He draws heavily on his cigarette but isn't impressed with the performance of the Tigers: "Trent was disappointing – a surprise after he got that 15-point maximum yesterday." With the meeting long since ended as a contest, the Glasgow riders race to a consolation maximum heat advantage that's won by Ksiezak, while Shane Parker's second place ensures his paid maximum. This is the signal for Jim to light a celebratory cigarette and smile, "Parker's a class act – that's two maximums on the trot for him, after months away through injury!"

The end of the Premier League meeting is the cue for Scunthorpe promoter Rob Godfrey to take to his tractor for an intensive track-grading session. Arguably Britain's tallest mechanic, Paul Harvey has finished his duties for the night with Magnus Karlsson and, therefore, is finally able to have a relaxing roll-up and a beer. On his way to the bar located on Scunthorpe's first bend, Paul stops for a brief chat. "I used to be a taxi driver and used to drive Norman Cook [Fat Boy Slim] around. I didn't know who he was at the time. He said to me once, 'I've met this fantastic bird Zoe [Ball] in Spain and I really fancy her! We spent the night dancing round a mirror ball. I want to get her a present and really impress her.' I said, 'Why not buy her the mirror ball?' So he did and had it shipped over! There's a story for you. I've got so many stories but, now I've seen you again, they've gone out of me head! Oh, I know, it must have been 15 years ago we used to drive Paul Heaton and all of them [The Beautiful South] round then. Erm, once we dared Kelly Moran to ride round the village on his bike with nothing on and, Kelly being Kelly, did, of course. But never came back because he got arrested! I might not be able to remember my stories but I know what would be a good title for the book, *Methanol and Mayhem*!" It's just 20 past 5 on a Bank Holiday Monday and the Conference League meeting is about to start. I take the chance to point out the start-line boy to Paul, "That's my next job after this! It'd be easier than being a mechanic!"

Scunthorpe v. Glasgow: *"We've not really beaten anyone by a big score"*

No sooner has the Saints v. Devils Conference League clash got under way than it's stopped again when the recent new addition to the Saints team – experienced James Birkinshaw – slides off on the second bend. Referee Graham Flint has no choice but to exclude him and, no sooner has the two-minute warning sounded, than stand-in announcer Graham informs us, "The two minutes are cancelled 'cause of a problem with the start gate." One of the loyal Glasgow Tigers fans doesn't really want to talk about the earlier Premier League meeting, "that was an embarrassment!" Someone who does want to talk about the meeting is Sheffield promoter Neil Machin who again evangelises on behalf of the Lincolnshire club. "This is consistently the best speedway track in this country! The worst is anywhere there's processional racing which is wherever the tracks are slick or, of course, the Elite League! Today, it wasn't brilliant but it was definitely entertaining!"

Rider Photos

The rerun of the first heat results in a win for Devils number 1, Mark Simmonds, who finishes ahead of Salford-born 17-year-old Ben Hopwood for the Saints. With Kyle Hughes in third, the visitors from Plymouth have taken an unexpected early 2-4 lead but this was to be the only time Plymouth were ahead during the meeting. The reply of the Saints is swift, immediate and arrives in the next race ("in memory of John Wilkins") won in some style by Gary Irving. Though my eyes occasionally deceive me, I distinctly see yellow-helmeted Devils rider Paul Starke finish second and, in blue, Adam Wrathall come in third. I'm perfectly capable of messing up my own programme without Graham's help in the announcer's box who ensures we all get the chance to make a comprehensive mess of our documents. His initial claim that third place went to the rider in a green helmet colour is rescinded after brief contemplation and he then claims it was a yellow helmet colour. The message that it probably isn't going to be a close contest hasn't quite percolated through to the Devils side of the pits by the time Tom Brown takes to the track for the third heat (which he wins in flamboyant fashion ahead of Scott Richardson and Jonathan Bethell for the Saints). Anything Tom can do Byron can do better, as demonstrated by the fourth heat where his all-action style makes the race look much faster than the official time would indicate. A glance at the scorecard prior to the meeting appeared to indicate that the Plymouth team were an unbalanced unit, in effect led by their heat leader trio of Mark Simmonds, Tom Brown and Seemond Stephens. Apart from these riders, the remainder of the team comprises Kyle Hughes (a Grade 5 rider) and three other members of the team on the lowest possible classification – Grade 1 – who, therefore, are always likely to appear on track as race fodder. Paul Starke somewhat belied these expectations when he managed 4 points from five rides. On the Saints side of the pits area only Jonathan Bethell (paid 6) and Adam Wrathall (paid 4) failed to gain at least one heat win. One of the many Scunthorpe heat winners, Gary Irving, bested the hard-riding Tom Brown in the seventh heat and, afterwards, gleefully described his win to club Press Officer, Richard Hollingsworth, as the best of his career.

Innovative face protection

Conference League meetings are frequently characterised by a never-say-die attitude to the racing that sometimes counterbalances the still slightly rough around the edges style of these emergent riders. Glasgow fan Jim Fleming is impressed with the spectacle and entertainment offered, "I haven't seen Conference League racing for quite a while and, though it's a bit gusty, the racing is better by far than the first meeting!" Apart from the high quality racing, to my mind Scunthorpe is definitely also the home of innovative face-protection equipment among the fans. On my first-ever visit to the club, I noticed that a computer screen guard had cleverly been pressed into service to protect its owner from flying shale and so it's no surprise when I spot a fan with a triangular clear Perspex faceguard that's a cross between a welder's face mask and a transparent beehive. It's definitely a speedway fact of life that you have to duck or, at least, sensibly avert your gaze whenever the riders' back wheels spray shale across the bends at any track. However, with this innovative piece of equipment, at least one Scunthorpe fan can stare at the race action safe in the knowledge that they're not going to get thwacked in the face by flying debris.

Arguably, Britain's nicest speedway couple, Shane and Anji Parker wander past en route for the bar. I congratulate Shane on his full maximum and paid maximum in successive days. "Yeah, two maximums – no one can complain about that! I was pleased with how it went. It was my first meeting here. I practised here in the winter so I had a good idea about it. The track was a little difficult at the start. It's a hard base here and there's slick and then you'd hit a ridge of dirt but, once they'd watered it, the slick got icier. But, it's hard to prepare a track for afternoon meetings – at the best of times! They usually race on an evening but, by half way through, it had really evened out!"

Back on the track, Plymouth endure some misfortune when Kyle Hughes suffers a puncture in the eighth heat to relegate him from the lead into second. The top-end strength of the Devils ensures that they had the race winners in three of the next four races, though equally their lack of depth in the team ensured that all of these were still only drawn. The decisive heat of the meeting looks on paper to be heat 13 and, with Simmonds and Stephens against Birkinshaw and Bekker, the visitors must have expected to narrow their 4- point deficit, But, sadly fatal for their outside chance of overall victory, Byron Bekker and James Birkinshaw proceed to give them a master-class in how to team ride. The nature of the beast is for one 5-1 to follow another so what had previously looked a close scoreline suddenly balloons to 48-36. Judged from the gloomy expressions of the riders stood in the pits viewing area, you'd have thought that Scunthorpe were the team that had ultimately struggled rather than Plymouth. Stood on his own by the ambulance in the pits, Jonathan Bethall looks into the distance with a forlorn expression that suggests he's in the midst of his own personal long dark teatime of the soul. I miss the last race to stand by my books table but as the large crowd streams to the car park but, keen to get elsewhere, no one lingers to make a purchase. Dave Hoggart has also been impressed by the quality of the entertainment on offer but scoffs at the latest speedway rumour that Eastbourne's Lewis Bridger may drop down to the Premier League. "He's on an average of 5.4 or something so the idea that anyone would take him on an 11-point average is fantasy thinking!" If I lived locally then I would attend Scunthorpe speedway on a regular basis particularly given that the locals assure me that this afternoon's double header contest didn't portray the excitement of this track in its best light. Nonetheless, it's hugely good value – Scunthorpe have offered their fans 30 heats of racing – without, it must be noted, any increase in their admission prices for this double-header meeting! With success on the track, all it needs is for the club to resolve some of their problems off the track to guarantee their continued bright future.[2]

25th August Scunthorpe v. Glasgow (Premier League) 54-39
25th August Scunthorpe v. Plymouth (Conference League) 51-39

---

[2] A couple of weeks after the August Bank Holiday double-header, Scunthorpe speedway announced in a press release:

Scunthorpe Speedway are delighted to announce that the travellers who have been camped on adjacent land for the last two months have finally been evicted by the council. The club would like to thank everyone who has taken time out to help the club win this battle but are warning against complacency as the council still have it as a potential site for a permanent camp. Relieved Promoter Rob Godfrey would still like as many people as possible to register their objection to the site being used. "Even if their site was supervised 24/7 I fear nothing but trouble if it is made permanent. I would urge anyone who hasn't already objected to do so. There is only a few more days left and it can be done on the North Lincs website. It is great that so many people want Scunthorpe Speedway to survive. I just hope the council listens because every time the site has been occupied we have had break-ins that have cost the club thousands of pounds and even had staff attacked verbally and physically. The worst incident was when our 70-year-old odd job guy had to seek sanctuary in the referee's box when he was pelted with rocks. These have been some of the worst days in the club's history and we can't afford for them to be a permanent problem."

Scunthorpe v. Glasgow: *"We've not really beaten anyone by a big score"*

CHAPTER 35.

Edinburgh v. Somerset:
"He actually gated ahead and then let the others through!"

29th August

When I arrive at the Edinburgh city centre meeting point for the regular Edinburgh Supporters' Club coach trip to Armadale organised by Ella MacDonald, there's already a long queue of keen Monarchs fans. The coach is often quite full but now that the Monarchs ride high at the top of the Premier League numbers have picked up further still. Tonight's meeting is notionally a top of the table clash between the Edinburgh Scotwaste Monarchs and the Somerset Sharp Rebels that follows on from their meeting two nights previously at the Oak Tree Arena. Somerset emerged victorious (48-44) that night. There are many knowledgeable men of a certain age and the consensus recognises that the Rebels aren't the best travellers to Armadale. I saw Somerset get comprehensively beaten at King's Lynn though a glance at the league table gives some cause for optimism because it shows they've already won four meetings away from home this season. Since it's August in Scotland and this is speedway, there's always the possibility of rain, though this seems unlikely after the city basked in tropical temperatures all afternoon. Rather gloomily one morose fan worries about possible meteorological intervention, "It's sticky today though you feel it could chuck it down at any time." Sheer weight of numbers dictate the almost full coach leaves fractionally late and its present popularity is based upon a potent combination: the lure of success, the attractiveness of the fixture against the Rebels along with the current exorbitant price of petrol. During the journey, Ella tries to solicit interest for three of the four remaining Monarchs away fixtures (at Stoke, Redcar and Newcastle) as well as with a trip to Glasgow for the David McAllan Farewell meeting. The regular fans on the bus are knowledgeable, comfortable in each other's company and unafraid to express blunt opinions. One fan echoes the general view, "I feel this will be more comfortable than we think it will!" Despite the demise of the aggregate bonus point, some hope is taken from the fact that Somerset only hold a 4-point lead going into tonight's meeting and, overall, the omens look good, "Fisher beat Doyle twice there – you've got to gate at Somerset but, at Armadale, it's possible to come from behind." Quite a few people also have an eye on tomorrow night's Premier League fixtures – aka Super Saturday – an evening which sees Berwick race against Somerset and Edinburgh travel to Stoke. There's intense debate over who will be Stoke's choice of guest tomorrow (it turned out to be Mark Lemon). There's broad agreement about the dynamics of the task ahead for the team: "We've got four away meetings left and, I reckon if we win two of them, we'll win the League!"

One of the Monarchs fans Jim has taken a brief nap and when he wakes up asks ironically, "Did I miss buying the winning ticket off Ella?" He's told, "You would'na win it anyway! You missed Hibs scoring two goals too." Jim isn't that credulous, "I was asleep for half an hour, not half a season!" Just before we draw into the stadium car park I walk to the front of the bus to make a quick exit since I've only got a narrow time window of opportunity to sell my books at the Scotwaste Arena. Though I've asked John Campbell's permission to do so, one of the older fans on the bus (John), has apparently confused the coach trip with the Queen's Garden Party and reacts badly to my perceived lack of etiquette (in moving to the front of the bus for a quick exit). News that I've travelled from Brighton doesn't impress him and he decides he'd prefer to welcome strangers with considerable anger and gratuitous hostility, "Get back to your seat! I don't care if you came from France! Get back to where you come from!" Coach trip organiser Ella tries to mediate ("calm down, John") only for John to continue his own unique 'Welcome to Scotland' initiative. Still irked he threatens to go to teacher, "I'll see Mr Campbell!" Ella shrugs: "He's seen Mr Campbell! You're getting ruder in your old age, John!"

Loyal Somerset Rebels fan and Programme Editor, Ian Belcher, has made the long journey from the South West of England to Scotland. He tells me straightaway, "We don't expect to win here!" He also corrects the misapprehension I'd just heard on the supporters' coach trip here, "Fisher only beat Doyle once. In his second ride, he has a tendency

to come off the inside gate and immediately shoot out wide for the dirt. Ryan just cut his nose off and that was it." Ian surveys his surroundings, "Paulco [Paul Colton] on the BSF knows this place as the Skipdome since it was renamed the Scotwaste Arena. The score flattered them the other night as they had a tactical ride and got a 5-1 in the last race when we put out Emil [Kramer] and Jordan [Frampton]." Shortly afterwards I speak to Gary Lough and our talk naturally turns to the probability that the Edinburgh Monarchs will be crowned the 2008 Premier League champions. Gary immortalised their last championship victory in print and, before that season started, had already read the runes, "the *Speedway Star* forecast 10th – it was a bit of an omen – I thought top four but I said top!" Conversation then turns to the subject of Tai Woffinden and, when it comes to the subject of passport choice, whether he's the Zola Budd of speedway. Gary's definitely not a big fan and wasn't impressed by some of his unguarded heat-of-the-moment statements when interviewed live during the recent *Sky* televised fixture at Armadale, "If he's not mature off the track, he shouldn't be on the track!" Before the tapes rise I catch a few words with Edinburgh promoter, John Campbell, and he notes the size of the huge attendance bucked the trend for *Sky* televised fixtures, "We had our biggest-ever crowd for the *Sky* meeting! Tonight isn't so large."

If it's Friday night in Scotland, then there's only one place for any speedway fan to be and that's at the Scotwaste Arena. In my case, preferably stood next to Dougie Copland and his father Bill. Pre-meeting talk that the Rebels aren't the greatest travellers is belied by a Jason Doyle win in the first heat though, given he's their top rider, this isn't exactly a shock. There's not much surprise for Dougie either when Monarchs guest Mark Lemon trails in third, "Lemon with his customary crap ride in heat 1." Dougie finds much to admire in the line up for the second race ("Aaron has his new helmet on") but also forecasts we might see some fight this evening from Rebels reserve Brent Werner, "he rides this track very well – it's probably his best track!" It sounds a shrewd judgement when Werner gates first but, by the second corner, he's already been relegated to third in a race comfortably won by Aaron Summers in 55.8 seconds ("that's his fastest time of the season, he's coming on is Aaron," notes Dougie approvingly). Among Monarchs fans conspiracy theories abound about the real reasons behind the recently postponement of the Glasgow versus Edinburgh Premier League meeting on August 17th. So far a date to rerun this fixture has yet to be arranged and a hypothetical concern has gained credence amongst Edinburgh fans. Namely, that it won't take place before the Premier League cut-off date and, therefore possibly, in a cruel world, these lost (deferred) points will cost them their rightful first place in the table. Dougie isn't impressed with the publicly stated grounds for this postponement, "It was called off at 10 with 6 hours to go!" But then he's even less impressed with the world of the Internet as it applies to Glasgow speedway, "They have a Glasgow forum that's full of tirades on Edinburgh and, they say, we're paranoid! They've closed it [postponement thread] now. It's full of venom anyway and, I think, the worst speedway forum!"[1] Talk of Glasgow Speedway reminds Dougie of the forthcoming David McAllan Farewell meeting, "Did you hear about what that Morris did to McAllan – it's a disgrace! I was there that day and it doesn't look any better on the DVD. He'd either be very brave or stupid to go back to Glasgow."

The third heat provides the second successive 5-1 for the Monarchs gained when Thomas H. Jonasson and Matthew Wethers storm home to victory. Dougie keeps his celebrations to a minimum and instead remarks, "Oh no, it's getting dusty!" After capitulation by the Rebels earlier in the season at King's Lynn, I'm already worried that this might not be anything like a close contest. Dougie doesn't share my anxiety and, in fact, relishes the prospect of a huge win, "I hope not – then we can go top!" The wonderful world of speedway as portrayed by *Sky* isn't quite Dougie's cup of tea, "*Sky* love Tai Woffinden. He's a golden child but ask any Edinburgh fan and they'll tell you he's a tosser! Not many people liked it when Tai took Matty's [Wethers] leg away and if, Kelvin says he took his leg away and he was stood right there, then he did! Everyone can admire him as a rider – as I have done in the past – but his head and ego are getting too big for him!" The lack of British riders with world championship credentials is also an ongoing concern particularly when our best prospect Scott Nicholls has endured yet another year of disappointment, "I think he's got worse since Kelvin [Tatum] started helping him."

The all-action Aaron Summers definitely doesn't know when he's beaten. Many riders would have settled for third place behind Jordan Frampton in heat 4 but, instead, on the penultimate lap, he telegraphs his desire to blast round

[1] Robin Goodall's match report on the postponement of this fixture in the *Speedway Star* noted, "The week-long deluge that had engulfed the West of Scotland claimed the eagerly anticipated Scottish Derby. The Glasgow track had taken a pounding, meaning there was always a doubt about the match. Work done on the track on Saturday proved to be in vain and, after overnight rain, an early decision was taken to postpone. Fairer weather later in the day may have made the postponement look like a premature decision but the damage had already been done to the track."

Edinburgh v. Somerset: *"He actually gated ahead and then let the others through!"*

the outside ("Ooh go on!"). Sadly, when confronted with the brute fact that Frampton has clearly read his intentions and acts to block this manoeuvre, the young Australian endures a sudden close encounter with the Armadale fourth-bend safety fence ("Ooh No! Unlucky, son"). Referee Stuart Wilson excludes Summers and awards the race and, with Ryan Fisher ahead at the time of the stoppage, the heat is drawn. Comparatively this counts as a minor triumph for Somerset and Dougie notes sardonically, "at least, Katt will get a point." Jason Doyle's second appearance on the track in heat 5 offers repeat medicine when he storms to a comfortable win without any real challenge from the Edinburgh pair of Matthew Wethers and Thomas H. Jonasson. "Jonasson can look really bad when he's third, Matthew Wethers is the man to be challenging. I suppose the track's made for Doyle tonight. He's not waved to anyone, that's good. Superstar!" Another topic close to Dougie's heart is the pronounced English bias of the *Sky Sports* speedway coverage. "I get pissed off with the media guys down South. They build up Adam Roynon – how many times did he ride this season? – yet William Lawson is a much better rider. It's so frustrating! Living down south, you probably don't notice it. When *Sky* came here you could see Nigel Pearson and Kelvin Tatum knew about five Scottish riders since 1970 and didn't even mention William Lawson. The first [televised] match after they came here was Poole versus Belle Vue and it was crap! Notice how, when it rained, Jason [Crump] ran the meeting. He didn't wait for the referee, he just signalled, 'OK, lads, back to the pits'. I actually like Jason Crump now – since he became world champion he's chilled out. Now, for me, Leigh Adams has become a tosser! Nicki Pedersen and Jason Crump both have the dedication to become world champions. So has Tomasz Gollob – I know he hasn't been world champion but he really wants it!"

Normal service returns in the next race when Mark Lemon and Derek Sneddon combine to race to a comfortable maximum heat advantage. The only real danger is complacency, "No! No! Don't team ride." Dougie has residual worries about exactly which version of Emil Kramer will line up at the tapes for the seventh heat. "Kramer is one of those frustrating riders – when he gets in front he looks really classy but see him at Berwick and he looks awful!" If the Edinburgh pair of Fisher and Tully have their eyes on the possibility that fast-gating Emil Kramer will zoom from gate 2 then, they completely blind-side themselves, since it's Matthias Kroger who roars away from the start. He manfully holds the lead until Fisher blasts past him on the third bend of the final lap. "You should have seen him [Fisher] pass Rymel from 15 metres back [at Berwick]. He flew past him! That was somewhat unexpected from Kroger who rode a good race. That's what I was talking about with Kramer." With Somerset already comprehensively adrift it was a question of 'when' rather than 'if' they would explore their tactical options. When the black-and-white helmet colour does appear, the joint Rebels team management of Steve Bishop and Garry May surprise everyone with their decision to bring Jason Doyle in as a tactical substitute off 15 metres in the eighth heat (along with Jordan Frampton for his rider replacement ride in place of Simon Walker). Dougie can't quite believe his eyes, "It's a big big gamble!" It's definitely the calculated decision of a serial optimist and, when it works (as it has previously for Somerset), then it looks inspired. However, when Aaron Summers and Derek Sneddon both decide to wear their metaphorical gating gloves in the same race, it suddenly looks altogether less wise. Though Jason Doyle quickly catches up with Derek Sneddon he's unable to find the gap required. "Derek's usual bloody awkward style is frustrating Doyle's attempts to get past him. He totally buggered him up. Whether he meant it or not I don't know! Derek was just throwing his bike around! My dad says he knew where Doyle was all the time and, as a speedway fan, I'd like to think so, but really I think he was just throwing the bike around!"

There's some delay while the track staff try to damp down the shale to stop the dust that has started to billow round the Armadale area. If, despite the scoreline, the racing so far this evening has been exciting, then Dougie isn't convinced I'll witness similar at Saracen Park on Sunday for the Glasgow versus Berwick Premier League meeting. "The racing at Glasgow is crap and, now they've got square corners it's even worse! I'll let you see that one for yourself." Keen to pre-identify problems on the horizon, Dougie also has some anxiety that Birmingham mightn't have the strongest team when they face Somerset at Perry Barr next Wednesday. "That's a good one Birmingham have done, they've signed Kenneth Hansen; he has to miss the first three matches so, when Somerset visit, they have to use a Conference League rider. He's some promoter that Graham Drury!"[2]

The BSPA website announced on the morning of the fixture that "Graham Drury has pulled the plug on the signing of Kenneth Hansen. The Dane was due to make his Brummies debut against Somerset but informed Drury he'd be riding for Slangerup in his home country instead. Said Drury: "Why should I sign a rider who can't ride on a Wednesday? He'd agreed to join a Wednesday night track and this happens. It's totally frustrating and I'm very annoyed about it."

Edinburgh v. Somerset: *"He actually gated ahead and then let the others through!"*

²We're then treated to a dramatic but extended ninth heat. The initial attempt to run the race ends on bend 2 when Jordan Frampton runs into Thomas H. Jonasson and, thereby, strips the chain from his machine. The Edinburgh fans react to the incident with loud disapproval ("he's getting booed like Woffinden!") before referee Stuart Wilson swiftly becomes the object of their collective ire. "Surely he interfered with him? Stuart Wilson is the referee so anything can happen!" The rerun has Thomas H. Jonasson come out on the diminutive Derek Sneddon's bike. Jordan Frampton then disproves the old adage ("once bitten, twice shy") when, on the second bend, he once again runs Thomas H. Jonasson wide – this time without mishap – before he escapes down the back straight only to then crash spectacularly on the third bend. Almost simultaneously Jonasson lays his bike down in a manner that makes it look like a fall. The referee excludes Frampton but a somewhat shaken and stirred Jonasson fails to make the re-rerun and so is excluded under the two-minute time allowance. His place in the race is taken by Andrew Tully who proceeds to win this protracted heat with some comfort.

If Asian betting syndicates could influence speedway, then you'd suspect their influence at work in heat 10 when Somerset nominate Emil Kramer to make a tactical ride in the black-and-white helmet. It's not the most auspicious decision and, rather predictably, it comes to naught when the Lemon/Sneddon partnership gain a maximum heat advantage to ensure that Kramer's solitary point isn't doubled. Dougie isn't quite sure what to think, "A bit of a strange one but never mind. He actually gated ahead and then let the others through! That was pretty piss poor wasn't it? Ha ha ha!" Edinburgh Monarchs meeting presenter Scott Wilson has had quite a bit to say about the race and/or the meeting so far though, quite what this is, is impossible to say as the loudspeaker system on the first bend gives off the sort of white noise you hear on radios when you're caught between stations late at night. With the tannoy subject to interference and with the stadium floodlights so dim that you'd think they were powered by energy-saving light bulbs, I wonder aloud, "Does the tannoy take power from the lights?" In the aggrieved but slightly heated manner you'd use to defend your sister if she slept round too much, Dougie is quick to riposte, "You could work for *Sky*, slagging the place off!"

In the latter stages of the meeting from race to race, suddenly one drama follows another. The 11th heat is no exception when, on the second bend, race leader Jason Doyle rears massively and immediately finds himself passed by Armadale's second-bend experts Ryan Fisher and Andrew Tully. They flash past in formation on either side of him before Doyle sets off in aggressive pursuit in a manner that causes Dougie to fear the worst, "He's never gonna stay on it like that! That's crazy riding – its not Somerset or Sheffield!" With the impetuousness of youth Doyle almost appears to ride on the wooden boards of the third- and fourth-bend fence before he zooms down the home straight only to then smash into the second-bend fence with tremendous force ("that looks bad!") While Doyle picks himself up and his crumpled bike is taken back to the pits I make my way out onto the centre green.

Earlier, Monarchs promoter John Campbell had asked me for some information on my book so that Scott Wilson could mention it over the loudspeakers during the meeting ("I'll put it in my pocket, either I'll give it to Scott or I'll find it tomorrow!") Even better than a plug over the speakers, I'm invited to the centre green for an interview. Whatever the track, it's a delight to watch any races from the centre green and I never get bored of the excitement of this experience. I'm not so keen on interviews, however, even though Scott conducts them with effortless professionalism – asking questions, genuinely faking interest, and generally making the book sound wonderfully exciting. Scott ends our interview to then segue effortlessly into his re-introduction of the riders. With his microphone switched off, Scott Wilson is a much easier man to talk to. He's taken to speedway with the fanaticism of a reformed smoker, "I was never into speedway till I came here!" Nowadays, he evangelises to everyone he meets and takes considerable delight and great pride in the Monarchs 2008 season performances so far. "This was the team no one fancied! The reserves have been magnificent tonight – look at Tully, he's been brilliant!" The rerun eventually takes place without the excluded Jason Doyle and the formality of yet another Monarchs 5-1 (their seventh in 11 heats) caps off this rerun race. It's won by Andrew Tully ahead of his team mate Ryan Fisher with, typical of the Somerset team tonight, Stephan Katt some distance behind them at the rear.

Viewed from the vantage point of the centre green the Armadale track is much more lavishly contoured than it appears from the stands. There's also a very notable slope that I hadn't previously appreciated. Like London buses, one Monarchs 5-1 follows another and the 12th heat is no exception. It's again won by Andrew Tully (this time partnered by Aaron Summers) and this fifth consecutive Monarchs maximum heat advantage takes the scoreline to a stupendous 53-19. The highlight of the race – though, when watched from the centre green, the whole race is a highlight – comes when Summers blasts past his much more experienced Swedish rival, Emil Kramer, on the back straight of the fourth lap. Like many Monarchs fans, Scott Wilson has worked out the complex set of mathematical permutations to do with the relative League positions of Edinburgh and Somerset. "We've got to beat them by 26. Of course, it counts for nothing 'cause we've still to go and win another one somewhere!" Scott is a fan of the tempestuous American in the number 5 Monarchs race tabard, "Ryan still wants to fight everyone and he can't team ride but he's always spectacular!" Like many other Edinburgh fans, the recent postponement of the keenly anticipated Derby fixture with Glasgow rankles with him: "That was freaking atrocious when they rained it off a fortnight ago – there was freak all wrong with it! If that costs us the League, there'll be bad blood!"

After he's won his first two races in some style, Jason Doyle suddenly appeared to think that he been invited along to engage in some form of speedway demolition derby. The first attempt to run heat 13 sees him knock Ryan Fisher from his bike. The race is stopped by the referee and adjudged as 'first-bend bunching'. The rerun sees Lemon fail to gate with the alacrity he had first time out but, instead, Jason Doyle leads the race until he falls spectacularly on the second bend of the second lap. Though he follows extremely close behind him, Ryan Fisher demonstrates exceptional reactions to immediately lay down his bike but, unfortunately, still smashes into his fallen rival. Behind them Jordan Frampton also lays down his machine yet also skids in slow motion into the melee of men and machinery already parked on the Armadale shale. A crowd of medical staff then surround the riders and the (unofficial) word from the centre green is that Jason Doyle has sustained a suspected broken wrist. Watched from the centre green, this is a spectacular and exhilarating pile up. Viewed from the first-bend terraces, the fence somewhat obscures the nuances of the action but, nonetheless, Dougie is in no doubt of the culprit: "Jason rode like a crazy man and Ryan did well to get it down so quickly!" Jordan Frampton wins the rerun but Dougie is much more absorbed pondering the permutations thrown up by the potential absence through injury of Jason Doyle due to his damaged wrist. "It's not really good for us, they'll still get a good guest and win at Birmingham and, of course, they'll still benefit from Kramer taking a rider replacement ride for Walker!"

Yet another 5-1 arrives for the Monarchs in heat 14 and it features a neat passing manoeuvre from Andrew Tully that Dougie admires, "Andrew just does it like Peter Carr – he's difficult to ride against so they just don't expect him to do it up the inside." The win is so straightforward that on the Edinburgh Monarchs website afterwards, Mike Hunter doesn't even bother to report all the race action, "The home team cut loose again with big 5-1 wins in the last two heats, clinching a victory large enough to take them to first place in the Premier League." Scott Wilson interviews John Campbell on the centre green and he's keen to acknowledge the win but studiously refuses to prematurely count any chickens, "I had hoped for a very big crowd and we got a very big crowd. We started in third place tonight and Somerset had a massive points advantage over us and we go top tonight! However, though it's a big win, it's no different to being beaten by 4 points, it's just the same. We now know King's Lynn can't catch us and, if we win at Stoke, Somerset need to win two away [meetings] to catch us." There's a post-meeting practice for William Lawson who's keen to regain match fitness after injury, try to hasten return to race action

Backstraight Grandstand at dusk

and again push on in his quest to wrest the title of Scotland's number 1 rider from James Grieves. After the majority of the fans have flooded away, Glasgow's keen speedway fan Heather McNeilly (aka Miss Green) arrives from work in Cumbernauld: "I have to go to get Jason Doyle's kitbag as he's staying with me tonight." News that he's probably broken his wrist merits a frown ("I wondered why he hadn't phoned me") and has Heather quicken her pace in the direction of the pits.

29th August Edinburgh v. Somerset (Premier League) 66-24

Edinburgh v. Somerset: *"He actually gated ahead and then let the others through!"*

CHAPTER 36.

Berwick v. Somerset:
"Oh, you've brought a bag to put your goggles in!"

30th August

When I arrive at Shielfield Park (technically in Tweedmouth) there's still a few Berwick Rangers fans stood outside the entrance turnstiles deep in discussion. All of them wear their distinctive gold and black scarves and tell me, "They drew 2s each with Forfar," but don't mention the game featured three penalties. The Anderson's Quality Butchers Berwick Bandits ply their trade at the stadium exclusively during June and July but the start and the end of the speedway season is topped and tailed with Saturdays where they share these facilities with the football club. After the match has finished, shortly afterwards the speedway commences. Though neither club attract a huge crowd, for local residents there's a brief period of the early evening when there's a queue of people and cars leaving the area followed shortly afterwards by a similar rush in the other direction.

Once inside the stadium, I immediately make my way to the pits area adjacent to the fourth bend to speak with perpetually cheerful Berwick promoter Peter Waite. Though diminutive in stature, his larger-than-life personality would be better suited to a 7-foot man. He's deep in conversation with a couple of groups of people. I learn they are sponsors when he instructs Graham Platten to make sure he gets their photographs on the centre green later. Peter is resplendent in his traditional race-night Berwick Bandits anorak with its distinctive design and vibrant black and yellow. Peter, like his southern-based Elite League counterpart Jon Cook, sports an impressive permatan that's all the more notable in this much less sunny part of the country. He clearly takes great pride in his stewardship of the club and its continued existence, but also clearly delights in the various tasks and duties of race day at Shielfield Park. "Look at the track, it looks lovely!" he says in his excited singsong voice. Whether I admire it or not, Peter certainly gives it a long, proud, lingeringly proprietorial stare. A few yards away from us Paul Clews and his fair-haired son (dressed in a sky blue sweatshirt top that bears the Clews Racing insignia) thoroughly inspect the sodden surface. While Paul Clews mooches about, young master Clews repeatedly gardens the fourth bend. Though Berwick-upon-Tweed is hardly famed as a drought region, Peter is keen to explain that dust isn't the reason he's doused the track. "We need it nice and wet for the home advantage and all the passing, when we don't make the start! You watch later, it will be wonderful and we'll get lots of passing! What's the point of speedway without passing?" Berwick's Premier League campaign has seen them move up the table though they're unlikely to make the top four places and, thereby, qualify for the notional glamour of the end-of-season play-offs. "Yeah, we're fifth. The only way is up. We need to win tonight and go to Glasgow tomorrow and beat them. That's the big one! It should be a fantastic meeting [gestures towards groups of sponsors pootling around the pits] we've got to keep cramming the sponsors in now. Else how are we going to pay for this lot? [Nods towards Berwick riders who unload and unpack their equipment in the pits] This season it doesn't matter if you win by 2 or 20, but we've had some big scores to pay for. That's speedway getting rid of the bonus point. They'll be back in the play-offs, otherwise how else will you know who's gone through? Think about it."

As well as his official track photographer duties, Graham Platten is also in charge of the trackshop[1]. I join him there while he sets out his merchandise in a small building close to the old-fashioned and austere toilet block they have at Shielfield Park (without hand-washing facilities). He's also keen to explain the soaked shale surface of the track that circles the football pitch here. "You can see that Peter has been watering the track. He loves to do it! You've probably read we've had the odd half-hour delay [this season] where they scrape the surface off to make it raceable!"

I base my table of books right next to the programme booth where Davina Johnston sells the Premier League's most

---

[1] Graham Platten (photographer and trackshop operator) was, over the winter months 2008-09 diagnosed suddenly and chillingly as having motor neurone disease and has had to give up his race-night occupations. He remains a good friend of the club, and comes to as many meetings as he can manage.

expensive programmes (£2.50) and also, in true speedway fashion, keeps meticulous records of her sales. Also close by is the raffle stall. They've no interest in the dampness or dryness of the track but, instead, all the talk is of the Edinburgh–Berwick meeting that took place at Armadale eight days previously. Feelings still run high about an incident in heat 15 that saw Michal Makovsky and Aaron Summers clash on the track and, then afterwards, have a follow-up incident that resulted in a smashed crash helmet. Ultimately no official action was taken after a severe case of the Arsene Wengers temporarily afflicted all the officials in the Scotwaste Arena pits area. Nonetheless, the incident was reported in copious detail by the Edinburgh *Evening News* under the headline 'There's no Summers Loving as Bandits' Ace Loses his Cool'[2]

Strangely, despite Michal Makovsky's exclusion from the race and subsequent attack upon Aaron Summers, discussions focus upon Ryan Fisher. Davina notes, "That Fisher is a dirty rat – he'll turn right on anybody! Speedway's a dangerous enough sport without doing anything silly but he doesn't care. Though, I have to say, his wife is lovely! Last week [when Ryan guested for Workington] she asked to look in my programme to see if Ryan would be out in heat 15. With all the abuse, she said she would be happy to just go back to the van! But him – that Nermark at Workington – will turn right on anyone."

[Raffle lady] (Laughing) "Did you hear Michal [Makovsky] has been invited to ride for Edinburgh at the David McAllan Testimonial?" There's incredulity all round and turnstile lady Muriel Ennis briefly stops rather earnestly eating her cheeseburger ("it's my tea").

[Raffle lady] "Michal had just got ahead of Fisher and Summers just came through and took him off!"

[Davina] "They say he [Summers] laughed in Michal's face in the pits. Who wouldn't react to that?"

[Raffle lady] "You see that the ref [Chris Durno] said the next day that he was wrong and if he knew what he knew now he'd make a different decision."

[Davina] "Who paid for the helmet then?"

[Raffle lady] "It was a collection."

[Davina] "Did you see what Fisher did to Paul Clews at Edinburgh when he took him to the fence? He could have really injured him!"

This conflab is briefly joined by Graham Platten who changes the topic of discussion to the recent Berwick Bandits away win at Workington (42-51). "They did well to get it on 'cause we drove over from Newcastle and, from Hexham, it rained all the way there. When we got there I was surprised to see Glyn Taylor doing the track and he said at 4 o'clock he was still thinking of watering it!"

[Raffle lady] "Tony Swales has done the track there since they first started."

---

[2] The report read as follows: "RAGING Berwick Bandits' star Michal Makovsky attacked Edinburgh Monarchs young Australian ace Aaron Summers in an amazing pits bust-up during last night's Premier League encounter. Makovsky clattered into the safety fence on the third bend in the heat-15 top scorers' race and accused Summers of knocking him off. But the referee thought otherwise and excluded the Bandits' rider from the rerun. The decision infuriated Makovsky, who returned to the pits and made straight for a startled Summers, shoving the 19-year-old Monarch against the wall and smashing the £400 racing helmet, which he was still wearing. Monarchs boss Alex Harkess dragged Makovsky off Summers and escorted him back to the opposition side of the pits. But Czech-born Makovsky will escape punishment because no licensed official witnessed the incident. Makovsky, who has a reputation of being something of a firebrand, was unapologetic afterwards. He said: "It was a dirty move by Summers. He dived up the inside of me and took my leg away and knocked me off. I've got a scar on my arm because he came straight at me on the bend. He could easily have apologised but he didn't even try to do that. If I do something dirty I apologise afterwards." Admitting that he damaged Summers' helmet, Makovsky added: "I blew up. It was down to pressure. It was definitely a dirty move by Summers yet I was excluded." A clearly shaken Summers said: "It was nothing to do with me. I was already in front in the race. He was the one who decided to turn left. He was already behind me because I had already passed him. When we went back to the pits before going out for the rerun, the next thing I knew he came straight across to me and shoved me against the wall. He has ruined my helmet, which is £400 down the drain. It came from Australia and it's something, which can't be replaced. I'm not very happy about it. It was purely a racing accident. It wasn't my fault." Match referee Chris Durno, who was summoned to the pits after the flare-up, said he was powerless to do anything. "I didn't see it because I was in the referee's box sixty metres away. I can't comment. I asked for witness statements and no one can give me any. Nobody saw it happen so I can only go on what I'm told. No licensed official saw the incident. It's obvious something happened. "I didn't witness it, my officials didn't witness it. I've got no evidence. I'm powerless to do anything unless a licensed official reports it to me." Durno will deliver Summers' helmet to the BSPA offices in Rugby for inspection and if it's deemed un-useable the straps will be cut and it will be returned to Summers. Makovsky's actions seemed so unnecessary because there was nothing riding on the last race, Monarchs having secured the match points with a powerhouse display in the first half.

[Graham] "I don't think he's there anymore. They say that Keith Denham is quite something – his own man, anyway!"

[Raffle lady] "If things weren't going well, Stoney would have a word and Tony Swales would change the track. Stoney's lost it now – maybe he's too old or he's lost his gumption. Perhaps it's all the extra weight but he's not the rider he was!"

[Graham] "Havvy is the same. If the gap is there, he'll take it but, when you get older, you get more sensible. In heat 14, Havvy [guest for Workington] was off 15 and he didn't even get close to Franchetti and Clews!"

[Davina] "Did you see the *Evening News* where John Campbell was moaning on about everyone? It's disgraceful! He was too snidey when he said he was cutting the grass [on the morning of the controversial Glasgow v. Edinburgh postponement]. He complained about the track at Workington too. Edinburgh is a trick track! Somerset will be a totally different kettle of fish here tonight! Brent rides this track really well and Adam McKinna [guest at reserve] is Adam."

Track watering

Somerset Programme Editor and Press Officer Ian Belcher has arrived with his friend Dave Thompson (who writes reports for the local paper). They've come via Robert Smith the highly regarded local fish and chip shop. "We've already had the battered haggis – excellent it was!" Ian also writes Somerset home-meeting reports for the *Speedway Star* to a strict word limit of 350 words. He doubts whether his friend Dave would be able to cope with this restriction, "Dave would never get it down to 350 words – that would be heat 1 for him!" Dave's keen to justify himself, "I wanna describe the heats as I see them and let people who haven't been know how it went. Sometimes you get carried away [last night] the first few heats were easy and, in the second half, there were all the real incidents so I've got into 20 or 30 lines per heat." Though Somerset don't always travel well, they're nonetheless definitely assured of their place in the play-offs and may even emerge triumphant to race against an Elite League team (and, thereby, possibly gain elevation to the upper tier of British speedway). Ian Belcher doesn't believe that this potential scenario is that likely, "Mike says he's not going to go up [to the Elite League] 'cause it'll quadruple his costs without really increasing his revenues. Sure if you get the parachute payment – well, the opposite 'cause parachutes come down [JS: "balloon payment"] Yeah that! Bet the Chapmans thought of that 'cause it's full of hot air. But, at Somerset, we struggle to break even 'cause Mike doesn't get the car parking or the bar receipts as Bill Hancock [stadium owner] gets that so we have to survive on advertisers, the club shop and what's taken through the turnstiles. Sure more people might come initially and, maybe advertisers will want to be seen on the telly but, if Mike says it won't work for us, he's been around so long he knows what's what!" Apart from his written work, Ian also takes to the airwaves on a regular basis. "I do five minutes on *Radio Somerset* every Friday. I send them the questions beforehand so they don't look stupid!"

Peter Waite, Paul Clews and young advisor

Though he's not here tonight, legendary speedway presenter Richard White Barrie (aka Dick Barrie) has left us a pre-recorded message that's played over the loudspeaker system. In the manner of flight safety briefings on an aeroplane, Dick tells us how to use the programme and specifically advises us to study the adverts contained within it because, "Anyone who supports our speedway club deserves to be supported!" This isn't the only pre-recorded message we receive from Dick but I'm distracted from the exact content of these important messages by a continual bustle of people drawn to the programme stall, raffle table and my book display. One lady comes up and asks if it's correct that one of my books has a picture of David McAllan in it as she'd been told that at Glasgow speedway. I show her his photograph on the back of *Concrete for Breakfast* and learn that this polite lady is his mum, Fiona McAllan. I donate a copy to his Farewell meeting. She stresses, "He wants it called a Farewell not a Testimonial meeting; [pauses to compose herself] He'll never ride again! Since he went to Denmark [for a GP] something switched off inside his head. Alun Biggart [the Denmark-based editor of the Glasgow Speedway Newsletter] invited him. He worried so much before he went about things like 'will my bag burst' [detail redacted]. The doctors says with all the metal in him in two years he'll be fine but…[trails off and looks pensive] anyway, thank you."

The idea of a Berwick meeting without the presence of Jim Brykajlo (and his son Steven) would be like rum without the Coke or Conference League version Wimbledon without Buzz Burrows. Jim has so many bees in his bonnet that, if only he could get them all into hives, he could make substantial quantities of honey. His job as a taxi driver in Edinburgh means that he gets to meet all sorts of people as well as various celebrities who also come to the city. "I had Michael Barrymore in the taxi this week. He's conceited. He asked me how his show on Spike Milligan was talked about. Two or three people in the weeks before had said it was a good show but doing that hasn't taken away the thing that's hanging over him. Was it the aura that hangs over him?" Talk of auras and honey brings up something not so sweet namely Jim's ongoing absence from the Scotwaste Arena on Friday night race night. "I've stopped going to Armadale 'cause of the West Lothian football mentality where every word is an 'f' and a 'c'. When I went to the Berwick KO cup match – a very fiery cup match – on April 25th – I didn't enjoy my visit. When some of the West Lothian football type people see a Berwick hat or colour, it's like a red rag to a bull. One of them saw my hat and told me to freak off back to England. He was one of the people who'd taken hospitality out on the night for him and his guests where they watch the speedway and drink too much. As well as the swearing someone spat on me." His son Steven interjects, "Slowly the football ned mentality is getting into speedway everywhere but getting worse at Edinburgh or it's more noticeable there." Jim is keen to be exact, "There are a huge number of really genuine Edinburgh fans who are on the back straight and all sorts of other places in the stadium but there is also a drinking culture where every word is an 'f' and a 'c'. In all my years of watching speedway, I've never heard such bad language as I've heard at Edinburgh this season. Stuff like 'go on Ryan knock the **** off!' when he dived under Makovsky. Do you hear that at Eastbourne when Scott Nicholls is racing against Adam Shields? That night this bloke was abusing all the Berwick fans and I said, 'Name me an Edinburgh rider from pre-Armadale days, à la Powderhall?' He said, "Huh, huh". He could have said Les Collins or Freddie Schott but he didn't know any riders from then. I said to that guy, 'I'm more of an Edinburgh fan than you are! Ignoring I'm Edinburgh born and bred! I was brought up following Edinburgh in the 60s – the old Meadowbank till 1967 and two years at Coatbridge'. I only started supporting Berwick 'cause Edinburgh closed down. It's not what you want but I don't like to make a fuss. I've been five times this season and three of them were Berwick matches. One of them was as a guest of Mike Hunter [for the Mildenhall meeting] and the other was a mistake – Birmingham in the Premier Trophy Final. Jason Lyons got 2 from five rides but the track was wet and heavy, mind. When a so-called nobody hospitality person can abuse people and behave like that it just puts you off. Gordon Fraser contacted them but I didn't hear anything. I felt they could have done something more quickly! I missed two or three months 'cause I didn't want to go back. Kenny Cricton did something. He knew me from when I used to go to watch the Dale Devils in 2006. Kenny commented, 'You, as a Berwick fan, were there every Saturday and we only had crowds of 80 or 90. You've been a supporter for years and shouldn't be treated like that'. Still can't say I'm happy with what happened that night but it certainly doesn't make you want to go. There are lots of people I really like there – but something like that doesn't make you feel good about them!"

With the meeting shortly about to get under way, we've wandered round to the open elevated section of the back straight that overlooks the spot where the riders exit the second bend before they generate huge speed along the narrow back straight into the sloped banking of the third and fourth bends. The recorded messages from Dick Barrie – that have haunted the meeting in the manner of someone who speaks beyond the grave in a séance – have been replaced with the dulcet tones of a live flesh-and-blood presenter in the form of Hugh Brown. Jim's son Steven Brykajlo tells me, "Dick Barrie isn't here tonight, not being nasty, but the parade might be a bit quicker!" Judged by Hugh's introduction of Scott Smith in the Bandits number 7 race tabard, this might be a forlorn hope, "It's Scud Scott, Scott Smith, Scott Scud Smith, get it right Hugh!" Steven grimaces, "Hugh Brown works for *Radio Borders*. Sometimes

Berwick v. Somerset: *"Oh, you've brought a bag to put your goggles in!"*

I'm not sure if I like him or not as it sounds like you're listening to a radio show." Jim is definitely sure about his feelings, "It's Hugh 'Disaster' Brown! He works for the Church of Scotland and *Radio Borders* – he disnae buy the *Speedway Star*, he just reads what's in front of him. It's amazing what he gets wrong. A couple of months ago when he was here on the centre green he said Rymel's 15 at Birmingham was the first away maximum since Richard Knight in 1992. But in fact, Makovsky had a maximum at Hull in 2003 and 2007 at Newport though the score was expunged! They had an illegal guest, Lee Complin. Stan Burza got a 14 paid 18 maximum, which was reduced to a 12 paid 15 maximum. Another time when Hugh did Long Eaton v. Glasgow at Shawfield in 1993, Jan Stæchmann – he looks distinctive – was in the pits doing his bike up so he wasn't on the parade. Hugh didn't notice this and carried on. Mike Hampson was introduced as Jan Stæchmann, he then carried on and got everyone out of sequence and when he got to the end, he thought, 'Hello there's no number 7'. Anyone else would have realised but not good old Hugh! Hugh is in administration for the Church of Scotland – he's not a Minister or anything!"

Funfair at the Pits Gate

Adrian Rymel opens his evening's work with a comfortable win in heat 1 that causes Steven Brykajlo to comment, "Rymel has been nigh on unbeatable here. Berwick should win, they've been going very well at home and that win at Workington should be enough to get us into the Young Shield." An unsatisfactory start requires that the second heat is rerun and the man with the most job titles in British speedway, Berwick's announcer/timekeeper/incident recorder/programme editor, Dennis McCleary, informs us, "Graham Flint has a message for Brent Werner, 'Can the rider in green sit still at the start please?'" The specificity of this message mustn't have got through to the LA-born American because, though he leads out of the second bend, he then slows dramatically on the back straight (almost to a standstill) and, thereby, lets the other three riders in the race past him even before they'd even entered the third bend. Over the tannoy Hugh Brown mistakes a Berwick 5-1 and Werner's lead bike for breathtaking excitement, "Oh, that was an incredible first lap – well, for the Bandits that is! That was incredible!" The third race provides another 5-1 for the Berwick Bandits though Paul Clews leaves it late when he manages to pass Emil Kramer on the final bend of the race. There's a brief delay for a track grade and I head back to the programme booth to find out what heat the interval will be this evening. Davina is not quite sure and, reading upside down, I notice on her diligently kept records that she's written the number 682 against tonight's date. This is probably the number of programmes sold (to produce revenues of £1,705) or, perhaps, is an early forecast of the number of points Berwick will score this evening. Fresh from her duties on the turnstiles, Lacey Louden already doesn't savour the prospect of the highly likely Bandits victory, "There's only one snag by winning – we help Edinburgh! We'll just have to grin and bear it." When Jordan Frampton leads the fourth race for three laps it looks as though Somerset might finally get a heat win but, instead, the Poole-born 23-year-old makes a real hash of his approach to the first bend of the final lap and loses the lead to the exotically named (but not everybody's first choice of speedway superstar) Tero Aarnio. Matthew Platten, son of Berwick photographer Graham, hopes that the Bandits form will carry on into tomorrow afternoon for their final away Premier League meeting of the season at Glasgow. The sound of his own confident talk and premature assumption of victory tonight against Somerset immediately spooks him, "We can throw away

Second bend action

a 10-point lead, we've done it before!" Jim Brykajlo marvels at the Finn's fortitude and application, "If you'd seen Tero on crutches last week you'd be surprised to see him riding tonight. He got a groin injury when he got knocked off by Fisher at Edinburgh. Fisher's a dirty bastard but, he's gonna get his comeuppance – Trent Leverington is going to get him!"

Heat 5 is a collector's item since it features the first win of the night by a Somerset rider. Predictably enough, it comes from Jason Doyle though, with Brent Werner marooned at the rear of the race, the heat is nonetheless drawn. Those that saw this as the signal for a concerted fightback by the Rebels were sadly misled and, many certainly wouldn't have predicted that Tero Aarnio would win the next (or any) race that featured both Adrian Rymel and Jordan Frampton (who finished last). Even less predictably, to follow up his unlikely victory, Aarnio then finished a creditable second in heat 7 behind Matthias Kroger. With Emil Kramer placed third, the Rebels actually gained a heat advantage to 'narrow' the deficit to 14 points (28-14). You have to harbour a vague worry about the long-term future of speedway as a sport when the potential League Champions can perform so execrably on the road! Admittedly, Edinburgh and Berwick are each technical tracks that have to be ridden in their own unique way, but clearly Somerset aren't really at the races at either location. While there's a rich speedway tradition of comprehensive home victories, at many meetings during the 2008 season the lack of an aggregate bonus point to 'spice up' the appeal of the contest has been noticeable. The eight heat sees Scott Smith aggressively ride Adam McKinna to the second-bend fence under the watchful but approving eye of Jim Brykajlo, "It's better when Scud misses the gate 'cause you never know what to expect!" Dennis McCleary updates the crowd on the latest news from Stoke where Edinburgh have already stretched into a comfortable lead (4-14). Jim suspects that the scoreline isn't solely down to Edinburgh's impressive away form, "It's not unknown that Mark Lemon wants to ride for Edinburgh when Reading close down. So it was a bad idea Stoke getting him to guest for them at number 1 after six or seven meetings for Edinburgh!"[3]

This season's Berwick star riders continue to excel on the track when Michal Makovsky wins the drawn heat 9 and Adrian Rymel combines with the exotically named Guglielmo Franchetti for a maximum heat advantage in the heat 10. Though he's captain, Berwick fans realise that this season is likely to be Rymel's swansong at the club. Jim predicts, "Peter will send him to Workington next year. Last Friday he said 'I love Berwick, I love riding here and the people but if Peter wants me to ride there he'll have to pay me more money now I'm a 10-point rider. I've had offers to go Elite League!'" Though the smart money is that Adrian will ultimately ply his trade somewhere else in the Premier League. Like many Berwick fans, Jim is happy with the careful financial husbandry that is the Peter Waite promotional blueprint for speedway at Shielfield Park, "Peter always gives them a chance – riders like Richie Hawkins and Carl Wilkinson – and when they do well, they always want more money!"

After the interval, we're treated to a dramatic first corner to start heat 11. Franchetti falls on the first corner and then gets up to have a pointed word with his team mate, Tero Aarnio. The rerun of this race then features another win for Jason Doyle – this time in the black-and-white helmet colour. One triumph often follows another and so it proves next time out with a surprise win for Emil Kramer who finishes ahead of Michal Makovsky and, the least exotically named member of the Berwick Bandits, Scott Smith. This newly found winning habit soon becomes addictive for the chequered flag starved Rebels and the 13th race of the night features Jason Doyle best the Bandits impressive Shielfield specialist, Adrian Rymel. The penultimate race line-up showcases the increasing internationalisation of the sport and also illustrates calibre of entertainment served up by contemporary Premier League speedway. In plain fact terms, Franchetti, Clews and Kroger take the points while Adam McKinna returns to the pits without payment. This bald statement doesn't really cover the thrills and excitement that they serve up in the process. The last race of the night is won in the fastest time of the meeting (66.1) by Adrian Rymel who easily defeats his erstwhile rival Jason Doyle for the second time this evening. It's a sight that causes Hugh Brown to express his delight, "In the battle of the number 1s there is only one number 1 – Adrian Rymel! Who was, of course, beaten by Jason when they met last time."

At 8.40 Dennis McCleary formally announces that the meeting is "officially closed" though, on the centre green, Hugh Brown seizes the opportunity to quiz some handy Berwick riders. First up is the "Entertainer of the Night" Paul Clews,

[3] Mark Lemon was second highest scorer for Stoke on the night with 7 points from five races.

Berwick v. Somerset: *"Oh, you've brought a bag to put your goggles in!"*

and Hugh plies him with an easy conversational opener, "They didn't look like a top of the League side to me." Matter-of-factly (in the tone of voice captured airmen usually use to assure us they've been treated well by their captors), Paul informs us that the Rebels have suffered "the rebound of the good performance at Workington". We would learn more from Paul but, instead, Hugh Brown interrupts to squeal with delight, "Oh, you've brought a bag to put your goggles in!"[4] Next to be subjected to a penetrating in-depth post-meeting interview is Scott Smith. Though tonight's performance by the Rebels doesn't merit praise Scott takes the philosophical view, "To get where they are they're a bloody good team!" Smith then proceeds to explain his early return to speedway from injury, "I probably shouldn't have rode at Workington but, my average is crap, so I did! It hurts like hell but that's speedway, you just have to ride through it!" The strain of these *ad hoc* interviews and the surprise sight of the goggle bag have left Hugh quite unsure what to think, "Well, there we are [small rider flashes past on the track] there's the mascot Kai Dempsey!" The post-meeting interviews conclude with Peter Waite who expresses some satisfaction at the recent turn of events. "The boys have come on fire too late in the season. I don't think we'll make the play-offs. We had an unfortunate couple of months and, now, it's too late to make the top four. We'll get close but we'll miss out by one point! The number fifth place will do us well in the Young Shield. We'd like a trophy and the team is on the edge of something brilliant!" Quizzed by Hugh on the likelihood of an away victory at Saracen Park tomorrow, Peter exudes confidence, "We're riding so well I think we can win there. We've won at top teams' home tracks like Workington and [struggles to remember]." A glance at the fixture list shows that the other allegedly powerhouse "top teams" Berwick defeated during their 2008 Premier League campaign were Birmingham and Mildenhall!

Over by the turnstiles Davina Johnston feels cheated by the prompt conclusion to the night, "The meeting was too quick! The public pay a lot of money to come in here and finishing at 20 to 9 isn't good enough!" Jim Brykajlo heads off for another night of taxi work in Edinburgh via a brief stop at the chip shop, "The new Czech at Newcastle [M. Hoavacek] is so bad that Bob Tasker [DVD film cameraman] can't even get him into the frame!" There's a healthy queue of fans from both teams at the renowned Robert Smith chip shop as well as some of the Somerset riders (who've collectively shown more speed to the chippie than to the first corner or finish line) and management. Such a scene typifies the community, collegiate nature of the sport and emphasises (once again) how the majority of the performers in the speedway world are usually easily accessible to the fans and also often drawn from a similar milieu. You can't imagine bumping into footballers at a chip shop after a match – not only do they live behind closed doors of their gated communities but sports science dictates they consume the gustatory equivalent of a calorie-counted and nutritionally rich macrobiotic diet (or similar weirdness) rather than some hearty deep-fried food. Somerset promoter Mike Golding and his partner Anita Lewis have already started to tuck into their fish and chip supper. This evening's Rebels top scorer Jason Doyle gained 16 points from five rides though it was a surprise to see him on the track at all after his bad crash the previous night at Armadale. After many years in the sport, Mike Golding has become something of an expert on the location and facilities of hospitals throughout the country. "Funny thing, the paramedic said, 'I can call an ambulance if you want. It'll be the County ambulance but it'll be better if you called it or if you went there yourselves'. They gave us directions to Edinburgh and we were on the M8 just about to pass Livingstone – where we were staying anyway – and Jason says, 'There's a hospital sign with an A&E Department!' I was in the outside lane and shot across. It was a lovely little place. I don't think the A&E Department is open 24 hours but we were seen straight away, X-rayed and everything and we were through so quick we were back in our hotel before the rest of the team had showered and driven back! It was excellent. Dunno why they didn't suggest it to us?" It's barely gone 9 o'clock when I find myself back in the reception area of my Berwick B&B where the diarrhoea suffered by the landlady's daughter's dog had prepared a special reception to cap off my early finish tonight.

30th August Berwick v. Somerset (Premier League) 58-35

---

[4] "The bag to put your goggles in" is a reference to a weekly sponsored presentation at Berwick of a set of new rider's goggles. These are awarded to the most exciting and entertaining rider (home or visitor). Referees often get asked to select the lucky winner. Paul Clews must have guessed or been tipped off he was going to be the selected winner so took his goggles bag out with him to put them straight into.

CHAPTER 37.

Glasgow v. Berwick:
"Hey, laddie, keep the throttle open more today!"

31st August

With many speedway clubs flung to obscure locales on the respective edges of their realms, it's often difficult to get there by public transport. Though the rise of the motorcar popularised out of town shopping, the incentives still don't appear to be quite there for casual fans to make the trip to speedway on a regular basis. Nowadays, noise and dust considerations ensure that the days of city centre speedway tracks have long since gone but, the ready availability of public transport links, should surely be one factor to be considered by any new promotional team when they construct their business plan. Saracen Park, home of the Glasgow Tigers is one of the few speedway tracks in Britain accessible by public transport. The mid morning train from Berwick to Glasgow Central Station, even with the restricted schedule of Sunday services, leaves you not far from the bus stop on Hope Street that can take you towards the rough vicinity of the speedway. This particular Sunday is an important tribal football day within the city limits of Glasgow since there's yet another old firm derby between intense rivals Celtic and Rangers. The need for extensive policing naturally ensures that this is an early afternoon kick-off and, as I exit the station, a group of scowling teenagers prompted by the sight of my luggage quiz me on the motivation for my journey and, more tellingly, my football allegiances. News that I'm a Sunderland fan and have no real interest in the Scottish Premier League just about reassures them. I omit to add that I've no desire to watch the match as regular exposure to Sunderland's style of play already gives me great familiarity with football matches where effort far outweighs skill. After a steep uphill walk, a slew of number 75 buses arrive at the bus stop and eventually one that goes from Hope Street to Milton arrives. My accent and bright purple coloured case definitively signals that I'm a stranger and I further confirm this when I ask the driver if he can tell me when we've arrived at the Gala Bingo in Hawthorn Street. For speed and convenience, Glasgow buses require that you have the exact change. Not that I know this but when I proffer my £5 note but I quickly discover this to be so. If this were London or any other English town (particularly those in the South East), at this point the driver would almost certainly tell me to get back off the bus and catch another one once I'd got the correct change. However, the generosity of strangers in Glasgow never ceases to amaze me and this is further confirmed when the driver lets me off my fare! Though I'd appreciate the view from upstairs on this double-decker bus, I sit downstairs with my bag, mindful of Ian Maclean's advice to "keep a close eye on my possessions."

It's hugely crowded downstairs, there's a number of smartly dressed old age pensioner women with full make-up and sprayed into position hairstyles. I sit with a young mum who looks barely aged 16, her hand firmly clasped to the handle of her pushchair. We pass an Irish pub with hoards of people in Celtic colours stood outside smoking close to the doorway while the game plays on the television screens inside. You quickly leave the imposing brick buildings of Glasgow city centre behind and, after a brief drive on some urban style dual carriageways, we start to wend our way through some of the outlying Glasgow estates that I doubt they advertise in the tourist brochures. We stop regularly and an ageing drunk gets on the bus. Though it's only 1pm he's totally slaughtered. His frequent, slurred attempts to engage everyone on the bus in conversation fall on deaf ears. Like everyone else, I say nothing. From the way I stand out with my case and earnest glances out of the windows, even though I haven't asked, prompts one of the smartly dressed older ladies a few seats away to advise, "We're not there yet – I shall tell you when we're getting near the Gala Bingo." Though they've ignored the drunk, some of the women on the bus strike up a conversation with me to establish if I'm on holiday or up to visit relatives. News that I'm here to watch the speedway elicits the traditional reactions of 'I used to go' or 'Is it still on then?' A couple of stops before I'm to get off, I'm given painstakingly detailed and very accurate directions to the stadium. Once off the bus, it's noticeable how few people walk around an area comprised of nearby high rise residential buildings or the much closer at hand new-build box units owned by multi-national companies that they've festooned with their distinctive logos. They're all closed and, though they're surrounded with recently erected fences and newly laid tarmac, they exude a forbidding air. After a brisk walk, I arrive at the Ashfield Bar outside Saracen Park. It's a building with a grandiose façade that betrays its historic wealth and significance at the time of its construction but, nowadays, with its faded glory and peculiar fencing it manages to look like a cross between a theatre and a nuclear bunker. Outside its entrance, there are an impressive number of dressed up women in high-heels smoking close to pushchairs. They're lost in conversation and have no interest in the speedway or need to glance up as a steady stream of cars and occasional pedestrians travel across the rough-hewn surface of the car park to the pits gate entrance.

Sunday @ 4pm

If I've encountered unexpected bonhomie on the bus here then the bloke on the gate quickly punctures the mood. Obviously well used to spending Sunday afternoons in summer listening to less than believable explanations from people who attempt to get into the speedway for free, he's singularly unconvinced by my story that I've come to sell my books or that my name should be down on his list as a guest of Alan Dick. A quick call on the walkie-talkie follows, "Alan, there's a man here who says he's come to sell his books and that you're expecting him." Alan crackles back his permission over the airwaves. Given the deprived area that surrounds the stadium, sceptical suspicion and a reluctance to accept statements at face value is understandable (especially from Sassenachs). Conditions aren't exactly ideal for speedway if judged by the jet black clouds overhead, though it is noticeable that these are being blown strongly away from the stadium and, off in the far distance, there's much brighter sky. I base myself in my usual position in front of the covered home-straight grandstand on the stepped terrace that overlooks the start-line but also close to the entrance and near to the adjacent programme stall. The track doesn't just look damp but is a sodden, deep earthy red colour. There's little activity except for Michael Max who slowly drives his blue Renault in the correct (anti-clockwise) direction from the pits round the track to park just by (albeit separated by the safety fence and a wall) the bar on the fourth bend. He unloads an impressive number of Tesco bags from the boot onto the edge of the terraces before he distractedly unloads two boxes of programmes which he takes off to the speedway office located in the white-painted bar building that overlooks the third and fourth bends of the speedway track. Keen to be helpful, I pick up the Tesco bags rammed full of white bread rolls and large plastic containers of milk to follow Michael in the general direction of the speedway office.

Berwick track walk

Inside the careworn but comfortable surrounding of the speedway office, Alan Dick answers the constantly ringing phone, "It's raining everywhere but here! Glasgow hasn't had a drop!" After he's advised another anxious punter Alan informs me that the bags are, in fact, "For the wee refreshment stall". I retreat re-laden with the bags, while Michael and Alan to discuss the important affairs of state, tactical matters and, quite possibly, the weather. Outside the office the tables are deserted but, from the open doorway that leads to the bar area, a portable CD/cassette player/radio loudly blares out the match commentary. Moments later there's many shouts after Rangers go 1-3 up, though it's hard to guess if these cries are of agony or ecstasy. I plonk the bags on the counter of the refreshment stall housed at the back of the low-roofed fourth-bend decked terraced grandstand. The kiosk is deserted though an impressive number of pies have already started to slowly warm in the heated glass-fronted pie cabinet and, by the not yet switched on hotplate, an impressive number of uncooked

Under orders

Glasgow v. Berwick: *"Hey, laddie, keep the throttle open more today!"*

burger patties are laid out ready to meet their maker. I wander back and stand by the safety fence to wait for Michael Max. He's reluctant to make weather forecasts but prefers the platitudes of polite speedway conversation, so affably claims that for Berwick, "Paul Cooper is a good choice of guest". I gesture at the track and ask, "So where are these famous square corners then?" With practised loyalty and his traditional effortless linguistic skill, Michael evades the intent of the question or the answer we both know with some brazen understatement, "I dunno! They've widened the pitch to give the football team a bit more room. In fact, the corners are wider and, perhaps, a little squarer but they look like bends to me!" Speedway bikes, tractors and bowsers all look spectacularly normal when you see them on a speedway track but the sight of a car on the Saracen Park red shale surface looks strangely incongruous as Michael Max drives off round the squarer corners to the pits to continue preparations for his race-day "Presentation/PR" Glasgow Tigers duties.

Back at the grandstand by the start-line, many of the staff have gathered to mooch or wait for the gates to open to allow the fans to flood into the stadium. The likely deluge will most probably come from the jet black clouds, though they continue to blow away and be replaced by white clouds that, hopefully, signal finer weather. Judged by the smoke that billows from a chimney in the distance, distant bright skies and the wind direction appears to indicate we might see some speedway action later. When the turnstiles open, ex Glasgow rider Jimmy Tannock stops for a brief chat. Later Ian Maclean tells me a little about him, "Rode as a reserve for the Ashfield Giants in 1952 – he'd be in his early twenties then. He subsequently rode for the Motherwell Lanarkshire Eagles and the Edinburgh Monarchs in the 60s and for a while rode at number 2 as partner for Douglas Templeton' he's an immensely popular and an infinitely nice guy". Jimmy's in expansive mood, "I think Edinburgh are going to win the League now. They've got a very good side – a team of heat leaders. Andrew Tully is excellent and, when William Lawson's back, think what a good team they'll have!" A young bloke passes eating chips covered in brown sauce and Jimmy breaks of his praise of the Monarchs to exclaim, "That's young Dale Lamb, the mascot! Hey, laddie, keep the throttle open more today!" Dale nods and Jimmy waves his fat fingered hands round in the air to emphasise his advice. Shortly afterwards, David McAllan's mum Fiona passes with a copy of the *Sunday Herald* held tightly in her hand. It contains a moving interview with her son conducted by Robert Philip. She's yet to find the opportunity to study its contents though it's a story she'd doubtless prefer had never had to be told. "I haven't read the article yet. £1.40 for a paper!"[1]

[1] The article reads: "I was paralysed. I put my hands down the front of my leathers and thought, 'Oh, God, my intestines are coming out. They weren't; I was actually holding my privates': David McAllan almost died after crashing on the speedway track, but he is now determined to live life to the full away from the sport he loves. The first time I saw a speedway rider, he looked like a spaceman to my seven-year-old eyes: the shiny black suit, the curious helmet and ungainly moonwalk gait (just try looking elegant in a pair of heavy boots, one of which has a two-inch steel plate attached to the sole to protect the left foot when sliding round corners.) By the time I reached my teens, I was completely hooked. American kids of the 1960s had Neil Armstrong to hero-worship, I had Charlie Monk of the Glasgow Tigers, surely the greatest rider never to win the World Championship. It may be four decades and more ago, but I can still hear the snarl of the bikes, the thunderous roars from the packed terraces of the White City and that intoxicating whiff of methanol fumes on the cinders the night my Australian idol pipped world champion Barry Briggs of the Swindon Robins on the line after a wheel-to-wheel duel worthy of the chariot race in Ben Hur. Though I had a vague notion girls might offer an interesting alternative in the years ahead, it was the most exciting 60-odd seconds of my early years. It was those unique sights, sounds and smells of speedway that captivated David McAllan the moment he made his first visit to the Berwick Bandits Shielfield Stadium at the age of seven to watch his uncle Kenny ride in a stars-of-the-future race. Thereafter, the sport would become McAllan's life. It would so very nearly also be the death of him. In heat 13 of Glasgow Tigers Premier League meeting against the Birmingham Brummies at Ashfield last October, McAllan was left paralysed from the waist down after being involved in a sickening pile-up on the fourth bend of the second lap. He learned to walk again and gets through life with the assistance of 22 various painkillers a day, plus a cocktail of other pills and potions to keep his bladder and bowels in a semblance of working order – not to mention the inconvenience of having to connect a regular round of catheters and bags – but, at 28, he will never ride a speedway bike again. The grounded spaceman is happy to be alive, even if he is now reduced to being a spectator at the sport he so loved. "If I skip breakfast I do tend to rattle like a tube of Smarties but it could have been so much worse," he says cheerfully. "All I ever wanted to be was a speedway rider. I knew I was never going to be the world champion but after years of struggle – years when I couldn't find a team or when I was riding with injuries – 2007 had been my best season. I was starting to put a lot of good scores together and I was really enjoying it. But, hey, it was meant to be. I'm not a great philosopher but obviously fate decided there was something else in life instead of speedway out there for me. It's hard, it's very hard knowing I'll never go to the tapes again but it was terrific fun while it lasted." Raised in Jim Clark's home town of Duns in the Borders, it was McAllan's uncle Kenny who encouraged the tot into the saddle. "He used to carve out an oval on Cockleburn Beach where he'd come down on his 500 cc racing machine, his son – my cousin – Bruce, would be on his 125 and there I'd be, eight years of age on my wee 50 cc red putt-putt. There could be up to 20 of us blasting round the sandy track having the times of our lives. "My mum Fiona worked as a part-time cleaner in a hotel while dad Charlie was a farm labourer; he knew how to drive a tractor, he could plough, he could sow, he's probably Britain's best employee. He's always up in the morning, he's never late, he puts in his full shift, he's always available to work a few extra hours, and that's something he fortunately gave to me. We never had much money but I was always given my pound to go to the speedway. My auntie Christine, cousin Bruce and me would pile into uncle Kenny's wee Toyota with his bike and tool box on a trailer at the back – the nose pointed up at the moon like a rocket." As their tiny offspring – he would grow to only 5'4" – became increasingly beguiled by uncle Kenny and his fellow daredevils, Charlie and Fiona McAllan bought a custom-made miniature speedway bike as a present for his ninth birthday. "It was identical to the machine world champion Hans Nielsen was riding but with smaller wheels and smaller frame powered by three 90 cc engines. It was absolutely fantastic. My dad stripped it all down and we painted it gold; today, to suggest painting a speedway bike would be criminal but when you're nine and you've just got a new toy" (On the subject of height, McAllan stands a good four inches taller than Peter Craven, the "Wizard of Balance" who won the world championship in 1955 and 1962, the year before he was killed in a crash at Meadowbank aged 29. So it

was not on the speedway track where no quarter is ever given or asked for that McAllan's lack of inches thwarted his ambitions. "Funnily, enough, I only remember it holding me back on holiday. We went to Great Yarmouth when I was 15 – at a time when I was riding a 500 cc speedway bike with no brakes – and feeling crushed when I wasn't allowed to drive a 50 cc go-kart because I wasn't deemed tall enough.") The nine-year-old McAllan took his new toy to the training track at Felton near Newcastle, a curious egg-shaped circuit where he gained renown as a young master of the art of hugging the white line on the inside of the bends. "I had a fascination with being able to turn really, really tight and crisp on that white line. Until the day I smacked a rock sticking out of the ground, head-butting the floor. I broke my nose, the blood flew everywhere but I never shed a tear. The only time I can recall crying in those days was when I caught my flesh in the zip of my fly." From Felton to Shielfield, Powderhall, Linlithgow and Shawfield, where McAllan, now astride a full-sized bike, would appear in the second-half of the programme after league meetings; as "Wee Dave "entered his teens, he won popularity among speedway fans for his style and never-say-die attitude. "I was still a midget but I think they recognised I had a big heart. Aye, may be too big. To me there is nothing as aesthetically pleasing to the eye as a newly-graded track. So one night at Shawfield – I was 14 – they'd just graded the track before my race and right from the tapes I was offski. From what I've been told, on the second lap I got a bit of a wobble and crashed in the corner. I knocked myself out and woke up in hospital four hours later. I came round with drips hanging out of me everywhere and gripping the bed because I was so out of it I thought I was up on the ceiling. My blood pressure had dropped to critical level but I was home the next day. The bike was too big for me, it was as simple as that, so my dad – and I still don't know what financial sacrifices my parents had to make all those years – got me a machine one inch shorter and lower. "When he graduated to the Premier League, McAllan made more appearances in ER departments than George Clooney. A cruciate ligament injury kept him out of action for over a year before he came a serious cropper in 2000 while riding for Stoke Potters on the Isle of Wight. "I was off gate one in my second ride when the Islanders Adam Shields came tearing up on my inside. He didn't hit me but I got a fright and came off – Bang! On the ambulance journey to hospital I had a burning sensation all over my body so they whisked me straight into X-Ray. When the radiographer looked at the result and muttered, 'Oh, no ...' I felt the fear of God. I had broken a vertebrae in my back and had to lie perfectly still for two weeks. It was pretty stressful but probably more so for my mum, and girlfriend (now wife) Lynn. Eventually, they put me on a ferry with a nurse to Portsmouth, ambulance to Gatwick then on to a BA flight to Edinburgh on a stretcher laid out across the back six seats." McAllan would make a full recovery but his luck finally ran out in the race jacket of the Glasgow Tigers on October 14 last year when, having scored 10 points from his previous four rides (two wins and two second places), he came out for heat 13. Understandably, his recollection of the end of his career is hazy but those who witnessed the crash will never forget the horror which unfolded. "It was a double-header meeting against Birmingham with Stoke to come so there wasn't a lot of dirt on the track, making it very slick. I went up wide at the corner looking for better grip and the guy came underneath me. I felt the front wheel go and I went down ..."

McAllan is far too decent a man to apportion blame but "the guy" in question – Birmingham's Phil Morris, who was due to "guest" for Stoke in the second fixture – was ejected not just from the rerun but from the entire meeting by the referee, a rare occurrence in speedway. "I felt I was lying on the ground wrapped up in a Fairly Liquid bubble with the sounds of those around me coming like shock waves. I told the first person on the scene, 'I've broken my back.' I knew I was in a mess so the best thing I did was just switch off and let the medics deal with me. And the reason I'm walking today is down to them for their speed and expertise in those first moments. In the ambulance, I was drifting in and out of consciousness and it was as though someone was sitting on my legs they felt so heavy. When I finally came round in the A&E department of the Royal Infirmary, I had no feeling from the waist down; I was paralysed. I put my hands down the front of my leathers and thought, 'Oh, God, my intestines are coming out of my stomach.' They weren't; when I managed to look down I was actually holding my privates. "On the trolley, every jolt sent waves of agonising pain down my back and I had the most incredible phantom pain in my right leg which I have to this day. Next morning I was in the operating theatre where they glued my broken vertebrae back together, drilled through the bones immediately above and below the break, and joined them all up with a metal plate. It took about seven hours and they did a fantastic job, absolutely fantastic." Such was the skill of the surgeon and the physio that 16 days later McAllan was not only back on his feet – however feebly and painfully – but was declared fit to be discharged. "It began with the tiniest bit of movement in one toe – even though I still had no feeling – but inch by agonising inch, they got me up and walking with the aid of a zimmer frame, then crutches, then sticks." By the beginning of November, McAllan was attending the out-patients' department where he told the physio that he intended walking unaided down the aisle on January 19, when he was to marry Lynn over the blacksmith's anvil in Gretna. "And I did, no crutches, no brace. Yes, it's been a change of life but I'm looking forward not back. I concentrate on what I can achieve, not what I can't. I'm alive and I intend living life to the full." David McAllan is walking proof that you do not need world titles to be a great champion. The David McAllan Farewell benefit meeting featuring 16 stars from around the world will be held at Ashfield on Sunday September 7th 2008, tapes up 4 p.m. For further details visit **www.davidmcallanracing.co.uk**

Meeting abandoned

Mitchell Davey signs autograph

Lifelong Tigers fan the rather modest and intelligent Ian Maclean always has his finger on the speedway pulse in this part of the world. "Mitchell Davey got taken off on a spinal board at Redcar on Thursday and yet he rode last night at Workington. Brave young man! Lee Dicken was so unfit at Workington last night that the doctor wouldn't let him ride 'cause he couldn't hold onto the bike! It's been a very poor season in many ways this year, never mind it's been a golden rule that it must be wet on a Sunday!" The lack silverware would never dim Ian's keenness to see his beloved Tigers race every week possible. Now that the contemporary rider he admires the most (Shane Parker) has returned to the team, all that's left to vaguely set his pulse racing this season is the possibility of a home win against Edinburgh in the Premier League ("I don't think that is likely") or the traditional end-of-season Tigers celebration. "I've just chosen to sit at Robert Ksiezak's table at the dinner dance. Everyone usually likes to sit at Shane's table."

Under leaden skies riders from both teams have commenced their track walk and avuncular promoter of the Berwick Bandits, Peter Waite, has joined his team as they painstakingly test the calibre of Saracen Park surface. Peter has the diminutive stature ideally suited to speedway racing though, sadly, he's no longer quite the right size. Paul Clews is out with his son who gardens at the start-line in determined almost frenzied fashion. Lenzie-based fanatical Tigers fan Alison Chalmers has arrived with her daughter, Laura, and takes some delight in the sight of one of the young Tigers Australians, Mitchell Davey, who's unseasonably dressed in shorts while he diligently surveys the start-line area. Though keen on all the Glasgow riders, Alison thinks highly of this particular young man, "Mitchell had a sorry start to the season at number 4 (due to his assessed average). He's only 18 but a lesser man would have given up! He often finished half a lap behind and had lots of falls but he's stuck at it!" Like for so many people at so many clubs round the country, speedway is a family affair that spans the generations for Alison who's here this afternoon with both her dad and her daughter. "My dad's been here – how old are the Tigers? 62 years. I went to Hampden to see my first meetings – I'm revealing my age now. We've got five Aussies out of seven riders this season. Did you hear Dicken couldn't hold his bike last night? What is our promotion on? No matter what happens Edinburgh will be champions! Some misguided people fancied Somerset but I saw us beat them here and we're not very good this season! Now you've seen them twice, you know what I meant!"

After the riders have all left the track, the tractor immediately comes round to the start gate area and starts to rip up the surface even more aggressively than Paul Clews's son did. Shortly afterwards, the riders head from the pits across the centre green with their giant kit bags slung over their shoulders en route to the old-fashioned changing rooms (with 1940s communal bathing pool) buried deep in the bowels of the home-straight grandstand. They glance quizzically at the latest bout of curatorial activity. Overhead the jet black clouds have changed to an even darker hue and the skies now look incredibly threatening though there's still 40 minutes left before the tapes are scheduled to rise. It's still possible to judge the direction of the wind by the smoke that billows from the chimney in the distance. This has completely reversed direction between 2 and 3 o'clock. Alison has only just commented, "I see Deek [Derek Sneddon] had fisticuffs again in the pits last night hitting Barker's mechanic" when we're interrupted by the Bandits posse of fans that includes Jim Brykajlo, Muriel Ennis and Lacey Louden amongst others. Jimmy B definitely isn't a Derek Sneddon fan but states bluntly, "Ryan Fisher is the dirtiest rider in the League!" Alison doesn't gainsay this opinion, "You should have seen what he did to Trent Leverington – twice!" Though Peter Waite himself isn't averse to completely ripping up the Shielfield Park track on his tractor just minutes before the start of the meeting, Muriel isn't that impressed with the ruffled look of the Glasgow track surface around the start gate area, "It looks a bit like a ploughed field – I think they're going to plant potatoes!" The rider introductions are kept to a minimum by Michael Max so we can move swiftly onto the meeting at the scheduled start time. Sadly, spits of rain soon turn heavier. It's not a sight that pleases Alison but, born of experience, she knows that water and the Glasgow Tigers don't exactly mix well. "Oh dear, it's raining! Neither Shane nor Trent like the wet – which isn't strange when you think they're Aussies – and what they have to ride on in Australia. If one of Robert, Shane or Trent doesn't perform, then we'll lose!" Despite the slippery surface (and the allegedly square corners) Adrian Rymel wins the first heat convincingly and, since Robert Ksiezak and Lee Dicken occupy the minor places, the heat is drawn. It's completely apparent to everyone in the stadium that, although the track is rideable, it's far from raceable. Nonetheless, the show must go on! Unfortunately, the rain suddenly becomes heavier as the riders line up at the gate for the second race of the meeting. When the tapes rose, on the outside gate Josh Grajczonek got no further than the first bend where he smashes dramatically into the fence. He lays prostrate on the track for some time in the rain. The mood of the fans is as dark as the sky but they don't have to endure the pain that clearly afflicts Josh.[2]

Glasgow v. Berwick: *"Hey, laddie, keep the throttle open more today!"*

Though rationally we all know that the meeting will be postponed, we all still wait optimistically until referee Mick Bates has made his final decision. Derek Sneddon swaggers past with a can in his hand apparently oblivious to the numerous critical glances thrown in his direction. "He can drink 'cause he's serving a driving ban. The Glasgow fans like to ask him who's driving him this week! Can you see Shane Parker doing that? Derek Sneddon is the Edinburgh captain and is supposed to lead by example. When Sheffield were here a few weeks ago and beat us Derek Sneddon, Aaron Summers and Andrew Tully came out of the bar and stood on the wall [of the fourth bend] to salute the Sheffield riders on their victory parade."

No sooner has Alison told me, "We've reached the 4.30 watershed" than over the loudspeakers the inevitable postponement is formally confirmed, "The weather's not been kind to us today!" The majority of the fans rush for the car park and I have the impression that more people appear to leave than actually arrived! Those that remain head off to the bar to drown their sorrows, reminisce or discuss the one heat of racing that we saw. The riders make the 150 yard or so dash from the pits to the grandstand changing rooms and a sodden Shane Parker calls out to me from the track, "You've jinxed us again, haven't you mate!" Tigers fan Jim Fleming is a seasoned smoker from this part of the world so won't let merely inclement weather get in the way of the joy of a much-needed cigarette. After he returns from the open first-bend terrace he stops for a word about Mitchell Davey, "I tell you who he reminds me off – Michael Lee! He's got the same sort of build. I remember hitching to see a British final at West Ham to see George Hunter ride – in 1965 maybe – but it was rained-off and I hitched all the way back. My mum wasn't pleased 'cause I'd been up all night and had my finals [chartered accountancy] the next day. I failed 'cause I could hardly keep my eyes open but passed when I took it again!"

31st August Glasgow v. Berwick (Premier League) 3-3 Abandoned

[2] Josh's altercation with the fence would result in a broken thumb and torn ligaments. This medical diagnosis required he mustn't ride a speedway bike for at least six weeks and, thereby, effectively ended his season. Still learning his craft, the last three crashes he was involved in – until the premature end to his 2008 campaign – were outside of his control and down to the fault of others or first-bend bunching.

CHAPTER 38.

Buxton v. Weymouth:
"We're the only track with such a varied selection of animal droppings"

14th September

The last time I visited Buxton speedway I came with my friend Stefan Usansky (to whom this book is dedicated) when he optimistically drove us over in torrential rain from Manchester. Sadly, we didn't get to see any racing although we were offered a cup of tea in the track staff kitchen that's inside one of the many recycled sea containers they have on site within the stadium. This time I arrive at noon nearly three hours before the tapes are scheduled to go up. Worryingly, drizzle spits on and, unusually, Buxton Speedway Club Chairman Jayne Moss isn't already sat in the booth at the entrance to the stadium. Buxton have the most beautiful location of any track within British speedway. It's almost postcard perfect set within rolling hills of a national park with panoramic views in all directions, provided dark low clouds don't hug the skyline and obscure the beauty of the countryside. It's an idyllic scene apart, of course, from when you look over the second-bend car park towards what appears to be a top-secret military-testing site with its strange shaped test chambers and underground bunkers (doubtless suitable for 'dark' activities like torture or nerve-gas experiments).

To look on the positive, the weak afternoon sun tries to break through the cloud cover and, laid out before me as I walk down towards the pits area, the track looks wonderfully pristine. Obviously if you base a speedway club in a national park, your activities may be subject to the whims of the weather but also the track will necessarily have to adapt to the contours of the land upon which it is set. Consequently, there's quite a dramatic slope if you compare the relative height of the back straight to that of the home straight. A small band of helpers are already hard at work within the stadium grounds. They're presently doing odd jobs in the pits (fixing a lamp), attend to the edges of the track or purposefully prepare the centre green with its essential furniture of flags and rakes. Nearby they check the toilets and do the other countless myriad of minor tasks that are essential to the smooth running of any speedway meeting. The club co-chairman Richard Moss, husband of Jayne and son of the man who founded the club (and, for a while, Hitmen rider), is very much a man of action rather than words. Though, today, I do get a smile and a handshake along with a few words before other essential tasks call him away again, "They say it'll be sunny later. We get all the weather imaginable here, usually in the space of 30 minutes!" The adjacent trackshop area is conspicuously deserted but the shop door is open true *Mary Celeste* fashion to reveal a couple of tables covered with retro-patterned tablecloths and an empty book display stand on which is hooked a sign that proudly announces in large letters "Buxton Hitmen Trackshop." Outside the large metal sea container that will shortly be packed with speedway merchandise, there's a small array of industrial style tables with fixed (water-laden) seating attached.

When I parked earlier in the almost deserted car park, the only other vehicle I could see was a speedway van must belong to Andrew Bargh as evidenced by his name spelt out in large letters upon its side. By the time I wander back up the hill Jayne Moss has arrived to open the kiosk that, on race day, serves as the customer services and parking office as well as turnstiles of Buxton speedway. Her eight-year-old son, Josh Moss, who's the energetic club mascot and also a keen footballer, accompanies her! "Josh scored four in his first game with his new football team. He was quite happy. They won 7-1 and 7-2 that's why we were late." Talk of football quickly moves onto the more mundane subject of waste products, "We're the only track with such a varied selection of animal droppings: rabbits and deer." Josh interjects, "and cows and sheep!" I head off for the warmth and comfort of my car just as half the Weymouth team arrive in a posse of vans. Close behind this convoy Weymouth Team Manager, Jem Dicken, in his heavily laden car wends its way up the slope through the drizzle. The Weymouth team are presently engaged on a Northern Tour but have suffered disruption from the weather. Jem remains philosophical, "We heard the Boston meeting was off when we were 30 miles outside Weymouth but, because we're on tour [Saturday at Redcar and Sunday at Buxton] we carried on and went to see Scunthorpe versus Rye House. But that was called off! We've done 500-odd miles already. It's 350 miles to Redcar and we were supposed to go back from here afterwards but Boston has been rearranged to tomorrow night." Brendan Johnson's dad Dave hops from his van and arrives to establish with Jem exactly how many rooms [five] they'll need when some of the Wildcats team stay over tonight (prior to the Boston meeting) at a place they know well from previous visits. Jem explains logistics to me, "some riders will go home before travelling to Boston and some are interested in going to Stoke to watch the speedway meeting against Redcar." A short distance away the riders are stood conspiratorially in a huddle having conversations unknown. I go over to question Brendan Johnson about whether they won last night. "Nah, we got thrashed 50 odd something or other!" I then wonder aloud if Weymouth might race against them again shortly in the play-offs. Brendan remains unsure, "Will we?"

Beware UXB

At Buxton there's a long tradition of watching the speedway from the comfort of your car and many fans arrive early in their vehicles to specifically claim their ideal parking spot. I chat to Jayne and Josh while she busies herself with a steady stream of fans in their vehicles. Though the surrounding area mostly looks wild, picturesque and unspoilt, apparently there's considerable danger from buried munitions. Jayne tells me about the unexploded bomb they found under the referee's box and Josh pipes up, "Me granddad and dad discovered it when they were moving the box. I wasn't born then!"

[Jayne] "You were!"

[Josh] "It's after 1999 then!"

[Jayne] "In World War II bombs were stored underground [points in the distance, though I can't really see without my glasses]. See the square boxes they have dotted around, they were under there."

[Josh] "There's 15 or so of them around here, we haven't found any bombs though!"

Josh Moss wheelie expert

[Jayne] "It's been a terrible summer with the rain. We have to be realistic about whether it's gonna be on or not!"

Josh tries to help his mum sell raffle tickets to the fans and a lady driver remarks, "It won't be long before he's in charge!"

[Jayne] "He'd overcharge everybody."

[Josh] "I wouldn't!"

[Lady] "How much change would I get from £20 if it was £15.20?"

[Josh] (thinks) "£4.80!"

[Lady drives off]

[Jayne] – "He's nine next week and the other one's two. I can't believe it! You know what it's like with kids, they get bored! Sometimes there's not a lot going on, as you know yourself, so it's not a surprise!"

The people who don't watch from their cars tend to congregate in the area round the referee's box start-line, the pits, the bar area on the bend or outside the nearby trackshop and catering kiosks. Though the rural surroundings make

Steve Miles and Charles McKay

this appear like a far-flung outpost of the Dave Rattenberry trackshop empire, in reality we're only an hour from Stoke where I'll head off to later. John Rich and I.C.A. Crook (aka Mushy Pea) will also be going there and John volunteers to show me the back roads route to the Loomer Road Industrial Estate. Earlier in the summer John had told me of his retirement plans that would have included giving up his work at speedway trackshops. However, he's had a change of mind, "By the way, I'm still going to be doing it next year." Once you become a senior citizen, you can pretty well say what you like. John needs no second invitation and briefly dons the metaphorical mantle of a literary (or artistic) critic. He has rigid views on the question that has vexed philosophers and artists for over two thousand years: namely, "What is literature?" With my speedway photo book *Shale Britannia* in his hand as an *aide memoire* and reference point, John states categorically, "Books are for reading not for looking at!" While I let that sink in John gently tries to point me in the direction where demand and profit would be higher than they are at present. "Why don't you do an A to Z of each track? The Elite League, Conference League and Premier League – put pictures of the track, a write up on each and a photo of the promoter. There'd definitely be demand and, with Exeter coming back and Bodmin, and Weymouth and Plymouth might go up to the Premier League – but their tracks are too small – it would be good." With John in charge of my publishing strategy, the Methanol Press publishing programme would certainly look a lot different and, if I was to adopt his suggested title for my next speedway book (*Round the Tracks*), the John Rich makeover would be complete. John and Mushy Pea remain nonchalantly confident that the meeting will go ahead despite the earlier drizzle and dark clouds. Mushy Pea explains the local climactic conditions, "It dries out sharpish. Three weeks ago they were packing it down with a van after they'd had tons of rain. After a few heats, the dust was flying and they were having to drag the shale back from the outside." A member of the track staff who dawdles in the shop for a few moments, Ian Baker ("I do odd jobs and track maintenance here") confirms Mushy's prognosis. He worries more about clubs elsewhere since Stoke speedway apparently might struggle to fit in all their various fixtures before the end of the season. "Dave at Stoke still has loads of meetings to run at home and away!"

Also in attendance at Buxton speedway, like he is pretty well every Sunday throughout the season, is passionate speedway supporter, Charles McKay. He's something of a thorn in the side of officialdom with his sometimes difficult but perceptive questions and observations based on an extensive knowledge of the sport (both past and present). Charles lives in Bradford and regularly attends speedway meetings throughout the country but particularly Stoke on a Saturday, Buxton on a Sunday and Belle Vue on a Monday. He's not a fan of pomposity, let alone arrogance never mind bureaucracy or mendacity in organisations and people. A keen researcher and critical thinker about any of the institutions of contemporary speedway, he's never at a loss for conversation. The topics range widely, whether it's the Speedway Grand Prix series run by "BSI – an IMG company" (under the auspices the FIM), organisations closer to home like the BSPA or, this afternoon's *bête noire*, the SRBF.

"Like most speedways fans I have given to the annual SRBF collection at my local track but knew nothing of what it did with the money. But, in the late 90's, I had heard stories that certain riders whose careers had been ended by injuries were finding life hard and the SRBF didn't seem concerned. In 2000 I went on the Charity Commission web page and was surprised – especially as the Charity Commission claim to update their records on a regular basis – that it had the name and details of someone who had died in February 1996 being the SRBF secretary/treasurer. In 2004, I contacted the Charity Commission asking for copy of latest set of accounts for SRBF and received copy of the accounts along with a letter telling me there would be no charge because the accounts were so old (being for the period up to Dec 1999). I was naturally concerned but wrote to SRBF asking for details of trustees so I could write to them with my concerns. I enclosed SAE to save them postage. After hearing nothing from SRBF, weeks later I received e-mail from friends with a copy of an Internet posting on *British Speedway Forum* by Mr Bernard Crapper of SRBF. In that posting, he stated that the Charity Commission were wrong and SRBF account was up to date. Having heard nothing directly from SRBF, I replied to Mr Crapper's posting with details of my many concerns and questions. Why no info on work done by SRBF? Or how to give to SRBF in the most tax effective way (e.g. Gift Aid) in programmes when SRBF collection held? Or why no details about SRBF in speedway press as it was in the 1940's and 1950's? Why no collection at British Grand Prix? Why no rider or ex rider as a trustee? After all, the Speedway Riders Association (SRA) had jointly set up SRBF in the 1940's. What were objectives of SRBF with regard to current riders and ex riders? Why so were their reserves (half a million pounds) so high? Would it not be better to give more help? This would, obviously, reduce their reserves but, if the possible coverage provided by these reserves became problem, they could increase income by better collections/fund raising!"

"Mr Crapper replied answering some of the concerns which, in turn, raised yet more questions. He said that my letter had been received and discussed at trustee meeting and it had been decided that I need to write to them care of Mr Crapper or the office at Wood Street, Rugby. Of course, no one had bothered to tell me this by letter! He stated again that the Charity Commission was wrong and that, in fact, accounts were up to date. Within a week, the accounts from 1999 to 2002 were shown on the Charity Commission web site and Mr Crapper told me the problem was he believed accountants submitting accounts and they, in turn, believed he was. There followed a long series of letters between SRBF and myself that got nowhere. I had contacted SRA and asked why they had no trustee on SRBF. Shane Parker replied and said it was because they had never been asked! At the SRA annual general meeting in October 2005, I was nominated to be their trustee on the SRBF and to act on their behalf. Prior to the annual general meeting , the SRA had meeting with SRBF about having a trustee. The SRBF said they felt that a rider would be suitable but they raised no objections when my name (as a non-rider) was mentioned. The day after Shane Parker formally submitted my name – as their appointed trustee – Chris Van Straaten contacted him to say that a "supporter" should not be in on SRBF meetings and the SRA should have nominated a rider. Since then I have washed my hands of the SRBF. After all, if I am not good enough neither is my money. I still have concerns and questions. For example, when riders are seriously injured fans organize benefits and fund raising etc. Shouldn't this be done by SRBF? They're the only legally recognised charity. They must provide (on time) accounts but do these one-off committees?"

Pesky tapes

Throughout our conversation Josh Moss repeatedly zooms up and down on his pushbike trying to pull wheelies. Some of these are extremely impressive to watch and others are even more vividly so in his imagination. Later some of his less skilled friends join him in this impromptu wheelie exhibition but they don't have his skill or bravery on the bike. Throughout his exhibition, Josh clings to the pushbike equivalent of a 'buyer beware' approach to trackside safety. Namely if you see him zooming in your direction then it's your responsibility to get out of the way while he perfects his bike craft. Buxton attracts a loyal following amongst its fans and they're all obviously well used to such displays of Josh's enthusiasm.

Pits scene

Earlier in the season I met keen Redcar fans Ken and Barbara Dolan when they were parked up waiting for the turnstiles to open on the waste ground that serves as the Smallmead Stadium car park. They live in Middlesbrough and, when not on the road following their beloved Redcar in their Premier and Conference League incarnations, they also exhibit roses and dahlias. Ken works as a mobile caretaker but, this afternoon, he's off duty and has driven over from Middlesbrough to Buxton (comparatively a much shorter journey than the 270 miles they'd driven to Reading in May). I'm disappointed that he hasn't brought along his giant St George's flag adapted with the Redcar name but then, since this is a fixture between Buxton and Weymouth, it would look out of place (assuming there was somewhere to hang it). Ken's appetite for speedway hadn't been slaked by a Conference League double header staged the previous night at the South Tees Motorsports Park which saw Redcar beat Weymouth (53-37) and then proceed to humble Sittingbourne (60-32). "I was disappointed with

Weymouth, though one rider scored 16 [Andrew Bargh scored 12], they didn't really turn up. I expected Sittingbourne to be poor. They started with six [riders], ended with four and we got 60 odd. I see Malcolm Saint [Vasey] or whatever he's called at Scunthorpe – who used to be Boston's boss until this season – is protesting about our team saying we've bent the rules. But it's only sour grapes! If the rules are bent by all people, you might as well also use them. Aaron Summers wasn't allowed to ride by Edinburgh and, the three riders we had in the squad weren't enough to ride, so we used rider replacement for Aaron against Weymouth though we had Leigh Boujos in against Sittingbourne but he didn't score many [3 from five rides]." After the meeting Ken and Barbara, like many others at Buxton speedway this afternoon, will then head off to the Potteries to see this evenings Stoke versus Redcar Premier League meeting.

Richard Moss's predictions about the variability of the weather prove correct and by 2.30 p.m. the bowser is out to copiously water the track. On the Weymouth side of the pits, they have the benefit of Laurence Rogers's experience to supplement that of their regular Team Manager, Jem Dicken. The purchase of Mildenhall speedway by the Chapmans of King's Lynn has suddenly left Laurence without any formal position within the sport. "It would have been nice to have had a phone call rather than read about it on the Internet. Then I could have said goodbye to the lads at Birmingham. Jonathan Chapman wouldn't let anyone put my name on the gate for the next Mildenhall meeting after and wouldn't recognise my BSPA pass, so I had to pay to get in! Lots of people were pleased to see me and, when I went to the bar afterwards, some of the riders were overjoyed! I just hope that it's not a play thing for Jonathan. It's a great little club and it would be a shame if it gets ruined if he gets bored! Huggy won't be doing the track unless he pays him £500 a meeting." Though interesting, this doesn't solve the mystery of what brings him to Buxton? "Phil Bartlett rang me and said, 'you put half of our team together so can you come along and help Jem out until the end of the season?' I've been on the Northern Tour. Last night after we said Lee [Herne] was going to go out in the black-and-white they [Redcar] stopped the meeting for track maintenance and totally flooded gate 4. I got Jem to ring up [referee Stuart Wilson] and protest and say we wouldn't ride until they graded the track. They did afterwards but it was too late! After our meeting, I helped Sittingbourne's Chris Hunt out at Redcar 'cause he lost Dean Felton after one race and Aaron Baseby after two and was in a panic. So I showed him what he could do to the programme over the remaining races." If I didn't expect to see Laurence Rogers at Buxton then I definitely didn't expect to see Sam Ermolenko there either. I ask Laurence, "What's Sam Ermolenko doing here?" and learn "He'll be helping out Lew [Lewis Dalloway] 'cause he lives close by." It transpires that he's also here to have some post-meeting practice to sharpen his ring rusty race skills for some testimonial appearances later in the season. Over the years, Newport-born Laurence Rogers has worn many hats within the sport and helped many people in their careers. One of these is Nigel 'Scoop' Pearson, "Around 1989, I knew Scoop when he was on Hospital Radio in Stourbridge and I said 'let's get that hospital radio bloke in to do the presenting at Cradley' so, it was me that started him off! He's gone back to shouting all the time again but, he doesn't listen to nobody, so there's no point saying anything!"

Round the corner from the pits, Charles McKay is deep in conversation with Peterborough Programme Editor, Steve Miles. As I arrive I hear Steve conclude their conversation about an unknown track with the words, "ever since they changed the track shape, the racing has been worse." Quite where this is remains a mystery but a few candidates spring to mind. However, the unexploded bombs that potentially litter the area are at the forefront of everyone's mind today. In an earnest tone of voice that you can imagine a doctor uses to deliver really bad news, Charles McKay rasps, "It killed a sheep – it had a name – stepped on the bomb and blew itself up down there! [Points to buildings in the distance] That's the Health and Safety Executive!" Probably not used to such untamed countryside, Steve looks suitably spooked, "It's scary that there's so much walking round here." Talk is interrupted by the sound of the *Thunderbirds* theme music that serenades both teams' as they head out onto parade. After we've had the introductions and learnt the line-ups, Charles wonders about the vexed subject of the precarious finances at Redcar speedway, "They boast that they have every meeting and every heat sponsored in the Premier League and Conference League. So where is all the money going? Glyn now has another job doing the track at Workington ever since they fired Tony Swales. He was told by Keith Denham, 'Your job is to turn up here on a Saturday and make sure there's no dust!' Other blokes work on it during the week. Still everyone's leaving or just hanging on by the skin of their teeth. The programme man left 'cause some programmes went missing and he was accused to stealing them. They found the box a few weeks later in the office. Then Birmingham visited and Keith's comments in the column had to be cut out of the programme!"

Buxton v. Weymouth: *"We're the only track with such a varied selection of animal droppings"*

John Branney wins the first race from the gate and it looked like Buxton might record a maximum heat advantage until Karl Mason ["he started out here"] passed Paul Burnett. Over the loudspeakers, the club announcer (named in the programme as) Graham Tagg lets us know that the winning time of 55.4 seconds is "John's fastest time of the season." Buxton like Sittingbourne, still adhere to the original founding philosophy of the Conference League – namely, to give riders their first steps on the speedway ladder and hopefully see them seize that chance before they progress on to greater things within the sport. Consequently, though Buxton are keen to win whenever possible, this isn't the be all and end all of the outlook that underlies their organisation on and off the track. That said, whatever the approach taken to team construction, most Conference League teams tend to have their most erratic or junior members at reserve. The second race showcases all the reserves in one race and this afternoon this race is won in a time that's five seconds slower than John Branney's previous benchmark from heat 1. Brendan Johnson is the winner and he's followed home by his comparatively less stylish team mate, Kyle Newman. Scott Whittington finishes comprehensively last with Buxton's solitary point picked up by Gareth Isherwood. Lee Smart wins the next race for Weymouth but honours are shared in a drawn heat.

Many riders play a significant role in the lengthy and often dramatic fourth race. First time up at the start-line John Branney breaks the tapes and, for his troubles, is put back 15 metres by referee Dave Dowling for the rerun. Immediately after this adjudication, the referee sounds the two-minute warning while Start Marshal Kev Tew and his helper frantically try to repair the tapes. This proves more complicated than they expected so the two-minute warning has to be cancelled to give them more repair time. When the racing resumes, there's only one strand of white start tape rather than the usual parallel two. The rerun of the race only lasts until the first bend where the high speed John Branney shows impressive reflex reaction to lay down when Kyle Newman locks up and gets out of shape in front of him. Almost simultaneously, some ladies by the start-line look up at Dave Dowling in the referee's box and shout, "Don't you dare!" If Dave had contemplated Kyle Newman's exclusion then he certainly didn't let on. Judged by his tone of voice, announcer Graham Tagg issues an apparently heartfelt request on behalf of the referee, "Would all riders come back to the tapes immediately!" The riders quickly do as they're told only to find, once they're back up at the start-line, that again, "The two-minutes time allowance has been cancelled!" More faff with the tapes then follows and predictably, in the rerun of the rerun (under the strict application of Sod's Law), the tapes then fail to rise and nearly strangle Kyle Newman on gate 1. Kyle survives his near strangulation and, when the race eventually gets under way, Jay Herne is determinedly chased all the way by Gareth Isherwood (who looks a totally different rider from the one that finished third two heats earlier). The battle for third place is equally keenly contested. Though much more experienced, John Branney has difficulty passing Kyle Newman because of the unpredictable trajectory and wildly varied lines that he utilises to progress round the track each time he circuits it. Branney eventually trusts speed, judgement and luck to nip past and ensure another drawn heat.

Without the added complication of time pressure, the start marshal team quickly repair the tapes back into their traditional arrangement before the start of the next race. As a concession to the range of climatic conditions seen at the track most weeks (and also not pander to the incipient male chauvinism of the average speedway fan), the Buxton Babes wear appropriately coloured University of Derby hoodies rather than the skin tight clothing sometimes favoured by start-line girls elsewhere. They clearly enjoy their jobs since they frequently have a laugh during their choreographed pre-race track walks and also when they're sat together on the centre green. They must also be passionate about their speedway since they all pay a great deal of attention to the racing as well as the completion of their programmes. Heat 6 has to be rerun without any exclusions after Paul Burnett unseats Brendan Johnson in the first corner. In the rerun, Burnett keeps the Weymouth Wildcat in his sights and pursues Johnson closely for two laps before he starts to ride an ever wider and wider racing line till the sheer additional distance that this involves comprehensively relegates him to last place. We're then treated to a lengthy track grade before the start of heat 7. The Buxton Babes take this interruption as the signal to head off and queue up at the burger van. Lots of other fans have had a similar idea and, by the time they've collected their food, the next race is due to start. They take the sensible but unilateral decision not to bother with a pre-race parade and instead concentrate on their burgers. They're back on the centre green in time for heat 8 but this has to be delayed after a bizarre turn of events that sees a member of track staff require attention from the private paramedic team who provide assistance at Buxton. Over the loudspeakers announcer Graham Tagg requests, "Can the Clerk of the Course [Clifton Mould] contact the ref immediately! Which he won't, of course, 'cause he's on the centre green at the moment." We're then treated to the sight of a man 'sprint' in noticeably stately (almost slow motion) fashion across the centre green, "There's our Clerk of the Course sprinting across the centre green [30-second pause] and, when he's got his breath back, can the Clerk of the Course contact the referee!" Shortly afterwards we learn that the cause of the medical emergency is a twisted knee and, in all likelihood, this is irrefutable medical confirmation they really do have considerable dirt on the track at Axe Edge. One fan near me isn't impressed, "It's daft! If it's not the tapes, it's the staff's knee!" They say little dogs bite hard and clearly this must be the case because the paramedics have to go and collect the stricken track staff member in the ambulance! During this enforced delay, Graham Tagg tries to drum up some custom for the food kiosk with a slightly over-detailed description of what's on offer, "Don't forget to visit the Burger Bar this afternoon – it's got cheese burgers and beef burgers!"

In football a striker known for his ability to poach goals has recently become known in modern parlance as "a fox in the box". This afternoon Buxton have the speedway equivalent with a 'Rocket at Reserve' in the form of Gareth Isherwood who wins the delayed heat 8 in some style. Each time he takes to the track this afternoon, Gareth appears to improve with every race. Elsewhere on the track during heat 8, the Battle of the Wildmen sees Kyle Newman fall and remount and so give sufficient delay for Paul Burnett to ensure that he gains his second point of the meeting with another third place. This Buxton heat advantage levels the score and they remain so after the next heat that features an attractive contest for third place between Brendan Johnson and Lewis Dallaway (in a race won by Ben Taylor). Stood in the pits, Jayne Moss manages my expectations, "We're running out of riders. It's close now but Weymouth have strength in depth! We've used our two strongest riders for rider replacement already and even Gareth, who has six, isn't having his best meeting. It's most unusual for him not to win heat 2. We beat Plymouth here and they weren't very happy! We've only lost once – to Boston – but I think today could be another defeat." Fresh from his comfortable victory in heat 9, Ben Taylor wandered over with a few questions for Jayne.

[Ben Taylor] "How many more meetings do we have here then?"

[Jane] "Well, that's the sixty-four thousand dollar question! – about two or three."

[Ben] "Not many then!"

[Jayne] "Nah."

[Ben] "When's the dinner dance?"

[Jayne] "15th"

In front of us, heat 10 is already under way and Jayne pedagogically draws Ben's attention to the on track action that unfolds in front of us, "Look at Lee Smart, how he goes round here!" We all intently watch Lee Smart ride with style and comfort round the track to win with some ease. This Weymouth heat advantage is immediately nullified in the next race won by Gareth Isherwood but, much more significantly, Lewis Dallaway finishes third ahead of Weymouth Wildcats [notional] number 1 Andrew Bargh who, again, finishes last to record a three race minimum. It's not his best performance and it would prove costly for his team. Lee Smart appeared likely to power to victory in heat 12 and this became a certainty when second placed Ben Taylor got completely out of shape on the fourth bend of lap one to relegate himself to the rear of the field. Traditionally the clash of the big guns, this afternoon's heat 13 proved to be a tactical battle between the clubs' respective team managers' Jack Lee for Buxton and Jem Dicken (with the help of Laurence Rogers) for Weymouth. Brendan Johnson came in to replace the out of sorts Bargh (and finished second) while for Buxton Scott Whittington took a rider replacement ride in place of Jack Roberts but finished last to record his own three ride race minimum. More significantly, in the penultimate heat Gareth Isherwood replaced his fellow reserve Scott Whittington and then won the race! With his partner Lewis Dallaway second, this suddenly took the Hitmen into the lead for the first time since the opening race of the meeting. By now, the sky had become both lighter and brighter to reflect the upbeat mood of the Buxton fans. At one stage during the final race of the meeting, it appeared the visitors – with Karl Mason up front and Lee Smart third (after he passed Ben Taylor) – had secured the 4-2 they needed to draw the meeting. However, it was only a temporary illusion for, at the very moment Smart passed Taylor, John Branney reciprocated overtaking manoeuvres to zoom into the lead past Mason. This revised race order didn't change again over the final two laps of the race and, with the last heat drawn, Buxton secured a narrow 2-point victory (46-44).

The Buxton team then went back out onto the track to enjoy a rather joyous victory celebration parade lap while, over the tannoy, we learnt that captain John Branney has been awarded Man of the Match for his paid 16 points from 6 rides (although personally I would have awarded this to Gareth Isherwood for his 15 points from 7 rides at reserve). Once the victory lap is over and the adulation has subsided, we're then treated to some impressive practice laps from a new rider in the Buxton number 5 race tabard. Instantly, he looks a class apart from the riders who've just competed in the Conference League meeting and, so he should, since he's ex World Champion Sam Ermolenko! John Rich and Mushy Pea pack up the trackshop with fastidious care aware that there could be questions later ("Dave Rattenberry asks more freaking questions than freaking anyone I know – maybe he was a policeman in a previous life?"). As we leave the burger van man calls out to John Rich, "Where were you for your burger today?"

[John] "It's alright."

[Burger van man] "I had no wastage today."

[John] "That's good isn't it?!"

14th September Buxton v. Weymouth (Conference League) 46-44

CHAPTER 39.

Stoke v. Redcar:

"Hit me! Big Ty? Big Ty! Hit it! Hit it! You gotta appreciate that!"

14th September

Though John Rich has kindly volunteered to lead the way from Buxton to Stoke, on our exit from the stadium car park we immediately get stuck behind the burger van man and his trailer. Our progress isn't helped by what looks like a slow puncture for one of the trailer wheels. Across the hills to the regular road network, it's mostly single-track roads. There are a number of opportunities to overtake but John is apparently oblivious to them despite the snail-like speed of the vehicle ahead. If we were to travel all the way to Stoke behind the burger van I worry that we'll actually miss the next weekend's meeting. A sudden rush of blood strikes John, who apparently forgets I don't know the route and/or I'm behind him, when he decides to suicidally overtake just at the moment the single-track road joins the junction of the winding, twisting, dangerous road to Stoke. Stuck behind this slow-moving vehicle, my choices appear to be to overtake suicidally or get lost. The contours of the road (in the general direction of Stoke Speedway) through these picturesque rolling hills are such that I can intermittently see John's car some way off in the distance. With double white lines, blind dips and hairpin bends rather than just become another road accident statistic, I crawl along and contemplate the meaning of life on a slow drive through this part of the Derbyshire Peak District on a road laid out like a ribbon before me. I manage a slightly less suicidal overtake to eventually catch up with John and follow him on an extremely complicated route that still requires I jump red lights and narrowly miss oncoming traffic. Eventually we arrive in the area known as the Loomer Road Industrial Estate. Stoke speedway have their home here and, since it's not long until tapes are due to rise, there's a substantial queue of cars that edge their way gingerly forward through the entrance gates into the Loomer Road car park.

Caroline Tattum along with her regular race-day team of Gaynor, Torty and Gabrielle are already hard at work. They welcome and banter with the fans, take their admission money, sell raffle tickets as well as also make sure they have their free official Stoke Easy-Rider Potters 2008 Matchday Magazine and Racecard. Caroline expected my visit but had forgotten about it. At the key revenue moment of the week, she doesn't have time to talk though does kindly give me a copy of the Matchday Magazine and Racecard that nowadays is included as part of the admission (or costs £2 for additional copies). The Premier League meeting against Redcar is a re-arranged fixture from Saturday July 12th and, consequently, the march of Time's winged chariot means that changes in rider averages, management cunning and injuries dictate the back-page racecard will need some amendment. This is particularly true of the Stoke line-up for tonight since there's been both injuries and some alteration to the allocation of team places. It's a task further complicated for the occasional visitor by all the similar-sounding 'foreign' names of some of their riders – Krister Jacobsen, Klaus Jakobsen and, of course, Jesper Kristiansen. The Redcar side of the racecard is altogether less complicated affair since Benji Compton replaces Daniel Giffardsson at number 6 in their team. Whatever the actual team compositions, I always relish my trips to Loomer Road since the racing has avoided dull or processional in favour of consistently entertaining each and every time I've visited.

The complimentary Stoke Matchday Magazine and Racecard shares some design elements of the "free" programme you get at Sheffield speedway though, the Loomer Road version not only has the bonus of greater length (12 pages) but more use of colour. As a document, it also shares some similarities with the excellent Matchday Magazine they produce at Newcastle speedway but, given that it's free, from a value point of view this will necessarily trump any document for which you pay £2.50. Inside the Stoke Matchday Magazine and Racecard, there's a column by Howard Jones – someone who, in artistic sensibility (rather than campness) terms, could be considered the Brian Sewell of Speedway. For many years, he has been the one-man driving force behind the end-of-season programme reviews that you find in the *Speedway Star*. The language and almost wilfully obscure criteria that Howard uses to analyse these programmes often leads you to wonder if he's somehow confused them with something altogether more complicated or artistic. His analytical criteria for 2008 has all the usual variables to help his rumination and discrimination. These include cover, design, research, racecard and value for money. They say beauty is in the eye of the beholder and, inevitably, with loosely defined categories of sensibility (rather than fact) there's a natural tendency for generalisation and interpretation. Howard is never happier than when he views a programme through the optic of its more technical aspects: namely proper paragraphing, indentation, photograph cropping and clarity, old-fashioned design, mediocre print quality, and so on. It would be a rare fan that over-engineers their enjoyment of any programme beyond the need for interesting articles and a reasonably accurate racecard. [1]

Keith McGhie prays for a win

The grandstand and terraces of the Loomer Road Stadium have an old-fashioned charm, despite the slightly worn nature of some of the fixtures and fittings. It also has a glass-fronted bar area that provides a panoramic view of the whole track except where your view is slightly obscured by the stanchions of the grandstand or the laudable safety feature of their air fence. If you're fortunate enough to be a sponsor (or arrive early) you can sit at a table right by the window and overlook the track. With little time to go before the action starts, there's a real buzz, urgency and hubbub of activity in the bar area, which also houses the trackshop and the popular refreshment kiosk. The general buzz of the atmosphere has been further improved by a large contingent of exuberant Redcar fans as always boisterously keen to watch their team ride. They abound with good-natured bonhomie, some are attired in fancy dress and collectively they enjoy their use of the terraces, bar and catering kiosk. The Croesus-like Dave Rattenberry is ensconced behind the tables of his trackshop that's located between the end of the bar and the wall of the gents toilets. He's got a cheery word for passing punters and, as owner of trackshops past and present dotted all over the country, he knows the majority of fans by sight if not by name. Prominently displayed on his stall, the latest edition of *Backtrack* catches my eye and I'm immediately excited by the breathless front-page promise of an article about Reading speedway in 1975 (the year they arrived at Smallmead). Disappointingly, this hasn't been specially written but is an extract from Arnie Gibbons' deservedly praised book *Tears and Glory*.

Track work

Though my books cover the minutiae and trivia of the people and places I encounter on my speedway tour around the tracks, Dave Rattenberry is always happy to suggest additional material for future books. He'd like them to become even more detailed than they already are, "Put in your book that you took a magazine off my stall and put it back when you'd read it!" If I were to religiously pursue this police statement-like line of coverage then, that way, madness would lie. Since he also runs the trackshop at the South Tees Motorsports Park, I grill Dave about the visitors. "Jason Pipe is a great bloke – he can't half talk though!" This sounds a bizarre criticism when it comes from

Pre-meeting pits

[1] Interestingly, the bright light of democracy shone through in the 2008 Speedway Star programme reviews when the veil of anonymity was lifted so much so that not only were the judges named (Howard Jones, Mike Berry and, for one issue, Chris Durno) but, when the Stoke programme came up for review, Howard magnanimously recused himself from the process and left the impartial analysis to his regular (2008) partner-in-crime Mike Berry. Nonetheless, it was still adjudged the fourth best programme in the Premier League and the 10th best programme in British speedway.

the chatty Dave Rattenberry. Dependent upon your point of view, it's either good or bad fortune that both Stoke and Redcar will finish outside the top four places in the 2008 Premier League. They definitely won't take part in the inaugural play-offs to determine who will race against an Elite League club for the honour of possible promotion to the upper echelon of British speedway. Such a promotion would signal (further) financial ruin for most Premier League clubs. Dave doesn't have much time for this new-fangled invention and believes it to be a charade. "There won't be any relegation from the Elite League – don't be daft! The only way there'll be a promotion is if King's Lynn were to come up 'cause you can't be a promoter of two teams in the same league." With an attractive display of Stoke Easy-Riders Potters anoraks hung behind him, you don't have to bother with much detective work to notice that an incredible stylistic similarity exists between the colour and design of the Stoke anoraks and those worn in greater numbers by the fans of the Redcar Bears who are stood drink in hand at the bar or *en masse* on the terraces. After many successful years in the trackshop business, Dave sensibly knows that once you've found a design that pleases people, at worst the teams you've provided them for will only meet each other a couple of times a season to spot their blatantly identikit anoraks. Dave didn't get where he is today with his burgeoning trackshop empire without business flair.

Potters presenter George Andrews is also in the bar and sits quietly at a table lost in deep study of the Matchday Magazine and Racecard. Given the substantial number of changes quite what this will tell him is unclear. Clearly George likes to take a few minutes of quiet contemplation to drink in the atmosphere and also psychologically prepare himself for his hours of breathlessly enthusiastic commentary ahead. Like speedway's slightly cynical version of Smashie and Nicey, George Andrews doesn't suffer from catagelophobia ("plenty of people write about me – not always nice things!") and, indeed, exudes the air and casually confident demeanour of a well-practised public performer. He's keen to draw my attention to the fact that the previous week's Stoke Matchday Magazine and Racecard saw club promoter Dave Tattum praise Nicki Pedersen in his 'The Potters' View' column. Apparently Nicki had practised at Loomer Road and, afterwards, pronounced it "awesome". Contrary to some people's perception of Nicki's attitude, Dave was keen to highlight that "unlike some others, Nicki always makes a point to thank people who've helped him!"

The Matchday Magazine and Racecard also features a regular column called 'Tracking the Visitors' written by Wimbledon uber-fan (and Internet Mr Angry) Derek Barclay. His predisposition towards the brilliance of all things Dons (particularly the Conference League version) means that his weekly snapshot of the racing career of every rider who appears for that week's visitors to Loomer Road is relentlessly viewed through the optic of their previous Stoke connections, tendentious "Wimbledon in London" 'roots' or their even more tangential Crayford connections. None of the Redcar Bears has any previous connection to the Potteries but they do have some connection with South-West London. Consequently we learn that Dan Giffard is a "one-time Wimbledon rider" (though tonight he's replaced by Benji Compton who has absolutely no connections to Stoke or Wimbledon even though he's already ridden for a substantial number of British speedway clubs) and also that Australian Scott James "like Giffard made a name for himself at the late-lamented Plough Lane track in "tennis country", Wimbledon in London!" This reads like Derek writes for the incredibly small number of foreign visitors to this country who somehow manage to venture to Stoke Speedway but haven't ever heard of Wimbledon. I'm unaware of Wimbledons elsewhere but, given our historic strong connections to our former colonies, they probably also have them in Australia and in the state of Massachusetts on the east coast of America. Derek was, of course, famously, the programme editor for the Conference League incarnation of the Dons and this season has converted to temporarily become passionate about Stoke Speedway. It's an admiration close to stalking brought on by his devotion for veteran speedway rider Dermot Mark 'Buzz' Burrows who now plies his trade in the Potteries. With the disproportionate mentions of a defunct speedway club, new arrivals could be forgiven for thinking that Newcastle-under-Lyme had been nominated as Wimbledon's twin town. Sadly, if Derek is here to watch tonight's encounter I don't bump into him so we all have to satisfy ourselves with a peculiar, blurry photograph that, from a quality point of view, I can't imagine satisfies the exacting standards Howard Jones usually applies to any image included in a speedway programme he analyses. This photo has the look of a snatched late-night webcam shot or grainy Crimewatch quality that fails to capture Derek's usual geography teacher look. In search of inspiration for his presentational work on the night of September 14th, George Andrews continues to avidly study the superseded Matchday Magazine and Racecard from July 12th! I expect his professionalism will dictate he'll keep spurious Wimbledon or Crayford mentions to a minimum.

Stoke v. Redcar: *"Hit me! Big Ty? Big Ty! Hit it! Hit it! You gotta appreciate that!"*

Like London buses or policemen, while there's never a speedway presenter when you want one, suddenly two come along together. Sat only a few seats away is off duty Redcar announcer Keith McGhie who chats amiably with a couple of other Redcar fans. The next time I come to the STMP Keith suggests that I search out and speak to "Sylvie who runs the office. Her husband is Clerk of the Course. They went to the first-ever Halifax meeting (they worked there) and then they went to every club meeting there and also at Bradford until it shut in 1997." Keith nods towards the crowded bar area, "I was just saying but for our fans, it would be empty here tonight." It's easy to pick out the Redcar fans on account of their anoraks, boisterousness, the musicality of their accents but also because there's a person in a bear suit as well as a posse of girls who, for reasons that completely escape me, have come along tonight wearing inflatable rubber rings! Sadly I don't learn the significance of their attire or its close connection to the club since it must (surely) be too obscure to be a widely practised North Eastern sexual fetish? Keith has read the chapter in my latest book *Concrete for Breakfast* that covers my visit to Redcar: "Having read your book I didn't realise that it was my job to promote Newcastle speedway! I always had the impression that that was George English's job and that mine was to promote Redcar speedway. I mentioned him last night but that's only because he's a Newcastle season-ticket holder." When I confess that I'm a Sunderland season-ticket holder, Keith retorts, "You've got just as many problems as him then!" With sight of the riders limping across the shale in their steel shoes from the pits gate on the fourth bend towards their parade in front of the home-straight grandstand, Keith quickly vacates the bar area to watch the racing from outside on the terraces.

I can't say that I blame him. The experience of speedway behind glass is equivalent of sex with a condom – it's definitely safer and the sensation is more or less the same but some indefinable quality remains noticeably absent. I've chosen to have a small display of my books on the table opposite Dave Rattenberry's trackshop and these have kindly been faithfully guarded by Mr I.C.A. Crook (aka Mushy Pea). He greets me with the news that there have been no sales. To my mind, this is the ideal location to attract attention. It's opposite the trackshop, by the well-trodden route that leads to the refreshment kiosk and a door that leads outside to the terraces (that overlooks the pits and fourth bend) and also directly opposite the gents toilet door so you can't avoid sight of my display as you exit the facilities. The lack of paper towels and soap is a hygiene issue I blank from my mind. The closest I get to a sale all day (given I also sold none at Buxton) is the Bears fan who comes up to inform me in a surprised tone of voice, "I've seen one of your books for sale in the [Waterstones] bookshop in Middlesbrough!" If my visit hasn't exactly been a success, then Stoke fan John Gerahty, who used to live only 10 yards from Sun Street, has a much superior tale of woe. "I've been made redundant, my catalytic converter has been stolen and I've just had to have my brakes done!"

On the centre green, George Andrews cranks up his trademark bluster and enthusiasm for the benefit of the fans though, the first time he runs through the changes to the Stoke team line up, he does it so quickly that you half suspect he's decided to practise his entry for a speed reading contest. After George's description of the changes to the Matchday Magazine and Racecard, it would be a brave man that could say who really would ride where or, even more complicatedly, how on earth you spelt the words Jacobsen, Jakobsen and Kristiansen. Years of experience and his innate sense of professionalism prompts George to read through the Stoke team once more, this time much more slowly, nonetheless we're all still left somewhere short of clarification. Collectively we definitively gather that Stoke have Jason Bunyan as a guest in the number 1 race tabard, club captain Ben Barker remains at number 3 (and is cheered loudly in the bar and on the terraces) while Andrew Moore continues to occupy the number 5 in a heat leader position (at least until his average drops further). When it comes to the other Easy-Riders Potters riders we'll just have to make it up as we go along. If George's fluency and familiarity with the rider names makes it hard to grasp the exact make-up of the Stoke team then things take an altogether more surreal turn when he recites the Redcar Bears rider line up in a manner that makes it sound like the hit parade. We learn "At number 5 it's Troy Proctor" and, just afterwards we're told "And at number 7 it's Arlo Badger."

The first race starts with promise for the Potters when Redcar's number 2, Josh Auty, is excluded under the two-minute time allowance and his place taken by Arlo 'Badgerman' Bugeja. When the race gets under way Gary Havelock wins easily with Stoke 'specialist' guest Jason Bunyan third. The Badgerman comes out in successive races and shows consistency to obtain his second consecutive last place. Up front by some margin, Stoke riders with complicated Danish names – Jakobsen (Klaus) and Kristiansen (Jesper) – cruise to a maximum heat advantage. Though the second race hasn't even finished, George Andrews's excitement levels quickly get close to ecstatically orgasmic. "And they're really milking it! Come on – let's hear it!" he implores the crowd who react with a sustained campaign of indifference, if judged by the lack of roar we don't hear over the speakers that pipe the rich sounds of the terraces into the bar area. Not interested enough to leave his gaggle of mates stood at the bar to watch the weirdly similarly named foreigners "milk it" for the Potters, ex-rider Paul Thorp swaggers past and into the toilets while an older star-struck Stoke fan calls out his (probably) regular suggestion, "It's about bloody time you got back on your bike!" Race night must exhaust the lady behind the bar based on the sheer number of times she rushes from behind her counter to briefly watch the race at the windows before she dashes back into position again. She does this each and every race unless she needs to serve someone more interested in beer than the race action.

The third race of the night showcases the canny track-craft that Buzz Burrows employed to such spectacular effect when he raced regularly against novices in the Conference League. As he crosses the line at the end of the first lap, third-placed Buzz glances over his shoulder at the close-following James Grieves before he then deliberately drifts wide to ostensibly cramp and disconcert his rival. Rather than shut off, the battle-hardened and always combative James Grieves twists his throttle yet further to round his erstwhile rival as they head deep into the apex of the bend and exits from the second bend easily ahead of Buzz to relegate him to last place. This showcases that experienced Premier League riders aren't as easily discombobulated unlike many novice Conference League riders were during the recent glory years for Burrows at Plough Lane when he rode so successfully for the Wimbledon Plc promotional team. Throughout the race a girl in the bar yells: "Go on Buzz!" with a frenzy and repetition that sadly fails to register with the rider through the glass, above the clamour of the race and the noise-cancelling effect of his crash helmet. Buzz trails home in last place. Up front his captain Ben Barker wins and a lady wearing an item of clothing emblazoned with the words "Ben Barker's Barmy Army" greets this victory with a joyful passion that approaches ecstasy. She'd been at Buxton earlier (though Ben hadn't) and, now that he has triumphed first time out, she can really let rip with her adulation. At the start of heat 4, Klaus Jakobsen has an engine failure at the tapes. It's a misfortune that indicates that this member of Ben Barker's Barmy Army is a relatively recent convert to speedway since she squeals "wha – hey!!" Only to be told by the girl next to her, "it's one of ours!" This temporarily punctures her mood and, if she could tell which side was which, Troy Proctor would have deflated it further when he powered past Andrew Moore as they exited the second bend second time round (after a neck-and-neck battle for the duration of the first lap). Taking another summer away from his job in the Mr Kipling factory, Andrew Moore tries to launch an immediate reply along the back straight but fails to catch up with, let alone pass, his opponent. With Arlo Bugeja third, the Bears have narrowed the overall points advantage for the Potters to 2 (13-11). On the centre green, George puts in an impressive plug for my book, apparently known locally as "Konker-reet furr berek-fust". Though in his excitement, George's explanations and accent might confuse, never mind that he delivers the odd hilarious malapropism, he's conscientious and professional enough to delivers his promised name check (something that is more than can be said for some other announcers/presenters). Those fans who are keen to learn the outcome of the GP Challenge and the identities of the three qualifiers discover this result is apparently, "Bay-ger, Wazz-e-lack [and some other mumbled Polish name followed by a few other random words in a statement that ends on a crescendo with] all them to 09 GP!"

Dave Rattenberry demonstrates that he's missed his calling as a "meeter and greeter" in the entrance of an out-of-town shopping centre or, perhaps, given their commendable employment record of senior citizens, he could don the orange apron they issue to their staff at B&Q. In fact, on race day Dave traditionally wears a pouch-cum-apron to keep some of his horde of money in. It's an unfortunately positioned garment since his almost continuous desire to ensure that his notes and coins haven't somehow been magically spirited away, lead you to suspect he's the reigning all-comers World Pocket Billiards Champion. Dave isn't impressed with the news of the results from the GP Challenge: "Did you hear George announce the result of the GP? It was Ulamek that won it, Walasek was second – how on earth did he say his name? – and Bjerre was third. He's abysmal! But not as bad as Mike Bennett though." When she doesn't rush from behind the counter to the windows, the occasionally underemployed younger girl stationed behind the bar uses her time to obsessively compulsively straighten all the bar towels. It's a lengthy bar and since customers repeatedly leave them in disarray they require endless obsessive attention. Outside on the centre green, it sounds as if George has unilaterally increased the number of heats in a speedway meeting to 20, "As we move to the end of the first quarter of tonight's meeting with the fifth heat!" However far we are through the actual meeting, George has definitely entered 'the zone' and, consequently, we're treated to a stream of consciousness style commentary

---

Stoke v. Redcar: *"Hit me! Big Ty? Big Ty! Hit it! Hit it! You gotta appreciate that!"*

that manages to be punk, post-modern and still vaguely echo Fred Flintstone's Yabba Dabba Doo. In George's case, this takes the form of an exhortation-cum-incantation, "Let's shift the shale! Let's burn some rubber! Let's go racing!"

It's an instruction that obviously has a deep and immediate psychological effect upon Gary Havelock who, no sooner has the referee put the riders under orders, touches the tapes and is excluded for his troubles. Benji Compton replaces Havvy in the rerun but the race only gets as far as the third bend before a determined Josh Auty (on the inside) battles with Buzz Burrows for second only for them to tangle and Buzz find himself plunged into the third-bend air-fence. In recent years there have been some severe injuries at Loomer Road – Craig Watson, Luke Priest and Dan Giffard spring to mind – so the addition of the inflatable safety furniture has been a godsend at this track. There's a substantial delay while Buzz lies prostrate on the shale (though he gets up immediately upon news that his bike has been repaired) though simultaneously, there's drama two tables away from me when Peter Oliver collapses. He's regularly accompanied to Stoke meetings by his brother, Clive, who sports a similar hairstyle but has Downs Syndrome. Clive must have the reverse Midas touch since it was only five minutes previously I noticed him affectionately stroke his brother on the back of the head. The medical staff have to split their duties between Buzz on the track and the prostrate Peter Oliver in the bar. Paramedics crowd round and minister oxygen while Clive howls anxiously. Incidents in grandstand bars, like those on motorways, instantly attract a crowd of rubberneckers. Having pulled "an edge" (as they say in the street demonstration business when there's a big crowd), Dave Rattenberry's innate salesmanship immediately kicks in and he repeatedly shouts above Clive's howls, "Reduced Stoke flags!" Despite the oxygen and the news of the price reductions, Peter doesn't look in a good way and, when the medical people decide to remove his brother from the building, Clive's howls reach a crescendo that he intersperses with frenzied tears and Rat intersperses with further exciting discount merchandise news. Clive is comforted by a kindly man with the most incredible pre-Raphaelite hairstyle (who I later learn is called Jeff). One of the country's most under-rated and politely solicitous promoters, Dave Tattum takes time out from his duties (albeit the meeting is substantially delayed and can't recommence without the medical staff) to personally check on the situation. Dave Rat is also worried about the brothers, "He's the best customer for DVDs I have! He buys them all – Redcar, Stoke, Wolves, everything!" Rat metaphorically crosses his fingers, blanks the tower of unsold DVDs from his mind and hopes that Peter will soon be safely out of hospital with his wallet. A man in the crowd knows the brothers well, "Peter's been mithered all week. First they're both diabetic but don't do it properly. Clive only eats beans and cake – he lives on beans and cake. Clive has day release but he's been sent home and they won't let him go back. They've shown him how to shower but he doesn't do as he's told! Peter would like to tidy his brother's place up as it's totally upside down [and full of DVDs] but he won't let him."

After a half-hour delay the full complement of paramedics are back on the centre green and the doctor has returned to be on call in the pits. The three rider re-rerun sees Benji Compton fly from the tapes and the sometimes ponderous Buzz Burrows also starts with alacrity but then, even though they're team mates, manages to hold back the ultra-fast Ben Barker with an almost telepathic series of blocking manoeuvres! After some delay, Barker eventually gets past Buzz to launch his pursuit of Benji Compton. Ben trails behind Benji for the third lap and most of the fourth until he draws level on the inside of the third bend of the final lap. With the race at his mercy and the majority of the hard work done, Barker then has a moment of madness and knocks Compton off on the fourth bend. The race is stopped and awarded to Compton with a second place for Buzz Burrows to create a bizarre 2-3 scoreline that takes the overall scores to 15-14. Veteran of the Stoke speedway scene, John Woolridge queries the fall, "He only frightened him to death, that's why he dropped off!" With still only five heats completed, George Andrews apologises for the delay before he engages in further public struggles with his fractions, "We've had the first quarter of the meeting elapse. Let's hope we can move things along from now!"

Heats 6 and 7 see an exchange of 5-1s, though the seventh heat should have been called back after a ragged start from which Redcar took full advantage. Andrew Moore trails in last. John Woolridge comments, "It's very, very slick out there tonight! Andrew Moore said that before the start and it's got worse!" According to George Andrews, the eighth heat features Scott Autrey in place of Josh Auty. In the bar Josh has his own cheerleader in the form of Sylvie who implores, "Come on Josh! Come on Josh!" The young rider is mounted on a rough-sounding bike (so rough we can even hear it in the bar) and, as he trails some distance behind in last place, Sylvie implores, "Oh Josh!" In mid-race she switches her Redcar allegiances and instead shouts, "Come on Benji! Come on Benji!" to encourage him into

Stoke v. Redcar: *"Hit me! Big Ty? Big Ty! Hit it! Hit it! You gotta appreciate that!"*

battle with Team Jacobsen/Jakobsen. The ninth race of the night treats us to the bargain spectacle of two races in one. Up front Ben Barker is closely pursued by Troy Proctor while, some way behind them, third placed Buzz Burrows leads Arlo Badger/Bugeja. As they swoop into the third bend for the second time, Bugeja pressures Buzz who practically swallow dives from his bike in a manner that suggests a professional foul but also hints at pantomime. Buzz smashes into the same section of the fence he'd previously tested in the fifth heat. The talk in the bar is that Buzz has been into that section of the fence so often this season that they'd had to double reinforce the panels and would soon name it after him! If the dive was intended as a professional foul then it had some merit since Proctor led the race at the moment of the stoppage. Though, that said, Barker had massively accelerated just as the riders entered the first bend of the third lap to draw neck-and-neck alongside his rival. Over the loudspeakers, George goes mental and, as far as I can make out, excitedly shouts, "Hit me! Big Ty? Big Ty! Hit it! Hit it! You gotta appreciate that!" John Woolridge informs me that Buzz's dedication to the Potters cause is such that he'd ride through the pain barrier for the club. "He's got quite a bad wrist injury. It's not broken but he took quite a chunk out of it and it's probably stiffening up!"[2] The marks Buzz gained for artistic merit are insufficient to render his exclusion as the primary cause of the stoppage, null and void. The race is rerun and, as the riders leave the second bend, Ben Barker is stone last. He then immediately passes Bugeja at lightning speed, tracks and passes Proctor on the third bend second time round and then powers onwards to win by some distance. He punches the air as he crosses the line, the home crowd go comparatively wild and the girl from the Ben Barker Barmy Army leaps up and down. George Andrews acclaims the win but again I can't quite make out the exact terms of his garbled, ecstatic praise. Potters guest, Jason Bunyan, suffers the mechanical misfortune of an engine failure in heat 10 to allow Redcar's James Grieves and Chris Kerr to record their second 5-1 together and take their team into a narrow 29-30 lead.

Before almost every race, George treats us to Stoke speedway's version of a Buddhist chant, "Your riders! Your colours! Your gate positions!" It's beautiful and mysterious in its own way! Out on the track – if we have an air fence, we might as well test it – appears to be the motto of some riders and heat 11 sees Josh Auty test the second-bend section with a dramatic fall that Mushy Pea puts down to the fact, "He had nowhere to go – only the fence!" Worth the admission money for his spectacular racing alone, Ben Barker makes yet another poor start in the 12th heat only to serve up the treat of another big race rush from the third place up to first past one of the many Jakobsens and Redcar's James Grieves. From the centre green a jubilant George Andrews burbles, "Come on – let's hear it!" If workshop hours are worth points on the track, then Potters guest Jason Bunyan hasn't quite spent enough time there this week. His spluttering equipment results in his exclusion under the two-minute time allowance in his final race of the night (heat 13). A score of 3 paid 5 won't be what the Stoke Easy-Riders Potters management expected when they booked him to be their number 1. When presented with an opportunity to transform your fortunes, you have to seize the moment and capitalise on your advantage. The Redcar partnership of Havvy and Troy do just that when they make no mistake in a race that now suddenly features weakened opposition in the form of reserve Klaus Jakobsen and the somewhat lacklustre Andrew Moore. What at the end of heat 12 had been a close meeting (36-35) suddenly becomes a struggle for the home team who trail 37-40 with only two heats to go. On a race night when anything that can go wrong does go wrong and any delay that can happen does happen, the 14th heat is rerun and finishes disastrously from a Stoke point of view when Burrows retires from the race and Kristiansen finishes third. These consecutive 5-1s for the visitors enable them to win the meeting with the luxury of one heat still to go. Judged from an entertainment and pence-per-hour point of view, the fans have witnessed a meeting to remember. The Redcar victory is built on a consistent team performance throughout with the exception of Josh Auty who rides to a four-race minimum (with two exclusions) and Arlo Bugeja who only manages paid 3. Jason Bunyan's disappointing performance for Stoke was arguably the difference between the two teams. Ben Barker excels as the most spectacular rider on show, while the Stoke top scorer with the popular surname Krister Jacobsen goes about his work unobtrusively to finish with 11 points from five rides. Overall, both on and off the track, I enjoy yet another enthralling visit at Loomer Road.

14th September Stoke v. Redcar (Premier League) 41-48

[2] Buzz would look back on the 2008 season with Neil Evans in the *Speedway Star*. "I've worn knee and ankle strapping for a while...you just don't shake off the bumps and bruises so easily as you get older. Deep down, you know that but there's no easy options when you are racing and you have to go in where it hurts. Start backing off and you let yourself, team mates and supporters down and that's when the rot sets in."

Stoke v. Redcar: *"Hit me! Big Ty? Big Ty! Hit it! Hit it! You gotta appreciate that!"*

CHAPTER 40.

Sheffield v. Scunthorpe:
"His wife Angie Collins used to cut my hair – when I had hair."

18th September

It's a gloriously sunny day and the fastest track in British speedway looks in perfect condition for tonight's local derby clash between the Sheffield Tigers and the Scunthorpe Scorpions. It's a timeless scene inside the Sheffield Speedway Office where Neil Machin and Janet both have a cigarette on the go and I'm just in time for a cup of tea. Janet always makes a lovely cup of tea and informs me "It's the soft water" that gives it its premium taste. Neil takes the opportunity to have a quick ride of one of his favourite hobbyhorses – namely, the modern lack of speedway coverage on the inside back pages of any tabloid newspaper you care to name. The solution is apparently simple, "We need someone who can take the small story and make it into something that the papers want to cover! The back pages every day are full of non-stories. We do have something to say, we take a big story [names some examples] and do nothing with it!" The anonymity of the sport does have its advantages though. "The BSPA bigwigs think we should be getting the coverage but, they don't realise, if we did we'd look even sillier than we do now! You're not going to attract people fiddling with rule changes or trying to bend them. That doesn't excite people! Imagine if people were paying attention to what went on in speedway, then they'd ask a few questions of these people. They might ask how people could represent their country and still be chasing two months later to be paid!" Talk of the media has Neil come over all wistful, "I like to remember that we started off Nigel Pearson[1] , even if he sometimes forgets it! He's a real technical detail man rather than human interest stories!" This will be a busy week at Owlerton Stadium since Sheffield will also stage the Premier League Riders' Championship on Sunday. Neil tells me, "We expect about 3,000." These are the numbers that any speedway club in the country would dream about on a regular race night. Though he has many years of experience of this speedway promotional lark, Neil still finds it difficult to estimate the number of programmes that he needs for any meeting. It's an awkward figure to guesstimate/estimate and Neil isn't going to be nominated for Environmentalist of the Year any time soon. "I haven't sold out of programmes any time this season. Every Monday I order 1,500 and then, every Thursday at 11 [p.m.], I feel gutted to have to throw them away! We don't recycle them – we throw them away! What's your book called again? [Scribbles away in a pad] I'm writing Dave's [Hoggart's] script tonight for him. You're not in the programme. If you'd sent something you would have been. But, as you didn't, it's not! Thank goodness it's your cock-up, not mine!"

In the hour before the turnstiles open the Sheffield speedway office is the nerve centre of operations as well as a real hubbub of activity as people come and go before the action eventually switches to the pits area. Scunthorpe promoter Rob Godfrey comes in half-way through our programme's discussion. "I like to sell out [the programmes] every meeting if I can! We've had our best August ever – great crowds – so you won't hear me complaining. That said we've not run for a couple of weeks so it's gone a bit flat." Talk among speedway promoters inevitably reverts to a set number of well-worn topics, usually the unreliability of riders, the iniquity of whatever recent referee's decision has gone against them or what BSPA ruling has been a travesty of natural justice and, of course, the all-time favourite, outrageous and/or spiralling costs (whatever their cause) compared to revenues. Rob and Neil soon involve themselves in a meaningful discussion about start-gate tape prices. Apparently, Alf Weedon used to do them. Nowadays Neil pays £10 for his while, comparative speedway new boy, Rob only pays a bargain £3. Rob Godfrey leaves and Neil conducts some *ad hoc* research. "Where would you say you'd seen the biggest crowds this season? I find that you often hear of massive crowds but, when you get there yourself, the situation looks very different! I remember hearing of massive numbers at Somerset when they were having the Conference League but, when I stood on the centre green, they hadn't turned up that night."

[1] Apparently it was Colin Pratt at Cradley. Though, many are keen to claim this honour.

Away in the cool shade of the home-straight grandstand, Mick Gregory has already set out the majority of his merchandise for his trackshop stall. He's read about himself in my book *Concrete for Breakfast* and has a few questions. "What's that in the book about Mike Hunter being dead [it was a false rumour Mick heard at a meeting I'd attended last season] he's obviously alive! I used to stay with him when I used to do the tracks up there. You worry whether Edinburgh would survive without him! I think every foreign rider who's ever rode for Edinburgh has stayed there and the Aussies! I used to stay there before Jane lived with him. I asked him if he still did his own ironing and he said, 'To be honest I buy my shirts a size smaller and then they're self-ironing!'" It's a top tip but it's not as half as good as the prize Mike Hunter scooped in Scotland when he won a newspaper competition to find Scotland's most loyal sports fan. "He's going to the West Indies – Barbados – to watch the cricket. I've known him all these years and I didn't even know he was a cricket fan!" Mike would be knowledgeable enough to answer my trivia question ("Who's Scotland's best-ever opening batsman?") but Mick isn't and so wouldn't have answered that it's Desmond Haynes.

Speedway is a community filled with obsessive collectors, whether it's of information, memorabilia or memories. The turnstiles have now opened and Mick quizzes a small knot of fans that linger by the trackshop. "See this table here [bangs on it theatrically for effect] [it sounds substantial] guess where that comes from?" Blank looks are exchanged and shoulders shrugged. "Belle Vue! I got it around 1981!" I think with the rich history behind Mick's ownership of this table we may have found the exciting speedway back-page story that Neil Machin earlier lamented the absence of in the modern media. Moments later, I'm distracted by matters of fashion when a couple of stylishly dressed Scunthorpe fans arrive. On a visit to the tasteless mountain mansion of one of my publishing customers, I was shown an extensive collection of hugely valuable treasures and *objets d'art* that included a 9-foot high 'work of art' made from diamonds, amethysts and other exotic stones that closely resembled a vagina. It had been specially commissioned and, inevitably, was distinctively unique. Though ultimately homogenous in their garishness, it appears most speedway anoraks embrace this approach to design flair and combine a concatenation of clashing patterns allied to bright colours within the same garment. Thankfully, some clubs buck the trend and one of these is Scunny who arguably have produced a stylish and understated speedway anorak. Well, they might also have the traditional super garish ones as well but, the one in evidence here tonight, is a cream affair with blue trim apparently sponsored by Hendersons. It's almost unobtrusive enough to be worn on a non-speedway night! Though the club is Lincolnshire based, this garment could become Alan Partridge smart casual if set off with a smart pair of open-backed driving gloves (and could, possibly, be a real babe magnet at your local Wetherspoons). Mick is in mid-grumble with one of his customers about the latest magazine to hit the speedway market. "The first edition of *Classic Speedway* sold well but it was only £2. The next is £3.50 and, I think, it'll struggle! Especially as they have stories copied from *Backtrack* in them." The man holds a copy of the second issue in his hand and it's clear that the editors have continued their unique tree and shrub themed rider colour photo on the back cover, "If you copy from one it's plagiarism and if you copy from more than one it's research!" If Mick isn't so sure about *Classic Speedway* magazine then he's definitely a huge fan of the main retro magazine from the Tony McDonald stable. "*Backtrack* is brilliant! I love that, I do! The one that came out last week, I had to read every page straight away. I stayed up till 2.30 a.m. to finish it all. The article on the Collins brothers was fantastic! It's even more interesting when you've known them! I saw Peter Collins have his first-ever ride at Crewe and I remember saying to people he'd be a future world champion! It was 1971 maybe? His wife Angie used to cut my hair – when I had hair – and I was over in Manchester, 'cause she was a hairdresser."

We're distracted from our conversation by the roar of the bikes or, to be exact, the irksome whine of some tinny engines created by two mascots as they do their practice laps. The sound is amplified in the grandstand and isn't appreciated by Mick, "There's bloody two of them tonight! You can't hear yourself think, never mind what the customers are saying!" My book display gets temporary interest when a man comes up, looks at the Sexy7even girls on the cover and demands, "What are they? Bloomin' speedway riders or someint?"

Mick's not happy with the meagre attendance 20 minutes before the scheduled start time. "Look at this, 10 past 7 and there's hardly anybody here! You'll be amazed at the number of gaps later. Even at half-seven there'll only be 200 here then there'll be a last-minute rush 35 minutes before start time. Last year I'd have been running up and down [behind his historic trackshop tables] but look at it! Even though Scunthorpe should be popular, many people won't come 'cause they won't have enough money for tonight and Sunday!" On the telly, there's an alternative attraction of Portsmouth playing in Europe in the UEFA Cup, "It doesn't help when football's on, I tell you!" A fan stood by the trackshop feels that the Sheffield promotion aren't helped by the lacklustre display often put up by visiting teams. "Big home wins – where we get 60 points – aren't going to get people rushing through the turnstiles, are they? We have had some good meetings – even some of the ones we lost – and if the speedway's good that's what excites me and would excite the neutrals. We know some people who came to the Garry Stead GP last year and they couldn't believe what they saw. I've seen it twice on DVD and I can't either! It's got them hooked enough to want to come back and see some more, but we all know that some meetings are boring and it's not all highlights. Then, we're fans and always come along! The casual visitor isn't going to." Earlier Sheffield Wednesday fan Terry Andrew who's been coming to the Owlerton for 48 years had expressed surprise at how long last week's meeting against Somerset took to complete. "A mate of mine, Gary, has been coming down here 30 years and says he's not gonna come again 'cause of how long the ref took to run the meeting. Craig Ackroyd didn't care, there was no urgency and it took so long! At the meeting before that [versus Rye House, August 28th] Ekberg made a perfect inside pass of Wilson and he bloody dropped it and that ref Margaret Vardy excluded him. It's the sort of thing that's killing speedway! Neil Street said, 'it was always a body contact sport' but he says nowadays 'you daren't touch anyone!' It was completely the wrong decision and we were winning easily anyway."

Mick Gregory with tigers

Rider introductions

Ruminations on the appeals and travails of speedway in Sheffield are interrupted by a pre-recorded message from Dave Hoggart played at ear-splitting volume over the speaker system, "Live and direct from the darkest depths of the imagination! This is Owlerton Stadium home of the Sheffield Tigers." This announcement is the signal for the riders to troop out onto the track for the parade. Instead of the pre-recorded Dave Hoggart, we're treated to him live and direct as he attempts to enthuse the crowd with some news, "The happy half-hours have been extended. It's £1.50 a pint but, as ever, please, please, drink responsibility!" Dave welcomes Scunthorpe co-promoter Kenny Smith and also rolls out the metaphorical red carpet for Rob and Paul Godfrey. Observational as ever, an alternative career in the police force could beckon for him, "Looking at the faces of the riders on the track – there's clearly some serious stuff going on!" The absence of Ricky Ashworth from the Sheffield side should only be a minor inconvenience and, I gather from the confident chatter among the Sheffield fans, that they expect an easy and comprehensive victory over their local rivals. The Scorpions riders clearly haven't read the runes since Richard Hall and Emiliano Sanchez immediately storm to an impressive 5-1 race win. Skilfully Dave Hoggart focuses our attention onto the magnificence of the track rather than the performance of the Sheffield riders, "Wow! Didn't that look fast for the first couple of laps! I can tell you track conditions have improved considerably since last week and a couple of tons of shale have been put down for the PLRC on Sunday!" Though it's hidden by his crash helmet, Dave still confidently asserts, "Emiliano Sanchez always with a smile on his face." If there is a smile, this doesn't last throughout the rest of the meeting since these will be the only points Sanchez gains all night. Sponsored by Bob and Debbie Wilson of Disraeli's pub in Worksop, heat 2 is drawn, while a race win for Andre Compton in the next race narrows the overall points deficit to 2 points. Viktor Bergstrom is last in the race, has his given name misspelt throughout in the programme but also belies the typesetting error in

Sheffield v. Scunthorpe: *"His wife Angie Collins used to cut my hair – when I had hair."*

the Scunthorpe team scores section that rechristens him as 'Victory' Bergstrom! The fourth heat sees the Sheffield Tigers resume normal service to take their first maximum heat advantage of the night (a win for Lee Smethills ahead of his team mate Ben Wilson). Though, notionally not in the best form and up against a Scunthorpe side bountifully packed with riders who aren't frightened of the fast wide open spaces of the Owlerton track, this gives the Tigers a lead they won't relinquish for the remainder of the meeting. The fifth heat sees another win for Andre Compton. Behind him, Paul Cooper comes under sustained pressure from Richard Hall who makes repeated attempts to pass his rival before he finally does so on the second bend of the last lap. Mick Gregory nods his approval, "That was spectacular!"

They know how to create a traditional speedway atmosphere at Sheffield and true to form Deep Purple's *Smoke on the Water* plays loudly. Last week's complaint that Craig Ackroyd ran a very slow meeting can't be levelled against SCB official Barbara Horley. She's so quick on the buttons that six races are completed within the first 33 minutes. A slim-line Mick Gregory confesses his dietary secrets: "I only have chips once a week here and at home I have steamed vegetables and fish. [Pats stomach] It's only the red wine that helps this!" The seventh heat sees Scorpions claw back some of the points deficit with a 4-2 score helped by a race win for Magnus Karlsson. Sheffield reserve Kyle Hughes suffers an engine failure and Mick Gregory rushes over to say, "Kyle actually won a race last week – his second, I think!" The meeting is definitively killed off when Sheffield race to consecutive 5-1s that progress the score to 32-22. The meeting is only 54 minutes old and we've already had nine races. Mick Gregory isn't enjoying himself, "God, it's boring when it's like this!" Another feature of the musical entertainment at Owlerton Stadium is the frequent distinctive sound of the Hawaii Five-O theme music and, given Sheffield's reputation at home, this disc must wear out on a regular basis. For the last race before the interval, Scorpions team manager Kenny Smith decides to grant Magnus Karlsson the honour of the black-and-white helmet colour (though this elicits a groan from Scunthorpe fans nearby to me who believes Hall should don this garment in the next race). It's all rendered academic when Joel Parsons gates – let alone when, on the third bend of the second lap, Magnus Karlsson falls. It's a sight that prompts an old age pensioner to rush up to Mick Gregory's table and screech triumphantly, "Same place, just about, as he fell last week! [although that was Jason Doyle on a tactical ride for Somerset]. The track was atrocious last week – hit a bump and it was straight into the fence!" After the race Dave Hoggart notes with some understatement, "That was a shame – Magnus was just trying too hard!" With their tactical options partially exhausted, it's a fall that confirms that the result of this meeting is beyond doubt. Though the meeting is only 59 minutes old, we've had 10 races and already it's the interval. We all have the chance to contemplate the meaning of our lives or be mesmerised by the large moon shrouded in cloud that hangs low in the back-straight sky. When he's not at the trackshop, Mick Gregory is a delivery driver. "I called in at Somerset on Tuesday. I couldn't believe how basic it was! You'd think they'd have got a stand up by now! On the back straight, they have five seats four deep but the track looked fantastic, though! I tell you what, it'll be cold at Exeter if they don't have a stand. It's way out of Exeter. They'll need to put buses on for the OAPs who don't drive. I saw three speedway tracks in one day. I spotted Plymouth's from the road – it looked really small!"

I finally get to see one of the mountain of orange umbrellas Mick Gregory stocks sold to a young boy happy to part with his £3.95. Notionally the brolly is emblazoned with a tiger but it definitely looks more Tigger-like than anything like the one the speedway club use as their logo. A man with the biggest programme board I've seen this season stands authoritatively by the trackshop proud to own some equipment appropriate to the uniquely large-sized Sheffield programme! Scunthorpe manager Kenny Smith takes the last tactical roll of his dice in heat 14 when he brings in Richard Hall as a tactical substitute off 15 metres. Off gate 1 Victor (aka Viktor) Bergstrom's task will be to clamp down on the Sheffield pair of Paul Cooper and Lee Smethills and, thereby, give his team mate the chance to catch up. Sadly, whatever the previously agreed plan, it's immediately scuppered when Bergstrom massively rears at the gate to allow the Sheffield pair to escape into the distance. However, the Scunny riders show great determination and eventually claw their way back to sweep past their rivals at the start of the last lap of the race. But then, just as suddenly as he reaches the front, Richard Hall gets becalmed as he exits of the second bend and slips back to fourth. Dave Hoggart explains this bizarre turn of events afterwards when he announces why Richard Hall won't compete in the final race, "He lost his steel shoe in his last race and twisted his leg below the knee. He is okay but not taking any further part in this meeting." That's a shame since the penultimate race of the night contained the most excitement in terms of passing. Though Sheffield have won comfortably, there's still some drama at the start of the final Premier

League race of the night when Joel Parsons gets his visor and facemask snagged on the start tape only for Magnus Karlsson to be penalised for this tapes offence by referee Barbara Horley. Even if you ignore the fact that Joel Parsons had the tapes wrapped round his head, even to my untutored eye he definitely seemed to be the rider at fault rather than the harshly penalised Karlsson. The always gently pedagogic Dave Hoggart informs us, "The only option in this race is to go off 15 metres [pause] I can confirm there will only be three riders in this race!" A bell then rings loudly – I assume to signal that the riders have two minutes to get to the start-line – but this fails to instil any urgency in the riders so we enjoy the luxury of a five-minute delay that ends when all four riders come back out on the track. Dave Hoggart tells us elliptically, "Well, as you can see, the situation has been resolved and we now have four riders again!" One of these riders is, indeed, Magnus Karlsson but he starts 15 metres away from the tapes and conspicuously fails to make any impression on the riders ahead of him. Positive to the last, Dave Hoggart is keen to rhetorically remind us, "as always with Scunthorpe, haven't we had a great night of speedway?"

After 105 minutes, Sheffield have emerged victorious 52-38 and, almost straightaway, a packed programme of second half racing commences. This is an Academy Challenge meeting between the Sheffield Tiger Cubs and the Scunthorpe Saints II comprised of four riders on each team (though Sheffield also have a reserve rider, Leigh Boujos). The teams comprise youngsters of wildly different/varied abilities and, they arguably, provide much greater excitement (and talking points) than their professional, much more experienced colleagues. The second race of the night features Montana Jowett who expects no special favours on account of her gender. She finishes three-quarters of a lap behind the third-placed Ben Hannon. Between some of the junior races the Sheffield reserve, Kyle Hughes, takes to the track "for some practice". Montana also rides in the third race but the question on everyone's lips is 'who or what on earth is the exotically named Leigh Boujos'? It's a question that isn't answered by his race victory. It's also a race that has Montana Jowett gain her first point of the night after Tom Hill is excluded. By heat 5 of the Academy Challenge mechanical difficulties, tiredness, bedtime and falls have decimated the teams to the extent that only three riders take to the track. They end up strung out like a line of washing. Though Owlerton boasts a big track, Adam Wrathall exaggerates the effect of this when he finishes half a lap ahead of Tom Hill who, in turn, crosses the line three-quarters of a lap ahead of Montana Jowett.

Not everyone stays to see these young riders compete but they should have since the last heat of the Academy meeting is far and away the most exciting race of the night, both in terms of the racing and its drama. Leigh Boujos flies from the tapes and, for nearly four laps, holds Ben Hopwood and Gary Irving at bay, even though the Scunthorpe riders have far greater experience than he does. It's pretty well neck-and-neck stuff but, as they enter the third corner on the final lap, Boujos and Irving tangle. Carnage ensues when the riders behind plough into their stricken fellow competitors. For a brief moment, bikes and riders appear to bunch together or fly through the air. Over the loudspeaker system, we're informed that Barbara Horley has excluded Goujos and awarded the race to the Scunthorpe pair to take the final score to 11-25. We're told the meeting is "officially closed at 22.16" while, away on the track, riders still lie prostrate under the watchful gaze of the medical staff. Their forlorn and battered machinery gets wheeled back to the pits. Mick Gregory is in no doubt that lack of tuition is the primary cause of the carnage. "They're not taught to lay a bike down nowadays! I tell you what, Ivan Mauger wouldn't let you ride until you'd learnt to lay a bike down!" It's certainly true that Ben Hopwood clattered over both Irving and Boujos after they'd come together. "I think that lad who was leading lost his nerve!"

Back in the Speedway Office Neil Machin is in reflective mood, "We didn't have a good night. It's very hard to make money in this game with the present climate. That's the three meetings in a week factor, of course! But, for meetings like this, I'd expect a much better crowd. That said, Scunthorpe didn't bring over any fans to speak of which isn't good when it's our local derby!"

18th September Sheffield v. Scunthorpe (Premier League) 52-38
18th September Sheffield Tiger Cubs v. Scunthorpe Saints II (Academy Challenge) 11-25

CHAPTER 41.

Scunthorpe v. Rye House:
"She certainly wasn't a full-fat Goth – perhaps a Goth-lite."

19th September

It's another sunny day in North Lincolnshire, far better than many during the summer. A train journey from Sheffield to Scunthorpe showcases the flat Lincolnshire countryside but once you arrive at the station, public transport choices are limited out to the speedway track. You can either pay for a taxi or walk there. To learn more about Scunthorpe, I elect to walk from the railway station to the track. Though just over two miles according to the RAC route planner, in the sunshine and with books to carry it feels a lot longer. The town centre is close by to the station and, with directions from passers by, I pick my way through some tight streets of residential houses. After I pass some bare patches of land created by council house clearances and wander past a school, eventually I find myself on Normanby Road. It's a busy route with residential housing on one side and light industrial buildings and various businesses on the other. I've never approached Scunthorpe speedway track from this direction previously and, apart from a mother walking home with her children in tow, this must be the Lincolnshire equivalent of LA since everyone else seems to drive. Perhaps they buy their cars from Scorpions stadium sponsor Eddie Wright. He's got a substantial building with a huge car park that's chock-a-block with unsold cars and a series of shouty signs that loudly proclaim "Eddie Wright – Car Supermarket of the Year". Nearby there's a half-built new housing estate rather grandiosely named Normanby Grange. It has an abandoned quality that verges on the derelict with foundations laid for houses that remain unbuilt. It looks like they'll be posher than the terraced houses I walked past in the town centre and, I suppose, I could have stumbled upon one of the new aspirational areas within Scunthorpe. When you approach a familiar place from a different direction, you gain a new perspective from the place. Normanby Road eventually gives way to fields on both sides just before the first recognisable landmark – a familiar roundabout! When I've driven from the motorway, this traffic island only seems a stone's throw away from the stadium. Obviously enough it feels far longer when you walk it, rather than drive it. Looks can be deceptive. In a different direction to the speedway track, there's a sign that points to Normanby Hall. David Cameron's wife, Samantha, once famously claimed that she grew up on an estate in Scunthorpe. Along with her flirtation with the Goth life-style, this would have added to the Woman of the People image Dave's advisors burnish. In fact her Baronet father, Sir Reginald Sheffield, owns more than 3,000 acres of Lincolnshire along with two of the region's finest stately homes. Understandable enough when you trace your family back to the 13th century.[1]

It's weird that Scunthorpe connects both speedway and the wife of the possible future Prime Minister of Britain. Whatever these notional inter-relationships, the location of the speedway track on the far-flung edges of Scunthorpe is indicative of the contemporary context when it comes to planning permission and the construction of speedway stadia in this country. If you're to gain permission, you need a forward thinking and positive council, a substantial area of land remote from the residents (that's also not really appropriate for commercial use) and, in an ideal world,

---

[1] Samantha grew up at Thealby Hall near Scunthorpe. One of two grand houses (the other home is Sutton Park) that remain in the Sheffield family's possession after their principal residence Normanby Hall was handed over to Lincolnshire council in lieu of death duties in the 1960s. Samantha went to £23,000 a year Marlborough College in Wiltshire. In the *Sun*, a friend recalls, "she certainly wasn't a full-fat Goth – perhaps a Goth-lite." The daughter of Sir Reginald Sheffield, the 8th Baronet and Viscountess Astor, it's alleged that Samantha has claimed that she was taught to play pool when at Bristol University by trip-hop musician Tricky. Several profiles have noted that the possible future Prime Minister, David "Dave" Cameron was attracted to Sam by the dolphin tattoo on her ankle and the fact that she taught him to "keep it real". Interviewed in the *Guardian* on their alleged friendship Tricky commented. "That's what she [Samantha Cameron] says and, though I don't remember it, I believe it. I used to hang out at the Montpelier pub in Bristol and she says that's where it happened. She was at college and the dates and times she mentioned match up. But then the tabloids got hold of it and they tried to make me say I smoked spliff with her. If I taught her pool then they [David & Samantha Cameron] should put something back. Seriously ... I'd like to meet him. I'd like to tell him my life was changed by music and by youth clubs. There's nothing now. Council estates are just entertainment material now – all cop shows and Asbo families. Cameron can help me take my portable studio in there and help kids create something. I got one question for him: Do you really give a shit?"

good public-transport links. With the support of the local council along with the hard work and determination of Rob Godfrey (and many volunteers), it's clear that you can build your own track from scratch and, with careful husbandry, then go on to make it succeed. The home of the Scorpions is definitely thrown to the periphery, both geographically and culturally. Though there are pavements, the route isn't best suited to pedestrians if judged by the volume of fast-moving traffic. There are definitely no public-transport links, though I'm passed by two coaches with school bus signs in the window along with a double-decker bus that proclaims it's hired under contract. There are identikit buildings dotted on either side of the road that have the soul-destroying 'box' uniformity associated with industrial areas everywhere. From the few signs outside or on their exteriors, it's a mystery what their main purpose of activity actually is. I could have tried to hitch a lift but the ongoing loss of trust and community spirit suffered in the modern age has, in most respects, sounded the death knell for this alternative means of travel. Dave Rattenberry and John Rich pass in their fully laden car but don't stop (afterwards Rat says they had no space). I eventually struggle with my box of books to the roundabout that leads down to the rough-hewn car park directly adjacent to the stadium perimeter. When approached on foot, the height and the extent of the security fencing is emphasised. There are numerous signs attached to the fence that warn of security patrols, something I suspect is the legacy of the recent problems the club have had with the nearby travellers' site. There's an impressively large dog by the entrance gate that looks like it could rip off my leg as soon as eat my sandwiches. Thankfully it appears docile if not exactly friendly. Though hours before the meeting, Ben Hopwood has already unloaded his bike from his van. He tries to run and start his bike – it fails to start – under the watchful gaze of his dad who shouts out helpful instructions. Out on the track Rob Godfrey, Graham Trollope and a smaller man with ferociously close-cropped hair slowly walk close together in a tight formation. They stare at the track with an intensity that suggests they're plain-clothes policemen on a painstaking hunt for forensic clues, though, in reality, they're clearing larger stones from the track surface by hand.

Eddie Wright - Car Supermarket of the Year

Club Archway

Over at the trackshop, there's the magisterial sight of the Ratmobile parked up outside. Dave Rattenberry clearly comes from the "why bark yourself" School of Trackshop Organisation since John Rich has already worked up a sweat carrying in and laying out the Scorpions merchandise. To the casual outside observer, John's job appears the speedway equivalent of being 'Employee of the Month' in an ice-cream van. Dave is full of the joys of late summer, "This is a place I love coming! It's a genuinely nice place to come. I wish more tracks were like this!" While John unpacks the bigger, heavier boxes; Dave sets out the programmes and photos. Fashion, as an Alan Bennett character once remarked about sex, is a wayward monarch. Living proof of this maxim, there are packets of coloured shirts (£18), coloured T-shirts in white, blue and black (£15), sweatshirts (£25), Scorpions baseball caps (£8) and beanie hats (£5). On hangers there are yet more differentially priced brightly coloured shirts. Though they're not visible to the untrained, naked eye, Dave explains their notional differences to me, "The £22 one is the Wulfsport Pits shirt and the £18 one is a dress shirt." After many years' experience Dave has strong ideas about how exactly his stock should be displayed by his staff, "The new coat needs to be right in front of their eyes! You can move those hoodies." John

Elle Fairbanks prepares

harrumphs, "I do it all then he freakin' messes about with it!" Also on the home straight and adjacent to the trackshop is the coffee shop. Already hard at work inside with preparations for a busy night ahead is the friendly, attractive Elle Fairbanks who shares coffee shop duties with Tai's nana, Cynthia Woffinden. Elle has worked in the coffee shop for the last two years, "I'm Tai's aunty – his mum's sister." One of the stars of tonight's Premier League visitors, Rye House, is ex-Scunthorpe rider Tai Woffinden. Like many Scunthorpe fans, his aunt has looked forward to his return since the fixture list was published. "Yeah, he's gonna be back! I don't travel much because it's too expensive. I follow Tai, of course, but he's never here 'cause he rides all over. I've been going since Tai's dad was riding. I went to Ashby Ville and Quibell Park. It was the '70s, late '70s, it's years ago! I'm a bigger football fan, I must admit and I didn't follow it when it weren't here! The atmosphere here is fantastic! I love the fastness of the bikes – just the thrill and Tai, of course, he's very fast! We're gonna be very busy tonight but, Cynthia and I, are gonna take 60 seconds out to watch him whenever he rides. When I'm not here, I work at the police station enquiry desk seeing to the public with all the troubles they've got."

Ben Hopwood arrives in the trackshop to try to get his copy of the DVD of the Saints versus Plymouth Conference League meeting recently held here on Bank Holiday Monday. He looks crestfallen when Dave Rattenberry says he's forgotten it ("John, have you left it in the Wolves box?"). Ben then gleefully describes the crash that ended the Academy League meeting last night at Owlerton Stadium. "Gary [Irving] nearly put me in the fence the night before. He's not great to ride with. Lee's primary chain snapped and Gary could have avoided him but ploughed right into him. Anyway I tried to go round them but hit them!" I sympathise and Ben asks excitedly, "Were you there? What was the crash like? Was it spectacular?" Ben Hopwood leaves without the DVD he'd expected and, shortly afterwards, Scunthorpe Press Officer and Programme Editor, Richard Hollingsworth, joins us in the trackshop. Tonight he also has close-cropped hair (though not as convict severe as the bloke on the track) and, much more unusually, sports a bright white collared shirt and tie. "I'm Clerk of the Course tonight. Everyone already knows what they're doing here so all I do is chat to the referee! Tonight it's Dave Dowling." Richard is modestly unassuming and doesn't have any airs and graces, despite his skill at his job and conscientious, hardworking approach to his Scunthorpe speedway club duties.

[Me] "Where were all the Scunthorpe fans last night?"

[Richard] "There were loads! More to the point, where were all the Sheffield fans? One of the big mysteries is what has happened to the travelling speedway fans nowadays? In the '80s, loads of fans used to go to away meetings everywhere and yet, nowadays, when everyone is more well to do and everyone has cars, they seem to have vanished! I know the days of supporter coaches has more or less passed but I just don't understand it."

[Me] [Points to slow-moving tractor] "Is that Graham TREE-LOW-PEE?"

[Richard] "Who?"

[Me] "Graham Tree-low-pee! That's how Neil Machin said he likes his name pronounced."

[Richard] "I think he's having you on. You don't say it like that here and, at Sheffield, I'm sure they don't either!" (leaves)

[Dave Rat] (shows remarkable turn of speed to rush from the trackshop clutching a ring in a clear plastic bag) "Is your wife here?"

[Richard] "Yes."

[Dave] "I've got one of these in and I know she'll want one as it's her favourite rider!" [Holds up a ring with the image of an extremely red-faced rider as if he's been horrifically sunburnt or, perhaps, as though he's an extra from a distant planet in an episode of *Star Trek*]

[Me] "Has he sustained severe burns to his face?"

[Dave] "That's Viktor Bergstrom!"

[Me] "Has he been sunbathing too much then?"

Scunthorpe v. Rye House: *"She certainly wasn't a full-fat Goth – perhaps a Goth-lite."*

[Dave] "Shut up! It's how the picture came out."

Later, by the programme stall they have just inside the entrance turnstiles at Scunthorpe, I wonder if there must be some dress code in operation this evening that's more suited to the Queen's Garden Party than speedway. Barry 'Bazski' Preston comes over to buy his programme and looks positively debonair dressed in a smart black shirt with large orange side panels. "These are the new shirts so I gotta wear it!" explains Baz. I'm not sure if it's going to catch on since it looks very RAC-man chic to my eyes. Quite a queue of fans builds up before the gates finally open and, once the turnstiles are unlocked, they stream into the stadium. There's much banter at the programme booth.

[Man] "I can't see anyone stopping Tai getting a maximum tonight."

[Small girl] "Tai'll be number 1 and Richard Hall number 2."

[Man] "Hey, you, Richard is our rider!"

[Girl] "But he won't beat Tai!"

Shortly afterwards an old age pensioner with a stick engages the programme lady in a heated debate about the track quality. He waves the stick around for additional effect, "It's a processional track. It's so fast, if you don't make the gate you're not going to catch up! We've been inconsistent all season and we were again last night. Sanchez was awful! I think he's got to the age when he doesn't try 'cause he might get hurt." Later Dave Rattenberry tells me in a conspiratorial stage whisper, "Rob Godfrey tells me he's definitely not here next year." Bazski's fresh-faced and thoughtful daughter Chloe Preston comes along to inspect her name in my book *Concrete for Breakfast*. Unusually, she's proud to parade around in a Rye House anorak.

[Me] "I thought you supported Scunthorpe? Why are you wearing a Rye House anorak?"

[Chloe] "My cousin rides for them."

[Me] "What's his name?"

[Chloe] "Tai Woffinden."

[Me] "He's pretty rubbish, isn't he?"

[Chloe] "No he's the best. (Pauses to inspect the book further) Am I the first kid in one of your books?"

The Scunthorpe start-line girls arrive but there's no sign of the recent revolutionary innovation of the start-line boy they had here on Bank Holiday Monday. Amazingly, although the ground they have to walk over is rough and stony, apparently the club is twinned with a beach since three of the start-line girls don't bother with shoes!

With the return of Tai Woffinden and the in-form Stefan Ekberg, many neutrals tip Rye House to pull off an away victory here this evening. Another possible factor is that Scunthorpe can't qualify for the end-of-season Premier League play-offs but, prior to this meeting, have already assured themselves of a Young Shield place. Whereas Rye House still have the motivation since they need victory to get into the play-offs. Premonitions that Rye House would be well up for this meeting prove well-founded when Ekberg and Neath hammer from the gate and, by the first corner, have established a dominance that they didn't relinquish. Sight of the rampant Rockets in control from the first bend prompts Sheffield promoter Neil Machin to exclaim, "Oh, here we go!" And, when Ekberg and Neath cross the line after barely 59 seconds, he expresses the thoughts of many Scunthorpe fans around him: "Freaking hell, they didn't need that!" Of even more concern for the home fans was the ding-dong battle for the third-place chip-shop money between Emiliano Sanchez and Richard Hall (after a battle royale, Sanchez triumphed). Though the Scorpions immediately hit back with a heat advantage, there's no real crowd reaction until the return of Tai Woffinden causes a buzz to surge through the crowd before he's even taken to the track. His comprehensive race victory brings broad smiles to many, particularly the faces of staff in the refreshment kiosk (Elle and Cynthia) but leaves many Scorpions fans in a quandary about where their true allegiances lie. Ultimately, these would always be with the Scorpions but, the sight of Tai in full flight and completely in his element, catches the eye and quickens the pulse amongst neutrals as well as the Normanby Road faithful. Scunthorpe announcer/presenter Shaun Leigh offers his congratulations over the loudspeakers, "Tell you what, he still knows the quickest way round here! It's another 5-1, they certainly haven't

Scunthorpe v. Rye House: *"She certainly wasn't a full-fat Goth – perhaps a Goth-lite."*

come for a haircut tonight!" Already 6 points ahead after three races, Ekberg wins the fourth with some ease to increase the Rockets lead (8-16). You'd hesitate to say that the meeting is already over as a contest but, with a spearhead of Woffinden and Ekberg ably supported by Rockets team mates with their gating gloves on, things already don't look so clever for Scunthorpe. By the fifth race the Rockets can even afford the luxury of a Chris Neath last place, mainly because Stefan Ekberg yet again flies round the track to record his third race win of the night. The sixth heat sees Richard Hall and Emiliano Sanchez finally decide to race the opposition and, pitted against the Rockets reserves, you'd expect them to gain the maximum advantage they deliver.

Veteran Rye House promoter, Len Silver has a forthcoming autobiography in process and his editor, Gareth Rogers, suggested I should grab a few words with him during his visit to North Lincolnshire. However, Len is nowhere to be seen, either in the pits, bar or grandstand. Sheffield co-promoter Dave Hoggart helpfully suggests, "Len will be in the stand – somewhere where he can see the programme!" Eventually I find Len plunged in darkness stood on his own midway down the back straight. It's just prior to the start of heat 7 when I stumble upon him and it's quickly apparent that Len only has eyes for his riders. He clutches his programme in rapt concentration as (once again) Tai Woffinden flies from the tapes. There's no doubt he would have continued to leave the rest of the field for dead if Scorpions reserve Ben Powell hadn't fallen off on the third bend after some pressure from Robert Mear and Carl Wilkinson. All three riders arrive together into the third bend and, though he is on the outside, Powell is adjudged to be cause of the stoppage and finds himself excluded by referee, Dave Dowling. Len peers into the distance understandably unable to make out the exact colour of the exclusion lights, "Is that the blue exclusion light on?" Experienced enough to wait for official confirmation of his judgement rather than transcribe it into the programme immediately, Len then squints at the programme racecard and carefully marks in Powell's failure to score. Judged by his own exalted standards, Tai is comparatively lacklustre in the rerun of the seventh heat since he's held back in second place until the fourth bend of the first lap. From this point, Tai accelerates to leave his erstwhile closest rival (Carl Wilkinson) considerable distance behind. Comfortably ahead by 6 points and with two riders on the top of their game and in complete mastery of track conditions at Scunthorpe, Len still remains cautiously guarded about the likely outcome. "It's looking good so far. Let's not count any chickens just yet!"

The Sheffield promotional massive have gathered by the refreshment kiosk for some much-needed sustenance and, in the case of Neil Machin, more cigarettes. Without the pressure of race night, Dave Hoggart can kick back and savour the spectacle, "It's the only chance I get to really watch a meeting properly!" And what a meeting to watch! With Ekberg programmed to ride at number 2 in the Rye House Rockets team, the eighth heat clearly won't provide any easy points for the Scorpions. Their cause isn't helped by Emiliano Sanchez's engine failure on the start-line and Ekberg duly completes the formality of his fourth win of the night (with still only eight races completed). To compound an evening of struggle for the home team, Robert Mear then becomes the third Rocket to win a race when (in heat 9) he bests Magnus Karlsson and Viktor Bergstrom. The 10th heat features a trademark Tai Woffinden overtake when he swoops round the entire field on the first corner before he powers away and proceeds to win by the proverbial country mile in a super smooth and stylish fashion. A Scunthorpe fan remarks, "We've just been totally outclassed! Against these we're just not good enough." It's not a prophecy but indubitably correct. It's not a surprise when Ekberg wins heat 11 closely followed by Chris Neath to further extend the Rockets lead to an impressive 14 points. The Scorpions torpor has had a hypnotic effect upon announcer/presenter Shaun Leigh in the referee's box. He inadvertently drifts off into a reverie of his own and completely forgets that he's actually on duty at Scunthorpe speedway. "Have I given you the result of heat 11 yet? I'm cracking up! The weekend starts here! [pause] You think you're having a bad week, I went to Reading on Tuesday!" The realisation that things might have got really out of kilter prompts a further realisation, "I won't have given you the line-up for heat 12 then?" Without need to glance at the programme, from the buzz in the crowd it's impossible not to know that Tai Woffinden will feature in this heat. For the second race in succession, Tai fails to make an inspirational start and this time remains stuck in second place until the third bend. As you'd expect, Tai then lengthens his lead but suddenly, to confound general expectations, Magnus Karlsson and the youngster vie for the lead until Magnus somehow snatches victory on the line. Shaun Leigh is ecstatic, "Whoa! Whoa! Fantastic! Old Chinese proverb say – look over shoulder!" It's a well-received victory and a good scalp for Magnus Karlsson though, when the results are read out moments later we learn, "Second – who did the last three-quarters of a lap on a flat tyre – Tai Woffinden." It's all so exciting that we're not told the winning race time [61.07]. In case I'd missed it, I ask the woman next to me, "Did he give us a time?" Only to be told, "He has a bit

Scunthorpe v. Rye House: *"She certainly wasn't a full-fat Goth – perhaps a Goth-lite."*

of, ah, you know, now and again!"

With the Scorpions suddenly on a roll, Shaun Leigh builds the suspense, "You know what we were just saying, 'I bet Magnus comes out in a black-and-white helmet colour' but he didn't. Well, Richard Hall will come out on a tactical ride in the next race!" In fact, he will win the race but this only serves to massage the scoreline rather than give the Scorpions any realistic chance of victory. Like London buses, one tactical option follows another and, the penultimate heat, has Viktor Bergstrom take a tactical substitution ride from 15 metres back. He manages to eclipse the challenge of Robert Mear but can't catch Rockets reserve Luke Bowen. The last race of the night features the Rye House dream partnership of Woffinden and Ekberg. Tai wins the race with ease but, rather surprisingly, Ekberg blots his copybook and spurns the opportunity to race to a notable six-ride maximum at Normanby Road. All that's left is for Shaun to tell us, "And third in blue was Stefan Ekberg, sorry Magnus Karlsson!" Afterwards Neil Machin enthuses, "Tai was a different class! It was an under-power performance [by Scunthorpe] but, quite why they had a slick track, I don't know! They can't even say the weather caught them out unless it was the sun. Fancy doing a slick track for Rye House when that's what they're used to all the time – slick track racing!"

19th September Scunthorpe v. Rye House (Premier League) 40-53

CHAPTER 42.

Sheffield/PLRC:
"I've no idea who's gonna win, mate! It could be any one of ten."

21st September

A bright sunny morning in the People's Republic of South Yorkshire finds a casually dressed Neil Machin in shorts, sandals and trademark unfashionable sunglasses. This year's PLRC will be held at Owlerton Stadium and, consequently, with proprietorial diligence Neil does some last-minute housekeeping around the place to make sure that it all looks perfectly spick and span for when the public (and other promoters) arrive. It's four and a half hours before the meeting when I catch Neil banging the dust from the speedway office doormats with a vigour that suggests it definitely has some therapeutic value. After it's suitably chastened, a still comparatively dust-free Neil moves over to the entranceway of the Panorama Suite and restaurant. Armed with a bar stool, paper towel and bottle of spray cleaner he gives a sign that proudly announces "Tigers Sheffield Window Centre" a vigorous clean before he hangs it back on its hooks over the doorway. The size and shape of this sign been adapted so that it can fit snugly over the greyhound graphics that also appears there. Neil's sign masks other greyhound messages but cleverly still leaves the words "Welcome to Owlerton Stadium" visible. Next stop on this Machin housekeeping tour is a proprietorial trip to the edge of the terraces to survey the extent of the activity on the speedway track itself. "I've no idea who's gonna win, mate! It could be any one of ten. People talk about Ostergaard but they forget about riders like Kevin Doolan, Andre Compton, Tai Woffinden, Shane Parker and Jason Lyons (he's never not had a rostrum finish here)." The track staff are hard at work on the surface but Neil has some anxiety about the fastidiousness of their work [points in direction of bends 1 and 2] "If they don't clean that safety fence, I'll go freakin' mad! When I speak to them, they'll give me all the reasons why they can't do it! On a wet day you can understand it but today, with the sun blazing down, there's no excuse for everything not looking lovely!"

On the subject of everything looking perfect, Neil proceeds to fuss over the Super7even plastic sign that's tied to the railings. On the way back to the speedway office, pleasantries are exchanged with trackshop man Mick Gregory who tells us, "I don't know who's gonna win and I don't freakin' care!" Back outside the speedway office, Neil decides the glass door could do with a last-minute wipe down before we go inside. The inner sanctum that is the Sheffield Speedway Office is already a hive of activity, albeit in the quietly confident under-stated manner that typifies Betty and Janet, the ladies who work there. The table is littered with papers, cups of tea, lit cigarettes along with champagne and flowers ready for the lucky rider who triumphs in the PLRC (or also, as consolation, for those who only gain a rostrum place). Always helpful, Neil suggests that I borrow a chair from the Panorama Room and base my small bookstall adjacent to the white table that will later serve as the programme stall, if based on the large sign attached to it that says "Souvenir Programmes £3". I take his suggestion as an instruction and, shortly afterwards, Neil walks past where I'm sat in the sunshine reading the Sunday papers on yet another tour of inspection. "That's good you sitting there. It'll act as a deterrent! Everything's on CCTV here but I've been here 16 years and I'm sure some people still sneak in, despite the security we have here. People will always manage no matter what you do! We have cameras everywhere. We have to have them in case there's an incident. Whenever we want to do something, we're reminded what 96 body bags looked like 'cause they had them down the road [Hillsborough]. It focuses the mind about safety! When people say to me 'Why can't we go on the back straight? They let us do it at Stoke and it's worse there'. I say 'that's freakin' Stoke and this is freakin' Sheffield!'" Sheffield co-promoter Dave Hoggart strides through the entrance gates with a broad grin on his face and is matter-of-factly greeted by Neil with, "The Mildenhall lad Truminski has dropped out! That's no great problem as he wasn't gonna freakin' win anyway! They've got Henning Loof instead. [pause] Right then, we've got Jeff Scott guarding the gate."

If the riders deliver the oodles of visual entertainment on the pristine stage that the Sheffield speedway management have prepared for them, then Shaun Leigh will provide this afternoon's oral entertainment. He's arrived four hours early to ensure that everything functions just perfectly. I quiz him about his work at Scunthorpe. "I've been doing Scunthorpe since it started. They know me and I just try to have a bit of fun! Some presenters think they have to tell you absolutely everything up to and including each rider's inside leg measurement. There's no point in doing that as 90 per cent of the crowd know more than you anyway! So best to keep them informed and just be yourself. Scunthorpe is always tons of fun, though I enjoyed it even more when it was on a Sunday afternoon. Last season in the Conference League it rained a lot but, otherwise, it seemed to be sunny every Sunday!" Shaun laughs off his inadvertent heat 11 mistake during the Rye House meeting. "I was being told in the headphones about rider replacement for heat 12 and passing on a message to the Start Marshal and, I thought, hold on, I wonder if I've given out the results for heat 11? That's why I asked!"

Betty Wilson in action

Many people arrive early and one of these early birds is Newcastle promoter George English. He encounters Neil Machin who's on yet another circuit round the stadium to check that everything remains ship shape and Bristol fashion. Almost as if they were next-door neighbours, they proceed to have a 'what's wrong with the world' conversation. These usually require a garden fence and frequent exclamations, "Oh, I know! I know!" It's soon apparent that there are frustrations when you regularly work with riders but also there are vicissitudes created by those that try to manage and/or advise you.

[Neil] "I don't know why the [BSPA] office puts out the shite that Topinka or Nieminen will be riding, if riders drop out. I've booked non-contracted Conference League riders as my reserves as I'm supposed to do! I'll tell you the only way Topinka will ride is if Doolan drops out! The only communication I've had about the meeting is just over a week ago when they asked how many rain-off tickets I wanted. I said 2,000. They rang back this week and said they didn't have any and to use my own! I do want to know from them if I'm supposed to have trophies to give out but I haven't heard! So I've bought them each a bottle of pop and some flowers. Though Ann did ring five times about the Super7even girls but, when I heard of how much they wanted, I wasn't prepared to spend the shared event money on such people!"

Janet makes another delicious cuppa

[George] "The Sexy Super7even girls earn more money from a shared event than the riders!"

[Neil] "Also, I didn't want to disrespect my girls who turn up every week and do that job here. They mightn't be seen as glamorous enough but they already work here doing that and we're proud to have them!"

Surprise is expressed that the field remains as per programme apart from the absence of Mildenhall's Seb Truminski.

[Neil] "That Truminski should be banned for a year. It's the second time he's failed to show and I hear that Mildenhall had no race jackets at Somerset on Friday 'cause he's got them. We're supposed to be running a professional sport! We want to get in the national media but can't even manage the simple things! I got given the Pairs jackets [race tabards] but they were all shitted up and with the wrong numbers on. I had to spend £94 getting them altered and cleaned.

House proud Neil Machin

Sheffield/PLRC: *"I've no idea who's gonna win, mate! It could be any one of ten."*

I did notice at the ELRC at King's Lynn on the telly that five so-called Elite League superstars had their numbers held on with gaffer tape. What's that about? I complained to Chris Van Straaten and said they should be fined £500 each then they'd never forget again but he bottled out and went for 50 quid.[1] That's hardly going to change behaviour and it's less than I've had to spend on the race jackets for this meeting! I give each of my riders their jacket at the start of the season and expect them to show up with it clean at every meeting!"

[George] "Me too! And I get a spare set just to be safe and sure. Plus some ones with black on the back for the Pairs and PLRC 'cause you know you've got those meetings! I dunno why others can't manage that."

The conversation moves on to shared frustrations on a variety of topics too specific (and damning) to repeat here and then returns to their respective plans for the remaining months/weeks of the season.

[Neil] "Can you tell me how the Young Shield draw will be made? As it was glossed over when we tried to talk specifics at the Conference. Is it, as I think, not on a commercially viable basis?"

[George] "Fifth gets to choose between the teams finishing ninth to twelfth."

[Neil] "I think whoever finishes fifth should be able to choose from anyone else."

[George] "So do I! It's irrelevant for me 'cause we had a shite year this year but the fifth team might want to race against the sixth as they're confident of knocking them straight out and clearing the way for themselves to win at an early stage."

[Neil] "They also might want to choose a local derby!"

Talk then ranges over some intractable problems that beset the Elite League as well as some irksome governance of the sport type issues, plus miscellaneous administrative matters. ("I was charged back for five tyres by Workington [after the PL Pairs] but not at the £19 rate!")

[Neil] (smirks) "I'll tell you what I'm doing, I'm asking each rider for their address and postcode as they arrive so I can work out the travel properly! The first rider through the gate – I'll give you three guesses who – refused to tell me!" George guesses correctly first time.

[Neil] "I see the [BSPA] office is wasting our resources sending out e-mails about the SRA end-of-season dinner."

[George] "I wouldn't ever go to one of those events."

Once the turnstiles open, the programme stall is a magnet for practically everyone who comes through the stadium gates. My bookstall is the inverse of a magnet. However, people stop to chat and one of them is Scunthorpe track photographer Steve Dixon, "I don't know why everyone was saying there was no dirt when there was tons on the outside – just no one went there! If Rye House wins next weekend against Newcastle, they'll now get in the play-offs but, strangely, I heard on Saturday they've already agreed the Young Shield dates against Workington who are presently still fourth! Still that's speedway." Everyone's favourite speedway nana, Cynthia Woffinden, again confesses to me that she can't always bear to watch the racing, "They think I'm looking 'cause I'm stood with my programme but, really, I have my eyes shut! I'm going to Pardubice to see Tai ride in a few weeks." Shortly afterwards Elle Fairbanks – who also works in the Scunthorpe refreshment kiosk – stops by and introduces me to her glamorous looking friend ("my sister Sue – Tai's mum"). Sue gives me a parent's natural reaction to the pressure and adulation her son experiences. "I wish people wouldn't build him up! It doesn't bother him but it bothers me! He's only young and still learning. The weight of expectation really can get to be something ridiculous!"[2]

Shortly afterwards, the always ebullient Wendy Jedrzejakski (aka Miss Fina Invader) arrives fresh from last night's Chris Neath Testimonial at Rye House. "They know me as The Rottweiler on the pit gate. Some of the Rye House riders

---

[1] Speedway Regulation 12.12.1 states that each race tabard should have a number on the front. Failure to comply with this regulation should result in a fine of £50 per rider per race. If this rule had been applied then the Sheffield Tigers would have been fined £1,500 per meeting during 2008.

[2] The weight of expectation among fans and the media alone with a dearth of British talent has meant Tai has taken centre stage at a young age. When Lewis Bridger won the Under-21 at Lakeside in 2009, Tai hinted at these pressures. "Good on Lewis – he deserves the limelight....I would rather they talk about him more than me and then it won't make everyone say 'Tai this, Tai that'. I'd rather have no one talk about me. If I had chosen to be Australian, I'd just be another one in the pack and nobody would be talking about me. I picked to be British and the weight is on my shoulders."

Sheffield/PLRC: *"I've no idea who's gonna win, mate! It could be any one of ten."*

turned up and said, 'we ride here we can come in'. I said, 'Only if you pay you can as it's a Testimonial so it's different!'" Wendy involves herself in the speedway community in a wide variety of ways, so it's only a slight surprise to learn that she's recently helped drive Danny King's bikes from Huntingdon to Poland with Danny's mechanic. "It took us 11 hours to Ostrow. We shared the driving. The roads are better than they were but are still a bit on the rough side! The Poles are wild drivers! You're continually looking and wondering what they're going to do. They just love to overtake. Usually when you think there's definitely no room. I think, 'Oh no! There's a car and a truck coming and no room!' but somehow they manage. There's some lovely tracks there and, when you go with a rider, you're treated like royalty! It took us 15 hours to get back 'cause we kept having to stop for Danny to be sick. He's got something wrong with his chest. He's going to the doctors so they can figure out what it is! There's nothing of him and his stomach is non-existent!" The sports reporter from Middlesbrough's *Evening Gazette*, Martin Neal looks forward to the forthcoming Redcar versus Boston Conference League play-off semi-final. "The trouble is no one is interested in the Conference League! Well, that's not true, Jason [Pike] is! About 200 diehards will turn up. All anyone is interested in is the Bears. Glyn Taylor is the white knight who's going to rescue Redcar. He's accepted an offer from a local businessman to keep the club going which is excellent news as it looked difficult for a while there!" Throughout these conversations, the programmes get unpacked from their boxes and, almost, fly off the stall. Minutes before the tapes rise I can count 13 empty PLRC programme boxes. Given each box contains 130 programmes and sell for £3 each that must mean the gross revenues from programme sales at this shared event will generate a minimum of £5,070.

Nerve centre of operations

Out on the centre green, the rider parade has started and Dave Hoggart gleefully informs the crowd that, "Each rider will be presented with a memento by the BSPA Chairman Peter Toogood. It's a bottle of specially brewed Sheffield Tigers beer from the Bradfield Brewery." Dave then briefly introduces each rider with a few words. We quickly learn, "Seb Truminski won't be here this afternoon as, unfortunately, he's decided to call a halt to his season." We're told Adrian Rymel has arrived at Owlerton Stadium, "fresh from the UEM European Pairs in the Czech Republic" and are warned that the highly fancied Ulrich Ostergaard "can be beaten around Owlerton as we saw, three weeks ago, when Reading visited." Edinburgh's Mike Hunter is a notable member of the crowd who's come along to see William Lawson represent his club, Edinburgh, in the PLRC. Mike doesn't expect William to emerge victorious but, instead, takes great satisfaction in the overall performance of the Monarchs team throughout their 2008 campaign. "At the start of the year, when crowds were poor, people said it was the credit crunch but, now we're doing well, crowds are up. So, it shows people have it when they want it. Unlike last time [Edinburgh won the Premier League], this year we've done it with a young team that's exciting to watch! They're just riding for fun and learning! We've got to savour it 'cause next season the powers that be will probably ensure we have to settle for mid-table mediocrity. Personally, success means I'm worked off my feet so, in one sense, a rest would be nice!"

Popular programmes

Jason Bunyan wins the first heat in a time of 59.4 seconds. It's a performance that Shaun Leigh hails, "It's the second fastest time ever round Owlerton!" Before the third heat the tapes are held for an eternity by referee Mick

Posselwhite, so much so that you'd think he may have lost the whereabouts of the start button on his control panel. It's a delay too far for Jason Lyons who is excluded for touching the tapes. As usual at Sheffield, Dave Hoggart is our meeting presenter but, out on the centre green, there's an interloper in the form of Mike Bennett who (fortunately) has swapped his microphone for a video camera. Before the fifth heat, news reaches the crowd that a season of misfortune and bad luck continues for Mildenhall riders (and fans), "A bit of bad news, I'm afraid Henning Loof has aggravated an old injury and had to withdraw from the remainder of the meeting." Heat 5 actually has the first overtake of the meeting and it happens when Jason Bunyan cuts underneath Kevin Doolan on the third bend of the second lap. After a third place in his first race, Gary Havelock retires from the eighth heat to effectively end any lingering outside chance he had of victory to the disappointment of a large contingent of Redcar fans here to support him. There's a dramatic heat 10 when home track expert Andre Compton pressures race leader Shane Parker on the second bend of the second lap before he falls back. Never one to give up the chase around Owlerton, Andre then tries to catch Shane Parker with a high-speed charge as they exit the fourth bend of the penultimate lap but, instead, strikes the fence and dramatically tumbles about half the length of the track before he comes to a painful standstill. His trademark big blasts round the outside traditionally thrill without either pain or exclusion. News that the race has to be rerun doesn't please Bill Gimbeth, "That'll bloody give [Ben] Barker an extra point!" Shane Parker wins the rerun and, as Bill predicted, Ben Barker now finishes second ahead of reserve Scott Richardson rather than retain the third place he originally occupied when the initial running of the race was stopped.

Knowledgeable Gordon Pairman of Belle Vue (and Glasgow) speedway is in typically dry, quick-witted form, "It's good to come to a meeting where I'm not losing money!" He takes some quiet satisfaction in the progress that Kauko Nieminen has made in recent years. "He's really moved up a level! I keep sending him congratulatory texts 'cause it's illegal to approach another team's rider. Now that Stoney's no longer the force he was, it's been a battle with Nermark for the hearts and minds of the Comets fans. He hasn't got as many points as Nermark but he's won the hearts and minds. He spent three years going nowhere with averages in the sixes before he got bounced out of Workington and ended up at Glasgow. He added a point and a half and that gave him confidence! He's lovely to deal with! Kauko will get a podium place here and he's already got the Pairs and the Four Team with Workington." Because of my involvement as Writer in Residence at Eastbourne, Gordon makes the assumption I saw the Eagles lose narrowly 46-47 at home to the Bees. "What happened at Eastbourne last night then? How much did Allen Trump have to pay for that one? Eastbourne led by 3 going into the last heat and, then, Coventry get a 5-1 to win! If Swindon win at Coventry tomorrow night, I'll be more of a subscriber to conspiracy theories!" After a slow start by his standards, Tai Woffinden wins heat 11 imperiously some distance ahead of Ulrich Ostergaard, Jason King and Magnus Karlsson. Until that heat, riders in the red or blue helmet colours (from gates 1 and 2) had won the first 10 races of the night. One thing that can definitely be said about the 2008 version of the PLRC is that the field is packed with a variety of talented riders who could all be genuine contenders for a place on the podium and, more importantly (unlike, say, the ELRC) they do appear to really want to excel. A case in point comes in heat 12, which features a brilliant ride from Kauko Nieminen who heads home three of his key rivals: Jason Doyle, Kevin Doolan and William Lawson. Brian Oldham stops for a brief word. "You misquoted me [in *Concrete for Breakfast*]. I would never have said that. My wife [Celia] has been to more British finals than me 'cause I don't know that! I did tell you off for not mentioning her, I admit! At least, I now know you write fiction."

If you'd studied the racecard beforehand, you'd have pre-identified heat 15 as one race that will really help determine who'll progress to the semi-final and grand final of this competition. Amusingly, Tai Woffinden tries to nudge Kauko Nieminen on the first bend and, given their comparative statures, it's no real surprise that his shove fails to generate sufficient force to create any meaningful effect upon his more substantial rival. Even though presently Kauko is presently at the top of his game and flies round Owlerton, Tai Woffinden still looks a class apart as he demonstrates effortless grace and incredible speed on his machine. Consequently, he really has no real need to push or shove but, instead, just blasts round the outside of his erstwhile rival on the back straight during the third lap before he eases away to victory. Dave Hoggart's impressed at the spectacle, "That young man never ceases to amaze me! You hear them praise him on *Sky* but look at that!" Ben Barker endures a torrid heat 16 and the sight of him at the rear of the field brings some satisfaction to Bill Gimbeth, "I'm glad the little bastard's at the back!" It's a safe place to be, given the severity of a tough last-bend clash between Adrian Rymel and Jason Doyle as they battle for the honour of the chequered flag. Ben Barker also rides in the next race. It's a 'do or die' race for him, though he seeks both a win and

Sheffield/PLRC: *"I've no idea who's gonna win, mate! It could be any one of ten."*

favourable results in the remainder of the meeting. You need skill and good fortune in order to win anything. Barker is certainly fortunate when in the initial attempt to run the heat has Kauko Nieminen smash into him and, justifiably, find himself excluded. Without this unexpected turn of events, Barker wouldn't progress to the semi-final race-off but, given a second opportunity, he makes no mistake in the rerun to pile pressure on his erstwhile rivals. Heat 19 is to prove decisive when Shane Parker's third place thwarts his own ambitions and robs him of any chance of a semi-final appearance. The race winner is Tai Woffinden (again in a class of his own) with Adrian Rymel second. If Rymel and Parker's positions had been reversed, both would have qualified.

Many newfangled ideas and approaches have beset contemporary speedway but, in my opinion, few are as iniquitous as the failure to award any championship to the person who finishes at the top of the points table after all the riders in any given field have completed their nominated number of rides. If this had been the case (and assuming no count back), then we would have, probably, been treated to a three-rider run-off between Tai Woffinden, Adrian Rymel and Jason Bunyan. However, the PLRC meeting format dictates that the top two riders automatically get seeded to the grand final (Woffinden and Rymel) while the next highest placed four riders all compete in a sudden death semi-final. In this elimination race, Nieminen gates from the inside while Doyle battles through the field to ensure that both Ben Barker and (rather unfairly) Jason Bunyan are cast aside. Predictably Tai Woffinden gates and wins the grand final. Jason Doyle provides some opposition but never looks likely to overhaul his young rival. Behind them Kauko Nieminen's engine failure deprives him of third place and saves the blushes of Adrian Rymel, who reserves his worst start of the night for the final race of the night.

21st September Premier League Riders Championship Winner: Tai Woffinden

CHAPTER 43.

Peterborough v. Wolverhampton:
"Please write any additional comments on reverse."

25th September

The 2008 season will be a memorable one for speedway fans who follow both Wolverhampton and Peterborough. Though it's been a season to try to forget in the basement for Wolves, at the East of England Showground it certainly can't be claimed that things are ever dull. In polite terms, it's been a rollercoaster season though arguably the defining moment of 2008 was the departure of the previous Peterborough speedway saviour/owner Colin Horton and the arrival of the club's latest "saviour", Rick Frost. He's a new man to the world of speedway and, whenever his name appears in the *Speedway Star*, you can guarantee that the phrases "Berkshire businessman" or "Speedboat Racing Champion" often also be mentioned. Apparently the league table doesn't lie and tells its own story. Peterborough have declined from the team that only a few short years ago were the Elite League champions and, instead, have become possible contenders for the inaugural relegation from the Elite League (though this is a possibility that very few people actually believe might happen).

If off-track goings on at the Panthers were a soap opera, then viewers could almost be guaranteed a cliffhanger every week. In a nutshell murmurs about finances developed from gentle susurration levels into almost a full-blown hurricane and, along the way, previously good friends – owner Colin Horton and promoter Mick Bratley – had a fall-out that saw the latter's departure. In pure soap opera terms, Bratley's management of Peterborough's number 1 star rider, Hans Andersen who, eventually, left the club allegedly because of unpaid wages and sponsorship monies, further deliciously complicated the situation and added to the drama. During these upheavals Rick Frost nearly bought the club but failed in his initial attempt to gain ownership before his persistence ensured that he was ultimately successful (though in the interim bankrolled the club in secret). If you then add to the mix, the return of East of England Showground crowd pleaser Ryan Sullivan for an all too brief spell (eight matches), allegedly on a huge points money deal even by recent Elite League standards. Let alone the return of Karol Zabik – who'd previously left the club in bad odour – who darkened their door at their hour of greatest need in September (2008), only then to be sacked and almost immediately rehired for the rest of the season and 2009 as well! Prodigal sons were the order of the day, off the track as well as on it, as shown when Mick Bratley also returned to the club under the new Rick Frost administration. Among the riders Daniel King came as close to being ever-present as anyone, while experienced speedway man, Trevor Swales, kept his humour and own counsel throughout.

Another constant at the club was trackshop owner Andy Griggs who continued to occupy the small glass-fronted office-cum-showroom on the ground floor of the home-straight grandstand that serves as the trackshop on race night. When I arrive Andy is already hard at work putting the merchandise out on display. Like many other trackshops in the country, at this stage of the season there's a sale on. Polo shirts have fallen in price (£13.99 to £10) as have rugby shirts (£20 to £15) and pit shirts (from £21.50 to £14.50). These price reductions should be sufficient to set Panthers fans hearts racing but, if not, Ryan Sullivan baseball hats at a bargain price of £5 should be enough to put the smile back on the grumpiest Peterborough supporters' face. Andy emphasises that he's taken a new approach to staff recruitment and, consequently, there's been a dramatic increase in IQ levels in the shop since the arrival of 17-year-old Laura Sawyn. Only a speedway regular for the last year and a half since her step dad, Nick Howlett, introduced her to the sport she's clearly already very much at home in the shop. Because of the irregular availability of the East of England Showground, this season Peterborough have (once again) struggled to race here consistently on their designated Thursday race night but, when they do, Laura serves to earn some much-needed cash. In between times, she studies for her four A levels in psychology, history, classic civilisation and English literature. If she gets the results that she wants, she'd like to do a BA in history at Cambridge University ("I've applied to Cambridge and, if I don't get in, I'll go to Leeds"). Andy's keen to point out with his tongue firmly in his cheek, "Mr Griggs does employ highly intelligent staff (make sure that's in bold print so my mate Dave Rattenberry can read it)." This week Laura has brought along her AS level psychology homework and studies summary information on the classic, path-breaking research famously undertaken in 1961 by Albert Bandur, Dorothea Ross and (no relation) Sheila A. Ross into aggression (*Transmission of Aggression through Imitation of Aggressive Models*). There's often quite a bit of that in the pits after a closely contested race and, if they were all still alive, I'm sure that this would be of interest to these psychologists who, Laura notes, were "observationists".

At the previous meeting, Laura had studied 16th-century history – in particular the Reformation and the Tudors – for her homework. Andy had enjoyed that too, "That was good. I helped! They cut your stomach open, while they're still alive! I enjoyed that more than I did the speedway. It was so good I can't recall who we rode against [it was Ipswich] and that was only on Monday!" Laura lives in the small town of Crowland situated midway between Peterborough and Spalding that's famous for its ruined medieval Abbey and its unique 14th-century three-sided bridge (Trinity Bridge). It isn't a place where there's much demand for Peterborough's speedway merchandise. "I'd buy a padded jacket if I was to buy anything. Generally in here, if they're kids they like bits and bobs whereas polo shirts and clothing goes well with adults." It's a shame the trackshop doesn't stay open during the winter because Andy would then have the chance to study the course texts on Laura's A-level English literature course – *Death of a Salesman*, *Othello* and *The Kite Runner*. Despite this lack of further study, Andy has turned into quite a literary critic, "I tell you something, that *Shale Britannia* is the worst book you've done! My mum – I'm not telling you her name, well, it's Beryl Griggs, mother of the aforementioned Andy – said, 'he doesn't take a very good photo does he?'" Fortunately, before my photographic skills can be subjected to further critique and analysis, Andy's warmly cuddled by Panthers rider Danny King and they immediately go outside for a private talk. At this moment, if this were a 1970s swimming pool changing room, I would point to the notice on the wall, ignore admonitions not to run or indulge in any bombing but, instead, point to the 'No Heavy Petting' advice.

Keen to protect the young and impressionable I venture outside but Andy and Danny are nowhere to be seen. Instead, Mick Bratley arrives in a rather swish motorcar that would immediately form a dashing impression at many locations, let alone the East of England Showground. Mick's distinctively coloured hair looks almost as sporty and dashing as his choice of motor vehicle. Even though he's management, I greet him warmly, "Welcome back! You weren't away long!" Mick nods, "I only missed one match. You're not writing another book, are you? Just put in it, 'Mick Bratley is a ******!'[1]" Pleased with his contribution to sports literature, Mick drives off with a throaty roar from the engine in his new 7 series BMW (sports version). Drat! I'd forgotten to check for Alan Partridge style driving gloves before the distant squeal of tyres on tarmac announced Mick Bratley's arrival elsewhere in the stadium. He's passionate about Peterborough Speedway and, if his posts on the Internet are any indicator, equally committed to policing the 'illegal' production of Peterborough Panthers Riders' photographs. It's a campaign that's all part of his ongoing quest to preserve the integrity and copyright of the highly sought-after and surprisingly evocative Panthers logo.

Keen to learn Laura Sawyn

Bargains galore

Claus Vissing gets advice

---

[1] A man who indulges in solo sexual practices that the government now claims delivers considerable health benefits.

Andy has returned to the trackshop and I overhear a lady exclaim, "So you are a Norfolk boy if you come from Norwich!" The trackshop is absolutely thronged this evening with people keen to hand in detailed market research otherwise known as the club questionnaire[2]. Fans can return these completed documents to ballot-box-like questionnaire receptacles either in the bar or the trackshop. Andy has kindly allowed me to display my books inside the trackshop at the far end of his many display tables. Consequently, I field a whole series of enquiries about Panthers branded items in sizes I can't find, for prices I'm not quite sure of. When I don't confuse the customers or test their patience, a steady stream of them thrust their completed questionnaires into my hand. The devil is in me sufficiently this evening to then ask them: "Actually, there was one question not included on the questionnaire. [this tended to then elicit a quizzical look] Where in the stadium should they put the statue of Colin Horton?" Some people take the trouble to make considered suggestions. Sadly, many of these would be anatomically impossible, even in the unlikely eventuality this statue were only a one-sixteenth scale model of the club's "saviour" before last.

The final interactive bit of the survey poses the question "What three improvements would you like to see at Peterborough speedway?" And reminds them, "Please write any additional comments on reverse." Given the notorious verbosity of speedway fans (and writers), luckily they're limited to only one side of paper (unless they've brought along additional supplies) to comment constructively or, as can be the case when a large number of speedway fans come together, have a good moan. Some respondents appear to have taken this request as an open invitation to indulge in a lengthy strategic plan and/or diatribe. Perhaps to speed up the consideration of these documents, the club could have had the foresight to request that the more risqué and left-field suggestions were colour-coded and written in red or green biro? Personally I would have paid to read these responses but, instead, had to satisfy myself with a subsequent report in the *Speedway Star* based on the 500 forms handed out at the entrance gates. Mark Plummer reported, "the responses threw up a wide range of interesting points, covering everything from a call for improved food to praising the introduction of softer toilet paper." Just as 9 out of 10 owners say their cats prefer it, apparently 91 per cent of the respondents applauded the club for their provision of the cheapest season ticket in the Elite League. 80 per cent of the fans surveyed apparently used the club website on a regular basis and just over a third of them had subscribed to the weather text service. Post-meeting press conferences were held in high esteem though some mardier types suggested additional seats should be laid on in the bar.

If the club wish to fully embrace modernity and provide entertainment appropriate to our technologically sophisticated age, then many suggestions were received about how to improve their service. These included, "Only running one home meeting per week/improvement in the food available on race nights/returning to Friday racing/bringing Hans Andersen back/better track preparation/starting meetings on time/better trackshop/introducing second half racing/improving the PA system/home style parade where riders are introduced in front of the grandstand." In fact, these were only the most popular suggestions. Other possible factors to consider, if the club wished to beef up the overall enjoyment of the speedway experience at the EoES, included a scoreboard on the centre green, better lighting, improved entertainment, more access to the riders, even softer toilet paper and shorter intervals. The survey also highlighted that Peterborough Panthers speedway club draw over 50 per cent of their fans from a geographically wide catchment area far outside Peterborough itself and its local environs. Loyal Panthers fans come from as far afield as Hastings and Felixstowe but are mainly residents of the counties of Lincolnshire, Northamptonshire, Bedfordshire and Hertfordshire. Some things really get the fans' collective goat, notably tactical rides, air horns, animals, the aggregate bonus point and the 10 p.m. curfew. The only response I actually saw myself (I couldn't avoid it since I had to fold it to get it into the box) was, "When Panthers win heats please can they all ride round for us to cheer!" In

---

[2] To give it its formal title, the "Peterborough Speedway Supporters' Survey 2008" asks a series of penetrating in-depth questions that include:
How many Panthers home meeting have you attended this season? (5 or less, 6-10, 11- 15, or, All);
Do you hold a season ticket? (Yes/No);
If YES to season ticket, do you think it's good value? (Yes/No);
If NO to a season ticket, would you consider one for next season? (Yes/No);
If NO, what would persuade you to buy one?
Do you buy a programme (Yes/No);
If NO, why?
Would you be interested in group admission discounts, party of 10 or more? (Yes/No);
Would you like more facilities for children e.g. play area etc?
Do you use the Peterborough website?
Did you use the weather text service this season?"
All respondents are also requested to provide their name, address, postcode, e-mail and mobile phone number.

Peterborough v. Wolverhampton: *"Please write any additional comments on reverse."*

2006 this could have got rather repetitive but, during the 2008 season, this would almost have a certain novelty value. It's great that the club actually consulted their fans! It certainly makes a refreshing change from attitudes held some places elsewhere where fans (like Victorian children) should be seen but not heard. We already know from Gil Scott-Heron that the revolution will not be televised (or will appear on *Sky*, which is more or less effectively the same thing). However, if Rick Frost wanted startling proposals that would take the club to the next level of profitability or popularity, then his research of fans' opinions combined with the expertise of his management along with his own entrepreneurial flair should be a truly potent mixture.

Every time I visit the East of England Showground, it's a pleasure to see Graham and Hilary Rouse, who are both fanatical Panthers fans with a love of their speedway. Talk of the inaugural promotion and relegation play-offs raises the question of whom exactly they'll have to face from the Premier League (should they lose to Wolverhampton). "There won't be many people here tonight 'cause we've had many meetings close together. Whatever happens tonight we'll be in the relegation zone. I think we'll be facing King's Lynn 'cause they're bound to get through 'cause they've got such a home advantage! Edinburgh will race Rye House and King's Lynn will race Somerset before that. When you see how many points King's Lynn win by every week it's bound to be them – and we don't go well at Wolves. I'm sure we'll only lose by 6 or so there [King's Lynn] then we'll win here." Though she supports a team with massive home advantage, Hilary isn't keen to watch astronomical scores elsewhere, "We haven't gone to either King's Lynn or Rye House this season as they're both set up for the home team and you don't want to watch that! Well, it's okay if it's your team as you put up with it! But, as a neutral, it's no fun." According to my calculations, Peterborough face an impossible task since they need to win by 100 points tonight to escape the relegation zone. My mathematics also assumes that other results all go in their favour – namely, that Coventry win at Belle Vue. Graham definitely doesn't expect miracles and dislikes the new-fangled end-of-season structure, "Coventry aren't going to try at Belle Vue, are they? The Elite League needs more teams – not to be relegating them!" The randomness of sport is inevitably built on 'ifs', 'ands', 'buts' and 'maybes'. We briefly savour the possible irony of a scenario where ex-Peterborough rider Hans Andersen lines up for his new club Coventry in heat 15 in the (theoretical) knowledge that a win will condemn his ex-employers to the play-offs while a last place would (theoretically) ensure that this fate awaits Belle Vue. We're interrupted from our hypothetical permutations by a man who has news of an apparently less than bright future for Sittingbourne speedway: "They're losing a thousand pounds a meeting and Graham Arnold has done his last-ever Sittingbourne meeting unless he has a change of heart. I reckon he's tired of battling the council and the idiot – someone who has a house that's way over a field – who complains about the noise. It's just gonna be a training track and for practising!" Hilary is sympathetic about the plight of this grass roots, community-based club but also has sartorial reservations about Ian Glover's fashion sense, "I wish that Start Marshal would change his trousers – he looks like a clown in them!" Though her husband Graham nods, in the manner of long-term couples everywhere, it's impossible to tell whether he approves or disapproves of Ian's fashion sense when he says, "He wears them at Lakeside too!"

Inside the trackshop, the deluge of surveys continues and I also learn that the East of England Showground is a venue that used to attract attractive lady television presenters in leather trousers. "I've met Suzi Perry twice – here and at Leicester Square. She was going out with an awful prat. She knows what she's talking about, that's why the riders respected her!" Andy Griggs isn't completely convinced that the survey will throw up that much useful information if judged by the calibre of some contributions from post-meeting fans' forums held in the bar area. "I took the flags to the Fans' Forum and some woman said, 'That's great, bring them out at the end of the season!' I said, 'They've been here since the first week so that tells me something'. She said, 'What?' I said, 'That you haven't been looking for them!' At the last meeting, there was about a hundred people at the fans' forum to meet the new owner, Rick Frost. I think they were curious and wanted to know what's going on. Someone asked, 'How much money do you get paid by *Sky*?' and when it was clear they weren't going to get an answer they said, Why won't you tell us?' Some people are unbelievable!" If you work in a trackshop (or any shop), you're part salesman, part entrepreneur and often, part therapist. Andy's approach is to keep a noncommittal expression on his face when fans tell him at great length about their opinions, travel or travails. Some Rye House fans arrive in the narrow confines of the shop and relate, in painstaking detail, their pilgrimage to watch Tai Woffinden race at a variety of locations last week. "We went to Scunthorpe and Sheffield and we're back at Rye House in between. We wanted to do it but we were exhausted, so imagine how Tai feels doing it every week?"

This season an evening in the Peterborough trackshop is the speedway equivalent of a guest appearance on *Mastermind*. Laura Sawyn has temporarily ditched her college homework in favour of some study of the *Driving Test Theory* booklet, "I've got my exam Saturday." [3] For people of a certain age, the idea that – in order to drive a car – you have to pass a theory test appears shockingly irrelevant. However, in *l'Ecole du trackshop*, Andy Griggs clearly thrives in his role as teacher and, under Laura's guidance, has gained polymathic knowledge of a wide variety of subjects. He's keen to quiz me, "Name three crossings named after animals?" It's definitely a teaser, "I know Pelican – that's a bird, mind – and Zebra, what's the other one?" Laura tells me, "There's two. A Puffin, that's for cycles and Pecan for I'm not sure!" I always thought pecan was a pie or a nut! [4] Before I can further reveal my ignorance, my refresher course on the Highway Code is mercifully cut short when announcer Kevin Moore arrives in the trackshop and wanders over with a request, "Just write something nice about me in your next book! Oh and I'm not Mike Bennett!" Obviously enough since, in the words of that famous speedway chant, "There's only one Mike Bennett!" Keen to complete his research before he heads off to his duties, Kevin kindly takes some key details about my book to use during the meeting when he announces my visit over the loudspeaker system. After Kevin departs, Andy comments, "Has he come and seen me? Have I got a sale on? [Andy has] If you weren't here, he'd be walking up and down here and go out again 'cause he hasn't figured out why he needs to come in here yet!"

Oxford trackman Nobby Hall has ventured cross-country to the East of England Showground for a much-needed dose of speedway action. Though, this season the Oxford Cheetahs sadly no longer require the use of Cowley Stadium, Nobby's old curatorial habits die hard. "I go to check it over every day! There were weeds growing on it and the dog people wanted it tidied up for TV. Best to look after it so that it doesn't take so much work when we need to use it again!" Nobby's come into the trackshop to buy a programme and is disappointed to learn that he has to go some distance back to the entrance turnstiles to purchase one. While he's there he kindly gets me one too so I immediately demonstrate my legendry lack of common sense and completely fail to understand how to use tonight's document. To be fair to myself, the scorecard in the centre of the programme is definitely only suitable for Monday night's Ipswich meeting and I feel hugely short-changed that it doesn't appear to be appropriate for tonight's meeting against Wolverhampton. In reality the relevant scorecard is found a few pages later in the programme but by then I've told the man widely considered to be the best speedway referee in the world, Tony Steele, that he's just bought an Ipswich programme. ("You're joking!") When I see him in the pits later, thankfully Tony has seen through my 'joke'/error, "Have you found it in the programme yet? I thought you were joking." Sadly, I was just being stupid.

It's always a privilege to be able to stand in the pits to watch proceedings and, from Edwin Overland's announcement, it's clear that the programme must actually contain a racecard for this meeting. "The Peterborough team is as per programme but there are a few changes to the other team." In fact, the opposite is the case since the Wolverhampton line-up is as per programme while Karol Zabik and Henning Bager swap positions. Zabik drops to reserve (number 6) while Bager takes his place in the main body of the team (number 4). The meeting effectively ends as a competitive contest when the first race is won by Lukas Dryml (whom Edwin Overland appears to calls Lukas Dribble) closely followed home by Peterborough's errant but prodigal son Ryan Sullivan. The difference in track shape and size between the East of England Showground and the Monmore Green stadium will be a significant hurdle to overcome for the visitors. Whatever the result tonight, Wolverhampton will still find themselves marooned and significantly adrift at the bottom of the Elite League table. To a certain extent, Peterborough still enjoy a measure of self-determination since they still (comparatively) control their own destiny and could avoid the end-of-season Elite League promotion/relegation play-

---

[3] When I worked in publishing, one of our sister companies made headline news in the *Sun* with the revelation that for [time period redacted] candidates who sat the driving theory test then were presented with some multiple-choice questions where there were no correct answers! Obviously, it's a reasonable assumption to expect when you're presented with four possible multiple choice answers to a driving theory question that one of them will be correct. This inadvertent error meant that all candidates who sat the exam had severely reduced chances of success. The 'heart rending' story in the *Sun* featured a man who'd allegedly (and foolishly) spent his life savings (around £900, I think) on a second-hand car to transport him to and from a job that he'd accepted. Given he had no licence to drive, he'd clearly got slightly ahead of himself but his failure to progress beyond the driving theory stage of the exam scuppered his chance to attain a licence and, subsequently, cost him his job offer. Unable to drive and without any income to allow him to insure his car, he'd taken drastic steps and got the car crushed. Personally the idea that you could sit down and take an exam and fail because there were sections with no right answers is, at least, farcical if not downright hysterically funny! However, it was no laughing matter for the Chief Executive of the testing company who, shortly after the article appeared, did the honourable thing and took responsibility for her actions.

[4] In fact, the wonderful world of pedestrian crossings now includes the following crossing types: Zebra, Pelican (Pedestrian Light Controlled Crossing) and Puffin (Pedestrian User-Friendly Intelligent crossings), along with Toucan's (Two-Can Cross) for cyclists and Pegasus crossings for horses!

Peterborough v. Wolverhampton: *"Please write any additional comments on reverse."*

off, if they were to win and Belle Vue were to lose their final Elite League fixture against Coventry.

An even greater pleasure than the opportunity to watch the race action from the pits is the opportunity to stand next to Peterborough Panthers Club Chaplain, the Reverend Michael Whawell. He watches the first race intently and afterwards, draws my attention to how much better the track is tonight than for the meeting against Ipswich, "It was faster than Monday with its 67s and 68s." If I hadn't written *Showered in Shale*, I would have never encountered Michael. He's done so much in his life it would be impossible to even attempt to live mine so richly though, nonetheless, my ambition remains to practise my writing enough so that I can write half as elegantly as he does. He has a sophisticated and quick wit, a frightening level of erudition on any topic you care to name and is a man of many passions. These include speedway, the church, people, and, of course, his wife Shirley and family, along with too many others to attempt to list. Speedway journalist and author, John Chaplin, highlighted Michael's resemblance to the Archbishop of Canterbury, Doctor Rowan Williams. I don't see that myself. John also bravely attempted to sum up Michael in an article that appeared in the *Speedway Star*.[5] "He is a man of many parts: speedway aficionado, soldier, qualified State Registered Nurse – a profession in which he reached the exalted heights of matron – rugby player, soccer player, cricketer, radio sports' commentator, he's run a dozen London marathons, he was a country parson, is a model railway enthusiast and is a freeman of the City of London." Nowadays Michael lives 18 minutes from the East of England Showground in Upper Glapthorn and told John Chaplin, "I've been so lucky to retire near Peterborough speedway because I think it's a great track. Big and fast, and I know people who pass other speedways to go to the Showground because of the sheer excitement of the racing. No dog track, nothing in the way, an old-fashioned racers' track. It's been an enormous privilege to be able to go there." In fact, Michael is the President of the Southern Track Riders in addition to his work as Peterborough Panthers Club Chaplain (he also holds this position for the World Speedway Riders' Association). "What I do is honorary. I must be the only Reverend with a BSPA pass." Michael has his own Weslake at home (along with a steel shoe) and to startle the neighbours, he occasionally fires it into life. Though retired, he still conducts a variety of ceremonies and tonight's speedway meeting contrasts sharply to events earlier in the day when he did the honours at "a funeral of a 39 year old suicide chap".

There's drama in the second heat when Claus 'the Crab' Vissing falls when second. He endures what Mark Plummer calls in his subsequent *Speedway Star* report "a nasty, but thankfully injury-free, smash". Dog collars (like uniforms everywhere) attract the confused, needy or angry, so it isn't a surprise when a man rushes over and asks Michael, "Will it be awarded?" With a hotline to the afterlife and the heavens, it's probably a reasonable assumption that Michael would automatically have some insight into the latest iteration of the SCB Rulebook as well as the considered thinking of tonight's official, Dale Entwistle. Michael is able to keep these powers secret and also help the man, "The definitive answer is on hand – the voice of authority – Tony Steele!" It's the man's lucky night since not only is Tony a justifiably highly acclaimed speedway referee but he's also patient enough to answer any queries, no matter how ridiculous (or complex). Tony then kindly proceeds to explain at length to the disgruntled man why this race has not been awarded. I'd have thought that his opening sentence explained it succinctly, "All four riders have to have done two laps before you can award it!" However, when you're disgruntled and you've got your dander up, like a waiverer stood on the ledge of a skyscraper, it can take some time to get talked back down and inside again.

Any conversation in the pits viewing area is somewhat difficult to hear above the noise of revving engines but, nonetheless, I catch Michael's wry comment upon Fredrik Lindgren's brother, "Ludvig Lindgren sounds like a philosopher or Nobel Prize winner!" During the break in proceedings for the rerun of the second heat Michael can bring up some of the more important events in life, "Have you noticed how Mansfield are on the slide?" They've suffered a points deduction but Michael, typically, takes a forgiving view, "Some player gave them false information." We're ideally placed in the frenetic hubbub of the pits to watch the riders as they prepare to go back out onto the track. Pleasure in the simple things of life and the sight of the three riders ready to go out through the pits gate prompts Michael to gleefully exclaim, "Here we go again!" Though a career in philosophy might beckon in the future, tonight Ludvig fishtails from the gate and struggles for control of his bike. However, since there are only three riders in the race, should he complete all four laps he's ensured of the third-place point, something he duly gets. When Edwin Overland announces the race

---

[5] Reactions to this article have varied. "The most common, and to me surprising, reaction has been 'Didn't know you had a model railway'. Even up to and including the estimable Tony Steele who revealed to me that he has several layouts from gauge 0 right down to Z – the most miniscule railway-in-a-briefcase job!"

results, he praises Ludvig for, "Showing good control to stay on". The race is won comfortably by Karol Zabik and, even though the meeting is only two races old, Michael has sussed out track conditions. "It seems once you're on the line – about two-thirds of the way out – you just stay on it! Danny [King] said it was like ice racing, very tricky – on by a whisker or you're completely off it! [Nods towards Rick Frost] Have you met the new owner? They all smoke, the whole family!"

Whatever the exact location of the racing line, it's like a clitoris to the Wolverhampton riders who collectively struggle to find it for most of the night! However, in the third heat they're unlucky when second-placed Niels-Kristian Iversen suffers an engine failure. Michael comments more politely upon this than you'd imagine the rider or the Wolverhampton team management do, "Oh dear, more gremlins!" If it's bad enough to drop easy points for mechanical reasons, then the situation is compounded by the resultant 5-1 for the Panthers. Wolverhampton's number 4, David Howe, finishes the race in lacklustre fashion massively trailed off at the back and, even though this looks poor, it will turn out to be a pinnacle since this will be his only point of the evening. With the scores already less than poised at 13-5, Edwin Overland tries desperately to inject some much-needed drama into proceedings with his theatrical announcement of the rider line-up for heat 4, "Jesper B. [pauses for effect] Monberg." Michael notes sardonically, "There's ex-Panthers all over the place tonight. I haven't seen old Jesper since he changed his name and haircut! Lukas has a rather flash suit on – is his usual in the wash?" Though he definitely knows his way round the best racing lines of the East of England Showground track, Jesper B. Monberg somehow manages to finish last while the Panthers zoom to their third 5-1 in the first four heats. Michael takes great satisfaction in the ongoing improvement of young Danish rider Claus Vissing, "Your friend Claus 'the crab' is now a Peterborough asset. He's come on a hell of a lot this season!"

Tony Steele tells me he's surprised to find himself at the East of England Showground this evening, "I've come here on autopilot. I wonder what I'm doing here?" Successful speedway riders have nightmare travel schedules during the speedway season but, then, so do referees of Tony's exalted standard. He's got a well-deserved holiday ahead but fits this around the demands of his work along with his duties as an international speedway official. "I'm on holiday then back two days at work, two days of business in Rome. It's a tight schedule and I'm flying from Rome to Gelsenkirchen for practice and then back on Sunday and Monday at Poole for the play-off final as TV steward. Poole versus Swindon would be the more thrilling final – I think they [Swindon] might win at Lakeside!" Tony is a thoughtful and knowledgeable man who speaks diplomatically about controversial incidents that involve his fellow speedway officials. He has great belief in communication to overcome misunderstandings and confusions. "Christian Froshauer, the referee at the Coventry World Cup, confused people because he didn't exclude people. I wish the ref had explained himself. It's always a shame when the ref doesn't explain his decisions!" A complex situation is further complicated by variations in the different Rulebooks that apply to speedway racing in Britain, Poland and Sweden, never mind the further differences contained in the FIM rule book. "The British Rulebook is clear – if any part of the machine or rider touches the tapes they're excluded. The FIM Rulebook says if the machine (only) touches it they're excluded. However, there's a second rule that says if you delay the start you're excluded though again Niels-Kristian Iversen would have been excluded." Tony enquires about how my book sales have gone going this season, nods interestedly, and observes, "People have no money! Jason Crump's book sold well initially and then died until they reduced the price to clear. Tempus reduced the price of tons of their books. That was because they needed to clear the warehouse for space. People don't have the money they once did!"

Previously sacked by Peterborough, tonight sees the return of Morten Risager to the East of England Showground – this time in a Wolverhampton race tabard. It's far from a memorable evening for him but he does, at least, finish second behind Kenneth Bjerre in heat 5 to record his only points of the evening (from four rides). With Fredrik Lindgren in third place this drawn heat briefly interrupts the ongoing sequence of 5-1s for the Panthers until this immediately resumes again in the next heat (6) won by Ryan Sullivan. David Howe retires in the seventh heat and, although Danny King wins the race, Niels-Kristian Iversen's second place, in comparative terms, represents something of a fightback for Wolverhampton who manage to only lose the heat 4-2. Nicolai Klindt obviously hasn't read the depressing Wolverhampton script and so emerges victorious at the end of heat 8 to become the first Wolves rider to win a race this evening at the Showground. Once Nicolai has tasted success, he just can't get enough of the chequered flag and so proceeds to win heat 9 as well!

Away to the left of the pits are some voluble and disgruntled Wolverhampton fans though, after the season they've endured, by now you would expect them to be stoically resigned to their fate or look to the future for succour. In his typically understated fashion, Tony sums the situation up: "Wolverhampton are a poor side. There's been a lot of good meetings here this season but this isn't inspiring!" Given his extensive travel over the years, it's hardly a surprise that Tony knows many of the quirky characters that make speedway what it is in so many countries where it's raced across Europe. The successful and eye-catching arrival of 19-year-old Jurica Pavlic to British speedway racing has brought Tony considerable pleasure on behalf of the Pavlic family. "He comes from Gorican in Croatia. It's a small town but they have a track there built by his dad in a hop field in the middle of nowhere. It's a real 'rags to riches' story. Jurica's a lovely boy from a lovely family. He looks a little odd but the mum and the sisters are stunning. His dad Zvonko, was a very good speedway rider whose career was cut short by injury when he crashed at Ljubljana. After he came out of hospital he collapsed and, when he went back in, they found a lump of wood still in him from the safety fence. It's a mystery how they missed it! Zvonko always said he'd build a track and we just laughed at him. After his career was cut short – he won the Yugoslavian national title a couple of times [in 1986 and 1988] – he had a real 'rags to riches' story. He was a small road mender, and once communism ended, they started building new roads. Zvonko's now the number one non-motorway road builder in Croatia – well, it's a road and aggregates company. There was nowhere safe for his son Jurica to ride so he built his own track. That's the thing about that country, you don't pass by – you have to visit! So, that means, if you want to ride you have to travel. We always said we'd go to the first meeting at his track and, you know when you say to somebody you'll do something, you have to do it! He built the track close to his house and, when I went the second time, he'd put up a back-straight grandstand. He's going to get a roof on it 'cause he wants to stage a GP there by the time he's 50.[6] Jurica has been very dedicated and has practised and practised. His father has driven him all over. Everywhere is a long way away from Croatia. He's come over here and it's amazing he has over a 100 points already! As I say, he's a lovely boy and they're a lovely family!"

The Wolves team collectively have a deflated look about them and, just before heat 10, the air fence joins them in sympathy when it punctures. Niels-Kristian Iversen wears the black-and-white helmet for this race and proceeds to beat both Lukas Dryml and the highly regarded (by himself) Ryan Sullivan. During the interval over at the trackshop, the Panthers fashion item of the season appears to be the Danny King black baseball cap with a very hip-hop metallic peak effect. The trackshop is crowded with people. Most of them have come along to hand in their surveys. Later Andy tells me, "There were well over a hundred surveys handed in here!" The racing resumes and heat 11 features the most exciting racing manoeuvre of the evening (so far) when Fredrik Lindgren thrillingly passes Danny King on the fourth bend of the first lap. He proceeds to streak away to win with some ease. Earlier Wolverhampton couldn't get a win for love nor money and yet, suddenly, the last four races have been won by Wolverhampton riders. The Reverend Michael Whawell has returned from a visit to the disabled fans in the home-straight grandstand, "It's so loud over there! I had to come back to the pits for some peace and quiet!" The 12th heat of the night features Claus Vissing's second fall of the meeting and, viewed from the pits, it's a hugely dramatic affair though our view is obscured by the air fence to the extent we can only see his bike handlebars appear above our sightline of the top of the fence. He must have come off his machine with some aplomb and ingenuity, since his handlebars twice bob above the fence sightline, almost as if he's organised his own one-man speedway tribute to the Dambusters. Once it's clear that Claus had survived (if not exactly thrived) from his encounter with the inflatable safety furniture, Michael can safely be sardonic, "Everybody keeps falling off and I want to go home!" We're joined in the pits by Oxford trackman Nobby Hall who's enjoyed his rare night at the speedway. He confides in Michael, "I first went when I was 8". He's now 66, so it's been in his blood for quite some time. They both know Bernard Crapper who'd retired last season from his role in charge of the Speedway Riders' Benevolent Fund. Michael reports, "Bernard's not at all well – he had his 50th wedding anniversary recently – I don't know what's wrong but he's not well." Bernard is praised as a stalwart before the conversation moves on to consider news that next season will see the introduction of "new mufflers – speedway will never sound the same again!" Michael has technical concerns, "Will it reduce the power of the bikes?" On a fast circuit like the East of England Showground any loss of power would be quite noticeable.

---

[6] Jurica Pavlic commented in the *Speedway Star*, "My father makes a beautiful stadium, one of the best in Europe. Now he makes the roof of the stadium to make it like in Cardiff. He wants the Grand Prix, I'm not sure yet, I think it'll be 2010 he will ask. And, of course, that would be a dream – to win the first Croatian Grand Prix!"

Peterborough v. Wolverhampton: *"Please write any additional comments on reverse."*

There's drama in the pits after Fredrik Lindgren has won heat 13. Ryan Sullivan comes back in high dudgeon. ("What happened there? Ryan looked ready to stop and get off!") Whatever has transpired definitely hasn't pleased a grumpy Ryan and, while Trevor Swales rings up the referee on the pits phone, Ryan stands next to him and gestures wildly. Dale Entwistle's reported response also doesn't meet with Ryan's approval and he continues to complain loudly. Wolverhampton team manager Peter Adams rings the tactical changes prior to the penultimate race of the night when he replaces David Howe with Ludvig Lindgren. After three rides for one point it's not exactly a controversial decision and doesn't surprise Michael Whawell, "David Howe never does well here – it's always something, bike problems or fisticuffs." The race itself features the manoeuvre of the meeting when Karol Zabik cuts inside two riders on the third bend at high speed to take the lead. Invariably taciturn, with eyes aglow Michael remarks, "It's nearly getting exciting." The drama has clearly seized guest presenter Kevin Moore who, possibly in unconscious tribute to *faux* orgasmic excitement showcased every week on *Sky* by Kelvin Tatum and Nigel Pearson, exclaims extremely loudly over the speaker, "All I can say is wow! That was one of the moves of the season." I can't quite put my finger on it but I suspect Kevin quite enjoyed that race. Though, to be fair, afterwards I learn the Panthers have a pre-recorded "wow!" message to be played to the fans.

Prior to heat 15, I notice that inside the first-bend building that houses the EoES bar area, that the front four rows of seats set out in preparation for the post-meeting press conference (led by Rick Frost) are already completely filled! These fans are so keen to learn more that they'll happily ignore the last race of the night to hang on his every word, sit close to celebrity or ensure they're ideally placed to ask questions. Unnoticed in the crowd, Tony Steele is stood between the home-straight grandstand and the bar building on a grass bank to savour the final race of the night. Just as the riders line up at the tapes the red lights come on and a bell sounds. Either one of the riders has won a prize or referee Dale Entwistle has noticed an infraction of the regulations. Tony provides an explanation, "I think he's just cottoned on to the fact that Zabik can't ride because he's not one of the three top scorers or in the top three averages – so he's not eligible!" There are many ways to skin a cat and, if injuries dictate, the track doctor can instruct a rider to withdraw from a meeting on medical grounds. Edwin Overland gives a bland description of the sudden medical ailment that has overcome one of the Panthers riders, "Danny King has just withdrawn and he's the second Panthers rider to get a sick note." Tony wonders aloud, "Has he just fallen over? I didn't hear that anyone had withdrawn. Maybe it was Vissing? But he wouldn't have been eligible, anyway!" Once the race is under way, after a slow start, Niels-Kristian Iversen appears determined to stamp his authority on proceedings. He overtakes his team mate Fredrik Lindgren on the third bend of the third lap and then nearly snatches the win on the line from Kenneth Bjerre though, with the naked eye (viewed for the first bend) it looks impossible to separate them. Dale Entwistle adjudicates that it's a win for the diminutive Bjerre. This ensures the Panthers win the meeting far more comfortably than the 56-37 scoreline suggests. Instead of the usual rush for the car park, significant numbers of fans crowd into the bar area for the fans' forum and post-meeting press conference. It's so full in there there's barely a spare square inch to be found. Health and safety appears ignored but, possibly more significantly, it's difficult to even get to the bar for a drink. It's also so crowded in the hallway outside the bar that you can barely get into the loos. Sadly I'm unable to get inside to listen to the account of the evening or to learn more about visions of the future but, whichever way you look at it, enthusiasm has returned to the club in spades after a difficult and tempestuous season. The role of any new management is always to look ahead and this, of course, is always where dreams can be fulfilled (even if the natural inclination of any speedway fan is to romanticise the glamour and thrills of the past). Sarah Miles' search for her missing other half has taken her into the trackshop and, as she comes through the door, she makes a point to highlight to me, "My husband is a sad bastard!" I know Steve is the Panthers Programme Editor, but this is news. Steve looks up from the not-so-secret pleasure of his thorough search through the discount Peterborough merchandise, "Don't put that in!"

25th September Peterborough v. Wolverhampton (Elite League) 56-37

Peterborough v. Wolverhampton: *"Please write any additional comments on reverse."*

CHAPTER 44.

Rye House/CLRC:
"'Ere Lisa, pose for a photo so you can be on the cover of his next book!"

27th September

The blue riband individual event of the Conference League season is the Conference League Riders' Championship this year staged in Hoddesdon, home of Rye House speedway club. Four hours before the scheduled start time the stadium car park is deserted and all the entrances to the stadium remain impregnably locked. It's remarkably quiet. Absolutely no sound of activity drifts over the stadium wall. The only course of action is to bang on the metal gate and eventually it's held ajar by a man (Little Pete) who looks out at me suspiciously. My question ("Can I come in?") gets a definite answer, "No, you can't! Not being funny – no! We're not open yet." I've arranged my visit with Len Silver but Little Pete is unable to check this because Len is presently asleep. After a bit more conversation, he relents and allows me to unload my boxes and take them into the stadium. Once inside, I find Andy Griggs hard at work unpacking his stock from his van. Pleased to have arrived inside the hallowed portals of Rye House speedway club, I tell Andy, "It's lucky that bloke let me in, otherwise I'd have been locked out still!"

[Andy] "You didn't ring the bell like everyone else?"

[JS] "I didn't know there was a bell. Where is it?"

[Andy] "By the door!"

Least said soonest mended is often the best course of action, so I set out my stall where Hazal Naylor suggested it would be best located last time I exhibited here. Although Hazal is away working in France, even when she's in another country, I'm keen to do exactly as Hazal suggests within Hoddesdon stadium. After I've laid out my stock, I explore the deserted stadium. The famous fish and chip area of the stadium looks resplendent with its shining sauna-effect wooden panels, though it appears slightly forlorn without its trademark lengthy queues (or any staff behind the counter). Slightly further on, sat on the wooden boards of the terraces that overlook the stop/finish line at Hoddesdon, Andy Griggs relaxes before work with Gaz. With proprietorial pride, Gaz surveys his nearby refreshment kiosk and tells me, "I like to get everything set up and all the dishcloths in place well before I start cooking!" The kiosk definitely looks conspicuously spick and span with its clean surfaces and glistening tea urn. Stacked at the front of the kiosk, there's an impressive array of circular and hotdog shaped buns bundled in plastic bags, next to a pile of napkins and a bowl full of wooden spoons. On the shelves at the rear of the compact kiosk, a variety of soft drink cans face neatly outwards adjacent to bulk quantities of Styrofoam containers that await yet-to-be-ordered hot food. Conical shaped clear plastic bags full of sweets hang from the ceiling, while the front of the kiosk is festooned with Coca-Cola posters that shoutily advise we "Play Refreshed!"

The kiosk's tall grey coloured fridge/freezer has an impressive array of cleaning liquids stacked on top and a large Flag of St. George takes pride of place stuck in the centre of its door. Gaz explains patriotically, "I'm English, not freakin' British!" Behind where Andy and Gaz sit, there's a half completed new building that turns out to be the new referee's box. Unlike the existing one, it will helpfully overlook the start/finish line rather than a spot five yards further down the track. Gaz explains, "They had to put the other one there [points away from the start/finish line] 'cause it was for the dogs. Now the dogs aren't running here anymore they can do it different!" In fact, this was a requirement for the club insisted upon by the FIM if the club were to continue to stage key Under-21 World Championship rounds since, at previous U21 qualifiers, referees had had to stand in a temporary shed in line with the tapes.

Andy confirms that Len is in the Land of Nod. Gaz suggests it might not be a good idea to go and wake him, "I wouldn't! He's 74 and he's been working here since 7 a.m., so he deserves a rest!" When questioned, Gaz explains

where he's from: "I live here! Well, I'm from the fairground over there!" He points to the caravan site on the back straight. On previous visits, I'd noticed a sign outside that says, "Showmen's Winter Quarters". The buildings there look much more like lodges than caravans. Judged by the glistening paintwork and impressive array of plants, it's clear the residents are anything but peripatetic. Proud to be English and proud to live locally, Gaz tells me with some pride, "30 or 40 families live there. We love it round here. Lorraine's [lady who works in the refreshment kiosk with Gaz] family has been there 53 years. It's really great and it's not Harlow!" Though it's only a few miles away Gaz emphasises that he doesn't hold the new town of Harlow in high regard. It hasn't been a great year to run the refreshment kiosk, "This season's been awful! The crowds are really down 'cause money is very tight! Everything's going up and up nowadays – petrol, food, gas – everything! No wonder no one's got any money! Speedway is much more exciting and better value than football but still people can't afford it." To add to these tales of recession in strong regional accents, Andy Griggs chips in, "When the CLRC first came here five years ago, there'd be coaches coming from all over – from really far away – but I don't think the crowd will be up to much tonight." Gaz nods, "I asked people last night [at the Rye House v. Newcastle Premier League meeting] if they were coming tonight and they say "Nah – I can only afford once a week now!"" Years before he started to work in his refreshment kiosk, Gaz had the chance to possibly play professional football. Back then football wasn't the glamorous highly paid activity it has now become. "I played for Chelsea for seven years and, when I was 16, they gave me a four-year contract. But, at 17, I walked away from it all when my mum died! You don't know what you want to do then never mind when something like that happens. Eddie McCready was the manager then. He used to smoke like a chimney. They all did – Peter Osgood, John Sparrow and Butch Wilkins. Eddie McCready came along to our youth training and said, 'I'm gonna make you run your guts out today!' The fag was hanging out of his mouth. 'And don't smoke 'cause it ain't good for you!' It was a difficult time. I'm still a Chelsea fan! I like your [Sunderland] manager, Roy Keane. If he don't like you, you're out. You know where you stand. Either do it his way or you can freak off!"

Back at my stall Andy Griggs returns some boxes of unsold books to me. "I've got Malcolm Vasey's to return too. I only sold two of his books on the Conference League. They're spiral bound and sealed in cling film." Though the turnstiles have yet to open, Andy's trackshop is a natural stop-off point for stadium staff as they arrive before they go elsewhere for their duties. Already completely prepared for the night ahead, Gaz is in playful conversation with a balding man in glasses who's distinctively dressed in white winklepickers, white trousers and a black shirt. It's an eye-catching style of dress that you don't see so much of nowadays. Still, he's well presented and wears the type of clothes that my mum would consider smart but, because he looks like a late-period balding Elvis Presley, she would probably also consider a bit "weirdy". Despite his memorable attire, the man bemoans the desert of his sex life to Gaz who's not exactly the most sympathetic audience, "I said to him earlier, 'your dad was a boxer [pause] and your mum was a greyhound!'" News that I'm a 'writer' prompts the man to tell me, "You should do my book – *Forty-Five Years Behind the Scenes at Speedway*." Gaz feigns astonishment, "No wonder we can never find you if you're behind the scenes!" Their banter and repartee is interrupted by the arrival of an attractive blonde-haired young woman. Gaz calls out, "'Ere Lisa, pose for a photo so you can be on the cover of his next book!"

[Lisa] (less than keen) "No way!"

[Gaz] "Why not?"

[Lisa] "'cause I'm ugly!"

[Gaz] "Oh right! I must have my ugly glasses on then! Come on Luscious Lisa – do you wanna be on the cover? (turns to me) She'd look good!" (she would)

While Lisa retreats to the bar, Gaz resumes upbraiding the man with the white trousers and winklepickers, "Anyway he's writing about you saying you're the twat at Rye House speedway!" The banter stops immediately with the arrival of Len Silver. After our recent meeting at Scunthorpe speedway, I shake Len's hand with some confidence only to find a quizzical look on his face. I remind him who I am. "Oh, I didn't recognise you. Last time I saw you it was dark!"

Once the turnstiles open, there's an initial rush of fans keen to secure their own ideal spot in the stadium from which to watch the CLRC action. Among these early arrivals are Graham and Hilary Rouse who've come with so much gear that I'm unsure whether they've here to watch the speedway or set up base camp before they mount an exploration

Rye House/CLRC: *'Ere Lisa, pose for a photo so you can be on the cover of his next book!"*

of the area. Graham admits with a smile, "We bring more gear than the riders!" Hilary picks up a copy of *Shale Britannia* from my table and pulls a face to signal she's about to give me her critical appraisal, "To be honest, I don't see anything in it!" They're a friendly couple who are speedway fans first and Peterborough fans second or vice versa. They're worried about the future of Boston speedway (who presently race at King's Lynn's Norfolk Arena). "Dale Allitt put on the forum that Boston's highest crowd – I think for the Trophy Final – was 283. The average was around 160 and the lowest was about 120! You can't survive on numbers like for too long, can you?" Talk moves on to something to do with Sheffield speedway and in particular, "The little one Dave Hogarth or Hogwart or something." Temporarily delayed from staking the claim to their favoured spot on the first bend, they quickly bustle off with their big tent-like chairs.

Gaz prepares

Club presenter Craig Saul arrives with his trademark banana and explains that he missed the Peterborough versus Wolverhampton Elite League B clash because of a business trip to Israel. Craig is a marketing manager for "A plastics company that makes garden sheds. You'll have seen them if ever you've been into Homebase, B&Q, Argos, Wicks, Costco and Focus amongst others." The company is owned by "the 14th richest man in Israel" who's also "the co-owner of Hapoel Tel Aviv (whom Chelsea might remember)." Craig has visited Israel many times and flies there with El Al who are famous for the rigour of their security checks. "I was asked all the usual security questions and the last one was: 'Where does your surname come from?' I can give many answers. I talked Torah. I told him about the book of Samuel where King Saul commits suicide rather than fall into the hands of his enemies. There's Mount Shaul (the Hebrew original for Saul) too – I try to keep my ego in check but I'm very proud of 'my' mountain. I also mentioned that my father originally came to this country [England] on the Kindertransport. He was one of the very first evacuation arrivals in 1938 (and actually captured in a photo in *Picture Post* magazine, which he and I still have) which seemed to close that [line of questioning] down."

Trophies ready

It's a big night for the riders and the opportunity to showcase their talents and/or further development. Tom Brown approaches the meeting in a confident frame of mind, "I just need five good starts tonight!" It wouldn't be a speedway meeting without gossip. An Oxford fan lets me know, "I went to Somerset and it was better racing there than at Oxford. They say Tony Mole is gonna take over." Another fan makes a prediction about the eventual winner, "Dean Felton said to us the other week he feels it's his year to win a CLRC. He says he just felt it was. Wow! What was that? A pig flying by?" It wouldn't really be a meeting at Rye House if George and Linda Barclay weren't present. They have a lot more time to attend Hoddesdon meetings nowadays since they no longer diligently fundraise on behalf of the Speedway Museum. George is always mild-mannered, quietly spoken and optimistically philosophical, "Health is luck, isn't it? I said that to a consultant and he looked surprised but agreed. You can do everything you think is right and still just get struck down! I'm tremendous! I've never felt better apart, of course, from the Alzheimer's, but I live with that." Linda Barclay is a huge fan of speedway racing at the Conference League level. "Sittingbourne is the grass roots of the sport! But, on crowds of 100, it's never going to do anything but lose money! I know Graham [Arnold] is worried that some of the riders go on to other things but

The shy Lisa

Rye House/CLRC: *'Ere Lisa, pose for a photo so you can be on the cover of his next book!"*

Sittingbourne is always going to be a stepping-stone. They should do more corporate days and training sessions as they'd make more money that way than running Conference League meetings!" Brendan Johnson passes and has a brief chat with George and Linda as well as myself. After he's gone George remarks, "He really is a very nice young man! People expect motorbike riders to be rough and ready but so many of them are nice!"

Anyone who is anyone within Conference League speedway has tried to be here tonight – whether riders, staff or fans. Plymouth Devils Programme Editor, Gary Spiller, has made the journey up from the South West, "Our crowds are down. We've had some below 500. I think the Best Pairs had 350 and, on the odd other wet Friday, we didn't get many. But then we've had a lot of rain this year!" Knowledgeable speedway fan, Charles McKay, is here to watch the meeting but also to swap some collectable programmes with fellow like-minded fans. "There's some sad bastards around – they want the rain-off programme and the meeting programme, even if it's the same programme! When Wimbledon went to Buxton it was rained off twice – people had to get three! I stopped at Peterborough Services on the way down to swap programmes. There's hardly any people here tonight. I had to look at my watch 'cause I've seen so few go by. I had to be here to get some money off people. Oh, and there is one I owe it to [Richard Hollingsworth]." After he's completed the transaction Charles returns and needs no second invitation to discuss the speedway Grand Prix series. "Who's progressing through the GPs each year? Hardly anyone! You only have to look through the results to see who never gets to the semi-finals or only does so once in a blue moon! There's also the sponsorship myth! Sure the top few riders attract good sponsorship but, if you're one of those riders who never gets to the semi-finals, why would you want to sponsor such a rider? Look at Andy Smith – you always knew he'd be in the GP challenge, and whenever he won he celebrated like he'd won the world final! In the old days they had a job and worked as well as being a speedway rider. Nowadays, they ride but often don't have a job. You can last 10 to 15 years riding a bike and, when you finish, you've got no trade behind you and probably no money! What are they going to do when they retire? Only so many can do engine tuning! I don't know the exact answer but what is the average age of Premier League riders? In the old days, they went on to better things. Nowadays if they go up to the Elite League, they often can't make as much money. I'm going to the German GP – James Easter says only 6,000 tickets have been sold for Gelsenkirchen! [spots Steve Miles] He's one of the sad bastards [who collects multiple copies of the same programme]."

Stood by my bookstall, tonight I must accidentally have my authority figure face on because John Goldsmith comes up and asks me some unanswerable questions about the track. "One thing I want to know is: how deep is the base? And what is it built of? And how much shale do they put down? As a teenager I rode on an old cinder track here. It was a 440-yard track but I just can't orientate myself. I'd like to know what's the base under the shale and how thick is the shale? I seem to pick up somewhere it's concrete but that wouldn't drain then, would it? The camber is definitely not as bad as it used to be! You used to drift half a yard out and fall off a precipice!" In my opinion, no speedway meeting would be complete (or so enjoyable) without the attendance of Arnie Gibbons. He fits an intense speedway travel schedule in around his accountancy work. His love of the sport takes him to a wide variety of glamorous locations. Last night he was in Scunthorpe ("Danny Warwick got paid 9 and put some effort in!) and he's here tonight in similarly glamorous Hoddesdon. The imminent demise of Reading speedway continues to play on Arnie's mind, "I have to say that the End of an Era meeting only looks worth going for the riders off the track rather than those on it! Shawn McConnell doesn't do it for me! Even if he's the best rider at Costa Mesa, which says more about the standard of their speedway than anything else! The most important thing is to see Mark Legg and to get my money [from the trackshop sales]. It's about 1500 quid. My book's going well. A purchaser by the name of Richard May said it was 'meticulous but awe inspiring' or something of that nature! And Bernie Leigh rang up for two more copies!" Arnie then gives me the news that the *Speedway Yearbook* editor Robert Bamford will take a sabbatical from his fastidious but time-consuming annual compilation of the British speedway statistics. "Rob Bamford isn't doing another year book!" Suddenly keen to find a quick positive after this surprise news, Arnie mentions that he prefers the *Yearbook* format to the *Almanac* one, "The *Almanac* was too clever by half. It was an A to Z listing. It was hopeless. All the info there was helpful but cut and pasted from the *Star*. If they wanted to do the referees they should have done a page and not scattered them throughout." We're interrupted in our conversation by the sound of Craig Saul's voice as it booms over the loudspeaker system to announce that the action – well, the rider parade – is about to start, "*The* most prestigious event in the Conference League – the Conference League Riders' Championship!" The riders parade around the track and afterwards are introduced in discount Noah's Ark fashion one by one to the

---

Rye House/CLRC: *'Ere Lisa, pose for a photo so you can be on the cover of his next book!"*

crowd. Arnie adds his own commentary: on Dean Felton ("he was in the Long Eaton team in 1993") and Ben Taylor ("the wonders of speedway! I've seen Ben Taylor about three times in four days and he rode for three different teams: Birmingham, for us, [Reading] last night and Buxton tonight!") This season [2008] Wolverhampton, Mildenhall and Sittingbourne have all made the basement position in their respective leagues their own. "Sittingbourne should finish with a not-perfect record three hours before Mildenhall! When they do the Mildenhall review, they'll pinpoint the highlight of the season when they nearly beat us [Reading]. 23-13 down to them and having to use a T/R was pretty embarrassing!"

Thankfully the CLRC has a traditional format. Consequently, if they remain uninjured, each rider will have five races and, at the end of the night, the person with the highest points will be the winner (unless there's a need for a run-off!). The meeting starts thrillingly when the 16-year-old Australian with the dashing, film-star first name – Darcy Ward – shows verve and determination when he zooms from the back of the field to the front. Although he rears and nearly falls at the start, over the course of the four laps he thrillingly picks his way through the field to emerge victorious! It's a performance that impresses the crowd and Craig Saul, "You know, I think we already have a contender for Race of the Night!" Maybe the second heat is also a thriller. However, I'm unable to see it when a group of portly bikers with receding hairlines arrive and stand on the fourth-bend wall to completely obscure my enjoyment of the racing, except for a small section of the track that comprises the entry to the third bend to the exit of the fourth. This does allow me to see Tom Brown's fall on the last bend of the last lap before he remounts to trundle home third. Throughout his commentary tonight, Craig Saul plays 'Spot the ex-Rye House rider' and the first sight of Rob Smith at the edge of the track (about to take to the shale for the third heat) gets him almost breathlessly excited, "and the second ex-rider on show here so far his evening is Rob Smith!" The third heat is so dramatic that it takes three attempts to complete and, almost, becomes a case of last man standing, wins. First time out the referee orders a rerun after Kyle Newman falls on the second bend. In the next attempt to run the race – when Rob Smith reaches the apex of bends three and four on the second lap – he smashes through the fence with virtuosity and some dramatic élan. Next to me a lady helpfully remarks to her friends (who've never been to speedway before), "I've seen them crash there before but never seen one [Rob Smith] go straight through the fence like that! The yellow one [Kyle Newman] had fallen off again and got up [only to be excluded for not being under power]" Eventually Lazarus-like, Rob Smith rises from the shale and as he trudges gingerly back to the pits he must have passed within sight of Craig's commentary position, "well, he has managed a smile on his face and he's had the appreciation of the home-straight crowd!" There's a short break for the track to receive some TLC and for the fence to be put back together by all the king's horses and all the king's men aka the smartly attired Rye House track staff. Craig fills the time with some promotional announcements. The owners of Paradise Wildlife Park are pronounced "very good friends of speedway" before he proceeds to compliment my work, "Jeff Scott the personification of speedway penmanship. I nearly called him the Stuart Hall of speedway but that would be unfair. Yes, it's all true, it's all in there – *Concrete of Breakfast*! And, of course, the book that started the whole odyssey, *Showered in Shale*. As I said earlier, talk to him, he doesn't bite – go and sample his wares!" Craig has a wry sense of humour and earlier he'd proudly told me "I've used tenacianos when interviewing Henning Bager – I warned him beforehand!"[1]

The line-up for heat 4 thrills Craig, "we've got a Devil, a Barracuda and two Crusaders lining up for this heat! The veteran of the field at 39 – appearing for the third time in the CLRC – Dean Felton!" Afterwards Pete Hill would say in his report on the meeting for the *Speedway Star*, "At 39, Felton cut a fatherly figure among a young field." Short of dad dancing or sight of an enormous beer gut, I'm not exactly sure how you cut a "fatherly figure" on a speedway bike! Whatever his style or age crimes, Dean was definitely involved in a exciting last lap when he diced for second place with the noticeably far-from-smooth Simon Lambert who rides his bike throughout the meeting in the manner of a bucking bronco. Though rougher than a rough thing, Simon hammers round the outside line for the whole lap and eventually gains second place on the line, just fractionally ahead of his fatherly older rival. By the time the race concludes, Aaron Baseby has retired after a spectacular tumble on the fourth bend of the second lap. This sight prompts the lady next to me to exclaim, "Ooh, look, there's another one falling off!" Apart from determined racing

---

[1] Kelvin Tatum frequently invents new words in the heat of the moment while he commentates live on a Monday night for *Sky Sports* at speedway meetings. Invariably he pitches his delivery at his traditional wildly excitable, close to orgasm level and simultaneously pulls his usual Botox 'surprise face'. Invariably, Kelvin also showcases an effortlessly virtuoso ability to mangle the English language. Arguably his new word "tenacianos" is the best example of his linguistic gift to the nation.

from pretty well all the riders, the other thing that you can definitely count upon at any CLRC is a fair share of crashes, falls and near misses. The fifth heat gets as far as the second bend of the third lap before Richard Lawson falls off his bike in virtuoso fashion and then, although he is thrown free from his machine, his riderless bike continues to be in the wars when Tom Brown smashes into it and appears to completely wreck it. Unusually for him, Craig suddenly gets a slight touch of the Kelvins and makes a minor howler, albeit of the lesser identity kind (rather than a malapropism), "and that certainly is a sight to see – William Lawson walking away to the pits!" In fact referee Dan Holt has excluded Richard Lawson and awarded the race. With only 3 points from two rides, things already look a bit dickey for Tom Brown and his pre-meeting requirement of just five good starts suddenly appears a mantra that fatally mixes wishful thinking, self-deception and blind optimism.

Given it's late September and that Rye House speedway stadium is located directly next to a canal, it's probably shouldn't be a surprise to find that my books have become completely sodden by 8 o'clock. The trackshop owner Andy Griggs treats me to the benefit of his experience on this dampness problem: "Yes, that's why we have all our books and clothes in plastic bags 'cause there will be dew and the books will be buggered!" If Darcy Ward thrilled us with his first ride then he quickly repeats the medicine in heat 6 when, once again, he makes a start poor enough to find himself marooned at the rear of the field. However, judged by this display, he's a born racer. Darcy's clever use of the inside line round bends three and four of the second lap sees him progress from third to the front. Heaven knows how well he would do if he could only gate well! Craig's admiration reaches a stratospheric cruising altitude "Another fourth to first performance for Darcy – we're going to run out of superlatives!" We all might soon run out of superlatives but, in the pits, Richard Lawson has run out of bikes or, to be exact, bike (singular) so he withdraws from the remainder of the meeting with "severe bike damage". Heat 7 has no sooner started than it's stopped again when Daniel Halsey and Scott Richardson decide to indulge in some formation safety fence demolition work. Craig sounds unimpressed, "Well, [humph] race number seven has been stopped." Rye House speedway has an old-fashioned safety fence that – to the untutored eye – has something of the look of strawberry bird-netting about it. It definitely doesn't appear as substantial as some safety fences you see in tracks around the UK but, given looks aren't everything, it really does its job every time I've seen a crash at this stadium. This year's crop of CLRC riders appear determined to give it a good test and the track staff definitely get plenty of practice putting it all back together again. After considerable industry on the second bend, we're told, "Well, the safety fence is up and running again".

The fence survives intact for the duration of heat 8, though a couple of unsatisfactory starts ensures that referee Daniel Holt has to issue warnings to riders overly keen to predict the rise of the tapes. The first stoppage sees the blue-helmeted Jay Herne warned about his future conduct and the second stoppage has the red-helmeted Byron Bekker similarly admonished. It strikes me as only fair and proper within the rules that Daniel attempts to eliminate movement at the start line. However, a man close to me remains distinctly unimpressed, "The ref's just trying to make a name for himself!" Once the race is under way, Kyle Newman provides some drama with a fall on the fourth bend though, for once, the fence isn't decimated. Kyle remounts but trails in last. Heat 9 stands out for the work of the Flag Marshal who decides to wave the chequered flag at the end of laps three and four. Fortunately, the riders can count better than he can and sensibly decide to continue to race for the full four laps. I fall into conversation with Tony Mint who's begun to view himself as something of a liability because any speedway club he decides to support invariably goes defunct, once they've properly excited his loyalty. So far he's seen off Rayleigh, Rye House, Crayford and Hackney and, given his previous record, his recent allegiance to Lakeside might cause the promotional team there some anxiety. "My first recollection of speedway was in 1967 at West Ham, where I went to a few meetings before it shut down. I can't remember a lot about it, really! Just the vastness of the crowds of 30,000 plus. I can remember the World Finals at Wembley – the old Wembley that was – and I used to go and watch the old National League Riders' Championship at Wimbledon."

The ongoing safety fence rebuilds have taken their toll upon the length of the meeting. Consequently, Craig Saul informs us that there won't be an interval. Heat 10 finds Tom Brown excluded for a fall and, shortly afterwards, he withdraws from the meeting. The race is won by the wonderfully impressive Darcy Ward to take his tally three wins from three races. The contemporary cultural need to find polite circumlocutions to disguise the base reality of situations has become all too prevalent nowadays. We're no longer passengers on trains (instead we're customers), the Bank of England doesn't print a lot more money (it indulges in quantitative easing), the SGP organisers respect

---

Rye House/CLRC: *'Ere Lisa, pose for a photo so you can be on the cover of his next book!"*

the disappointed Gelsenkirchen fans (really we're mug punters), and Craig Saul briefly decides to call the ambulance something else completely ("One of the falls necessitating the use of the Healthcare Vehicle!"). While our use of language changes beyond recognition, it's also safe to say speedway is full of idiosyncratic characters who, for reasons that may have something to do with the way we score in our programmes or keep detailed rider averages, often appear to have an obsessive interest with tabulation and comprehensive record keeping. This can manifest itself in a whole variety of compulsive ways and mannerisms from obsessive programme collecting to the development of ever larger, more complicated spreadsheets to record all the 'essential' data. Another marked characteristic of dedicated speedway fans is the sheer number of meetings that they attend in a season as well as over their lifetime. Though I'm absolutely positive that compared to some people, Nigel 'Noddy' Fordham's attendance record is merely a footnote in history, I'm extremely impressed by his dedication and fastidious record keeping. "This is my 41st year in going to speedway; I've been to 4,747 meetings in this is my 94th meeting of the season. I've been to 1,135 meetings at Ipswich and I have all the programmes from every meeting I've been to! I used to be an official but it was too much trouble and I gave up two or three years ago. You get treated like a piece of shit by the promoters who don't respect you and take everything for granted! You get promoters like Len Silver and Buster Chapman, they're genuine speedway people 'cause they put money back into the sport. Rye House, King's Lynn and Lakeside all do Juniors. None of us [unpaid helpers] get paid 'cause we don't want to be paid but respect would be nice. It's a word: RESPECT. Anyway, it means I can travel round more. I've been to most places in the world that stage speedway and this includes places like Russia, the Czech Republic and Italy. This year will be my 25th year going to the Czech Republic. It's basic speedway in the raw over there! The Golden Helmet is the star meeting. There's 32 heats and there's six riders in each race. It starts at 12 and there's tons and tons of passing. They even do moped speedway out there! Oh, you want to see it, it was funny! I haven't got a favourite rider although I used to follow Zdenek Tesar around everywhere. I went to see him one winter and stayed in a hotel nearby so I could see him play ice hockey. He told me, 'I'm a good goal minder!' After the first quarter he'd let none in and after the second quarter he'd let five in! Ha! Ha! I like all speedway riders 'cause they're supplying me with my sport that I enjoy. Plus, people don't realise how dangerous it is and that they put their lives on the line. I used to follow John Louis everywhere. In 1975 I had my hair dyed with tiger stripes when he went to Wembley. He came third. It once took me 61 hours to hitch to Lvov – which was Russia but is now the Ukraine – to see his son Chris Louis ride in the World Under-21 Final the year that he won it. The golden rule of hitching is never walk! Always stand in the same place under the lights or by a roundabout. It's rarer here but easy in Europe. This is a bad year, this year, as I've only been to 94 meetings. My best year was 1983, I think, I did 210 meetings that year. I've got a 632 page record book at home. I can tell you every mile I've done! Every track, every rider, every ref and, today, is my 948,000th mile. In the winter I rewrite it all again! There's train miles, tram miles, hitch-hiking miles, flight miles[2] – I always try to think of new things to record. It's been my life and I love it! I know too many promoters just take the money but, it's all about the riders and the racing really, so I'll always keep going." We're interrupted by news that Tom Brown has exited the Healthcare Vehicle and, after consultation with the track doctor, has withdrawn from the meeting. I'm not exactly sure why the doctor's note subsequently makes its way into Craig's possession (rather than the Incident Recorder's) but it allows him to tell us, "The doctor's note here says it's a weight-bearing injury!" According to Noddy some of the more-experienced riders should by now have won the CLRC, "Benji Compton should be up the top there. He's been riding too many years – he's been up and down. He ain't gonna make it! Tom [Brown] has tried too hard tonight and then you get out of control, don't you? That Darcy Ward does look good but I can't believe he's Australian – that's the worst thing!"

Darcy Ward's marvellous evening at Hoddesdon comes slightly unstuck when he falls on the first bend of the second lap in heat 14 and, since he's unable to clear the track, he's then excluded from the rerun. These lost points dent his championship ambitions. Suddenly, the permutations can boggle the mind. Heat 16 sees the safety fence take a further punishment – this time on the back straight – when Kyle Hughes gives it a good thump on his second lap. He is also excluded for his troubles. The vital race of the night turns out to be heat 17. A win for Jay Herne could take him into a run-off for first place with Benji Compton. However, if Benji finishes second or third, this would give Herne the outright title. To further complicate the situation, if Benji Compton wins heat 17, he will be crowned Conference

---

[2] A New York based graphic designer, Nicholas Felton, has pioneered an online version (www.feltron.com) of this will to tabulation. Called 'personal infomatics', Felton tracks and analyses the daily minutiae of his life (beers drunk, pages read, miles walked, photographs taken, cost per car mile, etc. etc.) to create his own personalised annual report. Fans like Nobby have blazed the trail with their own paper-based, speedway specific classificatory nomenclature that, years later and a continent away, Felton has apparently followed, formalised and, generally, gussied up a bit.

Rye House/CLRC: *'Ere Lisa, pose for a photo so you can be on the cover of his next book!'*

League Rider's Champion, no matter where Jay Herne finishes. Though Herne makes the gate, a hard move by Benji Compton on the second bend of the second lap takes him into a lead he fails to relinquish and (finally) secures him the CLRC crown. To take part in a run-off for third place, Darcy Ward needs to win his last outing and actually does so when the race is awarded (after Scott Richardson falls and is excluded by the referee). Daniel Halsey wins heat 19 to ensure the third place run-off is a three-way affair and Byron Bekker wins heat 20 to guarantee his podium place for second place in the championship. The additional three-way run-off race sees Darcy Ward make no mistake from the gate and his performance on the night gains favourable comment from Arnie Gibbons. "Darcy is an amazing talent for 16! It's the riders who experiment and fall off – who find that line and look for that extra 10 per cent who go all the way! Those that play safe mostly don't!"

27th September – Conference League Riders' Championship Winner: Benji Compton

Rye House/CLRC: 'Ere Lisa, pose for a photo so you can be on the cover of his next book!"

CHAPTER 45.
Sittingbourne v. Rye House:
"Poised on the brink of adequacy"

28th September

Sittingbourne head into their last meeting of the season at the Old Gun Site with the unenviable record of 13 meetings raced, 13 meetings lost. Notoriously, the Crusaders aren't the best travellers so it's no real surprise that they've lost all seven of their away meetings. So far this season, they've also lost six home meetings. However, given that the Rye House Cobras are only one place above them in the league table, this arguably represents their best hope of victory all season. Whether this will attract a great crowd of spectators down Raspberry Hill Lane is a mute point particularly as only 50 yards from the farm entrance that leads down to the track, there's a large sign advertising a rival attraction in the local area, namely, the "Allegro Owners' Spares Club". They say that the love of speedway is a specialist obsession but, we can safely say, the world of fanatical Allegro owners is arguably even smaller, just as obsessive but much more rarefied.

We've certainly got the weather to draw the numbers to this part of Kent though, given the flat lands that surround the stadium, there's still a definite chill in the air. As usual I position my stall by the ramp that leads up to the portacabin holding the tearoom that overlooks the first bend of Sittingbourne speedway track. This is such an intimate venue that there isn't really any need for advertising and promotion as people know that you're here. The usually taciturn Graham Arnold is stood proprietorially in his trademark but distinctive green overalls. They give him the appearance of a slightly scruffy paramedic as he enjoys an animated conversation with a small group of people about the future of the club. "We've literally survived this season! We lose £1,000 per meeting. We were let down by a sponsor! But this is our last season. There needs to be another level like the Academy League to develop the youngsters. The Conference League just costs too much to compete in for a club like ours!" The club can only operate speedway at this site on the outer reaches of Sittingbourne if they adhere to a strict set of conditions imposed by the local Magistrates Court. The scorecard in the programme hints at some of these conditions ("Please ensure that the Old Gun Site continues to be an air horn free zone") and I gather the frequent watering of the track here is partly driven by curatorial matters but also by the Terms and Conditions of the club's licence to operate here. Shortly afterwards a member of track staff tells me, "The last court case two months ago lasted an hour, they were questioning what they'd agreed in 2004!" Whatever the specific detail of these restrictions and the economic context of the club, the introductory column in the programme nonetheless strikes an optimistic note and, with the return of Mark Baseby from injury, apparently there are high hopes that the club might finally break its duck. The last meeting of the season is also the time for gratitude. "Now I would like to thank everyone who works tirelessly behind the scenes at the Old Gun Site. Without them there would be no Sittingbourne speedway. Volunteers are priceless, and we certainly value ours. Also highly valued are our sponsors. The Crusaders have made a loss this season, but many thanks to our sponsors, without whom that loss would be much bigger."

My prime location attracts conversations if not interest in my book. Club instructor Paul Heller professes shock at rumours of increased prices at Lakeside for the Play-off Semi-final meeting. "Graham was telling me Arena have put £5 extra on the admission for tomorrow's *Sky* meeting with Swindon! What's that about? I think *Sky* meetings should be free not extra. If you can watch it at home, what are you going to do? We haven't suffered with falling crowds – ours has stayed at around 100! We need more, of course! But elsewhere they say, pretty well everyone is down. Putting up the charges when it's expensive for a family anyway isn't the way to go!" Scunthorpe track photographer Steve Dixon has come along to the lunchtime meeting here with his always charming partner, Debbie. He was also at the CLRC last night. "Simon Lambert was struggling with a couple of injuries and didn't really want to ride. He looked like a novice but that was understandable. Len Silver always goes on about putting on a show but, last night, he just didn't seem interested! It was very low key. The night before they'd had Harleys and everything but there the riders just walked out [on parade] and walked off again. Even the catering has been getting bad comments on the Internet saying the fish and chips has gone downhill! People complain of soggy chips. That said, ours were lovely last night!" If the showmanship wasn't what was expected at Hoddesdon, then Steve believes things are even worse nowadays in the Speedway Grand Prix series run by BSI/IMG. "The GPs aren't what they were even a few years ago. The first corner used to be murder but now, it's almost boring! Riders like Nicki, Hans and Tomasz bring real excitement and I've got no problem with them. But, no one has that real aggression anymore! We're not going to Gelsenkirchen this year. Who would after last year? What with the queues to get in, the searches they abandoned and that stupid card system for paying for the drink and food? Plus, they'd shut the third and fourth bends so they could have the Speedway Grand Prix sign out. The track was awful! Just 'cause there's $200,000 on offer isn't going to get people to hop on the plane. Speedway riders aren't millionaires so are going to split the money." I'm shocked at the suggestion and ask if that is still what they do nowadays, only for Steve to reply, "What would you do?"

By the time of the first race, the trackside on the home straight is so crowded that I struggle to see the races. If only this number of fans were attracted to every Conference League meeting at the club. Presenter Derek Barclay strikes a positive note, "For once in a blue moon, we have no changes to the programme!" Things don't start well for the Crusaders when the Cobras race to a 4-2 heat advantage after Rob Smith wins and Lee Strudwick takes third. Lee's cousin, Niall (pronounced Neil), appears in the next race, though this has to be rerun after Dan Blake of the Cobras is warned for his movement at the start line by referee, Chris Gay. This admonishment makes no apparent difference to his concentration since he wins the rerun with some ease closely followed home by his team partner, Richard Franklin, for a 5-1 heat advantage that instantly takes the score to a comfortable 3-9. If Sittingbourne are to avoid an unwanted 100 per cent record, they'll have to stage a quick fight-back. It's a message that's got through loud and clear to the newly restored from injury Mark Baseby and his race partner Harland Cook. In the commentary booth Derek embraces the 5-1 for the Crusaders with enthusiasm, "Well, that's more like it!" On the subject of embraces, if judged by the loud teenybopper style screams that greet any mention of Mark Baseby's name, there's an enthusiastic female teenage fan-club element to this afternoon's support. By the end of the fourth heat, the Crusaders have restored the overall scoreline to parity after a race that features a last-gasp dash for the line by Richard Franklin that only just fails to gain him third place. Some of the riders appear to struggle with the track conditions and, as he passes by, Steve Dixon highlights the "two big holes on bend 1!"

SCB track inspector Colin Meredith is in the catering hut and, since he wears a collar and tie, I worry that they've recently introduced a new dress code at the Old Gun Site before they'll serve refreshments. Colin has come along this afternoon with his wife and is quick to explain his smart attire. "I'm here today to do an official track inspection. I have to go round and see everywhere once every three years. This is the true grassroots of the sport! What the future holds for Conference League speedway depends on how they decide to structure the organisation of speedway in Britain over the winter. If they go for Premier League 1 and Premier League 2, will teams like Plymouth be strong enough to take part? Probably not but, if there was, say, an Academy League – that Sittingbourne could take part in, for example – then this would bring on young riders and possibly attract teams of more equal strength. There needs to be a balance to get the best out of racing at that level. I don't know what they'll decide but something that needs to be addressed is payments. When a rider has been developed by a Conference club at the moment, they can't sign those riders but only register them. Maybe if another club signs such a rider, they should pay a fee of say £1,000 to the club that developed him. It would reward their work and help the finances, thereby protecting the club's ability to still develop more riders."

Out on the track the grading has finished and the racing restarts. The Mark Baseby/Harland Cook partnership immediately races to a maximum heat win for the second time in three races to take the Crusaders into a 17-13 lead that looked highly unlikely after the first two heats. Any mention of Mark Baseby or Harland Cook continues to attract teenybopper screams of acknowledgement. Though air horns might be banned, like the rest of us Derek Barclay has noted the adulation, "Mark's winning time there was the fastest of the meeting so far – 60.2 – surely that deserves a whoop?" Though more of a scream than a whoop, Derek's stagey reiteration of Mark and Harland's names attracts the enthusiastic response he requests. Another voice comes over the loudspeaker with some advice, "When the petition comes round about the running of speedway at Central Park, please consider signing it. It might seem strange for us to support this – as a rival venue – but we think it's good for speedway and Sittingbourne. So, please, support it like the Sittingbourne management does!"

Sittingbourne v. Rye House: *"Poised on the brink of adequacy"*

Heat number 6 takes four attempts to complete and goes on so long it begins to feel like its own mini speedway meeting. This afternoon's SCB official, Chris Gay, no matter what level of speedway he adjudicates is meticulously scrupulous about the need for a lack of movement at the start-line. First time out he stops the race because of movement at the line and, in the rerun, Dan Blake gets excluded for touching the tapes and is replaced by Richard Franklin. In the second rerun attempt, Mark Baseby's brother Aaron breaks through the tapes and is excluded while the green-helmeted Terry Day of the Cobras is warned about his twitchy movements. With Aaron Baseby starting from 15 metres back, the race finally gets run at the fourth attempt although there's still drama when on the back straight of the first lap when race leader Richard Franklin thumps into the fence, bounces off and continues on his way. Derek's amazed that Richard even held on, let alone raced away to victory, "That was amazing, Richard made heavy contact with the fence but still held on to win!"

Last minute preparations

If the Crusaders start to vaguely feel more confident of victory, then Andrew Aldridge and Gary Cottham quickly bring them back to earth with a 5-1 for the visitors. Heat 8 sees Aaron Baseby become the second member of the Baseby clan to win a race this afternoon. Anything one brother can do, the other brother can do better – as shown in the next race when Mark Baseby [loud teenybopper scream] and Harland Cook [teenybopper scream] combine for their third consecutive 5-1. Derek hails the triumph of the Crusaders super partnership: "There we go again – another 5-1, the third!" Though it's sunny this afternoon there's also a cool wind so Arnie Gibbons hasn't dressed in his favoured warm-weather gear (likened by Reading presenter Bob Radford as the colonial attire favoured during the last days of the Raj). Talk of three consecutive 5-1s prompts Arnie to remark, "There's a phrase you don't often hear at Sittingbourne!" With the Crusaders again back in the lead at 29-25, Arnie hails the Kent club as, "Poised on the brink of adequacy!"

Bend 1 from refs box

The bumps in the track surface begin to weigh into the equation and play much more of a factor in each race. During heat 10, Dean Felton loses control on his second lap when he hits a bump on the fourth bend but shows great aplomb just to remain seated on his bike never mind how he manages to retain his second place. Two laps later he hits the same bump in the track and once, again manages to stay on his machine but goes back to third place in the race to transform a possible Crusaders 5-1 into a 4-2. Heat 11 has Lee Strudwick take to the track for the Cobras and Niall Strudwick take to the track for the Crusaders for what I bill as "the race of the cousins." Arnie remarks (wrongly for once), "I thought they were brothers!" On this occasion, Lee beats Niall but the excitement is created during the first lap when Ricky Scarboro races side by side with Lee until he passes him on the exit from the fourth bend. The 12th heat is again stopped for movement at the start-line by referee Chris Gay. Arnie exclaims, "Not Blake moving again!" Over the loudspeakers Derek Barclay tells us, "The referee's decision is that previously having had a public warning, the rider in yellow [Dan Blake] is excluded." Though Rye House Cobras manager John Sampford could elect to bring in fellow reserve Richard Franklin in Dan Blake's place, he instead decides to have Blake take part in the rerun from 15 metres back. To my mind this fails to maximise the Cobras opportunity of race points, but Arnie explains, "He's already been excluded once so he has to stay in to have his three-ride minimum." Despite the handicap Dan Blake and Daniel

Kiosk view of rider parade

Sittingbourne v. Rye House: *"Poised on the brink of adequacy"*

Berwick enjoy a four-lap battle for third place that's eventually sees the Cobra triumph. The race winner is Harland Cook [teenybopper scream] who now has 9 (paid 12) from his four rides.

Arnie Gibbons is happy with SCB official Chris Gay's performance this afternoon, however, he believes that not all referees come up to Chris Gay's standard. "I'm perfectly prepared to accept referees using their judgement. It doesn't matter whether they're right and I'm wrong, it's just that they've come to a different conclusion. What I do object to is when they manifestly fail to interpret the rules correctly!" Heat 13 features a very close finish to the battle for second place but, with Rob Smith first and Terry Day third, Rye House have suddenly narrowed the score to 40-38. Once the Conference League meeting finishes there will then be a Junior Challenge meeting between Sittingbourne and Rye House as well as some Youth 250 cc races in the Sittingbourne Club Championship. In case we haven't spotted this in the programme Derek advises us, "Don't rush off after heat 15 'cause there's more racing, though I am! [to go to Mildenhall]" Unusually for Sittingbourne, where they like to grade and/or water the track at almost every opportunity, there is no track TLC before the penultimate race. Arnie remarks, "And again they're not grading – by Sittingbourne standards, Chris Gay is cracking through!" Heat 14 sees Dan Berwick replace Niall Strudwick but his participation only lasts roughly two laps (until the apex of the third and fourth bends) before he falls heavily from his machine. The race isn't awarded since the riders haven't completed two laps. This is unfortunate for Sittingbourne since Mark Baseby was holding the lead at the point the raced stopped. Sod's Law dictates that in the rerun Mark will perform less well but, for once, this immutable law of speedway doesn't apply when Mark wins in a time of 60.7 seconds. It's a victory greeted by yet more teenybopper screams as he crosses the finish line and again when the race results are subsequently confirmed! Arnie takes this moment to update me on the sales picture for his book: "Did I tell you I sold a copy at the Liberal Democrat Conference? I've [recently] sold two books to Europe – one to some bloke in Germany and another to some bloke in Sweden called Per Jonsson!"

With no bikes in the pit lane, the track staff poised to give the Old Gun Site shale some attention and, with the scores poised at 43-41, Mystic Arnie G announces his prognostication. "I'll write the script now – they'll water the track while they decide who's riding and Mark Baseby will slide off on the first corner!" While we wait to learn the line-ups Graham Arnold takes to the microphone, "As you can see [if you glance at the Junior Challenge racecard] Marc's [Owen] riding on a 500 cc. He's really one to watch! Let's hope we can keep things here next year. Every season, you never know what's happening. Let's hope we will be back! I'd just like to say a big thank you to everyone. They all do it voluntary, they're dedicated and I'm just pleased that they all give their help. We always say each year we're not going to run each year but then we do! Who can say? We have the refs' day out here on November 23rd so do come along and watch. Referee Chris [Gay] is always ready to race not ride. [pause] I must also thank Ivor Thomas, the guy who's responsible for everything we've done over here these last 38 years. Without him, it would never have happened! He's here today and we wouldn't be here without him. Well, we'll get on with heat 15 – let's hope we can win the last-heat decider!" After further examination of his imaginary tea leaves, Gypsy Arnie 'Petrolenko' Gibbons shines his metaphorical crystal ball and gazes hazily into the future, "Well Graham Arnold was a lot more upbeat than last year! All that's left is Sittingbourne's date with destiny!" All Sittingbourne need to do is draw the last heat and, when their talismanic Mark Baseby [teenybopper screams] hits the front, there's only ever likely to be one conclusion, particularly since Harland Cook occupies third place. However, there's a modicum of drama to come when Harland's chain comes adrift on the last lap to gift Andrew Aldridge third place. The drawn heat ensures a first Conference League win for Sittingbourne in their last meeting of the 2008 season. Like the majority of the crowd packed into the stadium, Derek Barclay is delighted, "At last we can say Sittingbourne are the winners! There was a hairy moment when Harland's chain went on the last lap but, it's been a real team performance – a brilliant, brilliant win for the Crusaders! Don't forget we now have an auction of a coat and a sweatshirt donated to the club by a lady in memory of her late husband. They're brand new. Never worn! They were bought at Cardiff and sadly her husband passed away before he could wear them! ... I'll leave you in John [Strong's] capable hands and see you again shortly."[1] Usually reticent, Graham Arnold must have had some form of truth serum in his coffee because he needs no second invitation to take to the microphone briefly once more, "As I've said, the season starts today!"

[1] During the close season Sittingbourne will announce that they will not take up a place in the newly created National League but, instead, will continue to run club meetings along with corporate events and training days. No longer Press Officer for Sittingbourne speedway, Derek Barclay's caustic comments on the *British Speedway Forum* about this decision appeared to indicate that the likelihood of his return to the commentary booth is unlikely.

After the meeting Mark Baseby, in a Team Baseby collared shirt, stands with his dad on the roadway adjacent to the wire pits fence and tucks into a bright white sliced sandwich. He chats to SCB Official, Chris Gay.

[Chris] "You were really holding the throttle open in heat 14."

[Mark] "I had to ride through the ruts."

[Chris] "You had quite a race with Rob Smith."

[Mark] "I don't like finishing second! But you don't mind who you have a close race like that with 'cause it's far better than a race you win easily, which is boring."

[Chris] "You were making the starts too!"

[Mark] "Yeah, it was some clutch plates I'd adjusted. Everything else was the same and it made all the difference. I think I've put myself in the window! [for the Premier League] I've come back a bit early sometimes from injury and that hasn't helped in the past."

[Chris] "Good for Sittingbourne to win too!"

[Mark] "Yeah, we could do with one."

[off-duty referee Dan Holt] "You didn't have your usual fall."

[Mark] "Did you miss that, then? Sorry to disappoint you!"

The Sittingbourne versus Rye House Junior Challenge meeting gets under way with a rider parade and some introductions by relief presenter John Strong. He has noticeable microphone problems, his notes get blown by the breeze and he stumbles over the riders' names. The way he introduces some riders, it sounds like he doesn't recognise them, even though some just appeared in the Conference League meeting. However, along with the younger riders who'll ride on their 250 cc machines these are the young riders of the future. Perhaps we all can't put names to faces (yet) but, their development, is the basis upon which Sittingbourne Speedway Club was founded and, hopefully, will continue to excel at in the future.

28th September – Sittingbourne v. Rye House (Conference League) 46-44

CHAPTER 46.

Reading v. Redcar:
"You know, in a year and a half here, I haven't actually met Barbara Horley."

6th October

The last-ever team meeting at Smallmead takes place less than a fortnight before the Smallmead gates are shut for the final time on speedway at this venue in Reading and sees the completion of the small matter of the second leg of the Young Shield quarter-final tie against the Redcar Bears. Should the Racers progress then there will be further meetings at the stadium before the End of an Era finale. However, already 12 points behind from the first leg at the South Tees Motorsports Park, a bizarre form of injury crisis that involves Tomas Suchanek plays havoc with the Reading line-up. Dave Wright's report in the *Speedway Star* sums up the situation succinctly, "Yet the writing was on the wall even before the tapes went up as Racers had to abandon their plans to use rider replacement for Tomas Suchanek, who was reported to be on the injured list. They [then] discovered that he had ridden in the Czech Golden Helmet the previous night and so, presumably, was fit enough to ride against Redcar. But he wasn't there for the start and, with no medical certificate, Reading had no rider replacement facility and so had to track only one rider in three of Suchanek's programmed rides." This is the sort of organisational snafu that simultaneously captures the magic of speedway and it's also the type of banal, bonkers but complex incident that can put off newcomers if you have to try and explain it to them.

When I arrive in the stadium there's a small gathering of Reading's Finest. This takes the form of Webmaster Andy Povey, Club Photographer Les Aubrey and Club Press Officer Robert Bamford. Long-time Reading supporter Andy would travel to watch the club race home and away even if he didn't have his duties to fulfil. His latest trip to Teesside hasn't filled him with confidence about the outcome of the meeting tonight. The writing was on the Teesside wall before the meeting when Chris Mills asked him, "Does this ride count towards my average?" [It doesn't] On the subject of averages Les Aubrey notes, "Mark Lemon has been trying to knock points off his average since mid season when he heard Exeter was reopening!" At this point, it would be traditional for us to commiserate with each other about the dashed hopes of our season that hasn't quite ended and, then, optimistically look towards a brighter future. Sadly, the future nowadays is counted out in days rather than years so, if as expected we lose this evening, all that will remain of speedway at Smallmead is the End of an Era meeting on Sunday October 19th. For such a milestone event, usually you'd expect that any club worth its salt would aim to go out with a bang rather than with a whimper. However, the line-up as it presently stands doesn't exactly set pulses racing. Press Officer, Robert Bamford, looks crestfallen when he considers the calibre of the field. "I was so embarrassed by the End of Era meeting line-up, I tried not to announce it but, just thought, 'sod it' in the end!" Les Aubrey is equally puzzled, "You'd think with three grand on offer [to the winner] more riders would want to ride!" Robert harrumphs, "Every time I suggest a rider – Jason Doyle or Tomas Topinka – Malcolm will say, 'Oh no, he does well here' or 'maybe not, he'll beat Ulrich'. It's really the Ulrich Ostergaard Benefit Meeting but it's not called that! There's even two semi-finals, just in case, to make sure he gets to the final!" When I enquire who the best riders on display are, apart from Ulrich, Robert replies, "Mads Korneliussen or Emil Kramer! The thing is that people will come along to see the old riders like Anders Michanek anyway." Without Reading's continued existence, Robert isn't quite sure of the teams that will take part in the Premier League for the 2009 season. "Five teams want to come up to the Premier League – Oxford, Newport, Exeter, Plymouth and Weymouth – they'll probably only allow the first three."

Our conversation is interrupted by the man from *Ideal Videos* who complains that the Marketing Department (aka the Commercial Admin team) staffed by Ross Marks and Paul Oughton don't want to help him put his centre-green advert into its correct grassy location. "It wasn't out at the last meeting and they said they couldn't help me as they had tickets to sell for the End of Era meeting!" In an attempt to be helpful I suggest to the *Ideal Videos* man, "Maybe you could ask the riders to crash into your air-fence sign?" Truth is often stranger than fiction judged by his reply, "We used to get Greg [Hancock] to come out for a race last and then stop and fiddle with his bike just in front of our sign for the televised meetings! You'd be surprised at what goes on!" One of the club's valued sponsors then leaves us with his friend in tow to make sure that his advert is in its proper place by the time the tapes rise for the last-ever team meeting at Smallmead.

Upstairs in the grandstand, Bob Radford is already in the commentary booth for his last-ever meeting on duty at the club. He has a prior engagement at a Manfred Mann concert that precludes his attendance the End of an Era final meeting. He's a veteran of the various incarnations of the Berkshire club and, if they were to list his various duties and job titles on a commemorative board, they'd need a very large lump of wood. Tonight, we're sadly without the services of Swindon-based club music man, Steve Gobey, who's elsewhere tonight on more notionally prestigious duties at Lakeside for the first leg of the Elite League Play-off final against Poole. On the subject of discarded pieces of wood, though the referee's box/commentary booth looks its usual comfortable, careworn self – in the adjacent small ante-room cum annexe that forms the other half of the grandstand roof box, it looks like burglars have been surprised half-way through their activities. All manner of chairs, tables, cabinets and assorted objects from many years of greyhounds and speedway at Smallmead have apparently been trashed and unceremoniously abandoned. Since we're high up in the grandstand you get a better view through its windows than that provided if you peer through the small frosted window above the urinals in the downstairs gents toilets. Despite this height advantage, nonetheless, the panoramic vista provided is uninspiring and roughly the same. Both overlook the rough-hewn potholed ground of the car park and the glamour of the nearby dual carriageway. Away in the distance, smarter low-rise box warehouse buildings of the industrial estate contrast massively with the twinkling much more monumental glories of Green Park or the Madejski Stadium.

Floodlit speedway

Start line

Continuing the statue theme I enjoyed at Peterborough, I enquire of Bob Radford, "Will they be erecting a statue of John Postlethwaite on the centre green at the End of an Era meeting?" Bob's quite definite, "There'll be no erections like that. You're young so you're okay but, when you get to my age, there's no erections! [sound of referee Christina Turnbull's footsteps on the steep wooden stairs] Shush! We better stop the men's talk if there's going to be ladies present!" Dressed in her trademark smart navy blue jacket, Christina sashays into the box. Bob would indulge in a luvvie bout of air kissing, if only he could be bothered to get out of his chair. Instead he holds out his hand in regal welcome, "You know, in a year and a half here, I haven't actually met Barbara Horley. Does she exist? And what's she like?" One part of a small coterie of three lady refs, Christina replies, "She's very nice. As soon as you meet her, you know that she's the RE teacher at a private girls' sixth form. Just from the way she looks over her glasses – like you do!" Bob would make an unlikely religious education teacher but then he also makes an unlikely weather forecaster for the End of an Era meeting, "There's a 33 per cent chance of rain and, possibly, not many people will come along!" Bob's in reflective mode, "Malcolm has actually done a bit of repair work up here but, then, all sorts of things can happen. For example, you can turn up and find the music man's not here and find we have to use the stadium microphone!" Quizzed by Christina on the calibre of the team this season, Bob remarks, "Ulrich Ostergaard has been a true number 1 this season for the Racers! Two of them haven't ridden well and two of them I wouldn't touch with a barge pole but, as they're still riding here, it would be wrong to name them, so, I won't!" Christina surveys the scene below from the referee's box and, although she can't see the people in the grandstand, there weren't many of them there when she walked up a few minutes ago, "It feels like the end of an era here – it's dead!"

This was to have been the season when Reading stormed (once again) to championship glory but then, it was also intended to be a campaign where you could set your watch by the precision of the rider parade and start time. "Look it's 25 to 8 already. Lucky it's 7.10 on parade and 7.30 tapes up! [Bob consults front of programme] It says "engines start" nowadays that's the politically correct way to put it!" When only three riders arrive at the tapes for the start of the first heat, you just know that it's almost certain to be one of those evenings for the Racers. And, so it proves, when Mark Lemon trails in some way behind Gary Havelock and Josh Auty. One maximum heat result often follows another. Sure enough, the Redcar combination of Benji Compton and Arlo Bugeja ride like respective future world champions to win the second heat sponsored by Dale Fontaine's Echoes of Elvis Tribute Show in a rather slow time of 66.65 seconds. With the aggregate score suddenly at a problematic 20 points deficit the sight of Ulrich Ostergaard on his way to the tapes lifts the spirits of the Smallmead faithful but then these are further dashed when James Grieves wins the race. It's all too much for some people and a disgruntled fan bellows the thoughts of many Racers supporters in the bar area after the shocker of the third successive poor heat, "Where the freak is Holloway?" In fact, Malcolm is elsewhere in the bar. He looks relaxed and dapper, though it's an appearance that belies the fact that the medical services had been called to attend him after he collapsed in the Speedway Office. "Before the meeting the ambulance came for Mad Wellie, he'd had a fit 'cause he hadn't had his diabetes tablets!"

With things not exactly going in favour of the home team, the track staff decide the sensible approach would be to indulge in a further track grade. Tonight these are almost more numerous than points since we've been treated to the sight of the tractor out on the Smallmead surface after two of the first three races. Though the shale looks carefully manicured, the performance of the Racers remains rough and patchy. In heat 4, Danny Warwick manages to have a sudden engine failure at a point on the third bend that leaves him the shortest possible walk back to the pits. After this execrable start, we've only reached heat 5 and already Ulrich Ostergaard appears with his helmet clad in the black-and-white. Fortunately he records the first race win of the night for the Racers but this really only massages the scoreline to a slightly more acceptable 12-21! Reading's mini-renaissance continues in the next race with a win for Mark Lemon. However, the overall impact of his triumph is lessened by the fact that again there are only three riders in the race. Since it's the last team meeting at Smallmead, I decide to savour some of the action from the centre green. It's always a treat to be close to the action and a pleasure to see Mark Lemon shrug his shoulders with insouciance to pass between Ty Proctor and Benji Compton to ensure his heat 6 race win. So far this evening, each race has been processional and, with the riders strung out like a line of washing, the opportunity for club photographer Les Aubrey to take any meaningful action shots that feature Reading riders together have been minimal. Instead he has amused himself with a count of the fans within the stadium. "I reckon 480. I've counted 280 people to the ref's box [waves his hand expansively from the second bend to the start-line],and in the bar and round there [waves hand expansively from the start-line past bends 4 and 3 to the pits area] there can't be more than 200 people!"

The seventh heat starts with some drama when, on the apex of bends one and two, Chris Kerr lays down his machine and immediately behind him Andrew Bargh also smartly lays down his bike. Rather than order a rerun, referee Christina Turnbull excludes the Reading reserve to impressively loud groans of derision from the scattering of Reading fans in the grandstand. Over the loudspeakers Bob Radford informs us, "And I can tell you Tim Sugar is on the phone!" However, it's all to no avail and, in the rerun, the Redcar riders reassert their authority when the Kerr/Grieves partnership races to a maximum heat advantage to take the meeting score to 16-29. Though more Large and Large than Little and Large, Smallmead race nights have been enlivened over the past two seasons by the repartee and chemistry over the tannoy of Bob Radford and Paul Hunsdon. All good things come to an end so we're treated to a last interview between the Two Amigos. Paul introduces his colleague as "an ex-team manager of the Reading Racers" and also "an advisor to Mrs Pat Bliss." Asked to take a trip down memory lane, Bob needs no second invitation but keeps his reminiscences of positive happenings at Smallmead on the brief side in case the shocking contrast with tonight's performance is thrown into even sharper relief. "All the way up to 1994 we had some good teams here!

Reading v. Redcar: *"You know, in a year and a half here, I haven't actually met Barbara Horley."*

Reading have won five championships, four at Smallmead and one at Tilehurst. Those are my happiest memories but if I had to pick one it would be 1990. That seemed to have everything – it was fantastic – we had a wonderful team spirit and riders like Per Jonsson, Jeremy Doncaster and Armando Castagna! Armando is probably the greatest showman of the Smallmead era! There's too many people and too many things to recall. When I saw the last meeting at Tilehurst, I wouldn't have guessed that we'd move to a purpose-built track. Obviously, my big hope is that we'll see the Reading Racers race again! That said, the greyhounds are struggling more than speedway so it's a big worry! And the council weren't that generous, they gave us a rubbish tip that took 25 years to settle! There are so many happy memories and it's been a privilege! I must say that Mark and Malcolm deserved a better effort from most in their team but, we have to thank them, because without them we wouldn't have had any speedway to enjoy recently." With a quiver in his voice Paul Hunsdon croaks, "On a personal note it's been a real pleasure to work with you! My confidence has grown through working with you for the last 18 months. Thank you!"

Whether the Reading Racers have a full complement of riders in each race or only one, it makes little difference to their performance on the track. The depressing run of results continues with the 2-4s in heat 8 and heat 9. The latter race sees Ulrich Ostergaard beaten for the second time this evening (this time by the impressively fast from the gate, Ty Proctor). Ulrich doesn't help his chances during the first lap since he strikes the fence on his exit from the second bend during an attempted blast round the outside from third place. With his camera slung round his neck, Les Aubrey remarks from the centre green, "I've given up [taking photos of the race action], I'm just messing about taking photos without flash and other things." Mark Lemon endures his third race as the solitary Racers representative in heat 10 and he finishes third to leave the scores less than poised at 21-42. Redcar often travel with an impressive number of fans and this evening is no exception. An impressive gaggle have made the journey from the North East to an industrial estate on the outskirts of Reading. It's a dedication that's much rarer nowadays in speedway. The Redcar fans do tend to celebrate in the manner of football fans but dress in the idiosyncratic fashion of speedway supporters. In front of the main grandstand there's a small group of five of them with a flag, a drum, a Mohican wig and also a multi-coloured wig. Completely accurately they gleefully chant "Easy! Easy!" In search of entertainment, Paul decides to solicit their opinions.

[Paul] "We're going to have a chat with the Redcar Barmy Army. Have you enjoyed yourself?"

[Redcar fan, loudly] "We're very satisfied!"[In a broad accent, he uses a variety of colloquial phrases to profess delight at seeing this meeting after a long journey down from Redcar].

[Paul] "You don't need a microphone! I'm just going to translate that into Southern! Will you be sampling the delights of Reading afterwards?"

[Redcar fan] "If we can find any!"

[Paul] "You could try the Red Light district!"

[Redcar fan] "If you can tell us about it!"

Though the evening hasn't quite progressed as Reading fans would have wanted it to, at least Bob Radford has the professionalism and sensitivity not to update us on the situation at Lakeside, "We do know the scores in the Elite League Play-off final but we're not going to tell you 'cause Tim Sugar has issued a decree 'cause we're both taping it at home!" Many races before the conclusion (or, even, the interval), it was painfully obvious that Redcar would progress to the semi-final stage of the Young Shield. Courteously Bob Radford praises their performance, "Congratulations to the Redcar Bears for going through to the semi-final and hopefully, Berwick will give them more of a meeting than we have!" No sooner have the Bears been applauded for their performance than Tom P. Madsen becomes the third Reading rider to win a race this evening when he triumphs in heat 11. Bob sounds a long way from the verge of ecstatic, "Tom P. Madsen wins that one and, let's face it, we haven't had a lot to cheer tonight!" Sadly, though Tom P. Madsen has vanquished ex-world champion Gary Havelock into second place the Racers can't build any advantage from his victory since Danny Warwick has another engine failure on the bend close to the pits gate. Yet to be cancelled due to poor ticket sales, Paul Hunsdon manfully bigs up the forthcoming dinner-dance at Windlesham Court the night before the End of an Era meeting. Interested fans can buy online or, for the princely sum of £45, "You can buy them off the Marketing team! Paul Oughton or ex Boy Band member Ross Marks, who I

Reading v. Redcar: *"You know, in a year and a half here, I haven't actually met Barbara Horley."*

keep expecting to see on *X-Factor!*" Before the turnstiles opened for tonight's meeting against Redcar, Paul Oughton reported that the club had sold 370 advance tickets for the last-ever meeting at Smallmead. Paul Hunsdon spins this to suggest we purchase our tickets early in order to avoid disappointment, "A huge number of tickets have been sold in advance and the Reading management are urging fans to buy them early because they warn the stadium has limited capacity!"[1] Ulrich Ostergaard wins the 12th heat in some style but sadly Danny Warwick again fails to finish when he falls on the third bend during the second lap. He clears the track promptly and, once again, has the shortest of possible walks back to the pits. By the standards set this evening, successive drawn heats represents almost huge success for the Racers though they still trail at the interval by 21 points on the night and 33 points on aggregate. Bob Radford tries to enthuse the small crowd, "The social highlight of the evening is coming up – the 50/50 draw!" Paul Hunsdon debates with himself what to do next, "Shall I venture over to the pits and find out why we're so bad tonight?" Ongoing technical problems with the microphone dictate that this idea is abandoned, "You can blame Malcolm Holloway – he forgot to tell the sound bloke it was off yesterday!" Instead of doom and gloom from the pits, Paul picks out some young fans to help with the draw and attempts to engage them in conversation:

[Paul] "What's your name?"

[Brandon] "Brandon"

[Paul] "Where are you from?"

[Brandon] "Muesli"

[Paul] "Where?"

[Brandon] "Muesli"

[Paul] "That's what I have for breakfast! Where are you from?"

[Brandon] [no answer]

[Paul] "Are you from Reading?"

[Brandon] "No"

[Paul, triumphant] "He's not from Reading!"

The mood in the Press Lounge during the interval isn't exactly upbeat. So much so that ultra loyal long-time Reading fan Nick Dyer complains that he's at the meeting! "I'm missing a concert in Oxford tonight for this!" When asked who's playing, we're none the wiser after the obscurity of his answer, "White Lies, they're going to be big! They have an Editors or Joy Division type sound." Club marketing guru, Paul Oughton, knows his musical trivia, "The first thing Ian Curtis wanted to be before being in a band was to be a speedway rider! Ivan Mauger was his hero!" Andy Povey is almost lost for words but mutters, "It's our worst home performance by a mile!" Robert Bamford bemoans the trials and tribulations of his life as a press officer as he packs away his laptop. "I watch the last three heats from the box. Not that I want to but I have to – so I can get the referee's memory stick and grind out yet another Press Release late into the night!"

With a sparse crowd that only really comprises the hardcore base of Reading Racers support, Paul Hunsdon nonetheless circuits the stadium in search of attractive female company. As usual, he lucks out on his quest but does manage to bump into unofficial club historian, Arnie Gibbons, before the final heat of the meeting, "I've just had a chat with Arnie and he tells me our heaviest home defeat was 26 points in 2000 against Swindon. We're already 29 points down. This is a pitiful way to end things here at Smallmead! Forget the score, get behind your boys – it's the last-ever team race at Smallmead!" Redcar have won so convincingly that they can afford send out Ty Proctor and Josh Auty for the experience to contest the nominated heat 15. While, for the last-ever team race at this stadium in Berkshire, Racers team manager Tim Sugar nominates Mark Lemon and Ulrich Ostergaard. The Redcar fans on the home straight concourse chant exuberantly, "We love you Redcar, we do! We love you Redcar, we do!" First time out the race only gets as far as the fourth bend where Josh Auty slams into the fence just as he attempts to exit the

[1] The Dinner/Dance was subsequently cancelled because unfortunately only 23 tickets were sold.

Reading v. Redcar: *"You know, in a year and a half here, I haven't actually met Barbara Horley."*

corner and accelerate down the back straight. Paul verbally winces on his behalf, "A very nasty looking spill for Josh Auty. We all wait for the referee's decision which is, obviously, the exclusion of Josh!" The whole evening, the tannoy system has broken up, creaked and groaned. For this last-ever team race at the Stadium, it sounds so bad that you'd be forgiven if you thought that Paul, in fact, broadcasted to us from a pirate radio station moored in the English Channel. The exclusion of Josh Auty from the rerun ensures that he'll be the first and only Redcar rider to fail to score in any race all evening! Not that this bothers the dozen or so members of the Redcar faithful who gleefully celebrate their triumph. The loudest of these fans is a really big one dressed in sandals with no socks, shortish combat trousers and what appears to be a giant hooded cassock made from a red dog blanket. Any police undercover operation in the Red Light district will immediately identify him as a potential punter should he get the directions and venture down there later. Ulrich Ostergaard ensures that some vestige of pride is retained when he wins the last-ever team race at Smallmead. Though, with a scoreline of 33-60, this still becomes the worst ever result at the stadium. Before the meeting Arnie Gibbons had been anxious about complex future fixture permutations if Reading managed to get to the final of the Young Shield. But, given we'd not even managed to get to the semi-final his anxiety proved academic. It's probably a relief to the promotional team since Arnie also noted, "The Young Shield is notoriously poorly attended." Nonetheless the magnitude of the defeat is a bitter pill to swallow so much so that the Racers unofficial club historian suddenly waxes lyrical and quotes T. S. Eliot, "This is the way the world ends not with a bang but a whimper."

Later that night, *Private Eye* editor, Ian Hislop, narrated a documentary on the British Railways that featured the closure of a huge number of regional railway lines following the publication of the Beeching Report. It was a highly controversial decision that required careful news management. So much so that Tony Hancock was paid £17,000 (for context, Beeching was paid a £34,000 salary) to make what were really propaganda sketches about the faults of the railway system dressed up as humour. Though that was the '60s and this is 2008, tonight the Reading Racers have notionally staged a speedway meeting but really conducted their own equivalent propaganda experiment in a final attempt to kill interest in and drive people away from team speedway in the Berkshire area.

6th October Reading v. Redcar (Young Shield) 33-60

CHAPTER 47.

Somerset v. Edinburgh:
"I've dug out an old hat in case we need it to celebrate!"

8th October

It's a lovely sunny autumn day in the South West for the Premier League Promotion Play-off Semi- Final Second Leg. The journey down is made better by the limited credit crunch volumes of traffic on the M4 and M5 en route to the Oak Tree Arena. The first person I meet is Mike Golding who is co-promoter at Somerset speedway with Peter Toogood (who's effectively only the sleeping partner in this relationship). You have to wear many hats as a speedway promoter and one of these is weatherman, "Once the sun goes down it'll get freezing here!". During the season, the riders have unenviable travel schedules and the same is often true of the promoters. Mike was at Armadale for the first leg where Somerset went down 56-37 and, afterwards, went to the Czech Republic. "We're just back from the World Under 21s at Par-doo-beece [Pardubice] and the Golden Helmet. On such a large track four riders [in the Under 21 heats] were rather lost on something prepared for six riders. We went to see Chris Holder win but, sadly, he came second after a run-off. He's too old to do it again! The Russian kiddie [Emil Sayfutdinov] who won, again, is so young he can do it for a couple more years. Of course, that never used to be the way 'cause the winner went straight through to the GPs but they don't anymore!" Qualification for the "BSI – An IMG Company" Speedway Grand Prix is primarily a closed shop with entry decided by what some fans view as the less than stellar management team of said organisation. The top eight finishers automatically re-qualify for the next season's competition and various other riders are 'selected' by the legendary BSI management (often for commercial rather than speedway reasons). There is also the chance to qualify to take part if riders find themselves on the podium at the conclusion of the GP Qualifying competition. Though he's hardly disinterested, BSI Press Officer and *Speedway Star* managing editor Philip Rising recently criticised (without apparent irony) the calibre of the riders in the final before a wheel had been turned. Apparently ignoring the present dull predictability of the present SGP field, he also raised doubts about whether the riders who would qualify would provide any "excitement" when they rode in the 2009 Speedway Grand Prix series. It's extremely rare that the *Speedway Star* criticises an event before it takes place (let alone afterwards) but Philip's pre-meeting report bucked that trend in highly sniffy fashion. Mike takes a pragmatic view of the vested interests this foregrounded, "It's probably 'cause it's a FIM event and one of the few not sewn up by BSI or IMG! They'd like to control everything if they could! At any GP you see 50 or 60 photographers but only the *Speedway Star* can take photos from the centre green. Around heat 19, you will see Dave Fairbrother put out the steps for Mike Patrick to stand on later. It's a closed shop!"

Nearby Mike's partner, Anita Lewis, tidies the entrance turnstiles booth to ready them for later and, as she does so, professes optimism about the prospects for the Rebels: "We're only 22 points down and anything can happen!" The ongoing development of the Oak Tree Arena stadium is a work-in-progress. There are noticeable infrastructure changes here every time I visit. Some of these have been undertaken to enhance the viewing pleasure of the speedway fans within the environs of the stadium but others, like the now fully operational clubhouse, obviously have commercial revenue potential throughout the whole year for the owner. Inaugurated at the club's dinner dance in November 2007, the clubhouse is available on a race night but also can be hired out to non-speedway patrons for various events such as business meetings or wedding receptions. From my glance round the stadium grounds, it appears that there's newly raised banking on the first bend and some extension of the grass banking that runs along the back straight. This provides panoramic views of the track and, in the other direction during any lull in proceedings, the sometimes stationary traffic of the M5 motorway. Mike Golding is justifiably proud and before the summer PL Pairs meeting commented proudly, "I'm a firm believer that looking down on a speedway race is the ideal viewing position to have at any meeting and I'm delighted that we've mostly been able to achieve my goal within the Oak Tree Arena. Almost wherever you watch from here, you can really see all the racing lines plus you're able to fully appreciate the action going on throughout the track. I genuinely feel that we have the highest views in speedway coupled with a wide choice of exceptional vantage points. This has to be the best way to experience speedway! It contrasts to some other tracks, where the fans have to watch from below the track level or through fencing that obscures the action. Improving the views was a priority when I arrived here and, now that we've completed that, we'll look to other improvements over the next year or so. We've gone for gradual and continuous improvement because we believe in careful management and have to cut our cloth according to the commercial environment in which we find ourselves. We feel we now almost have facilities to match the on-track excitement."

Somerset Programme Editor and Press Officer, Ian Belcher, also arrives early at the stadium. He too had made the trip to Armadale for the first leg and takes an optimistic view. "We did better at Edinburgh than last time 'cause Doyley survived to the end of the meeting! Jim [McGregor] excluded Sneddon for a tapes infringement [in heat 11] which he told us after was for spinning his wheel at the start. He'd been warned about that before. We put Stefan out in heat 14 'cause he'd just finished heat 9 by then. Before the race, I heard 'It's Deek in blue' and I thought I was about to see a band! Doyley said as we came out of the bar afterwards, 'Youse two [Ian Belcher and Najjer (aka Aron Whiting)] must be mad!" But it only cost £100 to fly and £30 for the car park. We stayed with Dennis Wallace who's Merlin on the forums. Only in speedway would you stay with another fan from another team! It was us two and Bish the team manager and, 'cause going to the stadium later isn't good for the team manager, Aaron Summers gave Bish a lift there. In what other sport would the opposition number 7 give the opposition team manager a lift there? I don't think Mike's that keen on it [the Premier League Play-offs] really, apart from the gate money! If the meeting's level on aggregate tonight there's three Golden heats – I think it's 3, 7 and 12? If they're still tied then, I don't know what happens![1] In the Cup, you'd run it again but not at this time of year. Next week, if we win, it'll be a double-header final of the Play-offs final as well as the final of the PL Knockout Cup. Obviously it's a big if! We'd do that so Mike can have the Elite League [promotion/relegation] meeting the next week before Doyley flies out. Given there's 21 points difference though, we're not counting our chickens! Of course, we have a very fair racing track here. We used to rip it up on the outside and leave it on the inside but Len Silver complained. He complained the sky was the wrong colour blue that night. He took photos to the BSPA management meeting and showed Rob Godfrey and said 'Look at that!' Rob said, 'God I'd love to get my track looking like that!' Mike said to Len, 'You don't do anything to yours except move the dust from one end to the other!' The riders know there's lots of different racing lines here!"

During my drive to the stadium, I listened to *BBC Radio 4's Thinking Allowed*. Presenter Laurie Taylor discussed the likely psychological outlook of the British population in the face of the current economic crisis with the famous sociologist, Professor Steven V. Lukes. To help our understanding, they looked closely at Durkheim's analysis of the Great Depression and identified that we're collectively in the stage before anomie sets in. Apparently during wartime, suicides drop because of the shared 'In It Together' nature of the experience. Presently we all watch the economic events unfold on the television together but have yet to feel the anger, depression, and violence that accompanies social

Walk this way

Di Phillips

High tech refs box

[1] Page 48 of the Rulebook (in an appendix) states that if the three Golden Heat races haven't produced a result then additional races are staged until a heat advantage is gained.

Somerset v. Edinburgh: *"I've dug out an old hat in case we need it to celebrate!"*

breakdown. Ian Belcher used to sell financial services but now just trains those people who do, so has his own more pragmatic definition of recession, "If manufacturing cost is greater than the retail price though it also depends on the level of the output." He also has a lift analogy about share price movements (which could also apply to house price fluctuations). "If you get in on the third floor, press the button and go up to the fifth but don't get out are you really on the fifth floor? The same applies when the lift goes down to the basement!" It's a truism in the world of finance that profits and losses are only crystallised at the point of sale so, effectively, the psychological impact of the perceived value of your paper assets can swing wildly from optimism to despair but you can only really assign their "true" value at the moment of sale. Fortunately, discussion of arcane financial matters quickly leads to speedway's equivalent, rider averages! Ian helpfully informs me, "Only group stage Trophy matches and league matches count towards a rider's averages in the Premier League. So no Play-offs, no Cup and no Young Shield meetings count! The only anomaly was one [Trophy] group had an extra team in the group stages but one extra match won't drastically affect your average."

We've slowly made our way to the new clubhouse and, though it looks a big building from the outside, inside it feels even larger. There are two brightly lit bowling alleys and seven large tables each surrounded by seven chairs (but no Snow White). Already this would be enough to stage a good-sized party, meeting or wedding reception yet, behind some green partitions, there's three more tables with white tablecloths surrounded by yet more chairs. The building benefits from a good-length bar (and serves bar food), some large TV screens and modern-style speakers dotted throughout to really blast out whatever they show on screen. Suspended from the ceiling is an impressive set of spotlights that create the feeling you could easily stage any play or theatrical extravaganza within the building. Some members of the track staff relax with coffees and a gossip at one of the tables. Tony Smith is the club Incident Reporter but there hasn't been much for him to report on at the Oak Tree Arena this season. This contrasts sharply to his experience when he did this job in Wales, "I did the first-ever meeting at Carmarthen and had two sheets of incidents!" Assistant Team Manager Garry May wears a distinctive red Somerset Rebels speedway anorak and worries that the speedway public have lost their appetite for the development level of British speedway. "They [Weymouth] put a British Junior meeting on for the British public and they don't come along!"

[Ian Belcher] "And the Aussie won it."

[Garry] (to Tony Smith) "Why weren't you there?"

[Tony Smith] "Traffic!"

[Garry] "Come on!"

[Ian] "The Crayford and Weymouth legend as featured in *Backtrack* magazine speaks!"

[Colin Carter] "When was it [you rode] then?"

[Garry] "'76!"

[Colin] "The one at Poole who's got no feet – he's a nutter he is!"

[Garry] "He came along to Weymouth and opened it full up and went whumpf into the fence. He didn't even turn! Lost both his legs."

[Colin] "Speedway goes in phases as we know. At the moment, it's in a dying phase. In four or five years, it'll rise up again!"

[Garry] "The Elite League needs more teams. The Premier League is the best with different teams. I don't watch the Elite League on the telly and the GPs are getting boring with the same riders doing well each week!"

Collectively this group aren't that impressed with the facilities at Stoke speedway club. "Dave Thompson loves going to Stoke. He says they found an unexploded bomb and blew it up and caused £50,000 worth of improvements. Someone said 'Stoke's a black hole' and someone else said 'I wouldn't talk it up so much!'" You should always speak as you find and, personally, I've always enjoyed a warm welcome as well as seen exciting meetings whenever I've visited Loomer Road.

Somerset v. Edinburgh: *"I've dug out an old hat in case we need it to celebrate!"*

At the other end of the home straight there's a small kiosk decorated in the red and blue of the Somerset speedway logo – well, it looks like version of the Confederate flag – to which a sign that announces "Di's Travel Centre" has been attached. Inside the kiosk is the indefatigable Di Phillips who often organises travel for the fans to the Rebels away meetings. "I hand-painted it myself – it took me ages." The inside wall of the kiosk is festooned in nearly as many flags than you'd find at the front of the United Nations building, "I've the flags of the nationalities of all our riders!" Tonight Di will sell tickets for the end-of-season presentation night. "For £25 you get a cabaret, nice food and obviously all the presentations. We'll probably get about 180 people!" She's a proud advocate of all things Somerset speedway, "We've got very loyal fans here who know their speedway!" Even closer to her heart is Magnus 'Zorro' Zetterstrom and, as is traditional (every time I see Di), she suggests that maybe now is the time for me to do a book on her hero. "Why not do a book on Zorro? There's a great story to tell! He's done so much, he broke his back – he's coming to the end of his career now but he's popular everywhere except Newcastle! He's a good lad and I'm looking forward to seeing him win the Elite League with Poole. I cheered him on the telly!" She expects that quite a few Rebels fans will make the journey over to Poole to watch the Elite League final. Di goes to as many meetings as she can but has had to cut back on some of her travels since her husband Roy's heart attack.

Along with Di, no trip to the Oak Tree Arena would be complete without sight of gentle giant Tiny Tim and his long-time friend Johnny Sometimes. Much taller than his ironic nickname Tiny Tim suggests, he invariably cuts a distinctive figure but tonight he wears a piece of headgear that attracts even more attention, "I've dug out an old hat in case we need it to celebrate!" Along with Speedway Dave, Tiny Tim and Johnny Sometimes formed their own Somerset equivalent of the Three Muskateers. Sadly, Speedway Dave has passed away. His loss is still felt strongly by his friends and all who knew him. Johnny isn't in the best of health but makes light of his situation as well as his recent need for crutches, "I can hardly grip anymore 'cause of my osteoarthritis. It's getting harder and harder to drive so I wear splints. But I'm living life to the full – the death of Speedway Dave taught me that!" Tiny Tim has man flu and, during our conversation, drops a half-eaten purple Locket onto the gravel floor that he then picks up and pops back into his mouth. "You're not talking about death again, are you?"

By now, the gates have opened so I've retreated to my book display table close by the entrance area. At the other end of the scale from Tiny Tim is "Mighty Atom" Judith Rourke who's come along tonight with her husband Colin. No sooner have they stopped for a chat than Brendan Johnson comes up and, because of her previous raffle ticket work, Judith is always the sales woman, "Are you going to buy one?" Brendan's already a loyal supporter of my books, "I've a whole bookshelf of them – I have them all!" In fact, Brendan was even name-checked in the lovely *Times* review of *Concrete for Breakfast* written by Ian McMillan. I warn Judith to behave herself because of Brendan's martial arts expertise, "If you misbehave, he'll throw you to the floor and into a headlock!" Judith is much more concerned with the back-straight stand, "The first part of the floor has collapsed on the back-straight stand. It's so old. It's so rotten. We've had it for years!" Judith bustles away and her husband Colin lingers to reveal the secret of a successful marriage, "After 38 years I don't bother trying to tell her what to do!" Brendan then briefly disappears to the refreshment kiosk (and kindly brings me back a cup of tea), "I've 10 meetings in the rest of October. I had a dip in mid-season but I'm back on top of things! I have a higher away average than a home one. I had hoped, if a reserve from Weymouth was picked [for the CLRC] it would have been me – but there you are!"

Avid speedway enthusiast, memorabilia collector, Coventry promoter and potential "Saviour" of Exeter speedway, Allen Trump has come along to the meeting. The last time the *Speedway Star* had featured news on the possible return of Exeter speedway club I'd gathered that the future looked bright. However, events happen, things change and I find Allen in extremely downbeat mood, "I'm having problems with the Jockey Club. I've got a 62-page contract with lots of clauses added into it that I didn't expect. It takes a long time to work through but, if we can, we will!" Later Mike Golding gives me his take on the revised version of the Exeter contract, "The big bosses of the Jockey Club in London have changed the goalposts at the last minute. They've added in 18 new clauses. One of which is that Allen has to return it to its initial condition, if speedway folds. That means knocking down the grandstand, re-grassing it and bringing back the lizards! That could be very expensive! It's a real shame with all the hard work he's put in to have all this come up at the last minute."

On raffle ticket duty tonight are Carol Dyer and Sheila Sabin. A steady stream of fans buy the 50/50 tickets and the enthusiasm of the ladies directly translates into increased sales. Though I spelt her name incorrectly in my latest book

("I'm not that worried") Sheila's more worried that I eat my sweets in an inappropriate fashion, "Did you enjoy your Love Hearts without sharing them?"

[Carol] "But do you read them? You've got to read them! What's the point otherwise?"

[Jeff] "Naw, they've got modern messages like, 'text me' nowadays."

[Sheila] "Have they?

Whatever the Love Hearts say or, indeed, whatever the weather, Carol and Sheila are keen to stress the enjoyment they get from selling the raffle tickets and generally meeting people, "We love standing here getting cold – we'll miss it all winter!"

Another notable aspect of presentation on race night at the Oak Tree Arena is the repartee between the presenter Nigel Thomas and announcer Rodney Cork based in the referee's box. Rodney keeps us updated on the team news: "Matthias Kroger has a fever and so will be replaced by Reading's Danny Warwick at reserve." Nigel advises us that Derek Sneddon will take a rider-replacement ride for Thomas H. Jonasson though, in fact, the Monarchs rider turns out to be Matthew Wethers. Rodney takes some delight that he isn't responsible for the first presentational error of the night, "I'm glad it was you that led them astray and messed up their programmes before the first heat!" Somerset Rebels number 1, Jason Doyle is nattily attired and presenter Nigel Thomas draws this to our attention, "In this race you'll see that Jason Doyle is wearing his new kevlars – you kindly donated – made in Poland." Once the tapes have been released by referee Dave Watters, Matthew Wethers of the Monarchs flies from the gate to lead the Rebels pairing for nearly four laps until Kramer dashes to the line and, in my opinion, narrowly fails to snatch the victory. However, I'm not stood in the ideal position to adjudicate on the race result since I'm stood a few yards away on the elevated bank that overlooks the entry into the first bend. Club announcer Rodney Cork is in no doubt of the result and burbles rhetorically, "I think you all know who won that one!" The lady next to me remarks, "I thought Wethers won but you can never tell from here." The referee's adjudication is that Emil Kramer has won and Rodney announces the result after he's fully savoured the quality of the racing on offer, "It was the sort of race we could have done with eight more laps off!" Surprisingly the Rebels talismanic number 1 Jason Doyle could only manage third place so Nigel Thomas wonders, "Perhaps they [his new kevlars] were pinching him a bit as he didn't ride like he usually does!"

Somerset co-promoter Mike Golding has apparently instituted his own race-night Keep Fit programme. If he hasn't then he certainly spends the initial part of the meeting on brief shuttle runs to and from the entrance turnstiles. Mike likes to meet and greet the fans as they arrive but also wants to watch the race action from the bank (where I'm stood) in addition to his other promotional duties. Somerset proceed to hammer home their second successive 4-2 of the night when Brent Werner wins heat 2 and guest Danny Warwick takes third place. Derek Sneddon separates the Rebels and immediately justifies the warning in the programme (from "Najjer's One to Watch" column) of his potentially match winning contribution for the Monarchs. This column also contains some relevant statistics on Derek Sneddon's Premier League record (1998-2008). Deek has ridden 926 times over 210 matches for a cumulative points total of 1,188 to result in a Premier League career average of 5.13. Nigel Thomas also has a layman's interest in all things mathematical, "We need 13 more of those [4-2s] but I can't see it happening!" The Rebels power partnership of the night appears to be Emil Kramer and Stephan Katt who power to three successive 5-1s when they ride together (in heats 3, 5 and 9). They enjoy some measure of good fortune on the third bend of the second lap of heat 3 when Ryan Fisher's chain snaps and he takes a sudden dramatic fall that earns him points for artistic merit plus an exclusion from referee Dave Watters. Mike Golding looks on phlegmatically, "They'd award that if they'd done two laps! I like to watch the racing but have to keep an eye on the turnstile too. I thought Wethers had won that first race. You don't mind to get decisions if they go for you!" When I note that it's hard to see from this angle, Mike retorts, "Oh no, I was stood on the patio [in front of the referee's box that overlooks the start/finish line] so I was dead in line and still thought he'd [Wethers] won!" Without Fisher in the rerun of heat 3, the result is a formality. The Rebels good form continues into the fourth heat and it features a win for Jordan Frampton who's followed home by Matthew Wethers with Brent Werner third ahead of an out-of-sorts Aaron Summers. Though the Rebels are already 10 points up (17-7) after four heats, Mike Golding studiously refuses to get carried away, "It was like this in the League match. Then they threw in a few tacticals and won the last half of the meeting to narrow the gap by four. We need them to throw a few chains more!" Alternatively, perhaps, Somerset need to track Emil Kramer and Stephan Katt in every race since, under clear skies and a perfectly formed half-moon, they race away to yet another comfortable win and extend the Somerset lead yet further (to 14 points on the night after only five heats). The Rebels resurgence comes to an abrupt halt when the Monarch most likely to win races tonight – Matthew Wethers – fires from the gate and is briefly joined up front by his partner Derek 'Deek' Sneddon. However, on the third bend of the first lap Jason Doyle and Jordan Frampton pass either side of Deek and, thereby, relegate him to last place, though they're unable to make any impression upon the Adelaide-born 23-year-old race leader.

Edinburgh Monarchs team manager and co-promoter John Campbell – dressed earlier tonight in a very smart Monarchs tracksuit top ("It's not very warm, I have to wear a jumper underneath") – seizes the tactical opportunity and sends out Ryan Fisher in the optional black-and-white helmet colour. This looks a wonderfully astute use of the regulations until the third bend of the first lap when race leader Ryan inexplicably slows. It's a manoeuvre that simultaneously blocks his race partner Andrew Tully but also allows Jordan Frampton to suddenly blast past to record an easy win. I'm stood on the banking next to a relatively recent convert to the world of speedway excitement Rebels fan, Mary Tottle. "I came with my daughter Reb as she'd just passed her test and didn't want to drive on her own. Well she doesn't like driving on the motorways and I got hooked! My husband doesn't come much. We also go to Poole – the atmosphere is great! I love the way they stand up and cheer! Reb's a mega speedway fan. We went to Poole on holiday and Jordan [Frampton] came to the campsite and picked the two girls up – Reb was with her friend Kate Ackerman. I'm not quite sure how it's spelt but she's her friend who got her into speedway. Jordan took them to Birmingham. He's got six seats in the van so there was Mike Golding, Garry May, Jordan and his dad and the two girls. It was rained off after they got there. I was watching at Poole and had to keep texting Mike the score. I suppose I've been coming just over a year now. Reb has been friendly with Danny [Warwick] for a while. He gave them a tour of Poole and Millionaires' Row. She's really mad keen and always happy to get lifts. You get to know the riders. Everyone is so approachable at speedway!"

John Campbell continues to exploit all his tactical options, so decides to send Ryan Fisher out again, this time for Thomas H. Jonasson's heat 8 rider replacement ride. He also replaces the lack-lustre Aaron Summers with fellow reserve Derek Sneddon. Predictably enough, Fisher wins the race and the points haul gained by the Monarchs would have been all the greater but for an engine failure for Derek Sneddon at the start of the second lap (when placed a comfortable third). After this drawn heat, the Rebels power partnership of Kramer and Katt again combine for their third consecutive 5-1 of the night and extend the Rebels race lead to 16 points and, thereby, narrow their aggregate deficit to only 6 points. This impressive partnership does come under considerable pressure when Matthew Wethers excitingly blasts round the outside of the third and fourth bend on the last lap but, nonetheless, narrowly fails to snatch second place on the line from the slightly complacent Stephan Katt. Honours remain even during heats 10 and 11. Fortuitously so from the point of view of the Monarchs, since Somerset see Brent Werner retire in one race with mechanical difficulties and Danny Warwick falls in the other.

During the interval, the fans are entertained by a genuinely insightful interview conducted by presenter Nigel Thomas with injured club captain Simon Walker. "I would like to be back, I'm just trying to get my head right!" Nigel wonders aloud, "Is it right now? If not, is the body?" "I dunno. I keep getting bad news. It's very depressing … the bottom of my spine is out of shape. I get the results [of a CAT scan] on Friday and learn whether I go under the knife or if they do something else. It's been described as a serious injury for everyday life. I've been speaking to Bish [Steve Bishop] about it. Today I'm okay, I've got back pain but another day the pain is such I can't get out of bed! If I had half the chance, if I get the all-clear on Friday, I'd be back Saturday!"

After 11 heats, the plain mathematics of the situation dictates that Somerset require four consecutive 4-2s to ensure their progression into the Premier League promotion Play-off final. Before the tapes rise on the first of these vital races, though the Rebels are 16 points up, Mike Golding remains cautiously downbeat when I enquire about their likely prospects, "It's too early to say we'll win! There's the heat 13s and 15s plus they'll have a tactical in heat 14. We'll put up a valiant effort and win by 18 in the end!" After two unsatisfactory starts the Monarchs duo of Ryan Fisher and Derek Sneddon fly from the tapes and, though they battle valiantly, the Rebels partnership of Emil Kramer and Brent Werner are unable to find any way past Deek. Ryan Fisher remains untroubled up front throughout and records the slowest time of the night at 60.16 seconds. Though it's the Monarchs only genuine heat advantage of the night (the other in heat 7 was tactically induced), the result of this race deals a body blow to the championship ambitions of the Somerset Rebels. The reaction of the crowd is muted, though we are told rather optimistically by Nigel, "The box says we need two 5-1s and a 4-2 from the last three heats!" If these results were to be obtained then the scores on aggregate would be tied and the count-back system over the three designated heats would come into effect. Just prior to heat 13, a low-flying military helicopter passes overhead and is some way into the distance before Jason Doyle wins heat 13. With Jordan Frampton in third, the Rebels have their 4-2 but now need consecutive 5-1s from the remainder of the meeting. Given they lead, Somerset have no tactical options open to them other than choice of which reserve rider to use (unless they wish to blood their number 8, Kyle Newman). In the end they decide to give Danny Warwick his programmed ride but, since both reserves have each finished last in their previous two races, whether it's Danny or Brent Werner who takes to the track makes little difference. The Monarchs riders are happy for Stephan Katt to take the race win while Andrew Tully and Derek Sneddon tuck in behind to ensure the heat is drawn and thereby ensure that Edinburgh guarantee their progression to the Play-off final. As the Edinburgh riders cross the line the result is greeted ecstatically in the pits area by the away contingent at work there. Elsewhere in the Oak Tree Arena, there's also brief strangulated cries of celebration from the scattering of Edinburgh fans who have made the long journey down to the South West of England. The last race of the night isn't relevant to the result but does showcase the Monarchs two key riders of the night – top scorer (by benefit of his tactical ride), Ryan Fisher and the Monarchs key performer at the Oak Tree Arena, Matthew Wethers. The top five of the Somerset 'Sharp' Rebels have performed to their averages or better (only Emil Kramer ran a last and that was in heat 15). Though Brent Werner scored a creditable 6 points, it was ultimately a weakness at reserve – along with the absence of club captain Simon Walker – that cost them the few significant points on the night that would prevent any extension of their league season.

8th October Somerset v. Edinburgh (Premier League Promotion Play-off Semi-Final, Second Leg) 53-39.

CHAPTER 48.

Reading:
"You must have very many happy memories?"

19th October

The impressive souvenir programme for the last-ever speedway meeting at Smallmead captures the bare bones of the situation concisely on its cover: "Reading Racers 40th Anniversary 1968-2008 End-of-an-Era also incorporating a celebration of 40 seasons of Reading Speedway Sunday 19th October 2008 engines start 6 p.m.". The typeface chosen for the words "Smallmead Stadium" look as though they have been written with a quill pen and employ calligraphy much more associated with the Elizabethan era of Shakespeare than the 21st century in this part of Berkshire. Apart from the fact that tears will be shed, it's guaranteed that one of the longest standing track records in British history will remain in perpetuity at 58.1 seconds. Racers legendary Per Jonsson recorded this time on the 12th October 1987 during a meeting against Coventry (in a year they went unbeaten in the league) that ended 39-39. Inside the programme edited by Robert Bamford, there are enough articles, memories and reminiscences to delight any reader, whether or not they're a Reading Racers fan. Communications Manager and Webmaster Andy Povey goes to the heart of the matter in the first few sentences of his article about his memories of the club. "This club means the world to me and I must admit it's very sad to have to face the fact that this will be our last-ever season at Smallmead. Admittedly, the stadium is showing its age now and is far from ideal but, over the years, we've come to love its quaint old ways." Without the help of the Reading Racers Commercial Team – Paul and Ross – I wouldn't have had an advert in the programme for this event.

Someone in his element on a day like today is Commercial Manager Paul Oughton who's taken up his usual watchful position by the turnstiles. Paul's work life could be likened to a bow with many strings and, as usual, though he's here physically he's also multi-tasking with the help of various modern technology gadgets. A short while later I find him crouched over his laptop with a complicated spreadsheet up on the screen. He helps to run "an Enduro text messaging service that gets sent to 120 riders. They used to get it the next day online but now, within 20 minutes of finishing, they all get the results. Yesterday I was at the ice hockey – Swindon Wildcats versus the Bracknell Bees – then in the evening I was at the boxing. Jamie Cox – the Commonwealth Gold Medallist – starred in the first professional fight in Swindon for 45 years and one of the biggest ever! Someone thought I was younger than Ross [Marks] yesterday and he's 21. I'm 30 but do you have to say that? Have you heard there's a few riders not here? Glen Phillips, Robert Mear's got injured, Chris Schramm and Chris Mills, plus reserve Paul Starke is riding at Boston, I think. We've sold 720 odd advance tickets and, I imagine, it's going to be hugely popular." The fresh-faced and friendly Ross Marks arrives to reveal emotions already run high elsewhere in the stadium, "There's already been some tears from the Winged Wheel girls!"

The Winged Wheel Boy, Arnie Gibbons, has just arrived with a stock of his acclaimed opus, *Tears and Glory: The Winged Wheel Story*. Given the subject matter of his book it would be a huge surprise if this last hurrah for the club didn't result in substantial sales. Sensibly he's brought many boxes but has yet to invest in a table to display them on. I lend him my battered pasting table and he stands in the cool wind on the sloping concrete walkway that leads from the turnstiles down towards the edge of the greyhound track. No sooner has Arnie set up his stall than he attracts significant interest from fans who mill round the entrance area. The topic on everyone's lips is the probable future for Reading Speedway club. Arnie isn't that hopeful: "I can't see anyone wanting to invest £8m [in a casino complex] just when there's a credit crunch on!" Something that the future definitely holds in 2009 is an exhibition about the speedway club at Reading Museum. "I'm coming back tomorrow with Reading Museum to get things like the green light and the referee's control panel. They're going to hold an exhibition next spring and they've already sourced lots of exciting exhibits. One of these that we are hoping to get is a vinyl copy of John Davis's non-hit single *Speedway Rider* – now there's a rare artefact!" I enquire about the location of Reading Speedway Museum, "Go to Marks and Sparks and see if you can spot where Eugeniusz Blaszak did his shoplifting and go out the back to the old Town Hall and it's in there!" I'm unclear whether it's tension or the cool wind but Arnie seems slightly giddy, so much so that he theatrically drops a copy of his book, "Whoops! A shop-soiled copy!"

The advance publicity for the event has led many fans to believe that the current Reading Racers Team Manager, Tim Sugar, will do the last four laps ever at Smallmead (though informed rumours have it that the rider will in fact be Dave Mullett). With the turnstiles fully operational, many fans congregate around the trackshop area where a number of famous and/or notable Reading Racers of yesteryear have gathered to sign autographs and pose for photographs. Many fans have brought their own battered-looking, well-used autograph books but others use the glossy souvenir programme which has a double-page section especially for autograph hunters entitled "The Reading Gallery". The Club Press Officer and Programme Editor, Robert Bamford, has the demeanour of someone who's done military service since he stands almost to attention and erectly surveys the scene in front of him. Next to the trackshop, Racers legend Anders Michanek is inundated with admirers. He still cuts a dashing figure casually dressed in a battered but stylish brown leather jacket with his grey hair resplendent but still quiffed flamboyantly. Anders smiles patiently while he poses for photographs and signs an endless stream of autographs for a long queue of keen men who all appear to be aged 50 or over. I nod towards Anders and ask Robert "Is that John Davis?" Rob half rises to the bait, "I sometimes wonder about you!" Like so many others I also join the line and ahead of me a lady who wears a distressed and aged Racers anorak says to Anders, "Did you enjoy your drive down the motorway with my brother?" Almost without missing a beat, Anders adapts his fluent replies to the subject at hand, "Was that your brother? He's a terrible driver!" Arnie Gibbons has specially kept aside a copy of his own book to get the photos inside it signed by the various individual riders of yesteryear in attendance tonight ("you just missed Richard May!"). The diminutive Andy Povey tootles about the area and occasionally stands to silently survey the scene. He's in a forlorn, reflective mood with an expression on his face that's part anxiety and part close to tears. Always an authority figure on all things Reading Speedway in my eyes I ask Andy, "Who are the replacement riders?" He weighs up my question thoughtfully, "I don't care about that! I'm worried about where all the old riders are and or what time they're coming or what they've been told! [Pause] It's Stoj for Phillips, Paul Clews and that Swede Linus Ludicvarm or whatever he's called!" [actually it's Linus Sundstrom]

Elsewhere in the stadium on the centre green local Elvis impersonator Dale Fontaine cranks up the pre-meeting atmosphere with a succession of his uniquely delivered Elvis covers. It sounds tonight like Dale has chosen to render only poignant numbers from Elvis's back catalogue and, thereby, subtly shift the emphasis from celebration to commiseration. Nonetheless some of the songs sound emblematically appropriate to the End-of-an-Era meeting, "Sweet Caroline … good times never fade away!" After the last of Dale's music has faded away Club Presenter, Paul Hunsdon, temporarily abandons his season-long quest for a slummy yummy mummy and instead conducts a series of consecutive interviews with many of the riders who are here because they've given service to Reading Racers speedway over the years. There's a sense of *déjà vu* all over again about some of the questions (and the answers) but, with a large crowd of the old-timers gathered in an informal cluster on the centre green, it's the ideal moment for us all to collectively bathe in memories of the riders, races and numerous (hopefully) happy recollections of the speedway served up at Tilehurst and Smallmead. First up is Bob Angel closely followed by John Hammond. I gather they both rode at Tilehurst. John Hammond definitely rode in 28 matches in 1970 (career average 5.05) and Bob Angel had been a second-halfer there.

[Paul] "You've got some happy memories of riding for Reading at Tilehurst?"

[John Hammond] "Yes I have!"

The still shockingly youthful Andrew Appleton (2002-2005; 163 matches; average 7.90) is introduced by Paul as "the only local rider who actually rode for Reading – for four seasons." Burghfield-born Andrew evades the question of his speedway comeback, "You never know … at the moment I'm going really well on the grass and the longtrack. I enjoyed growing up here. I've been coming since I was five years old. It's a bit unfortunate that it's finishing as there's been some brilliant riders over the years and there used to be some fantastic racing!"

Next into the spotlight is Petri Kokko – the Finnish rider with the glamorous but scientific sounding name who rode for the club from 1995- 1999 (141 matches; average 7.63).

Reading: *"You must have very many happy memories?"*

[Paul] "What is your happiest memory?"

[Petri] "'98 when we won the Cup was special. All the years were special – especially the ones we were winning."

[Paul] "You've flown in specially today." [Sound of female teenybopper-like adulation] (Pause – with a hint of jealousy in his voice) "It certainly sounds like you have lots of female fans over in the grandstand!"

On the crowded home straight, Peterborough Programme Editor, Steve Miles, theatrically glances round at the crowd thronged around him that fills the home-straight grandstand, "Not as many as I thought there'd be! The last meeting at Exeter really attracted a massive crowd!" Sadly Arnie is elsewhere, so can't give living proof of his accountancy skills but even he would struggle to accurately count this large sized crowd. Though your memory plays tricks over time, I'd definitely remember that the early era Smallmead crowds of my teenage years were often much bigger for workaday league meetings!

The next rider certainly needs no introduction but Paul provides one anyway.

[Paul] "438 appearances over 14 seasons. He won the Pairs title with Danny Bird, a warm welcome to the Welsh Wizard himself, Phil Morris! You've got some happy memories of riding for Reading but it must feel strange to be here tonight at Smallmead?"

[Phil Morris] "Yeah, it does! It's a special place! Not a good day to be here seeing it closing. It holds a place in my heart. The stadium closing as my career ends!"

[Paul] "What was your happiest memory?"

[Phil] "You'll probably think I'll say the Premier Pairs which was a big day – the last trophy to be won by Reading – but it's winning the League in my first year in 1992!"[1]

Speedway is well known for the geographic spread of its competitors so we don't have to wait long for Paul to display his widely admired foreign language skills.

[Paul] "His English and my Czech don't go well together – he made 117 appearances for the club [from 2005- 2007 he rode 113 matches for an average of 5.69] please welcome Sam [Zdenek] Simota.

[Sam] "Hello."

[Paul] "Sam was terribly injured in an accident this year."

[Sam] "The injury is getting much better."

[Paul] "You must have lots of happy memories?"

[Sam] "I like the people and fans here. Terrific! I very much like!"

With a crowd of ex-riders around him on the centre green, Paul struggles to

Tableless Arnie Gibbons

Reading stalwart Andy Povey

---

[1] Phil Morris rode for the club between 1991 and 2007, making his debut just six days after his 16th birthday. He is the only Reading rider to score a 21-point full maximum in a league match. Arnie Gibbons' Reading Speedway bible informs us that he rode 434 meetings for an average of 6.52. In his Racers points total of 3,047, Phil rode to four maximums and six paid maximums. Paul Hunsdon in his interview was, of course, using Rob Bamford's total of 438 meetings which also includes Premiership and Craven Shield fixtures.

identify some of the famous names of yesteryear by sight. And, once he's found them, he's got only limited time available to actually gain any really meaningful insights into their experiences

[Paul] "He didn't actually ride at Smallmead but rode at Tilehurst in 1969-70. Mike Vernam – have we got Mike Vernam here?"

[Mike] "I'm here!"

[Paul] "You rode a couple of years at Tilehurst. Did you enjoy that?"

[Mike] "Yes I did enjoy that."

[Paul] "Thank you very much, Mike Vernam."[2]

[Paul] "He rode two spells for the club from 1975 to 1981 and 1985 to 1987. He's the fourth highest points scorer ever on 3,115 points. He had an 8.94 average and rode to 32 full maximums – John Davis! Here is JD himself! How do you feel?"

[John] "Yeah, obviously very, very sad. I just hope the stadium does get rebuilt 'cause there hasn't been many people on the terraces which is a shame 'cause it's so exciting."

[Paul] "In 1980 you had a clause in your contract that said you weren't allowed to marry, do you want to tell us about that?"

[John] "It's all bullshit really!"

[Paul "You must have many happy memories from when you rode?"

[John] "There was lots of riders in the past who put bums on seats for whatever reasons; you could name 30 or so easily! [Lists many of them] Now you look across and you don't know who half the riders are!"

[Paul] "What was your highlight at Reading?"

[John] "The night we won the British League against Cradley Heath was very poignant! Actually, it was probably Wolves! I can't remember! [It was Wolves.] Sue Barker gave me a kiss which was a very special moment!"

From the cast of Reading Greats who mill about by him on the centre green, Paul Hunsdon next calls upon Tim Hunt who rode for the club from 1982 to 1985 ("he first came to the club in the mid '80s") in 161 matches for a Racers career average of 5.21.

[Paul] "Certainly I do know that you did taste the safety fence a few times as did a few other who tried to go round you!"

Tim makes light of his unofficial tour guide work that helpfully introduced many visitors to the Smallmead safety equipment but, instead, gleefully recalls the time his throttle stuck as he was crossing the centre green and sent his bike cart-wheeling away.

The rider interviews with their brief happy memories come thick and fast.

[Paul Hunsdon] "204 appearances, a very credible near 7 point average let's hear it for Richard 'Dickie' May!"[3] Paul quizzes Dickie about the very first ever night's speedway at Smallmead and whether he can still recall it as special. "Oh, it was! I remember it very well. We didn't think it would open on time. There were big queues of traffic." Questioned about the initial circuit itself, Richard recalls, "I liked the shape of the track – a bit bumpy it was – but I liked it!"

The only Reading rider to also be a shepherd, Paul welcomes as one of the true Reading legends.

[2] Arnie Gibbons' book indicates that during 1969 and 1970 Mike Vernam rode 62 meetings for the club for an average of 8.38 and rode to eight full maximums.

[3] An overnight sensation in 1969, he briefly held the Golden Helmet in 1972, riding for the Racers until 1975.

[Paul] "He rode for the club 568 times over 18 successive seasons from 1985. He needs no introduction [proceeds to list a huge number of trophies and accolades], the second highest points scorer of all time. Let's hear it for Dave Mullett!" [Huge cheer] [4]

[Dave] "It's great to be here but sad!"

[Paul] "Well Dave, mate, I was just reading out all those accolades."

[Dave] "I was just very fortunate to ride with so many good riders. I was very lucky!"

[Paul] "What was the highlight of your time at Reading?"

[Dave] "Riding with Per [Jonsson] was one of my highlights. A big highlight! There were just so many highlights!"

[Paul] "You must have a tinge of sadness?"

[Dave] "It is sad. I haven't made a habit of coming here since I retired. I've been probably three or four times. The crowd have always given me a warm reception when I didn't think they'd remember me!"

Tony Olsson rode for the club between 1986 and 1996. He took part in 278 meetings for a Reading career average of 6.86 that included three paid maximums.

[Paul] "He's flown over specially for today's meeting … Does Smallmead hold many happy memories for you?"

[Tony Olsson] "Of course it does! Nice to see so many people here today. It's sad but that's how it goes!"

[Paul] "You used to have quite a punk haircut."

[Tony] "I still have the punk but it's a bit shorter now!"

Shortly afterwards Paul is joined by Bernie Leigh who rode for the club at Tilehurst and Smallmead from 1969 to 1981. Bernie took part in 431 meetings and included two paid maximums in his Reading career average of 5.71.

[Paul] "It's good ole Bernie Leigh … Well, Bernie, I know you're a legend here. That must make you feel proud?"

[Bernie] "It does indeed and, to all the people who've turned up and supported Reading, thanks very much!" Bernie makes a point to recall, "team mate Bobby Schwartz – hence the walking stick!"

[Paul] "Well, ladies and gentlemen, we're coming to the end of our legends. He rode for the club from 1979 to 1992 – we call him 'Mr Reading Speedway'. He certainly deserves that tag – Jan Andersson! Thank you very much for flying over specially."

[Jan] "Very nice to be here and come back and see old friends and the track. Very nice."

[Paul] "These days are you involved in speedway?"

Reserved table in the VIP Lounge

The great Anders Michanek

[4] Dave rode for the club from 1985 until 2002. He made 561 appearances and scored 4,766 points. He had 12 full maximums, 19 paid maximums and finished his Reading with an average of 7.55. He holds the all-time record for Racers appearances and received testimonials in 1992 and 2001.

[Jan] "I'm involved in speedway engine tuning every day. I do work for a lot of Polish riders. I'm very pleased I work with Tomasz Gollob."

[Paul] "You must have very many happy memories?"

[Jan] "I must say I do miss seeing Bill Dore on the centre green with his pipe!"[5]

[Paul] "Is there anyone we've forgotten? Oh, yes! Championship winner in 1973, he kept the sport on the back pages in '74 when the club didn't race when he became World Champion – Anders Michanek! [Loud cheers – the second biggest cheer of the night, after Dave Mullett]. Does Reading have many special memories for you?"

[Anders] "Of course it has, I spent a lot of time on this track and around Reading."

[Paul] "Do you have happy memories of winning the World Championship?"

[Anders] "Of course! It doesn't matter if you score 15 points at Ullevi or at Smallmead – they're both good memories! It's always good to come back and always you're a bit nervous."

The early years at Smallmead arguably saw the club in its heyday from the point of view of its state of the art infrastructure and, of course, the size of the crowds. The club was also notable then for the high profile presenters it employed. One of these notables with the extended media profile was Dave Lanning. Tonight over the loudspeakers his voice sounds so quivery it's hard to decide whether it's emotion, age or, perhaps, a denture problem. "It's lovely to see so many old friends and it's very nostalgic to come back. I was here with Dave Hamilton for the first meeting! I really didn't want to miss it [tonight] and I hope speedway comes back to Reading! Can I thank you most severely, sincerely for your campaign to get me back to commentate on *Sky*. I did 50 World Finals starting in 1955. I think I've done enough, I think it's highly unlikely I'll come back!" Also glamourous but still inextricably linked to the early years at Smallmead is David 'Diddy' Hamilton who nowadays still works as a presenter at Fulham Football Club. Renowned for his work with the roving mic he modestly bats off compliments before he notes, "I was at Tilehurst in '73 when Anders won the title. I did the first season [at Smallmead] in 1975 with Dave Lanning. I did both stadiums and always love coming to Reading! It is a little bit sad. I wouldn't have guessed 33 years ago that the stadium would be closing, as it was a brand new stadium! I wish there were crowds like this every week!" The march of Time's winged chariot requires that the riders get back on to the parade truck and make their way round the Smallmead circuit one last time to salute the fans before the End-of-an-Era meeting itself can commence. "Ladies and gentlemen, we're just loading the last of the legends onto the truck – he's unable to get onto the truck – let's hear it for good ole Bernie Leigh!"

Arnie Gibbons has been busy with his books and, stood by my display table, he has the satisfied look of a man whose sales have been brisk. "They've sold 19 from the trackshop and I've sold 37 from here. I've got 8 with me and another 20 in the car. That's 350 total lifetime sales, so far! I have to say watching the racing is the least of my problems tonight!" For a brief moment I come over all "Paul Hunsdon" but rather than ask if Arnie has many happy memories of speedway at Smallmead, I wonder if doing his book this season as his beloved club (temporarily) closes has been a life-affirming experience? "It's been a great way to spend these last three hours otherwise I'd have been on the edge of a nervous breakdown! For someone who never expected to be an author, it's been a wonderful experience! My mother has read it and says it's 'well written!' So, that's great, as she's hard to please!" Given his sales success this evening it sounds like Arnie is more in need of a Brinks Mat bullion van than his wallet. My suggestion that he might like to lock the cash he has already in the boot of his car gets short shrift. Then his knowledge of all things Reading Speedway, let alone the Smallmead car park invariably trumps mine, "I'll be keeping my money in my pocket rather than taking it back to the car, thank you!" Though Arnie eschews the chance of an extra trip to the car park, I have to go back out there and, when I try to re-enter the stadium, the security guard on the reception cum turnstiles with the impressive nightclub style canopy outside asks, "Do you have a ticket? [Turns to the girl on reception] Can we let him back in?" I think she must have me confused with Arnie because she says, as if it were a heinous crime, "You're the writer are you?"

[5] Jan Andersson rode for the club from 1979-1992. He appeared in the Reading Racers tabard at 544 meetings and includes 46 full maximums and 20 paid maximums in his career points total of 5,519.5 to generate an impressive Reading career average of 9.07. He is Reading's all-time top point scorer and topped the club's averages six times in seven years.

While we wait for the action to start and the riders complete their last-minute preparations before they race for a first prize of £3,000, I wander to the VIP Lounge. Throughout the night appropriate or nostalgic music blasts out over the speaker system and, as the racing is about to commence, in apposite fashion the *Final Countdown* plays loudly. Hardly conducive to applied concentration, the music sounds really deafening in the VIP Lounge. Though we can hear the music and lyrics as clear as a bell it's much harder to distinguish the race results and times over the stadium sound system. The *Evening Post's* veteran speedway reporter Dave Wright is a fastidious journalist with a deserved reputation for the fluency of his writing as well as the accuracy of his copy and statistical information. He finds the inaudible nature of the changes to the race line-up something of a frustration. "It's bloody murder! You can't hear a thing on the speakers!" Commercial Manager Paul Oughton has also made his way to the nerve centre of press operations. As the sidecars noisily and pointlessly (in my opinion) race round the Smallmead track before heat 1, I wonder what impact they will have on the track's surface. Paul is equally mystified by their appearance, "I dunno why they're running them at all? If one of them crashes now, the air fence is dead!" Dave Wright has finally completed writing down the programme changes and is now sat with his laptop in his traditional section of the VIP Lounge a.k.a the Press Lounge (close to Robert Bamford and Andy Povey) only to find the commemorative trophies that will be presented to the riders later are kept there for their safety and conspire to block his view of the action. "I can't see 'cause of the trophies!" Conversation dramatically hushes when long-time Reading promoter Pat Bliss arrives in the VIP Lounge. She's warmly greeted by many people and soon is deep in conversation ("It's very, very sad"). She's brought quite an entourage with her. One member of Pat's End-of-an-Era massive is Petri Kokko who jokes that he won't be able to provide me with the autograph I've requested, "My photo isn't in there so I can't sign it!"

Press Conference backdrop

Crowded again!

Convivial conversation is briefly interrupted when the first race of the night loudly splatters shale upon the window of the hospitality lounge. Predictably enough Ulrich Ostergaard wins it. The second race of the night showcases a couple of possible stars of the future in the form of Richard Sweetman and Linus Sundstrom, who finish second and third respectively. Jordan Frampton leads the third heat before, on the second bend of the second lap, he decides to throw his bike in the air. However, he's so far ahead of meeting reserve Ben Read that he has enough time to remount and still trundle home in third place. Heat 4 features a couple of unforced falls from the veteran stateside rider Shawn McConnell as well as a tumble from the popular ex-Racer Paul Clews. Apart from the notional entertainment of the sidecar races, we're also treated to the sight of the famous Men in Black – veteran riders on veteran machines. Though only supposedly here to provide a gently 'contested' exhibition race as soon as the tapes rise they immediately treat it as a highly competitive contest. Over the speakers we're informed, "The man in red Jim Gregory is 81 years old!" He makes a couple of tentative corners before his dormant racing gene kicks back in again. After the additional 'entertainment' has subsided, Paul Clews takes to the track again for consecutive races and, this time, manages to gain his first point of the night in another race won by "Ul-rich Oos-ter-guard!"

Widely trailed in press reports beforehand was news that Dave Lanning would (once again) commentate on a speedway race and, as the widely acknowledged Voice of Speedway for so many years, it would allow many of those present to trip down memory lane and reminisce about the glory days of yesteryear. Beforehand Dave informs us, "Almost certainly it will be my last live commentary on a speedway race". The music played over the loudspeakers tonight is also evocative and nearly adds as much to the atmosphere as the sight of the various Reading legends. The canonical tune at Smallmead is course *Monday, Monday* by The Mammas and The Pappas. Like so many others, I only have to hear the first bars of this tune to immediately think of Monday race nights at Smallmead. Dave Lanning recalls, "*Monday, Monday* the only time we didn't play it was when we'd won the 1980 BL championship and [instead] played *We are the Champions*!" Happenstance dictates that the race Dave will commentate on is actually the first close and exhilarating contest of the night. I would like to report that Dave slipped back effortlessly into his excited but finely judged trademark commentary style but, sadly, just like the stadium infrastructure has rusted, faded and seen better days, so too has Dave's commentary. Though he sounds a little ring-rusty, he nonetheless enjoys himself, "My word, I'm having the best race of the night to commentate upon – wha'hey, it's the last lap! 300 metres to go!" If the technology had been available there would have been need for a photo finish and tonight's referee with impeccable Reading credentials, Dave Robinson, adjudicates that Jordan Frampton has won the race by a fraction from the impressive Linus Sundstrom. That isn't how I see the finish nor how I originally mark it in my programme and, shortly afterwards, it's no surprise when Announcer Dave Stallworthy tells us, "Jordan Frampton has rung the referee to say he was second – commendably honest of him!" Collectively across the stadium, this news makes a mess of the majority of the 1,200 commemorative programmes sold on the night. After the (incorrect) results have been announced, Dave Lanning pays tribute to absent friends, "One gentleman whose ghost still haunts Smallmead – Geoff Curtis – who was tragically killed. If you're looking down on us, Geoff, mate, we miss you!"[6]

On a night of some regrets and sadness, you can rely on John Davis to lighten the mood. "Nice to see lots of the old faces, and they are old, ha ha! Nice to see David Hamilton has OD'd on Botox!" Talk of the great ex Radio 1 DJ inevitably turns to his skin colour. Paul asks, "Suntanned isn't he?" and John needs no second invitation to gleefully reply, "Sprayed on, you'll find!" After a season-long quest led from the centre green, Paul Hunsdon finally captures a woman. She's not the MILF he searched for but it's "the lady who made it all possible, Pat Bliss". Paul eschews the chance to quiz her on her happy memories but instead leads with another one of his well used favourites – "An evening tinged with sadness". Obviously enough, given what the club means to her and her family, Pat is somewhat downbeat: "It's very, very sad today. It'll be awful to see the end after 34 good years!" Paul quizzes her about her arrival at Smallmead, "In 1980, I came to work behind the bar one night. I started promoting in 1981 and did more and more every year after that. 1990 has to be absolutely the greatest! We won absolutely everything and we've had a lovely team!" Though it's invidious to pick out favourites, nonetheless, Pat does so: "One thing you can say about Per was that he was such a safe rider, if you can say speedway riders are safe! He never had a wobble [pause] it was such a tragedy!"

[Paul] "It knocked the stuffing out of the club."

[Pat] (Pulls herself together) "Both Phil [Morris] and Danny [Bird] are really great but there have been so many great riders I don't want to pick any of them! It's unbelievable [to see so many of them here tonight], Bernie Leigh, for instance, it was 1980, I just can't believe it!"

Before the 10th heat we're treated to a burst of song from the Bay City Rollers and the sound of their famous anthem, *Bye, Bye Baby. Baby Goodbye* echoes throughout the stadium. Given my sister Jacq was a *huge* Bay City Rollers fan, I don't need to be told that this song was number 1 when Smallmead opened in April 1975! Paul Hunsdon tries to enthuse the crowd with the news that, after heat 12, Malcolm 'Mad Wellie' Holloway will take to the track. It's seven weeks since Malcolm's heart operation [triple bypass] and he's going to do four laps after heat 12!" Unfortunately for Jordan Frampton he doesn't get to take part in heat 10 when he falls foul of the time allowance. Dave Stallworthy notes, "The rider in red is excluded – just a minute ago the ref was congratulating him and now he's excluding him!"

[6] Geoff Curtis died after head injuries he received on track at the Sydney Showground on December 15th 1973 during heat 11 of the New South Wales Championship. Between 1971 and 1973, Geoff rode in 116 matches for the club to gain a 7.62 average that included two full maximums and 10 paid maximums. Along with Denny Pyeatt, Geoff Curtis's name deservedly lives on in Reading Speedway folklore. Arnie Gibbons' Tears and Glory is partly but proudly dedicated to "Geoff and Denny, proud wearers of the Winged Wheel"

Reading: *"You must have very many happy memories?"*

While we wait for the race to get under way Dave advises us, "Good news to hear Garry Stead is here for the final meeting at Smallmead. He always rode well here!" Before heat 12, Steve Harley and Cockney Rebels, *Come Up And See Me And Make Me Smile* blasts out and the race it presages features the collector's item of a win for Danny Warwick!

The interval features the last-ever chance for Paul Hunsdon to conduct the 50/50 draw at Smallmead and supervise the prize raffle with his trademark dexterity and innuendo. "172 on the white wins £155 – drawn by this lovely lady SUCKING her lolly!" Paul manages to contain his excitement to reveal, "The second prize is a bagful of merchandise they couldn't sell in the trackshop and [a gentleman] from Gaydar FM is doing the rest of the draw." Apparently this gentleman isn't from that institution, "Gaydar FM! You don't half talk some rubbish, Paul!" While we wait for Malcolm to take to the track for his four laps we're told that a collection is in progress for the British Heart Foundation and that "Malcolm has set himself a personal target of going round in less than 65 seconds – otherwise he'll donate £200 to the British Heart Foundation!" Other than pride at his handiwork, quite what Malcolm's surgeon Mr De Souza will make of the fact that Malcolm's about to race on a speedway track only seven weeks after his triple heart bypass isn't known. The crowd definitely have a collective sharp intake of breath when he falls on the third bend of the first lap. Malcolm quickly remounts to finish the race and Paul (slightly misleadingly) reports, "There you go – he wanted to beat 65 seconds – I think he did it in 64.99 seconds, I think you'll agree! Congratulations to Malcolm and our paramedic looks a relieved man as well!" The Men in Black then entertain us with another processional race during the interval. Paul Hunsdon takes the opportunity to interview selected people who come within range of his roving microphone. First up he finds, "Garry Stead – sadly a man who paid the ultimate price in a track crash at Somerset!" Garry remains poignantly stoic and understatedly positive, "Yeah, everything's a lot better now! I lost my speech for a while but I've got it back and people say I speak better! I still go round the tracks. Nothing's changed except I don't ride! I'm still involved on a day-to-day basis with speedway riders and everything! I always love to come to Reading. Pat Bliss used to ring up and say, 'Are you available to ride?' and I'd say, 'For you, I'm always available!' I was always happy to ride for and against them."

Paul also confirms to us all that, after the last race has been run on the Smallmead track, the celebrations will go on long into the night. "Afterwards there's going to be a disco and a race jackets auction. It's going to be a long, long night. It's 10 to 8 – the bar will stay open till 11 o'clock, when it will close for the last time! A disclaimer from a recent King's Lynn programme has been brought to my attention [by Chris Golding Incident Recorder at the Isle of Wight and King's Lynn]. It reads something along the lines of, 'Even though we organised the dinner dance, we cannot be held responsible for it being called off if the food is transported in an uncovered boat!'" Though there are still some races to go, the 2008 season has already effectively closed so Paul Hunsdon can quite safely conduct a brief post-mortem with Tom P. Madsen. "Things never clicked as a team! Some of us went well at one time and, sometimes, others went well at other times. You're right, mate, there are no excuses – we just didn't do it! It hasn't been a great year and it hasn't been a bad year. We didn't do as well as I thought we'd do for Mark and Wellie. We just didn't pick up many points on the road. My away average went up but it's all about what the team does. I want to be in the last four and the last race here doing the last four laps!" Sadly, Tom didn't get his wish. The crowd have noticeably quietened, possibly because the stark reality of the closure has collectively struck home. Announcer Dave Stallworthy tries to buck up the atmosphere, "You can cheer everybody, you can cheer your favourite riders!" Before heat 16, Dave Stallworthy reveals that race sponsor, "Dale Fontaine, used to be known as David 'Lightning' Howell when he was a mascot during the war years!" Maybe I misheard or it's an in joke?[7] Possibly it was this shock news (or similar distraction) that causes Cory Gathercole to crash spectacularly in heat 16 as he exits the second bend and starts to power down the back straight. During the delay Paul Hunsdon collars Paul Clews for a few brief thoughts about the demise of Reading Speedway at Smallmead, "It's a shame when any track closes. In the five years when I rode here you know, you know, you know [trails off]." To rescue the situation Paul trots out his "special memories" question only to learn, "I guess all the five years I rode here really." If this was an interrogation at Guantanamo Bay, then Paul would definitely be classified an unresponsive prisoner. But, since it's a speedway meeting in Berkshire, Paul Hunsdon takes control of the situation and effectively interviews himself, "We'll always remember you for your sweeps round the outside and your famous double fist bumping celebrations!"

[7] Actually, it turns out to be true, as described in the book *Warzone Speedway* by Trevor Davis.

Reading: *"You must have very many happy memories?"*

The rerun of heat 16 eventually gets under way and Tom P. Madsen makes a valiant and spectacular attempt to win Smallmead's soon to be retired 'Last Ditch Crash Closest To The Finish Line' Award. Placed second in the race, Tom somehow manages to slightly clip the safety fence approximately two or three yards from the finish line to get thrown from his machine and dumped in a heap on the track surface. Consequently, he conspicuously fails to finish the race. This gifts one of the meeting reserves, Marc Andrews, his only 2 points of the night. It also ensures that Tom's dream to take part in the last-ever race at Smallmead turns to dust. Dr Hunsdon is on hand to give his medical diagnosis, "Tom P. has come a real cropper there! I can tell you he has a little bit of discomfort in his left leg ... and he's up!" While the dust settles on a dramatic end to that race, it sinks in that race winner Mads Korneliussen is the only rider during the End-of-an-Era meeting to win a race from gate four. Ever vigilantly scanning the horizon for comely wenches, Paul Hunsdon's attentions are suddenly drawn elsewhere, "Can the disco in the bar turn their red light off! You have a ball going round and it's distracting the riders!"

The fifth Men in Black race of the night breaks its usual catatonic mould to provide more excitement in four laps than all the earlier races had managed to induce. 81-year-old Jim Gregory on his Rudge bike rides aggressively throughout. The object of his competitive streak is apparently John Taylor on his Douglas. However, he miscounts the laps and almost slows to a halt by the second bend of the fourth lap. It's a manoeuvre Dave Stallworthy greets with some sympathy from the commentary box, "He's slowed 'cause he thinks it's three laps!" It will be a decision that costs Jim the chance of victory but also his equanimity, if judged by how often he waves his fist at the completely innocent start marshal as he trails home in a distant fifth. Desire to get a lasting memento and souvenir of the Reading speedway era at Smallmead has suddenly got out of hand. Dave Stallworthy is forced to announce, "The Geoff Curtis sign has been taken from the bar! Could it be returned as it is the property of Reading Speedway! Could the person who has it return it or, if anyone sees it, please return it as it's the property of Reading Speedway!" Something hints to me that this might be the property of Reading Speedway? Though smaller items can be easily slipped into a bag or a pocket, it's a mystery how you could either walk around or think you could leave the stadium unnoticed in possession of a large Geoff Curtis sign.

Though there have been many Reading legends of yesteryear at the track this evening, there are numerous other riders who famously wore the winged wheel tabard with pride who sadly couldn't make the event. Some have sent messages instead. Per Jonsson takes pride in his track record and we learn that "Smallmead will always remain in my heart". Typical of the man, he looks positively to the future, "Hope to see you all when the new track is open!" Todd Wiltshire[8] sends his apologies for his absence since he was already "committed to a holiday in Queensland". We learn from Todd that "It's a shame to lose this little specialised track ... Per's track record will never be broken ... it's a true testament to Per and how good he was. I was only young but quickly gained the confidence to take my riding to the next level ... the track was fantastic to ride!" The next message Paul reads out is from Dene Davies (who, of course, rode for Reading from 1968 to 1970) who's now based in Adelaide, "As a former Reading rider I'd like to send my best wishes. I live 12,000 miles away and it's quite far to come." It's a shame that Dene couldn't spend this final evening at Smallmead to celebrate its closure. He rode 82 matches for the club to give him a career average of 5.65 that included a solitary but notable paid maximum.

Though security is obviously lax in the bar area, given the temporary loss of the Geoff Curtis sign, no one has yet bothered to pass on the full implications of the health and safety message to the musical entertainers about the danger caused by their rotating ball and coloured lighting equipment. Slightly exasperatedly, Paul Hunsdon pleads, "Can someone have a word with the band in the bar to turn off the fancy disco lights 'cause they're blinding us in the pit lane!" Shortly afterwards the good news that the Geoff Curtis sign that was traditionally found above the bar has now been returned to his girlfriend. She intends to treasure it until the club move into their next stadium and it can return to its rightful place in the bar! Bathed in nostalgia, the result of the meeting is to some extent an irrelevance but, as widely presaged beforehand, Ulrich Ostergaard gets his hands on both the trophy and the winner's cheque. The last-ever competitive race at Smallmead takes place at 9.35 p.m. on Sunday 19th October 2008. There's still plenty to look forward to in the bar including the auction of 18 race jackets but, suddenly surprisingly maudlin at the demise of my club and its home, I can't face the sadness of the final death throes and slip away into the darkness

---

[8] Had just two magnificent seasons with the Racers, riding for the club from 1990 to 1991 in 59 matches for a Reading career average of 8.76 that included one full maximum and three paid maximums. In 1990 he started the year as reserve but went on to finish 3rd in that year's World Final.

Reading: *"You must have very many happy memories?"*

of the car park. Consequently I miss Tim Sugar's (aka Dave Mullett) valedictory ride on the last four laps round Smallmead before the fans throng onto the surface for their own last-ever track walk. The next day, club historian Arnie Gibbons emails. "I've just returned from Smallmead this morning where I've been helping the Reading Museum team rescue Racers artefacts. I took a few unusual pictures. Last night's book sales (including 24 via the trackshop) were a staggering 89. Customers included David Hamilton, Petri Kokko and Tony Olsson. I gave my final copy to a woman I met while walking round the track at the end. She was Geoff Curtis's girlfriend – I got into conversation with her because she was holding the Geoff Curtis bar sign. I'm glad I had the book to occupy myself as it didn't give me too much time to dwell on the nature of the occasion!"

19th October – Reading Racers End-of-an-Era Winner: Ulrich Ostergaard

AFTERWORD

I hope that you enjoyed the journey.

Phew! What a fantastic year I had and what another brilliant experience. I was genuinely overwhelmed with the kindness of strangers and amazed how people went out of their way to help me.

Obviously all mistakes remain my own and I apologise if I have accidentally upset anyone. If you have any comments, of either persuasion, please get in touch via my website on **www.methanolpress.com**

Every effort has been made to get in touch with all copyright holders and many people featured in the photos but, again, I would be delighted to hear from you to make the appropriate credits or acknowledgements.

I mentioned earlier that I have been overwhelmed with help and kindness. I hesitate to name everyone as, inevitably, I will make a mistake and miss someone I'm extremely grateful to, so, with sincere apologies to those who I do manage to miss out I would like to thank the following people: Peter Adams, Rachael Adams, Mike Amos, Graham Arnold, Les Aubrey, Stephanie Babb, Mike Bacon, Andrew Baker, Robert Bamford, Nick, Johnny, Bev, Molly and Colin Barber, George and Linda Barclay, Derek Barclay, Dick Barrie, Phil Bartlett, Ian Belcher, Alun Biggart, Joyce and Malcolm Blythe, Tim Booler, Jim and Steven Brykajlo, Brian Burford, Peter Butcher, John Campbell, Alison Chalmers, Steve Chilton, Jon Cook, Graham Cooke, Kevin Coombes, Dougie Copland, Mick Corby, Lucy Cross, Dave Croucher, Jonathan, Keith and Cheryl Chapman, Martin Dadswell, Andrew Dalby, Paddy Davitt, Nick Dawson, Gordie Day, Anita Dennington, Alan Dick, Chris Durno, Graham and Denise Drury, Steve and Debbie Dixon, Neil Dyson, George and Joan English, Dave Fairbrother, Ben Findon, Jim Fleming, Richard Frost, Cory Gathercole, Chris Gay, Chris Geer, Trevor Geer, Arnie Gibbons, Bill Gimbeth, Darcia Gingell, Steve Gobey, Rob Godfrey, Mike and Anita Golding, Mick Gregory, George Grant, Andy Griggs, Nobby Hall, Keith Hamblin, Tim Hamblin, Steve Hilliard, Malcolm Holloway, Liz Hunt, John Hyam, John, Jordan, Karen, Mark and Judy Hazelden, Jim Henry, Andy Higgs, Richard Hollingsworth, Dave Hoggart, Paul Hunsdon, Lynn Hunt, Mike Hunter, Tony Jackson, Sue Jackson-Scott, Wendy Jedrzejakski, Billy Jenkins, Kayleigh Jones, Edward Kennett, Elvin King, Mark Lawton, Mark Legg, Sheila Le-Sage, Kevin Ling, Kevin Long, Gary Lough, John Louis, Michael Max, Tony and Susie MacDonald, Ella MacDonald, Ian and Jean Maclean, Neil Machin, Ross Marks, Julie Martin, Dennis McCleary, Charles McKay, Ian McMillan, Allan Melville, Steve and Sarah Miles, Jayne Moss, Hazal Naylor, Martin Neal, Bill Norris, Peter Oakes, Paul Oughton, Brian Owen, Gordon Pairman, Shane and Anji Parker, Dave Pavitt, Michael Payne, Jon Pearson, Nigel Pearson, Rob Peasley, Di Phillips, Graham Platten, Mark Poulton, Andy and Win Povey, Colin Pratt, Bob Radford, Dave Rattenberry, Julie Reading, Dave and Margaret Rice, John Rich, Giles Richards, Karl Roberts, Gareth Rogers, Laurence Rogers, Wayne Russell, Craig Saul, Mark Sawbridge, Chris Seaward, Sid Shine, Len Silver, Andrew Skeels, Phil Spence, Claudia Stæchmann, Tony Steele, Trevor Swales, Shaun Tacey, Bob Tasker, Dave Tattum, Caroline Tattum, Glyn Taylor, Peter Toogood, Stuart Towner, Ian Thomas, the late Stefan Usansky, Dave Valentine, Chris Van Stratten, Peter Waite, Barry Wallace, Nick Ward, Paul Watson, Alf Weedon, The Reverend Michael Whawell, Richard Whitehead, Bryn Williams, Scott Wilson, Steve Winter, Cameron Woodward, Ashley and Jane Wooller, Dave Wright and Malcolm Wright.

All quotes from the *Speedway Star*, speedway club programmes and various newspapers remain their copyright.

To pick out anyone in particular would be invidious. However, I owe so many 'thank you's'. The book wouldn't look as lovely as it does without Vicky Holtham's artistic skills. The look and feel of the covers, website and book layout were all originally conceived by Rachael Adams. There would be many more errors than there are without the help of Vy Shepherd. Graham Russel has shown tremendous pedantry and knowledge to wrangle with my words to convert them into some sort of sense. Robert Bamford also kindly copyedited the Reading chapters. Michael Payne and Billy Jenkins have continued to offer encouragement, while Ian McMillan wrote such a lovely review of my last book I was almost tempted to retire on the basis: 'how could things ever get any better?'. My true friend Sue Young has encouraged me often in so many things and really saved me when I needed that most – for which she has my eternal gratitude. Of course, without the love and guidance of my parents – Mary and Alan – none of this book or so many other things would ever have been possible. Finally, you can never have too many teachers and I was lucky enough to have been inspired to write my speedway books by a truly great teacher, poet, musician and wit – Michael Donaghy. He remains greatly missed.

Speedway for me has always been synonymous with Smallmead. I saw my first ever speedway meeting there and just to walk through the turnstiles was to find myself somewhere I truly felt comfortable and at home. I'm not the first speedway fan and, sadly, won't be last to have their club close down (possibly never to re-open). Since it was built in 1975, the transformation of the area around the stadium is a microcosm of the changes that have swept through British society since then and, peculiarly, to my mind symbolises the rapid transformations that have flung speedway (and its community values) to the periphery of our everyday cultural life. Though, somewhat careworn, Smallmead stadium retained a charm and character that (silly though it sounds) I cherished. I've grown from a boy to a man going to Smallmead and, like so many other things we hold dear, it has revealed the depth of its character while it aged. Luckily, we all have our memories of the people and places that are truly special to us and our lives and so, really, they'll never be lost but respectfully and lovingly burnished yet brighter over time.

It just remains to say: if you go to speedway already why not make a point of taking even more friends this year. And, if you haven't been for a while or have never been, now is as good a time as any to start!

Yours in speedway!

Thank you for coming on this journey round the tracks.

Brighton

10th June 2009

INFORMATION

Selected Speedway Sites

BSPA
www.british-speedway.co.uk

Blunsdon Blog
www.tattingermarsh.co.uk/blog/

British Speedway Forum
www.speedway-forum.co.uk

Speedway Plus
www.speedwayplus.com

Useful Sites

Macmillan Cancer Support
www.macmillan.org.uk

British Humanist Association
www.humanist.org.uk/home

Jazz Musicians

www.billyjenkins.com

The one and only Billy J – the incomparable speedway loving Bard of Bromley and progenitor of a distinctively British kitchen-sink jazz sound

Accommodation

All the following warmly welcome speedway fans and have special rates for them:

Waverley Hotel, Workington
01900 603246
www.waverley-hotel.com

Lower Farm, Harpley, King's Lynn
01485 520240

Welcomes visitors of Owlerton Stadium

Why not stay the night £55 per night double/twin including Bed & Breakfast?

Try our 2 main meals for £8 special offer
Mon-Thurs 6pm-9pm

The Garrison Hotel
Hillsborough Barracks, Penistone Road
Sheffield S6 2GB
0114 2499555
www.garrisonhotel.co.uk

IF IT HAPPENED – IT'S IN HERE!

Methanol Press Speedway Yearbook 2008
Edited by Robert Bamford

Was £14.99 now £5

The indispensable companion for the 2008 season for speedway fans everywhere – edited by respected speedway author and historian, Robert Bamford.

It's comprehensive, definitive and packed with useful information, covering all British Leagues – Elite, Premier and Conference – as well as all major meetings in Britain and Internationally along with complete coverage of the Speedway Grand Prix Series

**272 pages 74 Black and white photographs £5.00 Paperback
available from www.methanolpress.com**

Nominated for British Sports Book of the Year Award 2009

Concrete for Breakfast
More Tales from the Shale

The Times review by **Ian McMillan**

302 pages
223 Black & white photographs
£20.00 Paperback

THERE ARE CERTAIN sports that seem to be shaped by their histories and their settings just for the purpose of lyrical description: county cricket, with its long afternoons in the sun, its trundle to the pavilion as the rain threatens, its slowly changing scoreboards and its dozing gents and ladies reading the newspaper under hats made of straw; professional football, with its drama and its excitement and the painful way that glory can turn to farce in the instant it takes someone to miss a penalty under floodlights that glow like jewels.

There's a literature of mountaineering and sailing, and novels have been written about horse riding and rugby league and tennis. But speedway? Speedway as a source of poetic prose and philosophical discussion? There's certainly been a bit of a speedway-shaped gap in the shelves marked Sporting Literature. Until now, that is.

Jeff Scott's new book / **Concrete for Breakfast** is possibly Speedway's War and Peace, or its Ulysses, or, in some of the chapters, its local newspaper gossip page. It's the epic by which all other books on the sport (there aren't that many, let's be honest, and Scott has written most of them) will be judged.

Scott is writer-in-residence at Eastbourne Speedway and he has a love/hate (or more accurately obsession/exasperation) relationship with the sport. He has previously published a couple of fine volumes, **Showered in Shale** and **Shale Britannia**, that take us inside a society that often seems hidden from view unless you're a fan, and now in **Concrete for Breakfast**, he takes us on an odyssey across the 2007 season, to every stadium that staged the sport in a year that was blighted by the soaking summer and the inevitable feeling that here was a way of life heading for some kind of sunset.

As Scott explains in his foreword, **Concrete** continues his examination of the philosophical quest "What is speedway?" and the answers come tumbling out in a prose that possesses a kind of petrol-driven Dirty Realism, as though Raymond Carver had decided to turn up at a speedway meeting in Swindon on a dank March day with his notebook.

The picture that Scott paints is of a knowledgeable but shrinking community; as he writes: "the typical speedway supporter remains loyal but drawn from an ageing demographic that probably spells disaster for the longevity of the sport in the medium to long term". Later he talks of a particular enthusiast's "links to the salad days of the sport when it was wonderfully vibrant and truly a national pastime".

The book does seem at times to be simply a catalogue of one more rain-spattered visit to one more mist-covered stadium, where one more gang of self-deprecating and bantering volunteers are waiting to prepare the track for one more afternoon of minority sport. Did I mention the rain and the mist from Sittingbourne to Scunthorpe? I think I did. "Nowadays it's a minority sport served up in often decaying and poorly equipped stadia", as Scott writes, mistily.

If you persist with **Concrete** you come to love the people whom Scott writes about and you come to share his enthusiasm, and a little of his exasperation. You see that in the end this is more than a book about a pastime that happens to be down on its luck. It's a book about the persistence of the human spirit, about the odd juxtaposition of hours of hard physical work involving a family of volunteers who have been involved with speedway for years, and moments of extreme physical danger with fragile parts of the rider's body inches from the unforgiving ground.

What Scott is really good at is detail, sacks and sacks of gorgeous detail, and a love of the specific and precise language of speedway, with its lay downs and dirt deflectors and double point tactical rides. He has a keen and sympathetic eye for human failings that somehow seem to be magnified around the track.

In one chapter, for instance, he describes the visit of a well-meaning BBC team representing the Reading and Writing scheme to the Isle of Wight meeting. The BBC Radio Solent presenter's dress "indicated that she thought a speedway meeting might have something in common with a world premiere", and there's a splendid evocation of a race that Scott relates as "both a collector's item and typifies the rough-and-tumble, needs must, show-must-go-on attitude that is one of the enduring appeals of speedway racing at Conference League level".

Scott makes the sport seem somehow down to earth and heroic at the same time: "The initial running of the race has Brendan Johnson knocked off on the first bend and a rerun called by the referee for first-bend bunching...it would be safe to say that he appears not to be at all happy and, though normally a placid young man, it should be noted that he has martial arts expertise..."

Read this book for a glimpse of a lost tribe, for an examination of collectivism and individuality somehow working together, for endless descriptions of English weather, and for a brave attempt to pinpoint a particular branch of human endeavour that often seems to be far from the centre of things.

available rom www.methanolpress.com

ALSO AVAILABLE FROM METHANOL PRESS

Showered in Shale

One Man's Circuitous Journey Throughout the Country in Pursuit of An Obsession – British Speedway

"At the end of the month William Hill announces the shortlist for its sports book of 2006. If the author Jeff Scott's impulsively oddball doorstep is not already in pole position, then it jolly well should be."
FRANK KEATING, *Guardian*

"It's all here, in almost soap opera style proportions ... this is British Speedway stripped bare, this is how it really is and some of it isn't pretty ... many years into the future, historians will gladly hold this book to their bosom for its insight ... what the author has achieved – and it will be interesting to se how many people take this on board – is that he's provided a book that will stand-up as a fly on the wall type narrative of where and what our sport really is in the early millennium ... Showered in Shale is a quirky book, it's different and off-the-wall."
BRIAN BURFORD, *Speedway Star*

**508 pages 409 Black & white photographs
£20.00 Paperback**

When Eagles Dared

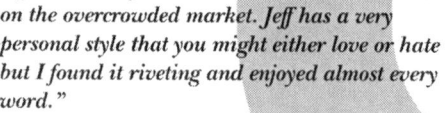

"A remarkable read and something completely different to any other books on the overcrowded market. Jeff has a very personal style that you might either love or hate but I found it riveting and enjoyed almost every word."
PETER OAKES, *Speedway Star*

**172 pages 158 Black white photographs
£10.00 Paperback**

Shifting Shale

2006 A Race Odyssey

Was £20 now £10

"Nobody else writing about speedway at the moment can capture the speedway experience in the way that Scott can. As always, the beauty of his work is in the description of the minutiae"
ALLAN MELVILLE, *Speedway Plus*

"Bill Bryonesque"
JIM HENRY, *Speedway-Researcher*

**354 pages 143 Black and white photographs
£10.00 Paperback**

Shale Britannia

A Sideways Glance at Speedway

Was £15 now £5

"A brilliantly quirky book"
Big Issue

"A marvellously evocative book"
JOHN INVERDALE, *Daily Telegraph*

"Superbly produced. I found it absolutely fascinating"
PETER OAKES, *Speedway Star*

256 pages 245 colour photographs £5.00 flexiback

All available from
www.methanolpress.com

methanol press